Also in the Variorum Collected Studies Series:

ROGER E. REYNOLDS
Law and Liturgy in the Latin Church, 5th–12th Centuries

KATHRYN L. REYERSON
Society, Law and Trade in Medieval Montpellier

ROBERT FEENSTRA
Legal Scholarship and Doctrines of Private Law, 13th–18th Centuries

RICHARD KAY
Councils and Clerical Culture in the Medieval West

BRIAN TIERNEY
Rights, Laws and Infallibility in Medieval Thought

UTA-RENATE BLUMENTHAL
Papal Reform and Canon Law in the 11th and 12th Centuries

ROBERT SOMERVILLE
Papacy, Councils and Canon Law in the 11th–12th Centuries

ANDRÉ GOURON
Juristes et droits savants: Bologne et la France médiévale

JEAN GAUDEMET
La doctrine canonique médiévale

PAUL FREEDMAN
Church, Law and Society in Catalonia, 900–1500

ROGER COLLINS
Law, Culture and Regionalism in Early Medieval Spain

KATHERINE FISCHER DREW
Law and Society in Early Medieval Europe: Studies in Legal History

JANE E. SAYERS
Law and Records in Medieval England: Studies on the Medieval Papacy, Monasteries and Records

VARIORUM COLLECTED STUDIES SERIES

Inquisitions and Other Trial Procedures in the Medieval West

For Sarah and Steve

Henry Ansgar Kelly

Inquisitions and Other Trial Procedures in the Medieval West

Routledge
Taylor & Francis Group
LONDON AND NEW YORK

First published 2001 by Ashgate Publishing

Published 2016 by Routledge
2 Park Square, Milton Park, Abingdon, Oxon OX14 4RN
605 Third Avenue, New York, NY 10017

Routledge is an imprint of the Taylor & Francis Group, an informa business

British Library Cataloguing-in-Publication Data
Kelly, Henry Ansgar, 1934–
Inquisitions and Other Trial Procedures in the Medieval West. – (Variorum Collected Studies Series).
1. Criminal procedure–England. 2. Law, Medieval–England.
I. Title.
345. 4 ' 2' 05

US Library of Congress Cataloging-in-Publication Data
Kelly, Henry Ansgar, 1934–
Inquisitions and Other Trial Procedures in the Medieval West / Henry Ansgar Kelly.
p. cm. – (Variorum Collected Studies Series: CS708).
ISBN 978-0-86078-839-3
1. Criminal procedure–Europe–History. 2. Inquisition–Europe–History. 3. Law, Medieval. I. Title. II. Collected Studies: CS708).
KJC9400. 5. I57 K45 2001
345. 4' 05–dc21 00–069004

VARIORUM COLLECTED STUDIES SERIES CS708

ISBN 978-0-86078-839-3 (hbk)

CONTENTS

This volume contains xxvi + 354 pages

PUBLISHER'S NOTE

The articles in this volume, as in all others in the Variorum Collected Studies Series, have not been given a new, continuous pagination. In order to avoid confusion, and to facilitate their use where these same studies have been referred to elsewhere, the original pagination has been maintained wherever possible.

Each article has been given a Roman number in order of appearance, as listed in the Contents. This number is repeated on each page and is quoted in the index entries.

Corrections noted in the Addenda and Corrigenda have been marked by an asterisk in the margin corresponding to the relevant text to be amended.

INTRODUCTION

The following essays deal mainly with the new form of criminal prosecution developed by Pope Innocent III and perfected at the Fourth Lateran Council in 1215, namely, *inquisitio*. As I note at the beginning of Essay V, I first developed an interest in the inquisitorial form of procedure while researching my book, *The Matrimonial Trials of Henry VIII*, which I started working on in 1969, on my first quarter sabbatical at UCLA. I also set forth some of elements of the procedure as practiced in the lower church courts of England in my *Love and Marriage in the Age of Chaucer*, mainly written in 1972 during a Guggenheim year.[1] The inquisitorial method, used in all courts, both ecclesiastical and secular, on the Continent and only in the ecclesiastical courts in England (except for a modified form in Chancery),[2] is to be contrasted, first of all, with other Roman-canonistic forms of criminal procedure, namely, *accusatio* and *denunciatio* (the latter also invented by Innocent III), and with the canonical process of *compurgatio*. I deal with all of these forms in passing in many of the essays below, especially Essay I, but I present a more extended treatment of *accusatio* in my *Canon Law and the Archpriest of Hita*.[3]

Inquisitio is also to be contrasted with the criminal procedures used in the secular courts of England. I begin the study of peculiarly English forms in Essays III and VI–VIII and continue more broadly in Essays IX and X when dealing with charges of 'rape'. In the last-named essays I also deal with English 'civil' procedures, in which one party sues another party for damages of some sort, or pleads for some sort of benefit from the court. Civil forms of trial in the Roman-canonistic tradition are similar, and are

---

1 H.A. Kelly, *The Matrimonial Trials of Henry VIII* (Stanford, 1976), *passim*; *Love and Marriage in the Age of Chaucer* (Ithaca, NY, 1975), esp. pp. 169, 200, 271–2.

2 See J.H. Baker, *An Introduction to English Legal History*, edn. 3 (London, 1990), pp. 119–20. The court of Chancery was probably established by the last quarter of the fourteenth century, but few records have survived from this period.

3 H.A. Kelly, *Canon Law and the Archpriest of Hita* (Binghamton, NY, 1984), Chapter 4: 'Procedure in the Court of Don Ximio' (pp. 89–112).

referred to from time to time in these studies (see the Index). Note that the word 'civil' is used in two ways, first, in contrast to 'criminal', and, second, referring to ancient Roman law (as studied in the medieval universities and applied in the courts) in contrast to canon law.

Even though the inquisitorial form of procedure is still used in most non-English European and European-based courts of the world, 'inquisition' has acquired a bad name because it is often thought of exclusively as the form of trial used in heresy cases. In fact, I myself have recently been manipulated into seeming to approve and authorize this mistaken understanding, in a television program, *The Inquisition*, which first aired in 1999.[4] The thrust of the two-hour interview that I gave for this program was that the inquisitorial system was first established with a sound array of defenses for defendants, with no thought of using it as a special method for prosecuting heresy. But the idea that the inquisitorial method was invented for combating heresy is the chief thesis of the program, and the few snippets extracted from my interview are introduced in a such a way as to support this notion and the conclusion that the papal heresy inquisitors were bound by few if any canons of due process. For instance, I am shown as saying that the heresy inquisitors needed only opinions rather than proofs, and nothing is said of the actual subsequent trial that was required. I trust that readers of the following essays will receive a more accurate understanding of my conclusions and the data supporting them.

In the first six essays, I examine the extent to which special procedures were allowed in heresy inquisitions and show how other procedures went counter to due process. This is the particular focus of Essay I, 'Inquisition and the Prosecution of Heresy: Misconceptions and Abuses'. It shows, as just noted, that the process of *inquisitio* was not developed with heresy in mind, and that in fact it was unsuitable for such prosecutions. Many of the abuses practiced by heresy inquisitors were resorted to because of the difficulty of following the rules in such cases. The essence of the inquisitorial system was that it could only deal with a public crime, and that, before a judge could proceed against a specific individual, he had to be able to establish 'probable cause', by reputable witnesses testifying to their belief that that person committed the crime. In other words, the rules did not permit 'fishing expeditions' obligating self-incrimination. The same is true of witnesses summoned to testify in 'general inquisitions': by law they should not be required to incriminate themselves.

---

[4] *The Inquisition*, copyright 1999, written by Steve Muscarella and Melissa Jo Peltier, shown periodically on the History Channel in the series, History's Mysteries.

This question is expanded upon in Essay II, 'Inquisitorial Due Process and the Status of Secret Crimes', which contrasts the external forum of the courts with the internal forum of sacramental confession and adduces the Spanish Inquisition to illustrate how the principles involved were observed or not observed in theory and practice. Further considerations of due process are presented in Essay III, 'The Right to Remain Silent: Before and After Joan of Arc'. This essay also compares the inquisitorial system with the procedures of English common and statute law. The 'right to remain silent' refers here to the right of a defendant not to be questioned before being charged with a specific crime, and before establishing the *fama publica* that is necessary before proceeding further. It also refers to the inquisitor's duty to inform the defendant of this right. The original trial of Joan of Arc at the hands of Bishop Cauchon provides an example of the denial of due process on this score. In the retrial of two decades later, which resulted in the nullification of Joan's condemnation, we can observe the extent to which violations of procedure were recognized or not recognized, and the same is true of the review that took place in the beatification trial beginning in the 1890s, analyzed in Essay IV, 'Joan of Arc's Last Trial: The Attack of the Devil's Advocates'. We also see here a modern example of another kind of medieval trial procedure, the canonization process, a species of civil trial in which the candidate is subjected to searching attempts at denigration by the 'promotor of the faith' and defended by the 'postulator'.

Essay V, 'Trial Procedures Against Wyclif and Wycliffites in England and at the Council of Constance', examines not only the abortive procedures against Wyclif in England and his posthumous inquisition and conviction at Constance, but also the peculiar inquisitions against his followers in England, in which they were not accused of crimes but were required to comment on condemned propositions attributed to Wyclif. It shows the same procedure being used on John Hus at Constance, followed by a standard form of inquisition (with some violations of due process) and the similar trial of Hus's follower, Jerome of Prague. The trial of the Pisan pope, John XXIII, is also detailed, as is the posthumous trial of John Petit, ably defended by Peter Cauchon, the episcopal inquisitor who later denied due defenses to Joan of Arc. Essay VI, 'Lollard Inquisitions: Due and Undue Process', studies the trials of lesser heresy suspects in England and examines how the rules of inquisitorial procedure were or were not followed. It also discusses the bull of Martin V, *Inter cunctas*, against the errors of Wyclif and Hus, issued at the end of the Council of Constance, and how it was received and implemented in England.

Essay VII, 'English Kings and the Fear of Sorcery', details various witchcraft scares or accusations in England from the time of Edward III to Henry VIII. It discusses inquisitions conducted by Archbishop Chichele of Canterbury, sometimes in Convocation (the formal gathering of the bishops and other delegates of the province of Canterbury), sometimes not, with Chichele acting as sole judge in both circumstances. The inquisition against Eleanor Cobham, Duchess of Gloucester, on sorcery (and heresy? treason?), is detailed at length; she was convicted of 'nigromancy', and her marriage to Duke Humphrey was annulled because the duke's consent was forced (effected by magical means). Her accomplices were tried in the secular courts; one of them, the priest Roger Bolinbroke, was condemned in King's Bench and executed. The article also discusses the allowability of torture in ecclesiastical courts and its alleged use by the King's Council (also discussed in Essay III). One witchcraft accusation treated here, against Edward IV's queen, Elizabeth Woodville, and her mother (bewitching Edward into marrying Elizabeth), is taken up again in Essay VIII, 'The Case Against Edward IV's Marriage and Offspring: Secrecy; Witchcraft; Secrecy; Precontract', as one of the reasons alleged to disqualify the children of Edward IV from succeeding to the throne. The case was tried, in effect, by Richard III's first Parliament, which, by judging in favor of the report, supported Richard's claim to the throne.

Essay IX, 'Statutes of Rapes and Alleged Ravishers of Wives: A Context for the Charges Against Thomas Malory, Knight', reviews the ways in which the sexual rape of women and the nonsexual rape (that is, abduction) of male and female heirs, married women, and widows were dealt with in the secular courts of England. It argues that many of the rape statutes, notably those of Westminster I (1275), Westminster II (1285), and 6 Richard II (1382), were not intended to modify the criminal prosecution of sexual rape but were rather aimed at charges of kidnapping, especially of wives. In actual cases, the abduction charge, with or without allegations of sexual violation, often turns out to be a fiction used by an ex-husband to gain compensation for losing his wife through annulment of the marriage (in the ecclesiastical court) or her voluntary departure. The defendant is sometimes the current husband of the woman, as in the case of Ralph Percy (Henry Hotspur's brother) in 1384 and the case investigated by Geoffrey Chaucer in 1387. In a sexual rape, the wronged woman can 'appeal' the perpetrator of felony (a capital offense), or a grand jury can 'present' the charge either as a felony or a trespass (noncapital crime). Abduction can be charged either as felony or criminal trespass, or a complainant (other than the alleged abductee) can bring it as a civil trespass. The commission given to Chaucer in 1387 did not specify felony, but it was returned as felony by the grand jury, whereupon one of the defendants, John Lording, established on the civil side of the King's Bench, in a countersuit against the complainants, that he was husband of the alleged abductee, who in fact had first been abducted by the complainants. Nevertheless, he was still required to plead ('not guilty') to the felony charge and ordered to stand trial before a jury. He remained as an accused felon for the next dozen years, during which time a jury failed to be assembled from term to term, until he finally managed to obtain (read 'purchase') a pardon from the king. When Thomas Malory was indicted for felonious rape and abduction of a wife in 1451, the alleged husband entered an appeal in virtue of the statute of 1382, which entailed an admission that the wife had consented to the abduction. His appeal had the effect of removing the case to the King's Bench and keeping Malory in prison until a jury was assembled for trial of this and the other charges that had been laid (perhaps trumped up) against him, and, as in the Lording case, no jury could be found for many terms. I state that he finally obtained a pardon and release from prison in 1460 (IX, p. 414), but in a corrected account in the Addenda and Corrigenda section at the end of this volume I show that the pardon he obtained in late 1455 resulted in his acquittal early in the next year, but that he was kept in prison until he could find further security.

Essay X, 'Meanings and Uses of *Raptus* in Chaucer's Time', begins by analyzing the two forms of quitclaim executed by Cecily Champain on May 1, 1380, releasing Geoffrey Chaucer from any further actions concerning her rape and any other cause (according to one text) and (according to the other text) from all actions of felonies, trespasses, accounts, debts, or other kinds or actions. It then discusses how 'rape', whether meaning sexual violation, on the one hand, or, on the other, abduction, without or without forced sex, could be charged, sometimes accurately, sometimes without basis in fact (as with the allegedly abducted wives noted above), in order to get a foothold in court; it also shows how fictitious charges of other kinds could be made in order to get a hearing about a real *raptus*. The article deals especially with the options that women of various conditions had in acting against male adversaries.

I hope that these studies not only throw light on how procedural jurisprudence developed and was practiced in the past but will also provide a background for study of present-day concerns about due process. English and American traditions of procedure have a pluralistic heritage, being based not only in English common law but also and especially in what has recently come to be called the pan-European common law or *jus commune*, which was a combination of medieval canon law and ancient Roman civil law. The two common laws are usually studied in opposition to each other, whether in their origins or their results – especially, on the criminal side, the inquisitorial Continental approach, on the one hand, and the adversarial Anglo-American approach, on the other. But I hope to have shown, especially in Essay III, when discussing Leonard Levy's *Origins of the Fifth Amendment*,[5] that since both systems were practiced at the same time in England, there was a real possibility of mutual influence. In the process, I counter claims that the Fourth Lateran Council incorporated 'a new oath that was self-incriminatory in nature', that Cardinal Otto of Tonengo introduced the self-incriminating oath into England in 1236, that Robert Grosseteste as bishop of Lincoln first used it in 1246, that his use of it was opposed by Henry III, that Archbishop Boniface of Canterbury revitalized it in 1272, and that Parliament under Edward II (1307–27) outlawed it. All of these conclusions are based on misunderstandings of the law and the records (see III, pp. 1005–7).

In fact, nothing was said at the Fourth Lateran Council about a requirement that the defendant in an inquisition take an oath to tell the truth (III, p. 996), but when it later became a part of the procedure, it was justified on the grounds that probable cause had been established by proving the existence of *fama publica*, that is, belief by reputable persons that the defendant was guilty (VII, p. 212n). It could thereby be compared to the process of compurgation: when a person was believed to be guilty of a crime, he was compelled to swear to his innocence under oath, and to assemble a stipulated number of character witnesses to swear to his good name. In the *inquisitio*, witnesses swear to the bad name of the charged person, and then he is forced to swear to his innocence or admission of guilt. This is a reasonable proceeding; it becomes unreasonable when the oath is administered before charges are levied or the requisite ill-fame is established.

A good example of due process in an inquisitorial proceeding has been documented recently by Richard Helmholz. In 1449 a married couple were cited before the consistory court of the bishop of Rochester and accused of killing their infant son. They denied that there was any legitimate *fama publica* against them, and when this was found to be the case, they

---

[5] Leonard W. Levy, *Origins of the Fifth Amendment: The Right Against Self-Incrimination* (New York, 1968; reprint with new preface, New York, 1986).

were dismissed, without having to take an oath or to answer the charge.[6] When Helmholz says, later on, that refusals to take the ex officio oath (by which he means an oath in an inquisitorial trial) 'are easy to find among the act books from the years after 1560', we cannot without further information tell whether the oath-refusers were justified, since as he says, the records 'reveal little about the specific legal grounds given for refusing the oath'.[7] In many of the cases cited in his essay, it is not clear whether the persons being required to swear were witnesses or defendants; and, if witnesses, whether they were required to tell the truth about themselves as well as others (*de se et aliis*), or, if defendants, whether due process had been followed before requiring the oath. I cannot do better than to bring forward here the conclusions of J.H. Wigmore (cited below, III, p. 1005), which have been wrongly impugned by commentators with less knowledge of the law than he possessed, and to recommend them to the attention of all legal historians. He states that the *ex officio* proceeding (insistence on an oath in an inquisition) was 'lawful enough on Innocent III's conditions about *clamosa insinuatio* and *fama publica*'. Later, however, abuses 'led to the matter being argued, in English courts and in popular discussion, as if this oath were either wholly lawful or wholly unlawful; though, in truth, by the theory of the canon law, it *might* be either, according to the circumstances of presentment'.

Another point that needs clarification is the question of the right of defendants in inquisitorial trials to be advised or defended by expert counsel. My main concern in the essays below is to insist that there was no prosecutorial privilege preventing heresy defendants from using lawyers. Here is what I say in Essay I:

> Persons accused of heresy had a right to be defended by legal counsel, just like persons accused of other crimes. Only actual heretics, that is, persons judicially convicted of heresy, were forbidden lawyers. If one want to find a legal system in which persons who were only charged with a felony were denied a trial lawyer, one can look to the English common law. This infringement of the defendant's rights was eliminated only in 1836 (I, p. 445).

I must elaborate on these statements, however, because it is claimed by invariably reliable historians that the *jus commune* (as defined above) was precisely similar to English common law in disallowing defense attorneys

---

[6] R.H. Helmholz, 'The Privilege and the *Ius Commune*: The Middle Ages to the Seventeenth Century', in Helmholz et al., *The Privilege Against Self-Incrimination: Its Origins and Development* (Chicago, 1997), pp. 16–46 at p. 34.

[7] Ibid., pp. 35–6.

in all criminal cases. Here, for instance, is what James Brundage says: 'A defendant in any canonical criminal proceeding was not permitted to engage a proctor to serve as his representative before the court, nor was he usually entitled to have legal advice from an advocate'. He adds: 'Although denial of access to legal representation and counsel strikes modern sensibilities as inherently unfair, it is important to keep in mind that this was the common law rule as well'.[8] And Richard Helmholz says:

> Like the common law courts, the medieval ecclesiastical tribunals denied criminal defendants the right to be represented by a lawyer in most circumstances. Professional lawyers, called *procuratores* or proctors, did represent most parties in civil litigation. Not so in ex officio proceedings. According to classical canon law, the presence of a proctor would interfere with the system's legitimate aim of dealing directly with offenders against the church's laws, and this was the rule put into practice in the English spiritual courts. The utility of lawyers was recognized in the *ius commune*, but it was felt that they would do more harm than good in criminal cases. There was no defense counsel.[9]

I respond first by noting Brundage's distinction between proctors and advocates: a proctor appeared in court *instead of* his client; an advocate appeared *with* the client (or his proctor) in court. (Of course, both proctors and advocates could advise clients and organize procedures beforehand outside court.) All of the authorities that Brundage cites deal exclusively with proctors. Furthermore, these authorities are not speaking of inquisitorial proceedings but of the ancient process of *accusatio*; this is true not only of the Gratian citations, which come from a time before the *inquisitio* was invented, but of the later discussions as well. We must be aware that in the *accusatio* the judge is not prosecuting the defendant but rather is moderating a charge levied by a private accuser (the *actor*) against a defendant (the *reus*), and the laws are insistent that both the accuser and the accused have to be present in court: that is, neither could be represented by a proctor.[10]

---

[8] James A. Brundage, *Medieval Canon Law* (London, 1995), p. 149 and n. 50.

[9] Helmholz, op. cit., pp. 42–3. He acknowledeges (p. 221, n. 128) that his conclusion about English procedure is based largely on negative evidence, but cites one case from 1377 in which the judge rejected a request for a proctor. However, as we will see below, in an inquisition it is at the judge's discretion whether the defendant must come to court personally or not.

[10] If the *actor* did send a proctor instead of showing up himself, and the *reus* did not object, it was the obligation of the judge to repel him; however, if the judge failed to do so, it was discussable whether the proctor's actions were valid. Of course, the final judgment had to be given with the accuser present. See John Andrew, Ordinary Gloss to *Sext* 2.2.1 v. *criminalis*, *Corpus juris canonici*, 3 vols. (Rome, 1582; repr. Lyons, 1606), 3:1:308.

When Innocent III in the decretal *Veniens*, issued in 1202 (three years after first outlining the inquisitorial procedure as an alternative to *accusatio*, in *Licet Heli*), says that proctors cannot be received in a criminal cause,[11] all of the commentators understand him to be speaking only of the *accusatio* mode, and they note that even here there are many exceptions to the rule. William Durant lists fourteen of them; and, though most of these exceptions are minor or obsolete, referring only to ancient conditions, some are (potentially) commonplace. For instance, proctors are allowed when the accusation concerns a noncapital crime, or when a crime is proceeded against in a noncriminal way, that is, civilly (seeking pecuniary damages).[12] Proctors may also be used when an accusation is made in a church court and a canonical penalty is sought.[13]

What about in an inquisition? Can a cited defendant send a proctor instead of appearing himself? The general answer is definitely yes, as is stated, for instance, by Cardinal Hostiensis in his *Summa*,[14] and by Innocent IV in his commentary on the *Decretals*,[15] though Durant transforms

---

[11] Innocent III, *Veniens* (1202), *X* (= *Decretales Gregorii IX*) 5.1.15, *Corpus iuris canonici*, ed. Emil Friedberg (Leipzig, 1879–1881) 2:737. For *Licet Heli* (1199), see 5.3.33 (2:760–61). The pope mentions conducting an *inquisitio* in an earlier letter, *Ut nostrum* (1198), but he does not elaborate on the method, and Raymund Pennafort omitted the pertinent references when he added the letter to the *Decretales* (*X* 3.12.1, Friedberg 2:509–12).

[12] William Durant, *Speculum judiciale*, lib. 1, pt. 2, *De procuratore* §1 *Ratione*, no. 10 (vol. 1, p. 207 of the Basel 1574 edition of the *Speculum*, repr. Aalen, 1975). The examples given above are exceptions no. 9 and 11.

[13] See *X* 1.38.5, *Tue* (2:214), and the commentary of Cardinal Hostiensis, *Commentaria in Decretales et Librum sextum* (Venice, 1581; repr. Turin, 1965), 1:186, no. 7.

[14] Hostiensis, *Summa aurea* (Venice, 1574; repr. Turin, 1963), *De procuratoribus*, no. 10, pp. 390–91: 'Sin autem questio criminalis est et pena major relegatione sit imponenda, non admittitur procurator, nisi ad allegandas causas absentie. . . . Secus, si agatur de crimine per inquisitionem: quia tunc potest constitui procurator' ('But if it is a criminal matter and a penalty greater than exile is to be imposed, a proctor is not admitted except to allege excuses. . . . But it is otherwise if a crime is prosecuted by way of inquisition, for then a proctor may be appointed'), giving examples in the *Decretales* (*X* 1.38.4 and 2.27.22). 'A penalty greater than exile' includes mutilation as well as death.

[15] Innocent IV on *X* 4.17.7 (*Causam que*), *In quinque libros Decretalium* (Venice, 1578), fol. 198, no. 11: 'In causa autem matrimoniali non est admittendum defensor nisi in eo casu si procederetur in causa [ac] si defensor non existeret. . . . Nec formabitur sententia in persona procuratoris vel defensoris, sed principalis persone, licet fuerit semper absens. . . . In inquisitione enim bene admittimus procuratorem' ('In a marriage cause, however, a defender is not to be admitted unless it were to proceed as if the defender did not exist. Nor is the sentence to be formulated in the person of the proctor or defender, but rather in terms of the principal person, even though he should be absent throughout. . . . For in an inquisition we certainly admit a proctor').

the latter's assertion by saying that a defender (*defensor*) is admissible in an inquisition.[16] He defines a defender as one who, without having been engaged to do so, guarantees to fulfill the judgment of the court (similar to the undertaking made by a proctor) and comes to the defense of a defendant in court.[17] John Andrew too says that Innocent IV is speaking of a defender, but he adds that there is no doubt that a proctor can be admitted in an inquisition, since, even though it deals with a crime, it does not constitute a criminal cause, as Cardinal Hostiensis notes in his commentary on inquisitorial procedure in the Lateran decree *Qualiter et quando*. Therefore, he says, a proctor can appear for the defendant unless he is cited to appear personally, or unless the case deals with a crime like homicide or simony that would prevent the defendant from 'fulfilling his order' (to which he has been or is to be ordained) or would result in the loss of his benefice, as noted in Innocent III's decretal *Inquisitionis*.[18] In other words, in some cases an inquisitor is required to insist that the defendant come to court in person, and in other cases he may allow or not allow the use of a proctor, as he chooses.

As is pointed out by Bartolus (d. 1357), the *inquisitio* was a new law (*jus novum*) not permitted in the *jus commune* (by which he means Roman civil law) but only in canon law (see below, VI, p. 301n). But secular judges nevertheless adopted the new method. From Anthony da Butrio, who died in 1408, we learn that the 'legists' (referring in this case to authorities on secular procedures) do not permit proctors in an inquisition, because the punishment remains the same as in an accusation for all crimes. The same

---

[16] Durant, *Speculum* 1.3, *De defensore*, no. 5 (1:232): 'In inquisitione autem bene admittimus defensorum, ut notatur secundum papam' ('In an inquisition however we certainly admit a defender, as is noted by the pope'), citing *X* 4.17.7, therefore referring to Innocent IV.

[17] Ibid., p. 231: 'Defensor est is qui, sine mandato, prestita cautione de judicato solvendo, alium in judicio defendit'.

[18] John Andrew, *Novella* on *X* 4.17.7 (Venice, 1581, repr. Turin, 1963), 4:56, no. 10: 'In inquisitione vero bene admittimus defensorem, secundum Innocentem. . . . De procuratore, non est dubium quin admittatur in causa inquisitionis', with the exceptions noted in his commentary on *Qualiter et quando* 2, *X* 5.1.24 (5:17, no. 24), where he cites Hostiensis. I give Hostiensis's own words (*Comm.* on *X* 5.1.24, 5:11A, no. 15, col. 2, v. *illi*): 'scilicet contra quem fit inquisitio venienti, vel procuratori suo, qui in hac causa intervenire potest, quia, etsi agatur de crimine, not tamen est causa criminalis, nisi quis personaliter sit citatus. . . vel nisi sit tale crimen quod executionem impediat' ('that is to the one against whom the inquisition is made, coming himself, or to his proctor, who can intervene in this case, since, even though it deals with a crime, nevertheless is not a criminal cause, . . . unless one is personally cited . . . or unless the crime is such that would impede fulfillment [of order, etc.]'). For Innocent III's *Inquisitionis* (1212), see *X* 5.1.21 (Friedberg, 2:741–2).

is true of canon law (that is, in ecclesiastical courts) in cases where the punishment remains the same, like those specified in *Inquisitionis*.[19] That is, to say, proctors are usually admitted in inquisitions. The distinction is made more simply by Bartholomew Bellencini (d. *ca.* 1478), who taught law at Ferrara and Bologna and served as an auditor of the Rota.[20] In his notes on Panormitanus's commentary on *Veniens*, he says: 'When a capital crime is prosecuted by inquisition, a proctor is admitted by the canons, but not by civil law'.[21]

It seems entirely reasonable that when defendants are charged with grave crimes they should be required to attend court in person. But in such instances were they permitted to be assisted or accompanied by an advocate? Or was there a body of law concerning advocates similar to the laws about proctors, prohibiting them in general but allowing them in exceptional cases? It seems not. Therefore, we must conclude that advocates were allowed. Albert Gandinus, a theorist contemporary with Durant (late thirteenth century) who was also a working judge, can guide us on this point. He says, when dealing with a different but related question (namely, whether an accused person being held in prison for homicide can be allowed a proctor for the preliminary matters of his case): 'It is conceded in civil cases and does not seem to be prohibited in criminal cases; therefore it seems to be conceded'.[22] Furthermore, Gandinus takes it for granted that advocates

---

19 Anthony da Butrio, *In libros Decretalium commentarii* on *X* 5.1.15 (*Veniens*) (Venice, 1578, repr. Turin, 1967), 5:7, no. 16: 'Si super crimine procedit per viam inquisitionis, legiste non admittunt procuratorem, quia ipsi non alterant penam ex modo procedendi; unde non intervenit, sicut non interveniret si ageretur per modum accusationis. . . . De jure autem canonico, ubi eadem est pena accusationis et inquisitionis, ut in criminibus exceptis de quibus in cap. *Inquisitionis*, . . . idem non intercedat'. Butrio should not be taken to imply that 'civilians' only worked in secular courts and canonists in the ecclesiastical forum; it was commonplace for both to serve in both venues.

20 L. Prosdocimi, 'Bellencini, Bartolomeo', *Dizionario biografico degli Italiani*, vol. 7 (Rome, 1965), p. 629.

21 Bartholomew Bellencini, comment added to the Venice 1592 edition of the works of Abbot Panormitanus (Nicholas Tudeschi), vol. 7 (on books 4–5 of the *Decretales*), fol. 70 note *g* (referring to the commentary on *X* 5.1.15, no. 11, fol. 67v): 'Quando agitur de crimine per viam inquisitionis, secundum canones admittitur procurator, secus de jure civili'. He adds that a defender can intervene in a crime that entails loss of benefice, and, similarly, in an inquisition a proctor or defender can intervene as long as the crime is not such as to impede fulfillment (of order), and the lords of the Rota have confirmed this by wide examination, in Decision 402 (I have not yet found the reference in question).

22 Albert Gandinus, *Tractatus de maleficiis*, ed. Hermann Kantorowicz, *Albertus Gandinus und das Strafrecht der Scholastik*, 2 vols. (Berlin, 1907), vol. 2: Rubric *Utrum procurator*

are allowed to serve in criminal cases, since he tells us how they should comport themselves in an *accusatio*. That is, they should be more cautious than in civil cases, because greater danger is involved.[23] His treatment of this subject, however, is surprisingly brief: it consists mainly of tactics to gain the favor of the judge for their clients.[24] We can see from this advice that advocates are able to speak in court for their clients, who are, of course, also present.

Other authorities of the time are even briefer in their pertinent references, but they say enough to assure us that advocates could and did engage in criminal prosecutions and defenses. For instance, Durant in his section *De advocato* says that no cleric can 'postulate' before a civil (that is, secular) judge in a criminal cause, except to supplicate for the accused.[25] He is clearly speaking of an *accusatio*, and is referring to the decree of the Fourth Lateran Council prohibiting clerics from participating in 'judgments of blood', that is, any court case that could result in death or mutilation.[26] Durant goes on to say that it would be safer to abstain from such a case altogether. Hostiensis agrees, because of the danger of incurring irregularity, whether one's client were convicted (and punished) or acquitted (and the accuser were punished).[27] The English jurists John Acton (writing in the 1340s) and William Lyndwood (writing in the 1420s) also concur.[28] But there would be no irregularity, according to Hostiensis, if the clerical advocate defended a client in a secular inquisition and secured an acquittal,

---

interveniat in maleficiis et quando, no. 3 (p. 114): 'Procurator ad predicta possit constitui, cum hoc concedatur in civilibus, nec in criminalibus videatur esse prohibitum, ergo videtur esse concessum', referring to Justinian, *Digest* 22.3.5, where the Ordinary Gloss says: 'Presumitur ergo licere omnia et fieri posse de jure et esse jure facta, nisi contra probetur'. See the edition of Johannes Fehius of Gailsdorf, *Corpus juris civilis cum glossa ordinaria*, 6 vols. (Lyons, 1627, repr. 1965–66), 1:2056, who sums up: 'Licita omnia jure presumuntur nisi illicita probentur'.

23 Gandinus, *Tractatus*, Rubric *Qualiter advocati circa accusationem se habere debeant* (p. 31): 'Et certe advocatus in his causis criminalibus debet se cautius habere quam in civilibus, nam ubi majus periculum vertitur, cautius est agendum'.

24 Ibid., pp. 31–34.

25 Durant, *Speculum* 1.3, *De advocato*, §1, *Objicitur*, no. 8 (1:261): 'In causa autem criminali, nullus clericus postulare potest coram judice civili, . . . nisi ut supplicet pro accusatis'.

26 Innocent III, *Sententiam sanguinis*, *X* 3.50. 9 (Friedberg, 2:659–60).

27 Hostiensis, *Comm.* on *X* 1.37.1 (1:182, no. 6): in defending the accused a cleric would be implicated in bloodshed (and therefore become irregular) if, because of his inexperience, the defendant were decapitated or mutilated, or if, because of his malice and cavillations, he were acquitted and the punishment unjustly inflicted on the accuser.

28 John Acton, *Annotationes in constitutiones legatinas* (appendix to Lyndwood), Const. Ottoboni tit. 7 v. *pro actoris parte* (p. 92); William Lyndwood, *Provinciale* 1.4.2 v. *advocatos in causa sanguinis* (Oxford, 1679, repr. Farnborough, 1968), pp. 29–30.

since in such a case there was no *talio* for an accuser.[29]

It follows that non-clerics are allowed and expected to participate in secular inquisitions and accusations, even serving as advocates for the accusers as well as the accused. There are other kinds of secular cases in which which clerics, especially those in major orders, were forbidden or discouraged from acting as advocates.[30] But they were able to partake in all trials in ecclesiastical courts, even accusations and inquisitions dealing with serious crimes, since judgments of blood were not to be found in that forum. As Acton says, it is the general custom of the Church not to prohibit clerics from acting as advocate or proctor before an ecclesiastical judge.[31] Durant observes that in criminal causes in which appeals can regularly be made, they can be made not only by the person condemned of a capital crime, but also by any outsider, even though the convicted defendant is unwilling.[32] How much more, then, could an advocate hired by or assigned to the defendant, make such an appeal.[33]

The decretal *Ex litteris* in the title, *De officio judicis,* was interpreted as requiring a judge to supply an advocate for a party that could not otherwise have one.[34] Though the case being dealt with is a civil litigation between two monasteries, in which the proctor of one asks the judge for an advocate, there seems to be no reason why the rule should not be also true of judges in accusations and inquisitions. John Andrew adds that it applies to certain persons who should be given advocates even if they do not ask, like women, orphans, the weak, those not of sound mind, and those who are

---

29 Hostiensis, *Comm.* on *X* 5.12.12 (5:47, no. 13 *in fine*). For the *talio*, or punishment of retaliation, see below, II, p. 407.

30 See the chapters of the title *De postulando*, *X* 1.37.1–3 (Friedberg, 2:210–11).

31 Acton, loc. cit., v. *exercere* (p. 91): 'Ille glosse dicunt contra, scilicet, illum clericum non prohiberi postulare vel procurare coram judice ecclesiastico. . . . Et hoc observat generalis ecclesie consuetudo'.

32 Durant, *Speculum* 2.3, *De appellationibus*, § 1, *Quis possit appellare*, no. 10 (1:829): 'In criminalibus autem, in quibus appellari potest regulariter, . . . non solum condemnatus de crimine capitali, sed etiam quilibet extraneus, etiam invito condemnato, admittitur ad appellandum pro eo'.

33 Hostiensis, loc. cit. in n. 27, makes this point about the clerical advocate: 'Immo et tali casu appellare posset etiam clericus a tali sententia, etiam invito reo, . . . et per consequens appellationem prosequi'.

34 Ordinary Gloss to *X* 1.32.1, *Ex litteris*, v. *implorando* (*Corpus juris canonici*, 2:420): 'Et hic patet quod ad officium judicis pertinet providere partibus de advocatis, si alias habere non possint. . . . Debet etiam attendere judex ut equa distributio advocatorum fiat'. See James Brundage, 'Legal Aid for the Poor and the Professionalization of Law in the Middle Ages', *Journal of Legal History* 9 (1988), 169–79.

unable to have them because of the power of their adversaries.[35]

Hostiensis deals with the problem of an advocate providing favor to someone 'in a condemned crime' and thereby falling under the same sentence of excommunication as the implicated criminal. He recommends that he continue to do his job, asking for absolution and arguing the injustice of the excommunication; for, he says, even an excommunicate deserves a legal offense. He goes on to say that the office of advocate is a just one and is granted as a means of defense; but if an advocate should act against justice and conscience in a condemned crime, then there is no doubt that the excommunication against the defendant includes the advocate as well.[36]

To leave the realm of theory, let me refer to cases of defense counsel being allowed in the following essays: a heresy conviction at Tours was overturned by the pope because the defendant, a man of military simplicity and ignorant of the law, was not given a *consiliarius* and lacked the counsel of *periti* (I, pp. 449–50). John Wyclif in his first trial was accompanied by four theologians and by other supporters (V, p. 4). At the Council of Rome, 1412–13, John XXIII called for defenders to give reason why Wyclif should not be posthumously condemned (V, p. 20), and the two proctors-promotors-instigators of the Council of Constance did the same (V, pp. 21, 23–24). At the latter council, defenders, including Peter Cauchon, were actually present in the posthumous trial of John Petit (III, pp. 1009–10; V, pp. 22–23). A proctor was admitted in the trial of John XXIII, though at the same time John Hus, who requested a proctor or advocate, was told that both were prohibited in heresy cases (V, p. 23). At the end of the council, Martin V ordered suspected heretics to be cited, 'with proctor and advocate removed' (V, p. 28; VI, p. 298). In both instances, there were legal grounds, as we have seen, for disallowing a proctor, but not for forbidding use of an advocate. In the trial of Joan of Arc, Cauchon, the expert defense attorney at Constance, belatedly offered to let her have the counsel of the judicial assessors (*consilium ab assistentibus*, *advis aux assistens*) (III, p. 1016), and he repeated the offer later: she could either choose one of them or he could

---

35 John Andrew, *Novella* on *X* 1.32.1 (1:261, no. 7).

36 Hostiensis, *Comm.* on *X* 5.27.8, *Proposuit* (5:68A, nos. 3–5): 'Vel potest intelligi quod tunc in crimine damnato prebebat ei consilium et favorem, et sic eadem fuit sententia involutus. . . . Quid ergo si quis in judicio, pro talibus scilicet, excommunicatus fuerit advocatus? Respondeo, si officium suum exequatur, ut debet, petendo scilicet absolutionem, sicut debet, vel defendendo ipsos et ostendendo quod injuste ligati sunt, sicut et verum est vel saltem verum putat, non accuso ipsum. Nam et excommunicato legitima defensio reservatur. . . . Et officium advocati justum est, et ad defensionem conceditur. . . . Si vero contra justitiam et conscientiam fovet ipsum in damnato crimine, haud dubium quin eadem sententia involvatur'.

appoint one himself (III, p. 1021). A proctor and defense lawyer were allowed to each defendant in the heresy inquisitions at Ciudad Real in 1483–85 (II, p. 421, n. 50). The concession of both proctor and advocate to a defendant in a heresy trial is one of the available defenses listed in the *Directorium inquisitorum* of Nicholas Eymerich (1376),[37] but only to be granted after due process has been violated by pre-arraignment interrogations (see III, pp. 1001–2). When Henry VIII was defendant in the inquisition trial of his marriage before Wolsey in 1527, he was represented by a proctor,[38] and in the famous legatine trial of 1529, both Henry and Catherine had proctors, though they sometimes appeared in person, and they were both assisted by counsellors.[39]

But the question of whether advocates were regularly used in criminal cases, or if not, why not, remains to be researched. In some cases, the answer is clear: they were unjustly prohibited, in a perversion of due process, as in the case of John Hus at the Council of Constance. On a more practical level, it seems likely that at least in the smaller courts there were few or no advocates to be found. Helmholz notes this for the diocesan consistory courts that he has studied in England, but he shows evidence that proctors were able to serve also as advocates.[40]

Sandrine Strobino has recently published an extant defense dossier that was submitted in a heresy (sorcery) case of 1467 in Sion (capital of the

---

[37] Nicholas Eymerich, *Directorium inquisitorum*, ed. Francisco Peña (Rome, 1578), pt. 3, § 117 (p. 296): 'Et sic concedetur sibi advocatus, probus tamen et de legalitate non suspectus, vir utriusque juris peritus et fidei zelator, et procurator pari forma' ('And so let an advocate be granted to him, but one who is upright and in no way legally suspect, a man learned in both laws and zealous for the faith, and, similarly, a proctor'). The formula of concession contained in § 120 (p. 298), in which the judge parries an appeal, indicates that the defendant can request specific persons for these roles: 'Ego reduco processum ad illum statum in quo talis petivit defensiones juris, et acquiesco petitioni sue, admittendo eum ad se defendendum; et concedo sibi juris defensiones, et mando sibi dari copiam processus, et concedo sibi talem quem petit in advocatum et talem in procuratorem, et sic ablato gravamine aufertur causa suspicionis, et recusatio jam sit nulla, juxta cap. *Cum cessante*, X *De appellationibus*' ('I restart the trial at the point when N. petitioned for legal defenses, and I consent to his petition by admitting him to defend himself; and I concede legal defenses to him and order the trial record given to him, and I grant him N., whom he has requested, for his advocate, and N. for his proctor; and so, with the grievance removed the cause of suspicion is taken away, and the recusal is null and void, in accord with *X* 2.28.60' [Friedberg 2:437]).

[38] Kelly, *Matrimonial Trials*, p. 25.

[39] Ibid., pp. 75–128; see pp. 79–80 for the proctors and p. 82 for the appointment of the queen's counsellors.

[40] R.H. Helmholz, *Marriage Litigation in Medieval England* (Cambridge, 1974), p. 150. He is speaking here, however, only of civil litigation, not of *ex officio* inquisitions.

modern canton of Valais in southern Switzerland). The procedure, which follows the general outlines of a 1428 ordinance of 'the Patriots', can be divined as follows from the dossier and the sentences of the prince-bishop, Walter Supersaxo. Upon accusation by three convicted persons and after a hearing (*cognitio*) of jurors (*jurati*) of the castellan, or judge of the first instance, the implicated person, in this case, a well-to-do widow named Fransa Bonvin, is put to torture by cord, after canonical admonitions, for several days; if she passes this ordeal, referred to as common purgation (*purgatio vulgaris*), then, at the instance (*clama*) of local parishioners, the castellan together with the bishop's notary-commissary can order a general inquest (*inquesta generalis*) on the basis of her *infamia* and other *indicia*. When the case comes to the bishop, the defendant asks to be admitted to her defenses, and the bishop by an interlocutory sentence assigns her a formal proctor (*legitimus procurator*), also called a defender (*defensorius*), who reviews and criticizes the accusations and formulates articles for defense witnesses to be questioned on. The witnesses (there were 67 in this instance) are also questioned on interrogatories attached to each article by the proctor of the faith. The bishop then gives sentence, in this case in favor of Fransa and against the proctor of the faith (*in odium procuratoris fidei*). Her acquittal is termed a canonical purgation. When Fransa was subsequently accused again by three other convicts, the same process was repeated, but her relatives and friends intervened after two general inquests had been conducted, and they petitioned the bishop to hold a *cognitio* to determine whether she should be tortured (further) or released. The castellan first presented the convicts' processes and the two inquests, and then the advocate (*advocatus*) of two supporters of Fransa (one of them being her former defender) successfully urged her release for various reasons, including lack of infamy and other *indicia*, discordant accusations, her previous canonical purgation, and her two common purgations.[41]

Another large defense dossier is to be found in the records of the inquisition against Cardinal John Morone in Rome in 1559, which also resulted in an acquittal. In this case, the defendant, who is variously represented by an advocate, a principal proctor, and lawyers designated as 'agentes, intercessores, et negotiorum gestores', formulated interrogatories to be attached to the articles of accusation before they were submitted to hostile witnesses, as well as forming articles of his own for defense witnesses (to which the prosecutor, that is, the proctor of the Apostolic Fisc,

---

[41] Sandrine Strobino, *Françoise sauvée des flammes? Une Valaisanne accusée de sorcellerie au XVe siècle* (Lausanne, 1996); see especially pp. 25, 114, 284–92.

attached interrogatories, as in the case of Fransa Bonvin).[42] In the related trial of the priest Dominic Morando, 1557–59, the defendant was interrogated many times without being charged; his requests for a proctor and advocate for defense were put off; finally, he was assigned a proctor, but then he was tortured, as a witness suspected of not having told the truth about others (his cries were recorded); finally, articles of accusation were culled from the interrogations, as in the case of Joan of Arc, and his proctor formulated interrogatories to accompany them.[43]

In the English common law, the criminal procedures were much different. Proctors were not used in any case. In 'private' criminal actions, that is, appeals of felony, which corresponded to the Roman *accusatio*, counsel was allowed to both accuser and accused. But when when the king was thought to be charging a felony *ex officio*, upon presentment by a jury, counsel was not allowed to the defendant (see IX, p. 388n, pp. 395–96). However, as David Seipp tells us, this latter rule was not always observed (IX, pp. 410–11). Nowadays, defendants in all criminal trials are still required to appear in court in person, but it is highly unusual for the defendant to act as his or her own defender (though he is ordinarily free to do so); usually, an attorney serves as defense counsel and speaks in the name of the defendant, much like the ecclesiastical (and civil-law) proctor of old, but in the defendant's presence, like Gandinus's criminal advocates. In common-law civil cases, however, attorneys did, and do, regularly act like proctors and represent their absent clients in court.

To sum up, I have tried to show in these studies that the rules of due process outlined at the Fourth Lateran Council for inquisitorial trials included safeguards comparable to those added to the United States Constitution in the Bill of Rights, and to demonstrate ways in which they were followed, ignored, abused, or modified in subsequent times, and how they compared with native-English systems. I hope that the data presented and analyzed here will stimulate more investigations into our common legal heritage.

None of these essays have been incorporated into my books, but have rather functioned as 'by-blows' of my larger projects. The earliest of them, Essay VII, combines my my interests in witchcraft and demonology[44] and

---

42 Massimo Firpo and Dario Marcatto, *Il processo inquisitoriale del Cardinal Giovanni Morone*, 6 vols. (Rome, 1981–95); see esp. 1:234; 2:150–51, 602–22; 3 (*I documenti difensivi*); 4 (*Il processo difensivo bolognese. La sentenza*) 83–145, 582.

43 Ibid., 5:61–223 (*Il processo di Domenico Morando*), esp. pp. 175, 187–89, 197–204.

44 H.A. Kelly, *The Devil, Demonology, and Witchcraft* (New York, 1968; rev. 1974); cf. *The Devil at Baptism* (Ithaca, 1985).

English history[45] with the study of the trials of Henry VIII, mentioned above. There is some repetition in the in the first six essays, and in Essays IX and X, because a certain amount of summary was necessary to make each article self-standing in its original form, but I hope that the summaries will prove helpful in focusing my arguments. In some articles I give a brief treatment of a subject that receives a fuller or more qualified treatment in a later article. For this reason, I have kept the articles in chronological order, with the notable exception of Essay VII, which I use as a transition from ecclesiastical to secular forms of procedure in England.

HENRY ANSGAR KELLY

UCLA, Los Angeles
December 2000

---

[45] H.A. Kelly, 'Canonical Implications of Richard III's Plan to Marry His Niece', *Traditio* 23 (1967), 269–311; *Divine Providence in the England of Shakespeare's Histories* (Cambridge, Mass., 1970).

ACKNOWLEDGEMENTS

Grateful acknowledgement is made to the following persons, journals, institutions and publishers for their kind permission to reproduce the papers included in this volume: the American Society of Church History, Duke University (I); Dr Peter Landau, Leopold-Wenger-Institut, Munich (II); the Medieval Academy of America, Cambridge, MA (III, V Addenda); Bonnie Wheeler (IV); Susan Green, Editor, *Huntington Library Quarterly* (V); E.J. Brill, Leiden (VI); the Pontifical Institute of Mediaeval Studes, Toronto (VII); Anne F. Sutton, Editor, *The Ricardian* (VIII); the Center for Medieval and Renaissance Studies, Los Angeles, CA (IX); Larry Scanlon, Editor, *Studies in the Age of Chaucer*.

I

Inquisition and the Prosecution of Heresy: Misconceptions and Abuses

The year 1988 marked the 100th anniversary of the publication of H. C. Lea's *A History of the Inquisition of the Middle Ages.* I would like to get the next century off to a good start by renaming his enterprise "A History of the Criminal Prosecution of Heretics in the Middle Ages."[1] The term *inquisition* has been widely misunderstood and misused by historians. There are two distinct abuses, one upper-case and the other lower-case.

When capitalized and given a definite article, as "the Inquisition" or "the Holy Office of the Inquisition," the term is often either personified and endowed with a diabolical omniscience or made to stand for a central intelligence agency with headquarters at the papal curia. Some authors clearly believe that there was a centralized Inquisition in the Middle Ages; others, such as Lea, know that this was not the case but frequently speak as if it were. Lea at times even uses the term "Holy Office" to mean "Holy Office-Building" or "Branch-Office-Building of the Holy Inquisition."[2]

In Lea's case the problem is faulty rhetoric rather than faulty knowledge; however, such misleading expressions are to be found not only in the writings of hostile polemicists but in those of "friendly witnesses" as well. For instance, Yves Dossat, an eminent historian of heresy prosecution of our own day, starts out his article on "Inquisition" in the *New Catholic Encyclopedia*

1. An earlier form of the present essay was delivered as a paper at a symposium organized by Edward Peters to mark the centenary of Lea's work, as part of the program of the Medieval Academy of America meeting held at the University of Pennsylvania, 7 April 1988. I should note that in my citation of medieval Latin (which was spelled and pronounced like the vernacular), I use *e* rather than the classical diphthong *ae*, in order to be more authentic and also to discourage the classical pronunciation of postclassical texts; for the same reasons I use *j* rather than consonantal *i*. See my "Lawyer's Latin: *Loquenda ut vulgus?*" *Journal of Legal Education* 38 (1988): 195–207, esp. 200–201. I also follow the convention of French and English historians of thirteenth-century heresy in translating proper names into the modern vernacular; for example, I render *Johannes Andree* as "John Andrew" (not "John of Andrew") rather than using the classicized form "Iohannes Andreae" or a medieval vernacular form.
2. Henry Charles Lea, *A History of the Inquisition of the Middle Ages*, 3 vols. (New York, 1888). Consider, for example, this passage: "The organization of the Inquisition was simple, yet effective. . . . The inquisitor wore the simple habits of his Order. . . . His principal scene of activity was in the recesses of the dreaded Holy Office, whence he issued his commands and decided the fate of whole populations in a silence and secrecy which impressed upon the people a mysterious awe a thousand times more potent than the external magnificence of the bishop. Every detail in the Inquisition was intended for work and not for show" (1:369).

thus: "The Inquisition was a special permanent tribunal established by Pope Gregory IX to combat heresy."[3] But elsewhere in the same encyclopedia it is pointed out that there was never a permanently constituted congregation and tribunal of inquisition against heresy until the sixteenth century.[4] Before then, there were only papal inquisitors, sometimes sporadically appointed, sometimes more permanently commissioned, but not organized over larger areas than individual dioceses, provinces, or kingdoms. Even the six *commissarii et inquisitores generales et generalissimi* appointed by Paul III in 1542, and their successors in the "Roman and Universal Inquisition" (the name given the congregation in 1588 by Sixtus V), functioned almost exclusively in Italy.[5] This point about the variety and diversity of medieval heresy inquisitions has been made especially by Richard Kieckhefer, who has rightly protested against referring collectively to these tribunals as the "the Inquisition." He has recently been joined in this campaign by Edward Peters, who has abundantly documented the development of the "the myth of *The Inquisition*."[6]

The remedying of this first abuse is in good hands, and I wish to turn my attention now to the lower-case abuse, to which even the upper-case opponents have sometimes fallen victim. I mean the use of the common noun "inquisition" by itself to designate a heresy prosecution, whereas historically it had a much wider meaning. This usage often stems from a confusion or misconception which is exemplified by the second sentence in Dossat's article. He writes: "It [the Inquisition] owed its name to the use of a new form of procedure created by Pope Innocent III, which permitted *ex officio* the searching out of persons accused of heresy."[7] This statement misleadingly suggests that the procedure of *inquisitio* instituted or formalized under Innocent III was primarily aimed at the suppression of heresy and was mainly used by the papally appointed inquisitors against heresy. Dossat acknowledges elsewhere that the procedure of inquisition was not invented for searching out heretics, but he maintains that it was admirably suited for that purpose.[8] Lea, too, was well aware that the *inquisitio* was not originally designed as a procedure against heresy or *only* against heresy, but he was clearly under the impression that it was rarely used outside of heresy

3. Yves Dossat, "Inquisition," *New Catholic Encyclopedia*, 16 vols. (New York, 1967), 7:535–541.
4. Ulric Beste, "Doctrine of the Faith, Congregation for the," *New Catholic Encyclopedia*, 4:944–946.
5. See Edward Peters, *Inquisition* (New York, 1988), pp. 105–121.
6. Ibid., pp. 1–7, 122–315; Richard Kieckhefer, *Repression of Heresy in Medieval Germany* (Philadelphia, 1979), pp. 3–7. Bernard Hamilton, *The Medieval Inquisition* (New York, 1981), p. 9, agrees with Kieckhefer's analysis, but not with his advice to abandon "the Inquisition" as a generic term to describe the work of medieval heresy tribunals.
7. Dossat, "Inquisition," pp. 535–536.
8. Yves Dossat, *Les crises de l'Inquisition toulousaine au xiiie siècle (1233–1273)* (Bordeaux, 1959), p. 107.

proceedings. He speaks of "this extraordinary power vested in the judge," that is, the bishop or ordinary. He seems to believe that of the three forms of procedure listed in the decretal *Qualiter et quando* from the Fourth Lateran Council in 1215, namely, *accusatio, denunciatio,* and *inquisitio*, the *denunciatio* was the usual method employed by the bishop as judge.[9] The reality is that the *inquisitio* was a new form of trial meant to replace the *accusatio*, which it did. The *denunciatio* was little more than an alternative method of starting an *inquisitio*; like the *accusatio*, it was rarely used, even though both *accusatio* and *denunciatio* continued to receive full treatment in canonistic commentaries.[10]

The *inquisitio ex officio* became the universal method of trial procedure in all ecclesiastical courts, except in "civil" actions or instance cases, where plaintiffs brought suits against defendants. The *inquisitio* was used at all levels, from the courts of archdeacons and rural archpriests or deans charging rustics with fornication or adultery to papally commissioned trials presided over by cardinals on charges brought against kings and queens.[11] For instance, all of Henry VIII's annulment trials were inquisitions.[12]

The medieval Latin sources always scrupulously distinguish between inquisition as a general process and inquisitio against heresy by referring to the latter as *inquisitio heretice pravitatis*, "inquisition of heretical depravity." But modern historians, especially English-speaking ones, have generally found this phrase too much of a mouthful and have used "inquisition" alone to do service for this specialized meaning, much as "therapy" in recent years has been used elliptically for "mental therapy," "chauvinism" for "male chauvinism," and "tenure" for "permanent tenure."[13] With all of these words

9. See Lea, *History*, 1:310. See *Decretales Gregorii IX* 5.1.24, *Qualiter et quando* no. 2, ed. Emil Friedberg, *Corpus iuris canonici*, 2 vols. (1879–81; reprint, Graz, 1959), 2:745–747. Hereafter, I will use the standard abbreviation *X* to refer to the *Decretales*. An early version of this decretal was issued in 1206, and it was also partially incorporated into Gregory IX's collection: *X* 5.1.17 *Qualiter et quando* no 1 (see n. 35 below). A still earlier decretal of Innocent III's, listing the three forms of procedure, deals with simony, namely *Licet Heli* (*X* 5.3.31), issued in 1199.
10. I intend to deal with these matters at greater length in a later study. For the time being, let me simply note that the trial records speak for themselves: accusations and denunciations are very scarce and inquisitions are the rule. For a rare example of a denunciation, from the year 1321 in the diocese of Rochester, see *Registrum Hamonis Hethe, Diocesis Roffensis, A.D. 1319–1352*, ed. Charles Johnson (Oxford, 1948), p. 218.
11. H. A. Kelly, *Love and Marriage in the Age of Chaucer* (Ithaca, N.Y., 1975), pp. 168–173; idem, *Canon Law and the Archpriest of Hita* (Binghamton, N.Y., 1984), pp. 51–54, 57–58, 91, 173.
12. H. A. Kelly, *The Matrimonial Trials of Henry VIII* (Stanford, 1976); idem, "English Kings and the Fear of Sorcery," *Mediaeval Studies* 39 (1977): 206–238.
13. The *Oxford English Dictionary*, 2d ed. (1989), gives the earliest instance of the restricted use of "tenure" as occurring in Vladimir Nabokov's 1957 novel *Pnin*. See my "Chaucer and Shakespeare on Tragedy," *Leeds Studies in English* 20 (1989), where I argue that the same phenomenon can be observed in the word "tragedy," which is often used elliptically for "great tragedy."

the ellipsis is often forgotten and the narrow meaning becomes primary. In my view, Peters would have been better advised to title his book *Heresy Inquisition* rather than *Inquisition*; as it is, he gives the impression, both in his title and throughout the book, that inquisition as a criminal procedure was specially designed for heresy trials.

But there is more to the matter than mere verbal abuse and confusion. Even the most careful historians of heresy prosecutions writing today sometimes seem to believe that heresy judges, especially papally appointed heresy inquisitors, had far greater legal powers—and heresy defendants were legally denied far more defenses—than was in fact the case. Thus, for example, we find Kieckhefer stating that "the inquisitors to whom the *officium inquisitionis* was entrusted had powers that other judges did not possess, as H. C. Lea and other scholars have repeatedly made clear."[14] My short response to this is a simple denial: the papal heresy judges did not have greater powers than other judges, and historians who have claimed otherwise (which does not include Lea) are mistaken. My more qualified response is that one must distinguish between powers that such "judges delegate" had *de jure* and powers that they exercised illegally, *de facto* but *contra jus*; and one must remember that papal inquisitors had no greater *procedural* powers than bishops in their dioceses. Lea himself admits that "technically there was no difference between the episcopal and papal Inquisitions."[15]

One should add that since the bishops were ordinary judges with jurisdictions not only over heresy but over every kind of offence, they had far more power than did the papal inquisitors, who had authority only over cases of heresy and were under the same restrictions as other delegated judges. But granted Lea's point that when bishops dealt with heresy they had the same powers as papal inquisitors, *were* these powers much greater than those allowed in other cases? Lea says yes: "The equitable system of procedure borrowed from the Roman law by the courts of the Ordinaries was cast aside, and the bishops were permitted and even instructed to follow the inquisitorial system, which was a standing mockery of justice—perhaps the most iniquitous that the arbitrary cruelty of man has ever devised."[16] In demonstrating his assertion, however, Lea constantly shifts between denouncing abusive laws and revealing abuses of laws. In other words, he is not clear on how far inquisitors were permitted by law to modify procedures in cases of heresy and how far they violated or distorted legal procedures.

More recent scholars have done little to clarify the confusion. For instance,

14. Richard Kieckhefer, review of A. Patschovsky, *Quellen zur bömische Inquisition im 14. Jahrhundert* (1979), in *Speculum* 56 (1981): 899–901. For a typical listing of these alleged
* special inquisitorial powers, see James Given, "The Inquisitors of Languedoc and the Medieval Technology of Power," *American Historical Review* 94 (1989): 336–359, esp. 339.

15. Lea, *History*, 1:364.

16. Ibid.

Bernard Hamilton, who says there are excellent studies of the judicial status of the papal heresy inquisitors, concludes from these studies that "on paper their powers were almost unlimited."[17] Some of the precisions and qualifications he goes on to make are accurate, but some are not, because he does not study the inquisitorial norms incumbent on all judges. The same is true even of Henri Maisonneuve, who provides valuable citations of canonistic commentaries on the title *De hereticis* in the *Decretals* of Gregory IX and the *Sext* of Boniface VIII but nothing on the title *De accusationibus, inquisitionibus, et denunciationibus* or on the general court procedures mandated for all kinds of cases.[18] For, once an inquisition moved beyond its initial phase, it was meant to follow pretty much the rules for other forms of trial. These rules were most abundantly set forth by William Durant, "the Speculator," in his massive handbook *Speculum judiciale* ("Judicial Mirror"), the final version of which was finished around 1289.

The thesis that I wish to propose is that there was not a single provision of the original *ordo juris* or rules of procedure for inquisition that privileged heresy cases over all other kinds of cases or limited due process for persons charged with heresy in ways that were not permitted for persons charged with other crimes. In later years two exceptions were made: the use of summary procedure and the suppression of the names of witnesses. But the first was soon defined out of existence, in effect, and only the second was given the force of permanent law.

Summary or abbreviated procedure was allowed or ordered in individual trials of various kinds. It was first permitted to papal heresy inquisitors as early as 1255, when Alexander IV authorized it for the Dominicans of Paris.[19] It was allowed by Boniface VIII in 1298 for all heresy trials (that is, whether conducted by bishops or by papally commissioned inquisitors).[20] The formula used by the pope, *simpliciter et de plano et absque advocatorum ac judiciorum strepitu et figura* ("simply and plainly and without the uproar and form of lawyers and judgments"), had been interpreted by some canonists as allowing the exclusion of lawyers and all rules of procedure.[21] But Clement V in 1314 decreed that no necessary proofs or defenses were to be excluded, and earlier, in 1312, he had permitted summary procedure in all sorts of cases, concerning benefices, tithes, marriage, and so on.[22]

17. Hamilton, *Medieval Inquisition*, p. 10.
18. See especially Maisonneuve's *Etudes sur les origines de l'Inquisition* (Paris, 1960), pp. 287–356.
19. See Alexander's bull *Cupientes* in Paul Frédéricq, *Corpus documentorum inquisitionis haereticae pravitatis neerlandicae*, vol. 1 (Ghent, 1889), pp. 123–124 no. 130.
20. *Sext* 5.2.20 *Statuta* (Friedberg 2:1078). An earlier use in a nonheresy case can be found in Gregory IX's decretal *Olim* (*X* 5.1.26; Friedberg 2:747).
21. See Charles Lefebvre, "Les origines romaines de la procédure sommaire aux XII et XIII s.," *Ephemerides iuris canonici* 12 (1956): 149–197, esp. 191–192.
22. *Clementines* 2.1.2 *Dispendiosam*, A.D. 1312, and 5.11.2 *Sepe*, A.D. 1314 (Friedberg 2:1145, 1200).

As for the concealment of the names and identities of witnesses from defendants in heresy trials, at least some authorities in the thirteenth century asserted that there was papal approval for this deviation from the *ordo juris*; this was the claim of the bishops of the provinces of Narbonne, Arles, and Aix at the Council of Narbonne around 1244.[23] Heresy judges did sometimes receive such approval, like the Dominican inquisitors addressed in 1254 by
* Innocent IV in the bull *Cum negotium*. But when a provision of this sort was eventually incorporated into canon law, it was in a much less rigorous form, in Boniface VIII's decretal *Statuta:* the names are to be suppressed only when revealing them would put the witnesses in real danger.[24] However, according to the *Repertorium inquisitorum,* the first edition of which was published in Valencia in 1494, the routine suppression of names in all heresy cases had become a "custom of inquisition," and support for this custom was found in Innocent's *Cum negotium*. A note to this effect is found in the 1582 official edition of the *Sext*.[25]

Other alleged privileges of heresy judges or restrictions on heresy defendants turn out to be nonexistent, either misinterpretations by historians or violations or distortions of the law by the judges themselves, "well-intentioned" or otherwise.

I dismiss without further ado the modern notion that defendants in any canonical process, inquisitorial or not, were presumed guilty until proven innocent. No one could be legally convicted of a crime without adequate proof. I should add, however, that if it was proven that a person was considered guilty in the community, he could be required to counter this opinion by compurgation, that is, by having acquaintances swear that they believed his denial of guilt. In the matter of heresy, one could be convicted on the lesser charge of suspicion of heresy if heretical connections were proved.

As for torture, it was the standard canonistic doctrine that all ecclesiastical

23. Council of Narbonne, chap. 22 (Mansi, *Concilia*, 23:362); this is also the claim of the *Processus inquisitionis*, ed. A. Tardif and F. Balme, "Document pour l'histoire de *processus per inquisitionem* et de l'*inquisitio heretice pravitatis*," *Nouvelle revue historique* 7 (1883): 669–678, p. 673, where the authorization of Gregory IX and Innocent IV is alleged. Dossat attributes the manual to the Dominicans Bernard Caux and John Saint-Pierre, inquisitors at Toulouse since 1245 and at Carcassonne as well since September 1248, dating it to the end of 1248 or beginning of 1249 (*Crises*, p. 167). It is listed as Manual number two by Antoine Dondaine, "Le manuel de l'inquisiteur (1230–1330)," *Archivum fratrum praedicatorum* 17 (1947): 85–194, esp. 97–101, and said to be unquestionably the work of the inquisitors of Narbonne, the Dominicans William Raymond and Peter Durant (Dossat maintains that this is a mistaken judgment). It is reprinted by Kurt-Victor Selge, *Texte zur Inquisition* (Gütersloh, 1967), pp. 70–76, using Dondaine's title, *Ordo processus Narbonnensis*, with no reference to Dossat's rival attribution.
24. *Sext* 5.2.20 (Friedberg 2:1078); Lea, *History*, 1:438.
25. *Corpus juris canonici*, 3 vols. (1582; reprint, Lyons, 1606), 3:1:645, note to *Sext* 5.2.20, referring to *Repertorium inquisitorum* (1575; reprint, Venice, 1588), pp. 360–361. The 1494 edition of this work, compiled by Michael Albert, J.U.D., of Valencia, was titled *Repertorium perutile de pravitate hereticorum et apostatarum*. The discussion in question is on Sig. Biiii^{rv}, in the entry *Nomina*.

judges were able to employ it, especially the torture of vacillating witnesses or those of "vile condition." Huguccio in the twelfth century formulated the rule that ecclesiastical judges should employ only moderate forms of torture, which John Andrew in the fourteenth century interpreted to mean rods or switches or leather whips rather than the rack or claws and cords.[26] Eventually, restrictions were placed on the use of torture by papally appointed heresy inquisitors because of reported abuses. Such restrictions were not specified for other judges.[27] *

Persons accused of heresy had a right to be defended by legal counsel, just * like persons accused of other crimes. Only actual heretics, that is, persons judicially convicted of heresy, were forbidden lawyers.[28] If one wants to find a legal system in which persons who were only charged with a felony were denied a trial lawyer, one can look to the English common law. This infringement of the defendant's rights was eliminated only in 1836.[29]

Defendants in heresy inquisitions had the right to appeal from the judge (whether bishop or papal inquisitor) to the pope himself at any point in the trial where they believed that their rights of defense were being violated. That such appeals could be made and actually were made and acted on during the fourteenth century can be seen in J. M. Vidal's *Bullaire*.[30] The idea that appeals were not allowable in heresy trials is a figment of historians caused by overreading phrases like *omni appellatione remota* ("every appeal removed") which appear in many papal letters to heresy inquisitors. The fact of the matter is that the same phrases commonly occur in other kinds of papal commissions, and they were explained by Innocent III in 1204 in the decretal *Pastoralis* as practically meaningless: they meant only that no *frivolous* appeals were to be allowed.[31] It is true that Boniface VIII's decretal *Ut inquisitionis* stipulated that appeals were forbidden to heretics, which could be interpreted to mean that once a trial was over the convicted persons could not enter an appeal against unfair proceedings (for example, a judge's refusal to allow an appeal *during* the trial). But such appeals were in fact made and accepted, as Vidal shows.[32]

26. See John Andrew's *Novella* (finished in 1338) on *X* 5.41.6 (1581, reprint, Turin, 1963), 5:161 no. 3, citing Huguccio, referring to Gratian, *Decretum* 2.23.5.1 *Circumcelliones* (Friedberg 1:928–929). See my *Canon Law and the Archpriest of Hita*, pp. 110–111, 184–185.
27. See *Clem.* 5.3.1 *Multorum querela* (Friedberg 2:1181–1182).
28. *X* 5.7.11 *Si adversus* (Friedberg 2:783–784). Even Peters alleges that heresy defendants were restricted in their use of lawyers (*Inquisition*, p. 67). Hamilton first says, rightly, that defendants could use lawyers (p. 44), but then he says that they were not allowed in certain conditions (p. 45). The latter may have been true in practice, but it contravened the *ordo juris*.
29. See David Mellinkoff, *The Conscience of a Lawyer* (St. Paul, 1973), pp. 47–62.
30. J. M. Vidal, *Bullaire de l'inquisition française au xive siècle et jusqu'à la fin du grand schisme* (Paris, 1913).
31. *X* 5.28.53 (Friedberg 2:432).
32. *Sext* 5.2.18 *Ut inquisitionis* (Friedberg 2:1077); Vidal, *Bullaire*, pp. lxxii–lxxiii.

The admission of tainted or criminous witnesses in heresy inquisitions was not peculiar to heresy cases but applied to other "exempt" crimes, namely, treason, or *lesa majestas*, and simony. It was justified by Innocent III for simony in the decretal *Licet Heli* of 1199.[33]

Now that we have dispersed these obfuscations, let us try to get a clear view of what constituted inquisition, the new general form of trial instituted by Innocent III, and see how heresy prosecutors adopted it, adapted it, and eventually abused it.

The essence, or "specific difference," of inquisition was that instead of an accuser the judge himself presented the charges against a defendant.[34] But Pope Innocent did not want it thought that the judge was somehow acting as an accuser in initiating the trial; rather, the action was to be started by public opinion: "non tanquam idem sit accusator et judex, sed, quasi deferente fama vel denunciante clamore, officii sui debitum exequatur" ("not as though the accuser and the judge are the same, but rather, with fame as it were serving as informant or outcry being the denouncer, the judge is to carry out the duty of his office").[35] According to this procedure, therefore, only public crimes publicly connected to a specific person were eligible for prosecution; the judge could inquire (that is, start an inquisition) *ex officio* only against someone who was "infamous" by reputation. The required procedure was that he charge an individual with committing a certain crime on the basis of *publica fama*, which he had to establish before proceeding to the charge itself. That is, he had to prove that trustworthy members of the community considered the defendant guilty before he could require him to plead guilty or not guilty, and if he pleaded not guilty, the judge had to offer proof of guilt. The person charged had to be present, and the chapters of inquiry (that is, the charges) had to be given and explained to him and all rights of defense allowed.

33. *X* 5.3.31, repeated and clarified in *Per tuas*, A.D. 1204, *X* 5.3.32 (Friedberg 2:760–762). The admission of *infames* and *criminosi* to testify against those who have left the faith antedates Innocent's invention of the inquisition; it is stated as permissible by Gratian in his dictum before 2.2.7.23 *Alieni erroris* (Friedberg 1:488). I should note that the rubric to canon 23 as Friedberg puts it, *Infames hereticos accusare non possunt* ("The infamous cannot accuse heretics"), belies Gratian's meaning; the older edition of the *Corpus juris canonici* cited above (n. 25), 1:691, gives a correct rubric: *Infames et haeretici homines bonae famae accusare non possunt* ("The infamous and heretics cannot accuse men of good fame").

34. In some cases there was a *promovens* who initiated and prosecuted the charges; examples can be found in the Rochester register (n. 10 above), pp. 479, 615, 784, 941, 1075 (compare 956). Eventually, there emerged two different kinds of *promotor*: an *ad hoc* assistant to the judge appointed in a specific case, called *promotor judicis officii*, who helped to formulate charges; and a permanent *promotor* who acted like an independent prosecuting attorney. For the former, see my "English Kings and the Fear of Sorcery," p. 225 n. 75, and my *Matrimonial Trials of Henry VIII*, pp. 23, 80, 89–90; for an example of the latter, see Vidal, *Bullaire*, p. 498.

35. Innocent III, *Qualiter et quando* no. 1 (see n. 9 above), a passage omitted by Raymund of Pennafort from *X* 5.1.17 but repeated in *Qualiter et quando* no. 2 (*X* 5.1.24; Friedberg 2:738, 746).

This procedure, which was allegedly so ideally suited for the prosecution of heresy, actually presented heresy-hunters with real puzzles, which Innocent III and subsequent commentators did little to solve, especially after Gregory IX in 1231 elevated "believers" to the category of "heretics."[36] There is a general prohibition in church law against the public prosecution of secret crimes—"Ecclesia de occultis non judicat"[37]—and a specific prohibition against it in inquisitorial procedure.[37a]

The bishops at the Council of Narbonne attempted to answer some of the questions posed by the Dominican heresy inquisitors. I have mentioned their allegation of papal permission for suppressing names of witnesses. They approved of another policy for which they did not claim an exemption, but which could be contrary to the *ordo juris*: in the preliminary information-gathering inquisitions the inquisitors could make persons testify "generaliter *de se* et de aliis" ("in a general way *about themselves* and about others").[38] Self-incriminatory testimony, especially if required under oath, would be regular only for a person who had voluntarily confessed to guilt. The bishops did warn the inquisitors not to condemn anyone without open and lucid proofs, and they specified the sort of external manifestations that were necessary to identify believers.[39] However, they did not indicate how suspected believers should be summoned and tried.

In an as yet unpublished collection of guidelines and procedures for heresy judges (which Antoine Dondaine lists as his fifth manual), to be dated shortly after 1265, though perhaps in its original form going back to Toulouse around 1256, the account of the preliminary inquisition matches that of the Council of Narbonne: all adults must say what they know "tam de se quam

36. *X* 5.7.15 *Excommunicamus* no. 2 (Friedburg 2:789). For the text of the whole letter, dated February 1231, see Selge, *Texte zur Inquisition*, pp. 41–42, who takes it from Lucien Auvray, *Les registres de Gregoire IX*, vol. 1 (Paris, 1896), no. 539. Friedberg gives only Raynaldi's date of 1229. This decretal declares "believers in the errors of heretics" to be themselves heretics, in contrast with the decree of the Fourth Lateran Council, *Excommunicamus* no. 1 (*X* 5.7.13), par. 5, where "believers of heretics" (this can be interpreted either as believers in the good character of heretics or believers in the good character of their teachings) are included in the lesser category of supporters of heretics. However, in a still earlier decretal, Lucius III's *Ad abolendam* (A.D. 1184), excommunication is decreed against the wrong thinker (*aliter sentiens*) as well as against the wrong teacher (Friedberg 2:780).

37. *X* 5.3.33 *Sicut* and 34 *Tua nos* (Friedberg 2:762–763), and see Stephen Kuttner, "Ecclesia de occultis non iudicat," *Acta congressus iuridici internationalis . . . 1934*, vol. 3 (Rome, 1936), pp. 225–246. Compare John Andrew, *Novella* on *X* 2.18.2 *Cum super* (2:108A nos. 4–5), who concludes: "Nulla ergo equitas potest movere judicem ut reum interroget de occultis. Equitate autem deficiente non est locus interrogationi judiciali."

37a. *X* 5.1.21 *Inquisitionis negotium* (Friedberg 2:741–742). I deal with this question at length in "The Inquisitorial Prosecution of Secret Crimes," forthcoming in the proceedings of the Eighth International Congress of Medieval Canon Law, held at the University of California, San Diego, in August of 1988, to be published in the Subsidia series of the Vatican Library's Monumenta iuris canonici.

38. Council of Narbonne, chap. 27.

39. Ibid., chaps. 23 and 29.

de aliis."[40] But in the formula for citing an individual to trial the person is said to labor under infamy, and the trial is to determine whether the infamy corresponds to the truth. The rest of the *ordo processus* is in accord with the rule of law.[41] However, the same manual contains an anonymous consultation that advises the inquisitor to use threats and deceit and even torture and imprisonment against defendants who deny heretical connection and who demand the opportunity of defending themselves *secundum juris ordinem*.[42]

From the fragmentary records of early trials, or from historians' fragmentary reports of more complete records, it is usually hard to tell exactly what procedures were being followed. But the records of the inquisitions held by the bishop of Carcassonne between 1250 and 1258, sometimes with the participation of the Dominican inquisitors, seem to indicate that care was taken not to bring suspects to trial without definite charges and proof and not to violate procedure in any other way.[43] But when we see the Dominicans operating again in the same city in the 1270s, as far as their practices can be deduced from Dondaine's sixth manual, the situation is much different.[44] Now confessions are secured by clearly irregular means, without establishing infamy, without giving chapters of charges, and by making defendants take an oath to testify *de se* on unspecified questions.

In 1291 the king of France, Philip the Fair, who would later oversee the inquisitorial extermination of the Knights Templar on outrageously bogus charges, intervened at Carcassonne and ordered the seneschal not to arrest or imprison anyone on the commands of the inquisitors unless he was a self-confessed heretic or was considered a heretic on the testimony of several trustworthy men.[45] Philip's insistence on the *ordo juris* does not seem to have affected the irregular trial procedures of the inquisitors, at least not for long, since the inquisitor of Carcassonne in the early 1300s, Geoffrey of Arblis, was still using a self-incriminatory oath, and a similar formula was used by James Fournier, bishop of Pamiers from 1318 to 1325 (he later became Pope Benedict XII).[46]

40. Manual 5, Vatican lat. MS 3978, fols. 17–38: chap. 9 (fol. 32). See Dondaine, "Le manuel de l'inquisiteur (1230–1330)," pp. 106–107, 141–146. For the dating, see Dossat, *Crises*, p. 199.
41. Manual 5, chap. 23 (fols. 35–36v).
42. Ibid., chap. 4 (fols. 25v–26).
43. Célestin Douais, ed., *Documents pour servir à l'histoire de l'Inquisition dans le Languedoc*, 2 vols. (Paris, 1900), 2:115–301.
44. Manual 6: *Doctrina de modo procedendi contra hereticos*, ed. Edmund Martène, *Thesaurus novorum anecdotorum*, vol. 5 (1717; reprint, New York, 1968), pp. 1795–1814. See Dossat, *Crises*, pp. 202–204.
45. See, for example, Malcolm Barber, *The Trial of the Templars* (Cambridge, 1978). For Philip's letter, see Claude de Vic and Joseph Vaissette, rev. Auguste Milinier et al., *Histoire generale de Languedoc*, 16 vols. (Toulouse, 1872–1904), 10:273–274. Philip's letter of 5 September 1298 supporting Boniface VIII's *Ut inquisitionis* (*Sext* 5.2.18), ibid., cols. 276–278, should not be taken as rescinding the 1291 cautions on due process.
46. L. Tanon, *Histoire des tribunaux de l'Inquisition en France* (Paris, 1893), p. 348 n. 1. Jean

In the meantime, in 1298, a change had occurred in the rules of procedure for inquisitions of all sorts (that is, not just against heretics). Earlier in the century, the authoritative Cardinal Hostiensis had declared that an inquisitory trial was void if the judge failed to charge a defendant or if he started to question witnesses about a suspect's guilt before the person's infamy was established. Boniface VIII in his *Liber sextus* (1298) issued two laws that invalidated Hostiensis's opinion and had the effect of removing part of the burden that Innocent III had placed on the judge's conscience and making it more a matter of the defendant's alertness or knowledge of the law. According to the first statute, *Postquam*, if a defendant confesses a crime to a delegated judge, he cannot then object that he was not first "defamed" or charged.[47] In other words, he must make his objection at the beginning (and if the judge fails to comply with the rules, he has the right to remain silent and to appeal). The second statute, *Si is*, similarly allows a delegated judge to proceed without establishing infamy if the defendant does not object.[48] Defendants still have the right to the proper *ordo juris*, and the judges have the obligation to follow it, but one can see that these laws might easily lessen a judge's concern for doing so. In one of Bishop Fournier's heresy trials, when a defendant, on being required to tell the truth about those things he had been charged with, asked to know exactly what the charges were, the bishop told him *de gratia* ("as a favor").[49] It therefore seems that Fournier, in this case at least, did not consider the specification of charges to be a right of the defendant but an option of the judge that he could exercise at his discretion.

It became standard procedure in many heresy tribunals that instead of following the canonical rules of charging the defendant with a public crime and offering him the chance to defend himself against all documentary and testimonial proofs that were produced, the inquisitors would make the defendant guess why he had been summoned to trial and would question him on his beliefs and actions in the hope of confirming their suspicions or uncovering new grounds for prosecution.

In one case that reached the pope on appeal in 1323 it was alleged that the

Duvernoy, *Le registre d'inquisition de Jacques Fournier, évêque de Pamiers (1318–1325)*, 3 vols. (Toulouse, 1965; a pamphlet of corrections was issued in 1972): see 1:40 for the formula used in the first recorded case, 9 August 1319. The Dominican vice-inquisitor is noted as assisting at the bishop's proceedings.

47. *Sext* 5.1.1 *Postquam* (Friedberg 2:1069). John Andrew, in the *Glossa ordinaria*, on the word *postquam*, *Corpus juris canonici*, 3:609–610, states explicitly that the opinions of Hostiensis are corrected by this decretal and the next. For Hostiensis on the failure to present charges, see his *Commentaria* to *X* 5.1.24 (1581; reprint, Turin, 1965), 5:11A no. 15.

48. *Sext* 5.1.2 *Si is* (Friedberg 2:1069). See Hostiensis on *X* 5.1.17, *Commentaria*, 5:5A–6 nos. 4–6. The canonists held that ordinary judges already had the power to proceed without establishing infamy; see John Andrew's gloss on this decretal at the word *fuerat* (col. 610), and see his *Novella* on *X* 5.1.25 (5:15A no. 10).

49. Duvernoy, *Registre*, 2:204, case of Arnaud Tesseyre. Later, after becoming Pope Benedict XII, Fournier accepted the appeal of a man who was denied the copy of the inquisitorial process held against him in his absence (Vidal, *Bullaire*, p. 44).

defendant, Jean l'Archévêque, lord of Parthenay, had been put into prison by the inquisitor of Tours and allowed no counsel to help him deal with the charges that were levied or intended to be levied against him, even though he was a man of military simplicity and ignorant of the law.[50] The same could have been said of Joan of Arc in 1431, who was imprisoned and grilled for a month without counsel before being charged.[51] In both cases there were hostile judges who refused appeals, but Parthenay's family managed to get the appeal sent directly to the papal curia, much as Catherine of Aragon's supporters would be able to do, even though her direct appeals were turned down by her legatine inquisitors in the trial of 1529. Joan of Arc could easily have been liberated from the Rouen inquisition (if not from the Rouen prison) if only her French allies had taken the trouble to have the case advoked to Rome. Eventually, a review of the trial was instituted by the pope, at the petition of Joan's mother and brothers, and their proctor submitted a list of 101 detailed objections to the proceedings.[52] Surprisingly, he made no objections to the violations of the inquisitorial process. Nor were such points raised by any of the other jurists who participated in the retrial—with the exception of a doctor of canon law named Jean de Montigny.[53] Things had come to a sorry pass when the very substance of the inquisitorial procedure was so routinely ignored that violations were no longer recognized as such.

The obligation of judges to establish *publica fama* and to make specific charges against defendants was still stipulated in canon law, however, and it received renewed emphasis in Elias Regnier's 1483 commentary on Boniface VIII's modifications of the *ordo juris* in the *Sext*. A few years later Regnier's comments were incorporated by Jean Chappuis into his editions of the *Sext*, and they remained enshrined in the *Corpus juris canonici*, including the papally authorized edition of 1582 and its reprints, for the following centuries.[54]

In conclusion, inquisition was a brilliant and much-needed innovation in trial procedure, instituted by the greatest lawyer-pope of the Middle Ages. It served the generality of church courts very well and formed the basis of modern Continental criminal procedure. The abusive practices that came to

50. Vidal, *Bullaire*, pp. 77–83.
51. Paul Doncoeur and Yvonne Lanhers, eds., *Instrument public des sentences portées les 24 et 30 mai 1431 par Pierre Cauchon et Jean le Maître, O.P., contre Jeanne la Pucelle* (Paris, 1954); and Pierre Tisset, ed. (with Yvonne Lahers), *Procès de condemnation de Jeanne d'Arc*, 3 vols. (Paris, 1960–1971). I follow the traditional vocabulary in considering the brief proceedings in which Joan was condemned as relapsed on 30 May to be part of the original trial.
52. Pierre Duparc, ed., *Procès en nullité de la condemnation de Jeanne d'Arc*, 4 vols to date (Paris, 1977–1986), 1:111–150 (modern French translation, 3:103–144).
53. Ibid., 2:266–317: *Opinio domini Johannis de Montigny, decretorum doctoris*; see esp. pp. 293–294. Duparc is preparing a fifth volume which will contain a commentary on the consultations.
54. I give details in the essay mentioned in n. 37a above.

prevail in the special heresy tribunals do not merit the name of inquisition, but rather should be identified as a perversion of the inquisitorial process caused by overzealous and underscrupulous judges. Part of the blame lay with the great canonistic commentators of the time, who failed to confront the theoretical and practical problems raised by the prosecution of heresy and who failed to instruct the inquisitors. Many of the inquisitors were trained in theology rather than in law, and they came by their ignorance honestly; and such honest ignorance has persisted to our own day.

II

Inquisitorial due process and the status of secret crimes

In this paper I will first review the laws of inquisitorial procedure in general, but with an emphasis upon the public aspects of the requirements. Then I will discuss some of the theoretical and practical difficulties posed by occult sins and crimes.*

I. Inquisitorial Procedure

The first title of the fifth book of the *Decretals of Gregory IX* deals with three kinds of criminal proceedings: accusation, denunciation, and inquisition. Accusation was the old Roman form, which required an accuser willing to bring charges against a defendant *sub pena talionis*. This meant that if he failed to prove the guilt of the accused, he himself would have to suffer the penalty assigned to the crime in question. Denunciation and inquisition were forms invented, for all practical purposes, by Innocent III as substitutes for accusation. In a denunciation, a specific person brought a charge against an alleged culprit after having first admonished him to amend his ways, without success. In an inquisition, the informant or informants were unacknowledged as such, and they would enter the case, if at all, only as witnesses, or, sometimes, as *promoventes*. In both denunciation and inquisition the judge conducted the case himself, and the denunciation became in effect an inquisition once the trial got under way. Denunciation as well as accusation pretty much faded away in practice, though both forms continued

---

* A note on texts and names: Since medieval Latin was pronounced like the vernacular, I transcribe it and spell it in the same way as the vernacular, using *j* and *v* for consonants and *i* and *u* only for vowels, and keeping *e* for the archaic diphthongs *ae* and *oe*; hence *Johannes Andree* rather than the classicized form *Iohannes Andreae*. See my 'Lawyers' Latin, *Loquenda ut Vulgus*?' *Journal of Legal Education* 38 (1988) 195-207, esp. 200-01. For proper personal names, I follow the example of modern historians of thirteenth-century heresy in translating them into the present-day vernacular: hence, in French, 'Jean André', and in English, 'John Andrew' (not 'Jean d'André' or 'John of Andrew'), rather than a Latin or medieval vernacular form.

to be fully treated by commentators;[1] and inquisition became the dominant form of criminal trial in all ecclesiastical courts, from the lowest to the highest, whether presided over by ordinary or delegated judges.

Antecedents or parallels to Innocent III's formulation of the inquisitorial system can be found both in ecclesiastical circles[2] and in secular governments.[3] But it was Innocent's legislation that was decisive and normative. The *ordo juris* of inquisition, as set forth in the decretals, was to be followed by every judge, including the papally delegated inquisitors into heresy. As judges delegate, these latter had no powers beyond other judges delegate; as judges of heresy cases, they had no powers greater than those of ordinary judges when hearing heresy cases. Contrary to what is often believed, the crime of heresy did not have a monopoly on torture or summary procedure, or even the use of criminous witnesses; such witnesses were also allowed for the other exempt crimes of simony and *lesa majestas*, whether the trials were inquisitorial or not. It is not true that defendants in heresy cases were forbidden counsel or the right of appeal. That they were sometimes denied these and other rights of due process, even in the name of the law, is a matter of record; but one should not think that these abuses were sanctioned by any legal approbation in the canons or other papal decrees. Eventually heresy did receive a unique exemption: when witnesses were endangered the judge could suppress their names.[4] I will return to the question of how heresy inquisitors were supposed to proceed and how they actually proceeded, especially in cases involving secret sins or 'unpublished' heretical beliefs.

---

[1] A full-fledged accusation with precisely described procedures is given in the fourteenth-century poem of Juan Ruiz, *El libro de buen amor*: Wolf accuses Fox of stealing and eating a chicken, and Judge Monkey gives a learned commentary on the canonical rules that had to be followed even in the secular courts. See my *Canon law and the archpriest of Hita* (Medieval and Renaissance Texts and Studies no. 27; Binghamton NY 1984) Chapter 4, 'Procedure in the court of Don Ximio'.

[2] Jehan Dahyot-Dolivet, 'La procédure judiciaire d'office dans l'Eglise jusqu'à l'avènement du pape Innocent III', *Apollinaris* 41 (1968) 443-55. See also n. 65 below.

[3] R.C. van Caenegem, 'Public prosecution of crime in twelfth-century England', in *Church and government in the middle ages, essays presented to C. R. Cheney*, ed. C.N.L. Brooke et al. (Cambridge 1976) 41-76. Many of the procedures detailed by van Caenegem, however, deal with the preliminary investigation of facts before the suspect is brought to trial, whereas I am dealing here with the rules to be followed once the suspect is constituted as defendant. For preliminary fact-finding procedures in the inquisitorial system, see below at n. 8.

[4] I deal with these points in 'Inquisition and the prosecution of heresy: misconceptions and abuses', *Church History* 58 (1989) 439-51. I describe the rules of inquisitorial procedure in *The matrimonial trials of Henry VIII* (Stanford 1976) and in 'English kings and the fear of sorcery', *Mediaeval Studies* 39 (1977) 206-38. The decretal allowing witnesses in heresy trials to be anonymous when they are thought to be in danger is Boniface VIII's *Statuta*, Sext. 5.2.20. The 1582 edition of the Sext. added a note that had the effect of allowing anonymity in all cases; see n. 52 below. For breaches of the *ordo juris* that were objects of appeal and reversal in the fourteenth century, see J.M. Vidal, *Bullaire de l'inquisition française au XIVe siècle et jusqu'à la fin du grand schisme* (Paris 1913).

Both accusation and denunciation dealt with crimes that were at least somewhat public, or not entirely occult, since they were known to the accuser or denouncer and they were brought forward with the expectation of having them proved in court by evidence, whether testimonial or documentary. In the case of inquisition, the very basis of the procedure rested on the idea of *publica fama.*

In the traditional kinds of civil and criminal proceedings, a trial consisted of a contest between a plaintiff or accuser and a defendant, with the judge acting as moderator. According to the inquisitorial form as established by Innocent III, the judge himself prefers charges, but not, the pope says, as if the same person is both accuser and judge; rather the *fama* serves as denouncer and the *clamor* as delator, while the judge merely carries out the duty of his office.[5] At the Fourth Lateran Council in 1215, the pope claims to have modeled the procedure upon the Gospel parable of the rich man whose steward was defamed to him as wasting his goods: 'And he called him and said to him, "How is it that I hear this of thee? Give an account of thy stewardship: for now thou canst be steward no longer"' (Luke 16.2). The pope also cites God's response to the ill repute of Sodom and Gomorrah (where God is obviously not portrayed as an omniscient deity but rather as a concerned magistrate): 'I will go down and see whether they have done according to the cry that is come to me' (Genesis 18.21).[6]

It is essential for an inquisition, then, that there be a public outcry before the trial can be inaugurated. But the scriptural examples cited by the pope illustrate two different situations: In the New Testament passage, specific crimes are reported about a specific person; in the Old Testament episode, general infamy has arisen about a whole population. In this decree, Innocent is concerned only about the former situation, and he explains the procedure to be followed. The *infamatus* is to be present before the judge when the inquisition is to be made, unless he has absented himself out of contumacy. The 'chapters' or specific points of inquiry are to be explained to him, in order that he may have the faculty of defending himself; the name and testimony of each witness against him is to

---

[5] X 5.1.24, *Qualiter et quando* no. 2 (canon 8 of the Fourth Lateran Council): 'Si per clamorem et famam ad aures superioris pervenerit, non quidem a malevolis et maledicis sed a providis et honestis, nec semel tantum sed sepe, quod clamor innuit et diffamatio manifestat debet coram ecclesie senioribus veritatem diligentius perscrutari, ut, si rei poposcerit qualitas, canonica districtio culpam feriat delinquentis, non tanquam idem sit accusator et judex, sed quasi denunciante fama vel deferente clamore officii sui debitum exsequatur'. Cf. X 5.1.17, *Qualiter et quando* no. 1, A.D. 1206, in a section omitted by Raymund of Peñafort in the *Decretales* (restored by Friedberg 2.738), and *Licet Heli*, A.D. 1199, where similar wording occurs. See also the decretal *Nos inter alios* of Alexander III (1159-81), X 5.34.6: the bishop can compel canonical purgation from his 'parishioner' even where accuser and witnesses are lacking, 'si de aliquo crimine publica laborat infamia'; the pope also uses the phrase, 'publica fama eum accusante', which Raymund omits (2.871).

[6] *Qualiter et quando* no. 2; in the similar discussion in *Licet Heli* the pope cites only the passage from Genesis.

be given to him, and he is to be allowed to enter exceptions or objections to all who testify.[7]

This *ordo* presupposes that the judge will have done a certain amount of preliminary investigation and evidence-gathering before bringing the charges against the *reus*. As William Durant notes, the general inquisition to be conducted by the bishop on his annual visitations will sometimes entail the taking of sworn testimony to ascertain whether certain persons labor under infamy.[8]

A specific inquisition, then, is to be made only against someone publicly defamed, and not at the petition of those who have submitted a *libellus* of defamation in secret. Innocent insists on this point in the decretal *Inquisitionis negotium* of 1212.[9] Cardinal Hostiensis was particularly determined to see that this law was upheld, and that judges should always be careful not to force anyone to lay bare 'occult infamy'.[10] It goes without saying that there would be an even stronger obligation not to uncover a completely occult crime or sin to which no infamy at all has attached. Hostiensis rejects the excuse that an inquisition cannot proceed unless all circumstances are revealed; he says that such exhaustive proceedings would often bring occult matters to public notice and impede the correction of sinners, contrary to the letter and intention of the laws.[11]

But let us suppose that, in lamentable contravention of these laws of procedure, a judge who has summoned a suspect on a specific charge of heresy decides for interest's sake to run him through all of the articles of the Apostles' Creed and finds him defective on a point not touched on in the chapters of inquisition. Can he treat this 'confession' as a prosecutable crime? This is the sort of question one would like to see posed and discussed by the commentators, because

---

[7] *Qualiter et quando* no. 2: 'Debet igitur esse presens is contra quem facienda est inquisitio, nisi se per contumaciam absentaverit; et exponenda sunt ei illa capitula de quibus fuerit inquirendum, ut facultatem habeat defendendi se ipsum. Et non solum dicta, sed etiam nomina ipsa testium sunt ei, ut quid et a quo sit dictum appareat, publicanda, necnon exceptiones et replicationes legitime admittende, ne per suppressionem nominum infamandi, per exceptionum vero exclusionem deponendi falsum audacia prebeatur'.

[8] William Durant, *Speculum judiciale* (Basiliae 1574; repr. Aalen 1975) book 3, part 1, title *De inquisitione*, para. 2, nos. 9 and 13 (vol. 2, p. 31).

[9] X 5.1.21, *Inquisitionis negotium*: 'Respondemus, nullum esse pro crimine super quo aliqua non laborat infamia, seu clamosa insinuatio non processerit ... puniendum ... cum inquisitio fieri debeat solummodo super illis de quibus clamores aliqui precesserunt. Nec ad petitionem eorum qui libellum infamationis porrigunt in occulto procedendum est'.

[10] Hostiensis, *Commentaria* (Venetiis 1581; repr. Turin 1965) on X 5.34.16, *Accepimus* (5.95 no. 23): 'Hoc enim semper est diligenter observandum, ne cogatur quis ad alicujus maxime occultam infamiam denudandam'.

[11] Ibid.: 'Alioquin si dicens de necessitate omnes circumstantias esse denudandas et quod aliter non posset procedere inquisitio, quandoque contingeret multa occulta publicari et plerumque correctiones peccatorum impediri, contra verba et mentem jurium predict[o]rum'.

such matters had painful relevance in their day; but I do not see that the great canonists concerned themselves about these practicalities.

Hostiensis, however, insisted that an inquisition was invalid if a judge started to question witnesses about a suspect's guilt before his infamy was established, or if he proceeded without formally charging the suspect. But Boniface VIII in 1298, in the statute *Postquam*, made it legal for a delegated judge to omit the infamy phase and the statement of charges if the defendant did not object or appeal, and he also decreed in the following statute, *Si is*, that if a person confessed to a crime he could not then object that he was not first charged. Canonists interpreted these laws to apply to ordinary as well as to delegated judges, and while they stressed that judges still had the obligation to establish infamy and specify charges, even if the defendant did not formally object, they did not discuss or insist on the judge's obligation to inform the defendant of his rights.[12] That is, commentators spelled out the rights of those who knew their rights, but not of those who did not know about the defenses stipulated by the *ordo juris*.

Thus, for instance, the Archdeacon notes that any such confession of a crime before a judge would be foolish, because it would prejudice or prejudge the case against him and would render the crime notorious.[13] To an objection based on

[12] Sext. 5.1.1-2, *Postquam* and *Si is*. *Postquam* specifies an *inquisitor deputatus*; but Archdeacon * Guy of Baysio, *Super Sexto ... commentaria* (Lugduni 1547) ad v. *deputatus*, says that it applies to the deputy of an ordinary judge as well (fol. 106v)—that is, as well as to the deputy of the pope. This view was followed by others, for instance, John Andrew, *Novella in Sextum* (Venetiis 1581; repr. Turin 1966) fol. 134. It is an easy step to apply the law to the ordinary himself. The *casus* of the sixteenth-century editions of the Sext., which is taken from Elias Regnier's *Casus longi super Sextum et Clementinas* (Pictaviae 1483), gives the case of a *judex ordinarius* who sets an inquisition in process against a subject on an occult crime (of theft or homicide), and the subject confesses. *Si is* deals with a *commissa inquisitio* to be done *simpliciter*; Regnier's *casus* has the pope commissioning an inquisition at the request of another, in which case 'it is certain that the inquisitor should do two processes, one on infamy and the other on the truth of the crime' (cols. 609-10 of the Roman edition of 1582; for John Chappuis's edition of 1500, see n. 52; for Regnier, I use the unfoliated edition of Strassburg 1488). John Andrew in his early *Apparatus super Sexto*, which became the *Glossa ordinaria*, ad v. *Postquam*, says that Hostiensis's opinions are being corrected here (cited in the Roman edition; checked against the Strassburg 1491 edition, Hain 3617, fol. 72). For Hostiensis on the failure to present charges, see *Commentaria* on X 5.1.24 (5.11A no. 15) and on failure to establish infamy, ibid., on X 5.1.17 (5.5A-6, nos. 4-6). See also n. 59 below.

[13] Archdeacon, loc. cit. ad v. *confessus*: 'sicut stultus et fatuus, nam contra se testificari potuit et ei creditur in sui prejudicium ... ; et postquam sic confessus fuit, factum est crimen notorium'. Geminian (Dominic of San Gimignano), *Lectura in Sextum* (Lugduni 1541) fol. 242v, expresses similar sentiments, following John Andrew, *Glossa ordinaria* ad v. *confessus*: 'Nulle igitur sunt partes judicis nisi ut ferat sententiam. Quid enim queremus de infamia vel capitulis ex quo claret de crimine? ... Jam enim est notorium crimen'. John Monk seems to say that a confession made in court would result in *infamia juris*, as opposed to the *infamia facti* that results from being found defamed of a crime. He notes that an extrajudicial confession does not defame by infamy of law ('Non tamen infamat infamia juris extra judicium facta confessio'). See *Glossa aurea Johannis Monachi Cardinalis super Sexto decretalium*, ed. Philip Probus (Parisiis 1535; repr. Aalen 1968) fol. 342 (= p. 803).

a law of the *Digest* ('Reorum confessiones pro exploratis criminibus non habentur'), he responds that the law applies only to confessions made under torture and not repeated after the torments cease.[14]

So far as I have been able to discover, the first commentator to discuss the defendant's right to know his rights in this context was Philip Probus, or Philippe Lepreux, a jurisconsult of Bourges, in his edition of John Monk's *Glossa aurea*, published in 1535.[15] John Monk himself had commented that, since the *ordo* requiring the establishing of fame and the detailing of charges was introduced in favor of the person against whom an inquisition was mandated, the person is to blame if he omits it; for one can renounce what has been introduced for one's own good, and one who does not use a defense in its proper order loses it.[16] Probus, however, insists that this is only true if one has been properly informed, or 'certified', about what one is renouncing. He alleges a number of authorities for this position, but none of them were addressing the rights of a defendant in court.[17] He adds that when there is a doubt one cannot presume that the proper certification has occurred, since certification is an external solemnity which is not to be presumed unless it is proved.[18] He notes, however, that certification is not

---

[14] Archdeacon, loc. cit., citing *Digest* 48.18.1.17, 27.

[15] See n. 13 above. Probus designates himself as 'Jurisc. Bituric.' in his edition of *De modo celebrandi concilii* of William Durant Junior, Paris 1545, which he dedicates to Paul III and the Fathers of the Council of Trent. In 1534 he published his edition of Arnoul Ruzé's *Tractatus juris regaliae*, to which he added a supplement. See Schulte, *Geschichte* 2.196 n.4; 3.553. Probus also published an edition of the *Pragmatica sanctio* in 1546 (*National Union Catalogue of Pre-1956 Imprints* 181.221).

[16] John Monk, *Glossa aurea*, fol. 342v (= p. 804), commenting on *Si is*: 'Cum ordo qui hic et supra, capitulo proximo, colligitur sit introductus in favorem illius contra quem mandatur inquiri, iste si omittat sibi imputet, cum quisque renunciare valeat his que pro se introducta sunt.... Et ille qui defensione suo ordine non utitur illam perdit'.

[17] Philip Probus, ibid., commenting on the word *renunciare* in John Monk's gloss: 'Id verum dicas dummodo ipse renuncians sit de hoc certificatus; ita dicunt Archidiaconus et Johannes Andree in cap. *Quamvis*, supra, *De pactis* [Sext. 1.18.2], allegando cap. *Placuit*, 38 Dist. [D.38 c.7], quos refert et sequitur Alexander [Tartagnus] de Imola [d.1477], consilio primo, col. 2, *Ponderatis his*, vol. 6, ubi concludit quod ut quis dicatur renunciasse beneficio, lege 2, *Cod.*, *De rescindenda venditione* [4.44.2], requiritur fuerit certioratus. Baldus in dictam legem 2, in 3 q., quem sequitur Johannes de Imola [d. 1436] in cap. penul., *De emptione et venditione* [X 3.17.6], pro quo facit glossa finalis in legem finalem *ff.*, *Ad [senatusconsultum] Velleyanum* [*Digest* 16.1.32]; glossa in *Auten.*, *Quomodo oporteat episcopos*, in para. *Sed etiam* [*Nov.* 6.1.8], in verbum *interroget*, col. prima; Bar[tolus] per illum textum in lege *An repudianda*, *ff.*, *De acquirenda [vel omittenda] hereditate* [29.2.23]; Jason post alios in legem *Sciendum*, *ff.*, *De verborum obligatione* [50.16.70]'.

[18] Ibid., fols. 342v-343 (= pp. 804-05): 'Et in dubio non est presumendum quod fuerit certificatus, cum certificatio sit solennitas extrinseca, que non presumitur nisi probetur, lege *Quecumque*, para. ult., *ff.*, *De publiciana* [6.2.13]. Notat Fredericus [Petruccius de Senis, d. ca. 1343], consilio 199, *Queritur an domina Margarita*, ubi unum notandum dicit quod, si notarius in instrumento attestatur se certificasse mulierem renunciantem hereditati paterne de virtute et effectu dicte renunciationis, quod per tale instrumentum non probatur renunciatio; arg. lex *Omnibus*, *Cod.*, *De testibus* [4.20.10], et quod notat

necessary when one has taken an oath, since in such a case it is assumed that one has come with due deliberation.[19] But he specifies that this does not apply where trickery has been used.[20] It is hard to see how a judge could escape a

---

Hostiensis in cap. *Quoniam contra*, super verba *per sententiam*, supra, *De probationibus* [X 2.19.11]. Quia secundum eum instrumentum facit fidem de his que inter partes geruntur, non de aliis; quod sequitur Antonius de Butrio in dicto cap. *Quoniam contra*, et Panormitanus in cap. *Cum causam*, supra, *De testibus* [X 2.20.37], et Roma. [?] in dictam legem *Sciendum*; Alexander, consiiio 10, in fine, vol. primo.

'Pro hoc ultimo dicto faciunt ea qua notat idem Alexander, consilio 20, no. 6, *Viso processu super causa vertente*, vol. 6, quod notarius rogatus de instrumento protestationis non potest conficere instrumentum nisi de his que vidit et audivit tempore quo conficiebatur contractus et instrumentum: Innocentius [IV] in cap. *Fraternitatis*, supra, *De hereticis* [X 5.7.4]; Baldus in rubricum *Cod.*, *De fide instrumentorum* [4.21], col. 5, et in legem *Cum precibus*, *Cod.*, *De probationibus* [4.19.8]; debet enim notarius conficere instrumentum de eo quod tempore contractus vidit vel audivit a partibus, ut ibi Alexander ipse hoc plene comprobat, et late consilio 191, *Perspecto instrumento*, vol. 6, ubi utrumque comprobat.

'Et quoad notarios seu tabelliones adde unum (incidenter tamen) quod citat Alexander, consilio 208 no. 3, *Ponderatis narratis*, dicto vol. 6, quod plerumque tabelliones non intelligunt significationes verborum; et sunt similes cantoribus qui bene cantant per practicam, sed non per rationem: Johannes de Imola in legem *Lucius*, *ff.*, *De vulgari et pupillari* [28.6.45], et in cap. *Raynutius*, supra, *De testamentis* [X 3.26.16]'.

[19] Ibid., fol. 343: 'Quod autem dicimus quod oportet renunciantem certificatum, debes intelligere verum et necessarium nisi intervenerit juramentum: quia tunc non requiritur certioratio, quia renuncians dicitur venire deliberatus: notant doctores post glossam in cap. *Ex rescripto*, supra, *De jurejurando* [2.24.9], ubi Balbus dicit quod quando juratur non de apicibus juris est disputandum. Hunc punctum late comprobat Alexander, consilio 146, col. 1, *Viso themate suprascripto*, vol. 7, ubi subdit quod illa virtus juramenti quoad robur contractus transit ad heredes jurantis: glossa finali in cap. *Quamvis*, supra, *De pactis*, hoc libro [Sext. 1.18.2], que reputatur sing. [?; see n. 20 below], secundum [Philippum] Franc[hum de Franchis, d. 1471], ibi; nam obligatio que oritur ex ipso contractu firmato debet transire in heredes, lege *Et* [= *Ex*] *depositi* et lege *Ex contractibus*, *ff.*, *De actionibus et obligationibus* [44.7.12, 49], licet quoad vinculum spirituale anime et quoad penam perjurii non transeat ipsum juramentum in heredes, ut per Innocentium in cap. *Veritatis*, supra, *De jurejurando* [X 2.24.14], et Johannem Andree in cap. finale, supra, *De foro competenti*, hoc libro [Sext. 2.2.3]; quod firmat latius idem Alexander, consilio 26 in fine, *Cumulatissime et eleganter*, et consilio 151 no. 10, *Viso themate suprascripto*, dicto vol. 7, ubi dicit quod tale vinculum non obligat heredem, quantum ad hoc ut habeat necesse petere relaxationem juramenti quam petere potuisset defunctus; allegat Balbum in legem 3, in versiculum *Querit*, Glossa *Codicis*, *Plus valere quod agitur* [4.22.3], et in *Auten.*, *Et qui* [?]; *Cod.*, *De bonis autoritate judicis possidendis* [7.72], col. ultima.

'Hec distinctio placet Neapo. [?], deci. 381[?], in fine, *Quondam Ypolita*'.

[20] Ibid.: 'Quod autem etiam supra proxime diximus, quod non requiritur certioratio ubi intervenerit juramentum, intelligas verum nisi dolo fuerit adhibitum; quia tunc nullam habet efficaciam, tam in principali quam in accessoriis; textus est in cap. *Licet*, *De jurejurando*, hoc libro [Sext. 2.11.2], ibi, *nec vi nec dolo*, qui reputatur singularis juncto [junctio?]; cap. 2, supra, *De pactis* [Sext. 1.18.2], secundum Philippum Franc[hum], ibi, quod licet contractus qui est nullus de jure civili approbetur per jus canonicum vigore juramenti, si tamen intervenit vis sive dolus redditur nullus. Facit quod citat Alexander, consilio 151 no. 3, *Viso themate suprascripto et statuto Veronensi*, vol. 7, quod quando statutum disponit quod contractus minorum, etiam juratus, non valeat sine consensu duorum consanguineorum, et quod talis contractus factus sine consensu dictorum duorum consanguineorum presumatur innitus dolo, seu

charge of using trickery if he demanded or even invited a confession from an unschooled defendant, who has been put under oath without having been offered the opportunity of legal counsel.

II. The Problem of Nonpublic Crimes

Heresy, like all other crimes, was routinely prosecuted by the inquisitorial method as soon as the procedure was formed. But even though many modern historians assume that the procedure was designed specifically for heresy, or at least admirably suited for the prosecution of heresy, a moment's reflection should make it obvious that the occult nature of heresy would make it particularly unsuitable for a trial procedure that depends essentially on *publica fama*. Of course, perpetrators of all sorts of crimes try to conceal their actions from the authorities; but unlike all other crimes heresy is primarily a sin of thought, and thoughts are by definition private. 'Belief' in heresy or heretics had long been designated as an offense in law, and Innocent III confirmed this status at the Fourth Lateran Council.[21] In 1231, Gregory IX made belief in heresy equivalent to heresy.[22] Both of these decretals were incorporated by Raymond of Peñafort in the *Decretals of Gregory IX*, and one might expect the commentators to give long and hard consideration to the question of how wrong believers could be brought to judgment by the inquisitorial method (or any other method). But they did not do so. Innocent IV and Bernard of Parma do not even note the difference effected by Gregory IX in the status of believers. Hostiensis does observe the change, and his observation is noted by John Andrew. John Andrew also follows Abbas Antiquus (Bernard of Montmirat) in distinguishing between persons who believe in the errors of heretics and those who simply believe that certain heretics are good men; the latter are not themselves heretics, and they still fall under the Lateran Council's canon against the supporters of heretics.[23] But neither he nor

---

intelligatur talis minor dolo inductus ad contrahendum, tunc valet statutum, et contractus non sortietur effectum; quia propter presumptum dolum juramentum potest contemni, cap. *Cum contingat*, supra, *De jurejurando* [X 2.24.28], et dicto cap. 2, supra, *De pactis*, et cap. *Licet*, *De jurejurando*, hoc libro'.

[21] Innocent III, *Excommunicamus* no. 1, X 5.7.13 para. 5: 'Credentes preterea, receptores, defensores, et fautores hereticorum excommunicationi decernimus subjacere'.

[22] Gregory IX, *Excommunicamus* no. 2, X 5.7.15, dated by Friedberg (following Raynaldi) A.D. 1229 (col. 789), while L. Auvray, *Les registres de Gregoire IX*, 1 (Paris 1896) no. 539 dates it February 1231. The pertinent phrase reads (para. 1): 'Credentes autem eorum erroribus hereticos similiter judicamus'.

[23] John Andrew, *Novella* on *X* 5.7.15 ad v. *erroribus* (Venetiis 1581; repr. Turin 1963, 5.52A no. 3). On Abbas Antiquus, see P. Legendre, 'Bernard of Montmirat', NCE 2.341; he wrote his commentary on the *Decretales* between 1259 and 1266.

the other commentators raise the question here of how one goes about indicting and prosecuting believers in heresy.

Durant's treatment of heresy in the *Speculum judiciale* is worse than useless. He copies out two *libelli* from Roffred, but they are cast in the nearly obsolete form of the formal accusation.[24] By the turn of the fourteenth century, as John Andrew points out in his *Additions* to the *Speculum*, one of these formulas was no longer valid, since it was designed for submission to a secular court; for Boniface VIII in the decretal *Ut inquisitionis* restricted heresy cases to the ecclesiastical courts.[25] Durant says that the same procedure is used against *credentes* and *receptatores*, who are accounted heretics if they remain excommunicated for a year. (This is the stipulation of the Lateran decretal. Apparently Durant did not realize the implications of Gregory IX's decretal.) The first move against such, then, is to petition that they be excommunicated.[26] But first they must be convicted, and he gives no advice on how this is to be done for believers.

In his general remarks on Durant's rubric, John Andrew says that Roffred is the only one of the *practici auctores* to treat heresy.[27] In fact, however, a good number of treatises on the prosecution of heresy had been produced by his time. Antoine Dondaine has described eleven of them, the first prepared by Peñafort himself.[28] The earlier of these treatises were fully in accord with the *ordo juris* of inquisition, but the later ones enjoined or approved of practices that abused the law in amateurish and dangerous ways. I wish to note specifically the procedure sanctioned by Dondaine's Manual no. 6, *Doctrina de modo procedendi contra hereticos*, which comes from the Dominican heresy inquisitors of Toulouse in the 1270s.[29] The inquisitors summon suspects and, without establishing infamy or presenting charges, put them under oath to testify about themselves and others concerning heresy. If they conceal or deny the truth, they are to be jailed until they confess. If they do confess the truth, they are to abjure the heresy.[30] It

---

[24] Roffred died shortly after 1243 (Schulte 2.76). See n. 65 below.

[25] William Durant, *Speculum*, book 4, part 4, title *De hereticis* nos. 1-2 (2.488); John Andrew's comment is in note *c* on the same page of this edition, with a garbled reference to Sext. 5.2.18, *Ut inquisitionis*.

[26] William Durant, loc. cit. no. 3.

[27] John Andrew, *Additiones* note *a* (4.488).

[28] A. Dondaine, 'Le manuel de l'inquisiteur (1230-1330)', *Archivum fratrum praedicatorum* 17 (1947) 85-194.

[29] The *Doctrina* is edited by E. Martène, *Thesaurus novorum anecdotorum*, 5 (Parisiis 1717; repr. New York 1968) cols. 1795-1814. See Y. Dossat, *Les crises de l'inquisition toulousaine au XIIIe siècle (1233-1273)* (Bordeaux 1959) 202-04.

[30] Martène 5.1795: 'Isto modo procedunt inquisitores in partibus Carcassonensibus et Tholosanis. Primo accusatus vel suspectus de heresi citatur, qui veniens jurat super sancta evangelia super crimine heresis vel Valdesie tam de se quam de aliis, tam vivis quam defunctis, dicere plenariam quam scit

became common for heresy inquisitors to proceed in this way. Specifically, instead of charging a summoned suspect, they would ask him to guess why he had been arrested and brought to trial, and then they would proceed to interrogate him about his beliefs and actions.

What was the canonical status of admissions of hitherto unknown crimes obtained in this way? After the publication of Boniface VIII's decrees, one would have the choice of agreeing with the Archdeacon's judgment that such a confession renders a crime notorious and punishable without further ado, or of anticipating Probus's implied conclusion that the confession should be invalidated by alleging that the defendant should have been properly apprised of his rights. There was, in fact, a successful appeal made on these grounds in 1323.[31] In the realm of theory, John Andrew says at one point that if one is forced to respond on hidden matters in an inquisition, it is grounds for appeal, whereas in an accusation the accused has an obligation to respond.[32] Elsewhere he says that the occult is not to be made public, but is to be left to God alone, and that there is no equity that can justify a judge's interrogating a *reus* on what is occult.[33] But even though he uses the term *reus* here he is dealing primarily not with a summoned defendant but with a witness who admits to a crime in the course of his testimony. The judge has no right to question him on a crime that he has committed; if he does, the witness does not have to reply. In the case at issue, the judge did question him, and the witness did reply and confess, and the pope punished him. John Andrew justifies the pope's action by saying that the witness answered without having been compelled to do so. (He contradicts this argument further on, perhaps, when he says that the oath to tell the truth on the principal matter of the case is understood to cover all contingent matters as well.) But he offers an alternative solution: when the question concerns the matter in hand, as

---

veritatem; et si celaverit vel negaverit, in carcere ponitur et detinetur donec fuerit confessus. Si autem dicit veritatem, diligenter ejus confessio per notarium publicum scribitur, et si errat in dicendo, ille qui confitetur potest se emendare, et ejus confessio corrigitur. Facta autem confessione vocantur due persone religiose, in quarum presentia ejus confessio sibi recitatur; qua recognita, et sic depositione facta, abjurat heresim'.

[31] Vidal (n. 4 supra) 77-83.

[32] John Andrew, *Novella* on X 5.1.24, *Qualiter* no. 2, ad v. *facultatem* (Venetiis 1581; repr. Turin 1963) 5.15 no. 25: 'Si ergo gravaretur, admittenda est justa appellatio.... Gravaretur autem si fieret inquisitio vel cogeretur respondere super occultis, et in hoc differt inquisitus ab accusato, qui super occultis respondere compellitur, quia jurat de calumnia'.

[33] Ibid., on X 2.18.2, *Cum super* (2.108A nos. 4-5): 'Si vero non esset defamatus, sive convictus, vel confessus, vel deprehensus, sed occultus, non deberet eum judex interrogare.... Occulta enim publicanda non sunt, sed soli Deo relinquenda.... Nulla ergo equitas potest movere judicem ut reum interroget de occultis. Equitate autem deficiente non est locus interrogationi judiciali'. Cf. *Novella* on X 2.1.13, *Novit* (2.9A no. 6): the denouncer should not denounce a sin entirely hidden but one that can be proved, 'quia omnino occulta sunt in Dei judicio'.

in this case where the witness was asked whether he was a partner to the simony that the defendant was charged with, the witness is required to answer—but only if he has been defamed on the point.[34] He follows Innocent IV in saying that a witness can be punished without further ado if he confessed to the crime that the main action is dealing with, but if he confesses to another crime, he cannot be punished unless the judge charges him in a new trial.[35]

We are left to conjecture what John Andrew would have thought of the case that I proposed above, where a judge elicits a confession of heterodox belief which corresponds to no antecedent crime and which, of course, labors under no infamy. But some of his thoughts on related subjects are pertinent. In the *Novella* on the Sext., he refers to the opinion of the Archdeacon[36] that the 'favor of the faith' is so great in the prosecution of heresy that even the pope can be accused of occult heresy. But John Andrew says that he is talking of a crime that can be proved, in other words a manifest crime; for something that is known to five people is sometimes said to be occult.[37] That is to say, it is a question of terminology. I will use the term 'quasi-occult' to designate matters which are known to some persons, but which are not the object of public infamy. Quasi-occult crimes can be brought to trial by way of accusation or denunciation; they cannot legally be brought to trial by inquisition without the consent of the alleged perpetrator.

John Andrew does touch indirectly on the prosecution of heresy when discussing the question of who has jurisdiction over heresy. In the *Ordinary Gloss* to Boniface VIII's decretal *Ut commissi*, he raises the problem of someone who has committed a crime of heresy in one place, say Ravenna, and then has moved to another place, say Milan. He makes a case for the position that any criminal can be prosecuted wherever he is found.[38] He clarifies his meaning in the *Novella*, giving examples of the sort punishable crimes the suspect might have committed in Ravenna, viz., 'adoring' or 'dogmatizing'.[39] He goes on to note that bad

---

[34] John Andrew on *Cum super* (no. 6).

[35] Ibid. (no. 9). See Innocent IV, *Commentaria* on X 2.18.2, *Cum Super* (Venetiis 1578) fol. 102 no. 3.

[36] The Archdeacon completed his commentary of the Sext. around 1311, but John Andrew in his own earlier apparatus attributes much of his own doctrine to the Archdeacon's teaching; see his first gloss to the Sext., given in the Roman edition.

[37] John Andrew, *Novella* on Sext. 5.2.5, *In fidei favorem*, ad v. *favorem* (fol. 136A).

[38] John Andrew, *Ordinary Gloss* on Sext. 5.2.12, *Ut commissi*, ad v. *procedendi*. See P. Tisset, 'Le tribunal ecclésiastique de Rouen que condamna Jeanne d'Arc, était-il compétent?', *Annales de la faculté de droit d'Aix* n.s. 43 (1950) 307-38, esp. 325-26.

[39] John Andrew, *Novella* on Sext. 5.2.12, *Ut commissi*, in glossam *Quid in casu* ad v. *peccavit* (fol. 139A no.7): 'forsan adorando vel dogmatizando'. The same reading occurs in the Venice 1499 edition (repr. Graz 1963) p. 254. The sixteenth-century editions of the Sext. in an *additio* modify and distort this gloss thus: 'Forsan peccavit adorando vel degradizando'. Tisset, p. 326, cites only this *additio*: he translates *degradizando* as 'manifestant sa vénération'.

belief is a different kind of offense, one that does not require a specific locale; a person carries it with him, and he sins wherever he is. He then alludes to two opinions cited by his friend Cino da Pistoia. One authority, James de Révigny, says that a heretic can be judged wherever he is found because insofar as he is a heretic he sins in every place. But the other authority, Peter de Belleperche, counters this position by saying that he is to be sent back to where he sinned the most and where his sins are notorious.[40] Presumably John Andrew, like Cino, prefers the latter opinion, but in either case the judge in Milan would not have been able, legally, to arrest or cite the subject unless he were *infamatus*—that is, 'defamed' of actual heretical deeds allegedly committed in Ravenna.

In the *Ordinary Gloss* to Clement V's decretal *Multorum*, John Andrew brings up the question of *ipso facto* censures--that is, censures automatically incurred upon the commission of a crime--as opposed to censures levied after a crime is proven in court. He says that *Multorum* shows that a constitution of the Church Militant can be binding on an entirely occult crime, as far as the punishments of excommunication and suspension are concerned. This was a principle that had been affirmed with regard to secret heretics by John of Faenza (Faventinus) in his *Summa* and *Glosses* on Gratian as well as by Goffred and by Raymund of Peñafort in his *Summa de penitentia*. But the Archdeacon had called it into doubt in his commentary on the Sext. John Andrew's solution is that the Church can bind entirely occult crimes, but a church court does not pass judgment on them *nominatim*.[41] Two centuries later Cardinal Cajetan raised the Archdeacon's question once again and countered John Andrew's solution with a remarkable subdistinction. Even a *hereticus perfectissimus* who is heretical only in his heart is not excommunicated or subjected to any other legal censures. But if such a heretic manifests his heresy externally, then he is immediately excommunicated. This is true, Cajetan says, even if the heretic should utter a word that no one hears, because then his heresy is occult not *per se* but only *per accidens*.[42]

---

[40] John Andrew, *Novella* on Sext. loc. cit., 'Hoc dico quia ubicumque sit male credens ibi peccat; et vide quod post Jacobum [Jacques de Révigny] et Petrum [Pierre de Belleperche] notat Cynus, *Cod.*, *De summa trinitate*, lege 1 in fine [1.1.1]. Dixit enim Jacobus hereticum alienigenam per Bon[oniam] transeuntem per Bon[oniensem] judicem puniendum, etiamsi judex proprius illum repetat, quia ex quo hereticus est omni loco delinquit; allegat legem *Ariani*, *Cod.*, *De hereticis* [1.5.5]. Petrus contra, quod remittendus est ad locum ubi plus deliquit et ubi notoria sunt ejus delicta, per legem *ff.*, *De accusatoribus, Si cui*, par. finali [*Digest* 48.2.7.5]'. See Cino, *In Codicem ... Commentaria*, 2 vols. (Francofurti 1578; repr. Turin 1964) 1.2r-v no. 12. On these jurists, see Tisset, p. 317 n.33 and 323 n.64. The *additio* followed by Tisset does not give John Andrew's citation from Cino, so that Tisset is forced to conjecture about the drift of John Andrew's reasoning.

[41] John Andrew, *Ordinary gloss* on Clem. 5.3.1, *Multorum*, ad v. *eo ipso* (cols. 268-69), referring to Archdeacon on Sext. 5.11.23, *Cum quis* (fol. 125v).

[42] Cajetan, *Commentaria* on Thomas Aquinas, *Summa theologie* 2-2.11.3, Leonine edition of the *Summa*, 8 (Rome 1895) 100-01.

In spite of various fine shadings, all authorities agreed on the principle, 'The Church does not judge hidden crimes'.[43] John Andrew quotes Hostiensis as saying, on the basis of this principle, that a man should not be judged according to conscience (that is, the judge's private knowledge or perception), but according to what is proved.[44] In contrast, we have Henry Charles Lea asserting that the inquisitor of heresy 'was a judge in the forum of conscience, bound by no statutes and limited by no rules, with his penitents at his mercy'.[45] While it may be true that some or even many heresy inquisitors acted as if they were bound by no statutes or rules, Lea is not correct in his assumption that they were legally exempted from the rules, and I cannot find that any of the inquisitors ever gave theoretical justification for invading the penitential forum.

III. Some Practices and Consequences

The matter of occult heresy is taken up in the first instructions issued by Thomas de Torquemada and his fellow inquisitors at Seville on 29 November 1484. Those who come of their own accord to confess their errors are to renounce them in public and do public penance. No one is to be admitted to secret abjuration and penance unless the sin was so occult that no other person knew of it or could have known except him to whom it was confessed, and no other person could have revealed it to the inquisitors. Any of the inquisitors in such a case can secretly absolve the sinner, 'for such action is in accord with the law'.[46] Torquemada does not quite say that the inquisitors are prohibited by law

---

[43] The principle is enunciated, for instance, by Innocent III in the decretal *Sicut*, A.D. 1199, X 5.3.33: 'Si excessus eorum esset ecclesie manifestus, que non judicat de occultis, pena essent canonica ferendi'; similarly, in *Tua nos*, A.D. 1207, X 5.3.34, he says, 'Nobis datum est de manifestis tantummodo judicare', as opposed to God, 'qui scrutator est cordium et cognitor secretorum'. For the earlier * history of the principle, see S. Kuttner, 'Ecclesia de occultis non iudicat', *Acta Congressus iuridici internationalis...Romae...1931*, 5 vols. (Rome 1935-37) 3.225-46.

[44] John Andrew, *Novella* on X 5.3.33, *Sicut* (5.32 no.8): 'Et per hoc arguit Hostiensis, non secundum conscientiam sed secundum probata judicari debet'. For this principle, see R.M. Fraher, 'Conviction according to conscience: the medieval jurists' debate concerning judicial discretion and the law of proof', LHR 7 (1989) 23-88, esp. 24, 52-53. When Fraher deals with secret crimes (e.g. pp. 47-49, 56), he usually means secretly committed crimes, like murder or theft, where the crimes are known, but perpetrators are not.

[45] Lea (n. 4 supra) 1.460. *

[46] *Instructions of Seville*, 29 November 1484, ed. E. Schäfer, 'Die älteste Instruktionen-Sammlung der spanischen Inquisitionen', *Archiv für Reformationsgeschichte* 2 (1904-05) 1-55, 109-77, on pp. 9-38, provision no. 5 (p. 17): 'E no deven recebir a ninguno a abjuracion, y pena secreta, salvo, si el pecado fuere tan oculto que no lo supo otra alguna persona, ni lo pudo saber, salvo aquel que lo confiessa, porque en tal caso podra qualquier de los inquisidores reconciliar, y absolver secretamente a la tal persona, cuyo error y delito fue, y es, oculto, y no es revelado, ni por otra persona se les podria revelar, porque assi es de derecho'.

from making such confessions public, but this may well be the meaning intended. We note that he takes 'occult' in its strictest sense. If anyone at all was privy to the sin, it would not qualify for private absolution, it seems. Of course, a sin or crime known to others might still be quasi-occult, as discussed above, and therefore not legitimately the subject of a formal inquisition.

Two and a half years earlier, Pope Sixtus IV in his bull *Gregis dominici* (dated 18 April 1482) had detailed what the cardinals of the Roman curia considered to be the proper procedure for dealing with heretics. Among other things, all offenses which were confessed before any *publica fama* had brought them to the attention of the bishops or the specially appointed heresy inquisitors, and before any summonses had been sent, were to be treated as occult and only secret penance given. Somewhat misleadingly, the pope speaks of this as a special concession, but then orders it to be followed.[47] A few months later the pope gave in to pressure from King Ferdinand and suspended the bull, but charged all ordinaries and inquisitors in the meantime to observe the 'common law'--that is, the *ordo juris* of the canons.[48] Of course, much of what the bull contained was simply a spelling out of the *ordo juris*, but the status of voluntarily confessed quasi-occult crimes was admittedly a grey area. We have seen that Torquemada's policy was to subject the confitents to public adjuration, and it would presumably have been perfectly legitimate to require an oath from them to testify *de se ac de aliis* and to elicit from them further details of heresy, at least insofar as they were manifest—which in Torquemada's view would include quasi-occult offenses.

But what about suspects who are formally cited to an inquisitorial trial? Torquemada does not specify any procedure, thereby leaving it to the inquisitors to follow the *ordo juris* of the decretal collections or whatever legitimate or abusive measures had evolved in practice. However, in the last directives issued under the supervision of Torquemada, the *Instructions of Avila*, dated 25 May 1498, which clearly respond to violations of the law on the part of some inquisitors, it is stipulated that the inquisitors are not to arrest anyone without sufficient proof, and they are to make a formal accusation within ten days of arrest and

---

[47] Sixtus IV, *Gregis dominici*, 18 April 1482, ed. H.C. Lea, *A history of the inquisition of Spain*, 4 vols. (New York 1906) 1.587-90, pp. 588-89: 'Ordinariis locorum ... ac inquisitoribus ... ut quorumcumque ... ad aliquem ex eis recurrentium, confessione diligenter audita, pro quibuscumque excessibus ... commississe fatebuntur ... auctoritate nostra in utroque foro, penitentiali et contentioso, absque abjuratione de absolutionis beneficio eisdem recurrentibus providendi, eisque penitentiam salutarem et occultam injungendi ... concedimus per presentes, ita quod in posterum ... contra eos inquirere non possint ... dum tamen ad inquisitionis processum super hujusmodi criminibus et inquisitorum personalem citationem executorii demandatam deventum non foret. ... Et insuper ... mandamus quatinus incolas ... qui ad eos ... pro confessione et absolutione predictis recurrerint absque aliqua dilatione seu mora eorum confessiones ... audiant et eis de absolutionis beneficio in utroque foro ut prefertur provideant'.

[48] Lea, *History of the inquisition of Spain* 1.234-36; the pope's order was dated 9 October 1482.

provide all of the admonitions that the case requires. They are to proceed in the trial with all diligence and not keep the defendant in jail in the hopes that more evidence will turn up, as has been done in the past, for delays of this sort are injurious both to persons and to property.[49]

As we have seen, Torquemada and his colleagues in effect defined as non-occult any crime that was known by someone other than the perpetrator, who could bring it to the attention of the inquisitors. Whether or not one sees in this a willingness to hold inquisitorial trials on such matters when they lack the required *publica fama*, at least one can be certain that there should be no place for the sort of 'fishing expeditions' that had become common in inquisitorial trials.[50]

The implied procedure in Torquemada's last instruction, cited above, is that the inquisitor will conduct a secret investigation and attempt to gather proof that a person is guilty of a specific crime. This can be compared to the procedure for establishing fame that had come into practice by this time, presumably in France, as described by Elias Regnier in his *Casus longi super Sexto et Clementinis*, published in Poitiers in 1483. In commenting on Boniface VIII's *Postquam*, he says: 'Nowadays the common procedure is that, before a person is cited *ex officio* and an inquisition takes place, there is a secret examination or information; and when the informations are completed, if it appears that the person has been defamed of the crime, the judge orders him to be personally cited'.[51] According to Regnier, the inquisitor was required to conduct the process on fame as well as the

---

[49] *Instructions of Avila*, 25 May 1498, ed. Schäfer, 109-14, 123-24, no. 3 (p. 110): 'Iten, que los inquisidores tengan tiento en el prender, y no prendan nunguno sin tener suficiente provança para ello, y despues de assi preso dentro de diez dias se le ponga la acusacion, y en este termino se le hagan las amonestaciones que in tal caso se requieren, y procedan en las causas y processos con toda diligencia y brevedad, sin esperar que sobreverna mas provança, porque a esta causa ha acaecito deternerse algunas personas in la carcel, y no den lugar a dilaciones, porque dello se siguen inconvenientes, assi a las personas como a las haziendas'.

[50] Perhaps I am taking too sanguine a view here. I suppose that ten days would be good enough time to interrogate a defendant before formally charging him, and it may be that some inquisitors did so. However, to judge from the early trials in Ciudad Real, in 1483-85, the procedure was entirely regular. See, for example, the case of Juan de Chinchilla, in H. Beinart, *Records of the trials of the Spanish inquisition in Ciudad Real*, 1 (Jerusalem 1984) 163-80: With no preliminary confession, he was brought to court and given detailed accusations and allowed to select a lawyer and a proctor before entering a plea of innocence, and so on. But according to the *Instructions of Toledo* of 1561, ed. P. Hinschius, 'Die Anweisungen für die spanische Inquisition vom Jahre 1561', *Deutsche Zeitschrift für Kirchenrecht* 7 (1897) 76-121, 203-47, each defendant is to be interrogated before being charged: He is put under oath, and after preliminary questions on family and on any previous encounters with the Inquisition, he is asked if he knows why he was arrested ('se le pregunte generalmente si sabe la causa de su prision'), and then questioned about 'other' points of Christian doctrine (no. 15, pp. 93-94).

[51] Regnier, loc. cit. (n. 12 supra): 'Et hodie communiter, prius aliquis citatur ex officio super crimine et fit inquisitio, et [*lege* fit] examinatio sive informatio secreta; et, factis informationibus, si constet judici quod talis est diffamatus super illo crimine, judex precipit ut citetur personaliter'.

process on the truth of the fame, that is, the person's guilt or innocence of the crime. And since the defendant had the right to insist that his ill fame be established, the judge would presumably have to present him with the records of whatever secret process had been conducted.

Regnier has been strangely neglected by historians of canon law, given his immediate and lasting success. His work was reprinted several times before the end of the century, and in 1500 John Chappuis made it a prominent part of the apparatus of his edition of the Sext. and Clementines. Chappuis is another unjustly neglected figure among canonists; for, apart from his being the first to gather and edit the post-Clementine extravagants, it was he who decided what additional commentary was to be added to the ordinary glosses of the earlier collections as well, and his apparatuses were taken over *en bloc* by subsequent editors, including the Roman correctors who produced the authorized 1582 edition. Thus, the *hodie* of Regnier's comment was enshrined as a *dies perpetuus*.[52]

In some quarters, such as England, the custom seems to have developed of incorporating an assertion of fame into the formal charges presented to the defendant. All of the articles in the inquisitions against Henry VIII's marriages end as follows: 'haecque fuerunt et sunt vera, publica, et notoria, ac de et super eisdem

---

[52] See n. 12 above and n. 59 below. I have consulted the Library of Congress copy of John Chappuis's first edition, Paris 1500-01, fol. 149; see *National union catalog* 99.618 (NC 0224981). Schulte, 2.374, gives only four lines to Regnier and misprints his name as 'Bognier' (corrected on p. 582). He lists the six editions noted by Hain, but not the incorporation of his work into the *Corpus juris canonici* made by Chappuis. He has no separate entry for Chappuis, and he deals with him only as the collector and editor of the extravagants (2.62-63). Another 'hodie' was added to the next title of the Sext., *De hereticis*, in the 1582 Roman edition, concerning Boniface VIII's decretal *Statuta*, which allowed the names of witnesses to be suppressed when they would be endangered (see n. 4 above): 'Hodie semper praesumitur imminere tale periculum et ideo indistincte solet observari, ut in crimine haeresis nunquam publicentur nomina accusatorum vel testium; vide extravagantem Innocentis Papae quam affert *Repertorium inquisitorum*, verbo *Nomina*'; Sext. 5.2.12 ad v. *imminere*, col. 645. The reference is to the *Repertorium inquisitorum pravitatis haereticae* (Venetiis 1575). I quote from the 1588 reprint, pp. 360-61: after Boniface's decree is explained this observation is made: 'Sed circa praedicta, nota quod de consuetudine inquisitionis nunquam nomina testium publicantur ipsi inquisito, nec de eis datur ipsi copia, quae consuetudo potest approbari per quandam extravagantem Innocentis, cujus tenor talis est'. There follows the text of Innocent IV's *Cum negotium*, addressed to Dominican heresy inquisitors, dated 10 March 1254. See *Bullae, diplomata, et privilegia sanctorum romanorum pontificum*, ed. A. Tomassetti, 26 vols. (Turin 1857-67) 3.585-86, where it is dated 9 March 1254. The *Repertorium* is a reprint, with additional notes, of the *Repertorium perutile de pravitate hereticorum et apostatarum* by Michael Albert, J.U.D. (Valentiae 1494). The quoted passage appears on sig. B iiii^{r-v}. Therefore, what may have been only a local Iberian abuse of the fifteenth century was universalized and, in effect, authorized as a legitimate *consuetudo* in the official edition of canon law a century later.

laborarunt et laborant publica vox et fama'. The proposal to prove the charges would therefore involve the proof of fame as well as proof of fact.[53]

The case of Joan of Arc is especially instructive in showing how the *ordo juris* that Torquemada was to insist on had fallen into neglect in the earlier part of the century in some circles. Joan was formally interrogated under oath for a month before she was charged, in spite of her repeated protests against the procedure. The citation issued against her seemed to promise that the trial would be conducted according to proper form: She was 'to be heard concerning articles and interrogatories to be given against her and made for her relating to matters of faith'.[54] When she was brought before the judge, Bishop Cauchon, he claimed that he had summoned her because of *fama publica* and certain informations, but, instead of presenting her with a list of charges, he insisted that she swear to tell the truth 'about these things which will be asked concerning matters of faith'.[55] Joan's response was entirely proper: 'I don't know what you want to question me about; maybe you could ask me things that I wouldn't tell you'.[56]

Many of the questions put to Joan concerned points of theology that she clearly had not considered previously. That is to say, even if her responses could have been considered sinfully heretical, they would not have been past sins, which could have been confessed and absolved in the sacrament of penance, but rather fresh sins committed on the spot, recorded and considered as public crimes, subject to public abjuration and punishment. When charges were finally leveled against her, they were all compiled from the responses that she had given under protest and without admitting any wrongdoing; no witnesses or documentary

---

[53] See Kelly, 'English kings' (n. 4 supra) 233 n.105, and *Matrimonial trials of Henry VIII* (n. 4 supra) 90. See also R.H. Helmholz, 'Crime, compurgation, and the courts of the medieval church', LHR 1 (1983) 1-26, at p. 14: 'Witnesses often testified to the existence of public fame, separating it from their perception of the truth of the underlying matter'. Most of the trials that Helmholz deals with are inquisitions, but he does not designate or analyze them as such, and he even translates the canonical term *inquisitio* as 'inquest' (p. 14 and n.64). Part of the confusion may come from the fact that English ecclesiastical courts generally imitated their secular counterparts in using the word *inquisitio* to refer only to noninquisitorial inquiries or inquests. See n. 61 below.

[54] P. Tisset and Y. Lanhers, eds., *Procès de condamnation de Jeanne d'Arc*, 3 vols. (Société de l'Histoire de France 466, 477, 479; Paris 1960-71) 1.34, citation of 20 February 1431: 'Decreverimus ipsam Johannam vocandam esse, citandam, et audiendam super articulis et interrogatoriis contra eam dandis et sibi faciendis fidei materiam concernentibus'.

[55] Ibid. 37-38: 'Caritative monuimus et requisivimus ut, pro acceleracione presentis negocii et exoneracione proprie consciencie, plenam veritatem super hiis diceret de quibus in materia fidei interrogaretur.... Insuper, ex officio nostro, ipsam Johannam judicialiter requisivimus quatinus juramentum in forma debita, tactis sacrosanctis evangeliis, prestaret de dicendo veritatem, ut premittitur, super hiis de quibus interrogaretur'.

[56] Ibid. 38: 'Je ne sçay sur quoy vous me voulez interroguer; aventure me pourriez-vous demander telles choses que je ne vous diray point'. The Latin translation reads, 'Nescio super quibus vultis me interrogare; forte vos poteritis a me talia petere que non dicam vobis'.

proofs were brought in evidence, and she was convicted entirely on the basis of her own words.

On the face of it, one might say that it was not surprising for Joan to have been convicted in violation of the laws of procedure, since her captors were determined to convict her. But Cauchon and his colleagues took all the pains they could to make the trial formally correct and impervious to appeal or reversal. Cauchon was greatly disturbed when John Lohier, who later became dean of the Roman Rota, on being asked his opinion about the trial when it was in its early stages, responded that he thought it was invalid. Among Lohier's reasons were the fact that the process was not 'ordinary' (probably meaning that no *infamia* had been established) and no charges had been presented to Joan.[57]

Cauchon was following what had become standard practice, at least in certain quarters. Proof of this can be had from studying the records of other trials, for instance those conducted by James Fournier, Bishop of Pamiers, a hundred years earlier. Here the defendant was summoned and routinely put under oath to tell the truth both about himself as 'principal' and about others as witness concerning what would be asked him touching on the catholic faith.[58] But confirmation can also be had from the judicial reviews of Joan's case, beginning with the commis-

[57] See P. Doncoeur and Y. Lanhers, *La rehabilitation de Jeanne la Pucelle*, vol. 2, *L'enquête ordonnée par Charles VI en 1450* (Documents et recherches relatifs à Jeanne la Pucelle, no. 3; Paris 1956) 48, testimony of William Manchon: 'Maistre Jehan Lohier, veu la procès, dist que ne valoit riens, pour plusieurs causes. Premierement, que n'y avoit point forme de procès ordinaire.... Item, que libelle n'avoit point esté baillé ne articles.... Desquelles choses monsieur de Beauvays fu indigné contre ledit Lohier'. Tisset, *Procès* 3.62 n. 3, 69-70, 213, assumes that Manchon was reporting Lohier as referring to the failure to establish infamy. Cf. the testimony of Thomas Courcelles in 1456, ed. P. Duparc, *Procès en nullité de la condemnation de Jeanne d'Arc*, 4 vols. to date (Société de l'Histoire de France 486, 491, 493, 498; Paris 1977-86) 1.356, who says that Lohier spoke of it to him: 'ipse dixit loquenti quod sibi videbatur quod non debebat procedi contra eamdem Johannem in materia fidei, nisi informatione precedente super infamia; et quod de jure requirebatur talis informatio'. Cf. pp. 216, 418-19, testimony of William Manchon, 1452 and 1456.

[58] J. Duvernoy, ed., *Le registre d'inquisition de Jacques Fournier, évêque de Pamiers (1318-1325)*, 3 vols. (Toulouse 1965; pamphlet of *Corrections*, 1972) 1.40: In the first case, Raymond de Sainte-Foy is summoned, 'cui constituto in judicio, oblato libro Evangeliorum, dixit [episcopus] et eundem monuit ut super hiis super quibus per eundem dominum episcopum fidem tangentibus catholicam interrogaretur, tam de se ut principalis quam de aliis, vivis et mortuis, ut testis plenam et meram sine diminutione veritatis et admixtione falsitatis diceret veritatem'. In this case the defendant objects to taking an oath or giving a promise, and so the bishop proceeds without insisting, but also without producing charges. In another case, the defendant, Arnaud Tesseyre, not only stoutly refuses to swear to such an oath, but also, when asked to tell the truth about those things he was accused of ('quod diceret veritatem super hiis de quibus acusabatur, tam de crimine heresis quam etiam de maleficiis per eum, ut dicitur, perpetratis'), he asked the bishop to say exactly what was said against him ('dictus Arnaldus rogaret dictum dominum episcopum quod ei diceret quod et que contra eum dicebantur'). The bishop then proceeded, 'de gratia' (as if he were doing the defendant a favor and not following the required *ordo*), to list the charges against him (2.204).

sion of Charles VII in 1450 and ending with the trial before the papal commissioners in 1455-56. Among the great number of objections that were made to the form and substance of her trial, including the hundred raised by the proctor of Joan's mother and brothers, there is only one complaint about the violation of inquisitorial procedure. It comes in the treatise of John de Montigny, a doctor of canon law, who says that there was no preparatory inquisition on infamy, as required even by Boniface VIII's decretals *Postquam* and *Si is*, and that Joan was wrongly made to respond under oath on a wide range of matters, even all sorts of occult questions.[59]

The failure of the other critics of Joan's trial to notice violations of inquisitorial procedure should not make us conclude that this procedure was a dead letter, even though still on the books. One need only look at the various trials that took place at the Council of Constance, in some of which Cauchon participated, to see the requisite forms being observed.[60] A more realistic and instructive example, perhaps, can be seen in the records of the heresy inquisitions conducted in Norwich from 1428 to 1431 by William Alnwick, Bishop of Norwich, and by his vicar general in his absence.[61] Alnwick, a doctor of civil law from Cambridge, was one

---

[59] *Opinio domini Johannis de Montigny, decretorum doctoris*, ed. Duparc, 2.266-317, esp. 293-94: 'In primis igitur deficit forma processus in eo quod non apparet de inquisitione preparatoria que permitti [*lege* premitti] debuit super infamia aut suspicione in materia fidei contra dictam Johannam; qua tamen pretermissa, licitum fuit dicte Puelle conqueri cum ad veritatem onerum impositorum sciendam seu inquirendam procedere vellent, prout et nisi sunt procedere, cap. *Cum oporteat* cum pluribus aliis, *De Accusationibus* [X 5.1.19 etc.] et cap. 1 et 2 eodem titulo, *Libro Sexto* [5.1.1-2]. Quod tamen fuit necesse, maxime cum dicta Puella non reperiatur apud bonos et graves fuisse de heresi diffamata aut in fide suspecta, sed potius fidelis et catholica. Secundo, in exactione juramenti gravata extitit, et ob hoc processus deffectivus, et hoc dupliciter, primo in eo quod cogebatur ad omnia inquisita, etiam quecumque et quantumque occulta, per juramentum respondere, et de respondendo generaliter et absolute quibuscumque interrogandis compellebatur, cum tamen de eis tantum debuisset per juramentum cogi ad respondendum de quibus erat diffamata seu in fide suspecta aut notata; unde locus fuit appellationi juxta ea que habentur in cap. *Qualiter et quando debeat* in par. *Debet* cum ibi notatis per doctores, *De accusationibus* [X 5.1.24]'. In notes after the *casus* to *Postquam*, Sext. 5.1.1, Elias Regnier states that the main effect of the decretal is to reinforce the proper procedure: 'Nota effectum principalem huius capituli quod judex non debet contra aliquem inquirere, nisi sit de crimine diffamatus; et potest ille contra quem inquiritur allegare et proponere quod non est diffamatus'. There follows the passage quoted above in n. 51: 'Et hodie communiter', etc. Montigny, a canon of Paris and counselor to the Parlement, wrote his treatise between 1452 and 1454 (Tisset, 'Tribunal' [n. 38 supra] 312).

[60] For Cauchon's participation, see Tisset and Lanhers, *Procès* 2.388; Mansi 27.819, 831, 834-36, 972, 1100, 1102, 1115; see also ibid. 28.167, 219, 804. Cauchon had a licentiate in canon law from Paris.

[61] N.P. Tanner, ed., *Heresy trials in the diocese of Norwich, 1428-1431* (Camden Society 4.20; London 1977). The term *inquisicio* is not applied to the trials proper, but is used only in connection with the proclamation made to the defendant's neighbors present in the courtroom when compurgation is about to be ordered, to inquire whether anyone can give reason why it should not be ordered (that is, by testifying to his actual guilt); see Tanner 104, 210, 216. Cf. Helmholz (n. 53 supra) 15. M.

of the English prelates involved in the Joan of Arc trial (he was present at her abjuration on 24 May 1431).[62] Many of his trials seem entirely regular, but a closer look suggests a pattern of deviations from the *ordo juris* similar to the deviations of Fournier and Cauchon: 'Diffamation' is simply asserted and not proved, followed by arrest and prolonged imprisonment and interrogation under a catch-all oath before formal charges are brought in court; there is no offer or explanation of defenses or opportunity given for defense counsel; compurgation is ordered without proof of ill fame or suspicion; and oaths against future false beliefs are exacted without having established past dereliction. On occasion, proper procedures appear to be followed--for instance, in charging a defendant before he is required to respond--but usually the formalities are observed only after the case has been engineered by contraventions of due inquisitorial process.[63] All of this demonstrates that the judges and attending jurists were aware

---

Aston, 'William White's Lollard followers', CHR 68 (1982) 469-97, objects to Tanner's calling all of the proceedings he edits 'trials' (p. 470), but in fact all of the records do pertain to trial records, and the term is entirely appropriate.

[62] Tisset and Lanhers, 1.385.

[63] I presume that the oath used in the preliminary examinations (see Tanner 72-74) was the same as that used in court, which is paraphrased on p. 41: 'Margeria ... prestitit juramentum veritatem quam sciverit et noverit super interrogandis ab eadem tangentibus materiam fidei dictura et depositura'. The case of the chaplain Robert Bert seems to be one in which the defendant was not subjected to interrogation until summoned to trial. He is characterized as, 'de heretica pravitate notatus, ut dicebatur, multipliciter et diffamatus, ac ea occasione coram dicto patre responsurus ad dictos diem et locum ad judicium evocatus' (p. 98). He denies all charges except that of owning a copy of *Dives et pauper*, but he denies that the book contained anything erroneous when he possessed it; in fact, before selling it, he had lent it to a Dominican friar to copy, for the use of a knight, whom he names (p. 99). The bishop orders compurgation, which Bert successfully performs, but then Alnwick says that in spite of his purgation he holds him to be vehemently suspect of heresy for having possessed *Dives et pauper*, which contains many errors and heresies (not specified by the bishop), of which he was *multipliciter diffamatus* in the diocese of Norwich. Bert is therefore ordered to swear that he will never hold errors or heresies in the future (p. 102). I take the phrase *ut dicebatur* to indicate that Bert's ill fame was never proved in court. It is true that according to the canonists ordinaries did not have to establish infamy before proceeding to make inquisition into the truth of the charges; see John Andrew, *Ordinary Gloss* to Sext. 5.1.2, *Si is*, ad v. *fuerat* (see n. 38 above), and *Novella* on X 5.1.24 (5.15A no. 10 and 5.17A no. 36) and see the discussion of William Lyndwood, *Provinciale* (Oxenforti 1679; repr. Farnborough 1968) 312 note *k*, and also the extensive treatment of John Acton in his glosses to the thirteenth-century legatine constitutions (published as an appendix to Lyndwood) p. 56, where he draws on John Andrew's *Novella* (therefore he is writing well after 1338; he was dead by November 1349). But purgation was never to be ordered without proving infamy. See William Durant, *Speculum*, book 3, part 1, title *De abolitione et purgatione.* para. 2, *Nunc de purgatione*, no. 1: 'Si infamatus non est, in nullo casu est ad purgationem cogendus' (2.55). Cf. X 5.34.6, cited in n. 5 above, and see Helmholz (n. 53 supra) 13-15. In the case of Joan of Arc, Cauchon could have claimed the privilege of proceeding without establishing infamy since he professes to be acting as Joan's ordinary. But even admitting this claim, and putting aside her justified attempts to recuse him as a hostile judge, she would have had the right to refuse to respond on all points set forth in chapters of inquiry on which infamy was not

of the required formalities, while not attaching much significance to their omission. No doubt the same could be said of jurists in the United States before the Supreme Court's 1966 decision in the case of *Ernesto A. Miranda versus the State of Arizona* on the constitutional right of a suspect to be apprised of his rights against self-incrimination. This right was neglected, especially in state and local courts, even though it is plainly stated in the Bill of Rights: 'No person ... shall be compelled in any criminal case to be a witness against himself' (Amendment 5). A related right follows: 'In all criminal prosecutions, the accused shall enjoy the right ... to be informed of the nature and cause of the accusation ... and to have the assistance of counsel for his defense' (Amendment 6).[64]

I suggest that historians of medieval jurisprudence need to be alerted to the fundamentals of inquisitorial procedure, so that they can assess, with greater accuracy than they have achieved in the past, the strengths and weaknesses of the law in theory and the uses and abuses of the same law in practice. In the absence of a canonical *Miranda* ruling, I hope that the present account will help to fill the need.[65]

---

proved. Alnwick was also one of the judges in the trial of Eleanor Cobham for witchcraft and heresy in 1441, which however was handled according to proper form. See my 'English kings' (n. 4 supra) 219-29. See also my account and notices of other trials there, especially those of William Russell for heresy, both in England and in Rome (pp. 213 n.18 and 225 n.75).

[64] The *Miranda* right to counsel is derived from the Fifth rather than the Sixth Amendment. See *McNeil v. Wisconsin* (13 June 1991), *U.S. Supreme Court Bulletin* 51 (1990-91) B2686-B2706.

[65] A good recent article is that by W. Trusen, 'Der Inquisitionsprozess: Seine historischen Grundlagen und frühen Formen', ZRG Kan. Abt. 74 (1988) 168-230. He discusses pre-inquisitorial forms (pp. 171-87), Innocent III (pp. 187-215), John Teuton's commentary on the Fourth Lateran decree *Qualiter et quando* no. 2 (pp. 215-18), and Roffred's views on inquisitorial procedure, as found in his *Libellus super jure pontificio*, ca. 1237 (pp. 220-29).

III

The Right to Remain Silent: Before and After Joan of Arc

The beginning of the typical Miranda warning—"You have the right to remain silent. Anything you say can be used against you in a court of law"[1]—is also a fair statement of the medieval right to silence that can be deduced from the canonical rules of due process, and such a warning could and should have been given to arrestees in inquisitorial proceedings. In such proceedings the judge was obliged to give any detained or summoned person a precise statement of the charged crime, to explain the nature of the charges, to allow or provide counsel and other defenses, and to prove that the person was considered guilty of the crime by respectable members of the community before insisting on a response to the charges or to any questioning. If the judge ignored these preliminary procedures and proceeded to interrogation, and persisted even after protest, the defendant could refuse to cooperate by declaring himself or herself aggrieved and entering an immediate appeal.[2] Remaining silent before being

A note on texts and names: Punctuation and capitalization are my own. In Latin texts I revert to the medieval spelling of *e* when editors use the classicized *ae* and *oe* (thus, for *Andreae* and *coelum* I put *Andree* and *celum*), and for both Latin and vernacular texts I use *j* and *v* for consonantal *i* and *u* (*juris* and *vobis* rather than *iuris* and *uobis*), to reflect the fact that medieval Latin was pronounced like the vernacular of the user, and also to remind present-day scholars not to adopt classical pronunciation (formulated specifically for the period 50 B.C.–A.D. 50) for postclassical Latin. See my "Lawyers' Latin: *Loquenda ut vulgus*?" *Journal of Legal Education* 38 (1988), 195–207. As for the rendering of names of medieval persons, one common method is to keep first and second names in the same language. This has the virtue of internal consistency but the drawback of external inconsistency, for it mixes classicized or medieval Latin names with modern English forms and medieval or modern versions of European vernacular names. For instance, one finds Ioannes or Johannes Andreae alongside John XXII and Jehan or Jean Le Moyne. I prefer another method, which has a long tradition in English historiography and hagiography: namely, rendering first names wherever possible into modern English, even when second names are left in another language: thus, Christopher rather than Christophorus Columbus and Charles rather than Carlo Borromeo. When second names in Latin texts are genitive patronymics, as in Johannes Andree, Bernardus Guidonis, and Gulielmus Duranti, I use the noninflected form seen in names like Augustus John, Samuel Daniel, and Dylan Thomas; thus, John Andrew, Bernard Guy, William Durant.

[1] This is the version that was adopted by the Phoenix Police Department; see Liva Baker, *Miranda: Crime, Law and Politics* (New York, 1983), pp. 177–78. Some recent variants of the second sentence are contrary-to-fact as they stand; for instance, the version currently used by the Los Angeles Police Department (dated March 1977) reads: "Anything you say can *and will* [my italics] be used against you in a court of law." A qualifying phrase like "if necessary" needs to be added. The U.S. Supreme Court opinion in the case of *Miranda v. Arizona*, 13 June 1966, did not give a formula to be followed by arresting officers but only a statement of what procedural safeguards were to be employed: "Prior to any questioning, the person must be warned that he has a right to remain silent, that any statement he does make may be used as evidence against him, and that he has a right to the presence of an attorney, either retained or appointed" (Baker, p. 142).

[2] I should note that when medieval jurists speak of a defendant's or litigant's rights they do not

formally charged was especially important in heresy cases, because one could be convicted not only for confessing a previously committed crime but also for expressing an opinion or belief that could be taken as a brand-new crime of false belief; it would become instantly notorious and require no further proof simply by being uttered in court.

In this study I wish to discuss the nature and implications of the right of refusal to answer questions before arraignment, and associated rights against self-incrimination, in connection with the case of Joan of Arc. Her case is particularly valuable because of the full, though biased, record of her condemnation trial in 1431[3] and the extensive formal review that led to her exoneration twenty-five years later, which included the depositions of 116 persons.[4] The juridical deficiencies of the records of Joan's condemnation have not been discussed as thoroughly or perspicaciously as the veridical questions of the trial record.[5]

---

limit themselves to the term *jus*. Thus, when Innocent III in the Fourth Lateran Council refers to the *facultas defendendi se ipsum* in an inquisition (see n. 10 below), the Ordinary Gloss speaks of the *ordo juris* (ad v. *presens*: "Ordo juris servandus est in inquisitione facienda") and the *casus* to this paragraph (*Debet*) speaks of *defensio* ("Omnis defensio sibi reservatur"): *Corpus juris canonici*, 3 vols. (Rome, 1582; repr. Lyons, 1606), 2:1598. When John Monachus discusses one of these rights, commenting on *Sext.* 5.1.2 (see n. 25 below), he refers to it as an *ordo introductus in favorem illius contra quem mandatur inquiri* and as a *defensio*; he says that it can be voluntarily renounced, or it can be lost if not used in its proper *ordo*, that is, in its stipulated procedural sequence ("Ille qui defensione suo ordine non utitur illam perdit"); and Monachus's sixteenth-century editor, Philip Probus or Lepreux, in commenting on his statements, speaks of such a right as a *beneficium*. For the *ordo juris* or *ordo judiciarius* in the older form of criminal proceedings, the *accusatio*, see Kenneth Pennington, *The Prince and the Law, 1200–1600: Sovereignty and Rights in the Western Legal Tradition* (Berkeley, 1993), p. 143. According to the earliest formulation, that of Stephen of Tournai, ca. 1165, the accused was to be properly summoned before a judge who had jurisdiction over him or her, legitimate delays were to be granted, the accusation was to be in writing, and legitimate witnesses were to be produced, so that sentence would be given only against a defendant who confessed or who was convicted. The sentence was to be in writing, except in brief cases and (especially) when the parties were "vile" persons.

[3] Pierre Tisset, ed., with Yvonne Lanhers, *Procès de condamnation de Jeanne d'Arc*, 3 vols. (Paris, 1960–71). The French text survives partially in the d'Urfé manuscript, from the second half of the fifteenth century; it begins midway through the testimony of 3 March 1431 (1:94). Some of the earlier material is covered by the Orléans manuscript, which is derived from the d'Urfé text but is the work of a faulty scribe (1:xxi–xxvi).

[4] Pierre Duparc, ed., *Procès en nullité de la condamnation de Jeanne d'Arc*, 5 vols. (Paris, 1977–88), rejects the term rehabilitation and substitutes, as is clear from his title, "nullification of the condemnation," to correspond to the juridical effect of the second trial (see the preface by Pierre Marot, 1:vii–viii). However, the sentence not only nullified the earlier processes but also expunged from Joan and her kin all marks of infamy that came from them (2:610).

[5] The notarized Latin form, called *Instrumentum sententie*, was compiled around 1435, that is, four years or so after Joan's execution; it consists in large part of a translation and adaptation of the original French text of the examinations of Joan. It was made by Thomas Courcelles, working with the principal notary, William Manchon, for the chief judge, Peter Cauchon, and cast in the form of a long official letter or public instrument in Cauchon's name and that of the deputy heresy inquisitor for France, John Lemaistre. But the first-person plural normally refers only to Cauchon: "Nos vero, episcopus predictus," etc. (Tisset, 1:2). Both Cauchon and Courcelles are highly suspect (Courcelles, who was rector of the University of Paris in 1430 and 1431, was one of only three assessors to urge that Joan be tortured; see Tisset, 2:394–95), but Manchon seems to have been conscientious and not inimical to Joan, and therefore some concerns about the record's accuracy can be allayed. We will see below, however, that we must be on our guard at all times.

Most objections against the trial procedure in the preliminary phases, both in the nullity trial and in our own era, center around the oppressive conditions of the interrogation, whereas the primary objection should have been against the interrogation itself.

In contrasting the inquisitorial system with Anglo-American traditions, I wish to claim somewhat more for the former than has ordinarily been given to it, since its beneficial aspects are frequently ignored or downplayed by historians. An example can be seen in Leonard Levy's study of the right against self-incrimination. He begins with the case of the priest John Lambert, who in a heresy inquisition in 1532 twice insisted that the principle "No man is bound to betray himself" was in the archbishop of Canterbury's own law, though he did not know precisely where; and he added that the principle "Cogitationis penam nemo patiatur" was also to be found there. Levy assumes that Lambert's "argument on illegality of the proceedings against him was founded on a system of trial that was antithetical to the inquisitorial system and older than Magna
* Carta."[6] But in fact Lambert was appealing to safeguards and defenses that were to be found in canon law,[7] and, as we will see, he was not objecting to the proceedings against himself, which he seems to have accepted as canonically regular, but to the practice of forcing persons to "detect" themselves in the absence of any proof or legally established infamy. Richard Helmholz has recently shown that many opponents of self-incrimination in later times made similar appeals to canonistic principles.[8] In what follows I will try to give an account of earlier theory and practice.

[6] Leonard W. Levy, *Origins of the Fifth Amendment: The Right against Self-Incrimination* (New York, 1968; repr. with new preface, New York, 1986), pp. 3–4, citing John Foxe, *Acts and Monuments*, 4th ed., ed. Josiah Pratt (London, 1877), 5:184, 221. For Lambert's trial, see below, nn. 74, 166. On p. 19 Levy characterizes the English criminal system in the middle of the fifteenth century thus: "Of course, trial by the local community could be trial by local prejudice, but at least the prisoner knew the charges against him, confronted his accuser, and had freedom to give his own explanation as well as question and argue with the prosecution's witnesses. He suffered from many disadvantages—lack of counsel, lack of witnesses on his own behalf, lack of time to prepare his defense—yet the trial was supremely fair, judged by any standard known in the western world of that day." But a few pages later he admits that the inquisitorial system, as still practiced in the ordinary episcopal courts, included a right to be informed of the charges, to know the names of the prosecution's witnesses and to have copies of their depositions, to have counsel, and to dispute and challenge charges and witnesses (p. 25).

[7] The axiom "Cogitationis penam nemo patiatur" was added to Gratian's *Decretum, De penitencia* 1.14, from Justinian, *Digest* 48.19.18: Emil Friedberg, ed., *Corpus iuris canonici* (Leipzig, 1879–81), 1:1161. The Latin version of the other adage, "Nemo tenetur prodere se[ipsum]," which is given by Foxe, is to be found in the Ordinary Gloss to the *Decretales Gregorii IX* 2.20.37, s.v. *de causis* (Roman ed., 2:736), as is pointed out by R. H. Helmholz in the article cited in the next note, p. 967. The glossator, Bernard of Parma, takes it to be the equivalent of Chrysostom's statement "non tibi dico ut te prodas in publicum," in Gratian, *De penitencia* 1, dictum post c. 87, §1 (Friedberg, 1:1184). Levy knows of Gratian's citation but assumes that the sentiment found no echo in later canonistic works (pp. 21, 70, 453 n. 40).

[8] R. H. Helmholz, "Origins of the Privilege against Self-Incrimination: The Role of the European *Ius commune*," *New York University Law Review* 65 (1990), 962–90.

1. Inquisition and the Right to Privacy

A restriction on unlimited inquiry was a fundamental principle of the new inquisitorial system set up by Innocent III at the Fourth Lateran Council in 1215; it was part of the "bill of rights," or guarantee of due process, that was then put in place, and it followed on the principle that "the Church does not judge secret matters."[9]

The pope designed the *inquisitio* to take the place of the procedure of *accusatio* in Roman civil law. In that older form of trial, an accuser brought a criminal charge against a certain individual and undertook to prove his guilt, agreeing to suffer the penalty of "retaliation" if he failed to offer sufficient proof: that is, he would undergo the same punishment that the accused would suffer if found guilty. One can readily understand the awkwardness of having to depend on the volunteering of good citizens willing to risk their own livelihood or even lives in order to have criminals brought to justice. For the vulnerable accuser Pope Innocent substituted trustworthy informants who could testify to their *belief* that a certain person had committed a crime. This collective belief the pope called *fama*, "fame," and on its basis an ecclesiastical judge (a bishop, say) could summon the suspect and *inquire*, that is, "make inquisition," as to whether the fame was true. The pope considered the fame, or public outcry, to be the equivalent of the accuser in the older system; this is how he forestalled the objection that the judge was acting as both accuser and judge.[10]

The judge's first obligation, when implicated persons were summoned to his court, was to give them, in writing, detailed points (chapters, or articles) of the charges against them and to explain the charges, thereby enabling them to defend themselves. He was also to give them both the names and the testimony of all the witnesses against them, and they in turn were allowed to enter objections both to the substance and to the persons of the witnesses.

This system required a certain amount of preliminary investigation. The pope envisaged that a judge would first be alerted by reports from afar and then go to the scene of the crime to see for himself. He modeled this procedure of "general inquisition" on Genesis 18.21, where God says of Sodom and Gomorrah, "I will go down and see whether they have done according to the cry that is come to me." The general inquisition was institutionalized in the regular episcopal and archidiaconal visitations, in which the ordinary prelate would interview substantial members of the local parish, sometimes called "synodal witnesses," on the facts of crimes and abuses and their opinions on the identity of the perpetrators. He would also gather whatever proofs of guilt were readily available or at least note the names of likely witnesses.

[9] Stephan Kuttner, "Ecclesia de occultis non iudicat," *Acta Congressus iuridici internationalis . . . Romae . . . 1931*, 5 vols. (Rome, 1935–37), 3:225–46.

[10] *Qualiter et quando, Decretales Gregorii IX* 5.1.24: Innocent III, canon 8 of the Fourth Lateran Council (Friedberg, 2:745–47); for the relevant text, see H. A. Kelly, "Inquisitorial Due Process and the Status of Secret Crimes," *Proceedings of the Eighth International Congress of Medieval Canon Law*, ed. Stanley Chodorow, Monumenta Iuris Canonici, Series C: Subsidia, 9 (Vatican City, 1992), pp. 407–27, esp. p. 410 n. 7.

As for the "specific inquisition," when an individual person was summoned to court, the judge could compel witnesses to testify both to the fame of the defendant and to his or her guilt.[11] Innocent himself would perhaps have considered it a violation of due process to force the defendant to respond directly to the question of guilt, whether under oath or not.[12] But as the thirteenth century proceeded, the self-inculpatory oath came to be justified both for accusatorial and inquisitorial processes, and it continued to be a feature of modern criminal procedure on the Continent.[13] Thus Cardinal Hostiensis in his *Summa Decretalium* (finished in 1253) wrote that the defendant should be forced to swear to tell the truth in an inquisition.[14] In the English common-law tradition, in contrast, charges were not answered under oath, and it was recognized that a plea of "Not guilty" could be made by a guilty person without perjury.[15]

In his *Commentary on the Decretals* (finished shortly before his death in 1271) Hostiensis maintained that the giving of chapters and the establishing of fame were absolutely essential to an inquisition and that a trial would be invalid if either procedure was omitted.[16] But Pope Boniface VIII in his *Liber sextus* of 1298 countered this position with two new laws. In *Postquam* he said that if you confess to a crime in an inquisition, you cannot invalidate your confession by claiming that you were never defamed of the crime or that charges were not

[11] *Decretales Gregorii IX* 2.21.8 (Innocent III, *Super his*, 1203): "Ceterum volumus et . . . mandamus ut super inquisitionis articulis, tam de fama electi quam literis contra eum sub nomine longe majoris et sanioris partis capituli destinatis, cogatis testes, qui nominati fuerint, perhibere testimonium veritati." The crime in this case was taken by commentators to be a case of counterfeiting letters (Friedberg, 2:343).

[12] However, in Innocent's decretal *Cum dilecti*, 1205, he rehearses with approval a case where *frequens clamor* against a bishop was investigated by papal legates who bound both the bishop and his canons by oath to tell the truth (or to answer questions) about the state of the local church (*Decretales* 5.1.18, Friedberg, 2:739–40).

[13] The history of this development is given by Adhémar Esmein, "Le serment des inculpés en droit canonique," *Bibliothèque de l'Ecole des hautes études, Sciences réligieuses* 7 (1896), 231–48.

[14] Hostiensis, *Summa aurea* (Venice, 1574; repr. Turin, 1963), *De inquisitionibus*, § *Et qualiter*, no. 6 (p. 1478), cited by Esmein, "Serment," p. 245.

[15] "Not guilty" therefore means nothing more than "Volo contendere." Cf. the plea "Nolo contendere," which began to be used in American criminal proceedings in the early 1870s: it subjects a defendant to conviction in a trial without admitting guilt and without precluding him from denying the truth of the charges in a different proceeding. The earliest citation of the plea of "Not guilty" given in the *Oxford English Dictionary*, s.v. Plead (v.), 7d, is from 1344 in the Law French form "plaider de rien coupable," and in English from 1454; but the *Dictionary of Medieval Latin from British Sources*, s.v. *acquietare*, 8, gives Latin examples from 1255 and 1315; the latter reads, "Acquietavit se quod non est culpabilis." Later in the fourteenth century the standard formula is, "Dicit quod ipse est in nullo inde culpabilis," as in some of the *raptus* cases from 3 Richard II (1380–81) referred to by Christopher Cannon, "*Raptus* in the Chaumpaigne Release and a Newly Discovered Document Concerning the Life of Geoffrey Chaucer," *Speculum* 68 (1993), 74–94, esp. p. 83 n. 46; the plea is to be found in the five citations from KB 29/32 (mm. 25, 8d, 32d, 38d, 61d). I should add that "Guilty" seems not to have been recognized as a plea until the seventeenth century (the first citation in the *OED*, s.v. Guilty and Plead, is 1681); before that, if a guilty person wished to admit guilt, he was simply said to confess.

[16] Hostiensis, *Commentaria in Decretales Gregorii IX* (Venice, 1581; repr. Turin, 1965), on 5.1.17 (5:5A–6, nos. 4–6) and 5.1.24 (5:11A, no. 15).

presented to you.[17] In *Si is* he said that if you are summoned to an inquisition and the judge proceeds to the business of inquiring into the truth of the charges without first establishing fame, if you are present and do not object, you cannot later impugn the trial on that basis.[18]

This legislation turned out to be a sinister development, because the pope said nothing about the judge's obligation to carry out the procedures for presenting charges and establishing fame or for alerting the defendant to his or her rights to these procedures; and he prescribed no penalty if a judge deliberately concealed these rights from unwitting defendants or insisted on proceeding without them.

According to the fourteenth-century canonist John Andrew, who composed the Ordinary Gloss on Boniface's *Liber sextus*, ordinary judges (as opposed to delegated judges) did not have to establish fame before proceeding to make inquisition into the truth of the charges.[19] But in his later *Novella* (finished in 1338) he noted the recommendation of Hostiensis that the ordinary judge should make inquiry and receive witnesses on infamy in order to avoid appeals; and this, he wrote, was the common practice in his own day.[20] He summed up by saying that when the defendant denies infamy but the infamy is notorious, the judge may omit the inquiry of fame and proceed to the inquiry of truth, though it would be safer to receive some witnesses to the infamy, because the defendant may in fact be wrongly defamed. Moreover, many things are said to be notorious which are not. Finally, if the defendant appeals, the process would be imperiled, because the judge would have to prove the infamy to his superior.[21]

[17] *Sext.* 5.1.1 (Friedberg, 2:1069): "Postquam coram eo qui contra te super certis criminibus inquisitor fuerat deputatus eadem crimina fuisti confessus, frustra confessionem tuam, quo minus puniaris ex ea prout justitia suadebit, eo pretextu impugnare contendis quod super eisdem criminibus non fueras antea diffamatus, vel quod per eundem inquisitorem capitula super quibus contra te volebat inquirere tibi tradita non fuerunt."

[18] *Sext.* 5.1.2 (ibid.): "Si is cui contra te commissa fuerat simpliciter inquisitio super certis criminibus facienda processerit, te presente nec reclamante aut quicquam super hoc excipiente, infamie inquisitione omissa, ad veritatem eorundem criminum inquirendam, processum hujusmodi ex eo, quod non fuit de infamia primitus inquisitum, ulterius impugnare nequibis."

[19] John Andrew, Ordinary Gloss to *Sext.* 5.1.2, ad v. *fuerat* (col. 610): "ad petitionem alicujus; quia si Papa proprio motu committit inquisitionem criminum alicujus, jam illum approbat infamatum, cum episcopus et metropolitanus procedant etiam ad inquisitionem, omisso tali art[iculo]"; see also his *Novella* on *Decretales* 5.1.24 (1581; repr. Turin, 1963), 5:15A, no. 15: "Sed quandoque fit inquisitio debito officii urgente, etsi nulla fama precedat, ut cum agitur de matrimonio contrahendo corporali . . . vel spirituali; . . . idem ubicunque ex mero et puro officio procedit judex, in his maxime in quibus vertitur periculum animarum."

[20] John Andrew, *Novella*, loc. cit., 5:17A, no. 36: "Consuluit tamen Hostiensis ibi [in *Decretales* 5.1.19] ordinarium, ut appellationes evitet, quod inquirat et testes prius recipiat super infamia; et sic communiter servatur."

[21] Ibid.: "Si negat utrunque, scilicet crimen et infamiam, vel solam infamiam, si notoria est infamia, potest procedere ad inquisitionem veritatis, non laborando tunc circa inquisitionem fame (*De accusationibus, Evidentia* [*Decretales* 5.1.9]), licet tutius sit aliquos testes ad cautelam recipere, ut est dictum: tum quia 'dictum [unius] facile sequitur multitudo' (infra, *De purgatione canonica, Cum in juventute* [5.34.12], §1); tum quia sequitur quod infamatus sit apud bonos et graves, nec ortum habuerit a malevolis, ut hic; tum quia multa dicuntur notoria que non sunt. Ergo ad cautelam testes recipiat (*De electione, Bone* [1.6.23]); alias, si appellaretur, in periculo esset processus, cum sit necesse coram superiore probari infamiam negatam, ut dixi."

As for the deliberate omission or postponing of formal charges, no responsible commentator justified the practice (I will note below that some writers of manuals for heresy inquisitors were exceptions). John Andrew noted that Hostiensis considered the defendant's silence about the omission of the fame process to be a sign of objection, but he said that such is not the case, and he invoked the rule of law that silence signifies consent.[22] However, it was an accepted principle that only an informed silence could be construed as consent;[23] and it does not seem to have entered the mind of Pope Boniface or any of the commentators on the *Sext* that defendants, and even defense attorneys, might be unaware of these rights. Presumably, they would all have admitted that the defendants had a right to know their rights—unlike American citizens before the *Miranda* ruling[24]—but it is only in the sixteenth century that I have found an author who insisted upon it. I refer to Philip Probus in his 1535 edition of Cardinal John Monachus's *Glossa super Sexto* (1301), commenting on the cardinal's explanation of *Si is* that one can renounce a procedure introduced in one's favor.[25] (I should note in regard to the cited rule of silence in response to an action that a companion rule of law provided that silence in response to a question signified neither admission nor denial.)[26]

The required order of procedures in an inquisition was made clear by Elias Regnier in his *Long Cases for the Sext and Clementines* (Poitiers, 1483), which was added to the Ordinary Gloss by John Chappuis in 1500. Although he limited his discussion of *Si is* to the case of an inquisition by a delegated judge initiated by his superior at the request of another person rather than ex officio, he explained *Postquam* as dealing with ordinary judges proceeding ex officio. In such cases there must first be infamy connecting a specific person to a specific crime; the person is then summoned, and the judge should give him chapters detailing the points on which he has been defamed. If he does not give him chapters, he is not bound to respond to the judge's interrogation.[27] If there is no antecedent infamy, he can say, "Lord judge, you cannot proceed against me

[22] John Andrew, Ordinary Gloss to *Sext.* 5.1.2, ad v. *reclamante* (cols. 610–11), referring to *Regula juris* 43, *Sext.* 5.12 (Friedberg, 2:1123): "Qui tacet, consentire videtur." See Christoph Krampe, " 'Qui tacet, consentire videtur': Über die Herkunft einer Rechtsregel," in *Staat, Kirche, Wissenschaft in einer pluralistischen Gesellschaft: Festschrift zum 65. Geburtstag von Paul Mikat*, ed. Dieter Schwab et al. (Berlin, 1989), pp. 367–80.

[23] See William Lyndwood, *Provinciale* (1432; Oxford, 1679, repr. Farnborough, 1968), 2.1.3, ad v. *aut permissionem* (p. 86 note *b*), dealing with alienation of property: "Absens namque et ignorans non videtur consentire; . . . imo nec quandoque sciens, maxime si sit absens. . . . Imo etsi presens esset, sciens et intelligens rem suam vel sue custodie commissam auferri, per solam taciturnitatem non videretur consentire." He cites Roman civil laws to make his points.

[24] So Levy, *Origins of the Fifth Amendment*, new preface (1986), p. xiii.

[25] Philip Probus, ed., *Glossa aurea Johannis Monachi Cardinalis super Sexto decretalium* (Paris, 1535; repr. Aalen, 1968), fols. 342v–343r (= pp. 804–5), on Monachus's statement "cum quisque renunciare valeat his que pro se introducta sunt"; for the text of Probus's arguments, see Kelly, "Inquisitorial Due Process," pp. 412–13.

[26] *Regula juris* 44: "Is qui tacet non fatetur, sed nec utique negare videtur."

[27] Elias Regnier, addition to the Ordinary Gloss to *Sext.* 5.1.1, headnote: "Judex debet exhibere capitula super quibus vult inquirere, ita quod ille contra quem proceditur non tenetur respondere ad interrogationem judicis nisi prius sibi traditis capitulis super quibus fuit diffamatus."

by way of inquisition, because I have not committed such a crime; or granted but not admitted that I did commit the crime, you still cannot proceed against me because I have not been defamed of it."[28] If the judge fails to take notice of either of these objections and fails to give chapters or establish fame, the defendant should make an appeal on the spot.[29]

Regnier concludes by saying that the usual practice of his own day was in conformity with these procedures, which were mandated by the Fourth Lateran Council: that is, before a person is cited ex officio, the judge conducts a secret investigation, and if it appears that fame of the person's connection with the crime exists, he is cited to appear in court; if he appears, he is to be given chapters.[30] A common way for judges to fulfill their procedural obligations once an implicated person was summoned, whether he or she obeyed the summons or not, was to present chapters that incorporated claims both of fame and of truth, together with an offer to prove both, if denied by the defendant.[31]

The Spanish Inquisition, which was getting under way at the time that Regnier was writing, seems to have had, at least at the beginning, a similar concern for observing the rule of law. In the trials held in Ciudad Real from 1483 to 1485, the procedure was to bring an unconfessed suspect to court and give him detailed charges and to allow him to select a lawyer and a proctor before denying the charges.[32] Undoubtedly, abuses did develop, especially in connection with holding suspects for a long period of time in the hope of generating proofs; but the Grand Inquisitor, Thomas de Torquemada, took steps to stop such irregularities. In the *Instructions of Avila*, dated 25 May 1498, he insisted that suspects were not to be arrested unless proof of specific crimes had been assembled, and the arrestees were to be formally charged within ten days.[33] He was also aware of the privileged status of completely secret crimes. According

[28] Ibid.: "Si judex procedat per viam inquisitionis contra aliquem non diffamatum, potest ille contra quem proceditur per inquisitionem dicere, 'Domine judex, non potestis procedere contra me per viam inquisitionis, quia non commisi tale crimen; et posito et non confesso quod tale crimen commisissem, adhuc non potestis procedere contra me, quia de tali crimine non sum diffamatus.' "

[29] Ibid., *casus*: "Antequam judex me interrogasset, debebam ista proponere, et si me noluisset me admittere, debebam appellare."

[30] Ibid., notes after the *casus*: "Hodie communiter prius aliquis citatur ex officio super crimine et fit inquisitio, et [*lege* fit] examinatio sive informatio secreta, et factis informationibus, si constet judici quod talis est diffamatus super illo crimine, judex precipit ut citetur ad comparendum personaliter; et si compareat, debent illi tradi capitula super his super quibus debet fieri inquisitio." See Kelly, "Inquisitorial Due Process," pp. 421–22.

[31] Kelly, "Inquisitorial Due Process," p. 423.

[32] Ibid., p. 421 n. 50, citing Haim Beinart, *Records of the Trials of the Spanish Inquisition in Ciudad Real*, 1: *The Trials of 1483–1485* (Jerusalem, 1974), pp. 163–80: case of Juan de Chinchilla. In his introduction Beinart speaks of confessions of defendants made in pretrial examinations (p. xxiv), but he gives no details, and none of the cases documented in this volume demonstrates any such procedure; perhaps he is speaking of cases in which the defendants are willing to confess. The Chinchilla case shows what happened when the defendant did not wish to confess but rather to maintain innocence.

[33] *Instructions of Avila*, 25 May 1948, ed. Ernst Schäfer, "Die älteste Instruktionen-Sammlung der spanischen Inquisitionen," *Archiv für Reformationsgeschichte* 2 (1904–5), 109–14, 123–24, no. 3 (p. 110); text in Kelly, "Inquisitorial Due Process," p. 421.

to the *Instructions of Seville*, issued in 1484, persons who confessed secret crimes could be admitted to secret abjuration and penance.[34]

Since, therefore, the law and commentaries clearly indicated that defendants in an inquisition were to be charged before being required to respond to questions about criminal activity publicly associated with them, and these requirements were carried out in practice, at least in some regions, how did it come about that Joan of Arc was forced to respond to an unlimited series of questions for a month before being charged, and that the points on which she was finally convicted were taken from her responses, most of them dealing with matters hitherto entirely secret? An obvious answer is that her prosecutors deliberately violated her rights in order to make her incriminate herself. But this answer is not satisfactory, because it is clear that not only Peter Cauchon and his associates but also virtually all of Joan's sympathizers, both at the time and later, believed it to be standard procedure to question a suspect under oath before any charges were stated. How did this extraordinary oblivion regarding correct procedure come about?

2. Prearraignment Interrogation and Instant Crimes of Thought

I have suggested elsewhere that such neglect or ignorance of the *ordo juris* was the result of an abuse first observable in the practices of papally appointed heresy inquisitors in southern France in the 1250s: witnesses summoned to swear to their knowledge of the heretical activities of others were also forced to testify concerning themselves—a procedure that would be proper only in the cases of persons who had already confessed their involvement in heresy. A reference to such an oath appears in the decretal *Accusatus* of Alexander IV (1254–61), which was incorporated into the *Liber sextus*.[35] It became customary to make not only the witnesses but also the principal suspects themselves swear such an oath and then to interrogate them without any charges being named; they would be required to guess why they had been summoned and to respond to questions about what they believed on points of Christian doctrine. Their misstatements would then be taken as confessed crimes of heresy.[36] Such abuses were undoubtedly rationalized by the excuse that certain heresy inquisitors were allowed to use summary procedure, which according to some canonists permitted the exclusion of lawyers and of all rules of procedure. In 1298, in a decretal newly

[34] *Instructions of Seville*, 29 November 1484, ed. Schäfer, pp. 1–55, 109–77, no. 5 (p. 17); text in Kelly, "Inquisitorial Due Process," pp. 419–20.

[35] *Sext.* 5.2.8, §3 *Licet* (Friedberg 2:1072). The pope says that the testimony of perjured witnesses in heresy cases can sometimes be admitted when their later "corrected" testimony implicates themselves as well as others: "Licet vero perjuri a testimonio etiam post penitentiam repellantur, si tamen ii qui coram inquisitoribus jurantes tam de se quam de aliis super facto heresis dicere veritatem eam celando dejerent et postmodum velint corrigere dictum suum contra se ac alios suos complices deponendo, . . . in favorem fidei, nisi aliud obsistat, stari debet tam contra se quam contra reliquos attestationibus eorundum." There is no comment on the form of the oath in John Andrew's Ordinary Gloss or his *Novella* or in the commentaries of the Archdeacon (Guy of Baysio) or Elias Regnier.

[36] H. A. Kelly, "Inquisition and the Prosecution of Heresy: Misconceptions and Abuses," *Church History* 58 (1989), 439–51, esp. pp. 447–49.

designed for the *Liber sextus*, Boniface VIII decreed that all heresy cases could employ summary procedure. In 1312, however, in the decretal *Dispendiosam*, Pope Clement V extended this privilege to many other kinds of cases, civil as well as criminal, and then, in 1314, at the urging of John Andrew, he issued the decretal *Sepe*, clarifying once and for all (supposedly) what could and could not be allowed under summary procedure; for one thing, no necessary proofs or defenses were to be excluded.[37]

The *Clementine Constitutions* was officially published by Pope John XXII in 1317, and the Dominican Bernard Guy, papal heresy inquisitor at Toulouse from 1306 to 1323, refers to one of the constitutions in the manual that he compiled in the early 1320s.[38] But he does not mention either *Dispendiosam* or *Sepe* when treating of summary procedure, which, according to his assertion, allows the inquisitor to reject all attempts by the defendants to make objections against witnesses, to demand a *libellus* (which he seems to take as an initial statement of charges), or to make appeals.[39] None of this was true, of course; heresy trials were privileged only in allowing the use of tainted witnesses (shared with cases of simony and *lesa majestas*—whatever that might be in an ecclesiastical court) and the suppression of the names of witnesses in cases where the defendant's knowledge of their identity would be likely to endanger them.[40] Guy did not eliminate all semblance of defenses for the defendant, however; he merely postponed them. Persons who are delated must first swear to tell the truth concerning themselves and others; if they confess, the judge proceeds accordingly. But if they refuse to tell the truth (Guy's assumption was that they are guilty), witnesses are received and chapters are culled from their testimony; these chapters, upon which they have been found culpable ("super quibus reperti sunt culpabiles"), are explained to the suspects and the witnesses' testimony given to them (without their names), and they are now given the ability to defend themselves, with objections and refutations allowed.[41]

The manual produced later in the century (1376) by Nicholas Eymerich, heresy inquisitor for Aragon, justifies a similar procedure, by referring, surprisingly,

[37] Ibid., p. 443; see *Sext.* 5.2.20 (Boniface's *Statuta*), *Clem.* 2.1.2 (*Dispendiosam*) and 5.11.2 (*Sepe*). John Andrew's Ordinary Gloss to the *Clementines*, published in 1322, describes his role in getting the pope to act in the matter (*Corpus juris canonici*, Lyons, 1606, 3/2:332, ad v. *Sepe contingit*). For a recent account of the provisions of *Dispendiosam* and *Sepe*, see Pennington, *Prince and the Law*, p. 189.

[38] Bernard Guy, *Tractatus de practica officii inquisicionis heretice pravitatis*, ed. C. Douais, *Practica inquisitionis heretice pravitatis auctore Bernardo Guidonis* (Paris, 1886), pt. 1, chap. 34 (p. 28): he gives a sample form letter dated August 1319 conforming to the constitution *Multorum* (*Clem.* 5.3.1), which requires papally delegated heresy inquisitors to work in conjunction with local bishops. Later on, in pt. 4, he complains of the inconveniences caused to the papal inquisitors by the constitution (pp. 174, 187–88). I take the title of Guy's treatise from his preface (p. 1). Pt. 5 of the treatise is edited and translated into French by Guillaume Mollat, *Manuel de l'inquisiteur*, 2 vols. (Paris, 1926–27).

[39] Guy, *Tractatus*, pt. 4 (p. 212).

[40] Kelly, "Inquisition and Heresy," pp. 443–46.

[41] Guy, *Tractatus*, pt. 4 (p. 229). See Mollat, 1:xliv–li, esp. p. xlvii, on the preliminary interrogation (he does not give any account of the actual procedure to be followed after the questioning; see p. xlix).

to Clement's *Sepe*. According to this constitution, he wrote, a *libellus* does not have to be submitted or the case contested. These are terms that refer to non-inquisitorial cases, where a plaintiff or accuser is present, but Eymerich said that it is the procedure to be used not only for persons who are accused (in an *accusatio*) but also for those who are only suspected (that is, we are to conclude, in an *inquisitio*). He recommended a subtle approach for the preliminary interrogation, starting with general questions and leading up gradually to the matter at hand.[42]

What was the status of statements made by defendants before being charged in an inquisition? According to Hostiensis, as we have seen, they should be thrown out. But the legislation of Boniface VIII nullified this approach and made fair game out of every admission that could be construed as the confession of a crime, whether it had been obtained by fair means or foul, and even though the crime had been entirely secret beforehand—or even nonexistent, as in the case of a faulty explanation of an article of the Apostles' Creed teased out under interrogation. For it was a principle that any confession made in court became instantly notorious, meaning that no further proof was necessary. This point was noted by the commentators on Boniface's statutes. Guy of Baysio observed that testifying against oneself in this way would be stupid and foolish.[43]

But what was one to do when one's bishop insisted that one had an obligation to respond to his questions? St. Thomas Aquinas, writing at the same time as Hostiensis, explained that a judge has no right to prosecute a crime unless there is an accuser or public infamy, or unless he witnesses the crime himself.[44] When the judge requires an accused person to respond to a charge against him, he is bound to reply, if it is done in accord with law, even though the response will convict him; his obligation to obey his superior overrules the obligation that he has against self-incrimination. However, if the question is asked against the rule of law, even though he may not answer with a lie, he is not required to answer at all; he may appeal or get out of it in some other licit way.[45] It is one thing to conceal the truth, and another to make false statements. No one is required to confess the whole truth but only what a judge can and should demand according to the rule of law: for example, when infamy or other clear evidence exists about a crime or even when a crime has been half-proved[46] (for

[42] Nicholas Eymerich, *Directorium inquisitorum*, ed. Francis Peña (Rome, 1578), pt. 3, §70 (p. 285) and §74 (p. 286).

[43] Kelly, "Inquisitorial Due Process," p. 411 n. 13, citing John Andrew, the Archdeacon, John Monachus, and Dominic of San Gimignano.

[44] Thomas Aquinas, *Summa theologie* 2-2.67.3 ad 2.

[45] Ibid. 2-2.69.1 corpus; ad 1. This article is cited by John Andrew in his *Additiones* to the *Speculum judiciale* of William Durant (Durandus), lib. 2, pt. 2, *De positionibus*, §7: *Positiones quibus modis reprobentur, et de cautelis circa eas*, no. 40, note *a* (vol. 1, p. 594 of the Basel 1574 edition of the *Speculum*; repr. Aalen, 1975).

[46] Aquinas, op. cit., 2-2.69.2 corpus: "Aliud est veritatem tacere, aliud est falsitatem proponere. Quorum primum in aliquo casu licet. Non enim aliquis tenetur omnem veritatem confiteri, sed illam solum quam ab eo potest et debet requirere judex secundum ordinem juris: puta, cum precessit infamia super aliquo crimine, vel aliqua expressa indicia apparuerunt, vel etiam cum precessit

instance, by the testimony of a single witness).[47]

One's only recourses, then, were deception by concealment or refusal to respond combined with a formal appeal. If the judge in turn refused to acknowledge or accept appeals and threatened punishment for failure to respond, one could either comply or accept the consequences of refusal, which, by right, should only have been conviction for contempt of court. Even the most unscrupulous judge could hardly have found a defendant guilty of unspecified crimes.[48] But any statements that defendants did make could and very likely would be used against them.

In a well-known series of heresy trials held in the diocese of Pamiers in southern France in the years 1318 to 1325—in other words, just after the promulgation of the *Clementines*—the procedure followed was like that advocated by Bernard Guy rather than that specified by Clement V and John Andrew. The situation was much like Joan of Arc's a hundred years later: the main judge was the bishop, James Fournier (the future Pope Benedict XII, 1334–42), working in collaboration with the deputy of the papal heresy inquisitor. Suspects were routinely required as the first matter of business to take an oath to tell the truth about themselves as principals and about others as witnesses in response to questions about matters of the faith. In instances where the defendants refused

---

probatio semiplena." It is interesting to note that in his response to the first objection Thomas says that there are many divine laws that have no punishment assigned to them by human laws, "sicut patet in simplici fornicatione." However, in England simple fornication was punished in the ecclesiastical courts.

[47] See Jean-Philippe Levy, "Le problème de la preuve dans les droits savants du moyen âge," *Recueils de la Société Jean Bodin* 17 (1965), 137–67, esp. pp. 156–59. Torture could be applied at this stage; for a recent study of the use of torture in heresy cases, see Johannes Fried, "Wille, Freiwilligkeit und Geständnis um 1300: Zur Beurteilung des letzten Templergrossmeisters Jacques de Molay," *Historisches Jahrbuch* 105 (1985), 388–425. We should recognize that torture was considered allowable in a wide variety of cases; see the extensive statement by John Teutonicus (ca. 1215) in the Ordinary Gloss to Gratian, *Decretum* 2.16.5, dictum ante c. 1, *Quod vero* (col. 1080).

[48] Helmholz, "Origins of the Privilege against Self-Incrimination," p. 983, likens medieval defendants to modern ones who face a "cruel trilemma," that is, "the unhappy choice among perjury, contempt, or conviction that faces all required to give evidence against themselves." He does not refer to the safeguards allowed defendants at the beginning of the inquisitorial process or the ability of defendants to enter an appeal each time that a prescribed procedure was not followed. I should note that Durant deals with the refusal to respond to questions in the context of noninquisitorial trials where there are two parties and there is a *litis contestatio*, as in civil suits and criminal accusations, and both parties have sworn to respond to "positions," or points of inquiry. See loc. cit. in n. 45 above, §9: *De pena non respondentis vel falso respondentis*, nos. 1–3, p. 596, and the accompanying additions of John Andrew; and see John Andrew's Ordinary Gloss to Boniface VIII's *Si post*, *Sext.* 2.9.2 (col. 346): a refusal to answer positions after swearing the "oath of calumny" is to be taken as a confession of the points asked, unless there is a reasonable cause for refusal (such as, John Andrew says, when the answer would entail the revelation of a hitherto unknown crime). Durant, in no. 2, cites Roffred, who says that, in an extrajudicial situation, one has no obligation to respond, but when one is silent *in judicio*, one is contumacious; however, Azo and others say that such silence or an obscure reply is equivalent to confession. But in no. 3, Durant cites Tancred as saying that a silent person neither confesses nor denies and therefore can only be punished as contumacious. In §7, no. 14 (p. 591), Durant says that one cannot be forced to reply when one is in doubt about one's rights or when the response would prove prejudicial to oneself: "Non est cogendus respondere quandiu dubitat de jure suo et quando ex responsione potest ei prejudicari."

to take such an oath,[49] Fournier proceeded to receive their statements unsworn, but these proved just as incriminatory as the sworn responses.

In one revealing case a defendant named Arnold Tesseyre, upon refusing to swear the oath, was asked simply to respond truthfully about those things of which he was accused, concerning both heresy and other misdeeds said to have been perpetrated by him. Arnold asked the bishop to tell him exactly what things were being said against him, and Fournier responded by listing the charges. However, he is said to have done it *de gratia*, as a favor, and not as giving the defendant something he deserved.[50]

Another case indicates that Fournier considered secret crimes to be within the province of inquisitorial proceedings. A carpenter's wife, Auda, who had come to have doubts about the Eucharist was summoned as publicly defamed of heresy;[51] but subsequent testimony indicates that the bishop summoned her as soon as he had been informed about her by a priest-infirmarian, who heard of it from a confidante of Auda's.[52] Auda's husband testified that when he first found out about her lack of faith, he was terrified and told her to go to confession, and he brought her to a priest for that purpose. Fournier then asked him why he had not reported his wife's words to him or to the heresy inquisitor. He responded that he thought she was raving because of illness, and furthermore she confessed it immediately; therefore he considered her to be excused and without fault.[53] If the husband had informed the bishop and this was his only source of information, he could not legally have proceeded against her by way of inquisition; but she could have been prosecuted by way of accusation if the husband had been willing to stand as a formal accuser.

It is noteworthy in this case that Fournier first interrogated Auda "simply," that is, without oath. He asked her if, as had been reported to him, she had erred in the articles of the faith and the sacraments of the church.[54] She was later questioned under oath concerning her earlier responses: she was made to swear to tell the full and plain truth and to say the truth in response to questions.[55] However, both her husband and her confidante, Emengard, were administered a form of the oath usually given to defendants; in the case of the husband, he was to tell the truth about himself as principal and about Auda as witness concerning the foregoing matters.[56] The infirmarian and other witnesses swore only to tell the truth concerning the foregoing.[57] After being questioned

[49] See the case of Raymond de Costa, *Le registre d'inquisition de Jacques Fournier, évêque de Pamiers (1318–1325)*, ed. Jean Duvernoy, 3 vols. (Toulouse, 1965; *Corrections*, 1972), 1:40–41, 48, 54, 106–7: he refused to swear on the grounds that oaths were prohibited. Another defendant refused because once when he was sick he had sworn not to take any oaths (1:511).

[50] Ibid., 2:204; text partially in Kelly, "Inquisitorial Due Process," pp. 424–25 n. 58.

[51] Ibid., 2:82.

[52] Ibid., 2:87–89.

[53] Ibid., 2:86.

[54] Ibid., 2:82.

[55] Ibid., 2:84.

[56] Ibid., 2:85; Emengard swore "super premissis de se ut principalis et de aliis ut testis puram et meram dicere veritatem."

[57] Ibid., 2:89–92, 97, 100.

about Auda, the husband was asked if he himself had had or still had any doubts about the articles or sacraments of the church, or if he had had any dealings with heretics. He responded negatively to both questions.[58] At the end of the case, after concurring with the majority of his assessors in sentencing Auda to penances that involved no humiliation,[59] Fournier announced that he retained the power to punish the female witnesses who had committed perjury during the course of the trial, and he passed a sentence absolving Auda's husband of any guilt in the affair.[60]

To sum up: if the practice noted in the previous section, of placing defendants in an inquisition under oath to respond to formal charges, led to procedural abuses, it was not nearly as detrimental as the practice that we have been studying here, of swearing in a suspect to answer questions before charges are explained and without any attempt to prove association with public crimes. Though post-arraignment oaths were never explicitly required by law, they did find justification and support among the canonistic commentators. But this was not true of prearraignment oaths and interrogations. Surprisingly, historians of self-incrimination, at least in the English tradition, rarely take note of the timing of inquisitorial proceedings but simply lump everything together under the rubric of "the oath ex officio." J. H. Wigmore notes that this frame of reference developed in Elizabethan and Jacobean England: the ex officio proceeding was "lawful enough on Innocent III's conditions about *clamosa insinuatio* and *fama publica*," but later abuses "led to the matter being argued, in English courts and in popular discussion, as if this oath were either wholly lawful or wholly unlawful; though, in truth, by the theory of the canon law, it *might* be either, according to the circumstances of presentment."[61]

In addition to failing to distinguish between proper and improper timing of oaths in ex officio inquisitions, historians have mixed up these oaths with those taken by witnesses in inquisitions and other kinds of trials, by the parties (plaintiffs and defendants) in suits or "instance" cases, or by persons delated to the King's Council, and they have created a spurious conflict between papal tyranny and plucky English resistance. Thus Levy is not only mistaken in saying that the Fourth Lateran Council incorporated "a new oath that was self-incriminatory in nature,"[62] he is also mistaken to claim, drawing upon generations of misleading sources, that Cardinal Otto of Tonengo introduced the self-incriminating oath into England in 1236; that Robert Grosseteste as bishop of Lincoln first used it in 1246; that his use of it was opposed by Henry III; that Archbishop Boniface of Canterbury revitalized it in 1272; and that Parliament under Edward

[58] Ibid., 2:86.

[59] Ibid., 2:101–5.

[60] Ibid., 2:105.

[61] John Henry Wigmore, "The Privilege against Self-Incrimination: Its History," *Harvard Law Review* 15 (1901–2), 610–37, esp. p. 617; this article is repeated largely unchanged in Wigmore's *Evidence in Trials at Common Law*, 8, last revised by him in 1940; in the revision by John T. McNaughton (Boston, 1961), see pp. 267–95, esp. p. 276. Later criticisms of Wigmore, noted by McNaughton on pp. 267–69, are largely unjustified.

[62] Levy, *Origins*, p. 20; cf. p. 23.

II (1307–27) outlawed it.[63] Otto in his legatine constitution—of 1237—was simply ordering litigants in ecclesiastical courts to take the oath of calumny in civil cases, while litigants in spiritual cases were to take the oath of telling the truth: "Jusjurandum calumpnie in causis ecclesiasticis civilibus, et de veritate dicenda in spiritualibus, quo et veritas aperiatur facilius et cause celerius terminentur, statuimus prestari decetero."[64] As for Grosseteste, he was conducting general inquisitions on the status of churches. The prescribed method was given in Innocent III's decretal *Qualiter et quando* (1206): the clerics of a church are to swear "to tell the inquisitors the plain and full truth about reforms which they know or believe are needed, both in the head and in the members, except for secret crimes."[65] Henry III's specific objection was against the bishop's unheard-of practice of compelling lay persons to reveal, not their own crimes, but those of others, and specifically private sins that were not publicly purgeable.[66] But he may also have been objecting against compulsory testimony in general.[67] Boniface of Savoy's constitutions were issued in 1261, not 1272 (he died in 1270); and, as William Lyndwood makes clear in his commentary (1430), he also was dealing with witnesses, not defendants: laymen can be forced to give sworn testimony in inquisitions.[68] Lyndwood says that in a general inquisition an oath should not be exacted from a person to reveal the hidden sin of someone; but in cases where crimes are brought forward for correction without an oath, the inquisitor can exact an oath concerning them.[69] That is, witnesses can be forced to testify to the fame and the truth of such crimes. Finally, the *Prohibitio formata de statuto "Articuli cleri"* of Edward II was simply another attempt to

[63] Ibid., pp. 46–48.

[64] *Councils and Synods with Other Documents Relating to the English Church*, ed. F. M. Powicke and C. R. Cheney, 1/2 (Oxford, 1984), p. 256. Cf. the somewhat different but still intelligible text in the first appendix to the Oxford 1679 edition of William Lyndwood's *Provinciale*, where the legatine constitutions of Otto and Ottobono are given with the gloss of John Acton (ca. 1345); see esp. p. 60.

[65] *Decretales* 5.1.17: "quod super his que sciunt vel credunt esse in sua ecclesia reformanda tam in capite quam in membris, exceptis occultis criminibus, meram et plenam dicant inquisitoribus veritatem" (Friedberg, 2:739).

[66] *Close Rolls of the Reign of Henry III*, 7 (London, 1927), pp. 224–25 (1252): "Et insuper, quod inauditum est, eos jurare compellunt predicti scrutatores vestri de privatis peccatis aliorum que non sunt, ut dicitur, publica cohercione purganda."

[67] For Grosseteste's visitations, beginning around 1238, and royal opposition to the procedure of the sworn inquest of laymen, see *Councils and Synods*, pp. 261–65. Sworn testimony in trials did not become a part of the common-law system until the time of Elizabeth I. See Charles M. Gray, "Prohibitions and the Privilege against Self-Incrimination," in *Tudor Rule and Revolution: Essays for G. R. Elton from His American Friends*, ed. DeLloyd J. Guth and John W. McKenna (Cambridge, Mass., 1982), pp. 345–67, esp. p. 346.

[68] For the original text, see the second appendix to Lyndwood, p. 21, and *Councils and Synods*, pp. 678–79, no. 14; as given by Lyndwood, pp. 109–10, the text is a summary paraphrase. His first sentence reads, "Statuimus quod laici, ubi de subditorum peccatis et excessibus corrigendis per prelatos et judices ecclesiasticos inquiritur, ad prestandum de veritate dicenda juramentum per excommunicationis sententias, si opus fuerit, compellantur."

[69] Lyndwood, *Provinciale*, p. 109, note *r*, ad v. *compelluntur*, citing John Andrew and Guy of Baysio on *Sext.* 3.20.1, §4: Innocent IV's 1245 decretal *Romana ecclesia* (in the Roman edition of John Andrew's Ordinary Gloss to this decretal, col. 570, ad v. *coactione*, a negative is missing; it should read: "A principio [non] exigetur juramentum per quod occultum prodere constringatur").

restrict the scope of church courts. It directed ecclesiastical judges not to permit the assembling of laymen to make recognitions by their oaths ("ad aliquas recognitiones per sacramenta sua facienda") except in matrimonial and testamentary cases.[70]

It turns out that the earliest evidence for the use of self-inculpatory oaths in England is to be found not in the ecclesiastical courts but in the King's Council under Edward II, where such oaths were imposed without any of the defenses of the inquisitorial system.[71] The council may have learned the technique from the papal heresy inquisitors who prosecuted the English Templars.[72] If so, there is no indication that the practice was carried over to the ecclesiastical courts, and the series of fourteenth-century statutes enforcing supposed Magna Carta guarantees of due process, culminating in that of 1368, were directed only towards the secular courts.[73]

The correct distinction between proper and improper oaths in inquisitorial proceedings was made by John Lambert in 1532, when he objected against judges who "sometimes, not knowing by any due proof that such as have to do before them are culpable, will enforce them, by an oath, to detect themselves, in opening before them their hearts." In such cases, he said, "I cannot see that men need to condescend to their requests." But it is otherwise when the proceedings are properly constituted: "I think it lawful, at the commandment of a judge, to make an oath to say the truth, especially if a judge requireth an oath duly, and in lawful wise; or to make an oath in any other case convenient; and that also for purgation of infamy, when any infamy is lawfully laid against a man."[74] By responding to the articles ministered against him, Lambert was

[70] *Statutes of the Realm*, 1 (London, 1810), p. 209. See *Councils and Synods*, p. 470, nos. 7–8, for the bishops' complaints in 1253 against similar efforts to limit their jurisdiction.

[71] See Levy, *Origins*, pp. 50–51.

[72] There is also a chance that the council was inspired by those inquisitors' use of torture; on this subject, see H. A. Kelly, "English Kings and the Fear of Sorcery," *Mediaeval Studies* 39 (1977), 206–38, esp. pp. 210 (n. 10), 212–13, 231, 233–37.

[73] See Levy, pp. 52–53, citing 25 Edward III (1352), st. 5, chap. 4; 28 Edward III (1354), chap. 3; 37 Edward III (1363), chap. 18; and 42 Edward III (1368), chap. 3; *Statutes of the Realm*, 1:321, 345, 382, 388. On p. 52 Levy repeats the statement of Mary Hume Maguire, "Attack of the Common Lawyers on the Oath *Ex officio* as Administered in the Ecclesiastical Courts in England," in *Essays in History and Political Theory in Honor of Charles Howard McIlwain* (Cambridge, Mass., 1936), pp. 199–229, esp. pp. 207–8: "We read a series of petitions from the Commons to the Crown referring to the distasteful practice of ecclesiastical courts of proving the case against the defendant by 'fishing interrogatories *viva voce*,' " but in a note (p. 450 n. 13) he points out that her references are to complaints made in 1347 and 1352 only against council practices and without any such language about interrogatories.

[74] Foxe, *Acts and Monuments*, 5:221. See n. 6 above. Levy, *Origins*, p. 62, might seem to be giving an accurate account of Lambert's position when he says: "Lambert, it should be remembered, meant only that he should not be compelled to detect himself or reveal crimes that were either unknown or unproved; he believed that one should answer under oath if properly accused by due process of law." But by "due process of law" Levy means only the English common-law system, for he thinks that Lambert was objecting to the process that was being applied to him: "He was the first person on record who, charged with heresy, objected to the oath procedure on ground that it was illegal to force a man to accuse himself" (p. 62). Rather, by responding to the charges against him, Lambert was acknowledging that infamy had lawfully been laid against him. See n. 166 below. Levy is also

presumably accepting the legitimacy of the process. But it is important to observe that in his case it was not simply a question of his denying that certain doctrines were preached or taught by him. To clear himself of the infamy that had been lawfully established against him, he was required to give his opinion on the doctrines, and he would be judged on the quality of his responses. This purgation procedure was used in the time of John Wyclif, for example in the actions against Philip Repingdon and others at Oxford in 1382.[75] It was carried over to the Council of Constance in the trial of John Hus, when he was first examined, not on his own views, but on Wyclif's doctrines.[76]

Lambert did not go so far as to say that judges were acting illegally in requiring prearraignment oaths. He moved from stating that the oaths were "enforced" to indicating that they were requested, and his point is that one does not have an obligation to comply with such requests. I should also note that modern historians have placed undue emphasis on the oath-taking process. The crucial point was the timing of the interrogation, with or without oaths, for even an unsworn confession of a crime would be witnessed by the judge and therefore rendered notorious. We have seen the results at Pamiers, under Bishop Fournier.

Proper inquisitional procedure was set forth and observed shortly before Lambert's trial in the papally commissioned inquisition against Henry VIII and Catherine of Aragon in 1529. One of the defendants, Catherine, exercised her rights of protest and appeal, and after her petitions were rejected by the inquisitors, Cardinals Campeggio and Wolsey, she refused to cooperate or respond (the trial was eventually stopped by an external appeal to the pope). Articles were administered against both defendants *ex officio mero* on 25 June, and ref-

---

mistaken in his characterization of the confrontation between Archbishop Arundel and the priest William Thorpe in 1407, which was recorded by Thorpe himself. It was not a formal inquisitorial proceeding, and there was no demand that he swear "to answer truly"; nor did Thorpe want "to know what he would be asked" before he would swear, as Levy thinks (*Origins*, p. 59). Rather, Arundel, who claimed to "know well" that Thorpe had been sowing false doctrine for twenty years, wanted him to take an oath to submit to his correction by renouncing specific opinions attributed to the Lollards: "I will shortly that now thou swear here to me that thou shalt forsake all the opinions which the sect of Lollards hold and is slandered with, so that after this time, neither privily nor apertly, thou hold any opinion which I shall (after thou hast sworn) rehearse to thee here"; from Bale's 1544 reprint of the ca. 1530 edition of *The Examination of Master William Thorpe*, in *Select Works of John Bale*, ed. Henry Christmas, Parker Society 36 (Cambridge, Eng., 1849), pp. 60–133, esp. pp. 70, 74–75. Anne Hudson has edited Thorpe's account for the Early English Text Society (O.S. 301) from an early-fifteenth-century manuscript: *Two Wycliffite Texts* (Oxford, 1993); see p. 34 for Arundel's statement: the Middle English text differs only slightly from the sixteenth-century modernization. Hudson discusses a partial Latin translation that Bale made of the modernization (pp. xxxi–xxxii) but does not mention his edition of the complete English text in 1544.

[75] Foxe, *Acts and Monuments*, 3:24–36.

[76] We are told that at first Hus refused to respond, but complied when told that his refusal might be regarded as a confession of guilt; see Matthew Spinka, *John Hus: A Biography* (Princeton, 1968), p. 236. Spinka does not cite his source for the specifics of the first day of interrogation, 6 December 1414, when Hus began his imprisonment in a Dominican friary. See also Spinka's *John Hus at the Council of Constance* (New York, 1965), p. 117 n. 21. David S. Schaff, *John Huss: His Life, Teachings, and Death, after 500 Years* (New York, 1915), says that according to John of Jesenice (the lawyer who had defended Hus in Rome), "Huss had committed a technical error in making any reply whatsoever as a prisoner" (p. 184, citing no source).

erence is made to the king's reply on 28 June. The prearranged schedule called for time to be given to the king to reply, and then for an oath to be administered to him and for him to be examined. Whether he did actually take such an oath is not stated in the court record prepared for the Rome appeal.[77] In the *causa inquisitionis ex officio mero* called by Archbishop Warham's successor, Thomas Cranmer, at Dunstable in 1533 on the same matter, responses to the articles were not made by Henry but by his proctor, without an oath, and without consulting Henry.[78]

3. Bishop Cauchon and the Interrogation of Joan of Arc

Peter Cauchon (ca. 1371–1442), the chief instigator and executor of the trial against Joan of Arc, was trained as an ecclesiastical lawyer: he had an advanced degree—a licentiate—in canon law from the University of Paris, where he served as rector in 1397 and 1403.[79] When he was at the Council of Constance, he witnessed a number of "causes of the faith," or heresy proceedings, two of which he participated in himself. They show that he was very familiar with inquisitorial procedures and defenses long before he came to try Joan of Arc.

Cauchon set out for the council on 8 January 1415, as one of the ambassadors of John the Fearless, duke of Burgundy, and legal counsel for him in the case of the doctrines of John Petit,[80] which was debated throughout the duration of the council.[81] Commissary judges were appointed at the thirteenth session, held on 15 June 1415, to make inquisition into it,[82] and Cauchon was one of a team

[77] H. A. Kelly, *The Matrimonial Trials of Henry VIII* (Stanford, 1976), pp. 89–95. For the directions to the proceedings, see *Letters and Papers, Foreign and Domestic, of the Reign of Henry VIII*, 21 vols. (corrected reprint, Vaduz, 1965), vol. 4, nos. 5613 and 5695.

[78] Kelly, *Matrimonial Trials*, pp. 205–7.

[79] Tisset, 2:388.

[80] See Alfred Colville, *Jean Petit: La question du tyrannicide au commencement du XVe siècle* (Paris, 1932; repr. Geneva, 1974), p. 512. In John Dominic Mansi, *Sacrorum conciliorum nova et amplissima collectio*, vols. 27–28 (Venice, 1784–85), his name is usually mistranscribed as "Canthon" (e.g., 27:819, 4 Feb. 1416). See Phillip Stump, "The Official Acta of the Council of Constance in the Edition of Mansi," in *The Two Laws: Studies in Medieval Legal History Dedicated to Stephan Kuttner*, ed. Laurent Mayali and Stephanie A. J. Tibbetts (Washington, D.C., 1990), pp. 221–39, who says that Mansi in spite of his misprints reproduces a text in some ways better than that in vol. 4 of Hermann von der Hardt, *Magnum oecumenicum Constantiense concilium*, 6 vols. (Frankfurt, 1697–1700, 1742). Stump does not point out that Mansi (or his sources) eliminates most of the rubrics of Hardt's edition and does not include other supplementary material. For a partially fictionalized account of the council, see Palémon Glorieux, *Le concil de Constance au jour le jour* (Tournai, 1964), told through the eyes of John Gerson's secretary. See also Glorieux's edition of Gerson's *Oeuvres complètes*, 10 vols. (Paris, 1960–73), esp. vol. 10, *L'oeuvre polémique*, pp. 511–30 ("Autour du tyrannicide"), with a chronological "Dossier" on pp. 164–70; and see the "Table chronologique" on pp. 583–98; pertinent documents are given on pp. 516–52.

[81] Heinrich Finke, *Acta concilii Constanciensis*, 4 vols. (Münster, 1896–1928), 4:239–40.

[82] Hardt, 4:335. The rubric reads: "Petiti judices commissarii pro inquisitione aliarum causarum fidei, presertim doctoris theologi Johannis Parvi, Galli, nuper defuncti, Burgundie ducis consiliarii" (not in Mansi, 27:729). One of the judges was Cardinal Peter d'Ailly, who was immediately recused by Burgundy's main lawyer, Martin Porée, bishop of Arras (Hardt, p. 336; not in Mansi). See Glorieux, *Concile*, pp. 87, 90–91; he reports Cauchon as also recusing d'Ailly on 17 June.

of lawyers who protested against an earlier sentence by the bishop of Paris and the deputy heresy inquisitor for France and who opposed its supporters at the council.

On 1 July 1415, Cauchon insisted that the "pretended writings" submitted by the council promotor Henry de Piro and by John Gerson "were and are false, mendacious, and fabricated in a false and deceitful fashion." He objected to the intervention of the promotor, since Gerson was a formal denunciator in the case and therefore the process was not an ex officio inquisition. The nine propositions, he asserted, had never been held or preached in this form by John Petit; if some words did appear to have been extracted from his work, the extraction was made in a false and truncated way by enemies of the duke. The sentence was null and void, because it was given in a cause of the faith in matters not condemned by the church; moreover, one of the affected parties (namely, the duke of Burgundy) had been allowed no voice in the trial, and the sentence was given by the bishop of Paris, who was a capital enemy of the duke and a participant in the war against him. The bishop in fact was plotting at the time to kill the duke, as was discovered from one of those whom he sent to Flanders for the purpose, who confessed to the crime and was decapitated. Furthermore, the trial was not held in a safe place, and university masters who were formal adversaries of the duke were admitted to the proceedings while others, motivated only by a zeal for justice, were repelled; the whole faculty of canon law was excluded, as was the Picardy and Savoy nation of the theology faculty, and the required approval of the faculty of medicine was not obtained.[83] In the following year, on 26 and 27 March, when it seemed that the judges were going to declare against the Burgundian position, Cauchon claimed grievances (reasons for appeal) and spoke of seeking the remedies of law.[84]

Other trials were held against the recalcitrant Pisan and Avignonese popes, John XXIII and Benedict XIII. In both cases formal charges were formulated and presented; some were supported by the testimony of witnesses, and others, especially the most outrageous, received no such support and were dropped.[85] As one of the witnesses against Benedict, referred to here by his prepapal name Peter de Luna, Cauchon was declared contumacious on one occasion for nonappearance. He did appear eventually,[86] as the trial proceeded in Benedict's absence. The sentence was read on 26 July, condemning him of numerous offenses including schism and heresy and violation of the article of faith *Unam sanctam catholicam ecclesiam*—which would also figure in the trial of Joan of Arc.[87]

The trial of John XXIII as well as that of Benedict XIII was conducted in his absence, and the proceedings concerning John Petit were posthumous, as were those dealing with the doctrines of John Wyclif. But the trials of the priest

[83] Finke, 4:264–66. Cauchon presented more arguments on 7 or 8 July (pp. 268–69) and on 9 July (pp. 269–71).

[84] Mansi, 28:835–36.

[85] This was especially true in the case of John XXIII.

[86] Hardt, 4:1271, 1275–76, 1306; Mansi, 27:1100, 1102, 1115.

[87] Hardt, 4:1373–77; Mansi, 27:1141–42; see Tisset, 1:278, 96, where the same form is used. It seems that in both cases the form of the Constantinopolitan-Nicene Creed used at mass has been unconsciously substituted for that of the Apostles' Creed (in which there is no *unam*).

John Hus and his lay follower Jerome of Prague took place in their presence. And though many procedural irregularities can be detected,[88] the defendants' own explanations of their positions under interrogation, which were accompanied with denials of wrongdoing, do not seem to have have been construed as evidence of new crimes of thought, but at most as confirmations of previous offenses, proofs of which were ostensibly established by documentary evidence and witnesses.[89] But there seems to have been no question of their exercising their right to call witnesses in their own defense.

Between the end of the Council of Constance and the trial of Joan of Arc, one can see a procedurally correct heresy trial in England in the case of the Franciscan William Russell, tried in 1425 under Archbishop Chichele, with an appeal heard in Rome in 1426.[90] But in the diocese of Norwich heresy trials were conducted from 1428 to 23 March 1431 by the bishop, William Alnwick, or his vicar general in his absence, which manifest some of the abuses observable in Cauchon's proceedings against Joan, including blanket oaths and interrogation without charges.[91] Alnwick served as one of Cauchon's assessors, being present at Joan's abjuration on 24 May 1431.[92] He was also one of three judges commissioned by Archbishop Chichele to hear the heresy and witchcraft trial of Eleanor Cobham, duchess of Gloucester, in 1441, but in this case the proper *ordo juris* was followed.[93]

Cauchon became bishop of Beauvais in 1420, and since Joan of Arc was captured in his diocese, on 23 May 1430, he claimed to be her ordinary judge. He asserted in his cover letter of 1435[94] that fame of her immodesty in wearing male clothes and of her making statements against the faith had arisen and

[88] I wish to amend the statement I made in "Inquisitorial Due Process," p. 425, that the requisite forms of procedure were observed in the trials that took place at the Council of Constance; they were notably lacking in the cases of Hus and Jerome. Space does not permit me to document my summaries of these trials, but I hope to do so elsewhere.

[89] According to the anonymous *De vita Magistri Jeronimi de Praga* (ed. Václav Novotny, *Fontes rerum Bohemicarum* [Prague, 1932], 8:335–38), Jerome was convicted of all the articles by witnesses: "Centum septem articuli . . . de novo fuerunt producti et subsequenter per sufficientes testes probati" (p. 335). "In quibus omnibus articulis . . . fuit omnino per testes convictus" (p. 336).

[90] *The Register of Henry Chichele, Archbishop of Canterbury, 1414–1443*, ed. E. F. Jacob, 4 vols. (Oxford, 1937–47), 3:126 ff.; see Kelly, "English Kings," pp. 213 (n. 18), 225 (n. 75).

[91] N. P. Tanner, ed., *Heresy Trials in the Diocese of Norwich, 1428–1431* (London, 1977), analyzed by Kelly, "Inquisitorial Due Process," pp. 425–26. The documents edited by Anne Hudson in "The Examination of the Lollards," in *Lollards and Their Books* (London, 1985), pp. 125–40, may show a degeneration in proper procedure. What seems to be the earliest *modus procedendi*, which was * added to the register of Bishop Clifford of London (1407–21), has no interrogatories (pp. 127, 129, 132, 139); the next, from the register of Bishop Polton of Worcester (1426–33), has interrogatories placed at the point at which the defendant has been charged and has denied the charges, and after witnesses have been received (pp. 132–37); the latest, in MSS Harley 2179 and Balliol College 158, gives the interrogatories at the beginning (pp. 132–35, 140). The interrogatories seem to have been formulated at the Canterbury Convocation of 1428 (see pp. 128–29).

[92] Tisset, 1:385.

[93] See Kelly, "English Kings," pp. 219–29; cf. Ralph A. Griffiths, "The Trial of Eleanor Cobham: An Episode in the Fall of Duke Humphrey of Gloucester," *Bulletin of the John Rylands Library* 51 (1969), 381–99.

[94] See n. 5 above.

grown in many circles, and that he accordingly decided to conduct an inquisition concerning her.[95] On the first recorded day of the trial, 9 January 1431, he shared his current information with assessors (advisers to a judge) and ordered further investigations to be made.[96] He appointed a promotor "of his office," John d'Estivet, to assist him; the promotor's duties were to submit articles, to introduce witnesses, and to accuse and denounce Joan and have her examined.[97] Notaries were appointed to hear and record the interrogations of Joan and of witnesses.[98]

Articles were ordered formulated on 13 January; they were read on 23 January but were not included in the record produced in 1435. A specially appointed commissary, John La Fontaine, was to interrogate witnesses.[99] Presumably the articles were intended to establish both Joan's ill fame and her culpability. The resulting depositions were read to Cauchon's assessors on 19 February, and all agreed that on the basis of this testimony she should be cited to an inquisition.[100] These depositions, or "informations," would often be referred to in the subsequent interrogations of Joan, but they were never exhibited to her or put in the later record.

According to the citation Joan was summoned to be heard on articles made against her and interrogatories put to her concerning the faith.[101] This is phrased to sound as if the right order would be followed: that is, charges would first be presented to her, and then she would be questioned on them. But when she was taken from prison and brought to court on 21 February,[102] Cauchon did not make detailed charges against her but told her only that she was there to answer questions. He explained that public fame had reported many of her deeds to be harmful to orthodox faith and that therefore it was incumbent on him to hold a trial concerning the faith. In the Latin proceedings he refers to "certain informations of which we made mention earlier." This is not to be taken to mean that he mentioned them to Joan; rather he is speaking from the retrospect of 1435. He told Joan that she had been "cited ex officio to respond truthfully to interrogatories in the matters of the faith to be proposed to her." (This, as we have seen, is not the way the actual text of the citation read, according to which articles were first to be given against her.) Accordingly, he charitably admonished her, "for the acceleration of the present case and the exoneration of her [or his own] conscience, that she tell the full truth about the things concerning the faith on which she would be questioned, not seeking subterfuges or defensive efforts to avoid confessing the plain truth."[103]

[95] Tisset, 1:1–2.

[96] Ibid., p. 3.

[97] Ibid., pp. 18–19. On the nature of the promotor, see n. 143 below.

[98] Ibid., p. 20.

[99] Ibid., p. 21.

[100] Ibid., pp. 25–26. The Orléans manuscript of the French text begins here (see n. 3 above).

[101] Tisset, 1:34: "citandam et audiendam super articulis et interrogatoriis contra eam dandis et sibi faciendis fidei materiam concernentibus."

[102] Her request to hear mass first was denied, in view of the crimes of which she had been defamed, and because of the male dress in which she still appeared.

[103] Ibid., p. 37: "Caritative monuimus et requisivimus ut, pro acceleracione presentis negocii et

This is the closest that Cauchon comes to saying that he was using summary process. But it is questionable whether he was consciously making such a claim, and even questionable whether he was conscious of violating the law of inquisitorial procedure by making her respond to questions before charging her, since, as I have already noted, even her sympathizers seem to have been unaware that this was a breach of correct procedure. However, he can hardly have been unaware of violating other rules of procedure, for they were of the sort that he himself had thrown up against the John Petit proceedings at Constance. Much would be made of these violations in the nullification trial.

Cauchon's next step was to require her to take what he called, in the Latin text, the standard oath ("juramentum in forma debita"):[104] while touching the holy Gospels, she was to swear to tell the truth about these things (French: "all the things") that would be asked of her. Joan responded, "I don't know what you want to ask me about. Maybe you could ask me things that I will not tell you."[105]

We might be tempted to conclude from that that Joan was able to divine in her unschooled way that neither Cauchon nor any judge had the right to force her to respond to unspecified questions and that she had a right to refuse to answer them. She clearly assumed, as we can tell from this response and some of her further answers, that there were certain questions pertaining to a trial of this sort that a judge did have the right to ask and that she had the duty to answer under oath, but she seems instinctively to have believed that she had a right to know what the questions were to deal with. However, it would be a mistake, I think, to suppose that she was primarily concerned with the question of her rights. Rather, she was concerned that the blanket oath being demanded of her would force her to violate previous oaths that she had made not to reveal certains aspects of her revelations.

Cauchon's response to her initial objection was not reassuring: "You will swear to say the truth about what will be asked you concerning the Catholic faith and

---

exoneracione proprie consciencie, plenam veritatem super hiis diceret de quibus in materia fidei interrogaretur, non querendo subterfugia vel cautelas ab ipsius veritatis confessione divertentes." According to the Orléans manuscript of the French text (which even in its original form may not have been an accurate record of the proceedings, but which, unlike the Latin, was at least contemporary with the proceedings), Cauchon told her that she was widely reputed to be accused of heresy and that she was delivered to him to have her "profess" in matters of the faith. Then the promotor told the bishop that at his request she had been cited to respond in matters of the faith, as would appear from letters and acts that he would exhibit presently, and he "requested that Joan be sworn to tell the truth and interrogated on the points that he would put to her" ("suppliant qu'elle fust adjuree de dire verité et interroguee sur les parties qu'il bailleroit," p. 36). The request was granted, and the bishop made the said Joan come to him, and he charitably admonished her and prayed her to tell the truth about things that would be asked of her, "tant pour l'abbreviacion de son procez que pour la descharge de sa conscience, sans querir subterfuges ne cautelles" (pp. 36–38).

[104] Ibid., p. 38; not in the French, which reads (continuing the sentence quoted in the previous note): "et qu'elle jurast sur les sainctes Euvangilles de dire verité de toutes les choses sur lesquelles elle seroit interroguee."

[105] Ibid.: "Je ne sçay sur quoy vous me voullez interroguer. Adventure me pourriez-vous demander telles choses que je ne vous diray point" ("Nescio super quibus vultis me interrogare. Forte vos poteritis a me talia petere que non dicam vobis").

concerning all other things that you know" (the Latin translation leaves out the "all other," making the statement somewhat less outrageous).[106] Joan replied that she would willingly swear to tell about her father and mother and what had happened since she came to France, but not about her secret visions or counsel; she would not reveal them even if her head were to be cut off. However, in eight days she would be able to say whether or not she should reveal them. The bishop then limited the oath to matters of the faith, and Joan swore to tell what she knew about what would be asked her concerning the faith, but would be silent about her revelations.[107] This oath in itself, which was much like the illegal oath of the heresy inquisitors, would undoubtedly have been enough to trap her into making dubious doctrinal statements, for instance about the precise meaning of her everyday prayers. But when Cauchon had quickly worked his way through questions about her parents and home and came to ask her to recite the Paternoster and Ave Maria, she stymied him by saying that she would recite them only in confession.[108] She thus showed that she was able to distinguish between the internal and external forums of the church.[109]

Cauchon concluded the first session by warning Joan not to leave the prison assigned to her under pain of conviction of the crime of heresy. She replied that she did not accept such a prohibition and that if she escaped she could not be accused of breaking her faith because she had never given it. When she complained about being held in chains and iron fetters, the bishop replied that it was because she had previously attempted to escape. She replied that it was licit for any incarcerated person to escape from captivity.[110] No response to this strong statement of prisoners' rights was recorded.

In the second session, of 22 February, at which forty-seven assessors were present in addition to La Fontaine and John Lemaistre, the deputy heresy inquisitor for Rouen, Cauchon required Joan to swear the oath that she swore on the previous day, but then he characterized it as an oath "to tell the truth about all that would be asked of her concerning the crimes and misdeeds of which she was accused and defamed."[111] This, of course, was much different from the terms that she had actually sworn to. The Latin makes it seem that she was required to swear the previous day's oath "and, in addition, to swear simply and absolutely to tell the truth to questions concerning the things about which she had been delated and defamed." The Latin adds, moreover, that she was required to swear under penalties of law.[112]

[106] Ibid.: "Vous jurerez de dire verité de ce que vous sera demand[é] qui concerne la foy catholicque et de toutes aultres choses que sçaurez" ("Vos jurabitis dicere veritatem de hiis que petentur a vobis fidei materiam concernentibus et que scietis").

[107] Ibid., pp. 38–39.

[108] Ibid., pp. 40–41.

[109] When she was asked later (on 12 March) how she could call herself a daughter of God and yet would not freely say the Paternoster, she replied that she did say it willingly, but when she refused, it was because she wanted to go to confession to the bishop (p. 126).

[110] Ibid., p. 42. The French text has nothing of this exchange.

[111] Ibid., pp. 44–45: "Jhenne premierement fut admonnestee et requise de faire le serment qu'elle avoit faict le jour precedent de dire verité de tout ce qui luy seroit demandé sur les crimes et malefices de quoy elle estoit accusee et diffamee."

[112] Ibid.: "Johannam . . . requisivimus et monuimus, sub penis juris, de faciendo juramentum

When Joan responded that her oath of the previous day should suffice, "she was once more admonished to swear absolutely to tell the truth concerning everything that would be asked of her, it being pointed out to her that not even a prince could or should refuse to take this oath to tell the truth in matters of the faith."[113] The Latin puts it in the active voice: "We again required her to swear; for no one, even a prince, who is required to swear an oath in a matter of the faith could refuse."[114] Joan replied, "I took it yesterday. You put too much of a burden on me."[115] But finally she took another oath in the form that she had used the day before (the Latin specifies rather that she finally swore to tell the truth in matters concerning the faith).[116]

This is the only time that Cauchon claims a special privilege for heresy inquisitions as opposed to other kinds of inquisitorial trials. There was certainly no justification in law for his statement, nor was such a privileged procedure in trials of the faith ever claimed, to my knowledge, in any of the manuals produced by heresy inquisitors, such as those of Bernard Guy and Nicholas Eymerich.[117] However, his claim was not contradicted in later proceedings.

A theologian named John Beaupere took over the questioning at this point. When he asked Joan if she would tell the truth, she replied that she would do so to some questions that he could ask, but not to others. That is, as the Latin makes clear, she would make no reply at all to certain questions.[118] Her usual method of refusing a question was to say, "Pass on," as when she was asked whether she received the Eucharist at any feasts other than Easter. She had already volunteered her practice of Communion at Easter after answering af-

---

quod die precedente prestiterat, quodque simpliciter et absolute juraret dicere veritatem ad ea que interrogarentur in materia de qua delata erat et diffamata."

[113] Ibid., p. 45: "Et derechef fut admonestee qu'elle jurast absolutement de dire verité de tout ce qui luy seroit demandé, en luy remonstrant qu'il n'y a prince qui peust ne deust refuser a faire ledit serment de dire verité en matiere de foy."

[114] Ibid.: "Iterum requisivimus quod juraret; nam quicumque, eciam princeps, requisitus in materia fidei non posset recusare facere juramentum."

[115] Ibid.: "Je le feis hier. Vous me chargez trop." Cf. the translation: "Ego feci heri vobis juramentum; bene debet vobis sufficere. Vos nimium oneratis me."

[116] Ibid.

[117] Cauchon's assertion is noted by Esmein, "Serment," p. 246 n. 1, but he does not advert to the crucial difference between swearing to answer charges truthfully and swearing to answer global interrogatories, nor does he point out that Cauchon was claiming a special exemption for heresy cases. According to J. Duncan M. Derrett, "The Trial of Sir Thomas More," *English Historical Review* 79 (1964), 449–77, repr. in *Essential Articles for the Study of Thomas More*, ed. R. S. Sylvester and G. P. Marc'hadour (Hamden, Conn., 1977), pp. 55–78, 591–96, esp. p. 65, Thomas More at his interrogation in the Tower on 3 June 1527 agreed with the lord chancellor, Thomas Audeley, that bishops could compel alleged heretics to say whether they believed the pope to be the supreme head of the church. He is referring to More's report of the confrontation: *The Correspondence of Sir Thomas More*, ed. Elizabeth Frances Rogers (Princeton, 1947), no. 216, pp. 555–59, esp. pp. 557–58. It would be more accurate to say, not that More agreed, but that he did not disagree and proceeded to make another point. In his detailed defense of the ex officio *inquisitio*, specifically as employed against suspected heretics, in *The Apology*, ed. J. B. Trapp, Complete Works of St. Thomas More (New Haven, 1979), esp. chap. 40, pp. 129–35, More made no such claim for the judges but described the procedures in strict accord with canon law.

[118] Tisset, 1:45–46.

firmatively that she went to confession every year. Herbert Thurston draws from this, rightly, I think, the following conclusion: "She was asked whether she fulfilled her Easter duties in the way in which the law of the Church required, and she said yes. When questioned about other Communions, she gave her judges to understand that that was a matter between herself and God and was no concern of theirs."[119]

At the next session, on 24 February, Cauchon again tried to make Joan take a completely unconditional oath: he admonished her three times to swear absolutely and without condition to tell the truth. She repeated her objection that he might ask her something that she would not give a true answer to, specifically concerning her revelations; and she added that he could ask her to tell about something that she had sworn not to speak of, and then she would be perjured—which, she said, the bishop should not wish to happen. She warned him that in calling himself her judge he had taken on a great burden, and she complained again that he was burdening her too much.[120]

When Cauchon persisted, Joan told him that she believed that not all the clergy of Rouen and Paris would know how to compel her if they had no right to do so.[121] This statement may have been intended as a claim that no ecclesiastics, especially those in territories hostile to her cause, could legally bind her to reveal her secrets. If she was referring to Cauchon and his clerical associates as enemies of Charles VII, he chose to miss her meaning, for he told her that she could consult with some of the assessors there present. When Joan ignored his offer, he took the tack of warning her that a refusal to swear would render her suspect.[122] When she still refused, he told her that she must swear under pain of being convicted of what was imputed to her (which, of course, he had not revealed to her). Joan responded, "I have sworn enough. Pass on." Finally Cauchon gave up his efforts to make her swear a wide-open oath, and he told her that she would expose herself to danger if she did not swear to tell the truth concerning whatever touched her process, that is, her trial, and she agreed.[123]

As the interrogation under Beaupere proceeded, she replied to a question concerning her voices, "I will not tell you everything, because I do not have permission, and besides my oath does not cover that matter. But I tell you that the voice is beautiful, good, and worthy; and I am not bound to respond concerning it." Then she asked to see in writing the points on which they intended

[119] Herbert Thurston, *Some Inexactitudes of Mr. G. G. Coulton* (London, 1927), p. 7. Thurston is responding to Coulton's assumption that Joan went to communion only once a year.

[120] Tisset, 1:55.

[121] Ibid., p. 56: "Et croy que tout le clergé de Rouen et de Paris ne m'y sauroyent contraindre se ilz ne avoyent tort." The Latin translation renders *contraindre* by *condempnare*, "condemn": "dicens ulterius quod totus clerus Rothomagensis vel Parisiensis nesciret eam condempnare nisi haberent in jus."

[122] Perhaps he was referring to heresy cases of the sort dealt with by Bishop Fournier (see above, n. 49), in which a refusal to swear indicated a belief that taking oaths was sinful.

[123] Tisset, 1:56–57.

to interrogate her.[124] From this request we can conclude that Joan came close to guessing what her rights were under the law: to have all the matters that had been alleged against her formally presented to her. And, of course, since it seems that she was not able to read, she was asking that they be explained to her, as was likewise required by law. She was also asking, in effect, for the help of a competent and sympathetic defense attorney, and this, too, was a requirement of the judicial process.

The French text is corrupt at this point,[125] which may be either a simple matter of scribal error or a sign of official skulduggery. The fact that the Latin translation radically changes the purport of her demand may incline us to the latter explanation. The text reads: "Again, she asked that she be given in writing those points on which she was not then responding."[126] In other words, instead of asking for all of the questions they were going to put to her, she was supposedly asking only for a reminder of the questions already asked but not answered, to which she was postponing her responses.

Joan's request was completely ignored (here the Latin and the French are in silent agreement), and another question was put to her: namely, did the voice from which she sought counsel have a face and eyes? She replied, "You won't have the answer to that yet"; and then she added a telling comment: little children had a saying that sometimes people were hanged for telling the truth.[127] When she was asked about this statement later, on 15 March (did she know of any crime or defect for which she could or should die?), she replied straightforwardly, "No."[128]

On 1 March, when asked whether she knew by her revelation that she would escape from her present prison, she told them to put the question to her again within three months and she would tell them then. This response might sound like a joke on Joan's part ("If I am no longer here, the answer is yes"). But the immediately subjoined demand makes it clear that she needed time to consult her voices: "Ask the assessors under their oath whether this touches the process."[129] The assessors were consulted, and all agreed that it did indeed touch the process. She then stated, "I have told you all along that you will not know everything. It must be that I will be freed one time. And I want to have permission, if I am to tell you. That is why I ask for a delay."[130] When asked whether

[124] Ibid., p. 62: "Respond: 'Je ne vous dys pas tout, car je n'en ay congié; et aussi mon serment ne touche pas cela; mais je vous dy qu'il y a voix bel, bonne, et digne; et n'en suis point tenue d'en respondre.' " The text is mistakenly interrupted at this point by the next interrogation; then Joan's previous response is continued, but now in indirect discourse, and with something plainly missing at the beginning: "Pour ce qu'elle demanda a veoir par escript les poins sur lesquelz on la vouloit interroguer."

[125] See the previous note.

[126] Ibid.: "Item petivit ut sibi darentur in scriptis illa puncta in quibus tunc non respondebat."

[127] Ibid.: "A quoy elle respond, 'Vous ne l'avez pas encoire'; item dit que le dict des petis enfans est que on pend bien aulcunes foys les gens pour dire verité."

[128] Ibid., p. 164.

[129] Ibid., p. 86: "Respondit: 'Loquamini mecum infra tres menses; ego de hoc respondebo vobis.' Dixit ultra: 'Petatis ab assistentibus sub juramento suo an istud tangat processum.' " There is no extant French text at this point to check the Latin against.

[130] Ibid.: "Ego semper bene vobis dixi quod vos nescietis totum. Et oportebit semel quod ego sim liberata. Et volo habere licenciam si ego dicam. Ideo peto dilacionem."

the voices forbade her to tell the truth, she replied, "Do you want me to tell you what concerns the king of France? There are many things that do not touch the process."[131] Two days later, when she was asked once again about escaping from prison, she asserted, in spite of the above opinion of the assessors, that it was not relevant to the case at hand: "That does not touch your process. Do you want me to speak against myself?"[132]

It turned out that in just under three months Joan did escape from her enemies once and for all by being put to death at their hands—which would be to their lasting ignominy and her lasting honor and glory.

4. Critical and Uncritical Reactions

We saw above that Cauchon himself made the distinction in the Petit process that some topics were not the proper subject for a judicial cause of the faith, and the fact that Joan's request was taken seriously and put to the assessors demonstrates the very point. Yet not only was there no complaint in the later nullification trial against Cauchon's forcing her to take an oath before being charged, there was also little objection to his making her swear new unconditional oaths to tell the truth on anything that would be asked of her. According to the notary, William Manchon, Cauchon himself clearly believed that, procedurely speaking, his handling of the trial was impeccable, and he was very much annoyed when he was told, probably on 17 March, that the distinguished canonist John Lohier considered the proceedings to be invalid. Lohier objected that the trial lacked the form of an ordinary process; that it was held under constraint, so that the assessors were not really free to make unbiased decisions; that, though it dealt with the honor of the king of France, no one from that quarter had a voice in the trial; that no *libellus* or articles had been submitted; and that no counsel had been provided to the defendant, who was a simple girl, to help her respond to questions posed by learned masters and doctors on difficult subjects. Privately, Lohier told Manchon that they were trying to trap her in her words, especially in asking about her apparitions. If only she would say, "it seems," rather than saying that she was certain, she would be in the clear. It was obvious that they were proceeding out of hatred for her, and therefore he refused to have anything more to do with the process.[133] Thomas Courcelles, one of the assessors, who was the author of the Latin translation of the proceedings, recalled in 1456 that Lohier's objection was that there had to be a preliminary process on infamy before there could be a formal process on the faith.[134]

According to Manchon, Cauchon said to some of his associates, including

[131] Ibid.: "Vultis vos quod vobis dicam id quod vadit ad regem Francie? Sunt multa que non tangunt processum."

[132] Ibid., p. 92: "Cela ne touche point vostre procez. Voulez vous que je parle contre moy?" ("Hoc non tangit processum vestrum. Vultis vos quod ego loquar contra me?")

[133] Paul Doncoeur and Yvonne Lanhers, *La rehabilitation de Jeanne la Pucelle*, 1: *La enquête ordonnée par Charles VI en 1450* (Paris, 1956), pp. 48–49.

[134] DuParc, 1:356. Tisset, 3:69–70, 213, mistakenly says that Manchon also mentioned this point.

Courcelles, "Look here, Lohier wants us to decree some fine interlocutories in our process! He wants to calumniate everything, and he says that it's worth nothing. To believe him, we would have to begin all over, and everything that we have done would be worthless!"[135] Presumably, Lohier was saying that Cauchon should issue interlocutory sentences admitting judicial errors.

Manchon reported that the bishop was determined to continue the process as it had begun.[136] In the event, however, it is clear that some of Lohier's criticisms were taken very seriously, and the course of the trial was modified accordingly. On 18 March Cauchon consulted with a larger group of assessors on how to proceed. He had extracts from Joan's responses read to them, and on their advice he ordered articles to be compiled from the interrogatories and responses, and these articles were to be presented against her in court.[137] On 22 March, after further consultation, he ordered that the earlier extracts which had been made "from the register of Joan's confessions" be reduced to fewer articles, to be submitted to doctors and masters for their deliberation. On the question of whether she should be further examined, he would proceed in such a way that their process would suffer no defect.[138] Joan's original responses were read to her on 24 March, so that she could not deny anything later, and she took an oath to add nothing to them except what was true. Furthermore, she agreed to accept what was read to her, except for any detail that she would contradict then and there, as true and confessed.[139]

It has been assumed that the articles commissioned on 18 March and 22 March were the same; but I believe that the 18 March order resulted in the seventy articles presented to Joan by the promotor on 27–28 March, and that the 22 March order resulted in the twelve articles upon which Joan was eventually convicted. The seventy articles do not draw extensively on her responses but are clearly based for the most part on wild hearsay; I take it that they incorporated the promotor's original interrogatory articles, which had been read to the court on 23 January. They are not addressed to Joan but to the two judges, Cauchon and Lemaistre. If Cauchon had proceeded according to canonical form, these original articles should have been presented to Joan as charges when she was first summoned.

Cauchon presented the twelve articles to the court on 2 April, claiming that they were compiled from Joan's responses to the seventy articles and the further questioning that ended on 31 March.[140] My supposition is that a draft of the articles had already been prepared, and that it was modified, especially in the first and twelfth articles on the question of submission to the church militant, to reflect her most recent responses. Joan was never shown these articles, which,

[135] Doncoeur and Lanhers, p. 49: "Vela Lohier qui nous veult bailler belles interlocutoyres in nostre procés! Il veut tout calompnier, et dit qu'il ne vault riens. Qui le vouldroit croire, il nous fauldroit tout commencer, et tout ce que nous avons fait ne vouldroit riens."

[136] Ibid. Manchon also testified in 1452 and 1456 about Lohier's objections: Duparc, 1:216, 418–19.

[137] Tisset, 1:179–80.

[138] Ibid., p. 180.

[139] Ibid., p. 181.

[140] Ibid., p. 289.

unlike the seventy, are in the form not of charges but of reported confessions. They were submitted to faculty members of the University of Paris, and it was on the basis of their responses that she was found guilty.[141]

My reconstruction of what happened is as follows. Cauchon remedied Lohier's major objection, that they had proceeded without instituting an ordinary process with formal charges, by proceeding to initiate such a process on 26 March. He professed to be opening a new phase of the trial: what had preceded, he said, was an ex officio preparatory process; now he was opening an "ordinary process," in which the promotor would present against Joan certain articles that Cauchon had ordered to be compiled.[142] Cauchon has been wrongly interpreted as saying that the ordinary process was not ex officio. In fact, it would have been readily recognized that the promotor was a part of the ex officio process from the beginning and remained so to the end.[143]

On the next day, 27 March, the promotor asked that Joan be sworn to reply by *credit* or *non credit* to the articles. This was equivalent to asking that she swear *de calumnia vitanda*, as to her belief, rather than *de veritate dicenda*, as to her certain knowledge.[144] Cauchon thereupon asked the advice of the assessors present how to proceed. The twenty-eight responses, which are preserved in the manuscript containing the French text of the interrogations but which were not included in the record prepared in 1435, reveal that there was considerable uncertainty about what the proper procedure should be: whether she should swear, and what kind of oath, how she was to answer on points of fact as opposed to law, how to respond if she was not certain, whether and what delays were to be granted or terms assigned for response, and so on.[145] Cauchon in the 1435

[141] The twelve articles are given on pp. 290–96 and the deliberations of the Parisian masters on pp. 297–327. One of the masters was Nicholas Midi (p. 297), who, according to Thomas Courcelles's surmise, was the actual author of the articles (Duparc, 1:357).

[142] Tisset, 1:184.

[143] Tisset mistakenly says that the process changed from ex officio to *cum promovente* (3:59–60). A *promovens* was an interested outside party to an inquisition, whereas Estivet was a *promotor officii judicis*, a promotor of the judge's office or assistant to the judge (see the letter of appointment, 1:18–19: "repperimus necessarium et conveniens esse habere promotorem generalem officii nostri in causa seu materia hujusmodi," etc.). See Kelly, "Inquisition and Heresy," p. 446 n. 34; idem, *Matrimonial Trials of Henry VIII*, pp. 23, 81, 89–90; and Adhémar Esmein, *A History of Continental Criminal Procedure with Special Reference to France*, trans. John Simpson (Boston, 1913), pp. 86–88 (the original version of Esmein's work, *Histoire de la procédure criminelle en France et spécialement de la procédure inquisitoire depuis le XIIIe siècle jusqu'à nos jours* [Paris, 1882], does not contain this discussion; one should note, however, that the Latin texts in the English version are riddled with errors). Tisset is right to state that only when articles are formally denied are witnesses to be produced to prove them; that is, in ordinary circumstances, depositions taken earlier cannot be used (3:61–62)—except for a defendant's self-incriminating testimony, which Boniface VIII allowed unless the defendant protested (which, of course, Joan did). But Tisset is mistaken in saying that in special cases it was not necessary to proceed as Lohier insisted, with a *libellus* of articles (3:62–63 n. 3); he cites Innocent IV (p. 60 n. 2), but whatever Innocent had had to say on the subject of summary process was superseded by Clement V's *Sepe* (see above, p. 1001).

[144] Tisset, 1:186 (Latin text). See Lyndwood's comment on Archbishop Boniface's constitution (above, n. 68), p. 109 note *p*, expanding on John Andrew's Ordinary Gloss to *Sext.* 2.1.1, ad v. *dicenda* (col. 309), for the distinction between the two oaths.

[145] Tisset, 1:187–88.

text says he decreed that she was to respond according to her knowledge to each of the articles, and if she requested a delay for any of her responses, it was to be given to her.[146]

Therefore, even though the promotor proceeded to swear an oath of calumny—asserting that he was acting in good faith and not out of any favor, rancor, fear, or hatred—Joan was told to take an oath of truth. She had to tell the truth concerning those things that touched on "fact." Cauchon then offered her the counsel of any of the assessors present that she wished to choose, or, if she wished, he would appoint some of them himself.[147] The 1435 text says that Joan was told that she had to take an oath before making her responses concerning fact; and this accords with Joan's response in the French text. She first thanked the bishop for the offer of counsel but said that she had no intention of abandoning the counsel of Our Lord; then she said, "As for the oath you want me to take, I am prepared to tell the truth concerning that which touches on your process." And this is how she was sworn.[148] The contents of the articles were explained to her, not by the promotor, but by Courcelles, a point omitted by Courcelles in preparing the 1435 text.[149]

By offering Joan counsel, Cauchon was paying lip service to another of Lohier's complaints, but it did not answer the latter's fundamental objection (perhaps unmentioned to Cauchon) that he and his assessors were enemies of Joan. Therefore, the offer of counsel from among her enemies was harmful rather than helpful. There was no attempt to meet the objection that there had been no process on fame, but in the final articles fame was asserted. Article 66 claimed that she had, at the instigation of the devil, offended God and the church in committing the above crimes and that she was scandalous and notoriously defamed of them (Joan responded that she was a good Christian, and as for the charges noted in the article, she referred herself to the Lord). Article 67 claimed that she committed all these things in the diocese of Beauvais and elsewhere (Joan simply denied the article). Article 68 stated that, because of clamorous insinuation, public fame, and information gathered, the judges found Joan suspect and vehemently defamed (Joan said that this article concerned the judges). Article 69 asserted that Joan had been and still was vehemently suspect and notoriously defamed among good and grave men and that she refused to correct herself in spite of charitable exhortations from the bishop and other notable clerics and honest persons (this is clearly the way in which her month-long interrogation was characterized; no other reference was made to it, except for the next article; Joan replied by denying all of the crimes the promotor attributed to her, saying that she did not believe that she had done anything against the Christian faith). Article 70 claimed that all of the previous articles were true, notorious, and manifest; that the public voice and fame had labored and still labored over them; and that she had confessed them both judicially and extra-

[146] Ibid., pp. 188–89.
[147] Ibid.
[148] Ibid., pp. 189–90.
[149] Ibid., p. 190.

judicially (Joan denied everything except what she had in fact confessed).[150] In other words, fame was simply asserted and not proved, even though denied by Joan. As for the truth of the charges, there was never any question of bringing in witnesses, since her own statements of her actions and beliefs were taken as confessions of crimes—and unrepented crimes, because in affirming her actions and beliefs she denied that she had done anything wrong.

Of all of the lawyers and consultants who attacked Cauchon's proceedings in the nullification trial, only one, a prominent ecclesiastical jurist and judge named John de Montigny,[151] censured the initial procedures on which everything else was based; but even he did not object to the fact that Joan was interrogated before she was charged. He noted that there was no preparatory process on infamy, as required by Boniface VIII's decretals *Postquam* and *Si is*. Joan was also judicially aggrieved in the exaction of the oath: first, because she was compelled by oath to respond to all subjects of inquiry, even the most occult ("ad omnia inquisita, etiam quecunque et quantumcunque occulta"), and she was compelled to respond generally and absolutely to all the things that were to be asked of her, whereas she should have been forced to reply by oath only concerning those points on which she had been defamed or found suspect in the faith; and, second, she was forced to swear repeatedly, whereas, according to law, the oath to tell the truth should be given only once.[152]

To recall Boniface's legislation: the decretal *Postquam* provided that a defendant who confessed immediately could not later invalidate the confession by claiming that he or she was not defamed of the crime, or that no articles of charges had been given; *Si is* stated that a judge could proceed without establishing fame if the defendant did not object. The corollaries noted by the commentators were that defendants who insisted on knowing the charges and seeing proof of fame had legitimate grievances if the judge proceeded without complying. I have argued that Joan's repeated desire to know the scope of the trial ("Is that part of your process?" and so on) constituted a demand to have the charges explained to her. Perhaps Montigny assumed that a process on fame could not be held without first giving chapters of charges.[153] But the fact that he does not mention the delay in presenting the chapters (the seventy articles) may indicate that he saw nothing irregular in the preliminary interrogation except its excessively broad scope, and that he did not fault Cauchon for the delay in spelling out the charges, but only for not holding a process on fame when Joan denied the final chapters that asserted fame and notoriety. But by then, as we have seen, all of Joan's responses to the previous interrogations

[150] Ibid., pp. 283–85.

[151] According to Duparc, 5:56, Montigny had studied at the University of Paris and taught canon law there from 1426 on (he obviously was not one of the masters consulted by Cauchon in 1431). In 1440 he became official of Paris, that is, the chief ecclesiastical judge under the bishop of Paris, and he was admitted as a doctor of canon law. Duparc says that he became dean in 1445, presumably meaning dean of Paris, but he goes on to characterize him as canon of Paris (a lesser title than dean). He was also a counselor for the secular high court, the Parlement of Paris.

[152] Duparc, 2:293–94.

[153] See the order insisted on by Hostiensis, at n. 16 above: first, chapters are given, and then the fame is proved.

were officially notorious, by virtue of the fact that she had made them under oath in open court.

Besides Montigny, two other consultants noted that Cauchon was at fault for questioning Joan on occult matters, namely, Robert Ciboule, who had studied and taught theology at the University of Paris, became rector of the university in 1437, and served as chancellor of Notre-Dame-de-Paris in 1451, and William Bouillé, master of theology and dean of the cathedral of Noyon, who became successively provisor of the College of Beauvais at Paris, procurator of the Nation of France, and rector of the university in 1439.[154] Ciboule cited some Scripture texts to establish his point,[155] and Bouillé invoked the principle that the church does not judge occult matters.[156]

In the beatification proceedings held for Joan of Arc beginning in 1892, the promotor of the faith, or "devil's advocate," Agostino Caprara, ridiculed all three of these authorities, Montigny, Ciboule, and Bouillé. He cited their opinions privileging occult matter from the scrutiny of the church as examples of defenses that were worse than Joan's crimes.[157] The postulator in his reply seems in effect to have agreed with his adversary; he said that he did not consider it necessary to defend the consultants' position on one's right to withhold occult matters from ecclesiastical judgment, since in fact Joan had offered to submit herself to the pope and a general council. In the case of Montigny, he says that it would have been better for him to have pointed out that Joan had not refused to explain her signs to the archbishop of Reims, and that by refusing to submit to the bishop of Beauvais she was not refusing the judgment of the church but the judgment of one wicked man.[158]

Thus we see that, by her strenuous objections to swearing blanket oaths and being required to answer all sorts of questions to unspecified charges, Joan showed herself to be a better lawyer than all, or almost all, of her legally trained defenders subsequently. We can conclude that the right to keep one's private thoughts and affairs to oneself, which was set forth clearly in the original rules of procedure for inquisitions, and repeated in later laws and commentaries and manuals of judicial order, was often badly neglected and lost sight of. But in the case of Joan of Arc, although her private thoughts were made the means of her condemnation and execution, we can rest assured that even if she had known the full extent of her rights, refused to respond, and appealed to Cau-

[154] Duparc, 5:57.

[155] Ibid., 2:387–88.

[156] Ibid., 2:334.

[157] *Sacra Rituum Congregatione, Eminentissimo ac Reverendissimo Domino Card. Lucido Maria Parocchi relatore: Aurelianen.: Beatificationis et canonizationis servae Dei Ioannae de Arc, Puellae Aurelianensis nuncupatae: Positio super introductione causae* (Rome, 1893), part 5 (= fifth pagination): *Animadversiones R. P. D. Promotoris Fidei super dubio, An sit signanda Commissio introductionis Causae, in casu et ad effectum de quo agitur?* §61–63, pp. 44–46. A complete set of the canonization proceedings of Joan of Arc is to be found in the Cardinal Wright collection of the Boston Public Library.

[158] Ibid., part 6: *Responsio ad animadversiones Promotoris Fidei*, §275–77, pp. 155–56. The response is "signed" by two postulators, Ilario Alibrandi and Giovanni Battista Minetti, but only one of them seems to have written it; see, e.g., §273, p. 154.

chon's immediate superior, the archbishop of Reims, or to the pope,[159] it would have done no good; her appeals on these grounds would have been rejected, as were her other implicit and explicit appeals. Even if there had been an attempt to follow the correct procedure at the beginning, thus foreclosing a ready supply of confessed material, Cauchon and his English paymasters would have found some other way to get rid of her.

Furthermore, we can take comfort in knowing that the extorted self-testimony, considered incriminating by her prosecutors, provided the chief means for laying open her heroic virtues to the judges in the final trial that opened in 1892. Her responses weathered the objections of successive promotors of the faith,[160] and she was beatified by St. Pius X on 11 April 1909 and canonized by Benedict XV on 9 May 1920. Herbert Thurston, writing in 1924, said, "If proof had been forthcoming that she surrendered herself unconditionally to the guidance of her voices, rejecting the authority of a properly constituted ecclesiastical tribunal, she would certainly never have been canonized."[161] This is no doubt true. That is, the cardinals and popes who judged her doubtless believed, like Thurston himself, it seems (at least for the moment), that an ecclesiastical tribunal could legitimately require the faithful to submit their private experiences to public examination; but this attitude went against both law and tradition.[162] For, even though persons who believed themselves to be receiving private revelations would be urged to confide in a competent spiritual director, they were not under an obligation to tell anything to anyone, except for thoughts or desires that they believed to be mortally sinful; and these were to be confided, not to the external forum of the church courts, but to the internal forum of confession in the sacrament of penance. We recall that Joan made this distinction when asked to recite the Lord's Prayer and the Hail Mary. This fundamental right to privacy extended to secret actions as well, actions like fornication, adultery, abortion, theft, and murder. Even when one was obliged to make amends to

[159] Pope Martin V died suddenly on 20 February 1431, the day before Joan first appeared in court; his successor, Eugene IV, was elected on 3 March.

[160] The first of these, Caprara, noted above, compared her to Christopher Columbus, whose cause for sainthood had recently been stalled. His conclusion was that she was a very fine woman up to the time that she was captured and subjected to judicial questioning; but then her greatness of mind failed, the splendor of divine revelations disappeared, and grave faults obscured her previous virtues: "Duo ergo stadia in puellae nostrae vita secernenda videntur; primum gloriosum, et admiratione plenum, usque ad suam captivitatem. . . . At, ubi capta illa fuit, et iudicialibus quaestionibus subiecta, defecit ea animi magnitudo, splendor ille divinarum revelationum disparuit, ac praegressas virtutes, quaecumque demum eae fuerint, graves culpae obscurasse visae sunt" (§70, pp. 52–53). In 1901 the promoter of the faith was Giovanni Battista Lugari: *Sacra Rituum*, etc., *Positio super virtutibus* (Rome, 1901), vol. 2, part 2: *Animadversiones R. P. D. Promotoris Fidei*; and in 1903 it was Alessandro Verde: *Nova positio super virtutibus* (Rome, 1903), part 1: *Novae animadversiones R. P. D. Promotoris Fidei*; and *Novissima positio super virtutibus* (Rome, 1903), part 2: *Novissimae animadversiones R. P. D. Promotoris Fidei*. The rest of the beatification and canonization proceedings concerned not her virtues but the modern miracles attributed to her intercession.

[161] Herbert Thurston, "Bernard Shaw on Saint Joan," *Studies: An Irish Quarterly Review* 13 (1924), 395–407, at p. 402.

[162] Regarding Thurston, we should recall his later statement made in response to G. G. Coulton that Joan had a right to keep some matters between God and herself (see above at n. 119).

injured parties, one could do so secretly; there was no obligation to turn oneself in to the church or civil authorities.

Thomas More has been taken to be the patron saint of our Fifth Amendment, which guarantees the right against self-incrimination, because of his refusal to speak his mind in court without a promise of immunity.[163] He also insisted upon the nonincriminating nature of silence, saying that there was no law in the whole world that permitted a person to be put to death for silence, and he appealed to the rule of law "Qui tacet, consentire videtur."[164] But even though More accepted that only God could be judge of what was secret in one's own heart,[165] and also indignantly denied that any convictions for heresy in England had been obtained on the basis of deceptive questioning or ambiguous charges,[166] he

[163] Richard Marius, *Thomas More* (New York, 1984), p. 462: "More made the legal point that was finally to be written into the Fifth Amendment of the United States Constitution: 'If I may not declare the causes without peril, then to leave them undeclared is no obstinancy' " (citing More's letter of ca. 17 April 1534 to his daughter Margaret Roper, *Correspondence of Sir Thomas More*, no. 200, pp. 501–7, esp. p. 505).

[164] Derrett, "Trial of Sir Thomas More" (n. 117 above), pp. 62–63. Derrett is mistaken in indicating (p. 593 n. 40) that Aquinas, *Sum. theol.* 1-2.71.5, supports the idea that silence is no crime; Thomas at this point is dealing with sins of omission, cases in which remaining silent would indeed be a crime; but see the passage quoted from Aquinas in n. 46 above. More invoked the rule that silence implies consent (see n. 22 above) to make the point that his refusal to take the statutory oath of supremacy could not be taken to signify his disapproval of the king's legislation. He could also have appealed to the rule that silence in response to questioning signifies neither affirmation nor denial (n. 26 above).

[165] Thomas More, *The Debellation of Salem and Byzance*, chap. 15, ed. John Guy et al. (New Haven, 1987), p. 86.

[166] More, *The Apology*, chap. 45, p. 148: "And he shall find whomsoever he will name, that hath been either punished or abjured, that the matters which have been layed unto them they have not been by any subtle questions induced to confess them, but they have been both well proved against them, and neither have been slight, nor light, nor so strange articles and unknown as they might therein of ignorance or simplicity so sore overshoot themself." For More and inquisitorial procedure, see n. 117 above. More no doubt had in mind articles like the forty-five that were ministered against John Lambert (above, nn. 6, 74), given by Foxe, together with Lambert's answers, in *Acts and Monuments*, 5:181–225. Foxe notes that it was More who had Lambert arrested. He suggests that he was released mainly because of Archbishop Warham's death. When Lambert got into trouble later, in 1538, Henry VIII himself sat in judgment on him and condemned him to death (pp. 227–36). An example of a question designed to entrap, based on no previous report or infamy, can be seen in the query put to Anne Askew after More's time, in 1545, by the mayor of London, namely, "whether a mouse eating the host received God, or no?" She says that she made no answer, but only smiled. See John Bale, *Examinations of Anne Askew* (1548), in *Select Works of John Bale* (n. 74 above), pp. 135–248, esp. p. 154. See Stephen Greenblatt, "The Mouse Trap," in *Objects and Subjects: Reconstructing Renaissance Culture*, ed. Margreta de Grazia et al. (Cambridge University Press, forthcoming). When a similar question was put to her later, she responded with a refusal: "Seeing ye have taken the pains to ask this question, I desire you also to take so much pain more as to assoil it yourself; for I will not do it, because I perceive ye come to tempt me" (p. 158). For earlier discussions of the host-eating mouse, see the Ordinary Gloss to Gratian, *Decretum* 3.2.94 (*Qui bene*), and references to it in the glosses on 2.1.1.54 (*Detrahe*) and 3.2.92 (*Accesserunt*); in the latter, the text should read, "Arg. hic quod mus non potest accipere corpus Christi." In the Roman edition (1606 reprint, col. 1963), "quod mus" has become "quãuis," i.e., "quamvis." See Gary Macy, "The 'Dogma of Transubstantiation' in the Middle Ages," *Journal of Ecclesiastical History* 45 (1994), n. 58; see also nn. 101–2 for a case prosecuted by Nicholas Eymerich, *Directorium inquisitorum*, pt. 1, p. 33 (see Peña's discussion in the appendix, scholion 14, p. 13).

defended the Star Chamber use of preliminary interrogations to elicit confessions of unknown crimes.[167] I suggest that an even better patron for the right against self-incrimination and for a global right to privacy is St. Joan of Arc. She was not principally concerned about defending her rights, of course, and one could hardly suppose that she managed to evolve a prototype of the Fifth Amendment; rather she was motivated by the need to protect personal loyalties and obligations. That is, she was not worried so much about self-incrimination as self-betrayal in the sight of God and the saints. Nevertheless, her legal rights were violated, and the self-testimony that was extorted from her in spite of her heroic efforts constituted a judicial rape that resulted in her death. Therefore, even though the church honors her not as a martyr but rather as a confessor of the faith, she can be considered a martyr in the cause of civil rights.

[167] More, *Debellation*, pp. 105–6. He is defending the practice in ex officio inquisitions of not revealing who the original delators were: "But why shall he not know them forthwith, when he is first convented? For it were not well done he should, no more than the King's Council, that many times call malefactors before them upon secret information first, use alway there by-and-by to disclose who told them the matter and what; which if they should, and by-and-by bring him forth, then though the suspect would confess haply some things thereby the sooner, yet should it be but that thing which he thought the tother knew; whereas while the thief knoweth not who hath given the information and yet thinketh by his examination that among his many fellows, though they be thieves all, yet some false shrews there be, he misguesseth among and weneth it were one where in deed it was another, and so in stead of one felony, to light there cometh twain." Perhaps we are to take it from this that similar preliminary interrogations of suspected heretics were in fact conducted by the bishops. Foxe notes that Lambert was first examined at Lambeth before being tried before the archbishop at Otford (p. 181); but it is likely that if any prearraignment interrogation had been attempted, Lambert would have alluded to it in his published responses. After the examinations of Anne Askew noted above, Edmund Bonner, bishop of London, examined her privately and asked her opinion about the matters laid against her and also urged her to utter the secrets of her heart, promising her immunity; but she declined, preferring to await the arrival of her friends (Bale, p. 163). She was eventually consigned to death by the King's Council, which she considered not a proper trial: "And so wę were condemned, without a quest" (p. 213). Criminal procedure in matters of heresy was up in the air after 1534; see Levy, *Origins*, pp. 69–73.

IV

JOAN OF ARC'S LAST TRIAL: THE ATTACK OF THE DEVIL'S ADVOCATES

In Joan of Arc's s canonization trial, the Devil's Advocates made serious charges against her modesty, temperance, humility, fortitude, perseverance, and military mission. In spite of fierce rebuttals by the defense team, the jury of Consultors found much merit in the accusations, but the judges (the cardinals and pope) gave her a resounding acquittal.

Joan of Arc has been subjected to many contradictory judgments over the ages, some of which must be characterized by unprejudiced observers (like you and me) as rash, being dictated by political, religious, or ideological biases. But in this paper I will uncover clashing opinions in a forum where we would expect most of the intellectual presuppositions and leanings to be fairly uniform, namely, the papal curia, in Joan's canonization trial. Of course, the accusatory format of the trial guaranteed basic differences of opinion, and the raw material for these opinions derived from the records of similar earlier trials.

Joan was a defendant in six ecclesiastical trials. The first occurred some time after she had made her vow of virginity at the age of thirteen: she was accused in the consistory court of her local bishop of having contracted marriage with a young man and then refusing to acknowledge it.[1] Her second trial was the examination by the dauphin's allies that took place in Poitiers.[2] Then came the trials of condemnation and relapse, and next the rehabilitation or nullification trial, ending in 1456. Finally, the canonization process for Joan began in 1869 and concluded in 1920, a period of over fifty years.[3]

In our consideration of this last trial, we will begin and end *in mediis rebus*, starting with the earliest Roman phase, dealing with Joan's reputation for sanctity, which opened in 1892, and ending with the sessions debating her actual practice of saintly virtues, concluding in 1903. But first a word on the preliminaries. As noted, the formal procedures began in 1869: with a petition to Rome from Felix Dupanloup, bishop of Orleans, on May 8.[4] Far from being inspired by the Franco-Prussian War, the process was in fact delayed by it, and the first local inquisition, held in Orleans, did not open until 1874.[5] The documents that resulted during the course of the process, both in France and in Rome, are remarkable for their lack of any reference to the military and political situations of the day. We must remember that the French garrison that had been preserving Rome from the Italian Republicans for a decade was forced to withdraw on the outbreak of the war in France, leaving Pius IX the "prisoner of the Vatican." His successor, Leo XIII, elected in 1878, continued his political aims of regaining the papal states. After 1887, he tried with mixed results to make an ally of France against the Alliance powers of Germany, Austria, and Italy. Pius X, elected on August 4, 1903, took a sterner line, which led to a break in diplomatic relations with France on July 30, 1904.[6] But the combatants in the spiritual battle over Joan's fate remained above the earthly fray.

The inquisition that opened in Orleans in November 1874 lasted for thirty-three sessions, ending in January 1876. Two further inquisitions were required under Dupanloup's successor, Bishop Coullié, the first in 1885, lasting also for thirty-three sessions (June to November), and the second in 1887–88, comprising twenty-five sessions (December to February),[7] after which the cause was admitted to the tribunal of the Sacred Congregation of Rites.

FIRST DEVIL'S ADVOCATE: AUGUSTINE CAPRARA

In 1892, then, the Devil's Advocate, or, as he was officially known, the Promotor of the Faith, began his assault upon Joan by saying:

> The history of the fifteenth century has consecrated two names especially for praise, for remembrance, and for perennial attention: Christopher Columbus and Joan d'Arc, or Joan Romée, called also the Maid of Orleans. Columbus is famous because of the New World that he sought and found, and Joan because of the recovered fortunes of her native land and its restored freedom and glory. Moreover, just as Columbus did not hesitate to conquer the "dark sea" and to thrust himself into every kind of vicissitude in order to acquire new shores for the Gospel and enter into their possession "in the name of Jesus Christ," so, too, the Virgin of Arc did not fear to take up arms and

commit herself to the perils and hardships of war in order to restore the kingdom of France, at that time almost destroyed, and to consecrate it "through the hands of the dauphin to the king of heaven, who is the king of France."[8]

The Promotor, a priest named Augustine Caprara,[9] elaborates on the problems that Columbus had and the far worse troubles of Joan, who fell into the hands of her enemies and died a relapsed heretic's death at the stake.[10] His final conclusion, however, is that she was no saint and that even her admirable human virtues did not survive her last ordeal: "It seems then that two stages are to be discerned in the life of our Maid. The first was glorious and full of admiration, up to her captivity. . . . But when she was captured and subjected to judicial questions, that greatness of soul gave out, that splendor of divine revelations vanished, and grave faults are seen to have obscured the aforesaid virtues, whatever, finally, they were."[11]

In the beginning of his discourse, the Promotor admits that Joan's execution as a heretic was the result of calumnies, but he refrains at this point from condemning the church authorities who were responsible for it; rather, he gives credit to the church for setting about the process of rehabilitating her: for hardly had Pope Calixtus III ascended the Roman see when, at the request of Joan's parents and kin, he appointed apostolic judges to consider the case anew and to declare what was just. It was entirely right for the church to protect the honor of such a virgin, for, as the present Holy Father, Leo XIII, wisely wrote in his recent letter on Christopher Columbus, the church willingly approves of whatever seems honorable and praiseworthy, and, while keeping its greatest honors for those virtues that pertain to eternal salvation, it does not for this reason disdain the other kind of virtues, "for the signs of divine power also appear in those in whom there shines forth a certain excellent forcefulness of spirit and mind."[12]

Not content with these "rather narrow limits," however, Joan's modern devotees have pressed for even greater honors, those reserved for the most outstanding virtues in the realm of morals. The Promotor says:

> I would not dare to say whether any more outstanding or more difficult case ever existed in previous times. I know, certainly, that in this preliminary seat of judgment it is only a question of the fame, or the "fume," of sanctity; that is, it must be decided whether or not it flourished in the past and still flourishes. But the documents that are submitted seem to prove this very clearly: that no age has been silent

about Joan's *political* virtues, joined certainly to piety and religion, indeed also to a prophetic spirit. But it is only in our own times that one has begun to think about her possession of true and heroic virtues befitting to saints.[13]

He refers to the great work on canonization produced by a Promotor of the Faith from the previous century, Prosper Lambertini, who later became Pope Benedict XIV: he used the example of Joan of Arc to demonstrate that the gift of prophecy could exist apart from sanctity, since in Joan's case there never had been any discussion or judgment concerning her sanctity and heroic virtues.[14]

By speaking of Joan in conjunction with Columbus, and saying that he could hardly think of a more celebrated or more difficult case for canonization than hers, the Promotor was clearly inviting * comparison with the recent elaborate attempts to have Columbus considered for sainthood. The formal process had begun in 1873, when Archbishop Donnet of Bordeaux officially requested the admiral's beatification; the petition was declined by the Sacred Congregation of Rites in October 1877, on grounds that the proofs for Columbus's marriage to Beatrice Enríquez de Arana, mother of his son Ferdinand, were insufficient.[15] The effort continued under Giuseppe Baldi, who was named Vice-Postulator of the cause, and he published three volumes of supporting petitions from nearly eight hundred bishops and archbishops, including even a prayer for Columbus's beatification by Pope Leo XIII himself,[16] but the cause never prospered, presumably because the opposition of the Devil's Advocate prevailed.

A similar number of episcopal testimonials had been gathered for Joan, including one from Cardinal Newman[17] (whose own cause for beatification was completed in 1991, except for a requisite miracle).[18] Promotor Caprara makes no reference to these postulatory letters, except indirectly, in alluding to the assertions of her sanctity that had only recently been forthcoming; these assertions, he adds, do not come from "probable causes."[19] That is, they are not based on historical evidence or on acceptable spiritual evidence (for instance, miracles attributed to her intercession).

Caprara proceeds to base his attack on the historical documents that the supporters for her canonization were using, namely, the full records of her trial of condemnation and her later posthumous trial of rehabilitation or nullification. He puts more faith in the records of the trials of condemnation and relapse, without, however, fully adverting to their questionable aspects. Specifically, he wants to establish that the redaction of Joan's responses into seventy articles by the judges' promotor was accurate: that is, that it corresponded truthfully to what Joan actually answered to the questions.[20]

This position was indignantly repudiated by the responding Defender, Hilary Alibrandi, an Advocate of the Congregation of Rites.[21] He rightly demonstrates that the seventy articles were not drawn primarily from her responses but were based largely on the unsubstantiated charges compiled against her before her interrogation began. Moreover, they were addressed not to her but to her judges.[22]

The portions of the records giving the responses that Joan allegedly made to interrogations, both before and after the presentation of the articles, have been generally accepted by historians with cautious confidence as accurately reflecting her words, and Promotor Caprara follows suit; he uses them to cast aspersions on her character. He shows himself critical of the inquisition begun in Orleans in 1874 and transferred to Paris without obtaining jurisdiction from the local archbishop, and he maintains that the deposition received there from De Wallon, the minister of public instruction, was invalid and should be thrown out. But he is less scrupulous about the illegality of the interrogation of Joan of Arc, and, as I have pointed out elsewhere, even Defender Alibrandi and his colleagues were not aware that a church court had no right to interrogate a defendant on anything but public crimes that had been publicly attributed to him or her.[23]

After the Promotor's first chapter, "On Proofs,"[24] he moves to his second major topic, Joan's reputation.[25] He cites Benedict XIV on the need to have a "common opinion" about the solid integrity of life and virtues of a candidate for sainthood, and he goes on to claim that up to the time of her capture she was admired for her military prowess, not for Christian virtue, and that she had no such fame for heroic virtue at the time of her rehabilitation trial.[26]

He wonders what can be considered spiritually heroic in her life. In her youth, she played games with the other little girls, and she loved to ride horses, which made her into a very strong woman. Later on, people took to giving her horses and costly clothes as gifts, and the dauphin ennobled her family. There was nothing wrong about any of this, of course, but it does not constitute heroic or even ordinary virtue.[27] She is to be praised for refusing the superstitious and almost divine honors that the people wished to bestow upon her, which, she protested, can be shown only to saints.[28] Here, Promotor Caprara seems to be admitting a common opinion about her sanctity without realizing it.

He continues: she boasted of her virginity, challenging her interrogators to have her inspected, but she was not always careful of modesty or free of imprudence, because the duc d'Alençon testified that he saw her beautiful breasts at times; nor did she keep herself from the anger that is customary with military persons, unlike holy martial figures like St. Louis and St. Ferdinand.[29]

As for her prophetic powers, and the divine mission they indicated, which her supporters claim as another *probable* indication of her reputation for sanctity, Benedict XIV has already been cited on the point that such charisms do not always go with sanctity, giving Joan as one example and Savonarola as another; furthermore, the Promotor adds, she did not always believe her voices or obey them.[30]

The third element in her holy reputation that her supporters claim for her is that of martyrdom. No one can fail to be moved at hearing of her death, the Promotor says, but the real reason she was killed, on the part of her enemies, was their rage that a woman had defeated them. On Joan's side, an incidental reason was that she had resumed male clothes to protect her modesty; but the principal reason was her constant insistence that she had been divinely sent to rescue France and her affirmation that her revelations and voices were true. Hence, some call her a martyr of modesty and a martyr of faith. But, as Benedict XIV points out, dying for a private revelation cannot be considered martyrdom. Moreover, our Heroine (*Virago nostra*) did not face death like a martyr but suffered it with great anguish and fear.[31] Finally, there is no fame of miracles.[32]

The Promotor's third and final chapter deals with obstacles to the beatification.[33] First of all, the sentence of the rehabilitation trial was not submitted to the pope or confirmed by him; furthermore, the judges did not pronounce her to be *de bono spiritu* but simply repudiated the twelve charges on which she was convicted and nullified her abjuration, without deciding anything about her virtue or sanctity.[34]

Moreover, the Promotor says, when he sees the miserable punishment that was visited upon Joan at Rouen; when he sees a cardinal of the holy church (Beaufort of Winchester), the bishop of

Beauvais (Cauchon), and many other prelates and ecclesiastical and religious men, as well as outstanding jurists and the whole faculty of the University of Paris, traduced as guilty of such a great crime (*tanti criminis reos traduci*); when especially he considers the shameful things the witnesses reported about Father Loyseleur, that he pretended to be St. Catherine and tried to get Joan to say what he wanted, and that he abused the very sanctity of the confessional in order to acquire her secrets and to persuade her to disobey the church, he seriously questions whether they should proceed further with such dishonor to the whole ecclesiastical estate. If the holy see were to add its force to her rehabilitation, what contempt can we imagine is in store for the clergy, what witticisms, especially in these times? For if the perennial enemies of the church reproached it for the ignorant censures of some clerics against Columbus, the imaginary cruelties inflicted on Galileo, and the deserved punishments visited on Bruno, what will they pour forth about the most wicked death by fire inflicted upon an innocent woman by clergymen? This was perhaps one of the reasons why the holy see, after constituting the judges of the posthumous trial of Joan, permanently refrained from passing a definitive sentence.[35]

There is a graver reason for silence. For even though she was declared innocent of the crime of heresy, and even though the judges of the rehabilitation trial admired her outstanding deeds and examples of her virtues, nevertheless, during her captivity she was gravely deficient in ways her defenders cannot excuse. First, there was her leap from the tower at Beaurevoir, which she herself admitted was wrong. She told her judges that she acted out of necessity, and she in no way repented the fault. This savors of heresy, denying free will. She was sorry only that she was injured.[36]

The Promotor will not judge whether Joan was really subject to the bishop of Beauvais's jurisdiction, but let it be admitted that she was not. She should nevertheless have followed Christ's example of submitting to an unjust judge. We need only read her responses to see how far she strayed from the footsteps of her mild Master. She refused to say the *Pater*, unless in confession; she was asked to swear several times and she refused, and when she finally obeyed she protested that she would not reveal everything to the judges. This contempt, joined with arrogance, was typical of her.[37] The Promotor may not have realized that Joan's behavior fell within the rights of a defendant in an inquisitorial trial. But if it had been pointed out to him, he would doubtless have retorted that standing on one's rights is not what one expects of a saint.

Joan did not hesitate to conceal the truth, and she came close to lying, the Promotor continues, quoting Quicherat's judgment that she did so to protect others and that she bent the truth about Charles's "angel," speaking truly only on the morning of her death. Joan's defenders try to interpret these lies as allegories, the Promotor says, but in fact, in confessing herself to be the angel, she called into question all of her revelations. He cites the argument of Theodore de Lellis, that distorting the truth because of pressure from the judges did not constitute perjury, a conclusion that the Promotor rejects.[38]

In her abjuration, she repudiated all of her visions. Her defenders excuse her as motivated by fear, but they do not dare to clear her of all blame. Let us grant that she did not understand the abjuration fully, but that does not excuse her of rashness, for she smiled contemptuously as she signed it.[39] One of the judges of her rehabilitation trial, John Brehal, the Inquisitor of France, compared her abjuration to St. Peter's denial of Christ and his subsequent affirmation of his Lord's divinity, and her modern defenders resort to the same comparison. But the Promotor does not accept their attenuations of her crime. Furthermore, on the day of her death she revoked her revocation of her abjuration. The upshot is that either Joan regarded her visions as true and gravely sinned when she retracted them out of fear; or she considered them to be false and she gravely sinned by affirming them so pertinaciously.[40]

The Promotor then raises what he calls a difficult question, whether Joan humbly submitted—or would submit—her visions and revelations to the church ("Arduam enim vero quaestionem obiici iam nobis video, utrum Ioanna suas visiones ac revelationes Ecclesiae humiliter submiserit"). He clearly believes that Joan had an obligation to submit her revelations to the church (which, of course, she did not), and he does not seem to realize that she had a right at any time to appeal her case to the pope, which the judges would have had to decide on the merits of her appeal, not on the current availability of the pope—and he seems to think that Joan would have known about the pope's difficult situation even before being told about it, since he alleges that she appealed to him only to delay the sentence. He concludes that, in his opinion, this is the main reason why Joan's cause could be prohibited from being heard in this court, since the rationalists maintain that Joan refused to submit to the church, and they hold her up as an example of freethinking. He wishes that the documents were clearer and stronger on the point. It is easier to assert than to prove that she did not understand what was meant by the term "Church Militant." The Promotor goes on to ridicule the three authorities in Joan's nullification trial who maintained that Joan was within her rights to withhold secrets in an ecclesiastical trial: William Bouillé, Robert Ciboule, and John de Montigny; he professes to consider their defense worse than Joan's opposing crime.[41] As I have shown in my essay on the right to silence, even the Defender in his reply shows that he is not aware of individuals' rights and sometimes obligations to confidentiality, which no church tribunal had the right to breach.[42]

As for Joan's boasted visions, how does one tell true from false revelations? The first criterion mentioned by the best authorities is the full and humble submission to the teaching church. The Promotor cites Benedict XIV's example of St. Teresa of Avila as one who constantly consulted with grave and prudent men about the graces and favors God bestowed on her in prayer and raptures (*raptus*). What a contrast with our Joan, who, when asked if she had ever spoken of them with her curate or any other ecclesiastical man, said no![43]

Then, the Promotor pronounces the judgment I cited above, about the two stages in Joan's life, one admirable and the other disappointing.[44] He goes on to admit that in recent times there has been a great surge of favor toward her, and that many persons, outstanding for learning and piety, have pressed for her canonization, almost—to quote her Jesuit champion Father Ayroles—to the point of imperiling the process with their enthusiasm.[45] He concludes:

> Such noble efforts of eminent men, such a universal concern for the Virgin of Arc, moves minds and urges the matter to be weighed more intimately and severely on the balances of the sanctuary, lest perhaps, as Benedict XIV writes in a very similar case, a worthy cause, acceptable to both God and man, should languish altogether neglected —especially if God be heard to invite his friend "to go higher" by means of clear signs and wonders from heaven. Therefore, that person will deserve extremely well not only of France but also of all Christendom who in our own day will bring the cause of the Maid, long suppressed or despised because of many circumstances, some

> caused by human malice, some by inactivity or carelessness, into the full light of day, having dispersed the darkness of all difficulties.[46]

In so saying, Caprara seems almost to regret that he has had to bring up the obstacles he has enumerated. We should also note that, far from objecting against Joan as a national heroine, he claims her as a figure of supranational significance.

To the fifty-four pages of animadversions of the Promotor and another forty-seven pages of documents, Defender Alibrandi makes a spirited and highly detailed reply of one hundred and seventy pages; he is often sharp and sarcastic, even indignant, in his reaction to what he takes to be the slurs made by his diabolical colleague against his beloved Maid. But he finds the Promotor's conclusion much to his liking in recognizing the universal desire for her canonization. Since this stage before the tribunal concerns her fame for sanctity, the Defender says, those who urge it must be declared victors. The Judges are also to decide whether there is some evident and insuperable obstacle to her cause, and the Promotor, whom he sometimes calls "Defender of the Faith" (*Vindex Fidei*) but here addresses as "Distinguished Censor" (*Censor Amplissimus*), has confessed that there is no such obstacle, when he intimates that someone could arise to disperse all of the difficulties and bring the cause to the full light of day.[47]

In all parts of the 1893 compilation, Joan is spoken of only as "Servant of God" (*Serva Dei*), but now she has the title of "Venerable Servant of God." She was given this designation somewhat earlier
* along the way to canonization than was Cardinal Newman, thereafter noted above, because as yet only her fame for sanctity had been established, not her practice of heroic virtue. One might suppose that this was because Newman's cause has proceeded under new rules, for in 1983 the adversarial trial system was eliminated and the Devil's Advocate cashiered—or, rather, the Promotor of the Faith was transformed into the "Prelate Theologian."[48] But the stage at which a candidate was to be declared Venerable remained where it had been specified in the 1917 *Code of Canon Law*, namely, after the establishing of heroic virtues,[49] and, according to Kenneth Woodward, the same thing is stated in Canon Macken's 1910 volume, *The Canonization of Saints*.[50] The *Code* also positively forbids the title of Venerable to be used at the time when the introduction of the cause is accepted.[51] Must we than conclude that Joan was given

the title exceptionally early? The answer is no,since Macken's account does not in fact agree with the *Code*. Rather, it matches the description of the beatification process, by Camillus Beccari, published in 1907, when Beccari was the Postulator General of Saints' Causes for the Jesuits, according to which the title of Venerable was juridically given to a Servant of God upon approval of the decree of introduction. The decision is arrived at after discussion and a vote by the Cardinals and the Officials of the Congregation, without vote or participation of Consultors.[52] Beccari's account, which must reflect the procedures in effect when Joan's case was being considered, differs substantially from that of the *Code* in other aspects as well, and I will conform to his outline in what follows.

The title of Venerable is first attributed to Joan in the decree of the Congregation of Rites approving of the introduction of her cause, "after the voice and writing of the Promotor of the Faith, Augustine Caprara, had been heard," a decree dated January 27, 1894, and signed by the pope himself on that day: "Sanctitas Sua rescriptum Sacrae ipsius Congregationis ratum habens, Commissionem Introductionis Causae Ven. Servae Dei Ioannae de Arc, Virginis, propria manu signare dignata est."[53] (This decree, by the way, makes the point that the iniquitous condemnation of Joan for heresy was pronounced by judges who were proponents of the schismatic Council of Basel,[54] which opened some six months after Joan's execution.)

Later in 1894, the Sacred Congregation of Rites published a longish history of Joan of Arc in which no whisper of blame is to be heard. For instance, in the account of the abjuration, we are told that "a small text of abjuration was read to her, according to which she was enjoined not to wear male clothing, not to bear arms, and the like" ("Tunc lecta ei est parva abiurationis schedula, qua ei iniungebatur ne virilem sumeret habitum, ne arma ferret, et alia huius generis"), which compromised her in no way.[55]

SECOND D.A.: JOHN BAPTIST LUGARI

The next records of Joan's process were published in 1901, in two volumes, both titled *Positio super virtutibus*, which I label 1901A and 1901B. The former contains two parts: first the testimony of forty-eight witnesses, dated July 6, 1898, reviewed by Alexander Verde, Subpromotor and Advocate of the Congregation,[56] and second a

Summarium additionale, with data taken from the nullification trial and other documents, mainly published by Quicherat, reviewed by Verde,[57] and a brief *Novum summarium additionale*, containing the formal request of the new Postulator, Xavier Hertzog, the current Procurator General of the Sulpicians, to the new Promotor, John Baptist Lugari, for the "compulsation" (formal authentication and submission) of the rehabilitation trial records. The Promotor first requires the Postulator to take the "oath of calumny," swearing he will act in good faith, and the Subpromotor, Verde, is present to examine all submissions for errors.[58]

In the 1901B *Positio super virtutibus*, there is first a long *Informatio* on the *dubium* in Joan's case, namely: "Is there certainty regarding the theological virtues of faith, hope, and charity toward God and neighbor and also concerning the cardinal virtues of prudence, justice, fortitude, and temperance, and associated virtues, to a heroic degree, in the matter and to the effect that is being investigated?"[59] The account is dated August 8, 1899, and signed by the Advocates John Baptist Minetti and Angel Mariani, and also by Adolph Guidi, and reviewed by Subpromotor Verde.[60] Next comes the *Animadversiones* of Promotor Lugari, dated 15 March 1901,[61] together with a packet of documents,[62] and finally the *Responsio ad Animadversiones*, dated 31 October 1901, signed by Minetti, Mariani, and Guidi.[63] Both the *Informatio* and the *Responsio* are in the first-person singular, and I take it that Minetti is the speaker.

The new Promotor divides his attack in the same way as his predecessor: after a prologue, he speaks first of proofs, then of the main subject under investigation, virtues this time rather than fame, and finally of the obstacles that he sees in the way of a positive response.[64] In the introduction, he willingly admits that Joan was a remarkable person who was moved by divine instinct to bring aid to her king and country. He, too, would rejoice if divine honors could be added to her earthly renown, but, unfortunately, it seems to him that the holy laws of the church stand in the way of such a result, and that for a number of reasons.[65]

In the first chapter, he says that the only valid proofs about the nature of Joan's virtues, so long after her lifetime, can come from historical documents. But the trial of rehabilitation was no less political than the trial of condemnation, except that it was prejudiced in her favor rather than against her. He impugns it in much the same way as his predecessor (though he makes no reference to his account).[66]

In the next chapter, he runs through the texts adduced by her supporters to prove her various virtues, and he finds all of them inadequate to the standard of the saints. Granted, she died a pious death, but, to start with the theological virtues, what was heroic about her faith? As for her possession of the virtue of hope, almost nothing is alleged, and what is said about her love of God and neighbor contains nothing remarkable. The same with the first two cardinal virtues, prudence and justice.[67]

He spends much time on the next cardinal virtue, fortitude. He admits that she suffered much but says that she did not do so willingly. One could, perhaps, speak of her tireless and unbroken fortitude in responding to her judges, but it would be more appropriate to praise her quickness of mind and wonderful memory. Moreover, since fortitude is the chief military virtue, it should be manifested especially in warlike deeds. But in Joan's case there is no testimony in support of such, and much to the contrary. When she received a slight wound, she carried on in a way unbefitting a *bellatrix*. Her fear of imprisonment was different from the attitudes of the saints of history, who positively desired to suffer out of love for God. The Promotor accepts that she was receiving genuine heavenly revelations, but he holds that she misinterpreted what her voices were telling her about being imprisoned and being released from captivity. He concludes that her saints did not speak more openly to her because of her weakness (*imbecillitas*). Therefore, she was far removed from the fortitude of the saints. He ends by telling of her fearful behavior on her death day. "Certainly, I am not one to censure these complaints, these groans of the Maid who was soon to die. For who would not be moved to pity her misery? I maintain only that she did not manifest heroic fortitude."[68]

It is surprising how little testimony there is to her temperance, the fourth cardinal virtue. On the other side, one can find testimony to her lack of the virtue: for instance, her anger toward the promotor of the trial, Estivet. Then, there is her love of luxurious clothing and gifts, much different from what is encountered in the lives of the saints. There are in fact no signs of any ascetic practices in her life. As for her chastity, it is true that she was found to be a virgin, but it was hardly consonant with modesty to boast of it and to offer her body for inspection. Sometimes, it is true, she showed prudent and necessary caution, by sleeping in her clothes when in the field with soldiers. But, Lugari adds, sometimes she acted otherwise. He brings up the duc d'Alençon's testimony again, about seeing her beautiful breasts. This was imprudent of her, and the fact that the duke did not have impure thoughts about her is attributable to the gift of God rather than to her precautions. The same is true of John d'Aulon, who could glimpse her nipples when helping her to arm or her bare legs when tending to her wounds. But the divine gift, if such it was, was not always in evidence. For, not to mention the gross attempts upon her by her captors, there was the case of the tailor who touched her breast and she had to beat him off, and the same with her familiar Raymond Macy when he would try to grope her. Finally, there is little evidence cited as to her humility, and many signs against it, such as, once again, her love of fine things.[69]

The Promotor begins his chapter on the obstacles to Joan's cause by in effect questioning the earlier decision of the Congregation that she had a sufficient reputation for sanctity over the years to be declared Venerable. He repeats Promotor Caprara's citation of Benedict XIV's characterization of Joan,[70] and he addresses Defender Alibrandi's response to it. Alibrandi maintained that Joan's gift of prophecy did in fact prove her sanctity, without considering the possibility that it proved only her divine mission. The Defender next alleged that many men saw in Benedict's words an invitation to submit her cause to the Congregation of Rites, but Lugari replies that this is hardly a probable interpretation of the pontiff's meaning. If he had meant anything of the sort, he would have spoken more clearly, as he did, for example, in the case of the martyrdom of Mary Queen of Scots. He gives Pope Benedict's laudatory history of Mary's life and his conclusion that there seemed nothing lacking in the requirements for a true martyrdom.[71]

Promotor Lugari continues: the principal obstacle to Joan's consideration for sainthood is her reliance on her own judgment in the matter of her revelations.[72] (In his response to this point, Defender Minetti spends a great deal of time showing that Joan consistently attempted to have her case removed from the prejudicial court of the bishop of Beauvais and brought to the pope.)[73] The Promotor's next animadversion is that, even though Joan has been praised for not pursuing her enemies on Sundays or holy days, she often did the contrary. He goes on to say that she was frequently lacking in due reverence toward her judges, even at Poitiers, but more so at Rouen.[74] Furthermore, she not only refused to answer her interrogating judges, she actively misled them with lies.[75] She also showed herself contemptuous of her voices, when she leaped from the tower against their prohibition, and she later admitted her sin. Should not this also stand in the way of her being offered to the faithful as a model of heroic virtue?[76] Finally, in her abjuration, she denied her divine mission. The fearful circumstances that she was in somewhat mitigate her guilt, but they do not entirely remove it. "Therefore, the Maid, in the supreme and gravest time of her life, betrayed the truth, abjuring and renouncing the mandate that she had received from God. Accordingly, even though she was a most noble heroine, even though she freed France from its enemies, even though she was pious and endowed with the most impeccable morals, still her virtues do not seem to be such as to make her worthy of being proposed by a decree of the holy see as an exemplar to be imitated by the Christian faithful."[77]

The above objections of Promotor Lugari and the response of Defender Minetti were prepared for the so-called "antepreparatory congregation," or preliminary meeting, held in the home of the Cardinal Relator, that is, the cardinal from the Congregation of Rites assigned to shepherd the cause through the juridical stages of the process, in this case, Cardinal Parocchi. Only the Consultors of the Congregation were allowed to vote.[78] According to the 1917 *Code*, the "Official Prelates" (whom I take to be the Promotor, Subpromotor, and Secretary) are also present and would seem to have the vote as well as the Consultors. Beccari states that a majority of the Consultors must decide "that the difficulties of the Promotor of the Faith have been satisfactorily solved" before the cause could proceed, whereas according to the *Code* the cause could go forward even with a negative majority, unless it amounted to two-thirds or more of those present, and even then the pope, after being informed by the Cardinal Prefect, might move it to the next stage.[79]

THIRD D.A.: ALEXANDER VERDE

The documents for the next two phases of the beatification process for Joan of Arc, the *congregatio praeparatoria* and the *congregatio generalis*, that is, the preparatory and general meetings, were both published in 1903. The first, which I label 1903A, has the overall title of *Nova positio super virtutibus.* It contains an attack against Joan by the new Promotor of the Faith, Alexander Verde, promoted from Subpromotor. His brief, titled *Novae animadversiones,* is dated April 19, 1902, and is only twenty-four pages long.[80] It is followed by the *Responsio* of the Defender, which fills three hundred and sixty-seven pages.[81] Like the previous response, it is signed by Minetti, Martini, and Guidi and cast in the singular voice, which I take to be Minetti's. Finally, there is an *Expositio virtutum,* unsigned but obviously prepared by the Defenders, of one hundred and ninety-eight pages.[82] Both second and third parts were reviewed by Subpromotor Mariani.

According to the 1917 *Code,* Promotor Verde's assignment in this stage would have been to bring up not only objections of his own but also any objections that he considered valid from the opinions of the Consultors who attended the antepreparatory session.[83] He refers to the Consultors as "PP. AA.," that is, *Patres Amplissimi,* "Distinguished Fathers," and his short treatise gains force because it is made up largely of their adverse opinions. The Promotor even presumes to be speaking for all of the Consultors, as in his opening statement:

> The Distinguished Fathers think that this is an outstanding and noble cause, but at the same time a most grave and very difficult one, in which they recognize the great absence of proofs, because the instruments for arriving at heroic virtues in the Venerable Servant of God seem to be altogether lacking. For there are neither contemporary witnesses available concerning these virtues nor legitimate and undoubted documents; nor does tradition exist. To begin with, witnesses are lacking. For the juridical inquests are encrusted with the five centuries elapsed since the actions occurred, and therefore the witnesses clearly rely on documents and histories; for which reason they do not even seem to deserve the name of witnesses. Add to this what one of the Distinguished Fathers says: "However upstanding they are as persons, they appear to be virtually in agreement with other defenders of this cause, among whom the celebrated Father Ayroles, S.J., is the most eminent, and to be excessively affected with partiality in favor of the Venerable candidate."[84]

He cites individual Consultors to object that the witnesses at the rehabilitation trial are not pertinent, or give contradictory testimony: for instance, about Joan's resumption of male clothing after her first sentence of condemnation. Contemporary documents stress only her military virtues.[85]

The Promotor himself objects that the Patrons of the cause (referring to the Response of the most recent Defender, Minetti, and his colleagues, which he quotes) rely on newspaper accounts and stage plays to establish her virtues, whereas such sources clearly have no weight.[86] Another Consultor notes that histories show her to be pious but not a saint. Tradition is also lacking, the Promotor adds, at least concerning the deeds of a saintly woman. Of the fifty-four witnesses in one of the Orleans tribunals, nineteen testified only concerning alleged miracles, and of the others the sixteen substantial witnesses drew only on hearsay. They are witnesses only to her general fame, not to specific virtues. After citing other Consultors on the inadequacy of the trial records, the Promotor speaks for all of them: "Nor do the Distinguished Fathers, in weighing the way of life of the Servant of God, judge it to have attained to the highest path of virtue, though they willingly acknowledge her to have been a good and pious adolescent." He proves this general conclusion by citing the words of only one Consultor.[87]

Promotor Verde moves on to the subject of Joan's mission to rescue France from its enemies. Whereas the earlier Devil's Advocates, especially Lugari, willingly admitted the divinely inspired and aided nature of this mission, while denying that it proved her to be a saint, Verde suggests for the first time that perhaps all of her voices were manifestations of hysteria, and he is able to cite a skeptical Consultor to back him up: "I find it surprising," says this Distinguished Father,

> to read that only Gabriel was sent to the Most Holy Virgin to announce the incarnation of the divine Redeemer, whereas two archangels, Gabriel and Michael, appeared to Joan, and in such a way that she really saw, heard, and even touched and adored them. Who knows whether she did not suffer some hallucination and cultivated it as consonant with her own genius. Certainly, she fell short of the "simplicity of a dove" when she concealed the matter from her father and mother, lest she be prevented from her enterprise; and, if indeed she revealed it to her curate, he seemed to have doubted her, and accordingly subjected her to exorcisms.[88]

When the Defender comes to refute these statements, he attributes them, as usual, to the Promotor (or Censor, as he calls him) rather than to the cited Consultor.[89] He has just noted that Leo XIII had already declared the divine nature of her mission in his decree of 1894, and he disposes of the hysteria hypothesis by showing that her case corresponds to none of the clinical descriptions of hysteria; then he takes up Cardinal Bona's signs for the "discernment of spirits," specifically for judging whether or not visions are the vain images of a childish mind.[90] As for the Consultor's remark about Joan's angels, Minetti urges the likelihood that the Virgin Mary was in constant communication with angels, and he goes on to detail the appearance of multiple angels to many holy individuals in history.[91] Regarding those who hold that Joan deliberately refrained from revealing her experiences to her parents in order not to jeopardize her mission, he says that they offer no proof. As for her curate, he distinguishes between her own parish priest in Domrémy, who she knew would hold in confidence all that she told him in confession, and the parish priest of Vaucouleurs, who, doubtless at the suggestion of Robert of Beaudricourt, came to her in surplice and stole and carrying holy water, commanding her to depart if she was evil and to approach if good. She approached, with great humility and devotion.[92] So much for the charge that exorcisms were used against her.

The Promotor goes on to say that her victory at Orleans need not be regarded as divinely assisted, and he balks at comparing her cause to those of Old Testament heroines; for they had the divine mission of preparing for the Messiah, whereas Joan's purpose was merely to liberate France—the country that would later produce Charles VIII, who brought such evils upon Italy; it was also the country from which Francis I emerged, and from which have issued the sophistical and seditious destroyers of all disciplines and good arts, who disturb the peace of almost the entire world. Nothing, therefore, that came before or followed upon her intervention shows her to have been sent from God.[93] This is the closest that any of the opponents of Joan's sainthood come to protesting against her cause on nationalistic grounds.

But if we should wish to grant that her mission was divine, Verde continues, it is nevertheless clear how difficult it is to find virtue in a young female warrior. One of the Consultors is impressed by Benedict XIV's characterization of Joan, cited by Promotor Caprara (and also, as we have seen, by Promotor Lugari), which neither Defender Alibrandi nor the present Defender could refute. In fact, the pope seems to have been gently rebuking those who put Joan's name into private martyrologies. Another Consultor considers her not heretical, indeed, but still not proved a saint. Still another judges her pious but also with some faults of frailty, and yet another finds her sometimes timid, proud, or angry.[94] The Defenders contend that not all eminent virtues need be sought in Joan but only those most appropriate to her life as a Servant of God. It follows, therefore, that she should be outstanding in chastity and employ all means to preserve it. But, as one Consultor says, there are some things in her life not consonant with modesty and insufficiently cautious; another finds it not congruous for her to boast of her virginity and to offer to prove it.[95] Similarly, what should be more proper to a female warrior than fortitude, in which Joan often failed? One Consultor sees weakness in her, especially in her leap from the tower of Beaurevoir. Another finds the Defense unconvincing: her hardships, which were predicted by her voices, were not only not borne joyfully, but not even patiently. He thinks that her constant desire to escape, against the counsel of her voices, completely removes her from the praise of heroic fortitude. She received her sentence of death with great complaining, which takes away from the perfection of her virtue. Add that she frequently made threats against her judges. It will not do to find her of lesser merit than those heroes who think it *dulce et decorum pro patria mori* (as Horace puts it). Still another Consultor finds her strong, not heroic; upright, but not a saint. She suffered, but only because she was forced to, and received word of her condemnation with great lamentation, invoking the divine judge against her human judge. That such human emotions are altogether foreign to the fortitude of saints is passed over in silence by her Defenders.[96]

In his response to this gibe, the Defender deviates from his usual practice and identifies it as coming from one of the Consultors rather than from the Promotor: "But if you listen to the 'other Distinguished Father' telling about the death of the Venerable Maid, you would not know whether he was speaking of a Christian Virgin beloved of God or the Vergilian Sybil" (he cites the mad ravings described in the *Aeneid*). He wonders where the "noble Man" (*Vir egregius*) finds his evidence that the Venerable Maid acted thus. Certainly, the first Promotor (Augustine Caprara) did not see it this way, since he said that even her executioner and bitter enemies were moved to wonder at her fortitude and piety in her last struggles.[97]

Moving on to Joan's lack of humility, the Promotor cites another Consultor, who believes that not enough has been made of the objections about Joan's love of luxurious clothing, her horses, and so on, and the not always humble way in which she dealt with her judges. It all shows an attitude much different from that of the saints. Two other Consultors complain of her lies or dissimulations, especially regarding her sign, and another is disturbed about her repeated refusals to submit to the church.[98]

So there are not only moral failings and a virtual absence of heroic virtue but also definite obstacles standing in the way of a positive decision, and the Consultors are surprised that the demand of the previous Promotor (Lugari) has not been answered, that a systematic list of her heroic virtues be produced. Promotor Verde cites two Consultors to this effect and adds his own view that the Defenders were not able to respond, and that it was presumably for this reason that Father Ayroles tried to make her out to be a martyr, in which case there would be no need to establish heroic virtue. He cites the requests of other Consultors for an organized layout of virtues accompanied with proof-texts, ending with one who speculates that if there had been an inquiry into her life shortly after her death, other obstacles might have come to light. The same Consultor concludes that her divine mission is not relevant, and once it is removed, he does not see what is left.[99]

The Promotor claims that the same is true for "the remaining Distinguished Fathers," who are concerned about the other objections that have been raised, especially her attempt to flee from the tower of Beaurevoir, against the will of her voices. No one can deny that she showed some weakness in thus trying to escape. Her defenders invented reasons, that she wanted to preserve her chastity and to bring aid to the citizens of Compiègne, but they could cite no evidence. Verde gives the words of one Consultor but says that the objections of the others (*reliqui*) are no less grave and severe, and he proceeds to cite the views of another, who finds her action not only one of disobedience but also a tempting of God. If one were to contend that the voices were only offering a counsel rather than making a command, another Consultor says, those especially favored by God cannot disregard heavenly counsels without at least some sin. Still another Consultor finds her rash as well as disobedient.[100]

Finally, the Promotor offers a number of Consultor objections concerning Joan's abjuration. The mildest of the objections is that the circumstances are not entirely clear and more light needs to be thrown on the point, but five other Consultors are more censorious: there is no doubt about the fact that she signed a retraction; true, she did nothing against the Faith, but she failed in heroic fortitude; it was hardly a light matter, since she so bitterly repented of it; after such long resistence, she should not have signed even to save her life; if the early Christians had done so, how could they have been considered martyrs? Repudiating her divine mission because of fear cannot be excused. This failing and her other faults make it impossible to conclude that the virtues of the Venerable Servant of God attained the heroic degree.[101]

The Promotor agrees, and he concludes with the words of two other *Patres Amplissimi*. One says that there still seem to be grave obstacles, and the other, no less gravely, declares:

> I persuade myself that one can never sufficiently condemn the unjust, even impious condemnation of the Venerable Joan of Arc, and, accordingly, one can never rejoice too much over the very thorough trial of rehabilitation that ensued. But from this it follows, in my humble opinion, only that the Venerable Maid can be proclaimed as admirable above measure and endowed with singular gifts, admired as a very chaste virgin and dear to God, and praised to the stars as the liberator of France, with deeds inspired by God Himself. But she cannot, at least not on the basis of evidence thus far adduced, be declared a saint, that is, one who practiced the virtues in a heroic degree.[102]

The fact that Promotor Verde was able to cite a substantial number of the Consultors on the antepreparatory panel with serious objections against Joan's advance to sainthood shows that his exercise was by no means entirely academic and routine. The massive response of Minetti and his colleagues must have done much to defuse these objections, but there was still a requirement for a final volley of doubts.

Minetti's response to Verde's attack of April 19, 1902 is dated February 12, 1903.[103] The preparatory meeting for which it was composed was to be attended by the Cardinals of the Congregation, chaired by the Cardinal Prefect, but, once again, only the Consultors were allowed to vote[104] (in contrast to the 1917 *Code*, according to which only the Cardinals voted, after hearing the new opinions of the Consultors present and any clarifications by the Secretary and Promotor).[105] The cause was clearly approved with dispatch, and a *Novissima positio* had to be prepared for a general meeting of the Congregation, presided over by the pope, with both Cardinals and Consultors voting[106] (according to the 1917 rules, judgment was to be reserved to the pope alone, after an advisory vote of the Cardinals, Official Prelates, and Consultors).[107]

The 1903B volume, *Novissima positio super virtutibus*, contains not only Verde's brief *Novissimae animadversiones*, dated May 9, 1903,[108] and the Minetti-Martini-Guidi *Responsio*, dated June 12, 1903,[109] but, to begin with, a brief *relatio* by the current Relator, Cardinal Ferrata.[110] Ferrata tells us among other things that there had been quite a mortality rate among his predecessors. Cardinal Bilio was first appointed as Relator, or *Ponens*, in 1876, and, on his death, an Englishman, Cardinal Howard, took his place, in January 1886. When Howard "departed from among the living," he was replaced on April 28, 1890 by Cardinal Parocchi. (Actually, Howard had only departed from living among the Italians. He took ill in 1887 and was brought to England in the spring of 1888; he died only in 1892, on September 16.)[111] Cardinal Ferrata was appointed on January 23, 1903, and the preparatory meeting, at which the *Nova positio* was discussed, was held on the following March 17.

Verde begins his *Novissimae animadversiones* by saying that more caution is needed in this sacred forum. He disputes the Defender's characterization of the nature and sufficiency of purely historical documents, adding similar doubts by the Consultors.[112] The last Consultor cited goes on to allege that the winesses to be found in the historical documents concerning Joan stress mainly her military virtues, a theme sounded in the previous exchanges, and another Consultor is cited to similar effect; the latter goes on specifically to question her heroic chastity, disturbed, like others before him, by the duc d'Alençon's report about seeing Joan's beautiful breasts. Moreover, she was *fortis* only when events were favorable, but timid in adversity. What about her flight from the tower, which was contrary to her divine voices, whatever the Defense says? And her abjuration? What of the fear and trembling in her final agony? One should forgive such behavior in a weak woman, but in a heroic woman, no way (*nullo modo*). Another Consultor has doubts about her divine mission; he will believe it only if she is first proved to be a saint.[113]

The Promotor himself disputes the Defender's response about the tower episode. If the articles of the condemnation trial were repudiated at the rehabilitation trial, the sentence of the latter tribunal was never confirmed by the pope; moreover, the facts are established not just from the articles but from Joan's own responses in the body of the trial record. Cauchon could not have so thoroughly tampered with the record as to produce such a consistent falsification. He in fact would have preferred to show her obeying her voices, as coming from the devil. The rehabilitation witnesses do not correct the account of the incident, and their silence confirms it; moreover, all contemporary documents support it, including the Cordeliers Chronicle.[114]

Minetti replies that the only rehabilitation witness who knew about the contents of the condemnation records was Courcelles, who wrote them at Cauchon's direction.[115] Moreover, the Cordeliers Chronicle is the only relevant contemporary document, and it clearly indicates that she did not leap from the tower but rather tried to escape by lowering herself on a rope, which broke and caused her to fall.[116]

As for the abjuration, Verde's predecessor Lugari cited nine witnesses who said that Joan signed some form of recantation. Verde now cites the formula reconstructed by the celebrated Canon Dunand in his *L'abjuration du Cimitière Saint-Ouen*, published at Paris in 1901, which includes the admission that she had committed *lèse-majesté* and seduced the people (p. 152), which in effect was a denial of her divine mission.[117] The Defender replies by showing how tenuous was the basis for that part of Dunand's formula, and by citing another book published by the same author in the following year, *Le problème de l'abjuration de Jeanne d'Arc et les derniers Congrès des Sociétés Savants*, in which he omits these words from the formula.[118]

The Promotor concludes by agreeing with the stong opinion of a Consultor, that at the time of her death Joan receded from the fortitude that she had shown earlier in her life. No one will say that one who behaves in such a way should be proposed as an example for others to imitate, and it is only on such persons that the honors of the altar are to be bestowed in this forum.[119]

The result of the three rounds of debate on the virtues of Joan of Arc was much the same that the Congregation had arrived at in its 1894 synopsis of her life, after dismissing the objections of the first Devil's Advocate. But, as we have seen, it was not without a great deal of soul searching, not only on the part of the two following Devil's Advocates, who had a professional stake in being contrary, but also on the part of the Consultors assigned to the case, who can be thought to have had some genuine concerns. We may not think much of some of these concerns—for instance, their unwillingness to admit of any lapses in persons of genuine holiness or their straitlaced ideals of feminine modesty. But it is gratifying to see that more generous spirits prevailed in the face of persistently repeated objections from functionaries who, it was decided, were living up to their reputation of supporting the devil more than promoting the Faith.

The general meeting of the Sacred Congregation of Rites at which the *Novissima positio* was debated was held on November 15, 1903, presided over by the new pope, Pius X. After the Cardinals and the Consultors voted, Pius postponed making a decision and asked all present to pray for divine light in so difficult a matter. He would make similar statements in subsequent beatification cases,[120] though he seems more concerned in this case than in the others to request prayers from the judges of the tribunal. His decision was formally announced on the Feast of the Epiphany, January 6, 1904, which was also the birthday of Joan of Arc. He summoned to his side Cardinal Cretoni, Prefect of the Congregation, Cardinal Ferrata, the Relator of the Cause, Promotor Verde, and Secretary Panici, and solemnly announced that Joan's practice of all the virtues in a heroic degree was established, and he authorized the move to the next stage, the discussion of four miracles.[121] In the event, three miracles were approved for her beatification, in a meeting held on January 12, 1909, and after another delay for prayerful consideration Pope Pius announced, in the presence of the same four dignitaries, on the following January 24, that she could proceed to beatification.[122] In the actual decree of beatification issued on April 11, 1909, the pope revealed that the vote of the Cardinals and Consultors on January 12 was unanimous.[123] One can only conjecture whether the Devil's Advocate also concurred.

NOTES

1. The marriage seems to have been arranged by her parents; see Pierre Tisset, ed., with Yvonne Lanhers, *Procès de condamnation de Jeanne d'Arc*, 3 vols. (Paris, 1960–71), vol. 1, pp. 123, 127. Joan may have been charged with having given not only future but present consent (i.e., actually

marrying the boy), though actions to enforce mere betrothals seem to have been common in France; see Charles Donahue, "The Canon Law on the Formation of Marriage and Social Practice in the Late Middle Ages," *Journal of Family Practice* 8 (1983), 144–58, esp. 150, 154, contrary to English practice: see R.H. Helmholz, *Marriage Litigation in Medieval England* (Cambridge, 1974), pp. 35–36, especially n. 37.

2. See Charles T. Wood's essay in this volume.

3. A complete set of the beatification and canonization proceedings of Joan of Arc is to be found in Cardinal John Wright's Joan of Arc collection in the Boston Public Library, Bishop Cheverus Room. A copy of the 1893 volume described in n. 8 is also to be found at Harvard.

4. For the French text, see A. Mouchard, *Les fêtes de la béatification de Jeanne d'Arc, Rome-Orléans-la France (1909): souvenirs et documents* (Paris, n.d.), pp. 25–26. Copies of this book are in Cardinal Wright's collection (see previous note) and in the Library of Congress.

5. Ibid., p. 27.

6. A brief account of such matters can be found in J.N.D. Kelly, *The Oxford Dictionary of Popes* (Oxford, 1986), pp. 309–14.

7. Mouchard, p. 29.

8. *Sacra Rituum Congregatione, eminentissimo ac reverendissimo domino Cardinale Lucido Maria Parocchi Relatore: Aurelianen.: Beatificationis et canonizationis Servae Dei Ioannae de Arc, Puellae Aurelianensis nuncupatae, Positio super introductione causae* (Rome: Typis S. C. de Propaganda Fide, 1893) [hereafter referred to as *SRC* (1893)], part 5 (= fifth pagination): *Animadversiones reverendi patris domini Promotoris Fidei super dubio, An sit signanda commissio introductionis causae, in casu et ad effectum de quo agitur?*, pp. 1-2, §1: "Due praecipue nomina ad laudem, ad memoriam, ac perennitatem historia saeculi XV consecravit: Christophori Columbi, et Ioannae d'Arc, seu Romee, quae Aurelianensis puella etiam nuncupatur. Celebris ille namque propter novum ab se quaesitum repertumque Orbem: haec ob restitutas patriae sortes, adsertamque libertatem et gloriam. Accedit: quemadmodum Columbus *tenebrosum mare* conquirere, seseque omnigenis obiicere casibus non dubitavit, ut novas oras Evangelio acquireret, earumque possessionem *in nomine Iesu Christi* iniret; ita Darciensis virgo arma sumere, seseque bellorum periculis laboribusque committere non timuit, ut Galliae regnum tunc prope eversum restitueret, illudque consecraret, *per manus Delphini, caelorum regi, qui est Rex Franciae.*"

The parts of *SRC* (1893) are:

> Part 1: *Informatio super dubio, An sit signanda*, etc., by John Baptist Minetti, 76 pp., reviewed by Subpromotor Gustave Persiani.
>
> Part 2: *Summarium super dubio, An sit signanda*, etc., 212 pp., reviewed by Subpromotor Augustine Caprara. (This must be of an earlier date than part 1, since Persiani succeeded Caprara as Subpromotor when the latter became Promotor.)

Part 3: *Summarium additionale: Excerptum ex processu Aureliae condito anno 1885, super dubio, An sit signanda*, etc., 401 pp., reviewed by Subpromotor Persiani.

Part 4: *Summarium additionale novissimum super dubio, An sit signanda*, etc., 11 pp., reviewed by Subpromotor Persiani.

Part 5: *Animadversiones r. p. d. Promotoris* , as above, 101 pp.

Part 6: *Responsio ad Animadversiones Promotoris Fidei super dubio, An sit signanda*, etc., 170 pp., signed by Hilary Alibrandi and John Baptist Minetti, reviewed by Subpromotor Persiani.

9. He signs himself as "Augustinus Caprara, S. C. Adv. s. [that is, Advocate of the Sacred Congregation of Rites] Fidei Promotor," 5:54; he signed his review of part 2 as "Augustinus Adv. Caprara S. R. C. Assessor et S. Fidei Sub-Promotor" (p. 212). He appends to his *Animadversiones* a series of longer proof-documents, called *Summarium obiectionale* (pp. 55–101), to which he refers as appropriate in the body of his discourse.

10. Promotor Caprara, *SRC* (1893), 5:2, §2.

11. Ibid., pp. 52–53, § 70: "Duo ergo stadia in puellae nostrae vita secernenda videntur; primum gloriosum, et admiratione plenum, usque ad suam captivitatem. . . . At, ubi capta illa fuit, et iudicialibus quaestionibus subiecta, defecit ea animi magnitudo, splendor ille divinarum revelationum disparuit, ac praegressas virtutes, quaecumque demum eae fuerint, graves culpae obscurasse visae sunt."

12. Ibid., pp. 2–3, §3, quoting Leo XIII's encyclical on the Columbus Quadricentennial, *Quarto abeunte saeculo*, July 16, 1892, *Acta Sanctae Sedis* 25 (1892–93), 3-7.

13. *SCR* (1893), 5:4, §5: "Hisce instructa praesidiis tandem Causa Darciensis Virginis Sacri huius Fori limen attingit: qua utrum anteactis temporibus alia praestantior simul ac diffficilior extiterit affirmare non ausim. Novi quidem in hac praeliminari iudicii Sede nonnisi de Fama, seu de *fumo* sanctitatis agi: utrum scilicet ea nec ne viguerit ac in praesens vigeat disceptandum esse. At documenta ipsa, quae in medium afferuntur, hoc probare apertissime videntur: de Iohannae *politicis* virtutibus, pietati utique ac religioni, immo prophetico etiam spiritui coniunctis, nullam aetatem conticuisse; de veris tamen heroicisque illius virtutibus, prouti Sanctos decet, nonnisi aetate nostra cogitari coeptum esse."

14. Ibid. See *Benedicti XIV, pont. opt. max., olim Prosperi cardinalis de Lambertinis, Opus de servorum Dei beatificatione et beatorum canonizatione* 3.45.9 (Prato, 1839–42, 7 vols.), 3:526: after giving a very favorable account of her life, Lambertini concludes: "Cum tamen de puellae sanctitate et heroicis virtutibus nunquam factus sit sermo, nedum judicium de eis prolatum, hinc inferre licet, prophetiae donum posse a sanctitate esse sejunctum." Caprara cites Lambertini's treatment more fully later, pp. 20–23, §29.

15. See "Colón (Cristóbal)," *Enciclopedia universal ilustrada* (n.d., but published shortly after 1907), vol. 14, pp. 196–243, especially 232.

16. Giuseppe di G.B. Baldi, *La glorificazione del genio cattolico: Sentimenti dell' episcopato ed una postulazione inedita di monsignor Rocco Cocchia, arcivescovo delegato e vicario apostolico a Sua Santità, il sommo pontefice Leone XIII, per la causa di beatificazione dell' incomparabile servo di Dio Cristoforo Colombo* (Genoa, 1879); *Il voto dell' episcopato cattolico per la glorificazione del genio cristiano: Adesioni episcopali alla causa del servo di Dio, Cristoforo Colombo, aggiuntavi una lettera del conte Roselly de Lorgues ed altre testimonianze della cattolica stampa: Seconda raccolta di documenti* (Genoa, 1880); *Cristoforo Colombo glorificato dal voto dell' episcopato cattolico: Terza raccolta di documenti . . . aggiuntovi un articolo del conte Roselly de Lorgues sull' opportunità della causa* (Genoa, 1881). All three of these volumes are in the Library of the University of Michigan. The prayer of Leo XIII is given in the final volume, p. 128. See also Antoine François Félix Roselly de Lorgues, *Histoire posthume de Christophe Colomb* (Paris, 1885), pp. 376-452. Baldi's pamphlet, *Degli avviamenti alla causa di beatificazione di Cristoforo Colombo* (Genoa, 1877; also at the University of Michigan), announces his intention of publishing the results of agitation for Columbus's canonization, in which he gives the place of honor to the sentiments expressed by the celebrated bishop of Orleans, Felix Dupanloup, in a letter written on September 12, 1866 (pp. 12-13).

17. Cardinal Newman, *SRC* (1893), 3:358-59. Only a few of the letters are to be found in the printed file. Newman's letter, like most of the others, is undated, but the dates that are given range from 1879 (p. 357) to 1889 (p. 379).

18. He is therefore entitled to be called "Venerable." See the article by the postulator of his cause, Vincent Ferrer Blehl, "Where Does Cardinal Newman's Cause Stand?" *America* (September 25, 1993), 15-17, and his earlier article, "Prelude to the Making of a Saint," *America* (March 11, 1989). See also Kenneth L. Woodward, *Making Saints: How the Catholic Church Determines Who Becomes a Saint, Who Doesn't, and Why* (New York, 1990), pp. 355-73.

19. Promotor Caprara, *SRC* (1893), 5:4, §5.

20. Ibid., pp.5-7, §§ 7-10.

21. Defender Alibrandi, *SRC* (1893), 6:9-19, §§ 14-30. The Response is "signed" by Hilarius Alibrandi S.C. Adv. and by Iohannes Baptista Minetti, but the first person singular is used throughout (see, e.g., p. 2, §§2-4, and p. 154, § 273), and Alibrandi is repeatedly identified as the author in subsequent exchanges. According to the account of Camillus Beccari, "Beatification and Canonization," in *The Catholic Encyclopedia*, 2(1907), 364-69, each candidate for sainthood has an Advocate of the Cause, whom I take to be Alibrandi, and a Procurator (Proctor) of the Cause, presumably Minetti. Minetti was the author of part 1: *Informatio super dubio, An sit signanda commisio*, etc. As we will see below, Minetti, now an Advocate, is

listed first in the signatures to the Response to the next Promotor (*SRC* [1901B], 4:206), which is also couched in the first person singular.

22. See my account, "The Right to Remain Silent: Before and After Joan of Arc," *Speculum* 68 (1993), 992–1020, especially 1019. Alibrandi was a celebrated professor of ancient Roman law, who had been an advocate for saints' causes since 1863; see E. Volterra, "Alibrandi, Ilario," in *Dizionario biografico degli Italiani* (1960), vol.2, pp. 370–71. He had in fact been appointed by Bishop Dupanloup as Joan's Defender at the end of the first process held in Orleans in 1874–76, but, after Dupanloup's death in 1878, he resigned, exhausted from his labors in what he foresaw would be a strenuous enterprise. His replacement, Lauri, was promoted to the ranks of the opposition, being appointed Devil's Advocate, and his successor as Defender, the poet and artist Tosti, died in the midst of his labors (Mouchard, pp. 27–28), whereupon the task was taken up by Alibrandi once more.

23. Kelly, "Right to Remain Silent," p. 1023.

24. Promotor Caprara, *SRC* (1893), 5, chap. 1, "De probationibus," pp. 5–11, §§6–15.

25. Ibid., chap. 2, "De fama," pp. 12–28, §§16–39.

26. Ibid., pp. 12–14, §§16–19.

27. Ibid., pp. 15–18, §§21–24bis.

28. Ibid., p. 18, §24bis: "Laudanda quidem, quod superstitiosos ac pene divinos sibi a plebe tributos honores declinaret, ac nonnisi Sanctis eos adhiberi posse protestaretur."

29. Ibid., pp. 19–20, §§25–27.

30. Ibid., pp. 20–24, §§28–32.

31. Ibid., pp. 26–27, §§35–37.

32. Ibid., pp. 27–28, §§38–39.

33. Ibid., chap. 3, "De obstaculis," pp. 28–54, §§40–72.

34. Ibid., pp. 28–29, §40.

35. Ibid., p. 30, §42.

36. Ibid., pp. 31–32, §§43–44. The episode of Joan's attempted escape from Beaurevoir will be returned to several times below.

37. Ibid., pp. 32–33, §45.

38. Ibid., pp. 33–35, §§46–49.

39. Ibid., pp. 35–37, §§50–51.

40. Ibid., pp. 37–40, §§51–55.

41. Ibid., pp. 41–46, §§57–63.

42. Kelly, "Right to Remain Silent," pp. 1022–23.

43. Promotor Caprara, *SRC* (1893), 5: 51–52, §68–69.

44. Ibid., pp. 52–53, §70.

45. Ibid., p. 53, §71.

46. Ibid., p. 54, §72: "Tam nobiles praestantium virorum conatus, adeo universale in Darciensem virginem studium, commovent animos, ac

rem intimius ac severius ad sanctuarii lancem perpendere suadent, ne forte, uti persimili in thesi scribit Benedictus XIV, causam Dei et hominum iudicio promoveri dignam iacere omnino et perpetuo derelictam manere contingat; praesertim si claris de caelo signis et prodigiis, Deus amicam suam ut superius ascendat invitare audiatur. Optime itaque non de Gallia tantum, sed universim de re christiana ille merebitur, qui Puellae causam, per tot vicissitudines hominum partim malitia, partim desidia et incuria sive oppressam, sive despectam, aetate demum nostra, disiectis omnino difficultatum tenebris, ad plenam meridiem adducat."

47. *SRC* (1893), 6:170, §307.

48. See Woodward, pp. 90–91.

49. *Codex iuris canonici*, (Rome 1922) canon 2115.

50. Woodward, pp. 77, 83, citing Thomas F. Macken, *The Canonisation of Saints* (Dublin 1910). Woodward recommends Macken's book for those who cannot read the Latin of the *Code*.

51. *Codex iuris canonici*, canon 2084.

52. Camillus Beccari, "Beatification and Canonization" (see n. 28 above), p. 367; Macken, pp. 37, 4–42, 133.

53. "AURELIANEN. Decretum Beatificationis et Canonizationis ven. Servae Dei Ioannae de Arc virginis aurelianensis puellae nuncupatae," *Acta Sanctae Sedis* 26 (1893–94), 500–03. A grammatical note: since *Sanctitas* is feminine, we would have to render the action by saying that "the Holiness of the Pope deigned to sign with *her* own hand," if we wished to follow gender of the original, or "*its* own hand," if we make it neuter. The use of the regal and papal plural in Latin causes similar grammatical awkwardnesses.

54. Ibid., p. 501.

55. "AURELIANEN. Beatificationis et canonizationis Ven. Servae Dei Ioannae de Arco. Synopsis vitae," *Acta Sanctae Sedis* 27 (1894–95), 488–510, especially 504. No date is given; but the document of the Congregation immediately preceeding is dated August 11, 1894, and others before it have the date of September 1, 1894. The document immediately following the "Synopsis vitae" is dated January 29, 1895.

56. *SRC* (1901A), part 1; p. 1 is missing from my copy, but it doubtless carried the title *Summarium super dubio, An constet*, etc. (as below). The introductory letter is signed on p. 2 by the Substitute Secretary, Philip di Fava, and dated July 6, 1898. At the end, p. 527, "Alexander Adv. Verde, S.R.C. Assessor et S. Fidei Subpromotor" indicates that he has reviewed the material.

57. *SRC* (1901A), 2:1–169.

58. *SRC* (1901A), 2:171–75. The original Postulator, appointed by Bishop Dupanloup in 1876, was Albert Jules Captier (Mouchard, p. 27), Hertzog's predecessor as Procurator General of the Sulpician Order.

59. *SRC* (1901B), 1: *Informatio super dubio, An constet de virtutibus theologalibus fide, spe, et caritate in Deum et proximum; nec non de cardinalibus prudentia, iustitia, fortitudine, ac temperantia, earumque adnexis, in gradu heroico, in casu et ad effectum de quo agitur?*

60. Ibid., p. 110.

61. Promotor Lugari, *SRC* (1901B), 2: *Animadversiones r.p.d. Promotoris Fidei super dubio, An constet de virtutibus*, etc., pp. 1–60.

62. Promotor Lugari, *SRC* (1901B), 3: *Summarium obiectionale*, pp. 1–28.

63. Defender Minetti, *SRC* (1901B), 4: *Responsio ad Animadversiones ... super dubio, An constet*, etc., pp. 1–206.

64. Promotor Lugari, *SRC* (1901B), 2: *Animadversiones*, chap. 1, "De probationibus," pp. 2–7; chap. 2, "De virtutibus," pp. 7–27; chap. 3, "De obstaculis," pp. 27–60.

65. Ibid., pp. 1–2, §1.

66. Ibid., pp. 2–7, §§2–10.

67. Ibid., pp. 7–15, §§11–24.

68. Ibid., pp. 15–20, §§25–37. The last passage reads: "Profecto non is sum ego, qui has querelas, hos gemitus mox moriturae Puellae exprobrem. Quis enim misellae misericordia non teneatur? Id unum contendo, eam heroicam fortitudinem non ostendisse."

69. Ibid., pp. 20–27, §§38–49.

70. Ibid., pp. 27–30, §§51–54

71. Ibid., pp. 30–32, §§55–57, citing Benedict XIV, *Opus* 3.13.10 (3:119). Benedict also publishes, for the first time, he believes, the letter that Mary wrote to Pius V just before she died, which he discovered in the Castel Sant' Angelo and translated from French into Latin (3:617–19).

72. Promotor Lugari, *SRC* (1901B), 2:33–41, §§59–71.

73. Defender Minetti, *SRC* (1901B), 4:130–47.

74. Promotor Lugari, *SRC* (1901B), 2:41–47, §§72–80.

75. Ibid., pp. 47–53, §§81–86.

76. Ibid., pp. 53–56, §§87–90.

77. Ibid., pp. 56–60, §§91–95. The final passage reads: "Ergo Puella in supremo gravissimoque vitae suae tempore veritatem prodidit, divinitus receptum madatum ejuravit atque abnegavit. Quamvis igitur nobilissima virago ipsa fuerit, quamvis ab hostibus Galliam liberaverit, quamvis pia fuerit atque innocentissimis moribus praedita; attamen eius virtutes tales non fuisse videntur, quibus digna sit quae exemplar christifidelibus imitandum, Apostolicae Sedis decreto, proponatur."

78. Beccari, "Beatification," p. 368.

79. *Codex iuris canonici*, canons 2105–07.

80. Promotor Verde, *SRC* (1903A), 1: *Novae animadversiones r.p.d. Promotoris Fidei super dubio, An constet de virtutibus*, etc.

81. Defender Minetti, *SRC* (1903A), 2: *Responsio ad Novas animadversiones*, etc.

82. Ibid., 3: *Expositio virtutum*. It is preceded by a table of contents.

83. *Codex iuris canonici*, canons 2108-09.

84. Promotor Verde, *SRC* (1903A), 1:1-2, §1: "Conspicuam sane et nobilem causam agi AA. PP. arbitrantur, eamdem vero gravem admodum perarduamque: in qua nempe magnam agnoscunt inopiam probationum, quum instrumenta quibus Ven. Famulae Dei conficiantur heroicae virtutes omnino deesse videantur. Nec enim de his virtutibus aequales testes praesto sunt, nec legitima et comperta documenta, nec traditio. Testes quidem desunt: nam ornatae sunt iuridicae quaestiones quinque saeculis postquam actae res erant, proptereaque testes documentis et historiis plane innituntur: quare ne testium quidem nomine videntur decorandi. Adde quod ipsi, ut quidam e PP. AA. numero ait, 'quamvis spectatissimi sint, apparent et ipsi veluti totidem alii causae huius vindices, quos inter eminet cl. p. Ayroles S. I., et a nimis studio partium abrepti videntur favore Venerabilis.'"

85. Ibid., pp. 2-3, §§2-5.

86. Ibid., pp. 3-4, §6, citing Defender Minetti, *SRC* (1901B), 4:3.

87. Promotor Verde, *SRC* (1903A), 1:4-7, §§7-13. The quoted text reads (pp. 6-7, §13): "Nec vero vivendi rationem Ancillae Dei PP. AA. perpendentes, quamvis eam bonam piamque adolescentem ultro fatentur, censent tamen ad summum virtutum fastigium eamdem prevenisse."

88. Ibid., p. 7, §§14-15; the quoted text reads (§15): "Dicam enim verbis cuiusdam P. A.: 'Miror quod cum pro annuncianda Sanctissimae Virginis Redemptoris divini incarnatione solus Gabriel missus legatur, Ioannae et Gabriel et Michael Archangeli apparuerint, et ita ut eos ipsa realiter viderit, audierit, imo et tetigerit et adoraverit. Quis scit, eam passam non fuisse quandam hallucinationem, talemque coluisse, utpote suo consonam genio? Certe, citra columbae simplicitatem, ne a proposito impediretur, patri et matri rem occultavit, et, si quidem in confessione curato indicavit, ipsi dubitasse videtur, ex quo exorcismis eam subiecit.'"

89. Defender Minetti, *Ad Novas*, *SRC* (1903A), 2:109.

90. Ibid., pp. 98-109.

91. Ibid., pp. 109-15.

92. Ibid., pp. 116-17.

93. Promotor Verde, *Novae*, *SRC* (1903A), 1:7-8, §§16-17.

94. Ibid., pp. 8-10, §§18-21.

95. Ibid., pp. 10-11, §22.

96. Ibid., pp. 11-13, §§23-24.

97. Defender Minetti, *Ad Novas*, *SRC* (1903A), 2:169, citing *Aeneid* 6.45 and Promotor Caprara, *SRC* (1893), 5:26, §35.

98. Promotor Verde, *SRC* (1903A), 1:13-15, §§25-27.

99. Ibid., pp. 15-18, §§28-32.

100. Ibid., pp. 18-20, §§33-36.

101. Ibid, pp. 20–23, §§37–42.

102. Ibid., pp. 23–24, §43: "Nec minus graviter alius P. A.: 'Mihi suadeo,' ait, 'numquam satis reprobandam esse iniustam, imo impiam Ven. Ioannae d'Arc condemnationem; unde nec satis laetandum de ipsius rehabilitationis processu amplissimo. Ex iis tamen tantummodo (meo humili iudicio) sequitur, admirabilem supra modum Ven. Puellam, singularibus ditatam dotibus, praedicari posse: virginem pudicissimam Deoque caram admirari, Galliae liberatricem, operibus ab ipso Deo inspiratis, ad astra laudibus attolli; sanctam vero, idest quae virtutes in gradu heroico exercuerit, saltem ex adductis usque nunc, minime proclamari posse.'"

103. Defender Minetti, *Ad Novas*, *SRC* (1903A), 2:367.

104. Beccari, "Beatification," p. 168.

105. *Codex iuris canonici*, canons 2108–10.

106. Beccari, loc. cit.

107. *Codex iuris canonici*, canons 2112–14.

108. Promotor Verde, *SRC* (1903B), 2: *Novissimae animadversiones r. p. d. Promotoris Fidei super Dubio, An constet de virtutibus*, etc., 16 pages.

109. Defender Minetti, *SRC* (1903B), 3: *Responsio ad Novissimas animadversiones r. p. d. Promotoris Fidei super Dubio, An constet de virtutibus*, etc., 102 pages.

110. Relator Ferrata, *SRC* (1903B), 1: *Factum concordatum*, pp. 3–7.

111. "Howard, Edward Henry (1829–1892)," in *Dictionary of National Biography*, suppl. vol. 1 (1901), repr. as vol. 22 (Oxford, 1921–22), pp. 874–75; p. 2431 of the *Compact Edition* (Oxford 1975).

112. Promotor Verde, *Novissimae*, *SRC* (1903B), 2:1–9, §§1–18

113. Ibid., pp. 9–10, §§19–23.

114. Ibid., pp. 10–13, §§24–30.

115. Defender Minetti, *Ad Novissimas*, *SRC* (1903B), 3:72–74.

116. Ibid., pp. 65, 74–76.

117. Promotor Verde, *Novissimae*, *SRC* (1903B), 2:15, §§35–36.

118. Defender Minetti, *Ad Novissimas*, *SRC* (1903B), 3:86–88.

119. Promotor Verde, *Novissimae*, *SRC* (1903B), 2:16, §37.

120. See, for instance, *Acta Sanctae Sedis* 36 (1903–04), 495, 623, 631, 693, 696.

121. "Decretum Beatificationis et Canonizationis Venerabilis Servae Dei Ioannae D'Arc, Virginis, vulgo dictae puellae Aurelianen.," *Acta Sanctae Sedis* 36 (1903–04), 429-32. He praises her in an allocution delivered the same day, January 6, 1904 (ibid., pp. 464–65).

122. "AURELIENEN. Decretum Beatificationis et Canonizationis Ven. Servae Dei Ioannae de Arc, Virginis, Aurelianensis puellae nuncupatae," *Acta Apostolicae Sedis* 1 (1909), 167–69.

123. "Venerabilis Ioanna de 'Arc' Virgo, Aurelianensis puella nuncupata, renunciatur Beata," ibid., pp. 390–94, especially 393.

V

Trial Procedures against Wyclif and Wycliffites in England and at the Council of Constance

I began my study of inquisitorial procedure in connection with my investigations into the marriages of Henry VIII, for, much to my surprise, I found that the trials conducted by Cardinal Wolsey, the papal curia, and Archbishop Cranmer were inquisitions, the form of trial invented by Innocent III and institutionalized at the Fourth Lateran Council in 1215. This meant that Henry was not a plaintiff in civil suits but a defendant in criminal trials.[1]

Innocent devised the inquisition to supplement or replace the "accusation," which required a public-spirited accuser to take upon himself the burden of proof against a defendant, and, in case of failure to prove the charge, to receive the punishment that would have been meted out if guilt had been found. In an inquisition, respectable public opinion, *publica fama*, took the place of the accuser, and the judge himself served as prosecutor. On the basis of a plausible report that someone had committed a crime, the judge would summon him and explain the charges so that he could defend himself. The judge was first obliged to prove, by the testimony of reputable witnesses, that the defendant was believed to be guilty. The next step was to prove, by other witnesses, the truth of the charge. Defendants were to be told not only the content of the testimony but also the names of the witnesses, so that they could make whatever objections against them they wished.[2] Defendants therefore had no obligation to respond to any questioning before they were charged, and no obligation to plead if no public infamy

A version of this paper was read at the Twenty-Fourth Medieval Workshop at the University of British Columbia, "Heresies and Heretics in the Middle Ages," 18–19 November 1994. I would like to thank Margaret Aston, Anne Hudson, and Alison McHardy for their comments and suggestions.

1. H. A. Kelly, *The Matrimonial Trials of Henry VIII* (Stanford, Calif., 1976).
2. Innocent III, *Qualiter et quando* (1215), in *Decretales Gregorii IX*, ed. Emil Friedberg, *Corpus iuris canonici*, 2 vols. (Leipzig, 1879–81), 2:746. See n. 47 below for a partial citation of the text.

were established. They had the right to counsel, and the right of appeal, not only at the end of a trial but also at any stage at which they believed their rights were being infringed.[3]

There is a widespread but mistaken belief that the inquisitorial procedure was devised to facilitate the prosecution of heresy. But it does not take much thought to realize that, on the contrary, this system was particularly ill suited for heresy cases, since it was designed to prosecute only public crimes publicly associated with definite persons; that is, there was no provision for examining what persons thought about given doctrines, unless there was evidence that they had preached, taught, or written erroneous opinions on them. Even in such cases where there was evidence of the public manifestation of heresy, the rules were to be followed.[4]

Therefore, because heresy prosecutors were hampered by the rules of inquisitorial procedure, they were under pressure to bend or violate them. One of the most flagrant abuses of due process devised by the papal *inquisitores hereticae pravitatis* (inquisitors of papal depravity) in the thirteenth century was the transformation of witnesses into defendants: persons summoned as general witnesses to local heresy were forced to testify not only about others but also about themselves—*de se et aliis;* and any doctrinal misstatement they might make—after being required, for instance, to explain their understanding of the Creed—constituted an instant notorious crime that could be charged against them. After irreparable damage to the defendants had been done, the inquisitors could then make a show of following the *ordo juris,*[5] the order of law.

This abuse of pre-arraignment interrogation became widespread on the Continent. I originally supposed that England was free of it, since not only were Wolsey's and Cranmer's matrimonial inquisitions canonically regular,[6] but the same was true of the trials of heresy, sorcery, and other offenses conducted by

3. See H. A. Kelly, "The Right to Remain Silent: Before and after Joan of Arc," *Speculum* 68 (1993): 992–1026.
4. I deal with this subject in "Inquisition and the Prosecution of Heresy: Misconceptions and Abuses," *Church History* 58 (1989): 439–51.
5. Ibid., 447–48; see also H. A. Kelly, "Inquisitorial Due Process and the Status of Secret Crimes," in Stanley Chodorow, ed., *Proceedings of the Eighth International Congress of Medieval Canon Law,* Monumenta iuris canonici, Series C: Subsidia, vol. 9 (Vatican City, 1992), 407–27 at 415–16; and Kelly, "Right to Remain Silent," 1000.
6. Another regular trial held (or planned) by Wolsey in his capacity as legate *a latere* was that against George Crompton, knight, for adultery; the articled charges against him are in Public Record Office SP 1/49 mm. 39–41, calendared in *Letters and Papers, Foreign and Domestic, of the Reign of Henry VIII,* 21 vols. (corrected reprint, Vaduz, Liechtenstein, 1965), 3:1944, no. 4442 (7). This case is treated by Mary L. Robertson, "Court Careers and County Quarrels: George Lord Hastings and Leicestershire Unrest, 1509–1529," in Charles Carlton et al., eds., *State, Sovereigns, and Society in Early Modern England: Essays in Honour of A. J. Slavin* (Gloucester, 1998), 153–68, esp. 158.

Henry Chichele, archbishop of Canterbury from 1414 to 1443. Due process under Chichele was only to be expected, since he was guided by his chancellor William Lyndwood, later his chief judge, a notorious stickler for the rule of law.[7] However, I saw signs of this abuse in the heresy trials conducted from 1428 to 1431 under Bishop William Alnwick in Norwich,[8] and evidence of a somewhat similar practice in a trial allegedly held in 1532 under Wolsey's fellow-archbishop, William Warham (Cranmer's predecessor as archbishop of Canterbury). In this proceeding, according to John Foxe, John Lambert was required to give his views on a series of articles listing mainly Lollard or Wycliffite doctrines without being charged with actually having preached or written about them. I observed that the same kind of procedure had been used in prosecuting followers of Wyclif in England in 1382 and at the Council of Constance in 1415.[9]

In the present essay I propose to look further into these last-named prosecutions. Other actions against suspects accused of taking their inspiration from Wyclif were carried out in more expected inquisitorial procedures, whether regular or abusive, and I have treated them elsewhere.[10] Here I will concentrate on the academic followers of Wyclif who in 1382 were required to give their opinions on condemned propositions of Wyclif without having been charged with teaching them; and then I will examine the similar procedure used against John Hus

7. H. A. Kelly, "English Kings and the Fear of Sorcery," *Mediaeval Studies* 39 (1977): 206–38, esp. 212–14, 218–29, drawing on *The Register of Henry Chichele, Archbishop of Canterbury, 1414–1443*, ed. E. F. Jacob, 4 vols. (Oxford, 1932–47); and William Lyndwood, *Provinciale* (1432; Oxford, 1679; reprint, Farnborough, England, 1968).
8. N. P. Tanner, ed., *Heresy Trials in the Diocese of Norwich, 1428–1431* (London, 1977); and Kelly, "Inquisitorial Due Process," 425–26.
9. Kelly, "Right to Remain Silent," 994, 1008, 1025 n. 166. On Lambert, see John Foxe, *Acts and Monuments*, 4th ed., ed. Josiah Pratt (London, 1877), 5:181–225. In characterizing Lambert's case, I was following Foxe's account on p. 181, according to which, after being brought from Antwerp to London, "he was brought to examination first at Lambeth, then at the bishop's house at Otford, having five and forty articles ministered against him, whereunto he rendered answer again by writing." But Lambert's remarks in his response to the first article contradict this account, at least in showing that there was a long delay between the Lambeth examination and the current one: he indicates that he was first charged with offenses, but even though the archbishop could not find him guilty, he was not released, but new matters were imagined against him, and he would not have been found guilty of those charges either, "had it not been that by long imprisonment you enforced me to tell what I thought in them, which I have and will freely do" (p. 184), which may indicate a previous session of responses after the Lambeth examination. In his response to the twelfth article, he notes that the archbishop ordered him examined by Doctor Lesse and others, who told him that the question of the sufficiency of Scripture was "the head and content of all others objected against me" (p. 198). I therefore mischaracterized the case when I said that Lambert was not objecting to the proceedings against him (p. 994), and that in answering the charges against him he was acknowledging that infamy had lawfully been laid against him (p. 1007 n. 74).
10. H. A. Kelly, "Lollard Inquisitions: Due and Undue Process," in Alberto Ferreiro, ed., *The Devil, Heresy, and Witchcraft in the Middle Ages: Essays in Honor of Jeffrey B. Russell* (Leiden, 1998), 279–303.

in Constance. In addition, I will discuss measures taken against Wyclif himself, both in England during his lifetime and in England and Constance even after his death, as well as other associated prosecutions in Constance.

The first action taken against Wyclif that we know of began with a summons issued sometime around the beginning of 1377, ordering him to appear before the archbishop of Canterbury, Simon Sudbury, during Convocation at St. Paul's in London. He answered the summons on 19 February and appeared in the company of four theologians from each of the four orders of friars, appointed by John of Gaunt to assist him, and accompanied as well by Gaunt and by Henry Percy, earl of Northumberland.[11] The proceedings were unusual, since a defendant in an inquisition would normally appear alone, advised, if at all, by lawyers rather than theologians, and certainly not by the high nobility. Nevertheless, the trial was conceived of as a standard episcopal inquisition; its nature is summed up by Bishop Courteney of London: Wyclif was "cited to respond to his ordinary concerning allegations against him."[12] In other words, he was not being tried by the bishops as a body but by Sudbury as Wyclif's "metropolitan" ordinary (that is, the archbishop as having jurisdiction over all fourteen dioceses of the province of Canterbury), with the other bishops serving as his assessors.[13]

In the event, Wyclif's trial was broken up by a riot, sparked by a quarrel between Courteney and Gaunt as to whether Wyclif should be seated or remain standing,[14] and apparently not reconvened and concluded. The next action came from Rome in a series of bulls from Pope Gregory XI, all dated 22 May 1377. Because the letters chide the archbishop of Canterbury and the bishop of London, as well as other bishops, for doing nothing against Wyclif, it has been assumed that the pope had not been informed of the proceedings at St. Paul's.[15] But it is possible that his informants, simply identified as "many trustworthy persons,"[16] did tell him of the event but stressed its abortive result.

11. Thomas Walsingham, *Chronicon Angliae*, ed. Edward Maunde Thompson, Rolls Series 64 (London, 1874), 117–18. See Joseph H. Dahmus, *The Prosecution of John Wyclyf* (New Haven, Conn., 1952), esp. 26–28. Dahmus reminds us of the virulently anti-Gaunt attitude of Walsingham (p. 16).
12. Walsingham, *Chronicon Angliae*, 119; Courteney argues against Gaunt that Wyclif should stand, "qui illuc citatus advenerat, responsurus coram suo ordinario et depositis contra eum."
13. See Kelly, "English Kings," 222 n. 64.
14. Dahmus, *Prosecution of Wyclyf*, 28–29.
15. Ibid., 35.
16. See Gregory XI, letter 1, *Regnum Anglie gloriosum*, 22 May 1377, addressed to Sudbury and Courteney. It is translated by Dahmus, *Prosecution of Wyclyf*, 39–41, following the text of Sudbury's unpublished register, which is given by Pratt in Foxe, *Acts and Monuments*, 3:6–7, n. 1; the text is also given by

The usual papal commission of this sort ordered the commissioners to try the suspect on the charges and arrive at a definitive sentence. But we find deviations here from such a procedure. In the first bull, *Regnum Anglie gloriosum*, the pope orders Sudbury and Courteney to inform themselves secretly about the matter, and if they find it true that Wyclif has been holding and preaching the reported propositions, a list of which the pope encloses, they are to arrest and imprison him and endeavor to receive a confession from him concerning the propositions; then, revealing their actions to no one, they are to send to the pope a copy of such confession and of whatever else he may have said or written to "induce," or prove, the propositions, and to send as well an account of all else they have done in the matter, while keeping Wyclif in chains and awaiting further instructions.[17]

In order to follow these instructions, the prelates would presumably have had to initiate a formal inquisition by charging Wyclif with having held the propositions, and asking him to respond: either to acknowledge and confess them, or to deny them or explain away any objectionable sense. If he admitted them without further ado, the judges would normally have proceeded to convict and sentence him, but in this case the pope seems to have wished them to stop short of such a conclusion. We need not fear that the pope was contemplating the sort of violation of due process that I alluded to at the beginning, of attempting to secure statements of heterodox beliefs from a defendant without making formal charges. Not that the pope or his advisers would necessarily be above using such a ploy—it was standard procedure for Gregory's predecessor Benedict XII when he conducted heresy inquisitions as bishop of Pamiers fifty years earlier.[18] But this was suitable only for unsophisticated and inexperienced persons, not for someone like Wyclif, who would doubtless have been well aware of the proper procedures and his right to counsel. Furthermore, in his case it was a question of propositions

Walsingham, *Chronicon*, 178–80, and in his revised account, *Historia anglicana*, Rolls Series, 28.1 (London, 1864), 1:350–52.

17. Ibid. The Latin reads: "vos secrete informantes, si inveneritis ita esse, prefatum Johannem faciatis auctoritate nostra capi et carceribus mancipari, ejusque confessionem super eisdem propositionibus seu conclusionibus recipere [Dahmus translates as "extort," but more accurately as "secure" in the bull to Edward III; *Prosecution of Wyclyf*, 46] studeatis, ac ipsam confessionem et quecumque dictus Johannes dixerit seu scripserit super earundem propositionum et conclusionum inductione ac probatione, et quicquid feceritis in premissis, sub vestris sigillis clausa et nemini revelata, nobis per fidelem nuncium transmissuri, eundemque Johannem sub fideli custodia teneatis in vinculis, donec a nobis super hoc aliud receperitis in mandatis." In the "boilerplate" that follows, omitted in the Walsingham texts but included in the Foxe edition, the phrase "appellatione postposita" ("all appeal set aside") was taken to refer only to frivolous appeals; see Kelly, "Inquisition and the Prosecution of Heresy," 445. Note: In all Latin citations, I re-medievalize *ae* to *e*.

18. *Le registre d'inquisition de Jacques Fournier, évêque de Pamiers (1318–1325)*, ed. Jean Duvernoy, 3 vols. (Toulouse, 1965; *Corrections*, 1972); see Kelly, "Right to Remain Silent," 1003–5.

excerpted from one of his writings, *De civili dominio*, and it would have been necessary to put the implicated statements to him verbatim.

In a supplementary commission, *Nuper per nos*, the pope reviewed the contents of the first letter, but omitted the point about receiving a confession and sending it along with other proofs to Rome.[19] Therefore, no trial need take place at all to fulfill this second commission. But since the letter refers to the previous letter for fuller details, perhaps no such significance should be read into the omission of the passage. The letter continues with instructions on what to do if Wyclif should elude capture: the prelates are to cite him publicly to appear before the pope himself within three months, with a warning that whether he appears or not, the pope will proceed against him and convict him in accordance with his demerits.[20]

The pope's third letter, *Super periculosis*, instructs the prelates to warn the king and other prominent figures in England of the danger posed by Wyclif's reported teachings.[21] Another letter, *Regnum Anglie quod altissimus*, is addressed directly to Edward III.[22] In it the pope recounts the commission he gave to the archbishop and bishop in his first letter: investigating Wyclif's alleged preaching of the propositions and imprisoning him, if they determined he had so preached; receiving a confession from him; and then sending it and other statements of Wyclif on to the pope.[23] Omitted are the two instructions about secrecy.

Finally, Gregory sent a letter, *Mirari cogimur*, to the chancellor and university of Oxford, in which he ordered them to prohibit the further teaching of all

19. Gregory XI, letter 2, *Nuper per nos*, 22 May 1377, Foxe, *Acts and Monuments*, 3:7 n. 1, from David Wilkins, *Concilia Magnae Britanniae* (London, 1737; reprint ed., Brussels, 1964), 3:117–18, corrected from Walsingham, *Chronicon*, 176–78; *Hist. angl.*, 1:348–50; translated by Dahmus, *Prosecution of Wyclyf*, 41–43. The relevant text reads: "vos secreto informantes, si ita esse inveneritis, predictum Johannem auctoritate nostra capi et carceribus mancipari faceretis, eumque sub bona custodia teneretis in vinculis, donec a nobis super hoc receperitis alium in mandatis, prout in dictis literis plenius continetur."
20. Ibid.: "nos super premissis, et contra eum, usque ad debitam condemnationem ipsius inclusive procedemus, prout ejus demerita exigent, ac nobis secundum Deum et conservationem dicte fidei videbitur expedire."
21. Gregory XI, letter 3, *Super periculosis*, 22 May 1377, text in Foxe, *Acts and Monuments*, 3:7 n. 1, from Sudbury's Register; also in Walsingham, *Chronicon*, 175–76; *Hist. angl.*, 1:347–48; trans. Dahmus, *Prosecution of Wyclyf*, 44–45.
22. Gregory IX, letter 4, *Regnum Anglie quod altissimus*, 22 May 1377, text in Walsingham, *Chronicon*, 180–81; *Hist. angl.*, 1:352–53; trans. Dahmus, *Prosecution of Wyclyf*, 46–47; partially translated by Foxe (as opposed to his editor), *Acts and Monuments*, 3:8–9.
23. Ibid.: "se informantes, si invenirent ita esse, facerent prefatum Johannem auctoritate nostra capi et carceribus mancipari, ejus confessionem super eisdem propositionibus seu conclusionibus recipere studerent, ac ipsam confessionem, et quecumque dictus Johannes dixerit vel scripserit super earundem propositionum et conclusionum inductione et probatione, nobis per fidum nuncium transmittere non postponant."

such suspect propositions, no matter how phrased or defended, and to arrest Wyclif and turn him over to the archbishop of Canterbury and the bishop of London. No mention is made of any preliminary investigation and there is no warning about secrecy. Furthermore, the chancellor and university were to proceed against those who objected to these actions, if such individuals were under their jurisdiction and were tainted with the same errors, and if they persisted in these errors; the chancellor was to arrest and transfer these individuals to the archbishop or bishop, and were to proceed in other ways as well, as chancellor and university deemed best.[24]

There seems to have been a delay in the transmittal of these bulls, perhaps because of the death of Edward III on 7 June, but the letter to him was nevertheless not readdressed to Richard II. Preliminary word of the letters seems to have arrived in England before the closing of Parliament on 28 November, since Wyclif says in *De ecclesia* that the bishop of Rochester boasted to him that Wyclif's conclusions had been condemned, citing a notarial document from the curia. Wyclif indicates that the reaction of "many" (presumably others at the Parliament) was one of incredulity: Rochester's statement was taken to be a defamation of the Roman curia, a scandal to king and realm, and a manifestation of concerted suspicion against Wyclif on the part of the bishops.[25]

The letter directed to Oxford was received only shortly before Christmas of 1377, whereupon Wyclif was placed under house arrest by the vice-chancellor.[26] Meanwhile, Archbishop Sudbury responded to the pope's letters by sending a mandate to the chancellor of Oxford on 18 December 1377 ordering a secret examination of the propositions attributed to Wyclif, and ordering the chancellor also to cite Wyclif to appear before the archbishop at St. Paul's within thirty days.

24. Gregory XI, letter 5, *Mirari cogimur*, 22 May 1377, text in Walsingham, *Chronicon*, 174–75; *Historia anglicana*, 1:346–47; trans. Dahmus, *Prosecution of Wyclyf*, 47–49; trans. Foxe, *Acts and Monuments*, 3:5–6. The pertinent text reads: "mandamus quatenus conclusiones et propositiones in bonis operibus et fide male sentientes, licet eas proponentes sub quadam verborum sive terminorum curiosa implicatione nitantur defendere, de cetero non permittatis asseri vel proponi; dictumque Johannem auctoritate nostra capiatis, seu capi faciatis, et ipsum venerabilibus fratribus nostris, archiepiscopo Cantuariensi et episcopo Londoniensi, aut eorum alteri, sub fida custodia transmittatis. Contradictores quoque de dicto studio vestre jurisdictioni subjectos, si qui forsan, quod Deus avertat, essent hujusmodi erroribus maculati, si in illis pertinaciter perstiterint, ad similem captionem et missionem, aliasque, prout ad vos spectat, firmiter et sollicite procedatis."

25. Wyclif, *Tractatus de ecclesia* 15v, ed. Johann Loserth (London, 1886; reprint ed., New York, 1966), 354: "Unde episcopus Roffensis dixit mihi in publico parlamento stomachante spiritu quod conclusiones mee sunt dampnate, sicut testificatum est sibi de curia per instrumentum notarii. Et visum est multis quod fuit assercio indiscreta, primo quia vergebat ad curie Romane defamacionem, secundo quia implicabat regis nostri et regni scandalizacionem, et tercio quia ostendebat sui et fratrum suorum consentaneam suspicionem." Cf. K. B. McFarlane, *John Wycliffe and the Beginnings of English Nonconformity* (London, 1952), 80.

26. Dahmus, *Prosecution of Wyclyf*, 62–64.

Wyclif was to be warned that whether he presented himself or not, the process would go forward against him, as the papal letters directed and required.[27] We note that the archbishop was following the pope's first letter to the extent of ordering a secret investigation, but his conformity ended there. Rather than awaiting the result of the investigation, and, if it turned out to verify the allegations against Wyclif, having him arrested and transfered under guard—or, if he became suspicious and escaped, to cite him to appear before the pope—the archbishop ordered him cited to appear by his own volition for a local trial, while alleging that this was what the pope had ordered.

According to one chronicler, the vice-chancellor of Oxford was imprisoned for having imprisoned Wyclif, and Wyclif was released; moreover, the chancellor held a public examination of the impugned theses, in Wyclif's presence (perhaps by way of a formal inquisition; the chancellor served as judge over those subject to the university's jurisdiction); the result was that the propositions were declared orthodox, though faultily formulated.[28]

Sometime early in the next year, 1378, Wyclif appeared as defendant in an inquisition not at St. Paul's but at Lambeth, where he was questioned on the propositions that the pope had enclosed in his first letter. Sudbury, Courteney, and their assessors—it is not clear from Walsingham's account if other bishops were present for the trial—seem to have come to the same conclusion as the Oxford investigators. Walsingham first gives a different impression: he says that the prelates were much disturbed by an emissary from Richard II's mother forbidding them to come to a definitive sentence and that subsequently a group of London supporters of Wyclif broke up the trial, with the result that Wyclif did not appear again before the death of Pope Gregory (which occurred on 27 March 1378). But then Walsingham proceeds to give Wyclif's formal explanation of each of the propositions, and he says that Wyclif succeeded in deluding his examiners and evading conviction, being let off with an order not to treat of such propositions in teaching or preaching, on account of scandal to the laity.[29]

In May of 1382, Courteney, now archbishop of Canterbury (Sudbury having been killed during the Peasants' Revolt), held a council at Blackfriars, the Dominican headquarters in London, consisting of a selection of bishops, theologians, canonists, and "civilians" (experts in Roman civil law) to examine a

27. Sudbury, mandate of 18 December 1377, trans. Dahmus, *Prosecution of Wyclyf,* 64–66, from Sudbury's register, noting errors in Wilkins, *Concilia*, 3:123–24.

28. Dahmus, *Prosecution of Wyclyf,* 64, 66, drawing on the *Eulogium historiarum sive temporis*, Rolls Series 9, ed. Frank Scott Haydon, 3 vols. (London, 1858), 3:348–49.

29. Walsingham, *Chronicon*, 183–90; *Hist. angl.*, 1:356–63; see Dahmus, *Prosecution of Wyclyf,* 66–71.

series of conclusions. The conclusions were not specifically attributed to Wyclif, but were simply said to have been publicly preached in the realm. The council condemned ten of the conclusions as heretical, including statements about the Eucharist, and fourteen as erroneous.[30] Scholars have concluded that almost all of them were in fact derived from Wyclif's writings or teachings, including the bizarre thesis "that God must obey the devil" ("Quod Deus debet obedire diabolo").[31] This is said to have been one of Wyclif's proudest conclusions,[32] and, as we will see below, his chief disciple, Nicholas Hereford, was passionate in defending it. However, Wyclif himself understood that the condemned proposition stated only that God had in fact obeyed the devil, "Deus obedivit diabolo," and he defends the idea in a sermon, not as something that he has held in the past, but as a fact derivable from the Bible (Jesus ministered to Judas, washing his feet when he was the devil, and Jesus also allowed himself to be carried by the devil at the Temptation).[33] In the same sermon Wyclif goes on to single out this proposition as a slander, in a passage cited by the current Carmelite compiler of the *Fasciculi zizaniorum magistri Johannis Wyclif cum tritico* ("Bundles of Master John Wyclif's Weeds, with Wheat").[34] He observes that some of the decisions taken at this "earthquake council" (so called because an earthquake occurred during the Blackfriars meeting) were orthodox but others were plainly heretical. They were orthodox in condemning heresies that mendacious men invented with the help of their father [the devil, of course], which no orthodox person would wish to hold: "They falsely attribute such things to orthodox men in order to denigrate their reputation, as if they were hereticizing that God is the devil, or some other manifest heresy; consequently

30. Courteney's report of the proceedings is given by Wilkins, *Concilia,* 3:157–58; trans. Dahmus, *Prosecution of Wyclyf,* 89–90, 93–95.

31. This is the wording in Wilkins, *Concilia,* 3:157, and the *Fasciculi zizaniorum* (full citation at n. 34, below), 278, 494, and also in Foxe's Latin edition, though the thesis is omitted entirely from the English; see *Acts and Monuments,* 3:21 and n. 2. But "debeat" appears for "debet" in Walsingham, *Chronicon,* 343; in *Hist. angl.,* 2:58, there was some tampering with the text, apparently, with "Quod debent" replacing "Quod Deus debeat" (making it an obligation of Christians rather than of God to obey the devil).

32. Dahmus, *Prosecution of Wyclyf,* 97, 116. The thesis has been taken to mean nothing other than that one must obey a legitimate civil ruler even though he is sinful; this is in contrast to Wyclif's idea that sinfulness in the spiritual realm invalidated one's authority. See Reginald Lane Poole, *Illustrations of the History of Medieval Thought and Learning,* 2d ed. (London, 1920; reprint ed., New York, 1960), 262–63.

33. Wyclif, *Sermones,* 3.54, ed. Johann Loserth (London, 1889; reprint ed., New York, 1966), 3:467–68.

34. *Fasciculi zizaniorum magistri Johannis Wyclif cum tritico,* ed. Walter Waddington Shirley, Rolls Series 5 (London, 1858). The manuscript, only half of which was edited and published by Shirley, seems to have been compiled over the years by the provincials of the Carmelite friars. It was put into final shape and copied in 1439. See James Crompton, "Fasciculi Zizaniorum," *Journal of Ecclesiastical History* 12 (1961): 34–45, 155–66, esp. 158–66.

they are prepared to use false witnesses to impute such heresies to faithful men, as if they were their perfidious inventors."[35]

It is noteworthy that Wyclif refers to the use of false witnesses, which one would normally think of in a trial context, but it is not clear that formal depositions of witnesses, as opposed to the reports of confidential informants, were used in prosecuting his chief followers in England. There was, however, some use of witnesses in other trials.[36]

In his mandate to the bishops sent on 30 May 1382, Archbishop Courteney reminded them that each of them by canon law was to serve as heresy inquisitor in his diocese, and they were to proceed against anyone who held the condemned propositions.[37] But the first trials to take place under the provisions of this mandate were held by Courteney himself as metropolitan against Robert Rigg, chancellor of Oxford University, and other proctors of the university. Unfortunately, neither the archbishop's register nor the *Fasciculi* gives a full record of the proceedings. Some of the formalities may have been omitted, of course, but there must at least have been official citations of the defendants to the archbishop's presence.

According to the *Fasciculi*, on 12 June 1382 Rigg and two proctors, Walter Dasch and John Hunteman, were formally convicted as "vehemently suspect" of favoring heresies and errors, especially those of Philip Repingdon, Nicholas Hereford, and Wyclif, on the basis of seven "evidences"—that is, detailed statements of actions. These doubtless constituted the schedule of charges levied against them, to which they must have confessed guilt, since no further *ordo juris* seems to have been followed. Rigg was thereupon examined on the two dozen

35. *Fasciculi*, 283: "'Quantum,' ait, 'ad damnationem et catholicationem factas in isto concilio terremotus, patet ex dictis quomodo alique sunt catholice, et alique plene heretice. Catholice sunt ille que sunt de heresibus quas mendaces ex se et patre suo finxerant, quas nullus catholicus vult tenere. Talia enim fingunt de viris catholicis, ut suam famam denigrent, ac si hereticarent quod Deus est diabolus, vel quamcunque aliam heresim manifestam; parati consequenter per falsos testes hereses tales imponere fidelibus, ac si ipsi forent earum perfidi inventores.'" In the last sentence, for *per falsos testes hereses tales imponere* Loserth reads *per falsos apocryphos testes imponere*, while noting the manuscript reading of *falsos apostolos*.
36. For instance, the trial of the Irish Cistercian Henry Crump in 1392 (*Fasciculi*, 343–48); see Kelly, "Lollard Inquisitions," 285.
37. Wilkins, *Concilia*, 3:158–59; trans. Dahmus, *Prosecution of Wyclyf*, 101–3. The passage about bishops serving as heresy inquisitors reads: "cum juxta sacrorum canonum instituta quilibet eorundem in suis civitate et diocesi heretice pravitatis inquisitor existat" [since each of them is the inquisitor of heretical depravity in his city and diocese, according to the provisions of the sacred canons]. Dahmus takes the clause to be an exhortation rather than a simple statement of fact (p. 103).

implicated propositions, and he agreed that they had been rightly condemned. Finally, Rigg was accused of contempt for failing to carry out the archbishop's mandate. He pleaded guilty and asked for forgiveness, which Courteney granted.[38] Thomas Brightwell, who had also been convicted as a suspect, and another bachelor (of theology, presumably) debated some of the propositions before they too finally agreed to their condemnation.[39]

Courteney then gave Rigg a mandate, dated that day, 12 June, in which he ordered that no teaching or preaching was to be allowed to Wyclif, Hereford, and Repingdon, or to John Aston and Laurence Bedeman, all of whom were vehemently and notoriously suspect of heresy, or to anyone else so suspect or defamed; and he suspended the said suspects until they could "purge their innocence before him."[40] Unlike Rigg, these persons were not as yet convicted but only suspect by public fame, and they were required to defend themselves in the archbishop's court. Courteney on this occasion also gave Rigg a monitory letter in which he said that he had learned from the testimony of trustworthy men and from his own experience that Rigg had been somewhat inclined to the articles condemned at Blackfriars and was still inclining to them, and that he suspected him of intending to molest the clerics who approved of the condemnation. He solemnly warned him not to do so, and he repeated the instructions of the first letters about not allowing any of the named suspects to teach at Oxford.[41]

There is no indication that Wyclif himself was issued a formal citation to appear before the archbishop. As for Repingdon and Hereford, the *Fasciculi* says that they were assigned 18 June to respond, and, since the archbishop's register says that John Aston also appeared with them, the same must have been true of him. As we will see, they do not seem to have been formally charged with holding the condemned theses. In a normal inquisition (one that followed the *ordo juris*), the defendant would either confess or deny the charges; if he denied them, the judge would attempt to prove them by documents or by the written testimony of witnesses; and if he lacked sufficient evidence of actual guilt, but could establish only the *fama* of guilt—that is, testimony of trustworthy persons who

38. *Fasciculi*, 304–8.

39. Wilkins, *Concilia*, 3:159, reproducing Courteney's register.

40. Ibid., 3:159–60; it reads in part: "Inhibeatis . . . quod nullus de cetero . . . Johannem Wycliff, Nicolaum Hereford, Philippum Rappyngdon, canonicum regularem, seu Johannem Asshton, vel Laurentium Bedeman, qui de heresi vehementer et notorie sunt suspecti, vel quemcunque alium sic suspectum vel defamatum, ad predicandum admittat, audiat, vel auscultet, aut eis faveat publice vel occulte, sed statim, tanquam serpentem venenum pestiferum emittentem, fugiat et evitet. Et preterea dictos suspectos ab omni actu scholastico, donec suam in ea parte innocentiam coram nobis purgaverint, suspendimus, et sic per nos suspensos fuisse et esse, publice denuncient," etc. See below for the process of purgation.

41. Ibid., 3:160.

believed him guilty—the judge could order purgation. This meant that the defendant was required to swear, not to his orthodox belief or to agreement with actions taken by a synod or tribunal, but rather to his innocence of the offenses charged against him. He would also have to find a stipulated number of neighbors or associates who would swear to his credibility and good reputation.[42]

However, when the Oxford suspects appeared before Courteney in his role as heresy inquisitor for the entire province of Canterbury, he had a new kind of purgation in mind. From the decree that he issued against Repingdon and Hereford on 20 June, we get a notion of the nature of the proceedings, which was made known to the defendants and perhaps even agreed to by them. He says that both defendants by their own consent appeared before him as heresy inquisitor on the day fixed by him to respond under oath and declare fully and plainly their understanding (*sentire*) of certain conclusions.[43] In other words, the archbishop was not interested in finding out whether they had committed crimes of heresy or erroneous teaching in the past; he was solely concerned to know what their current belief was on certain points, and he was willing to accept their sworn word in the matter.

He goes on in the decree to say that, because the defendants contemptuously refused, without any reasonable or legitimate cause, to respond to some of the conclusions, and responded heretically to others and erroneously and less than fully to still others, he gives them another chance to reply to the propositions—which are to be understood in the senses precisely defined by him—or else suffer the penalty of being declared to have confessed them and being considered convicted upon them.[44] Of course, the defendants could have given one reasonable

42. Purgation was not to be ordered unless *fama* was established; see Kelly, "Inquisitorial Due Process," 426 n. 63, citing William Durant, *Speculum judiciale*, Lib. 3, pt. 1, tit. *De abolitione et purgatione*, §2: *Nunc de purgatione*, no. 1 (vol. 2, p. 55 of the Basel 1574 edition of the *Speculum*, reprint ed., Aalen, 1975).

43. Wilkins, *Concilia*, 3:163: "Christi nomine invocato, nos Willielmus, permissione divina archiepiscopus Cantuariensis, totius Anglie primas, et apostolice sedis legatus, ac per totam nostram provinciam Cantuariensem inquisitor heretice pravitatis, vos, Nicolaum Hereford et Philippum Reppyngdon, sacre pagine professores, habentes hos diem et locum de consensu vestro expresso ex prefixione nostra ad peremptorie respondendum et dicendum plene et plane sentire vestrum super conclusionibus istis ad quas nos referimus, subductis verbis subtilibus et sophisticalibus aut logicis, et ad id juratos, monitos, atque jussos."

44. Ibid.: "quia absque causa rationabili seu legitima quacunque noluistis, nec vultis, immo recusastis et recusatis, ad conclusiones aliquas illarum coram nobis judicialiter, juxta nostras monitionem et jussionem predictas, contemptibiliter respondere; verum ad nonnullas illarum heretice, et ad nonnullas erronee et minus plene, respondistis; ex abundanti monemus, primo, secundo, et tertio, ac peremptorie, quod vos plene et plane, subductis quibuscunque verbis subtilibus, sophisticalibus, aut logicis, repondeatis, et quilibet vestrum respondeat, ad conclusiones easdem, et ad sensus per nos limitatos, sub pena quod alias hujusmodi conclusiones habeantur per vos pro confessatis, et vos super eisdem

and legitimate cause for not responding to any of the propositions—namely, that the external forum of the Church had no right to judge thoughts or secret crimes.[45]

At the first session of the trial on 18 June, after Courteney put the three defendants under oath and required them to give their opinion about the propositions, Repingdon and Hereford asked for a copy of the propositions and for time to respond in writing, which was granted.[46] As I noted at the beginning of this essay, it was a requirement of the *ordo juris* set forth by Innocent III at the Fourth Lateran Council to give the defendant a copy of charges. (Repingdon and Hereford cited another decree of this council, as we will see below.) The allowance of time to respond could be considered to fall within the general requirement that the defendant was to be given all defenses.[47] Courteney asked Aston if he too wished a delay, but Aston declined and said that he would respond immediately. He gave a general answer to all the conclusions—namely, that his opinion was to keep silent on them.[48] I take it that he was not, as Joseph Dahmus thinks, promising to refrain from discussing or teaching them in the future;[49] rather, he was refusing to say what he thought about the propositions. This was his right, according to the due-process principles of inquisitorial procedure, but the archbishop and his assessors clearly did not take this view. Courteney's response was to find him suspect in the matter, and he issued a decree declaring him vehemently suspect of heresy, having previously been *defamatus* of heresy (that is, guilty of heresy in the opinion of trustworthy men), and he forbade him to preach

conclusionibus haberi debeatis pro convictis." In this text, *contemptibiliter* is awkwardly placed and might indicate that the defendants were being accused of failing to give a contemptuous response (that is, failing to repudiate the propositions with due contempt). But in my view this is an unlikely interpretation; see n. 71 below for a proper placing of *contemptibiliter*.

45. Stephan Kuttner, "Ecclesia de occultis non iudicat," *Acta Congressus iuridici internationalis . . . Romae . . .* 1931, 5 vols. (Rome, 1935–37), 3:225–46; Kelly, "Right to Remain Silent," 995; and for some of the pertinent pronouncements on this subject, by Innocent III and others, see Kelly, "Lollard Inquisitions," 299 n. 68.
46. Wilkins, *Concilia,* 3:160–61: "et prestito per eosdem corporali juramento, tacto libro, de dicendo sentire suum super conclusionibus antedictis, iidem Nicolaus et Philippus der dictum dominum archiepiscopum, inquisitorem heretice pravitatis per totam suam provinciam, in ea parte examinati, singillatim petierunt diem ad deliberandum super conclusionibus antedictis, et ad respondendum eisdem in scriptis, ac sibi copiam conclusionum hujusmodi ministrari; quam copiam iidem Nicolaus et Philippus tunc ibidem lectam publice receperunt."
47. Innocent III in the Fourth Lateran Council, canon 8, decretal *Qualiter et quando, Decretales Gregorii IX* 5.1.24 (Friedberg edition, 2:746): "Exponenda sunt ei illa capitula de quibus fuerit inquirendum, ut facultatem habeat defendendi se ipsum." In the *casus* to this decretal accompanying the Ordinary Gloss, this passage is summed up thus: "Omnis defensio sibi reservatur"; *Corpus juris canonici,* 3 vols. (Rome, 1582; reprint ed., Lyons, 1606), 2:1598. See also "Right to Remain Silent," 993 n. 2.
48. Wilkins, *Concilia,* 3:161: "Dixit itaque pro finali responso ad omnes conclusiones hujusmodi sub unico contextu, quod sentire suum est in ea parte subticere."
49. Dahmus, *Prosecution of Wyclyf,* 115.

in the future. Then Courteney interrogated him further, and Aston confessed that he had heard of the archbishop's earlier mandate prohibiting him from preaching, but that he had preached in spite of it. By the terms of the mandate, this meant that he had incurred excommunication, and Courteney set the date of 20 June for Aston to offer any reasons against decreeing the excommunication and against his being pronounced a heretic. He set the same date for Repingdon and Hereford to produce their responses.[50]

That Courteney was ready to pronounce Aston a heretic might seem surprising, since the register does not indicate that the man had been charged with heresy or had confessed to heresy, or that any testimony or other evidence proving him guilty of heresy had been published in the trial. But if we look ahead to the archbishop's decree of 20 June, we can see that a failure to agree with the findings of the archbishop's council was considered sufficient grounds to be convicted of heresy.

On the specified date, 20 June, Repingdon and Hereford submitted a joint response to the twenty-four articles, now presented as twenty-five and given in a different order.[51] Their response was prefaced by a declaration of willingness to be corrected if found to be erroneous in any way. Addressing the first conclusion—that the substance of the bread and wine remains in the sacrament of the altar after consecration—they concede that it is a heresy, if understood in a sense contrary to the decretal *Firmiter credimus*.[52] The latter was the creed of the Fourth Lateran Council; Raymond of Pennafort placed it at the beginning of the *Decretals of Gregory IX*. The pertinent text reads, "the body and blood of Jesus Christ are contained in the sacrament of the altar under the appearances of bread and wine, with the bread having been transubstantiated into the body and the wine into the blood by the divine power."[53] The two defendants comment similarly on the second and third propositions, which also deal with the Eucharist. The second—that accidents do not remain without a subject in the Eucharist—is a heresy, they say, if taken in a sense contrary to the decretal *Cum Marthe* (a

50. Wilkins, *Concilia*, 3:161.
51. Ibid., 3:161–62, contrasted with the list on 3:157–58. The second list is not numbered in the response, but numbers are used when the archbishop refers to them. No. 5 of the first list is now no. 7, meaning that the article on obeying the devil has changed from no. 7 to no. 6; no. 17 of the original list is divided into two, nos. 17–18, with other changes as follows: 18 to 19, 19 to 20, 20 to 22, 21 to 23, 22 to 24, 23 to 25, 24 to 21. At the Council of Constance, the 45 Wycliffian propositions condemned begin with the 24 Blackfriars theses in the following order: 1–4 = 1–4; 5 = 7; 6–7 = 5–6; 8–10 = 8–10; 11–12 = 11; 13–16 = 12–15; 17 = 16–17; 18–19 = 18–19; 20–23 = 21–24; 24 = 20.
52. Wilkins, *Concilia*, 3:161: "'Quod substantia panis materialis et vini manet in sacramento altaris post consecrationem'; ad sensum contrarium illi decretali, *Firmiter credimus*, concedimus quod est heresis."
53. *Decretales Gregorii IX* 1.1.1 (Friedberg edition, 2:5).

decretal letter of Innocent III dating from 1202);[54] and the third proposition, that Christ is not in the sacrament in his proper corporal presence, is also a heresy if taken in a sense contrary to the Clementine decretal *Si Dominum* (which is Clement V's renewal at the Council of Vienne, in 1312, of the 1264 decree of Urban IV about the feast of Corpus Christi).[55] Of all three propositions they say that in everything concerning the sacrament of the altar they profess that they wish to agree with the words and sense of Holy Scripture, along with the determinations of the Church and the sayings of the holy doctors.[56] They are ostensibly agreeing with papal law, but by by referring to *Firmiter* and *Si Dominum* simply as decretals rather than also as pronouncements of ecumenical councils, they may be reflecting a belief that these recent conciliar decrees did not constitute determinations of the Church.[57]

Since their response concerning the first thesis spoke of a sense different from the decretal *Firmiter*, Courteney asked them what that sense was (that is, he asked them to explain in what sense the proposition was heretical), but they were unwilling to answer. He then explained to them the sense of the condemned proposition, putting it in the form of a question to them: "Does the same material bread, that is, the same by number that is placed on the altar before the consecration, remain according to its own substance or nature after consecration in the sacrament of the altar, and is the same true of the wine?" They answered that they did not know how to make a better reply to this sense, for the time being,[58] and they responded similarly to questions about the second and third articles. To

54. Ibid., 3.41.6 (2:636–39).
55. *Constitutiones Clementinae* 3.16.1 (Friedberg edition, 2:1174–77).
56. Wilkins, *Concilia*, 3:161.
57. One of the heresies of John Purvey, which he recanted in 1400, is the rejection of the determinations of Innocent III and the general council held at Lyons (confusing the second council of Lyons, held by Gregory X in 1274, with the Fourth Lateran Council in Rome, 1215); see Wilkins, *Concilia*, 3:261–62.
58. Ibid., 3:162: "Quibus responsionibus dicto domino Cantuariensi datis, iidem Nicolaus et Philippus, eo quod ad sensum et verba prime conclusionis non responderunt expresse, sed ad contrarium sensum illi decretali, *Firmiter credimus*, interrogati tunc ibidem judicialiter, quis esset ille sensus, noluerunt illum exprimere. Quesitum igitur ab eis, juxta sensum ejusdem conclusionis, ex parte dicti domini Cantuariensis declaratum: 'An idem panis materialis in numero qui ante consecrationem ponitur in altari remaneat secundum propriam substantiam vel naturam post consecrationem in sacramento altaris?' et de vino similiter. Ad hunc vero sensum illi Nicolaus et Philippus dixerunt se nescire protunc melius respondere, quia respondebant, ut prefertur, in scriptis." The last part would seem to mean, literally, "they did not know how to respond better, for the moment, because they were responding, as noted above, in writing." But since there is no reference above to any further response in writing, no doubt "quia respondebant" is a mistake for "quam responderant," so that the meaning is, "they did not know how to respond better, for now, than they had already responded, as noted above, in writing." This is confirmed in the language of the second and third conclusions, 163: "quam, ut premittitur, respondebant" and "quam responderunt, ut prefertur."

the sixth conclusion (formerly the seventh), on God obeying the devil, they replied that it was heresy when taken to mean that God in his own person or essence should obey the devil by the obedience of necessity. Because they did not answer fully and expressly, the archbishop asked if God owed some kind of obedience to the devil, and they said yes—namely, the obedience of charity, because God loves the devil and punishes him, as He should. And one of them (Hereford, according to the *Fasciculi*) offered to prove this sense of the article to anyone, under pain of burning.[59] In so saying, he may simply have been asserting his willingness to risk the death penalty, but his mode of expression may indicate an offer to undergo the ordeal of fire along with a champion who held the opposite view.[60]

Repingdon and Hereford were also interrogated on article 11 (on excommunication), number 20 (on special prayers; 19 in the first list), and number 25 (on mendicant friars; 23 in the first list). The archbishop's assessors found their answers to some of the articles (1–3 and 6) to be heretical and to others, namely, 19 (they mean 20, in the current list) and 25, to be erroneous. As a result, Courteney issued the decree cited above, and after the two defendants declined to make a further response, he set 27 June for them to appear and hear his disposition of the case.[61]

Courteney then addressed a separate admonition to Aston, rehearsing all that had proceeded, and giving him another chance to submit his views on the articles; if he refused to answer, he would be judged to have confessed them (that is, acknowledged them as true rather than false). The archbishop read the first

59. Wilkins, *Concilia*, 3:163: "Ad sensum insuper et textum sexte conclusionis, quia non responderunt plene et expresse, interrogati an Deus debeat aliquem modum obedientie diabolo, dixerunt quod sic, scilicet obedientiam charitatis, quia diligit eum et punit eum, ut debet. Et ad probandum, quod Deus debet taliter obedire diabolo, obtulit se sub pena incendii ad quemcunque." Cf. *Fasciculi*, 328: "Et ad hoc probandum se obtulit sponte sua magister Nicolaus sub pena incendii."

60. Although ordeals were outlawed by the Fourth Lateran Council in 1215, some forms of the *judicium Dei* were still practiced in England—we all know of the trial by combat ordered by Richard II between the dukes of Norfolk and Hereford, as portrayed by Shakespeare; see J. H. Baker, *An Introduction to English Legal History*, 3d ed. (London, 1990), 87. More to the point, a challenge by fire was offered a hundred years later by a Franciscan opponent of Savonarola; it was accepted by a Dominican colleague of the latter, and undertaken by the city of Florence, where an elaborate "fire trail" was set up. See Roberto Ridolfi, *The Life of Girolamo Savonarola*, trans. Cecil Grayson (Westport, Conn., 1959), 236–42. The event was set for 7 April 1498: "In the Piazza dei Signori a great platform had been erected, about seven feet high, ninety feet long, and sixteen feet wide, covered with rocks, so that it would not catch fire. On this was built a great bonfire of wood treated with oil, resin, and gunpowder, so that the fire might spread faster and more dreadfully. Down the length of the platform ran a narrow path through the bonfire, barely more than two feet wide, and through this the two friars were to pass, entering at the same time from opposite ends." In the event, the Franciscan party lost nerve, and the test did not take place. For Ridolfi's notes to chapter 22, in which this account occurs, see the Italian edition, *Vita di Girolamo Savonarola*, 2 vols. (Rome, 1952), 2:205–11.

61. Wilkins, *Concilia*, 3:163.

article and asked Aston to reply in Latin, because of the laymen present. Aston, however, spoke in English, to incite the people against the archbishop, "as it seemed." He answered nothing pertinent to any of the articles, but only subterfuges, often stating, "as if he were a layman" (*sicut laicus*),[62] that it was sufficient for him to believe as Holy Church believed. On the first article, concerning the material bread, he said that that matter exceeded his intellect, and, as if deriding the archbishop, he said that he could take that word "material" and put it in his purse, if he had one. The archbishop, after consulting his assessors, considered his response inappropriate, and therefore he held Aston as confessed and convicted of all of the propositions and accordingly declared him to have been and still to be a heretic, concerning the heretical propositions, and erroneous, concerning the erroneous propositions.[63]

According to the *Fasciculi*, Aston was delivered to secular custody, where he wrote and broadcast an account in Latin and English of his examination by the archbishop at Blackfriars, which he says took place on 19 June (the two encounters actually occurred on 18 June and 20 June).[64] He says that he confessed his belief in the real presence of Christ in the sacrament of the altar, accepting what Scripture and Holy Church determined. He states that when questioned on the proposition that the material bread remained in the sacrament, he protested that he had never held, taught, or preached it—this matter, or speculation about it, transcends his intellect; and therefore he believes whatever Scripture explicitly teaches must be believed, and whatever else touching faith that is not in Scripture he believes as Holy Mother Church believes.[65]

Such a denial of having held or taught heresy, together with a confession of orthodox belief, should have been enough for him to have been acquitted, in the absence of contrary evidence; or, at the most, he should simply have been required to undergo canonical purgation. However, Courteney and his associates

62. Doubtless the text is not saying that Aston was claiming to be a layman, but that he was responding like a layman, whereas he was almost certainly at least a cleric in minor orders; the archbishop identifies him as a master of arts and scholar in theology and distinguishes him from the laymen present. Aston calls himself a priest in his own account of his examination by the archbishop, treated below.

63. Wilkins, *Concilia*, 3:164.

64. Margaret Aston ("Wyclif and the Vernacular," in Anne Hudson and Michael Wilks, eds., *From Ockham to Wyclif* [Oxford, 1987], 281–330), edits the English version of the manifesto (pp. 229–30), as found in *Knighton's Chronicle* and a Wycliffite collection, MS. Bodley 647, together with another alleged account by Hereford and Repingdon or Hereford and his fellow-priests (Knighton) of their responses to the archbishop. But rather than taking the accounts to refer to an actual distribution of their statements on 19 June ("Wyclif and the Vernacular," 297), I assume that the *Fasciculi* chronology is accurate, and that John Aston mistook 19 June for 20 June. The Hereford-Repingdon statement (entirely orthodox because it skirts all of the problematic questions) strikes me as spurious, since it has the same mistaken date of 19 June; perhaps it too was composed by John Aston.

65. *Fasciculi*, 329–30.

did not see it Aston's way, and an anonymous refutation of his statement was promulgated: Aston was condemned as a heretic, not because he confessed, as he claims, that the bread truly becomes the body of Christ, but because he refused to confess, as Holy Church teaches, that the body of Christ is truly there in its own corporal presence, and for holding that the substance of material bread or wine remains after consecration; moreover, he contemptuously refused to declare his faith concerning the twenty-four heresies and errors solemnly condemned by the Church and publicly required by the heresy inquisitor, having been canonically admonished.[66]

It is clear that the authorities believed they had a judicial right to require a statement of faith on specific points of faith, especially from those who had been delated as teaching the opposite. As I have noted, Courteney did not insist on an explanation if the defendants were willing simply to accept his council's condemnation of the propositions. It goes without saying that Courteney considered the original condemnation of the twenty-four articles to be the voice of Holy Mother Church, whereas Aston obviously did not.

Another defendant, Thomas Hilman, had been summoned on 20 June because he was suspected of favoring Aston somewhat. He too was required to respond to the articled propositions; he asked for time and was given until 27 June. He appeared on that day, along with Repingdon and Hereford, but Courteney continued the trials until 1 July because his assessors were not present. On 1 July, the three defendants did not appear at the appointed time, but Hilman finally showed up in the afternoon. After some hesitation over the propositions, he finally agreed that they were all heretical and erroneous, and he promised to teach the contrary as long as he lived. The archbishop then declared Repingdon and Hereford contumacious and, accordingly, he excommunicated them. The two defendants thereupon drew up a formal appeal to the pope, which they nailed to the doors of St. Paul's and St. Mary's churches in London; Courteney formally rejected the appeal as frivolous on 12 July. It is not clear what grievances were alleged by the two appellants.[67] It would be interesting to know if they included Aston's implicit objection, that the Church authorities had no business judging secret thoughts or forcing a person to speculate on matters that one could not be proved to have written or spoken about in the past. If so, how would the appeal have been treated if it had been accepted by the archbishop and forwarded to the papal curia; or if, instead of posting it in London, the defendants had sent it to

66. Ibid., 331.

67. Wilkins, *Concilia,* 3:164–65. Wilkins gives only the text of Courteney's *apostoli*, or formal response to the appeal. It is Dahmus, drawing on the archbishop's register, who says that the appeal was against the sentence of excommunication and was nailed to the church doors (*Prosecution of Wyclyf,* 120).

the pope on their own and circumvented the court? The archbishop's determination that his subjects could be required to make formal assent to what he had determined to be Church teaching might have appeared a very reasonable procedure to the curia; but it would be hard to justify in the light of the *ordo juris* required in a formal inquisition.

Our query need not remain entirely speculative, for in the event Hereford left England for Rome to present his case personally before the pope. But our only account of this effort is provided by the unreliable Henry Knighton, who seems to suggest that Hereford held all of the two dozen theses condemned at Blackfriars—including, of course, the heretical Eucharistic propositions. He has Hereford presenting "the aforesaid conclusions" before the pope in full consistory, saying that he would defend them against everyone even to the danger of death, "usque ad mortis periclitationem." The pope, with the consent of the consistory, condemned some of the conclusions as heresies, some as errors, and committed Hereford to perpetual prison, not wanting to run the risk of offending the English people by having an Englishman, even though a defender of heresy, consumed by fire.[68]

Hereford later escaped and returned to England, where he finally recanted in 1390.[69] Repingdon, however, capitulated much earlier. In the decree restoring him to his position at the university, dated 23 October 1382, Courteney gave a selective rehearsal of the previous proceedings, omitting all reference to his faulty answers and saying only that he had suspended Repingdon, being suspect of heresy, until he could purge his innocence, and that he was guilty of contempt for not appearing in court on the day specified.[70] In contrast, when Courteney restored Aston on 27 November 1382, he said that Aston had been vehemently suspect of heresy, having been gravely defamed of holding certain propositions; had contemptuously refused to respond concerning them; and had been condemned as a heretic.[71] But a few days earlier, on 18 November, at the Oxford convocation, Aston had used the same formula of abjuration as Repingdon: he

68. *Knighton's Chronicle, 1337–1396,* ed. G. H. Martin (Oxford, 1995), 276–81. The Roman pope at this time was Urban VI (elected in 1378, after which the French contingent elected Clement VII); shortly after the latter's death on 15 October 1389, Boniface IX was elected.

69. See Dahmus, *Prosecution of Wyclyf,* 128.

70. Wilkins, *Concilia,* 3:169 (23 October 1382).

71. Ibid., 3:169 (27 November 1382): "de heretica pravitate vehementer suspectus, per nos fungentes officio inquisitoris heretice pravitatis, fuisset ab omni actu scholastico, justitia exigente, rite suspensus, et proper suam manifestam contumaciam pariter et offensam coram nobis judicialiter contractas, eo quod certis conclusionibus, quibusdam hereticis, quibusdam vero erroneis, per sacrorum canonum instituta, et nos de quamplurium suffraganeorum nostrorum ac aliorum sacre theologie, juris canonici et civilis doctorum, jurisque peritorum consilio et assensu damnatis, de quibus extitit graviter defamatus, respondere per nos monitus atque jussus, id facere noluit, sed contemptibiliter recusavit, pro heretico et errante ac ut hereticus atque errans legitime condamnatus."

repudiated all the heresies and errors that the clergy had condemned and of which he until that time had been defamed.[72]

It is true that both Repingdon and Hereford had been defamed of holding the twenty-four propositions, or at least some of them, from the time that they refused to repudiate them before the archbishop. But the archbishop's statement, in the mandate reconciling Hereford, that Hereford had been defamed of the propositions beforehand, and that that was the reason he had been cited to an inquisition, looks like a retrospective attempt to make his irregular proceeding (of interrogating defendants on heresies without first accusing them of having publicly held them) into a regular inquisition.

Now let us look at the ways in which Wyclif was dealt with at the Council of Constance, especially in connection with his Bohemian admirers. We should first note that in 1409, Thomas Arundel, the current archbishop of Canterbury, ordered the University of Oxford to set up a committee of twelve persons to comb the works of Wyclif for possible heresies and errors, and two years later the committee produced a list of 267 heresies and errors, omitting many other conclusions that they noted were badly expressed and could be upheld as orthodox by means of sophistical debate.[73] Arundel condemned the theses in a Canterbury synod and forwarded them in March 1411 to the Pisan Pope John XXIII in Rome.[74] Late in 1412, the pope convened a council in Rome in which Wyclif's books were condemned, and in a decree of 2 February 1413 he ordered them burned, and he summoned any defenders of Wyclif's memory to appear at the Holy See within nine months to give reasons why Wyclif should not be posthumously condemned for heresy.[75]

72. Wilkins, *Concilia,* 3:172.
73. Dahmus, *Prosecution of Wyclyf,* 152–53, citing Wilkins, *Concilia,* 3:322, 339–49.
74. Dahmus, *Prosecution of Wyclyf,* 153.
75. John XXIII, *In generali concilio,* given in *Annales ecclesiastici,* year 1413, §§1–3, ed. Augustinus Theiner, 37 vols. (Bar-le-Duc, 1864–83), 27:345–46, Dahmus mistakenly puts the Roman Council in 1411–12. The first Pisan pope, Alexander V, had previously denounced Wyclif as a damned heresiarch in a decretal sent to the archbishop of Prague, *Sedis apostolice,* dated 20 December; see *Annales,* year 1409, §89, 37:298–99. Both Alexander V and John XXIII are considered authentic popes in the *Bullarium romanum*; or, to give it its formal title, *Bullarum, diplomatum, et privilegiorum sanctorum romanorum pontificum taurinensis editio,* edited by Bishop Tomassetti, blessed by Pope Pius IX, and sponsored by Cardinal Gaude, 25 vols. (Turin, 1857–85); see 4:655–56. Alexander's status is still debated; but John has been more firmly relegated to the rank of an antipope since the modern John XXIII assumed his name and number.

In December of 1413, John XXIII announced that a general council would meet at Constance in November of 1414. At the first general session, on 16 November 1414, following the precedent of the Council of Pisa, the pope appointed two "proctors and promotors," John de Scribanis and Henry de Piro.[76] Thereafter they, and especially Henry de Piro, would be responsible for preparing the prosecution of the trials that took place at Constance. For instance, in the session of 2 May 1415, the promotors (or "instigators," as they are also called) ask for and receive orders for citations, not only of Jerome of Prague, but also of John XXIII, who had now become the object of a vindictive conciliar inquisition.[77] On the same day, the eighth session was set up for the purpose of condemning the memory of John Wyclif, and, accordingly, on 4 May, Piro presented a citation that had been affixed to the doors of churches calling for persons to come forward to say why the memory and teaching of Wyclif should not be condemned. Since no one had shown up, Piro accused all such potential defenders of contumacy for their failure to appear. Then he requested that Wyclif be condemned, in particular a set of 45 of his theses that had previously been condemned by the University of Paris (beginning with the 24 propositions condemned at Blackfriars),[78] along with a list of 260 collected by the University of Oxford, some of them overlapping with the first list. The 45 articles were condemned, but a complete reading and condemnation of the 260 theses was postponed until the next session. No one appeared to defend Wyclif's memory, but witnesses examined by commissioners appointed by John XXIII and the present council testified to Wyclif's final impenitence. His impenitence was declared proved by the *ordo juris* (a claim that due process for condemning an absent defendant—or in this case, a dead one—had been followed), and the sentence of condemnation was passed.[79]

76. For the acts of the council, I use Hermann von der Hardt, *Magnum oecumenicum constantiense concilium*, 6 vols. (Frankfurt, 1697–1700, 1742), vol. 4; and John Dominic Mansi, *Sacrorum conciliorum nova et amplissima collectio*, vols. 27–28 (Venice, 1784–85). According to Phillip Stump ("The Official Acta of the Council of Constance in the Edition of Mansi," in *The Two Laws: Studies in Medieval Legal History Dedicated to Stephan Kuttner*, ed. Laurent Mayali and Stephanie A. J. Tibbetts [Washington, D.C., 1990], 221–39), Mansi, in spite of his misprints, reproduces a text in some ways better than that in Hardt. Stump, however, does not point out that Mansi (or his sources) eliminates most of the rubrics of Hardt's edition and does not include other supplementary material. For the acts from the pope's arrival to the appointment of the promotors, see Hardt, 4:6–19; and Mansi, 27:531–40.
77. Hardt, *Magnum oecumenicum*, 4:140–49; Mansi, *Sacrorum conciliorum*, 27:623–29. Pope John went to Constance with the expectation that the acts of the Council of Pisa would be ratified, which would mean that the Roman and Avignonese claimants to the papacy (Gregory XII and Benedict XIII, respectively) would be deposed and he would remain as pope. But after succumbing to pressure for his own abdication, he changed his mind and fled Constance (on 20 March).
78. See n. 51 above.
79. Hardt, *Magnum oecumenicum*, 4:150–57; Mansi, *Sacrorum conciliorum*, 27:629–36.

Other actions taken against heresy and associated crimes at Constance, apart from the condemnation of Wyclif, were, of course, the trials of John Hus and his lay follower Jerome of Prague, and the examination of the doctrines of John Petit.[80] Heresy charges also figured in the trials of John XXIII and the Avignonese pope, Benedict XIII. The proceedings concerning John Petit were posthumous, as were those dealing with the doctrines of John Wyclif, and the trials of John XXIII and Benedict XIII were conducted in their absence.[81] But the trials of Hus and Jerome of Prague took place in their presence. Petit's writings were defended by the ambassadors of John the Fearless, duke of Burgundy—including Peter Cauchon, the future inquisitor of Joan of Arc—and the tactics they used show what legal resources were available in an inquisition when the defendant was supported by able counsel.[82]

In the case of Hus, the official record, which is quite piecemeal, gives the impression that the trial was procedurally correct. The charges on which he was convicted were based on his writings (which he acknowledged to be his) and on the testimony of witnesses to his preaching, after his protestations, denials, and qualifications were heard and rejected. His condemnation was confirmed by the full council on 6 July 1415;[83] on the same day, he was burned at the stake.

But there were irregularities. He had been given assurances of safe conduct, and after his arrival at Constance, Pope John XXIII had lifted the sentences of excommunication and interdict issued against him two years earlier at Rome (for nonappearance after having been summoned by a papal commission); but then he was arrested, placed under harsh imprisonment,[84] and subjected to interrogation by a newly appointed commission—without, it seems, his having been

80. For Petit, see Heinrich Finke, *Acta concilii constanciensis*, 4 vols. (Münster, 1896–1928), 4:239–40.

81. Kelly, "Right to Remain Silent," 1010.

82. Ibid., 1009–10.

83. Hardt, *Magnum oecumenicum*, 4:389–40; Mansi, *Sacrorum conciliorum*, 27:747–65 (Session 15). The sentence (Hardt, 435–40; Mansi, 752–53) includes a summary account of his trial, but only from the time of his personal appearance before the council. The letter addressed by the council to the Bohemians on 26 July (Hardt, 485–90; Mansi, 781–83) speaks of opening a *judicium* concerning him after he arrived at Constance ("Verum de Johanne Huss, qui primum huc venit, judicium orsi") by examining his books and gathering the testimony of witnesses. Then they listened to him, to ascertain his understanding of matters, first by means of an *examen* before deputies of the council and then at a public audience of the whole council, all arranged with the help of King Sigismund: "Scitote autem nos eundem Johannem Hus primo ex reverendissimis dominis cardinalibus, ex prelatorum et magistrorum excellentissimorum quampluribus, examini suo deputatis, demum data sibi publica audientia, serenissimo Romanorum semper Augusto ac Ungarie rege assistente, quemadmodum intelligeret auscultasse."

84. A letter of protest by Bohemian noblemen, dated 14 May 1415, was addressed to the council Fathers, charging that Hus's safe conduct had been violated and that he was arrested and put in fetters on a starvation diet (Mansi, *Sacrorum conciliorum*, 27:655–59). The council issued a decree justifying its action

issued a new summons or given chapters of charges. Moreover, instead of being examined directly on his own views, he was asked to give his opinion on the alleged views of Wyclif. We are told that at first he refused to respond, but complied when informed that his refusal might be regarded as a confession of guilt.[85]

Hus was eventually presented with formal charges concerning his own views and activities.[86] According to the account by Peter of Mladonovice, one of Hus's followers, the commissioners, headed by John de Rupescissa, patriarch of Constantinople, did not conceal the identities of witnesses from him but brought them before him in prison so that he could see them sworn in. However, when he asked for a proctor or advocate to defend himself from the witnesses, many of whom were his mortal enemies, he was told that it was prohibited by law to defend a man suspected of heresy.[87] Legally speaking, of course, only convicted heretics were forbidden lawyers, but the prohibition was often illegitimately extended to persons who were only charged with heresy.[88] However, remaining excommunicated for a year for nonappearance rendered a suspect guilty of heresy,[89] and it may have been on this pretext that he was denied counsel. But John XXIII was allowed to appear by proctor, and, as mentioned above, lawyers were allowed for the trial of Petit's writings, which had been previously condemned in an inquisitorial court, and defenders were summoned for the trial of

on the grounds that Hus was an impugner of the Faith: "Cum tamen dictus Johannes Huss, fidem orthodoxam pertinaciter impugnans, se ab omni conductu et privilegio reddiderit alienum" (Hardt, *Magnum oecumenicum,* 4:521–22). In other words, the council prejudged him to be guilty of the charges on which he was to be tried. The decree is undated, but Hardt conjectures that it came after the abjuration of Jerome of Prague on 23 September 1415. It should be noted that canon law, in a decree issued by Clement V at the Council of Vienne (1312) against the abuses of papally appointed heresy inquisitors, cautioned against severe imprisonment that seemed more like punishment than custody ("duro . . . tradere carceri sive arcto qui magis ad penam quam ad custodiam videatur"), *Const. Clem.* 5.3.1, *Multorum querela* (Friedberg edition, 2:1181).

85. Matthew Spinka, *John Hus: A Biography* (Princeton, N.J., 1968), 236. Spinka does not cite his source for the specifics of the first day of interrogation, 6 December 1414, when Hus began his imprisonment in a Dominican friary. See also Spinka's *John Hus at the Council of Constance* (New York, 1965), 117 n. 21. David S. Schaff, in *John Huss: His Life, Teachings, and Death, after 500 Years* (New York, 1915), says that according to John of Jesenice (the lawyer who had defended Hus in Rome), "Huss had committed a technical error in making any reply whatsoever as a prisoner" (p. 184, citing no source).

86. See Hus's letter of 4 January 1415 to John of Chlum, *The Letters of John Hus,* trans. Matthew Spinka (Manchester, 1972), 140–41.

87. Peter of Mladonovice, *An Account of the Trial and Condemnation of Master John Hus in Constance,* English translation of *Relatio de magistri Joannis Hus causa* by Spinka, *John Hus at the Council of Constance,* 87–234, esp. 117–18; the Latin text is edited in *Fontes rerum bohemicarum,* vol. 8, ed. Václav Novotny (Prague, 1932), 25–120, esp. 41.

88. *Decretals* 5.7.11 (Innocent III, *Si adversus*); Kelly, "Inquisition and the Prosecution of Heresy," 445.

89. *Sext* 5.2.7 (Alexander IV, *Cum contumacia*).

Wyclif's writings and memory. Later, on 5 June, an attempt to deny Hus his right to be present at the council's considerations of the charges against him was foiled.[90] The question of his right to call witnesses or submit documentation on his own behalf seems not to have come up.

As for Jerome of Prague, none of the proceedings against him are contained in the surviving acts of the council until his abjuration on 23 September 1415. But Peter of Mladonovice preserved the text of the citation issued against Jerome on 17 April 1415, as multiply defamed of errors and heresy, ordering him to appear in public session of the council to respond to allegations against him, being assured of the council's safe conduct. Soon afterward he was captured and imprisoned, and on 23 May he was brought before the council and asked why he had not obeyed the citation. He responded that he would have obeyed it if he had known of it. After he answered various accusations orally, he was returned to custody.[91] In his abjuration of 23 September, in which he referred to an earlier statement (made on 11 September), he did not admit any heresy on his own part: he simply denounced all heresy of which he had been "infamed," and specifically the doctrines ascribed to Wyclif and Hus.[92] He remained in prison, and on 24 February 1416 the council promotor announced that a commission consisting of the patriarch of Constantinople and a professor of theology named Nicholas Dinckelspuel had been appointed to examine witnesses concerning him. On 27 April the results were published, with the number and names, or stations, of witnesses being announced and the kind of proof that each gave for each article specified (hearsay—that is, public fame—or notoriety, or belief, or knowledge, or otherwise); and Jerome's written responses to each were exhibited (no response is recorded to the last, no. 45, which asserted that *publica vox et fama* existed

90. Spinka, *John Hus: A Biography*, 258–59.

91. Peter of Mladonovice, *Narracio de magistro Hieronymo Pragensi, pro Christi nomine Constancie exusto*, ed. Novotny, *Fontes* 8:339–50, esp. 340–43. For a brief account of Jerome's arrest, imprisonment, and trial, see Spinka, *John Hus: A Biography*, 246–47, 291–96; he draws mainly on František Šmahel, *Jeroným Pražský* (Prague, 1966), who unfortunately does not document his account. The promised safe conduct in the citation, which reads "Ad quod a violencia, justicia semper salva, omnem tibi salvum conductum nostrum, quantum in nobis est et fides exigit orthodoxa, tenore presencium offerimus et assignamus plenius," was perhaps held to be nonoperative because Jerome had not responded of his own free will; or it may be that it was a deliberate ruse and not intended to apply to him, if his guilt was already taken for granted, as in the case of Hus.

92. Hardt, *Magnum oecumenicum*, 4:499–514; Mansi, *Sacrorum conciliorum*, 27:791–93; 28:160–61. Spinka, in *John Hus: A Biography* (p. 393), following Šmahel's Czech translation (p. 168), uses the word "befouled" for *infamatus* and agrees with Šmahel that Jerome was admitting guilt. *Infamatus* is used in the council's citation of Jerome as a synonym of *diffamatus* ("de quibus apud nos multipliciter infamatus existis"; "personam tuam tamquam suspectam et multipliciter diffamatam evocamus"); see Peter of Mladonovice, *Narracio*, 341.

concerning all of the other articles).[93] On the same day, the promotor submitted 102 more articles, with claims of proof (for example, "proved by four witnesses").[94] In addition, the promotor indignantly complained that Jerome was eating and drinking better in prison than if he were free. He asked, rhetorically, "Did not Christ fast for forty days before His Passion?"[95] He then mentioned other salutary examples of fasting and he requested the council fathers to afflict Jerome similarly with fasting and to make him respond to the earlier articles under torture, with a *credit* or *non credit*, so that he would not be able to escape by hypocritical responses; and if he denied anything that was legally proved, he was to be handed over to the secular court.[96]

Jerome gave public oral responses to the second set of articles on 23 May and 26 May. On the first occasion he refused to respond under oath because, he said, he wished to speak freely; if given permission to speak freely later, he would swear. On the second day, he refused to swear once again, this time because the proceeding was against him ("ordo esset sibi perversus"). The promotors had to be content to have his responses entered unsworn.[97] According to the report of Poggio Bracciolini, who was present, Jerome refused to make any answers to their questions unless he could plead his own case first. He complained that he had been kept in prison for 350 days without having been given any means of defending himself, while his enemies had been given free rein to slander him; but he finally agreed to answer the charges first and speak his mind afterward.[98] When his responses were completed, John de Rupescissa reviewed the evidence, which showed Jerome to be quadruply convicted of heresy (this conclusion is not explained). However, the patriarch continued, since the defendant had often insisted on a public audience, he would be allowed to speak, in order to forestall any inane objection (presumably of the sort already made by the Bohemians and the Moravians).[99] After giving a long history of the situation in Prague and his

93. Hardt, *Magnum oecumenicum,* 4:615–16, 630–46; Mansi, *Sacrorum conciliorum,* 27:837–38, 840–48.

94. Hardt, *Magnum oecumenicum,* 4:646–91, cf. 748–62; Mansi, *Sacrorum conciliorum,* 27:848–63, cf. 887–93.

95. The answer, of course, is no: his forty-day fast was some three years earlier, and on the night before the Passion he had a rather lavish Last Supper.

96. Hardt, *Magnum oecumenicum,* 4:689–90; Mansi, *Sacrorum conciliorum,* 27:863–64. Since churchmen were not allowed to shed blood, defendants convicted of capital crimes were entrusted to a secular court for execution.

97. Hardt, *Magnum oecumenicum,* 4:748–56; Mansi, *Sacrorum conciliorum,* 27: 887–90.

98. *Poggii florentini ad Leonardum Aretinum epistola de M. Hieronymi de Praga supplicio,* ed. Novotny, *Fontes* 8, 323–34, esp. 324–26. The anonymous *De vita Magistri Jeronimi de Praga* (ed. Novotny, 335–38) says that Jerome had refused to respond to the 107 articles put to him by the two commissioners while in prison or anywhere but a public and open audience (p. 335). But, as we have seen, he did respond to the original set of 45 articles in private, and only balked at responding to the additional 102 articles.

99. Hardt, *Magnum oecumenicum,* 4:756; Mansi, *Sacrorum conciliorum,* 27:890; see next note.

coming to Constance, Jerome stated that he had agreed to the condemnation of Wyclif and Hus only because he feared burning.[100] He repudiated his earlier abjuration, and asserted his belief that the two men and their teaching were holy, except for what they said about the sacrament of the altar against the opinions of Church doctors.[101]

Formal sentencing was set for 30 May. On that day, a sermon was preached against Jerome, and he made a response in which he explained that he refused to respond to the articles under oath because there had been a change of judges in his trial; and he complained that not all of the articles had been read by them. The patriarch then delivered the sentence against him, summarizing the course of the trial: Jerome was proved to have held many of the false doctrines of Wyclif and Hus; he had repudiated his own denunciation of Wyclif and Hus and asserted that he had never read any error or heresy in them (Jerome's exception of their Eucharistic doctrines in his final speech was ignored); he was therefore condemned as a heretic and as relapsed into heresy. The sentence was approved by the council, and he was delivered to the secular authorities for execution. Jerome thereupon commended his soul to God and started to sing the Creed, and he was led bound through the squares to the place of execution, where he was burned.[102]

In the cases of both John Hus and Jerome of Prague, their own explanations of their positions in court, which were accompanied with denials of wrongdoing, do not seem to have have been construed as confessions, but at most as confirmations of previous offenses, proofs of which were ostensibly established by documentary and testimonial evidence.[103] But the initial procedure used against Hus—having him comment on propositions attributed to Wyclif—resembles the form of trial devised by the archbishop of Canterbury in 1382 for use against Repingdon, Hereford, and other followers of Wyclif. Its employment at Constance may have been influenced by the English precedent, even though the

100. The threat of condemnation must have been forceful, for word had spread that a death sentence had already been passed against him; such was the belief of the Bohemian and Moravian noblemen who in a letter of 2 September 1415 protested to the council against the execution of Hus (Hardt, *Magnum oecumenicum,* 4:495–97; Mansi, *Sacrorum conciliorum,* 27:788–791).

101. Hardt, *Magnum oecumenicum,* 4:756–62; Mansi, *Sacrorum conciliorum,* 27:890–93.

102. Hardt, *Magnum oecumenicum,* 4:764–71; Mansi, *Sacrorum conciliorum,* 27:893–97.

103. According to *De vita magistri Jeronimi,* Jerome was convicted of all the articles by witnesses: "Centum septem articuli . . . de novo fuerunt producti et subsequenter per sufficientes testes probati" (p. 335). "In quibus omnibus articulis . . . fuit omnino per testes convictus" (p. 336).

English were apparently no longer using it. Although the procedure could be compared to the Continental abuse of grilling suspects *de se et aliis*, especially where the inquisitors were armed with lists of heresies to guide their questions,[104] it was more likely inspired by scholastic practices in the universities of England, France, and elsewhere, where it had long been the custom to write commentaries on unorthodox as well as orthodox propositions. As William Courtenay points out, lists of censured propositions, like those of Paris of 1277, "acted as guidelines for further students and bachelors on the appropriate wording of statements for debate or conclusions."[105]

It is not clear what the purpose was of having Hus write a commentary on Wyclif's propositions. Perhaps the promotors regarded him as a belated defender of the sort they had called for earlier. At any rate, nothing seems to have been made of his responses. However, since Hus had publicly defended some of Wyclif's articles in 1412,[106] there would have been good reason to have formally charged him with holding them; if this had happened, the inquisitional procedure would have been regular.

The 1382 procedure, however, was intended as a new kind of purgation, not of past offenses against orthodoxy, but of present unorthodox belief. John Aston's desire to remain silent should have been honored, but it was not. He did not think of Joan of Arc's brilliant defense, when Bishop Cauchon required her to recite the Our Father and Hail Mary. She replied that she would only do so in confession.[107] Only a confessor had the right to inquire into one's thoughts and beliefs, and whatever was disclosed had to remain under the seal of secrecy.

The last word on procedure at Constance comes in the bull of Martin V, *Inter cunctas pastoralis cure solicitudines*, issued on 22 February 1418 and addressed to all archbishops, bishops, and inquisitors of heretical depravity, but especially those in Bohemia and Moravia, where the errors of Wyclif, Hus, and Jerome were still flourishing. The pope orders suspects to be examined on the forty-five

104. See, for instance, the catalogue of twenty errors of the Waldensians and "Roncarolians" (followers of John de Ronco) in "Inquisitorial Manual no. 5," dated shortly after 1265, in Vatican MS. lat. 3978, fol. 50. Antoine Dondaine ("Le manuel de l'inquisiteur [1230–1330]," *Archivum fratrum praedicatorum* 17 [1947]: 85–194), says that this list is common in the inquisitorial manuscripts (p. 148).

105. William J. Courtenay, "Inquiry and Inquisition: Academic Freedom in Medieval Universities," *Church History* 58 (1989): 168–81, 179–80. In formal trials, however, defendants were never required to comment on lists of previously condemned propositions of others, but only on suspect propositions allegedly found in their own writings. See J. M. M. H. Thijssen, *Censure and Heresy at the University of Paris, 1200–1400* (Phila- * delphia, 1998), esp. 76–77, 87–88.

106. Gordon Leff, "Wycliff and Hus: A Doctrinal Comparison," in Anthony Kenny, ed., *Wyclif in His Times*, (Oxford, 1986), 105–25, esp. 123–24.

107. Kelly, "Right to Remain Silent," 1014.

articles of Wyclif and the thirty articles of Hus condemned at the council, according to a set of interrogatories that he provides.[108] I deal with this bull, and its possible connection with the formulation of interrogatories against suspected heretics in the Canterbury convocation of 1428, in my study of more usual inquisitorial procedures against Lollards.[109] But let me add here that the pope's provision that suspects are to be examined "with proctor and advocate removed" ("semotis procuratore et advocato")[110] may mean only that the proctor would not be allowed to answer for the suspect (this was typical of criminal proceedings) and that the suspect could not respond in the presence of his advocate; but it could easily have been interpreted to mean that the suspect was not allowed to consult with an advocate. Where the bull more clearly violates due process is that, as in the cases we have examined, it forces one to say what one thinks about matters of doctrine, thereby going counter to the rule that the Church does not judge secret matters except in the secrecy of the sacrament of confession.

108. Martin V, *Inter cunctas*, Hardt, *Magnum oecumenicum*, 4:1518–31; Mansi, *Sacrorum conciliorum*, 27:1204–15.
109. Kelly, "Lollard Inquisitions," 296–303.
110. Ibid., 298; Hardt, 4:1529; Mansi, 27:1213C.

LOLLARD INQUISITIONS: DUE AND UNDUE PROCESS

Inquisition, or inquisitorial procedure, was a new form of criminal trial developed by Pope Innocent III at the turn of the thirteenth century; he established it in its definitive form at the Fourth Lateran Council in 1215.[1] It enjoyed an immediate success, and it became the basis of procedure not only in all of the ecclesiastical courts of the Western world, but also in all of the secular courts, with the exception of England. I am particularly interested in studying the rights of defendants in the inquisitorial system as practiced in the English ecclesiastical courts, in comparison with defenses permitted in secular courts at the same time. In this paper I will concentrate on one aspect of this subject, namely, church actions taken against the dissidents known as Lollards in the last decades of the fourteenth century and the first half of the fifteenth century.

The early campaign against John Wyclif and his Oxford followers culminated in 1382 in an unusual form of proceeding that deviated from the normal format of trials "in matters of faith," in that, instead of responding to formal charges of having preached or taught erroneous doctrine, the defendants were required to comment on a series of twenty-four propositions condemned as heretical or erroneous by a council of bishops, theologians, and canon lawyers. I have shown elsewhere the details of this procedure and of a similar procedure employed against John Hus at the Council of Constance in 1415.[2] Here I wish to detail other kinds of trials that were used during the same time.

---

[1] *Qualiter et quando* no. 2, *Decretales Gregorii IX* 5.1.24: Innocent III, canon 8 of the Fourth Lateran Council, A.D. 1215, ed. Emil Friedberg, *Corpus iuris canonici*, 2 vols. (Leipzig, 1879–81; repr. Graz, 1959), 2:745–47; for the relevant text, see my "Inquisitorial Due Process and the Status of Secret Crimes," *Proceedings of the Eighth International Congress of Medieval Canon Law*, ed. Stanley Chodorow, Monumenta iuris canonici, Series C: Subsidia, vol. 9 (Vatican City, 1992), pp. 407–27, esp. 410 n. 7.

[2] H.A. Kelly, "Trial Procedures Against Wyclif and Wycliffites in England and at the Council of Constance," forthcoming in the *Huntington Library Quarterly* 61 (1999).

In a normal inquisition (one that followed the *ordo juris*), the defendant would either confess or deny the charges; if he denied them, the judge would attempt to prove them by documents or by the written testimony of witnesses; and if he lacked sufficient evidence of actual guilt, but could establish only the *fama* of guilt that triggered the charges—that is, testimony of trustworthy persons who believed him guilty—the judge could order purgation. This meant that the defendant was required to declare his innocence of the charges under oath, and also to find a stipulated number of neighbors or associates who would swear to his credibility and good reputation. A trial of this sort is set forth in the formal summary by John Buckingham, bishop of Lincoln, of the process he conducted against William Swinderby, concluded on July 11, 1382. Swinderby, suspect of preaching heresy and delated by public fame, was cited to appear before the bishop's commissaries, who leveled charges against him and gave him a term to respond; his response was to deny all wrongdoing. Because of the vehement fame against him, the commissaries fixed a date for canonical purgation and also to allow opponents of the purgation to prosecute the charges. Three friars appeared as denouncers to prove the charges; they produced witnesses whose testimony was published by the bishop and his commissaries, whereupon the bishop convicted him of five errors and six heresies, which he abjured.[3]

We should note that the denouncers in the above case do not function according to the mode of *denuntiatio* set up by Innocent III, according to which a denouncer brings a fault to the judge's attention for the purpose of fraternal correction.[4] Rather, their function seems to be a combination of the earlier *promovens*, or interested aggrieved party who initiates the action, and the *promotor officii judicis*, or judge's assistant.[5] But rather than being appointed by the judge, in this case volunteers for the position were solicited and accepted by the judge.

---

[3] *Fasciculi zizaniorum magistri Johannis Wyclif cum tritico*, ed. Walter Waddington Shirley, Rolls Series 5 (London, 1858), pp. 334–37; the text of the bishop's letter was doubtless taken by the compiler from Bishop Trefnant's register, where it appears, in a transmittal letter from Buckingham dated 10 February 1390, at the beginning of the 1391 process against Swinderby. See *Registrum Johannis Trefnant, episcopi Herefordensis, A.D. 1389–1404*, ed. William W. Capes (London, 1916), p. 231.

[4] *Decretales Gregorii IX* 2.1.13; 5.1.16; 5.3.31 (Friedberg, 2:242–44, 737–38, 760).

[5] Both of these functions are to be distinguished from the independent prosecutor, or *promotor fiscalis*, that was soon to develop in France. See my "Inquisition and the Prosecution of Heresy: Misconceptions and Abuses," *Church History* 58 (1989), 439–51, p. 446 n. 34.

Or at least this is the way Bishop Buckingham presents the matter in his summary. But in his own register it is recorded that the same three friars had presented the original charges, to the number of sixteen, against Swinderby.[6] Furthermore, since the bishop instructed the clergy of the archdeaconry of Leicester "to cause all and sundry who were willing to speak against Swinderby at the time of his purgation to come forward and to denounce him,"[7] are we to conclude that no other denouncers appeared and that the three promotors were obliged to step in again? In his later trial, held in 1391, Swynderby asserted that more than three opponents did come forward: as he was about to make his purgation, "there stooden forth five friars or more, that some of them never saw me before nor heard me, and three lecherous priests." But his account is compatible with there being only three denouncers, with the others functioning as witnesses: "Some of these they cleppeden denunciators, and some were clepped comprobators, that were there falsely forsworn, pursuing busily and crying, with many another friar, with great instance, to give the doom upon me, to burn me," and so on.[8]

On May 14, 1391, the archbishop of Canterbury, William Courteney, notified his province, especially the dioceses of St. David's and Llandaff, that in his recent metropolitan visitation of the Lincoln diocese, he had established by the testimony of witnesses as well as by public fame and the notoriety of the fact itself that, after his abjuration, Swinderby had relapsed, or at least "prolapsed," from bad to worse ("de malo in pejus prolapsus") by preaching the same and other doctrines repugnant to the Faith, and he forbade anyone, under pain of major excommunication, to allow or attend the preaching of one thus convicted of heretical depravity.[9]

---

[6] See Anne Hudson, *The Premature Reformation: Wycliffite Texts and Lollard History* (Oxford 1988), p. 74, citing Lincoln Archives Office, Episcopal Register XII, fols. 242–44, and see also K.B. McFarlane, *John Wycliffe and the Beginnings of English Nonconformity* (London, 1952), p. 122. I assume that the friars were the same: in the bishop's letter they are identified as the Franciscan Roger Frysby, the Augustinian John Hunchay, and the Dominican Thomas Blakstone. McFarlane says that they were masters of theology from these three orders.

[7] McFarlane, p. 123.

[8] *Registrum Trefnant*, pp. 238–39 (spelling modernized).

[9] David Wilkins, *Concilia Magnae Britanniae* (London, 1737; repr. Brussels, 1964), 3:215. His statement of proof is: "prout nuper coram nobis in visitatione nostra metropolitica prefate Lincolniensis diocesis ex plurimorum fide dignorum attestatione, ac alias fama publica et facti notorietate, que nulla poterant tergiversatione celari, referente, informationem accepimus evidentem" (in my citations of Latin, I remedievalize *ae* to *e*).

Before this time, however, action was being contemplated against Swinderby elsewhere, namely, in the diocese of Hereford, for on November 10, 1388, the sheriff had been ordered to hand Swinderby over to the bishop, John Gilbert.[10] No action seems to have been taken at that time, and he only came to trial later in 1391, under Gilbert's successor, John Trefnant, with no notice being taken of the archbishop's pronouncement that he was already re-convicted. However, the trial record is preceded by a letter of Bishop Buckingham, dated February 10, transmitting his 1382 "sentence," or account of Swinderby's conviction and abjuration,[11] which presumably Trefnant solicited in preparation for a trial of relapse.

In his official account of the trial, Trefnant says that Swinderby appeared before him on June 14, 1391, having been summoned as vehemently defamed of schismatic heresy and of perverse doctrines, both public and occult, to answer charges formulated by *nonnulli Christifideles fideique catholice zelatores*, which had been presented to the bishop for the purpose of informing his office ("ad informandum officium nostrum"). The articles as administered to Swinderby are still addressed to Trefnant and speak of the defendant in the third person. The formulators promise (in the passive voice) that if he should deny the articles, they will be proved by trustworthy witnesses and legitimate documents.[12] When Swynderby submitted an elaborate denial of the articles, after he failed to answer further citations, the anonymous *nonnulli* continued to prosecute the case by bringing in witnesses, awkwardly referred to as *testes pro parte nonnullorum Christifidelium.*[13] Some time after Swynderby's final appearance in court on October 3 (the bishop's account does not give a date), Trefnant declared him a heretic, schismatic, and false informer and seducer of the people, to be shunned by all until he deserved to be reconciled to the Church.[14] There is no explanation of why he was not convicted as relapsed into heresy. Perhaps the bishop and his assessors accepted Swinderby's argument that his abjuration in Lincoln had been forced. At any rate, his sentence ends, in effect, with a mere invitation to

---

[10] McFarlane, p. 129.

[11] See n. 2 above.

[12] Ibid., p. 233. See the translation by John Foxe, *Acts and Monuments*, ed. 4, ed. Josiah Pratt (London, 1877), 3:111. Foxe refers to the charges as "articles by the promoters laid against him" (p. 112).

[13] *Registrum Trefnant*, p. 255.

[14] Ibid., p. 271.

abjure, whereas Swinderby himself, in his subsequent appeal to the king's justices and to the knights of Parliament, pointed out that a heresy conviction entailed the death penalty,[15] and, as we saw above, he claimed to have been threatened by death in the 1382 trial. The archbishop's letter of May 4, cited above, alludes to the death penalty when it says he wishes to prevent Swinderby from infecting other people, lest their blood be required at his hands in an extreme judgment ("ne ipsorum sanguis in extremo judicio, quod absit, de nostris manibus requiratur"), but it pronounced no penalty against Swinderby himself. It may be that the authorities were as yet reluctant to impose the ultimate sanction demanded by Church law.[16]

Trefnant also reports on the trial of Walter Brute, which began soon after Swynderby trial. According to the rubric, the process was promoted from the bishop's own office and also at the instance of certain Christian faithful ("ex officio promotus ac eciam ad instanciam quorundam Christifidelium").[17] This terminology is in contrast to the later common formula, according to which it was the judge's office that was promoted, not the trial.[18] This time we are shown the *quidam Christifideles* presenting the charges to the bishop and taking an active-voice role: "We give and exhibit and intend to prove" first of all that Brute, being gravely defamed, was cited to appear several times before Trefnant's predecessor, Bishop Gilbert, and so on.[19]

Trefnant then reveals the chief of the *quidam* as Walter Pryde, penitentiary of the Hereford Cathedral, when he recounts that Pryde and his colleagues presented to him, formally sitting in judgment, two public instruments against Brute: one was a witnessed statement made by him on October 14, 1391, that Swynderby had been wrongly convicted on the preceeding October 3; the second was a notarized

---

[15] Ibid., p. 272. McFarlane, p. 133, says that there is no record of any reaction to this appeal. But the *Fasciculi* reports that Swinderby made an appeal to Richard II and to the audience of the duke of Lancaster (John of Gaunt) during his 1382 trial; as a result, the trial was recessed and the matter committed to Parliament, which decreed that it should be sent back to the bishop (p. 340).

[16] On the theoretical availability of the death penalty for heresy before the 1401 legislation, see Alison McHardy, "*De heretico comburendo,* 1401," *Lollardy and the Gentry in the Later Middle Ages*, ed. Margaret Aston and Colin Richmond (1997, forthcoming).

[17] *Registrum Trefnant*, p. 278.

[18] I discuss these matters in *The Matrimonial Trials of Henry VIII* (Stanford, 1976), p. 266, where I cite the commission given to the vicar-general of the bishop of Winchester in 1535: he is authorized to proceed "ad alicujus partis procurationem, promotionem, sive instantiam, etiam ex officio mero, mixto, vel promoto."

[19] *Registrum Trefnant*, p. 279.

statement of Brute's assertions to the bishop on January 19, 1392 against tithes and the taking of oaths, and his admission that earlier in the month he had eaten and communicated with Swynderby. The bishop then ordered the two conclusions to be put in writing and given to Brute.[20] The second document seems to be an official report of a session of the trial not otherwise recorded. In fact nothing else of the trial is recorded until the end. We are not told how Brute was originally summoned and charged with the articles formulated by the *quidam*, nor how he responded. But it is clear from the report of the January 19 session that at least in part of his response he stated his present belief rather than answering charges of past actions or statements (which was all that was required by the *ordo juris*).

We do not know whether he was forced to speak his mind on his beliefs, rather than addressing the previously listed charges of committed offenses. The bishop simply says that Brute presented to him, partly in person and partly through messengers, various papers written in his own hand in reply to the conclusions and articles which Trefnant had assigned to him at various times and places for his response.[21] The resulting prolix treatise does not refer directly to any objected article but simply details his views on various points, enveloped in clouds of personal philosophy.[22]

The final days of the trial are not recounted as part of letters patent from the bishop, like the first part, but rather are described in a third-person narrative. By the time that Brute finished his response, the trial had gone on for almost two years, to the latter half of 1393. The bishop set October 3 and the days following for his sentence, but no sentence is recorded. Rather, we are told that, in the presence of seventeen theologians (including Nicholas Hereford, who had been tried for heresy in 1382 and excommunicated as a fugitive from justice, and who finally abjured in 1390) and two canonists, three days were spent in showing Brute the heresies and errors in his writings. On October 6 he read a simple statement submitting himself to the Gospel, the Church, the four Latin Fathers, and Bishop Trefnant, whereupon a theologian preached on St. Paul's text, "Noli altum sapere, sed time" ("Be not high-minded, but fear," Rom. 11:20).[23] There follows a list of the "conclusions, heresies and errors condemned

[20] Ibid., pp. 283–85.
[21] Ibid., p. 285.
[22] Ibid., pp. 285–358.
[23] Ibid., pp. 395–60.

by Bishop John and his assessors on October 6,"[24] but Brute himself does not seem to have been convicted of heresy, and his submission to the bishop's correction does not look like an abjuration. In his opening statement, Brute had said that he would willingly accept correction from anyone who would show him his errors by scriptural reasons,[25] so that perhaps he was exonerated of formal heresy. Heresy is defined later in the register, at the end of the "sentences" of the chancellor of Cambridge and other Cambridge scholars against Swinderby's doctrines, thus: "Heresy is a false dogma contrary to the Catholic faith and the determination of the Church, which is pertinaciously defended," and a heretic is defined as one who invents such a new doctrine or who follows and pertinaciously defends one invented by others.[26] The crucial element of pertinacity must have been judged lacking in Brute.

A promoted trial, reported by the Carmelite John Langton in *Fasciculi zizaniorum*, was conducted by Archbishop Courteney in 1392 against the Irish Cistercian Henry Crump. Crump was examined by the archbishop on ten questionable conclusions that he had allegedly defended at Oxford, which he denied. But on three of the conclusions he was accused by way of denunciation ("per modum denuntiationis accusatus") by a Dominican friar named John Paris, acting on the occasion as promotor for the archbishop ("tanquam per promotorem officii domini Cantuariensis in hac parte"), and he was convicted by the depositions of nine witnesses and compelled to abjure.[27]

Courteney's successor, Archbishop Arundel, used his chancellor, Robert Hallum, to serve in effect as his promotor in the trial of the Lollard William Sawtrey in 1401, calling him the "organ of his voice," and employing him to read the articles and the sentence.[28] In the same year Hallum served as promotor in the trial of a London parish

---

[24] Ibid., pp. 360–65.

[25] Ibid., pp. 285–86.

[26] Ibid., p. 393. The Cambridge sentences are given immediately after the list of Brute's condemned views, on pp. 365–93. On p. 394, *error, blasphemia*, and *scisma* are defined.

[27] *Fasciculi*, pp. 343–48. Langton identifies himself on p. 348; he adds that a little later there was discovered a letter from the bishop of Meath to the University of Oxford, dated 1 April 1385, recounting the trial in which he had found Crump guilty as an impenitent and obstinate heretic on 18 March of the same year; the letter follows on pp. 349–56; then he appends a letter from Richard II to Oxford, dated 30 March 1393, suspending Crump from teaching and summoning him to his council to respond to charges of spreading heresy—but with no mention of his previous convictions (pp. 358–59).

[28] Wilkins, 3:256. For a chronology of Sawtrey's trial, see McHardy, "*De heretico.*"

priest, Robert Bowelond, who was delated to Arundel during his visitation of the diocese of Coventry and Lichfield, for "incest" and grave incontinence with a nun from a priory in the diocese. Bowelond may have been the man of this name identified by William Thorpe as an early follower of Wyclif;[29] he chose for his judge Philip Repingdon, one of the Oxford Wycliffites convicted and rehabilitated in 1382, now the abbot of his monastery of canons regular at Leicester. He denied the charge, and proofs of witnesses and other evidences sufficient for conviction were produced at the promotion of Hallum and in the presence of the archbishop's commissary and other clerics deputed by the archbishop for the purpose.[30]

We have seen that Archbishop Courteney considered Swynderby convicted a second time by notoriety in 1391. When Courteney conducted a visitation of the Lincoln diocese in 1391, he established by the testimony of witnesses as well as by public fame and the notoriety of the fact itself that Swinderby had relapsed.[31] In 1389 he had used visitation witnesses not only to establish the initial public fame of alleged heretics at Leicester, but also to convict them by notoriety. However, when they subsequently appeared before him to be tried in person, he clearly did not consider them to have been convicted and then relapsed; rather, he received their confession of heresies and errors as a first conviction.[32] On the same day that he convicted the Lollards of Leicester as notorious heretics, Courteney also dealt with an anchorite named Matilda (Maud) who had been reported as infected with Lollard doctrines. She was first examined (at her hermitage, according to Wilkins's interpretation) on the same questionable conclusions that the others had been accused of,[33] and, because her

---

[29] William Thorpe, *The Testimony of William Thorpe*, ed. Anne Hudson, *Two Wycliffite Texts* (Oxford, 1993), p. 93; see notes, p. 111.

[30] Wilkins, 3:262–63.

[31] Wilkins, 3:215: "prout nuper coram nobis in visitatione nostra metropolitica prefate Lincolniensis diocesis ex plurimorum fide dignorum attestatione, ac alias fama publica et facti notorietate, que nulla poterant tergiversatione celari, referente, informationem accepimus evidentem."

[32] Ibid., pp. 208–12; see the more recent edition by Joseph Henry Dahmus, *The Metropolitan Visitations of William Courteney, Arbishop of Canterbury, 1381–1396* (Urbana, 1950), pp. 164–72; see esp. p. 171 (Wilkins, p. 211 col. 1): "de heresibus et erroribus per viam notoriam convictos, excommunicatos denunciavimus, a Christi fidelibus evitandos." Their subsequent appearance in court, confession, abjuration, and reception of penance follow.

[33] Wilkins, p. 209: "Dominus archiepiscopus ad eandem Matildem sic reclusam *misit, et* ipsam super conclusionibus, heresibus, et erroribus predictis diligenter examinavit"; Dahmus, *Metropolitan*, p. 166, omits the italicized words, and assumes that

answers to the *interrogata* were not clear but rather sophistical, the archbishop assigned a day and time for her to appear before him and respond "concerning certain articles and interrogatories about the aforesaid heresies and errors to be objected to her for the correction and salvation of her soul."[34] In other words, an informal interrogation preceded a formal presentation of charges and interrogations in an inquisitory trial. She confessed her errors, and asked for and received pardon.[35]

After the condemnations of 1382, there was still concern in England with identifying and condemning Wycliffian errors, but there is no clear example of their being used *en bloc* in court in the way in which they were administered to Repingdon and others. However, Archbishop Arundel did seem to have some such list of errors ready to apply to the priest William Thorpe when he confronted him in 1407. According to Thorpe's autobiographical account, Arundel considered his reputation as a Lollard well established, and he urged a streamlined process: "I will, shortly, that thou swear now here to me that thou shalt forsake all the opinions which the sect of Lollers holdeth and is slandered with, so that after this time, neither privily nor apertly, thou hold none opinion which I shall, after that thou hast sworn, rehearse here to thee."[36] When Thorpe declined this invitation to abjure, the archbishop produced certified testimony from Shrewsbury that Thorpe had preached five specific errors there, which Thorpe denied. Then, at the suggestion of one of his assistants, Arundel asked him to explain then and there what he held about each of the five alleged errors. At another clerk's urging, Thorpe was asked to explicate a dubious-sounding assertion ("It is a sin to swear well") from a sermon of St. John Chrysostom, which was found in the possession of one of Thorpe's associates. Thorpe reports, "I was some deal aghast to answer hereto, for I had not busied me to study about the wit thereof," but he says that the archbishop was satisfied with his impromptu explanation.[37]

Courteney summoned the recluse to him (p. 49); but something is clearly missing from the text as he gives it.

[34] "Super articulis et interrogatoriis predictas hereses et errores concernentibus sibi ad anime sue correctionem et salutem objiciendis."

[35] Dahmus, *Metropolitan*, p. 49.

[36] Thorpe, *Testimony*, p. 34 (I modernize the spelling); see H.A. Kelly, "The Right to Remain Silent: Before and After Joan of Arc," *Speculum* 68 (1993), 992–1026, esp. p. 1008 n. 74.

[37] Thorpe, pp. 76–77.

In the Canterbury Convocation of 1407, held at Oxford, Archbishop Arundel prohibited the reading (teaching) of any work by Wyclif or anyone else since his time without first being officially approved, and no translation of the Scriptures made in the time of Wyclif or later was to be read without episcopal or provincial license.[38] The constitutions were officially published in 1409, and in the same year Arundel set about compiling a new list of Wycliffian heresies and errors. His Oxford committee emerged with 267 propositions, which were condemned in a Canterbury synod in 1411. The list was for-

---

[38] See Joseph H. Dahmus, *The Prosecution of John Wyclyf* (New Haven, 1952), p. 152; but Dahmus errs in saying that the archbishop's constitutions dealt only with Wyclif's translations of the Bible; rather, they dealt with all translations of the Bible. For the text, see Wilkins, 3:317, and also William Lyndwood, *Provinciale* 5.4.3 (1432; Oxford, 1679; repr. Farnborough, 1968), p. 286, and in the final appendix, p. 66: "nec legatur aliquis hujusmodi liber, libellus, aut tractatus [containing translations] jam noviter, tempore dicti Johannis Wickliff, sive citra, compositus, sive componendus in posterum," etc. Nicholas Watson, "Censorship and Cultural Change in Late-Medieval England: Vernacular Theology, the Oxford Translation Debate, and Arundel's Constitutions of 1409," *Speculum* 70 (1995) 822–64, p. 825, cites C.R. Cheney, "William Lyndwood's *Provinciale*," *Medieval Texts and Studies* (Oxford, 1973), pp. 158–84 at 172 n. 7, as saying that the constitutions were issued in 1409, two years after their "first drafting"; but what Cheney says is that they were first *issued* in 1407 and finally published in 1409. Watson's characterization of the constitutions on pp. 827–28 contains a number of errors, some induced by reliance on John Foxe's paraphrase. The constitutions do not "impose limits on the discussion of theological questions in the schools," as long as articles determined by the Church are not called into question (no. 9); they do not require a monthly inquiry "into the views of every student at the university" but only an inquiry as to whether any student is holding suspect doctrines (no. 11); they do not prohibit the study of Wyclif's works altogether, but only such as are not approved by a panel of twelve censors; the panel is not to be appointed by the archbishop but by one or both universities, as the archbishop thinks best (no. 6); not all authorized preachers are required to present themselves for examination by the ordinary, for the parochial clergy are exempt (no. 1); preachers are forbidden to discuss the sins of the clergy only when no clergy are in the audience, and similarly they are not to discuss lay sins before an entirely clerical audience (no. 3); there is no prohibition against preaching the sacraments, as long as orthodox doctrine is followed (no. 4); only temporary parochial clergy are ordered to restrict themselves to preaching what is expressly contained in Peckham's *Ignorantia sacerdotum* (no. 1); no ban of subject matter is extended to schoolmasters—except, of course, anything contrary to the determinations of the Church! (no. 5)—and there is no prohibition of "all argument over matters of faith outside universities"; there is a prohibition against the unauthorized reading, not ownership, of new translations of Scripture (no. 7). Finally, Watson's assertion (p. 892 n. 16) that *translatio* in medieval texts "routinely refers to acts of interpretation or exegesis or to 'the exposition of meaning in another language'" is dubious, and is supported only by reference to a twelfth-century Italian dictionary; no such usage has been recorded in England: see R.E. Latham, *Revised Medieval Latin Word-List from British and Irish Sources, with Supplement* (Oxford, 1980).

warded to Rome for further condemnation.[39] But in two high-profile cases dealt with by Arundel, those of the tailor John Badby in 1410 and the knight John Oldcastle in 1413, the defendants were interrogated only on the specific charges against them. In both cases, however, the questions were aimed not at establishing the truth of the charges, that they had propagated heretical ideas, but at determining whether they currently endorsed those ideas. In Badby's case, he had already been convicted in the previous year, after being delated to Bishop Peverel of Worcester for having held, taught, and publicly maintained a heretical view of the Eucharist. In that original trial also, instead of requiring him to confess or deny his guilt of the charged crime, the bishop simply asked him what he believed on the subject. Under Peverel's interrogation, Badby readily acknowledged that he firmly held the implicated doctrine, and his response served as the basis of Arundel's review in Convocation. Arundel urged Badby to revoke his assertion of belief, and, when he refused, his previous conviction was ratified.[40]

Oldcastle was delated directly to Archbishop Arundel, who summoned him to trial on five charges. After being excommunicated for defying the summons, he was arrested and brought before the archbishop, who recited the charges and offered to absolve him of the excommunication. Oldcastle responded by reading a prepared statement of his beliefs. Upon consultation with assessors, Arundel said that he must respond to the articles. But rather than asking him whether he had committed the specified crimes, he said that Oldcastle must say whether he believed that material bread remained after consecration and whether it was necessary to confess to a priest. When Oldcastle refused to respond (as was his right), Arundel said that if he did not make a clear response he could declare him a heretic. Then, "taking pity on him," the archbishop gave him a set of four articles in English, all concerning present belief: "How believe ye this article?" or "How feel ye this article?" After hearing his responses, Arundel declared him a heretic, saying that he was unwilling to confess his error or purge himself of it or to renounce it ("errorem suum noluerit confiteri, aut se purgare de eodem, nec etiam detestari").[41] We note that Oldcastle was not put under oath, perhaps because

---

[39] Wilkins, 3:322, 339–51; Dahmus, *Prosecution*, pp. 152–53.
[40] Wilkins, 3:325–28.
[41] Ibid., 3:353–56.

he refused to be absolved of excommunication, and, in spite of the archbishop's implied claim in the sentence, he was not offered compurgation.

A group of eight suspected heretics from Bristol, some of whom had connections with Oldcastle, were treated differently. The record is rather complicated and needs an overview. The suspects were indicted before royal commissioners in 1413 or 1414 on charges of Lollardy and turned over to the local ordinary, Nicholas Bubwith, bishop of Bath and Wells, for ecclesiastical trial. They successfully purged themselves in mid-1414 and early 1415, but it was only on June 18, 1417, that the king requested verification of the suspects' claim of purgation; presumably the suspects had been kept in prison in the meantime. On October 4, the bishop's office replied with an account of seven of the defendants. The king inquired again on November 28 about the other suspect, Christina More, and reply was made on January 10, 1418.[42]

Four of the suspects were delivered on June 28, 1414, to Bubwith's commissioners. On July 5, they were brought before the bishop himself to "respond upon matter of Lollardy and to other articles concerning the Catholic faith and the determination of Holy Church." They took an oath to tell the truth to all interrogations ("ad omnia interroganda"). Bishop Bubwith first interrogated Edmund Brown on the fourteen articles of faith, the ten commandments, the seven sacraments, the seven works of mercy, and the "seven cardinal virtues," asking him how he thought ("interrogavit qualiter sentiit") about each. Brown responded that he thought well and as a Catholic about them, and that he had never thought or held the contrary and never would do so. Similarly, when asked about the seven mortal sins, he replied that they were all to be avoided. The other three defendants responded in the same way.[43] We note that they were not required to expound upon any of the articles and risk making damaging misstatements of doctrine.

Then the bishop objected to them *ex officio* and interrogated them, under their oath, asking them to say whether they were Lollards, or had read any books of Lollards, and so on, and whether the articles

---

[42] *The Register of Nicholas Bubwith, Bishop of Bath and Wells, 1417–1424*, ed. Thomas Scott Holmes, 2 vols. (London, 1914), 1:283–90 (no. 716), 298 (no. 745). See John A.F. Thomson, *The Later Lollards, 1414–1520* (Oxford, 1965), pp. 22–24.

[43] *Register of Bubwith*, pp. 284–86.

upon which they had been indicted (before the royal commissioners) were true, and whether the fame about them in Bristol, that they were Lollards, was true or false. They all declared their innocence, and offered to purge themselves. Purgation with twelve compurgators each was ordered on July 23, and a call was put out for volunteers to come forth and speak against the defendants and impede the compurgation. But no such opponents appeared, and the purgation was successfully performed before the bishop's official, John Welles. However, in spite of the fact that they succeeded in clearing themselves, they "abjured in the form of law" (that is, no doubt, they were forced to abjure) all heresy and all Lollardy, declaring that from then on ("decetero") they would abstain from all suspect gatherings. Those present included the mayor and one of the sheriffs of Bristol.[44] On the same day, July 23, Christina More's trial took place, with the same result. She made her purgation on October 23 before John Storthwayt, the bishop's commissary general.[45]

The other three suspects were delivered from the king's prison in Bristol by the mayor and a sheriff, acting on a royal writ, on January 30, 1415, to Storthwayt, and he held their trial on the same day (Bishop Bubwith was by now at the Council of Constance).[46] Concerning the articles of faith, virtues, and so on they made responses similar to those of the the first four. Then the commissary, acting "*ex officio* and in the forum of mere correction of soul," objected to them the crime of heresy and error, in general and in particular, and especially concerning the chapters and articles of Lollardy on which they had been indicted and defamed; all objections met with constant denials.[47] When asked about the fame of the crime of Lollardy that labored against them, they responded with a strong declaration that it was true, *penitus animis* ("to the depths of minds"?), and they earnestly and humbly asked to clear themselves by purgation or any other reasonable and legal means. Purgation was set for February 25 in the same way as before, except that this time fifteen compurgators

[44] Ibid., pp. 286–88.

[45] Ibid., p. 298.

[46] A.B. Emden, *Biographical Register of the University of Oxford to A.D. 1500* (Oxford, 1957, repr. with additions, 1989), 1:295.

[47] *Register Bubwith*, 1:288–89: "Crimen heresis et erroris, tam in genere quam in specie, ac presertim capitula et articulos Lollardie super quibus, ut premittitur, fuerunt indictati et publice diffamati, eis et eorum cuilibet ex officio in foro mere correccionis anime per dictum commissarium objectum et objecta, constanter negarunt et negavit quilibet eorundem."

were required of each. The suspects were all cleared, and after making their abjuration, they were restored to good fame.[48]

We see, then, that the trials of the Bristol suspects did not follow the inquisitorial procedure of summoning defamed persons, listing and explaining the charges on which they were defamed, proving that the bad fame against them really existed, and then, when the truth of the charges could not be proved by confessions or documents or witnesses, subjecting them to purgation. Instead, they were interrogated under oath about their beliefs, then required to respond to the truth of the charges on which they had been indicted in the secular court, and finally required to say whether the fame against them was true. If they had denied the truth of the fame, then the bishop and his delegates would haved been obliged by law to prove the existence of the fame before receiving witnesses to the truth of the charges or ordering purgation. But since the defendants admitted that they were defamed, but groundlessly, and they themselves requested purgation, the ordering of purgation could be considered procedurally regular. But what about the abjuration?

William Lyndwood, writing between 1423 and 1430,[49] sets forth the law on abjuration in his commentary on the 1407/07 legislation of Archbishop Arundel: "You should know that everyone who is gravely suspect of heresy and wishes to return to the unity of the Church can be compelled to abjure heresy."[50] But Lyndwood is speaking of convicted suspects, of those who, by means of witnesses or other lawful proofs, are convicted of having said or done something suggestive of heresy (in this case, holding that the Church cannot make laws restricting preaching) and formally pronounced by the judge to be, not heretics, but suspected of heresy. Then, unless these suspects repudiate the proved opinion or action, they are to be declared heretics.[51] But in addition to such repudiation, Arundel also

[48] Ibid., p. 289.

[49] C.R. Cheney, "William Lyndwood's *Provinciale*," *Medieval Texts and Studies* (Oxford 1973), pp. 158–84, at 160.

[50] William Lyndwood, *Provinciale* (1432; Oxford, 1679; repr. Farnborough, 1968), 5.5.1, p. 292, v. *abjuraverint* (note *h*): "Scire enim debes quod omnis qui est graviter suspectus de heresi, volens redire ad unitatem ecclesie, potest compelli heresim abjurare," citing Alexander IV, *Accusatus, Sext* 5.2.8 (Friedberg, 2:1071–72).

[51] Lyndwood, loc. cit., v *convicti* (note *f*): "Per testes vel alias probationes legitimas, et in hac convictione requiritur pronunciatio, ut dixi supra, *De simonia*, c. *Nulli*, v. *convictus* [p. 281 note *o*], et debet hec pronunciatio esse, non scilicet ut pronuncietur hereticus, sed ut pronuncietur sic dixisse verbo, actuve fecisse, per quod satis apparet

requires them to make an abjuration in due form, and it is here that Lyndwood makes the above statement.[52]

According to the law, then, since the Bristol defendants were not convicted, they were wrongly required to make an abjuration, and it should follow that if they were later convicted of falling into heresy it ought not be considered a relapse but rather a first conviction. There is a good chance that this would have been the judgment if the case had arisen in Convocation, because Lyndwood was now effectively in charge of defining Church law in the province of Canterbury. Three months or so before the first of the Bristol suspects were delivered for trial, Henry Chichele had taken over as archbishop of Canterbury, and on August 1, 1414, he appointed Lyndwood his chancellor and auditor of causes. By 1417 he was the official of Canterbury, the chief judge of the province under the archbishop. His views on relapse can be seen in the 1421 trial of William Taylor in convocation. The archbishop turned towards the jurists present and asked them to consult their books on what was to be done in a case of relapse. Lyndwood replied immediately (*incontinenti*) with a written response: 1) A suspect of heresy, cited and absent through contumacy, becomes vehemently suspect, but this is not sufficient for a criminal conviction. 2) Deliberate continuance such contumacy changes the vehement presumption of guilt to violent presumption, which suffices for automatic conviction. 3) If such a person returns before condemnation and is ready to abjure, he should be allowed to do so. 4) A person who abjures heresy in a general way and later falls into a species of heresy is considered relapsed. 5) A relapsed heretic is to be left to the secular court without hope of remission.[53] He does not make it clear in this statement, as he does in his later gloss, that before such a defendant is required to make an abjuration he must be formally sentenced as vehemently suspect (in this case,

---

eum sentire quod ecclesia non posset sic statuere, et sic per consequens de heresi suspectum esse: et nisi resipiscat, pro heretico damnandum fore."

[52] Further on, 5.5.2, p. 296, v. *simpliciter* (note *d*), Lyndwood asks whether a person who abjured one form of heresy and later fell into another form of heresy should be considered relapsed. He cites John Andrew as saying no, Archdeacon Guy of Baysio as saying yes; he finds an argument to support Andrew, and then notes that Andrew himself in another gloss supports the positive response, which is also that of Geminianus (Dominic of San Gimignano), an exact contemporary of Lyndwood's (he died before 1436). Geminianus says that a person who abjures one form of heresy can be seen to abjure all forms because they are all connected.

[53] *The Register of Henry Chichele, Archbishop of Canterbury, 1414–1443*, ed. E.F. Jacob, 4 vols. (Oxford, 1983–47), 3:168.

for contemptuously refusing to appear in court). In his commentary, he defines relapse as the repetition of the same fault (*iteratio ejusdem delicti*).[54] He goes on to distinguish between true relapse (one conviction of heresy followed abjuration and then by another conviction of heresy) from fictitious relapse, drawing on the decretal *Accusatus* of Alexander IV, according to which one of the convictions, before or after abjuration, is not of heresy but of vehement suspicion of heresy (like proven association with heretics).[55]

An early case of relapse held before the archbishop in which Lyndwood served as examiner and assessor was the trial of John Claydon on August 17, 1415. The form of the trial is not entirely clear. Only one item is objected to him, namely, that he had been and still was notoriously defamed of heresy and also vehemently and notoriously suspect. He responded by publicly and judicially confessing that for twenty years he had been reputed in the view of the common people to be vehemently suspect of Lollardy and heretical depravity, and notoriously defamed of the same, such that in the time of Bishop Braybrook of London (1381–1404) he was kept in prison for five years, until in the time of Henry IV he made an abjuration before the king's chancellor John Scarle (in office until March 9, 1401). The rest of the trial seems to consist of interrogations. Chichele asked him if he had ever abjured heresy before anyone else, and he publicly and judically confessed that he had made a solemn abjuration before Archbishop Arundel about two years later ("circa biennium elapsum") in a Convocation of the clergy at St. Paul's, when, because of the aforesaid vehement suspicion and infamy he was charged with articles allegedly savoring of heresy and error and contrary to the determination of the Church. Included in the abjuration was a promise to abstain from all communication with men defamed and suspect of these opinions.[56] This was apparently not considered a second conviction, perhaps because his earlier abjuration was not preceded by a trial or because Chancellor Scarle had no ecclesiastical jurisdiction over him.

Archbishop Chichele then asked Claydon if he possessed any books written in English. He responded that he could not deny that he had possessed several English books, for it was because of these books that

---

[54] Lyndwood, loc. cit., v. *relapsus* (p. 296 note *l*).
[55] Ibid., v. *relapso* (note *n*); see n. 28 above for *Accusatus*.
[56] *Register of Chichele*, 4:132–33.

he was arrested by the mayor of London, and he believed that the mayor had the books in his custody. The mayor, who was present, testified that this was so, and in his opinion they were the worst books he had ever read. Regarding one of the books, Claydon confessed that he had had it copied and had heard about a fourth of it read. On being questioned whether he thought the content of the book was good and Catholic, he answered that much of what he had heard was very salutary, and that he particularly liked a sermon that was copied there. Finally, Claydon was questioned about Richard Baker, and he confessed that he had had frequent communication with him, even though he knew that he was suspected or defamed of heresy.[57]

After these confessions, Chichele committed the books to Robert Gilbert, master of theology, to Lyndwood, doctor of both laws, and to other clerics for examination, and he ordered the admission of three witnesses. The first, David Berde, a twenty-three-year-old servant of Claydon's, illiterate, like his master, was asked three questions: Did he know the book exhibited to him by the examiner, which certain persons vehemently suspect of heresy called *The Lantern of Light*? Did he know that Claydon read this book or had it read to him? Did he know if Claydon approved, held, or taught the contents of the book as good and Catholic? Berde responded that he did know the book and knew that it contained the ten commandments in English and other matters which he could not remember. He said that Claydon listened to it and commended it and never rejected anything he heard in it as suspect. But Berde could remember nothing more than the first commandment being read from the book. The second witness, another illiterate servant, Saundre Phelip, aged fifteen, on being asked the same three questions, testified that the book was copied and corrected in Claydon's house and in his presence, and that Richard Baker and a person named Montfort, who were held to be vehemently suspect of Lollardy, on several days came and discussed the book with Claydon. The third witness, Baltazar Mero, aged thirty, concorded with Berde, except that he could not remember anything of the content of the book. He added that he had seen Claydon often communicate on articles of Sacred Scripture with Baker and Montfort, who he said were held to be suspect of Lollardy.[58]

Then a committee consisting neither of Gilbert nor Lyndwood but

[57] Ibid., p. 133.
[58] Ibid., pp. 133–36.

of four friars, all masters of theology, reported on the books: they all contained many heresies and errors, and fifteen in the *Lantern* were singled out. Finally, after consulting with Lyndwood and other assessors, Chichele decreed that the books were to be burned, and, because the assessors believed Claydon to have relapsed into abjured heresy, because of what had been confessed and testified to and proved by the evidence of facts and deeds, he read the definitive sentence against him, delivering him to the secular judge.[59]

Apart from the severity of the conclusion, the procedure in this case seems regular enough. Claydon was not quizzed about his present beliefs, except in an attempt to discover whether he had knowingly supported heresy in the past, but it would seem that the results were inconclusive, since he did not admit to supporting any specific doctrine, either then or in the past. The evidence presented about his possession of suspect books and consorting with a suspected Lollard should have led only to a conviction of vehement suspicion of heresy, and, according to Lyndwood's later explication of Alexander IV's decretal, this would not have been sufficient even for a fictitious conclusion of relapse, if his first conviction under Arundel was also for no more than suspicion.

The finding of heresies and errors in Claydon's books is not said to have contributed to his condemnation, but only to the decision to have them burned. The possession of suspect English books was not covered in the constitutions of 1407/09, but it was incorporated into the constitution that Chichele issued in the year following the Claydon trial.[60]

Meanwhile, at Constance, the posthumous trial of John Wyclif took place in 1415, as did the trials and condemnations of two of his Bohemian admirers, John Hus and Jerome of Prague. The proceedings against Hus were notable above all in his first being required to write his opinion of propositions ascribed to Wyclif.[61] But though Hus's examination on Wycliffite doctrines does not seem to have played a part in his formal trial, it may have influenced the procedure set forth in the bull of Martin V, *Inter cunctas pastoralis cure solicitudines*,

---

59 Ibid., pp. 136–38.

60 Ibid., 3:18–19, *Statutum editum contra hereticos*, 1 July 1416: archeacons and episcopal judges are to make inquisition not only into those holding heresies and errors but also "those possessing suspect books written in the common English tongue." For the procedures called for in this statute, see Jacob's introduction, 1:cxxxii, but see also my correction of his account, in my "English Kings and the Fear of Sorcery," *Mediaeval Studies* 39 (1977), 206–38, pp. 222–23 n. 64.

61 For details, see my "Trial Procedures."

issued on February 22, 1418, and addressed to all archbishops, bishops, and inquisitors of heretical depravity, especially those in Bohemia and Moravia, where, the pope says, the errors of Wyclif, Hus, and Jerome are still flourishing. The prelates of those regions are like silent watchdogs, unable bark, not being ready, with the Apostle, "to revenge all disobedience" (2 Cor. 10:6).[62] The remedies that he first enjoins are entirely standard and in accord with the established *ordo juris*. All persons who are found by a competent ecclesiastical judge to be "suspect by suspicion alone," specifically of favoring the doctrine or any article of the above-named heresiarchs, are to undergo canonical purgation, and, if they fail, to be condemned as heretics. It should go without saying, though in fact the pope goes ahead and says it, that if anyone is actually found guilty of such an offense, he is to be canonically punished.[63] But then Pope Martin orders a method of dealing with suspects that goes beyond previously approved inquisitorial procedure. Lest prejudice and scandal should befall the orthodox faith on the pretext of ignorance, he says, he rehearses the forty-five articles of Wyclif originally condemned at the council, together with the thirty condemned articles of Hus, and orders them transmitted to the kingdom of Bohemia and to other places where this doctrine has festered; he requires bishops and inquisitors to compel all persons defamed or suspected of such pestiferous taint to respond under oath to the individual articles according to interrogatories, given below, that are suitable to each article, under pain of *confessatum crimen*, excommunication, suspension, interdict, or other formidable canonical or legal penalties, when and however they see fit and the nature of the circumstances requires.[64] The thirty-seven questions that follow

[62] Martin V, *Inter cunctas*, ed. Hermann von der Hardt, *Magnum oecumenicum constantiense concilium*, 6 vols. (Frankfurt, 1697–1700, 1742) 4:1518–31, and John Dominic Mansi, *Sacrorum conciliorum nova et amplissima collectio*, 27 (Venice, 1784) 1204–15; I follow the text and numbered sections of the *Bullarium romanum*, 26 vols. (Turin, 1857–67), 4:665–67, here citing the salutation, introduction, and §1, p. 665 (Hardt, 1518–20, Mansi, 1204).

[63] Ibid., §9, pp. 667–68 (Hardt, 1522, Mansi, 1206).

[64] Ibid., §11, pp. 668–69 (Hardt, 1522–23, Mansi, 1207). The last part of the text reads: "Precipimus et mandamus ut quilibet eorum . . . omnes infamatos seu suspectos de tam pestifera labe sub confessati criminis, excommunicationis, suspensionis, interdicti, aut alia formidabili pena canonica vel legali, prout, quando et quemadmodum eis videatur expedire et facti requireret qualitas, ad singulos hujusmodi articulos per juramentum corporaliter prestitum, . . . juxta infrascripta interrogatoria ad quemlibet articulum convenientia, respondere compellant." Wyclif's articles are given in §12, pp. 669–71 (Hardt, 1523–25, Mansi, 1207–09), and Hus's in §13, pp. 671–73 (Hardt, 1525–27, Mansi, 1209–11), condemned at the council on 4 May

the articles are headed by the instruction: "Upon the aforesaid articles, each person suspected of them or arrested for asserting them is to be interrogated according to the following method" ("Super premissis autem articulis, quilibet de eis suspectus seu in eorum assertione deprehensus juxta modum interrogetur"). The first questions concern the suspect's personal knowledge of the three heresiarchs (1–2), whether he honored them after their death (3–4), and whether he believes in the authority of the Council of Constance and its condemnations (5–8). Does he possess their books? (9–10). Especially if he is literate, he is to be asked if he believes (that is, approves and considers valid) the sentence of the council on the 45 articles of Wyclif and the 30 of Hus (11). The next questions concern the lawfulness of swearing, and the sinfulness of perjury (12–14). The remaining questions concern matters of faith connected with the heresiarchs' errors, but phrased positively, so that a "yes" answer would be an assertion of orthodoxy: for instance, "Whether he believes that a Christian who contemns the reception of the sacraments of confirmation or extreme unction or the solemnization of matrimony commits a mortal sin" (19).[65]

The pope continues: If anyone is found defamed or suspect by secret information or otherwise of the doctrine of these heresiarchs, he is to be cited to appear before the bishop or other ecclesiastical judge with jurisdiction over him, with no proctor or advocate, to respond on oath concerning the aforesaid articles or on other appropriate ones. This letter is to be published, minus the articles and interrogatories (!), and all such heretics are to be denounced as excommunicated.[66] All bishops and other inquisitors are to diligently search out all offenders, and those whom they find to be defamed of such heresy and error, or whom they find, by their own confession or factual evidence, or by other means, to be infected by such taint, they are to punish by excommunication, suspension, interdict, or other appropriate penalties ("eos quos per inquisitionem hujusmodi diffamatos, vel per confessionem eorum seu per facti evidentiam, vel alias, hujusmodi heresis et erroris labe respersos reperietis, auctoritate

---

1215 (Hardt, 4:153–55; Mansi, 27:632–34) and 6 July 1415 (Hardt, 4:407–12; Mansi, 27:754–55), respectively.

[65] Ibid., §14, pp. 673–75 (Hardt, 1527–29, Mansi, 1211–13). The *Bullarium* skips one of the questions, which we can label 28a: "Item, utrum credat religiones ab ecclesia approbatas a sanctis patribus rite et rationabiliter introductas" (last item on p. 1528 of Hardt, 3rd from bottom of col. 1212 of Mansi).

[66] Ibid., §§15–16, pp. 675–76 (Hardt, 1529–30, Mansi, 1213).

predicta etiam per excommunicationis, suspensionis, et interdicti . . . [penas] et per alias penas . . . corrigatis et puniatis"). This sounds as if the merely defamed are to be punished in the same way as those found guilty; but the pope goes on to specify that persons who are defamed of the articles are bound to purge themselves, while those who are convicted of the articles by witnesses or their own confession or other legitimate proofs are to be forced to abjure and undergo fitting punishment, and if they refuse to comply, the judges are to proceed against them *ex officio*, all appeals ceasing, as against heretics, and punish them, even consigning them to the secular court.[67]

At first glance, it might seem that the pope has gone beyond traditional procedure, in allowing defamed defendants who refuse to answer questions to be convicted as if they had confessed the crime. However, though he does not quite say so, he seems to consider the interrogation as part of the purgation process, as incorporated into inquisitorial procedure. According to standard due process, the judge should cite a suspect and charge him with, say, having preached the doctrine of Wyclif and Hus, on the basis of public fame to that effect. If the judge can prove no more than the existence of the fame, then he can require the defendant to purge himself by affirming his innocence under oath. Pope Martin has added the requirement, in order to make the charge and the purgatory assertion perfectly clear, of having the defendant respond to clear questions of heterodoxy and orthodoxy, which require only positive or negative answers to establish the defendant's orthodoxy. It would seem to be a reasonable procedure. What was wrong with it, and why shouldn't the pope impose it? After all, he was in charge!

The answer to what was wrong with the procedure is that it violated the principle that the Church does not judge secret matters,[68] since

---

[67] Ibid., §17, p. 676 (Hardt, 1530, Mansi, 1213–14).

[68] Enunciated, for example, in the Ordinary Gloss to Gratian, D. 32 c. 11, *Erubescant,* where Urban II says, "de manifestis quidem loquimur; secretorum autem cognitor et judex est Deus" ("We are speaking of manifest thing, whereas of secret things God is the one who know and judges") (Friedberg, 1:120). The Gloss says, "Ex hoc patet quod ecclesia non judicat de occultis" ("From this it is clear that the Church does not judge concerning hidden things"); see *Corpus juris canonici,* 3 vols. (Rome, 1582; repr. Lyons, 1606), 1:131, v. *secretorum.* Innocent III, writing in two decretals on simony, dated 1199 and 1207, states the principle thus: "Si excessus eorum esset ecclesie manifestus, que non judicat de occultis, pena essent canonica feriendi" ("If their excess were manifest to the Church, which does not judge concerning hidden things, they would deserve canonical punishment"), *Decretales* 5.3.33 (Friedberg, 2:763); "Nobis datum est de manifestis tantummodo judicare. . . . Sine

the questions go beyond the effort to establish specific past crimes to force statements of present belief. This is the sort of thing that only a confessor should be able to ask a penitent within the secrecy of the confessional.

There is extant a copy of *Inter cunctas* addressed to all of the bishops of England,[69] and the whole text was copied into the *Fasciculi zizaniorum.* The bull may have been influential in formulating a somewhat similar system of interrogation of Lollards, which was approved at the Canterbury Convocation of 1428.[70] However, Lyndwood, who participated in the convocation and who vetted at least the *Modus et forma procedendi et processus faciendi contra hereticos* formulated there,[71] did not draw on *Inter cunctas* in when commenting on such matters in the *Provinciale* (in his glosses on the constitutions of 1407/09). He did, however, draw on Continental Imperial law to justify some aspects of the stipulated procedure, namely the extravagant *Ad reprimendum* of Henry VII, Holy Roman Emperor from 1308 to 1313. When Arundell says that "indications" are sufficient for conviction ("sufficit convincere per indicia"), Lyndwood explains *indicia* as slight—though sufficient—demonstrations of guilt, and adds that the word can also be understood as sanctioning procedure not only by accusation and inquisition but also by denunciation, as in the extravagant.[72] When Arundell decrees that the

---

dubio . . . isti apud districtum judicem qui scrutator est cordium et cognitor secretorum culpabiles judicantur" ("It is given to us to judge only concerning manifest things. . . . Without doubt those [who acted with simoniacal intention] are judged guilty by that strict judge who is the scrutinizer of hearts and the knower of secrets"), ibid., 5.3.34.

[69] Hardt, 4:1518–19.

[70] *The Register of Henry Chichele, Archbishop of Canterbury, 1414–1443*, ed. E.F. Jacob, 4 vols. (Oxford, 1983–47), 3:191–92. See Anne Hudson, "The Examination of Lollards," *Bulletin of the Institute of Historical Research* 46 (1973), 145–59, repr. with an appendix in *Lollards and Their Books* (London, 1985), pp. 125–40, at 128–30. *Inter cunctas* is not given in the printed excerpts of the *Fasciculi* manuscript, Oxford, Bodleian MS E. Musaeo 86; it is contained on ff. 138rb–145ra, as Professor Hudson informs me. In her article she deals only with the interrogatories, §14.

[71] *Register of Chichele*, 3:191–92. I accept the identification of the *Modus* with the *Informacio ad procedendum contra hereticos* edited by Hudson, "Examination," pp. 136–39; see Thomson, *Later Lollards*, pp. 224–25, and Hudson, p. 128. The rules of procedure are correct, as far as they go, except that the suspect is wrongly called *hereticus*, as if already convicted, and no mention is made of the need to establish *fama* (which could be omitted by ordinaries, unless the defendant insisted on it).

[72] Lyndwood 5.5.4, p. 302 note *x*: "i.e., per demonstrationes leves, sufficientes tamen. . . . Et potes intelligere *indicia*, ut scilicet non solum procedat contra tales per accusationem vel inquisitionem, sed etiam per denunciationem, sic quod aliqua via data possit constare de commisso crimine, ut patet in extravagante que incipit *Ad reprimendum*, Collatione 11." See *Corpus juris civilis*, ed. John Fehius, 6 vols. (Lyons

trial can proceed even in the defendant's absence, without the case being contested (*lite non contestata*), Lyndwood says that this is founded on *Ad reprimendum*.[73]

A form of abjuration was also approved with the *Modus et forma procedendi*, and in two of the three extant copies of the two documents, including a collection from Lichfield, two lists of articles "upon which heretics or Lollards should be examined" precede the abjuration. Since the articles are in the form of questions rather than propositions, they could only be employed to ascertain present belief, not past teaching, and the only procedurally orthodox use for them (taking the procedure of *Inter cunctas* to be unorthodox) would be to examine suspects who have agreed to abjure all errors previously held, taught, and affirmed, in order to add articles to the formula of abjuration. As the text of the abjuration is given, only two examples are given, followed by an *et cetera*.[74] However, in the register of Thomas Polton, Bishop of Worcester (1426–33), the lists appear in the middle of the manual, after defendants have denied the charges and witnesses have been deposed. There is no procedural justification for interrogating defendants on their beliefs at this stage, and Lyndwood would hardly have sanctioned it on the basis of formal law. Its placement here therefore probably signals an abuse of due process, possibly inspired by *Inter cunctas*.[75] But even the Lichfield sequence would have been a ready

1627, repr. Osnabrück 1966), 5:2:141–67 at 145–46. Bartolus in his gloss to *inquisitio* (col. 145) calls inquisition a *jus novum* not permitted in common law (*de jure communi*) but allowed in canon law when there is *publica fama*. But here he says it is allowed even when there is no fame, referring to Henry VII's second extravagant, *Quoniam nuper*, ad v. *publice vel occulte* (col. 171).

[73] Lyndwood, loc. cit., note *c*: "Istud fundatur in dicta extravagante *Ad reprimendum*."

[74] Hudson, "Examination," p. 136: "ante hanc horam nonnullos articulos et opiniones fidei catholice et determinacioni sancte romane ecclesie repugnantes tenui, docui, et affirmavi, videlicet, quod venerabiles ymagines non sunt venerande seu adorande, ac eciam quod peregrinaciones ad gloriosum Thomam martirem et alia loca pia non sunt licite, etc." These examples correspond roughly to nos. 26 and 28 of the jurist's list (p. 134). The lists appear before the abjuration in the Harley MS (from Lichfield) and the Balliol MS (see pp. 132, 140).

[75] In "Right to Remain Silent," p. 1011 n. 91, I suggested that the Polton sequence was the original placement, but I now agree with Hudson that the Lichfield order makes more sense. In the Polton register, the lists come after section VIII (p. 138), just before the guideline on the use of torture for half-proved crimes. On this latter point, Lyndwood in his *Provinciale* (5.5.4 ad v. *non obstante*, p. 305 note *f*) cites the same laws as the manual, namely, the Clementine *Multorum* (n. 87 above) and Gratian's *Imprimis* (C.2 q.1 c.7, Friedberg, 1:442); see Kelly, "English Kings," p. 213 (cf. pp. 231, 237). Thomson's objection that *Multorum* was not relevant to England because "the inquisition" had not been introduced there (p. 230 n. 3) is not to the point,

invitation to abuse suspects' rights, by quizzing them on their beliefs before charging them with public crimes, or in lieu of charging them.

The 1382 policy of requiring suspects to give opinions on Wycliffite views was used to examine university-trained scholars, and though it could be compared to the Continental abuse of grilling suspects *de se et aliis*, especially when the inquisitors were armed with lists of heresies to guide their questions, it was more likely inspired by scholastic practices in the universities.[76] The final examination of Walter Brute in 1393 also seems to resemble a scholastic discussion. In contrast, the lists of questions attached to the abjuration formula of 1428 may have been primarily devised for the examination of the unlearned. This is John Thomson's assumption: "As many of the Lollards were ignorant and illiterate it would *a priori* seem the only effective way of eliciting their views."[77] If this was indeed their purpose, we can easily see how they could be used to circumvent and not assist due process. In the only case we know of in which one of the lists was used, in the diocese of Bath and Wells in 1448, the articles were put to a very old and blind chaplain named John Yonge, and his responses were later made the basis of accusation before the bishop, who declared him a heretic.[78] It does not appear to have been a fair trial, but the result may have been regarded as educative rather than punitive, for the "mere correction of soul," as Commissary Storthwayt put it in Bristol in 1415. We can perhaps see something of the sort in the 1389 case of Matilda, the recluse of Leicester, treated above, where an informal interrogation gave rise to formal charges along with accompanying questions: *certi articuli et interrogatoria*. But though the outcome might seem benign in these cases, where the suspects were willing to comply, in others they proved not so harmless, for

---

since the decretal sets forth the rights and limitations of bishops as well as papal delegates in conducting heresy inquisitions. Moreover, torture was available to ecclesiastical judges in other kinds of cases, including civil suits; see especially John Teutonicus, Ordinary Gloss to Gratian, C.15 q.6 dictum ante c.1 ad v. *Quod vero* (*Corpus juris canonici*, 3 vols., Lyons, 1606, 1:1080), and see my *Canon Law and the Archpriest of Hita* (Binghamton, 1984), pp. 110–11, 184–85.

[76] See my "Trial Procedures." The decretal *Accusatus* of Alexander IV mentioned above, when it refers to an oath that witnesses take to tell the truth *tam de se quam de aliis* (Friedberg, 2:1072, §3 of the decretal), reflects a stage in the self-incriminatory interrogation of defendants, as practiced on the Continent. See "Right to Remain Silent," p. 1000.

[77] Thomson, p. 226.

[78] *The Register of Thomas Bekynton, Bishop of Bath and Wells, 1443–1465*, ed. H.C. Maxwell-Lyte and M.C.B. Dawes (London, 1934–35), 1:120–27.

instance, in Bishop Alnwick's trials in Norwich.[79] The fact remains that these methods were used to force persons to expose themselves to criminal charges, and to create punishable crimes where none existed before. As Thomson points out, "Examination by questioning could serve to systematize beliefs into a more rigid form than that in which they were in the mind of the accused."[80] To be legal, examinations of this sort should have been confined to the realm of the internal forum in the sacrament of confession. To use such procedures in the external forum was fundamentally contrary to the "Magna Carta of ecclesiastical civil rights" established at the Fourth Lateran Council, which allowed inquisitorial prosecution only for previously committed public crimes. The only concession made later to heresy inquisitors, duly noted in the *Modus et forma procedendi*, was that the identity of endangered witnesses might be concealed.[81]

But it was inevitable that defenders of the faith would find the defense safeguards too confining and would seek ways of bending or ignoring them, with or without the realization that they were going counter to the law. The most ingenious solution to the problem that I know of in England is that encountered in the reign of Queen Mary, where Cranmer, Ridley, and Latimer seem to have been ordered to engage in a formal debate on disputed questions of the nature of the Eucharist before they were tried.[82] Since they acquiesced, all the incriminating evidence that was needed was obtained without violating the canons of due process—except in spirit! But that story remains to be researched and told.

---

[79] N.P. Tanner, ed., *Heresy Trials in the Diocese of Norwich, 1428–1431* (London, 1977); see my "Inquisitorial Due Process," pp. 425–26.

[80] Thomson, p. 229.

[81] Hudson, p. 138, section VIII; Kelly, "Inquisition," pp. 443–44. The text in Hudson should read, "si *tamen* viderit quod ex donacione copie *imineret* periculum," etc. The defendant is allowed to name persons who he suspects may be biased for some reason, say enmity ("puta *inimicicie*").

[82] Foxe, *Acts and Monuments*, 6:439, 767.

VII

ENGLISH KINGS AND THE FEAR OF SORCERY*

In this essay on English kings and the fear of sorcery, I will be dealing chiefly with the monarchs of fifteenth-century England, most of whom are familiar to us from Shakespeare's eight connected history plays, from *Richard II* to *Richard III*. In keeping with the practice of my historical sources, I will use the terms sorcery, magic, and witchcraft to mean the same thing, namely the attempt to foretell or control events either by natural occult powers or by supernatural agency — that is, by recourse to spiritual beings. Even the invocation of God himself could be considered magical, when, for instance, his name appeared in charms; but simple appeals to divine assistance were permitted, even, for example, in the practice of herbal medicine.[1] Sometimes the devil and other evil spirits of Christian theology were specified as active ingredients in the mix of magic, sometimes not. But it can be assumed that all orthodox and learned Christians of the time would explain any instance of what appeared to be effective supernatural magic (any event, therefore, beyond the powers of nature which could not be considered miraculous because of suspect circumstances) as brought about by diabolical or demonic agency. Furthermore, even when the magic was thought to be effected by natural means (for example, the use of poisons or aphrodisiacs), the devil's instigation would easily suggest itself; and even magic that was thought to be totally ineffectual was often attributed to the devil's illusions.[2]

* This essay is an expanded form of a paper read at a symposium on 'Witchcraft and the Occult in History and Art' held at the University of California at Davis on 16-17 February 1974. Another version was read at the Pacific Coast Conference on British Studies, Stanford University, 10 April 1976.

1 See William Lyndwood, writing between 1422 and 1430, glossing the word *incantationes* in Archbishop Pecham's constitution *Ignorantia sacerdotum*: 'Utputa, in collectionibus herbarum, quae medicinales sunt aliquas observationes attendendo, nisi symbolum vel orationem dominicam.' That is to say, the first commandment forbids the use of incantations such as those found in herbals to make the herbs medicinal, unless it is simply a matter of reciting the creed or the Lord's Prayer. See Lyndwood, *Provinciale* 1.11.1 gl. v. *incantationes* (Oxford, 1679; rpt. Farnborough, 1968), p. 55.

2 At the beginning of the chapter on 'Demonic Witchcraft' in my book, ***The Devil, Demonology, and Witchcraft*** (New York, 1968; 2nd ed. Garden City, N.Y., 1974), I limited my discussion of

In spite of what any given magician or witch might think, the orthodox view was that God and the angels would never participate in magical activities, and that the only other spirits in existence available for such participation were the fallen angels — that is Satan and the other devils or demons.[3] Assistance by the devil did not necessarily involve the idea of a pact with the devil or of worshiping the devil. Devil worship was a patristic concept that was revived on the Continent in the Middle Ages, but it only rarely enters into accounts of English witchcraft. I consider it unfortunate that some historians have decided to reserve the peculiarly English term 'witchcraft', which has no Latin or Continental-vernacular equivalent, for the Continental notion of 'sorcery combined with devil worship'.[4]

England's importance in the history of European witchcraft is well known: it serves as a kind of control in a scientific investigation. Much of the Continent was infected with a virulent disease, but England got off lightly, and historians have long been trying to determine why. Many of the factors that went into the spread of witch persecution on the Continent were present in England during the fifteenth century: there was a large dose of heresy (the Lollards), much social unrest and civil war, ecclesiastical inquisitions against suspected witches, and much secular concern about sorcery. It is, in fact, from the secular government that many of the serious alarms against sorcery during this time are first raised, usually in connection with plots, imagined or real, against the life or state of the reigning king.

Prominent among my sources are the chronicle histories of the age — the annual records of events compiled by monks or friars, or by citizens of London or other cities. For such historiographers, supernatural causation was always a very important factor. Since one of the main purposes of history was to teach lessons for the present from the past, it was thought especially worthwhile to draw attention to the workings of divine providence, whenever possible. The interventions of the devil were not as important, perhaps, but they too were underlined as often as they were perceived.

Anyone who has had experience in analyzing 'rules for the discernment of spirits', in attempting, for instance, to distinguish demonic possession from false

witchcraft-sorcery-magic to diabolically assisted activity, without going into the question of the 'legitimate science' of natural magic.

3 In the New Testament, there is only one devil, Satan; the Gospel demons or unclean spirits do not tempt, but only cause illness by corporeal possession; and neither the devil nor the demons are fallen angels. But in patristic times and later these subtleties were not recognized: there was no longer any real distinction between diabolical and demonic activity. For documentation of the biblical data, see the book cited in the previous note, and also my article, 'The Devil in the Desert', *Catholic Biblical Quarterly* 26 (1964) 190-220, esp. 202-13.

4 This is the terminology favored especially by Jeffrey Burton Russell, *Witchcraft in the Middle Ages* (Ithaca, 1972), who holds that 'European witchcraft is best viewed as a religious cult of the Devil' (p. 17).

possession, will have come to the conclusion that it is very difficult even on the level of accepted faith to separate natural from supernatural influences. In a way, of course, the doctrine of Providence makes things very easy: everything is brought about ultimately by God's causation or permission. But the problem remains of assigning motives to God for particular events: motives of reward, punishment, trial, discipline, and so on.

It is obvious that a given historian's personal likes and dislikes, especially his political affiliations, would play a large role in forming his opinion as to who was on the side of God and who had the support of the devil. For the past generation (since 1944), students of English literature have accepted, virtually without exception, the existence of one such politically motivated providential schema: namely, the Tudor myth, as formulated by the late E. M. W. Tillyard in his *Shakespeare's History Plays*. According to Tillyard, the Tudor historians sought to establish the legitimacy of the Tudor dynasty by regarding almost the whole of the fifteenth century as a time of divine displeasure and punishment brought about by the deposition of Richard II in 1399. But finally, according to the theory, the supernal wrath was satisfied, and there was a man sent from God whose name was Henry who brought redemption to the land: Henry Tudor, crowned King Henry VII in 1485.

Even *a priori*, there is something odd about this picture of Henry VII, whose chief claim to the throne was that of the last of the Lancastrians, heir to Henry IV, Henry V, and Henry VI. Why should he foster a mystique of divine punishment against his Lancastrian forerunners? In point of fact, a close reading of the chronicles demonstrates that he did no such thing. Instead, he upheld the Henrys, and even made serious attempts to procure the canonization of Henry VI. There was, nevertheless, a Tudor 'myth' or party line, but it took an extremely simple and obvious pattern. Henry VII was indeed sent by God, but his purpose was not to rescue England from divine punishment, but to rescue her from the diabolical rule of the Yorkist King Richard III.

Looking back into still earlier chronicles, we find similar patterns: it was the historians writing under Richard III's brother, Edward IV, the first Yorkist king, who saw Henry VI and the house of Lancaster as divinely overthrown, and Edward IV as divinely supported; this we could term the York myth. A Lancaster myth was created at the beginning of the century: God raised up Henry IV to overcome the evils of Richard II. King Richard's supporters, of course, took an opposite view. In the sixteenth century, fragments of all of these myths were preserved and incorporated into works of literature and drama — for instance, into Shakespeare's plays.[5]

5 For more details, see my *Divine Providence in the England of Shakespeare's Histories* (Cambridge, Mass., 1970).

The early sources also reveal that it was not only the chroniclers who thought in this way but often the kings themselves, and not simply for the purposes of propaganda. They sincerely believed that God was on their side, and it was easy for them to think that their opponents were minions of the devil, however much these minions might protest that it was they who had divine support.

In the late fourteenth and early fifteenth century especially, England was filled with prophets who claimed to be divinely inspired.[6] And while it was normally not feasible to proceed against someone for consorting with God, it was simple enough to accuse a man of uttering false prophecies, and charge him with treasonous sedition. One such prophet, the hermit William of Norham, was imprisoned by Richard II for his pains, and he seems to be the same northern hermit who later had unpleasant information for Henry IV — but this time he was rewarded with decapitation.[7]

It is only a short step from the denial of divine inspiration to the charge of magical or diabolical divining, and of using sorcery to oppose or influence the king in some way. As we shall see, it is a step that was often taken.

Another step that is not so short is the identification of sorcery with heresy. As is well known, this identification became commonplace on the Continent, and is most strongly asserted in the *Malleus maleficarum* (1486).[8] Some scholars have too easily assumed that the same was true of England.[9] In fact, however, witchcraft in England was almost never formally associated with heresy, as a perusal of the myriad cases of witchcraft cited by G. L. Kittredge will reveal.[10] In the con-

6 See Morton W. Bloomfield, *Piers Plowman as a Fourteenth-Century Apocalypse* (New Brunswick, N.J., 1962), and see the index of Kelly, *Divine Providence* s.v. 'Prophecies'.

7 Continuation of the *Eulogium (historiarum sive temporis)*, ed. F. S. Haydon (RS 9.3; London, 1863), pp. 380, 397; cf. Kelly, *Divine Providence*, p. 12 n. 10. See George Lyman Kittredge, *Witchcraft in Old and New England* (Cambridge, Mass., 1929), chap. 14: 'The Seer' (pp. 226 ff.).

8 Russell, *Witchcraft*, pp. 219-33. I am speaking only of the views of the theoreticians and prosecutors of witchcraft. Russell elsewhere in his book goes on to conclude that heretical witches such as the prosecutors described really existed. For a recent critique of this position, see Norman Cohn, *Europe's Inner Demons* (London, 1975), excerpts of which appear in the December 1974 and January 1975 issues of *Encounter*.

9 Russell, *Witchcraft*, p. 204, in speaking of the 1401 statute on the burning of heretics, makes it clear that he believes it to apply to witches, for he takes it as evidence that magic was considered a civil crime. I shall discuss the significance of the 1401 statute below, at nn. 25 and 38.

10 The only cases I have found in Kittredge in which heresy figures are the following:

(1) 1441: Eleanor Cobham (pp. 81-83); see my treatment below.

(2) 1457: Thomas Hull of Hertford confessed to the bishop of Lincoln that he had aided Thomas Curteys in using nigromancy and heresy (p. 38).

(3) 1467: William Byg, a crystal-gazer, was accused of heresy and sorcery in the court of the archbishop of York (pp. 187-88).

(4) 1492: Margaret Geffrey was summoned on charges touching on the crime of heresy and sor-

stitution *Ignorantia sacerdotum* of Archbishop Pecham, issued in 1281, sorcery, incantations, and other superstitions are said to be implicitly forbidden under the first commandment's prohibition of idolatry, whereas heresy is forbidden by the second commandment. Pecham's distinction was enshrined in the ***Provinciale*** of * William Lyndwood,[11] who, as official of the court of the province of Canterbury (1417-*c.* 1429), was the ranking ecclesiastical judge and canonist of his time.

Lyndwood himself clearly does not regard sorcery as seriously as he does heresy. In his only references to the subject, apart from his commentary on Pecham's decree, he says simply that clerics who are proven to be sorcerers are to be deposed;[12] and, when speaking of the rule that baptismal fonts are to be kept locked on account of witchcraft, he declares it better to be silent than to speak about such things.[13] Heresy was another matter. When commenting on the 1409 constitutions of Archbishop Arundel against the Lollards, he insists that only two judges have jurisdiction over cases of heresy: the bishop of the area and a

cery to the court of the bishop of London's commissary, for using a cunning-man to secure a rich husband (pp. 61-62); see below, n. 16 no. 7.

(5) 1510: a priest, James Richardson, of the diocese of Lincoln was arrested as a person publicly defamed of heresy or sorcery (pp. 207-208).

It should be noted, however, that Kittredge does not hold himself bound to report all charges of heresy, as is evident from his failure to mention the heretical character of the witchcraft charged against Alice Kyteler and her associates in the notorious inquisition instituted by Richard Ledrede, bishop of Ossory, at Kilkenny in 1324. See *A Contemporary Narrative of the Proceedings against Dame Alice Kyteler*, ed. Thomas Wright (Camden Society 1.24; London, 1843). Ledrede was an English Franciscan who, however, had been made bishop in France by Pope John XXII at a time when the trials of the Templars as heretical sorcerers were still fresh; see Cohn (n. 8 above) 202. In fact, Edward II, at the urging of John XXII's predecessor Clement V, had allowed papal inquisitors into England to bring similar charges against the Templars there; but, contrary to what happened under Ledrede in Ireland, there was no conviction and no burning. See Frederick Pollock and Frederic W. Maitland, *The History of English Law before the Time of Edward I*, 2nd. ed., 2 (1898, rpt. Cambridge, 1952), pp. 550-51; John G. Bellamy, *Crime and Public Order in England in the Later Middle Ages* (London, 1973), pp. 139-40.

11 Lyndwood, *Provinciale* 1.11.1 (see n. 1 above), pp. 54-55 (cf. appendix, pp. 28-29). According to G. R. Owst, '*Sortilegium* in English Homiletic Literature of the Fourteenth Century' in *Studies Presented to Sir Hilary Jenkinson*, ed. J. Conway Davies (London, 1957), pp. 272-303, especially 274, Pecham's analysis 'set a precedent for all future tracts and sermons on the Decalogue which was zealously followed.' In his commentary on Pecham's constitution, Lyndwood says that the concept of idolatry can include not only infidels but heretics and bad Christians as well (gl. v. *omnis idolatria*); but he goes on to define *sortilegia, incantationes, superstitiosum*, and the rest with no reference to heresy. For instance gl. v. *cum superstitionibus*: 'Superstitiosum est omne illud quod ab hominibus fit ad colendam creaturam vel partem creaturae sicut Deum, vel ad invocationem daemonum, vel ad exercendas magicas artes ... et generaliter omne illud quod ponit spem in aliud praeterquam in Deum'.

12 Lyndwood, *Provinciale* 1.4.2 gl. v. *sortilegos* (p. 32).

13 ibid. 3.25.1 gl. v. *propter sortilegia* (p. 247): 'Quae honestius est tacere quam dicere'.

specially delegated papal inquisitor. It has never, he says, been permitted to anyone inferior to the bishop, or to the bishop's official or vicar general. 'For the matter of heresy is one of the major matters that pertain to the bishops alone.'[14]

In contrast, the offense of witchcraft was one of the minor matters that fell within the jurisdiction not only of the bishops' officials, but of the courts of the archdeacons as well. We are told in Chaucer's *Friar's Tale* that the archdeacon 'boldely dide execucioun In punysshynge of fornicacioun, Of wicchecraft, and eek of bawderye', and so on.[15] But the normal form of trial even in these lower courts, except where suit was brought by a third person (usually for the restitution of spouse or property), was the *ex officio* inquisition, which was basically the same procedure as that employed by the Roman Inquisition.[16] In *

14 ibid. 5.5.2 gl. v. *ordinarii* (p. 296): 'Cognitio namque haeresis duobus tantum iudicibus in iure permittitur, viz. episcopo loci, et inquisitori haereticae pravitatis a sede apostolica deputato .... Non enim reperies aliquem textum, ut credo, qui hanc cognitionem concedat inferiori episcopo, vel eius officiali sive vicario generali. Est enim causa haeresis una de maioribus causis quae pertinent ad solos episcopos'. Later (5.5.4 gl. v. *idem ordinarius*, p. 304) Lyndwood gives his opinion that the ordinary can allow delegated judges to initiate heresy trials, but that only he is to give sentence.

15 Chaucer, *Canterbury Tales* III (D) 1302 ff., ed. F. N. Robinson, *Works*, 2nd ed. (Boston, 1957), p. 89. It is interesting that magic in both Chaucer and John Gower seems usually, perhaps always, to be natural and not diabolical; even in the *Franklin's Tale*, where natural magic is denounced as an illusion from the viewpoint of the Christian faith, it is not said to be effected by evil spirits. Cf. Kittredge, *Witchcraft*, pp. 56-58.

16 See R. Naz, 'Inquisition', *Dictionnaire de droit canonique* 6.1418-1426, and see the influential *Speculum iudiciale* of William Durantis (late thirteenth century; ed. Basel, 1563), book 3, part 1, pp. 25 ff.: *De inquisitione*. For rather full records of such inquisitions, see the *Registrum Hamonis Hethe diocesis Roffensis, A.D. 1319-1352*, ed. Charles Johnson (Canterbury and York Society 49; Oxford, 1948), pp. 911-1043: Acts of the Consistory Court of Rochester for 1347-1348. Examples of the kinds of witchcraft offenses brought before a bishop's vicar can be seen in the sixteen cases reported from the records of the court of the Commissary of the bishop of London from 1475 to 1539, in William Hale Hale, *A Series of Precedents and Proceedings in Criminal Causes Extending from the Year 1475 to 1640* (London, 1847). (I have not seen the edition by R. W. Dunning, Edinburgh, 1973.) Following each case I give Hale's number and the relevant page in Kittredge: *

(1) 1475/6: Nazareth Jarbrey admitted using a crystal-gazer to find a thief (H 43, K 188).
(2) 1476/7: John Bere, accused of defamation and belief in sorcery (probably for finding stolen goods), cleared himself (H 65, K 36).
(3) 1480: 'John Stokys uses incantations of sorcery for fevers' (H 10, K 36).
(4) 1481/2: Joan Beverley, witch, solicited two other witches to make two men love her (H 27, K 107).
(5) 1489: Joan Corbett, accused of being a witch, cleared herself (H 70).
(6) 1490: Joan Benet, witch, was accused of attempting to kill a man by using a wax candle (H 82, K 85).
(7) 1492: Richard Laukiston and Margaret Geffrey were summoned on charges touching the crime of heresy and sorcery ('de et super certis articulis crimen haeresiae tangentibus et sorseriae'). Laukiston took a fee from Geffrey to give to a cunning-man, who was to find a husband for her worth £ 1000. Upon admission of guilt, Laukiston was ordered to restore the fee to Geffrey, and Geffrey was ordered to do public penance, by walking barefoot and candle

such trials, summonses were issued on the basis of accusations by unnamed persons; the presiding official functioned as both accuser and judge; the accused was bound under oath to answer to charges;[17] and conviction did not necessarily depend on the confession of the accused, but on the judge's negative assessment of the evidence.

In cases of heresy, modifications were permitted: other heretics or suspect persons could serve as accusers or witnesses, and names of accusers and witnesses could be withheld from the accused when fear of recrimination was present; summary procedure could be used, as could torture. Often no advantage of these con- * cessions was taken; but the papal canons allowing them were normally addressed not only to specially delegated inquisitors but to local bishops as well; and, what is more, they were recognized in England as applying to the diocesan ordinaries. Archbishop Arundel in 1409 specifies that bishops are to proceed summarily (*summarie et de plano absque strepitu et figura iudicii*),[18] and Lyndwood explains

in hand on three successive Sundays before the procession of the cross (H 123, K 61-62, 107).

(8) 1493: Elena Dalok was accused of being a slanderer and a quasi enchantress who cursed people and predicted their death (H 137, K 130, 228).

(9) 1497: John White confessed to using magic art, namely the finding of stolen goods by using a psalter and key (H 207, K 196).

(10) 1497: Sir Robert, rector of St. Mary at Nax, was accused of defamation by means of his sortilegious arts (another case of thief-finding) (H 216, K 196).

(11) 1502: Eleanor Dulyne, accused of attempting to poison her husband by divinatory arts, cleared herself (H 264, K 62).

(12) 1509: Alice Ancetyr consulted a magician to recover stolen goods and slanderously accused Christopher Sandon (H 284, K 188-189).

(13) 1526: Margaret Williamson was accused of using an amatory drink, and of having suspected books (H 325, K 107).

(14) 1527: William Browne confessed to using magical art and incantations to cure horses (H 326, K 36).

(15) 1528: Margaret Hunt and her compurgators asserted that she accompanied the use of herbs in her cures with prayers, like the creed, the Lord's Prayer, and the Ave Maria (H 337, K 36-37). Cf. Lyndwood's remark in n. 1 above.

(16) 1528: Elizabeth Fotman admitted to healing a horse by making crosses on it with a rod (H 338, K 37).

From the case of Richard Laukiston and Margaret Geffrey in 1492, it is clear that the commissary considered himself competent at least to inquire into matters of heresy, though it is not clear why this case and not the others was thought to touch upon heresy. Another case involving heresy occurred in 1490: David Chirke was suspected of heresy for not attending church (H 84).

17 Cf. Durantis, *Speculum iudiciale*, p. 33: 'Ubi vero nullo prosequente sed ex superioris officio inquiritur, tunc [reus] iurabit propter infamiam contra eum ortam.'

18 See Lyndwood, *Provinciale* 5.5.4 (pp. 302-305) and appendix, p. 68. Cf. E. F. Jacob, *The Register of Henry Chichele, Archbishop of Canterbury, 1414-1443*, 4 vols. (Canterbury and York Society 42, 45-47; Oxford, 1937-1947), I. cxxxv-cxxxvi, who, in discussing the case of the Franciscan friar William Russell, mistakenly intimates that the words calling for summary procedure

at length the methods allowed. For instance, if a witness vacillates he can be put *in quaestionibus*, as long as no blood is shed ('dum tamen sanguinem per hoc non eliciat').[19] If guilt is proven only by one witness of good reputation, the accused may be tortured, in order that the truth might appear ('tunc inquisitus poterit torqueri, ut eruatur veritas'); for, as Lyndwood remarks, sterner action is always called for when a convicted person refuses to confess.[20]

It might be thought that one reason why heresy was not often associated with witchcraft in England is that Lollardry, which was the regnant heresy there, had no resemblance to the dualist heresies that allegedly first gave witchcraft its heretical qualifications; it was, on the contrary, a proto-Protestant sort of puritanism, and it outdid the orthodox Church in its condemnation of sorcery by denouncing such things as the use of amulets with gospel texts written on them. But it was in fact not only dualist heretics who had been associated with the diabolical witch-cult on the Continent; and dualists like the Cathars were even more opposed to material things than the Lollards, and 'so far from worshipping the devil they were passionately concerned to escape from his clutches'.[21]

An example of the judicial distinction between sorcery and heresy can be seen in the cases brought before Archbishop Henry Chichele and the convocation of the clergy in early November 1419. Richard Walker, a chaplain, was strongly suspected of sorcery, and admitted his magical attempts under oath. He was made to appear at Paul's Cross with his magic books and instruments before a great crowd. After listening to a sermon by the bishop of Llandaff, he abjured his practice and went in penitential procession through Chepe Street, after which his materials were burned; and he was allowed to go free.[22] Walker had declared in

distinguish a type of inquisitorial trial not used or allowed in England. It was in fact permitted in heresy proceedings to all bishops by Boniface VIII, *Sext.* 5.2.20 (*Statuta quaedam*), and in cases of benefices, tithes, matrimony, and usury by Clement V, *Clem.* 2.1.2 (*Dispendiosam*). The phrase is defined in *Clem.* 5.11.2 (*Saepe contingit*). In all these decretals the word *simpliciter* is used instead of *summarie*, the term favored in later documents, as, for instance, in Martin V's mandate to Cardinal Branda to proceed against Friar Russell (*Register of Henry Chichele* 3.139), though in the pope's recollection of the order later he uses both terms: 'summarie, simpliciter, et de plano sine strepitu et figura iudicii' (3.148). Russell's trials, by the way, both in England (1425) and in Rome (1426), provide a good illustration of how the option and even the mandate to use summary justice could be ignored and all the full forms of the ecclesiastical inquisition employed.

19 Lyndwood, *Provinciale* 5.5.4 (p. 304) gl. v. *testium receptionem*.

20 ibid. (p. 305) gl. v. *non obstante*. Torture was used in the Templar and Kyteler cases (n. 10 above), though in the former torturers had to be imported from the Continent, and in the latter whipping was used, which was a common form of ecclesiastical punishment in England. See also nn. 101 and 120 below.

21 Cohn, *Europe's Inner Demons* (n. 8 above), p. 58. For the Lollard views cited, see Kittredge, *Witchcraft*, p. 52 and Owst, '*Sortilegium*' (n. 11 above), pp. 301-302; Owst (p. 292) quotes the Dominican John Bromyard as giving a qualified approval to the wearing of gospel texts.

22 *Register of Henry Chichele* 3.54-56; also in David Wilkins, *Concilia Magnae Britanniae et*

convocation that he had come to the conclusion that his magic operations were false because none of them had taken effect. Kittredge assumes that this form of confession cleared him of heresy.[23] But in fact there had never been any question of his having been suspected of heresy, unlike three other men who were accused of heresy at the same convocation. One was sent to prison for further deliberation, and the other two abjured their errors. They were released, and warned of the punishment for relapse.[24]

According to a statute passed by Parliament in 1401, the penalty for relapse into heresy was, or could be, at the discretion of the bishop, burning by the secular authorities.[25] Before that time, burning was commonly used as a means of capital punishment only for women convicted of high treason, an offense for which men were hanged and quartered, unless the sentence was mitigated to decapitation.[26] It has been supposed that only after 1401 could men as well as women be burned, and not only for heresy but also for witchcraft. But, apart from the fact that, as we have just seen, heresy and witchcraft were regarded as separate crimes, burning was specified as a punishment for both heresy and witchcraft in the legal textbooks produced in the latter part of the reign of Edward I (1272-1307), namely *Fleta* and *Britton*.[27] In 1279, the body of a woman thought to have been a witch was burned by the judgment of the whole clergy in Northumberland.[28] Whether or not they were acting on the rule stipulated later in *Fleta* and *Britton* is not clear. But the fact that some of the lords of Parliament in 1376 insisted that Alice Perrers' Dominican accomplice should be burned for his magical practices suggests that the law was by no means a dead letter. The same may well be true of heresy, though without question the statute of 1401 made burning easier.

* * *

Hiberniae 3 (London, 1737), pp. 393-95. Cf. *Register* 3.67-68 for another example of a non-heresy trial (forgery in this case) sandwiched between heresy proceedings.

23 Kittredge, *Witchcraft*, p. 80.

24 *Register of Henry Chichele* 3.55-57; Wilkins, *Concilia* 3.393-95.

25 The statute on the new sect of heretics, 2 Henry IV, c. 15 (1401), *Statutes of the Realm* 2 (1816, rpt. London, 1963), pp. 125-28, gave any bishop the power to hand over any person who refused to abjure his heresy, or who was convicted of heresy for a second time, to the secular authorities to be burned, without need for a secular trial or order from the king. In the statute of 2 Henry V, 1 c. 7 (1414), the heretical doctrines in question are termed 'Lollardries' (*Statutes* 2.181-84). See James FitzJames Stephen, *A History of the Criminal Law in England*, 3 vols. (London, 1883), 2.444-50, and Jacob, *Register of Henry Chichele* 1.cxxx.

26 See Stephen, ibid. 1.475-76. Women were sometimes also burned for felony, e.g. arson: Pollock and Maitland, *History of English Law* 2.552.

27 *Fleta* 1.35, ed. H. G. Richardson and G. O. Sayles, vol. 2 (Selden Society 72; London, 1955), p. 90; *Britton* 1.10, trans. Francis Morgan Nichols, ed. Simeon E. Baldwin (Washington, D.C., 1901), p. 35, with a later gloss (n. 2) defining the relation between ecclesiastical and royal courts. See Pollock and Maitland, ibid. 2.552.

28 Pollock and Maitland, ibid.; Kittredge, *Witchcraft*, pp. 47-48.

The Alice Perrers case can serve as a useful starting point for our survey of royal witchcraft scares. In 1376, the last year of the reign of Edward III, Edward's mistress Alice Perrers was formally charged by the Commons with having gained the affections, procured the madness, and enervated the strength of the king through magical arts. The magic was said to be the work of an iniquitous Dominican friar who, according to the Benedictine chronicler Thomas Walsingham, achieved his effects through the use of wax images, powerful herbs, and incantations like those of the famous magician Nectanebus, king of Egypt; he was also accused of giving Alice magical rings of remembrance and forgetfulness, like those which Moses had made, for the king to wear. When the friar was captured by stratagem, a maid asked him why he did not foresee his fate, since he was able to predict the future for others. He answered that he did indeed foresee it, but did not know when it would happen. Walsingham reports further that the archbishop of Canterbury, who was the protector of the Order of Preachers, was able only with great difficulty to deliver the friar from the duke of Lancaster (John of Gaunt) and the other magnates, some of whom insisted that he should be executed by burning. As it was, the Dominicans took charge of him and kept him in close custody.[29]

After Henry IV was crowned king in the autumn of 1399, he handed over to Parliament a scroll 'containing magical arts', which had been found in a chest belonging to one of Richard II's priests, John Magdalene. Being an ecclesiastic, Magdalene was not immediately arrested but was summoned on the next day before a convocation of the clergy at St. Paul's. He declared that he knew nothing of the contents of the scroll but was only keeping it for the king, and so he was released. But the Commons in their turn demanded that Richard's evil counsellors, both ecclesiastic and lay, be arrested, especially those who had demented the said king 'by sortilege or false and fallible calculations'. Henry replied that some of them were already in custody, and asked for others to be named specifically so that appropriate measures could be taken against them.[30] *

It seems that Henry IV himself was not above suspicion in the matter of witchcraft. We learn from the report of Burgundian chroniclers that when the duke of Orléans protested against Henry's right to the throne, he sought to prove his point by challenging the new king to single combat; but he stipulated that no charms were to be used in the contest, nor any invocations forbidden by the

29 Thomas Walsingham, *Chronicon Angliae*, ed. Edward Maunde Thompson (RS 64; London, 1874), pp. 97-99; cf. Kelly, *Divine Providence*, p. 23 n. 65; Kittredge, *Witchcraft*, p. 105; and George Holmes, *The Good Parliament* (Oxford, 1975), pp. 135-37.

30 Thomas Walsingham, *Annales Ricardi secundi et Henrici quarti*, ed. Henry T. Riley in *Chronica monasterii sancti Albani* (RS 28.3; London, 1866), pp. 301, 309.

Church. Wariness of this sort in trials by combat was fairly commonplace.[31] But Henry seems to have sensed a larger charge of witchcraft, especially upon receipt of the duke's second letter, in which he denied that divine virtue had placed Henry on the throne. In his reply, Henry insisted upon his providential backing, and asserted that diabolical magic could never have achieved such results: 'Our Lord God, to whom we ever give praise, hath shown us his divine grace more than we are worthy to receive or have, if it were not that of his mercy and goodness it hath pleased him to give to us that which surely all the sorcerers and devils could not have known how or been able to give, nor all those who meddle with their arts'.[32]

Walsingham's treatment of Edward III and Richard II and their brushes with sorcery has nothing to say about diabolical magic. However, when he comes to detail Henry IV's troublesome campaigns against Owen Glendower in Wales, he reports that many believed the bad weather to have been caused by the evil art of the Franciscan friars favorable to the Welsh. 'But far be it', he piously says, 'from men who profess such a holy rule to contract such great familiarity with demons'.[33] His words might be taken, at least by later readers, to imply the notion of acquiring 'familiar spirits' by means of a diabolical compact.

A very interesting comment on the same subject comes from a Cistercian chronicler, who, like Walsingham, was quite favorably disposed to Henry IV's takeover of the throne from Richard. He says it is true that such storms could be caused by the sortilege that Owen's magicians are thought to perform, and that it is not impossible to put the air into motion through the power of unclean spirits; but nevertheless the true answer in the opinion of the discreet is that the English failed in their venture because they have no right to Wales.[34] Which is as much as to say that it was the just disposition of God's providence that was the ultimate cause of the storms.

The chronicler John Hardyng says simply that everyone thought witches were to blame for the weather.[35] Hardyng also reports that among the many means

31 See Kittredge, *Witchcraft*, pp. 53-54.

32 John de Waurin, *A Collection of the Chronicles and Ancient Histories of Great Britain, now Called England*, trans. William Hardy and Edward L. C. P. Hardy (RS 40.2; London, 1887), pp. 65, 75, 81; cf. Enguerrand de Monstrelet, *Chronicles*, trans. Thomas Johnes (London, 1867), pp. 16-23.

33 Walsingham, *Annales*, pp. 343-44: 'Sed absit hoc ab hominibus tam sanctam professis regulam, ut cum daemonibus tantam contraherent familiaritatem'.

34 Author 'B' of the *Chronicle of Dieulacres Abbey, 1381-1403*, ed. M. V. Clarke and V. H. Galbraith in *Bulletin of the John Rylands Library* 14 (1930) 176.

35 John Hardyng, *Chronicle*, ed. Henry Ellis (London, 1812), p. 360. A later chronicler, John Rous, discusses Glendower himself as a magician: he is said to have had a stone which could render him invisible; it had belonged to the earl of Arundel, who had had a raven, or a spirit in the

that were used in plots against King Henry's life, there were enchantments made 'to waste him out and utterly destroy' him.[36]

In 1406, Henry IV through his Council ordered a full-scale ecclesiastical inquisition against sorcerers of various kinds in the diocese of Lincoln who were causing injury to the people.[37] There is, however, nothing in the order to Bishop Repingdon to indicate that the king feared any attempt against his own person, or indeed that the magic was connected with the devil or with heresy, though it was said to be subversive of the faith. It is instructive to compare Henry's 1406 writ against witchcraft in Lincoln with the statute against heresy issued five years earlier.[38] Those convicted of witchcraft are to be kept in prison until they renounce their arts, whereas convicted heretics who refuse to abjure are to be burned. *

It is also worth noting that there is a great deal of evidence for campaigns against heresy in the diocese of Lincoln during the tenure of Bishop Repingdon,[39] but no evidence of any concern on his part for the discovery of witches. Only one case of sorcery is recorded in his register: in 1417, John Smith of Alconbury was accused of practising necromancy, sorcery, and illicit conjurations, and of invoking evil spirits.[40]

form of a raven, that one day had belched it up. See Rous's *Historia regum Angliae*, ed. Thomas Hearne (Oxford, 1716), pp. 206-207; Kittredge, *Witchcraft*, p. 176; Kelly, *Divine Providence*, p. 69 n. 19. Shakespeare describes Glendower as professing, much to Henry Hotspur's disbelief and disgust, to be able to summon spirits from 'the vasty deep' (*1 Henry IV* 3.3.53). Hotspur replies, 'Why, so can I, or so can any man; But will they come when you do call for them?'

36 Hardyng, *Chronicle*, p. 370; Kelly, *Divine Providence*, pp. 44, 311.

37 Thomas Rymer, *Foedera*, 2nd ed. (London, 1704-1732), 8.427-28 (2 January 1406): the suspected culprits are designated as *sortilegii, magici, incantatores, nigromantici, divinitores, arioli,* and *phitones*. They disturb the people and scandalize the Church and the faith by their manifest subversion. The king proceeds as defender of the faith against those who thus impugn it, and orders their imprisonment until they reform ('quousque a suis maleficiis huiusmodi respiciant') or until he orders otherwise for their deliverance. For the moralistic habit of piling up synonyms for malefactors, see Dino Bigongiari, 'Were There Theaters in the Twelfth and Thirteenth Centuries?', *Romanic Review* 37 (1946) 201-24, especially 202.

38 See n. 25 above.

39 Margaret Archer, ed., *The Register of Bishop Philip Repingdon, 1405-1419*, vol. 1: *Memoranda 1405-1411* (Publications of the Lincoln Record Society 57; Hereford, 1963), pp. xxxiv-xxxvii. Repingdon himself was tried and convicted of heresy in 1382.

40 ibid., p. xxxiii. Archer reports that a full account of Smith's activities and of his defence is given on fol. 177r-v, which of course falls beyond the portion that she has edited. I should perhaps mention here that very few episcopal registers of the fourteenth and fifteenth centuries have been published; see the list of those falling in the first half of the fifteenth century given by E. F. Jacob, *Archbishop Henry Chichele* (London, 1967), pp. 117-18. Furthermore, such registers as survive only rarely contain the records of the consistory courts, and of course never include those of the archdeacons' courts. These latter records, when not missing, are almost all unpublished; see G. R.

The reign of Henry V (1413-1422) produced a striking case of royal witchcraft jitters, which was joined to the motif of the wicked stepmother. In 1419, Henry IV's widow, Joan of Navarre, was taken into custody, so Walsingham reported, after having been 'defamed' for practising witchcraft ('de quodam maleficio') aimed at harming the king. According to the London chronicles, the dowager queen instigated a certain Franciscan, John Randolph, master of divinity, to kill King Henry by sorcery and necromancy.[41] But the Rolls of Parliament record only that the friar, identified as the queen's confessor but not said to be implicated himself, brought a charge against her of attempting to murder the king, without specifying sorcery as the means.[42] Whatever the truth of the matter, the queen was kept in confinement for almost three years (though allowed to live on a lavish scale), and her property remained confiscated. She was apparently at liberty by 13 July 1422, when her royal stepson, on his deathbed in

Elton, *England 1200-1640* (Ithaca-London, 1969), pp. 103-106, and especially Richard H. Helmholz, *Marriage Litigation in Medieval England*, Cambridge Studies in English Legal History (Cambridge, 1974).

41 Walsingham, *The St. Albans Chronicle, 1406-1420*, ed. V. H. Galbraith (Oxford, 1937), p. 123; *A Chronicle of London, from 1089 to 1827* [ed. Nicholas Harris Nicolas and Edward Tyrrell] (London, 1827), p. 107; *Chronicles of London*, ed. C. L. Kingsford (Oxford, 1905), p. 73.

42 According to this report, made on 16 October 1419, the queen's schemes 'are openly published throughout the whole realm of England'. See *Rotuli parliamentorum*, 6 vols. (London, 1767-1777), 4.118. A month earlier (25 September), Archbishop Chichele of Canterbury informed the bishop of London that King Henry wished to have prayers and processions for himself and his army in France, so that God may protect him from all of the wicked plots of his enemies and from the 'superstitious operations of necromancers, especially such as (according to report) have lately been devised by some persons for the destruction of his person'. The king ascribed the detection of these evil operations and the preservation of his person from them solely to God's goodness and the devout prayers that his people had offered for him. See the *Register of Henry Chichele* 4.206-207 and Wilkins, *Concilia* 3.392-93. The archbishop may be referring to the matter of Queen Joan and Friar Randolph; two days later (i.e. 27 September) the King's Council ordered the queen deprived of her dowry and other revenues and possessions, and four days after that she was arrested. See A. R. Myers, 'The Captivity of a Royal Witch: The Household Accounts of Queen Joan of Navarre, 1419-21', *Bulletin of the John Rylands Library* 24 (1940) 263-84, especially 264. Kittredge, *Witchcraft*, p. 80, takes the mandate simply as evidence that Henry's prelates as well as Henry himself were worried about witchcraft. However, earlier letters of the archbishop requiring prayers for peace, unity, good weather, and victory against England's enemies show no such concern; see *Register of Henry Chichele* 3.323-25 and 4.123-24 (9 April 1415); 3.435-37 and 4.127 (7 June 1415); 4.158-59 (2 August 1416); 4.167-68 (8 May 1417). In the letter of 9 April 1415, Chichele does give a certain role to the devil: the dissension, scandal, and ancient schism that afflict them have been stirred up by the enemy of the human race, but their own demerits have also deserved it all; and he sees the famine, pestilence, and other disasters that have been visited upon the usually pleasant realm of England to be the result of divine punishment (not, therefore, caused by witches). Finally, it should be noted that shortly after the queen was denounced in Parliament, Archbishop Chichele took up a witchcraft case in convocation in which no connection was made with plots against the king's life: namely the trial of Richard Walker, held on 8-9 November (discussed above at n. 22).

France, ordered her dowry restored to her, in order to clear his conscience in the matter.[43]

It has been assumed that the friar in this case was the same Friar Randolph who, after having been committed to prison for treason, was delivered therefrom by Henry V's brother, Humphrey, duke of Gloucester, in 1425.[44] There is evidence that Humphrey was interested in 'natural magic', in the form of astrology and alchemy.[45] But sixteen years later, in 1441, he would be connected with magic in its less acceptable forms, in the most sensational witchcraft trial of the century, that of Eleanor Cobham, Humphrey's second wife. *

One of the charges against Eleanor upon which she was convicted was that she 'had enforced the foresaid duke of Gloucester to love her and wed her'.[46] Gloucester first became involved with Eleanor, it seems, in 1425, the same year in which he secured Randolph's release from the Tower. At first she was only his mistress, since he was still married to Jacqueline, countess of Hainault. But when Pope Martin V in 1428 declared the marriage null and void, Humphrey hastened to marry Eleanor.[47]

43 Kittredge, *Witchcraft*, p. 80; Myers, 'Captivity', 265-71.

44 K. H. Vickers, *Humphrey Duke of Gloucester* (London, 1907), pp. 276, 278. Randolph must have been sent back to the Tower in fairly short order (perhaps at the insistence of Cardinal Beaufort, Gloucester's uncle, who violently objected to the release), for it is reported that he was murdered there in 1429 by the mad 'parson of the Tower'. See W. Paley Baildon, 'The Inventory of the Goods of Brother John Randolf', *Archaeologia* 61 (1908) 166-74; Kittredge, *Witchcraft*, pp. 79-80.

45 Vickers, *Humphrey*, pp. 276, 322-23.

46 *An English Chronicle of the Reigns of Richard II, Henry IV, Henry V, and Henry VI Written before the Year 1471*, ed. John Silvester Davies (Camden Society 1.64; London, 1856), pp. 58-59; *The Brut, or, The Chronicles of England*, ed. Friedrich W. D. Brie, 2 (EETS 136; London, 1908), MS. F, pp. 480-81. These two records, both of them based on London chronicles, give the fullest account of the case, and I will be relying chiefly on them (pp. 57-60 of *English Chronicle* and pp. 477-82 of *Brut*). For a complete list of sources, see Kittredge, *Witchcraft*, pp. 416-17 n. 40.

47 Vickers, *Humphrey*, pp. 165, 204-205. A charge of witchcraft leveled at the time of Humphrey's alienation from the Countess Jacqueline is to be found in the deliberately anonymous 'A Complaint for My Lady of Gloucester and Holland'. According to the poet, a mermaid resembling an enchantress and surrounded by witches strove to make the duke's heart 'double' in love, and to estrange him from Jacqueline. One stanza goes:

This cirenes nuwe crafft oute sought
 By thayre fals incantacyouns
And fals medecynes they wrought
 To tempre theyre confeccyouns
 In metys and dyvers pocyouns,
The prynces hert agaynst al lawe
From his promesse his hande to drawe. (ll. 64-70)

The poem has in the past been confidently ascribed to John Lydgate, a major recipient of Humphrey's patronage, and the piece appears in the Early English Text Society's edition of Lydgate's

Eleanor's accomplice in this matter was proven to be one Margery Jourdemayne, who came from the manor of Eye near Westminster — 'the Witch of Eye, whose sorcery and witchcraft the said Dame Eleanor had long time used'; Eleanor allegedly won Gloucester 'by such medicines and drinks as the said witch made'. Because of this, 'and also for cause of relapse, the same witch was burned in Smithfield', on Friday, 27 October 1441.[48] As was noted above, burning was the penalty for female traitors; some of Eleanor's other associates in magic were accused of high treason, and one of them, Roger Bolingbroke, underwent execution by hanging and quartering. But Margery is not specifically associated in the sources with treason or the alleged plots against Henry VI. Burning was also the possible penalty for relapsed or recalcitrant heretics, and heresy was one of the charges reportedly leveled against Eleanor. One well informed source says that Margery was 'burned for her false belief and witchcraft that she had used of long time'.[49] But, as we know from the canonist Lyndwood (who in 1441 was Keeper of the Privy Seal), the false beliefs or superstitions of witchcraft were not automatically labeled as heresy in England; and burning was a known penalty for witches. Perhaps, as with heresy, a second conviction for witchcraft would bring it into force. Margery had been arrested for sorcery before, in 1430, along with two clerical associates, John Virley and Friar John Asshewell, and imprisoned in Windsor Castle. They were released in 1432, Margery on her husband's bond.[50]

Also arrested in London in 1430, according to the report of one chronicler, were seven female witches (*maleficae*) from various parts of the realm, for plotting the death of young Henry VI. They were imprisoned in the Fleet,[51] and no more is heard of them. There is nothing to suggest that Margery and her companions were connected with such a plot, but it was a time of national apprehension on the point of witchcraft, if only because of the reverses that the English were suffering in France at the hands of the Maid of Orléans. She was denounced by another brother of Henry V, John, duke of Bedford, as 'a disciple and limb of the fiend', who 'used false enchantments and sorcery'.[52] She was captured and delivered to the English in 1430, and burned in the next year. She was notorious as a 'false witch',[53] and sent to her punishment 'tanquam male-

Minor Poems 2 (London, 1934), pp. 608-13; but Derek Pearsall, *John Lydgate* (London, 1970), p. 166, strongly opposes the attribution.

48 *English Chronicle*, pp. 58-59.

49 *Brut*, p. 480.

50 Kittredge, *Witchcraft*, p. 83.

51 *Chronicon rerum gestarum in monasterio sancti Albani (A.D. 1422-1431)*, ed. H. T. Riley (RS 28/3.1; London, 1870), pp. 56-57.

52 Rymer, *Foedera* 10.408, assigns Bedford's statement to 1428 (for 1429?). *Rot. parl.* 5.435-38 puts it in 1434.

53 *Chronicles of London*, pp. 96, 133.

fica'.[54] Joan would therefore serve as a precedent for taking the same action against the Witch of Eye.

According to one continuator of the *Brut*, the charges against Eleanor Cobham came in the aftermath of an outbreak of bad weather which endangered King Henry VI on his visit to London on 15 July 1441: 'And so it was spoken amongst the people that there were some wicked fiends and spirits areared out of hell by conjuration for to noy the people in the realm and to put them to trouble, dissension, and unrest. And then it was known that certain clerks and women that are called witches had made their operation and their craft to destroy men and women, or whom they list, unto death by their false craft and working. Whereof Dame Eleanor Cobham, which was the Duchess of Gloucester, was named principally of these acts and false deeds for to destroy the king, whom God save and keep!'[55]

The first to be 'taken as conspirators of the king's death' were two clerics, Roger Bolingbroke and Thomas Southwell, for allegedly attempting 'to consume the king's person by way of nigromancy'. Specifically, Southwell was to say Mass in a forbidden place (the lodge of Harnesey Park near London) upon certain instruments with which Bolingbroke used 'his said craft of nigromancy against the faith and good belief'.[56] This alleged plot was in fact uncovered before King Henry's London visit, to judge from a record of Southwell's confinement to the Tower on 10 July.[57] Presumably the two clerics were first subjected to an ecclesiastical inquisition, for Bolingbroke was made to undergo the same kind of penance as that assigned to Richard Walker in 1419.[58] On Sunday, 23 July, he was displayed on a high stage at St. Paul's Cross in the midst of all of his magical properties, which included 'images of silver, of wax, and of other metals, and swords, with many other diverse instruments of this false craft of nigromancy and the devil's power'.[59] After the sermon,[60] 'he abjured all manner articles longing in any wise to the said craft of nigromancy or missowning [discordant] to the Christian faith.'[61] It was done in the presence of Henry Chichele, archbishop of Canterbury; Cardinal Henry Beaufort, bishop of Winchester (uncle of

54 *Chronicon Angliae de regnis trium regum lancastrensium*, ed. J. A. Giles (London, 1848), reign of Henry VI, p. 11.

55 *Brut*, pp. 477-78.

56 *English Chronicle*, p. 57.

57 *Calendar of the Close Rolls: Henry VI* 3 (London, 1937), p. 422.

58 See above at n. 22. No records of trials before Archbishop Chichele appear in his register after 1428.

59 *Brut*, p. 478.

60 According to Giles's chronicle (n. 54 above), the sermon was preached by John Low, bishop of Rochester (p. 31), though in fact at this time Low was still bishop of St. Asaph.

61 *English Chronicle*, p. 57.

Gloucester and his deadly enemy); Robert Gilbert, bishop of London; William Ayscough, bishop of Salisbury; 'and many other great clerks', and lords temporal: 'the Earl of Huntingdon, the Earl of Northumberland, and the Earl of Stafford, and more other lords of the King's Council, and the mayor and aldermen with the commons of the City of London, and many more people of divers parts, and strangers of the realm, and aliens of other strange lands beyond the sea, being in the City of London at that time.'[62]

* It was only after this public ceremony, it seems, that Bolingbroke was examined by the King's Council, before whom he confessed that he had worked his nigromancy at the instigation of Dame Eleanor Cobham, who had desired 'to know what should fall of her, and to what estate she should come.' Such a desire could easily be taken, and obviously was so taken, to mean that she wanted to know when Henry VI would die, and whether her husband would succeed him as king. She was clearly also suspected of attempting to shorten the king's life. Eleanor was accordingly summoned to appear before Archbishop Chichele and other prelates (among them were Cardinal Beaufort, Cardinal Kemp of York, and Bishop Ayscough), who no doubt functioned as the archbishop's assessors, or judicial assistants. The duchess was to answer the charges contained in certain articles 'of nigromancy, of witchcraft or sorcery, of heresy, and of treason'.[63] It was clearly an *ex officio* inquisition, with the charges being leveled by the archbishop himself.[64] The chroniclers are no doubt misleading in indicating that she

62 *Brut*, p. 478.

63 *English Chronicle*, p. 58. *Brut*, p. 479 adds to the list of attending prelates the bishop of London and the bishop of Bath (John Stafford). Eleanor was examined on 'twenty-eight divers points both of felony and treason'.

64 Even when accused persons are tried in provincial councils, that is the convocations of the Province of Canterbury, it is Archbishop Chichele himself, as metropolitan of the province, who is the sole judge. In contrast, when grants of money are given, the archbishop and the other bishops and clergy make the concession jointly (see, for example, *Register* 3.87, 113). Sometimes the language of the register suggests that the whole council also acts in sentencing and punishing offenders; for instance, the punishment of the sorcerer Richard Walker, discussed above at n. 22, was ordained 'auctoritate totius concilii' (3.55; cf. 56, 68, 204). But whenever the register provides the word-for-word formulas by which the archbishop convenes trials or articulates objections or gives sentence, it is clear that the other participants in the convocation have a purely advisory role. For instance, though the archbishop and his brethren seem to be placed on equal terms in ordering the punishment of the counterfeiter John Wathe ('per avisamentum domini et confratrum suorum punitus', 3.92), Chichele describes himself in the formula of sentence as 'iudex unicus' (3.100). The other bishops present at such trials, in contrast to the lower clergy, are always described in the verbatim formulas as *assidentes* to the archbishop (see 3.124, 126, 133, 205); and the same is true
* of the single non-convocation trial recorded in the register, convened *ex officio mero* (3.171). On the point of heresy trials before convocation, I question E. F. Jacob's interpretation of Chichele's 1416 constitution (*Register of Henry Chichele* 3.18-19). According to Jacob, the archbishop gives the diocesans the choice, when Lollardy is proven, of condemning the offenders to prison or of bringing the accused before the provincial council (I. cxxxii). In fact, what the archbishop says is that if the bishops do not hand convicted heretics over to the secular court, they are to imprison

was formally charged with treason, which was not an ecclesiastical or 'clergyable' offense, but nevertheless it is likely that her allegedly treasonable motives would have been detailed in the articles.

Before she could be apprehended, Eleanor had fled to sanctuary at Westminster,[65] but she answered the summons and appeared at St. Stephen's chapel in the king's palace at Westminster, on Tuesday, 25 July. She pleaded 'not guilty' to the twenty-eight charges objected against her, 'and so they let her go safe again to the sanctuary until the morrow, that was St. Anne's Day.' On that day, she came again, as cited, and Bolingbroke was brought forth as a witness. He 'vouched all these points upon her that were showed the day abovesaid to her, whereof she knowledged some points at that time, the number of five'.[66]

The trial was adjourned until the autumn, and the bishops in due course ordered Eleanor kept in Leeds Castle in Kent until the process reconvened. She, however, was unwilling to leave sanctuary and pretended to be ill. She then attempted to leave secretly on the river, but was apprehended and taken to the castle.[67]

them for life or at least until the next provincial council. At the provincial council, *anyone interested* in the further execution of the various heresy trials conducted by the bishops can avail himself of the records deposited with the official of Canterbury by the bishops. The constitution therefore does not lay the sole or primary charge of further execution upon the bishops. Nor is it only for such appealed or prolonged cases that reports are to be submitted to convocation. Jacob arrived at this latter conclusion through an unfortunate *lapsus oculi* (or, more technically, proleptic ellipsis arising from homoeoarchon), as is demonstrated from his translation on I. cxxxii n. 1, which omits several lines of the text on 3.19. The relevant Latin passage, with Jacob's omission in brackets, reads as follows: 'Ac de [omnibus et singulis supradictis, quo videlicet inquisierunt, reperierunt, ac in processubus se habuerunt, personas huiusmodi convictas custodiri fecerunt, diligentiisque aut negligentiis archidiaconorum sive commissariorum praedictorum, aliisque] omnibus et singulis circumstantiis praemissis quomodolibet concernentibus, ac praesertim de abiurationibus, si quos interim haereses abiurare contingat, in proxima praelatorum et cleri convocatione sub forma publica distincte et aperte nos et successores nostros certificare curent; et eosdem processus officiali curiae nostrae Cant. effectualiter liberent penes eundem seu in registro curiae nostrae Cant. remansuros, sic videlicet quod quilibet cuius interest pro executione ulteriori eorundem processuum ad eundem officialem recursum habere poterit cum effectu.' That is to say, the bishops are to make a formal report concerning *all* of the above-stated measures ordered against heretics, including the inquiries to be undertaken at least semi-annually by the bishops and archdeacons or their commissaries; and the trial records to be filed with the official of Canterbury are not restricted to those cases where the convicted heretics have been imprisoned only temporarily.

65 *English Chronicle*, p. 57. The dates given in this report are unreliable. Bolingbroke's disgrace is said to have occurred on Sunday, '25 July' (meaning 23 July), Eleanor's flight on the night of the next Tuesday, and her citation as for Monday, '22 July' (meaning 24 July). According to William Worcester, *Annales rerum anglicarum*, Eleanor fled to sanctuary on the eve of St. Margaret, that is, on the previous Wednesday, 19 July. See the editions by Thomas Hearne in *Liber niger scaccarii* 2 (Oxford, 1774), p. 460 and by Joseph Stevenson in *Letters and Papers Illustrative of the Wars of the English in France* (RS 22/2.2; London, 1864), p. 762.

66 *Brut*, pp. 478-79.

67 *English Chronicle*, p. 58. *Brut*, p. 497 says she was taken into custody on 11 August.

Meanwhile, on the same day as Eleanor's second appearance in court, namely, 26 July, the young king (he was still only nineteen years old) took action himself, or at least action was taken in his name: he ordered a comprehensive investigation to be made into this 'false deed and cursed imagination to the king and to the realm',[68] and an inquiry into 'all manner treasons, sorcery, and all other things that might in any wise touch or concern harmfully the king's person'.[69] Four inquests were ordained in the City of London, and other inquests were held throughout Middlesex. Eleanor was indicted for felony and treason in both jurisdictions.[70] The indictment handed down in the Guildhall of London named Bolingbroke and Southwell as principals and Eleanor as accessory, according to one chronicle, which adds immediately: 'And this same time was taken a woman called the Witch of Eye', on the charges I discussed earlier.[71]

The indictment of the London jurors is still extant in the Public Record Office, and it has recently been summarized and partially transcribed. Eleanor was accused of plotting to make herself queen, and because Henry VI's prosperity stood in the way she sought the assistance of Roger Bolingbroke, a clerk of her household, a great astronomer famous for his knowledge of the black arts. Bolingbroke was said to have contacted demons and other malign spirits in earth and air on several occasions between 29 June 1440 and 23 March 1441; and during this time, through the assent and command of Eleanor and of Thomas Southwell, to have assiduously labored over the king's horoscope to see when he would die — even though according to the determination of Holy Church and the teaching of divers doctors it was forbidden to any liege of the king to make such calculations about kings and princes without their consent. It was charged further that on 27 October 1440 Bolingbroke, with Southwell's assent, feloniously and traitorously revealed to Sir John Solers and many others that according to his calculations he knew well that the king would soon die; his alleged motives for this revelation were to take away from the king the cordial love (of

68 *Brut*, p. 479: the king entrusted the investigation to the mayor, aldermen, and commons of London; the earls of Huntingdon, Stafford, and Northumberland; Sir Ralph Cromwell, treasurer of England; Lord Fanhope (Sir John Cornwall); Sir Walter Hungerford and other knights and squires.

69 *English Chronicle*, p. 58: the commission was directed to the earls of Huntingdon, Stafford, and Suffolk, 'and to certain judges of both benches'.

70 *Brut*, p. 479. After mentioning that Eleanor was delivered to custody on 11 August, the *Brut* speaks of 'other of her counsel and affinity ... both men, women, witches, and other', who are to be kept in the Tower at the king's command. The order to keep her in Leeds Castle must have been delayed until she could be indicted in the secular courts (see below). It was only on 9 August that King Henry ordered her held in custody at Leeds, because of certain crimes, defects, and causes that had been laid against her by the archbishop of Canterbury on 25 July (Rymer, *Foedera* 10.851).

71 *English Chronicle*, p. 58.

the people), and to cause the king by his very knowledge of the revelation to become so overwrought by sorrow that he would more quickly die.[72]

On 19 October, Eleanor was brought back to Westminster, and her ecclesiastical trial resumed on the next day, when she appeared to be 'examined of her sorcery, and witchcraft, and treason'.[73] A more circumstantial account of this day in court says that certain articles were objected against her 'of sorcery and nigromancy', with no mention of treason — or of heresy.[74] Perhaps the charges against her had been reduced; or it may be that the chronicler is being more accurate here than he was before, and that there never was a formal charge of heresy against her (I have already noted the unlikelihood that she would have been directly accused of treason in such a court). The articles were read by 'Master Adam Moleyns, then clerk of the King's Council' (he later became bishop of Chichester), who apparently served as the 'promoter' or judicial aide.[75] Because of illness, Archbishop Chichele was not able to preside over the court himself, but committed his power to Bishops Gilbert of London, William Alnwick of Lincoln, and Thomas Brown of Norwich.[76]

72 Public Record Office, King's Bench 9 (Ancient Indictments)/ 72/ 14, as given in J. G. Bellamy, *The Law of Treason in England in the Later Middle Ages*, Cambridge Studies in English Legal History (Cambridge, 1970), pp. 126-27, 236-37 (and cf. pp. 153-54). This is the first clear case that Bellamy can cite of witchcraft or necromancy being regarded specifically as treasonous. As a contrast, he refers to the case of John de Nottingham in 1324; he had agreed to kill the king and others by his arts and had made seven wax images for the purpose, but was appealed merely for felony (p. 126 n. 1, citing *Select Cases in the Court of the King's Bench*, ed. G. O. Sayles (Selden Society 75; London, 1955), pp. 154-57). But it is noteworthy that when Parliament finally passed a statute against calculating the sovereign's life, the offense was made a felony, not treason: 23 Elizabeth I c. 2 (1580-1581), *Statutes of the Realm* (1810-1828, rpt. London, 1963), 4.1.659-60. On wax images, I should point out that it is only according to a later historian, Robert Fabyan, in his *New Chronicles of England and France*, ed. Henry Ellis (London, 1811), p. 614, that Eleanor and her associates were charged with having used a wax image of Henry VI in order to kill him. Fabyan died in 1513, and his work was first published in 1516.

73 *Brut*, p. 480. *English Chronicle*, p. 59 says that the trial reconvened on Saturday the 21st.

74 *English Chronicle*, p. 59.

75 See R. Naz, 'Promoteur de justice', *Dictionnaire de droit canonique* 7.357-58. The promoter was not an independent 'prosecuting attorney', but simply filled the judge's accusatorial role. The promoter of Cardinals Campeggio and Wolsey in the legatine trial of 1529 was John Hughes, who has left a memorandum of his duties. See *Letters and Papers, Foreign and Domestic, of the Reign of Henry VIII*, ed. J. S. Brewer et al., 22 vols. (London, 1856-1929; corr. rpt. Vaduz, 1965), 4, no. 5613.7. I describe his activities at length in *The Matrimonial Trials of Henry VIII* (Stanford, 1976). It was customary for the judge himself to level the first set of charges, and to assign this function to a promoter only in certain contested or complicated cases, where further formulations of charges were necessary. The Chichele register provides examples in the English and Roman trials of William Russell (3.126 ff. and 139 ff.). In the English trial, held before convocation, two promoters were appointed, but after their first appearance only one of them, namely Richard Collyng, vicar of St. Laurence Jewry, continued to function in the case. It is noteworthy that Collyng is said to have been appointed *by the clergy* to promote the archbishop's office against Russell (3.146; cf. p. 126).

76 *English Chronicle*, p. 59; *Brut*, p. 480 adds the bishop of Salisbury. There is an instance in

According to one report, Eleanor denied all of the charges now objected against her;[77] according to another, 'some she denied and some she granted', but on the next day of trial, Monday the 23rd, she 'was convict of the said articles', and had nothing to say when given the opportunity to impugn the witnesses brought against her, but simply submitted to the bishops' correction.[78] The *Brut* gives details of the witnesses who appeared on that day. First of all, Bolingbroke and his instruments were brought before her. She denied the intent that had been placed on her activity, and said 'that she did it for to have borne a child by her lord, the Duke of Gloucester'.[79] Southwell too testified against her, as did Margery Jourdemayne, who said that 'she was causer and doer of all this work and deed'.[80]

On the following day, Friday, 27 October, 'the said Eleanor abjured before the bishops the articles abovesaid. And then she was enjoined for to appear before the said Archbishop of Canterbury or his foresaid commissioners the Thursday, the ninth day of November next following, for to receive her penance.'[81] Margery Jourdemayne met her fate on the day of Eleanor's abjuration, which was also the day on which Southwell was to be arraigned.[82] But he died in the Tower the night before, in accord with his prophecy 'that he should die in his bed, and not by justice'.[83] For some reason the secular trial of Bolingbroke and others involved in the case was not held for some weeks.

On the final day of Eleanor's trial, Thursday, 9 November, Archbishop Chichele himself appeared to deliver the sentence, in the company of Cardinals Beaufort and Kemp, Bishops Gilbert, Alnwick, Ayscough, and Brown, 'with divers doctors and masters of divinity'; he 'divorced and departed the Duke of Gloucester and Dame Eleanor Cobham, as for matrimony made before between them two'.[84] Historians have not always noticed this important conclusion of the Cobham witchcraft trial, namely that the court upheld the charge that Eleanor

Chichele's register (3.198-200) of his temporarily committing the conduct of a trial in convocation to another bishop.

77 *Brut*, p. 480.

78 *English Chronicle*, p. 59.

79 It seems that Eleanor had borne two children to Gloucester before he married her (Vickers, *Humphrey*, p. 205), but none after.

80 *Brut*, p. 480.

81 *English Chronicle*, p. 59.

82 *Brut*, p. 509 (MS. G, the version that Caxton printed in 1480). Another chronicler speaks of this Friday as the day of his condemnation; see C. L. Kingsford, 'Brief Notes for 1440-1443' in his *English Historical Literature in the Fifteenth Century* (Oxford, 1913; rpt. New York, n.d.), p. 340; in *Chronicon Angliae* (n. 54 above), p. 31, it is the day of his punishment. But, as we shall see from the case of Roger Bolingbroke, it seems that all of these actions could occur on the same day.

83 *Brut*, p. 509.

84 *Brut*, pp. 480-81. *English Chronicle*, p. 59 gives the date correctly (*Brut* says 6 November).

had coerced the duke into marrying her by means of sorcery, and that therefore they found the marriage null and void from the beginning. The accuracy of this reported annulment is confirmed by the findings of Humphrey's biographer; though unaware of the sentence of 'divorce', he noticed that after her trial, 'her rank was not recognized, for she is described in all official documents as "Eleanor, lately called Duchess of Gloucester"'.[85]

Secondly, on the day of sentence, 'Dame Eleanor Cobham, by ordinance and charge of the Archbishop of Canterbury and his brethren, was joined to her penance for the great offence and trespass that she had done against God and holy Church and for the false sorcery and witchcraft that she used and long time had wrought'.[86] This wording seems to confirm my earlier speculation that the charges of heresy and treason allegedly brought against her in her first appearance in the archbishop's court were either dropped or never levied in the first place. We have seen, of course, that she was indicted of treason and felony in the secular courts, but the fact that we hear nothing of her arraignment before them suggests that the case was abandoned. Perhaps it was felt that the punishment to be meted out by the church court was sufficient, though J. G. Bellamy notes the possibility that she was not put on trial because there were no satisfactory precedents for trying peeresses on such crimes — a lack that was remedied in the Parliament of January-March 1442.[87]

In one account, an abbreviated London chronicle, Eleanor is said to have been condemned as a heretic as well as a witch: 'adiudicata et damnata pro haeretica et nigromantica'. Furthermore, part of the penance she received, namely to go in pilgrimage, taper in hand, to different churches on three market days of the following week, resembles the penalty enjoined forty years later on another woman, Margaret Geffrey. In her case too there was the rare union of heresy and sorcery in the charges against her, and she, like Eleanor, sought to win a wealthy husband by means of magic. But this form of penance was confined neither to sorcery nor heresy, but was in fact a common punishment visited upon convicted adulterers and fornicators.[88]

85 Vickers, *Humphrey*, p. 274. Cf. Rymer, *Foedera* 11.45, for the order of 26 October 1443 'de conducendo Alianoram Cobeham'; here her former title is not even referred to. When, shortly after Gloucester's death in February 1447, Eleanor was prevented by King Henry from inheriting any of his goods, she is described as having been his uncle's wife: 'quae fuit uxor avunculi sui nuper ducis Gloucestr.' (*Rot. parl.* 5.135). See Kingsford, *English Historical Literature*, p. 93, for other implications of the annulment.

86 *Brut*, p. 481.

87 Bellamy, *Law of Treason* (n. 72 above), p. 154 and note, citing *Rot. parl.* 5.56.

88 The Latin chronicle is MS. Rawlinson B 355, ed. Ralph Flenley in *Six Town Chronicles of England* (Oxford, 1911), p. 102; see Kingsford, *English Historical Literature*, pp. 79-81, 112 (addendum). For Margaret Geffrey, see above, n. 10 (no. 4) and n. 16 (no. 7). On penances for adultery and fornication, see Helmholz, *Marriage Litigation* (n. 40 above), p. 182.

Eleanor's offences, of course, were much more serious than Margaret Geffrey's; not only did she, unlike Margaret, succeed in her magical matrimonial scheme, but her experiments with the occult must also, in the judgment of the ecclesiastical and secular authorities, have touched somehow on the life expectancy of the king. Accordingly, after her three days of public penance, 'she was committed again to the ward of Sir Thomas Stanley, wherein she was all her life after, having yearly 100 mark assigned to her for her finding and costs; whose pride, false coveteise, and lechery were cause of her confusion.'[89]

On the day after Eleanor's final day of public humiliation, that is on Saturday, 18 November, Roger Bolingbroke 'was brought to the Guildhall with Sir John Hom, priest, and William Wodham, squire', but Hom and Wodham were pardoned.[90] Hom, or Hune, is identified as one of Eleanor's chaplains in another chronicle, according to which he was condemned for treason and sentenced to death before being pardoned by the king.[91] Bolingbroke, however, was not so fortunate. He was arraigned before the lords and justices 'of the foresaid articles of treason against the king's person, and thereof by twelve men of London he was found guilty. Wherefore by the judgment of Sir John Hody, that time Chief Justice of the King's Bench, he was drawn from the Tower of London unto Tyburn; and there he was hanged and let down half alive, and his bowels taken out and burned, and his head smitten off and set on London Bridge, and his body quartered and sent to certain towns of England, that is to say, Oxford, Cambridge, York, and Hereford. And when the said Master Roger should die, he confessed that he was never guilty of any treason against the king's person; but he presumed too far in his cunning, as he said, whereof he cried God mercy; and the justice that gave on him judgment lived not long after.'[92]

Perhaps by this last detail the chronicler is implying that Bolingbroke's punishment was more severe than his guilt warranted. Another chronicler, William Worcester, testifies that many made great lamentation over his death, though admittedly he had been Eleanor's counsellor in the magic art; but he speaks of him in seemingly praiseworthy terms as one of the most famous scholars in the world in astronomy and the nigromantic art.[93]

The long account of Eleanor in the *Brut* ends as it began, with a fierce attack of weather that seems somehow attributable to her: she was kept in ward in the constabulary of Westminster until Wednesday, 24 January 1442; and when she

89 *English Chronicle*, p. 60.

90 *Chronicles of London* (n. 41 above), p. 149; *A Chronicle of London* (n. 41 above), pp. 129-30.

91 *Brut*, p. 509 (MS. G).

92 *English Chronicle*, p. 60.

93 Worcester, ed. Stevenson, *Letters and Papers* (n. 65 above), p. 763.

was brought out to begin her journey to the Isle of Man, 'there was such weathering of thunder, lightning, hail, and rain that the people were sore adread and aghast of the great noise and hideous of the weather, that suddenly was done and showed there at their passage at that time.'[94]

I have gone into such great detail in this case, not only because it has not been done before, but also because of its importance as an illustration of the moderation and due process which the English courts, both ecclesiastical and secular, could bring even to a witchcraft scare of nationwide scope. After widespread investigations and inquests, only a handful of people were brought to justice, and no doubt all of them were truly implicated to some extent in the forbidden arts. This is not to say that political and private prejudice played no part in the prosecutions; it undoubtedly did. But the authorities never lost control of the machinery of justice; and, though such simple phenomena as electrical storms could create something of a panic among the people, there seems never to have been any real danger of a large-scale persecution of suspected witches.

The case is also interesting because of the picture it gives of the interplay between secular and ecclesiastical courts. Unfortunately, the picture is only a very partial one. Without the actual trial records we cannot tell the precise official relationship between the two systems, let alone determine whether or not there was any cynical manipulation of one jurisdiction by the other. We cannot even tell whether the church courts always had priority in witchcraft cases, or whether it was left to the discretion of the secular and/or ecclesiastical authorities. It may be that all of the implicated persons in the affair were given an ecclesiastical trial before any secular judgment upon them was passed, even though for some of them no records of such proceedings have yet been uncovered.

The exposure that the Cobham case gave to witchcraft as a threat to government does not appear to have inspired apprehensions of this sort during the generation that followed, even though the country was torn by the respective claims of the Lancastrians and Yorkists. Similarly, little mention is made of the devil's opposition during the Wars of the Roses, though there is an abundance of assertions of divine support.

It is only at the end of the long contest between the allies of Henry VI and the party of the duke of York that I have found any reference to the influence of occult powers. But it is simply a matter of vague allegations implicating Friar * Bungay, who seems to have ranked with Roger Bolingbroke as (in Worcester's words) 'quidam clericus famosissimus unus illorum in toto mundo in astronomia et arte nigromantica'. He was implicated on the basis of that by now familiar form of spectral evidence, unfavorable weather. When Queen Margaret, wife of

94 *Brut*, p. 482.

Henry VI, was prevented for a long time from crossing the English Channel to join in the attack against the Yorkist Edward IV, it was said to be God's will by her enemies, and by others, who bore her good will, 'that it was done by some sorcery or witchcraft of one named at that days Bungay or such other'.[95] When in the next year (1471) the Lancastrian lords were hampered by mists and other impediments at the battle of Barnet, the rumor was that they were caused by the incantations of Friar Bungay.[96]

Witchcraft came seriously to the fore again only within the York family itself, in connection with Edward IV's brothers, George duke of Clarence and Richard III, and Edward's queen, Elizabeth Woodville.

Clarence was convicted of treason early in 1478, and apparently executed in secret. The chronicler John Rous, writing a decade later, maintains that he met his fate because credence was given to a prophecy to the effect that after 'E' 'G' would reign; Rous also reported that Humphrey of Gloucester was said to have been killed in order to forestall a similar prophecy (viz., that Gloucester would kill Henry VI). Both prophecies, he said, were fulfilled by Richard, duke of Gloucester (that is, Richard III).[97] A generation later Polydore Vergil discounted the prophecy as motive for Clarence's conviction, though he attributed the idea of its fulfillment in Richard to the illusions of demons. After writing the first draft of his history, Vergil apparently read some form of the Croyland Chronicle, where he found a more plausible reason for Clarence's downfall, namely the duke's complaints after one of his servants was put to death for practising *veneficium*.[98]

95 *The Great Chronicle of London*, ed. A. H. Thomas and I. D. Thornley (London, 1938), p. 214.

96 Fabyan, *English Chronicles* (n. 74 above), p. 661. Kittredge, *Witchcraft*, p. 153, mistakenly says that it was the Yorkist lords who were so impeded.

97 Rous, *Historia regum* (n. 35 above), p. 215; Kelly, *Divine Providence*, p. 70. Alison Hanham, *Richard III and His Early Historians, 1483-1535* (Oxford, 1975), p. 121, badly mangles Rous's meaning in her translation of the manuscript text (a plate of which appears opposite p. 121): she renders the phrase *nempe quod dux Gloucestriae ipsum interficeret* as 'but undoubtedly that Duke of Gloucester killed himself', whereas it means 'namely, that the Duke of Gloucester would kill him', i.e. Henry VI.

98 For Vergil's dependence on the Croyland Chronicle materials, see Kelly, *Divine Providence*, p. 90 and note, and cf. Hanham, ibid., pp. 96, 135-51; Hanham, however, is hampered in her analysis not only by her imperfect hold on the Latin language, but also by her failure to use Vergil's draft history, Vatican MS. Urb. lat. 498. In his first version, Vergil said that he inquired into the cause of Clarence's downfall from many authorities still living, but could find nothing certain; and after dismissing the 'G' prophecy he indulged in some reflections on providential justice (for which, see Kelly, *Divine Providence*, pp. 98-99, 325), which he later cancelled, and added the Croyland story on an inserted page (namely fol. 211). Hanham suggests that Vergil did not read the Croyland Chronicle in its present form, but rather the 'Ur-text' probably written by John Russell (see the next note). For Vergil's added account of Clarence's fall as he kept it in his printed editions, see the early English translation of his second edition (1546), ed. Henry Ellis, *Three Books of Polydore Vergil's English History* (Camden Society 1.29; London, 1844), pp. 167-68.

The Croyland report of this last-named incident may come from one of Edward IV's councillors, John Russell, at that time bishop of Rochester.[99] He identifies the servant in question as Thomas Burdett, who was allegedly in league with 'Master John Stacy, a person who was called an astronomer, when in reality he was rather a great sorcerer' (*necromanticus*). Stacy first came to the attention of the authorities in 1477, when he was accused of attempting to murder Richard Lord Beauchamp by sorcery. His connection with Burdett was brought out during an *acerrimum examen* — literally 'a very severe examination'. Kittredge assumes from this phrase that Stacy was 'examined under torture'.[100] He is doubtless correct. As we have seen, William Lyndwood considered the use of torture even by the ecclesiastical authorities in proceedings against heretics to be approved by canon law; and though there may have been no clear sanction of its use by the secular arm, it would be surprising if it were not employed on occasion at the call of convenience or necessity. We know for certain that it was used by the King's Council in the sixteenth and seventeeth centuries; and William Worcester reports a case of the same thing under Edward IV, some years before the Stacy affair. Much earlier still, Geoffrey Chaucer adds details of torture to his sources so casually as to suppose a familiarity with the procedures among his listeners and readers.[101] *

99 Bishop Russell's connection with the Croyland Chronicle was suggested by Paul Murray Kendall, *Richard III* (London, 1956), p. 432, which I discussed in my 'Canonical Implications of Richard III's Plan to Marry His Niece', *Traditio* 23 (1967) 269-311, especially 272-73. But J. G. Edwards, 'The "Second" Continuation of the Crowland Chronicle: Was It Written "in Ten Days"?', *Bulletin of the Institute of Historical Research* 39 (1966) 117-29, shows that the ten days of April 1486 mentioned at the end of the continuation refers not to the writing of the chronicle but to a legal action presided over by Russell as bishop of Lincoln. He also calls Russell's part in the compilation of the chronicle into question, but Hanham, ibid., pp. 86-96, defends Russell as the most likely candidate. I agree, and would add that even if the bishop did not compose his history at Croyland at that time (when, we are told, he spent not just ten days but a whole month at the abbey), it is a likely time for his account to have been left at Croyland. For the passage dealing with the duke of Clarence's downfall, see the *Continuatio historiae croylandensis*, ed. William Fulman, *Rerum anglicarum scriptores veteres* 1 (Oxford, 1684), pp. 561-62, and the translation of Henry T. Riley, *Ingulph's Chronicle of the Abbey of Croyland, with the Continuations by Peter of Blois and Anonymous Writers* (London, 1854), pp. 478-79.

100 Kittredge, *Witchcraft*, p. 139. Hanham, ibid., p. 137 gives the same rendering.

101 For Lyndwood, see above at nn. 19-20; on torture under the Tudors and Stuarts, see Stephen, *History of Criminal Law* (n. 25 above), 1.222. Worcester, ed. Stevenson, *Letters and Papers* (n. 65 above), pp. 789-90, says that in 1468 a certain shoemaker named Cornelius, servant of Sir Robert Whittingham, was arrested for carrying letters from Margaret of Anjou; in the Tower, he was forced to implicate others by having fire applied to him while his feet were being racked or squeezed: 'Ibidem comburitur pedibus in tormentis dictus Cornelius ad confitendum multa'. Bellamy, *Crime* (n. 10 above), p. 140, cites John Stow as saying that John Hawkins, one of the men implicated by Cornelius, was put on the rack: 'He was brought to the brake, called the Duke of Exeter's daughter.' The Duke of Exeter in question is John Holland, constable of the Tower under Henry VI, who according to Coke introduced the rack as part of a plan to bring imperial civil

Stacy and Burdett were accordingly brought to trial at the order of the king, and there was allegedly uncovered a witchcraft plot against the king. The two were convicted of treasonably imagining and compassing the death of King Edward by necromancy and other means at various times during the previous three years.[102] Both protested their innocence, but they were nevertheless hanged, drawn, and quartered on 20 May 1477.

Clarence made his protest almost immediately after the executions, and within

law to England (ibid., p. 139). On Cornelius and Hawkins, see also Bellamy, *Law of Treason* (n. 72 above), pp. 140-41, 147, 164. As for Chaucer, he has Theseus tell Palamon (*Knight's Tale*, ll. 1744-1747):

> Youre owene mouth, by youre confessioun,
> Hath dampned yow, and I wol it recorde;
> It nedeth noght to pyne yow with the corde.
> Ye shal be deed, by myghty Mars the rede!

Earlier, Palamon told Arcite that they had agreed not to hinder each other in love, even though they had to die 'in the peyne' (line 1133), and Pandarus uses the same expression in *Troilus and Criseyde*, 1.764. It clearly does not refer to the 'strong and hard prison' (*peine forte et dure*) inflicted on those who refused trial by jury (i.e. refused to plead guilty or not guilty), which led to the practice of 'pressing' beginning under Henry IV. See Ralph B. Pugh, *Imprisonment in Medieval England* (Cambridge, 1968), pp. 24-25; Stephen, *History of Criminal Law* (n. 25 above), 1.299-300; Bellamy, *Crime*, pp. 138-39, 141-42. In the *Stanzaic Morte Arthur* (late fourteenth century, surviving in a late fifteenth-century manuscript), the author uses the term 'hard pain' to mean torture, in an episode added to the story of the poisoned apple in the French *Mort Artu*: the squires who served at the table are taken into custody, 'and thay ar put in harde payne'; one of them confesses: 'There he grauntyd amonge hem alle, It myght no lenger be to layne [i.e., hidden] How in an appelle he dede the galle'; ed. J. Douglas Bruce, EETS, ES 88 (London, 1903; rpt. Millwood, N.Y., 1975), p. 48. lines 1648-1654. In Chaucer's *Nun's Priest's Tale* Chanticleer tells Partlet of the fate of two murderers:

> And right anon, ministres of that toun
> Han hent the carter and so soore hym pyned,
> and eek the hostiler so soore engyned,
> That they biknewe hire wikkednesse anon,
> And were anhanged by the nekke-bon. (ll. 3058-3062)

In the year 1433 a merchant complained to Commons that the lord of the port city of Gildo in Brittany had imprisoned a servant of his 'and engined him so that he was in point of death' (*Rot. parl.* 4.475). In the Wakefield Cycle play of the Crucifixion (late fourteenth or early fifteenth century, preserved in a late fifteenth-century manuscript), the attendants, called torturers (*tortores*), say that Christ would have done another trick if he had had the rack:

> He wold have turnyd an othere croke
> Myght he have had the rake.

See *The Townley Plays*, ed. George England, EETS, ES 71 (London, 1897; rpt. 1966), p. 260, ll. 87-88.

102 J. R. Lander, 'The Treason and Death of the Duke of Clarence: A Reinterpretation', *Canadian Journal of History* 2.2 (1967) 1-28, especially 8, citing the *Third Report of the Deputy Keeper of the Public Records*, app. 2 (London, 1842), pp. 213-14.

a few weeks he himself was arrested. Among the charges upon which he was convicted in February 1478 was that he had accused King Edward himself of using sorcery: Clarence 'said and labored also to be noised by such his servants apt for that work that the king our sovereign lord wrought by nigromancy and used craft to poison his subjects, such as him pleased'. He was also charged with having accused Edward of designs upon his own life, and perhaps it was meant as an illustration of the way in which the king used witchcraft: he declared 'that the king intended to consume him [Clarence] in like wise as a candle consumeth in burning'.[103]

Edward IV had been connected with another familiar sort of witchcraft plot some years earlier, when his mother-in-law, Jacquetta of Luxemburg, duchess of Bedford, was accused by one Thomas Wake of making magic images — specifically an image of the king and one of her daughter, Elizabeth Woodville Grey.[104] Presumably the purport of the accusation was that the duchess had by her witchcraft engineered the king's infatuation with her daughter, which led to his at first secret, then public, marriage to her.

Edward's union to Elizabeth was made public in 1464, and Wake's accusation came only several years later: Jacquetta was cleared of the charge on 22 January 1470. Whether or not Wake was attempting to impugn the king's marriage at this time can only be conjectured; but that was clearly the intent of the charge when the matter was taken up again after Edward's death in 1483, in support of Richard III's claim to the throne. The parliamentary statement of the accusation is couched in terms of notoriety resembling those of articles in an *ex officio* inquisition: 'The said pretensed marriage ... was made ... by sorcery and witchcraft, committed by the said Elizabeth and her mother Jacquetta, duchess of Bedford, as the common opinion of the people and the public voice and fame is through all this land, and hereafter, if and as the case shall require, shall be proved sufficiently in time and place convenient'.[105]

103 *Rot. parl.* 6.194; Kittredge, *Witchcraft*, p. 140.

104 Kittredge, *Witchcraft*, p. 84.

105 *Rot. parl.* 6.240-42, reprinted by Mortimer Levine in *Tudor Dynastic Problems, 1460-1571*, Historical Problems, Studies and Documents 21, ed. G. R. Elton (London, 1973), pp. 135-37. The declaration was first presented to Richard late in June (by the 26th) of 1483, and then ratified under his parliament early in 1484 (see Levine, pp. 28-29). Cf. the language of the articles in the legatine trial of 1529. The first article, as given in Cambridge University Library MS. Dd. 13.26, fol. 6, reads: 'In primis vobis, illustrissimo principi Henrico octavo, ad effectum supradictum obiicimus, exponimus, articulamus, et ministramus: Quod vos et celeberrimae memoriae Arthurus, perennis famae Henrici septimi nuper regis Angliae et dominae Elisabeth consortis suae primogenitus, fratres ex eisdem parentibus geniti eratis ac pro talibus in regno Angliae et alibi communiter habiti et reputati fuistis sicuti estis de praesenti, haecque fuerunt et sunt vera, publica, et notoria, ac de et super eisdem laborarunt et laborant publica vox et fama, ac obiicimus coniunctim et divisim et de quolibet'.

In this charge Queen Elizabeth herself is included in the practice of witchcraft, which perhaps reflects the fact that a short time before (on 19 June 1483) Richard, according to Polydore Vergil, had accused that witch (*illa maga*) Queen Elizabeth of afflicting his body with her *veneficia*. Thomas More, who, according to Alison Hanham's plausible argument, was drawing on an early version of Vergil's history, gives the queen an unlikely associate, Edward IV's mistress: 'That sorceress and that other witch of her counsel, Shore's wife, with their affinity, have by their sorcery and witchcraft wasted my body'.[106]

The traditional view, which Hanham opposes, is that More's chief informant was John Morton, who in 1483 was bishop of Ely. In More's narration, Richard's charge occurred just after Morton had sent for some strawberries from his garden at Richard's request. It has been suggested that Richard deliberately simulated a witchcraft attack by eating strawberries, to which he knew he was allergic.[107] Or, taking a less villainous view of Richard and assuming some basis in fact for More's story (a dangerous assumption), we might conjecture that the Protector was genuinely frightened by some consequence of the bishop's gift. Be that as it may, I know of no direct evidence associating Morton with a witchcraft plot against Richard.[108] He was, however, linked with a 'nigromancer', one Thomas Nandyk, who joined Buckingham's rebellion against Richard in the autumn of 1483. But in Richard's strange proclamation of 23 October, in which he goes out of his way to condemn sexual immorality (in particular, he denounces the ex-Marquess Dorset, Queen Elizabeth's son, for 'holding the unshameful and mischievous woman called Shore's wife in adultery'), he does not bring up the matter of witchcraft.[109] When the participants in the revolt were attainted by Parliament early in 1484, five instigators of the treason were named, including

106 Thomas More, *The History of King Richard III*, ed. Richard S. Sylvester, *Complete Works of St. Thomas More* 2 (New Haven, 1963), pp. 47-48; see ibid., pp. 218-19 for the text of Vergil's account (from the Ellis ed., n. 98 above, pp. 180-81). See Hanham, *Richard III* (n. 97 above), pp. 152 ff.: 'Sir Thomas More's Satirical Drama'. As I noted above in connection with the Croyland Chronicle, Hanham must be faulted for neglecting to consult Vergil's manuscript, in this case in order to determine the precise state of the *Anglica historia* when More presumably got hold of a copy of it and, as Hanham thinks, deliberately satirized the Italian's methods. In the instance under discussion, namely Richard's charge of witchcraft against the queen, it does in fact occur in the earliest layer of Vergil's manuscript, on fols. 217v-218.

107 John Dover Wilson, 'A Note on *Richard III*: The Bishop of Ely's Strawberries', *Modern Language Review* 52 (1957) 563-64, following Dr. J. Swift Joly.

108 Rossell Hope Robbins, *The Encyclopedia of Witchcraft and Demonology* (New York, 1959), p. 162, says that Morton, the countess of Richmond (i.e., the mother of Henry VII), and other Lancastrians were tried for using sorcery in 1483, but I cannot find any report of such trials, and Professor Robbins informs me that he is unable to locate the source for his statement.

109 Rymer, *Foedera* 12.204-205.

Buckingham, Morton, and 'Thomas Nandyk, late of Cambridge, nigromancer'.[110] The black art is simply listed as Nandyk's profession, and no account is taken of his making use of it in his treason. He was referred to in the same way in Henry VII's first Parliament, in which all those so attainted were pardoned.[111]

The context of this last named parliamentary act did not of course allow any opprobrious comment to be made on Nandyk's necromancy, but it could perhaps be taken as an augury of Henry VII's attitude toward witchcraft that a publicly proclaimed sorcerer could be set at large without let upon his practices. Henry Tudor's disputed title to the throne gave rise to the same kind of plots and insurrections that had aroused fears of sorcery among his predecessors. But I can find no evidence of such concern in him; nor is there any association of witchcraft with his name, with one exception, an exception that seems to confirm the above impression. In 1496, a multiple murder-by-witchcraft plot against the king and his family and councillors was alleged in a confession by one Bernard de Vignolles, who implicated, among others, John Kendal, grand prior of the Knights Hospitallers of St. John of Jerusalem. Kendal's supposed motive, apparently, was to advance the pretender Perkin Warbeck.[112] Bernard's confession is endorsed by Henry VII in his own hand, so the king must have read the series of charges against the prior; but, as Kittredge says, 'he seems to have made light of it', for Kendal received a general pardon on 18 June 1496.[113]

As for Henry VII's sixteenth-century Tudor successors, they seem to have inherited his lack of serious concern for the magical arts as such, in connection with their own persons. In the case of Henry VIII, witchcraft seems to have touched his conscience directly only at one point, and that a sore one: he came to the conclusion that Anne Boleyn had bewitched him into loving her. This view of the matter crystallized after his attraction towards her had long since waned, when he was seeking a way out of his marriage to her. But he did not publicize his conviction that witchcraft had been used; he simply spoke of it to someone as a great secret, as if he were going to confession. The someone, however, broke the seal of confession, as it were, and revealed it to one of the king's principal

110 *Rot. parl.* 6.245-47.

111 ibid., p. 273: but 'Nandyk' (or 'Nandik' or 'Nandike') has metamorphosed into 'Vandyke'.

112 James Gairdner, *Letters and Papers Illustrative of the Reigns of Richard III and Henry VII* 2 (London, 1863), pp. 318-23. The magic involved the use of a special ointment to be spread on a doorway through which the king was to pass; it was to have the effect of inciting the king's friends to kill him. Vignolles claimed that Kendal eventually refused to make use of the ointment, not because of a change of heart, it seems, but because he feared that the virulent substance might endanger his own life (in fact, Vignolles said, the ointment was harmless, for he had surreptitiously replaced the magic brew with a concoction of his own).

113 Kittredge, *Witchcraft*, p. 50, citing the Calendar of Patent Rolls.

courtiers, who in turn passed it on to Lord and Lady Exeter, whence it came to the ears of the emperor's ambassador, Eustace Chapuys. Chapuys found it difficult to believe that the king could be serious, but he accepted the report as true because it came from a good source.[114]

Apart from this single instance of amatory witchcraft, the occult arts seem to have encroached upon royalty in the sixteenth century mainly by way of prophecy. For instance, the duke of Buckingham, like Macbeth, was told that he would one day be king, a hope that led to his execution in 1521.[115] One of the offenses for which Lord Hungerford was attainted and executed in 1540 was his inquiry by conjuration into the duration of the king's life.[116] In 1532, the King's Council investigated Sir William Neville for giving voice to certain prophecies about the king.[117] In Edward VI's time a man confessed to calculating the death date of that king, but Edward dismissed the matter as insignificant. He did, however, order the offender to the Tower, where he was kept for a year.[118] During Queen Elizabeth's reign, there was a whole series of charges of such calculations of the life expectancy of the sovereign, which led to parliamentary action against it.[119] Now the matter was taken seriously, and rightly so, because of the numerous real plots against the queen with which such activities were often connected. Yet, in spite of this, and in spite of the unquestionable growth of popular interest in witchcraft, there was no panic, no witchhunting worthy of comparison with that which occurred in other lands, no reaction like that of King James VI and his Scottish subjects in 1590 and the years following.

As we have seen, most of the theoretical, judicial, and motivational ingredients for a witchcraft epidemic were available in England during the fourteenth, fifteenth, and sixteenth centuries, but they did not occur in an explosive combination. The reality of witchcraft's power for evil was admitted, but it was not singled out for undue attention. Attempted murder and treason by witchcraft were not prosecuted with greater vigor than other forms of murder and treason. If torture was used in England, it was no doubt used as 'judiciously' for ferreting out other crimes as for investigating possible instances of sorcery. Witchcraft was sometimes felt to be connected with heresy (though burning was a possible

114 Chapuys to Charles V, 29 January 1536, given in Paul Friedmann, *Anne Boleyn* 2 (London, 1884), pp. 202-203.

115 Kittredge, *Witchcraft*, pp. 228-29.

116 ibid., p. 65.

117 ibid., p. 63.

118 Wallace Notestein, *A History of Witchcraft in England from 1558 to 1718* (Washington, D.C., 1911; rpt. New York, 1968), p. 13.

119 ibid., pp. 25-27; cf. Alan Macfarlane, *Witchcraft in Tudor and Stuart England* (London, 1970), pp. 77-78, and see n. 72 above.

penalty for witchcraft apart from any consideration of heresy); but it was not formally identified with it, and in spite of the Templar and Kyteler cases in the early fourteenth century there was no acceptance of the idea of the heretical cult of witchcraft.

The ecclesiastical inquisition was used as well against witchcraft as against heresy (where torture was allowed but probably not practised) and other offenses, but similar due process was observed in all cases. No doubt a papal inquisition could have been had for the asking, if an English monarch had deemed it necessary or advisable, as did Edward II in the case of the Templars, but the need was not felt.[120] Of course, church inquisitions, papal or otherwise, were not necessary for the successful mounting of a good-sized witch hunt; but nothing of the sort occurred, even in the sixteenth century, when England shared the kind of religious dissent that allegedly provided the occasion for witch burnings on the Continent.[121]

The devil, in short, was given his due in England; but it was rarely more of a due than was warranted by traditional theology and common sense. Perhaps the English faith in divine providence was so strong that repression of the devil and

120 For Edward II, see above, nn. 10 and 20. Edward at first prohibited the inquisitors from using torture, as being contrary to the laws of his kingdom. Beginning at least with Henry VIII, or even Edward IV (see n. 101 above), the English rulers had no such scruples, at any rate for Council investigations; but they did not attempt to impose the practice in either ecclesiastical or secular trials. It is noteworthy that in the papal inquisition into Henry VIII's first marriage, the legatine trial of 1529, instituted at the king's invitation, the normal forms were observed, in spite of the fact that the papal commission allowed for summary procedure. The *ex officio* inquisition was still used in England even after the break with Rome. For example, Cranmer employed it in the trial of Henry's second marriage, to Anne Boleyn, in 1536, and Archbishop Whitgift was using it in the 1580's — see J. B. Black, *The Reign of Elizabeth*, Oxford History of England 8, 2nd ed. (Oxford, 1959), p. 199 (in the same series, J. D. Mackie, *The Earlier Tudors*, 1952, pp. 549-52, describes the papal inquisition against Cranmer and other heresy trials under Queen Mary: even here torture was not used). The *ex officio* procedure was also still being used in the archdeacons' courts; see E. R. Brinkworth, *The Archdeacon's Court: Liber actorum, 1584* (Oxfordshire Record Society 23; Oxford, 1942); Brinkworth points out, both here (p. v) and in 'The Study and Use of Archdeacons' Court Records, Illustrated from the Oxford Records (1566-1759)', *Royal Historical Society, Transactions*, 4th Ser., 25 (1943) 93-119, especially 101, that basically the same procedure was followed until 1640. See, for example, Claude Jenkins, *Act Book of the Archdeacon of Taunton* [for 1623-1624], in *Collectanea* 2, ed. T. F. Palmer (Somerset Record Society 43; London, 1928), pp. 1-175.

121 This is the thesis of H. R. Trevor-Roper, 'The European Witch-Craze of the Sixteenth and Seventeenth Centuries' in *Religion, Reformation, and Social Change* (London, 1967), pp. 90-192. The causal implications are questioned by H. C. Erik Midelfort, *Witch Hunting in Southwestern Germany, 1562-1684* (Stanford, 1972), p. 6: 'In attempting to explain why witch hunts broke out at specific times, scholars have pointed to their temporal conjunction with wars of religion and outbreaks of heresy hunting. There is no doubt some validity in correlating witch hunts with periods of religious conflict and renewal, but the correlation is still incomplete, and the reasons for the beginnings of large-scale witch hunting remain unclear.'

his co-workers could be safely left to God. At any rate, it was clearly providential that at the time when the *Malleus maleficarum* was published on the Continent, an extremely levelheaded sovereign had begun to rule across the English Channel.[122]

122 I wish to thank Professor Norman Cohn for giving this essay a last-minute reading and thereby saving me from several questionable generalizations.

VIII

The Case Against Edward IV's Marriage and Offspring: Secrecy; Witchcraft; Secrecy; Precontract

John Ashdown-Hill's recent article, 'Edward IV's Uncrowned Queen',[1] is very illuminating on the life of Eleanor Butler. But some of the legal subjects that he treats need clarification. This is particularly true of his opening paragraph:

> Richard III's accession to the throne was based on the claim that the children of Edward IV were illegitimate. His case was that Edward IV's marriage with Elizabeth Woodville was both clandestine and bigamous and therefore invalid. If the two premises of clandestinity and bigamy were provable, Richard's case was a good one.

He cites as his authority Richard Helmholz's article on 'The sons of Edward IV'.[2] But Helmholz does not consider the full parliamentary justification in the so-called *Titulus regius*, specifically the charge of witchcraft. Furthermore, he does not claim that clandestinity would invalidate Edward's marriage. Secrecy made a marriage illicit but not invalid. Charles Ross is quite correct in saying that Edward IV's marriage 'was not made invalid because the lords had not assented, nor by the fact that it had been celebrated privately'.[3] Helmholz does say, however, that the secrecy of a marriage, even though the marriage is valid, could have the effect of illegitimating any children born to it.

Secrecy was, nevertheless, relevant to the marriage as well as to the question of legitimacy of offspring. Parliament in fact alleged two secret marriages of the king, the first to Eleanor Butler and the second to Elizabeth Woodville. If the first marriage could be proved to have taken place — that is, if it were not so secret that there were no witnesses to it — then it could be alleged as an impediment, the impediment of 'precontract', to the second marriage. This, of course, is where the bigamy would come in. 'Precontract', by the way, means *previous marriage*, when alleged as a challenge to a subsequent marriage. Any previous marriage would do, whether secret or public. The word does *not* mean 'preliminary contract' or 'betrothal'. A betrothal to one person did not invalidate a subsequent marriage to another person.

As noted, the *Titulus regius* alleged another impediment besides bigamy to the validity of the marriage between Edward and Elizabeth: namely, witchcraft. Secrecy, of course, was relevant to both of these impediments, because, as we will soon see, the purpose of non-secrecy was to make sure that any impediments to a proposed marriage could be brought to light and thereby prevent the marriage from taking place.

I have made some of these points earlier in *The Ricardian*, in my articles on the *Croyland Chronicle* (1985, 1987, 1990),[4] but I think it is time to dust them off and expand upon them.

Titulus Regius: Four Premises and Two Conclusions

The Parliament held at the beginning of 1484 did not add any arguments to the 'roll of parchment' (the *Titulus regius*) that was presented to Richard six months earlier, just before his coronation, but simply made a formal endorsement of it. The document makes four statements or premises about Edward IV's 'ungracious pretensed marriage' to Elizabeth Grey.[5] They are as follows:

Premises:

1. *Secrecy from the Lords:* 'And here also we consider how that the said pretensed marriage betwixt the above-named King Edward and Elizabeth Grey was made of great presumption, without the knowing and assent of the lords of this land'.
2. *Witchcraft:* 'And also by sorcery and witchcraft committed by the said Elizabeth and her mother Jaquette, Duchess of Bedford, as the common opinion of the people and the public voice and fame is through all this land, and hereafter, if and as the case shall require, shall be proved sufficiently in time and place convenient'.
3. *Secrecy from the Church:* 'And here also we consider how that the said pretensed marriage was made prively and secretly, without edition of banns, in a private chamber, a profane place, and not openly in the face of the Church, after the law of God's Church, but contrary thereunto and the laudable custom of the Church of England'.
4. *Precontract:* 'And how also that at the time of contract of the same pretensed marriage, and before and long time after, the said King Edward was and stood married and trothplight to one Dame Eleanor Butler, daughter of the old earl of

Shrewsbury, with whom the same King Edward had made a precontract of matrimony, long time before he made the said pretensed marriage with the said Elizabeth Grey in manner and form abovesaid'.
These statements are then asserted to be true — 'Which premises being true, as in very truth they been true' — with the following effects.
Conclusions:
1. *Invalidity of Marriage:* 'It appeareth and followeth evidently that the said King Edward during his life and the said Elizabeth lived together sinfully and damnably in adultery, against the law of God and of His Church; and therefore no marvel that, the sovereign lord and the head of this land being of such ungodly disposition and provoking the ire and indignation of our Lord God, such heinous mischiefs and inconvenients, as is above remembered, were used and committed in the realm amongst the subjects'.
2. *Illegitimacy of Offspring:* 'Also it appeareth evidently and followeth that all the issue and children of the said King Edward been bastards and unable to inherit or to claim anything by inheritance, by the law and custom of England'.

The accepted view is that Robert Stillington, Bishop of Bath and Wells, was the author of the petition. He was a trained canonist, having received his doctorate in Roman civil law (which included, of course, the mastery of canon law) from Oxford by June 1443.[6] His case is made carefully, and each element should be given due weight. We should note especially that there is no claim that each of the two conclusions depends on all four of the premises. The claim is only that, given the four premises, the two conclusions follow.

The Church Law on Clandestine Marriage

If it was true that Edward concealed his marriage to Elizabeth from the lords of the land, this circumstance had no effect whatsoever on the validity or invalidity of the union. This was a question reserved to the Church courts, which followed canon law. If it was also true that he disobeyed canon law and married without the reading of banns and not *in facie ecclesiae*, 'in the face of the Church', as canon law phrased it, he was liable to punishment; but the marriage was not therefore invalid.

The law on the point was given in the title *De clandestina desponsatione* of the *Liber Extra* of Gregory IX (1234). The third chapter in this title, *Cum inhibitio*, one of the decrees of the Fourth Lateran Council (1215), confirmed earlier strictures against secret marriage and required that notice of any forthcoming marriage be posted in church, so that any possible impediments could be raised by anyone who knew about them (for instance, a person already married to one of the proposed spouses). Fitting penances were to be imposed on all who violated these rules. The first chapter of the title, *Si quis clam*, decreed that if one of the parties to a secret marriage denied it, the burden of proof would be on the one who asserted it. The second chapter, *Quod nobis*, provided that if one or both secret spouses deny the marriage, it cannot be enforced without proof that it took place; if both spouses make the secret marriage public, then it must be approved by the Church as if contracted in the view of the church *(in ecclesiae conspectu)* from the beginning.[7]

Acceptance and enforcement of the Lateran decree was immediate in England. Diocesan statutes from the 1220s say that the notices, or banns, of marriage were to be published on three successive Sundays or holydays before the public marriage was to take place. William Lyndwood, writing in the 1420s, attributed this rule to the Council of Oxford in 1322, and excerpted it in his *Provinciale* in the first title of book 4, *De sponsalibus et matrimonio*.[8] In title 3, *De clandestina desponsatione*, he excerpts the constitutions of Archbishop Simon Mepham, 1329, ordering the Lateran decree to be made known to all the faithful. He decreed that priests who participated in marriages without publication of banns or outside of the spouses' parish were to be suspended, and the spouses themselves duly punished as well.[9] Lyndwood then presents an excerpt from the 1342 constitution of Archbishop Stratford, *Humana concupiscentia*, imposing *ipso facto* excommunication on all who forced priests to conduct a wedding service for a secret marriage, and ordering other penalties against all who celebrated marriage clandestinely.[10] Lyndwood's work, with his glosses and index (dated 1433), was one of the first books to be printed at Oxford in the 1480s (and the largest book to be printed there for a hundred years more),[11] and it was undoubtedly a standard reference work in 1483.

Witchcraft as an Impediment to Marriage

Witchcraft could be an impediment in one of two ways: as causing impotence and as affecting marital consent. The first impediment was included in a title of Book 4 of the *Liber Extra:* title 15, *De frigidis et maleficiatis, et impotentia coeundi* ('Concerning the frigid and the bewitched, and inability to have intercourse'); and though none of the eight chapters of the title deal explicitly with witchcraft, the Ordinary Gloss does treat the matter.[12] The Gloss also refers us to Gratian's *Decretum:* Case 33 is about a man who cannot render the debt to his wife because impeded by witchcraft; and chapter 4, *Si per sortiarias* ('If by witchcraft'), of the first question, along with Gratian's comment before it, deals explicitly with the matter.[13] The accepted law was that, if a man was impotent with respect to all women, it was diagnosed as a natural defect; if, however, he was impotent only with one woman, that is, his wife, the conclusion was that witchcraft was the cause, and the marriage could be annulled.

The canons and canonists do not speak to the second kind of invalidity caused by witchcraft, but it would fall under the category of 'force and fear,' which prevents adequate consent. The decretal *Cum locum* begins: 'Since consent does not take place where there is fear or coercion, it is necessary for all coercion to be eliminated when someone's assent is required. Now marriage is contracted by consent alone, and, when it is sought, the person whose intentions are in question should enjoy full security, lest he say out of fear that he is pleased by something he hates, with the result that usually follows from unwilling nuptials'.[14]

Royal Witchcraft Encounters in England

In my 1977 essay in *Mediaeval Studies*, 'English Kings and the Fear of Sorcery', I showed that every sovereign from Edward III to Elizabeth I was affected by witchcraft claims or charges.[15] The most significant episode for our purposes here is the alleged plot against the life of Edward IV's immediate predecessor, Henry VI, by Eleanor Cobham, Duchess of Gloucester, and her accomplices. In the ecclesiastical trial of Eleanor that took place in 1441, one of the charges upon which she was convicted was that she 'had enforced the foresaid duke of Gloucester to love her and wed her.' Accordingly, the judge, Archbishop Chichele, 'divorced and departed the duke of Gloucester and Dame Eleanor Cobham, as for matrimony made before between them two'. Accompanying the archbishop when he passed sentence was Cardinal Beaufort, Bishop of Winchester (1404-47); Cardinal Kemp, Archbishop of York, who eventually became archbishop of Canterbury (1452-54); the three bishops who had conducted the trial by Chichele's appointment, namely, Robert Gilbert, Bishop of London (1436-48), William Alnwick, Bishop of Lincoln (1436-49), and Thomas Brown, Bishop of Norwich (1436-45); and also William Ayscough, Bishop of Salisbury (1438-50), 'with divers doctors and masters of divinity', including Adam Moleyns, the judges' 'promotor' during the trial, who later became bishop of Chichester (1445-50).[16]

I detail all the prelates who participated in the trial and approved of the sentence of annulment, on grounds that it was coerced by witchcraft, to show that annulment by reason of witchcraft was considered a real possibility. We must remember that Robert Stillington at this time was coming to to the end of his doctoral studies in canon and civil law. This trial occurred not long before the time that Jacquetta of Luxemburg allegedly used witchcraft to induce Edward IV to marry her daughter, Elizabeth, in 1464, even though he was already allegedly married to Eleanor Butler. Jacquetta was no stranger to secret marriages. A year after her first husband, John of Lancaster, Duke of Bedford, died in 1435, she surreptitiously married Richard Woodville, and had to pay the large fine of £1000 for marrying without the king's license.[17] A witchcraft charge was brought against Jacquetta a few years after Edward IV's marriage to Elizabeth had been made public. A man named Thomas Wake accused her of making magic images, specifically an image of Edward IV and another of her daughter Elizabeth. She was cleared of the charge on 22 January 1470,[18] and she died on 30 May 1472.

We note that the author or authors of the *Titulus regius* offer to prove the claim against her, if the need should arise in the future, an offer not made with respect to the claim that Edward had previously married Eleanor Butler. We may also note that witchcraft was taken seriously just before this time. The Croyland Chronicler, a doctor of canon law whom I previously took to be John Russell, Bishop of Lincoln, but whom I now identify as Richard Lavender, Archdeacon of Leicester and Official of the Consistory Court in Lincoln,[19] in discussing George, Duke of Clarence, says that Clarence's servant, Thomas Burdett, was in league with Master John Stacy, a person who was called an astronomer but was also a great necromancer ('dictus astronomus cum etiam magnus necromanticus extiterat'); when Stacy was examined under torture concerning his damned art, on a charge of attempting to murder Richard Lord Beauchamp by means of leaden images, he implicated Burdett, and both were executed; Clarence protested the next day, and finally he himself was convicted of treason.[20]

Stacy and Burdett were convicted of witchcraft plots against the life of the king; they were executed on 20 May 1477. Among the charges that Clarence was convicted upon in February of 1478 was that he had accused Edward of himself using lethal witchcraft against his subjects.[21] Robert Stillington was also implicated in his treason and imprisoned in the Tower, being released in June only after paying a large sum of money. When historians assert that Stillington impugned Edward's marriage to Elizabeth out of motives of revenge,[22] we are doubtless being invited to question the existence of the alleged previous marriage between Edward and Eleanor.

As we have seen, the *Titulus regius* accuses Elizabeth as well as her mother Jacquetta of the witchcraft that led to Elizabeth's marriage to Edward. This circumstance may lend credence to Polydore Vergil's report that on 19 June 1483, that is, just about the time that the *Titulus* was presented to him, Richard accused Elizabeth of being a witch (*illa maga*) and afflicting his body with witching-poisons (*veneficia*). Thomas More has a different version of the incident, in having Richard associate Elizabeth with Shore's wife and other witches (*praestigiatrices)* in making his body bewitched (*fascinatum*) with their magic poisons *(magica veneficia)*. I have discussed in my early article whether Bishop Morton was somehow implicated in a witchcraft plot, noting that the 1484 Parliament condemned Morton along with a 'nigromancer', Thomas Nandyk, late of Cambridge, for instigating Buckingham's rebellion.[23]

Finally, let me recall that an argument against the validity of marriage because of witchcraft was contemplated by Henry VIII, shortly after the death of Catherine of Aragon in 1536, but with regard to his second marriage, to Anne Boleyn. Eustace Chapuys reported on good authority that Henry had confided to one of his intimates at court, like a man going to confession, that 'he had entered into this marriage seduced and constrained by witchcraft, and for this reason he believed that he was able to take another wife', which he desired to do; moreover, God had proved the invalidity of the marriage (as He had with his first marriage) by refusing to grant him any male children.[24]

The Impediment of Previous Marriage

The Croyland Chronicler, when reporting on the original presentation of the *Titulus regius* (he says that everyone knew the identity of the author), sums up the claim against Edward IV's sons by mentioning only the precontract with Eleanor Butler, with no allusion to the witchcraft charge.[25] When he reports the ratification by Parliament at the beginning of 1484, he simply says that that the validity of marriage was denied, without mentioning the impediment or impediments at issue. He does say, however, that it was beyond the power of that lay court ('*curia illa laicalis*') to decide the matter — meaning, of course, that it fell within the jurisdiction of the ecclesiastical courts. But in spite of their lack of jurisdiction, he says, Parliament went ahead and acted, 'because of the great fear that affected the most constant men' ('*propter ingentem in constantissimos cadentem metum*').[26] He is alluding to the canonistic criterion that invalidates matrimonial consent. The decretals *Veniens* and *Consultationi* specify *metus qui posset in virum constantem cadere*, 'fear that could affect a constant man'.[27]

Ross, following Mortimer Levine, is mistaken to attack the parliamentary case against the marriage on the grounds that 'if a precontract existed, making the marriage of 1464 invalid, there was nothing to prevent Edward and Elizabeth going through another ceremony of marriage after the death of Eleanor Butler in 1468'. If no such validation of marriage took place, then the marriage would still be invalid.[28] (Helmholz notes that a remarriage could only have taken place validly if Elizabeth had been unaware of Edward's first marriage when she married him.) In short, if Edward had made a present-tense contract of marriage with Eleanor Butler, even if he had not consummated it, he would not have been able to marry Elizabeth Woodville while Eleanor was still alive, and he would not have been considered married to her after Eleanor died.[29]

Conclusion

It follows, then, that, as the *Titulus regius* asserts, if Edward IV married Elizabeth Woodville when already married or when befuddled by the aphrodisiacs or other bewitching devices of Elizabeth and her mother, the marriage was not valid, and the three sons and seven daughters that Elizabeth bore the king were illegitimate. Helmholz notes that the clandestinity of the invalid marriage between Edward and Elizabeth would have prevented the automatic legitimation of the children born after Eleanor's death. He concludes that the lack of jurisdiction, pointed out by the

Croyland Chronicler, is the strongest argument against the parliamentary case, and he believes that the statement that the marriage's invalidity was common knowledge throughout the land, coupled with an offer of proof, 'was evidently meant to anticipate the argument that Parliament was without authority to decide the question of legitimacy'. But in fact the statement of common knowledge and offer of proof was the standard formula in charges made in an ecclesiastical tribunal.[30] Furthermore, this formula is used only concerning the witchcraft charge and not the precontract allegation.

By the time that the claim for the illegitimacy of Edward's offspring was ratified in the Parliament of 1484, the two princes were assumed to be dead, so that the argument at that time would affect only the five surviving daughters. It may have been partially Richard's worry over the legitimacy of the parliamentary declaration, because not supported by a decision of the competent church court, that lay behind his plan to annul his marriage to Anne Neville and marry Edward's eldest daughter, his niece Elizabeth. Then it would not matter whether they were to be considered legitimate. He could have graciously legitimized all of the daughters, with regard to temporal affairs, even without applying to the pope for spiritual legitimation.[31] A century earlier, Richard II had thus legitimized his cousins the Beauforts, illegitimate children of his uncle John of Gaunt by Catherine Swinford.

The Croyland Chronicler knew that a papal dispensation was possible for an uncle-niece marriage (which did not fall among the Levitical degrees), but he reported that Catesby and Ratcliffe persuaded Richard it was not, for fear that young Elizabeth would take revenge upon them for causing the death of her uncle Anthony and her brother Richard.[32] Therefore, since Richard abandoned any thought of annulling his marriage to Anne and marrying Elizabeth, the question of the legitimacy of Elizabeth and her surviving siblings (that is, her four sisters), was not revisited, not by Richard III and certainly not by Henry VII, whose claim rested on his descent from one of the Beaufort bastards; for Henry knew only of their re-legitimation by their half-brother Henry IV, who added the rider that their rehabilitated status did not include the right to inherit the throne. Elizabeth's bastardization by Parliament was therefore ignored by Henry VII's first Parliament, and it continued to be ignored when Henry married her with a papal dispensation for consanguinity.

Something similar happened in the case of Elizabeth I. Henry VIII had gone ahead and effected an annulment between himself and Anne Boleyn, and, though the grounds for the action were left unstated in Cranmer's sentence of divorce, the judgment was taken as sufficient to bastardize young Elizabeth, and Parliament accordingly declared her illegitimate. The first Parliament convened by Elizabeth I left this act of 1536 unrepealed, not deliberately, as perhaps was the case with Henry VII's Parliament, but by way of oversight. By another oversight, they resurrected the act of 1540, as emended under Edward VI, which included yet another declaration of the queen's illegitimacy.[33]

NOTES AND REFERENCES

1. John Ashdown-Hill, "Edward IV's uncrowned queen: the Lady Eleanor Talbot, Lady Butler," *The Ricardian*, vol. 11 no. 139, December 1997, pp. 166-90.
2. Richard Helmholz, 'The sons of Edward IV: a canonical assessment of the claim that they were illegitimate', in P. W. Hammond, ed., *Richard III: Loyalty Lordship and Law*, London 1986, pp. 91-103.
3. Charles Ross, *Richard III*, Berkeley 1981, p. 91.
4. H. A. Kelly, 'The last chroniclers of Croyland', *The Ricardian*, vol. 7 no 91, December 1985, pp. 142-77, see esp. pp. 145-47 and 166-67, nn. 33, 43; 'The Croyland Chronicle tragedies', vol. 7, no. 99 December 1987, pp. 498-515; and 'Croyland observations', vol. 8 no. 108, March 1990, pp. 334-41, esp. pp. 340-41.

   I should mention with respect to Alison Hanham's article, 'Author! Author! Crowland Revisited', *The Ricardian* vol. 11 no. 140, March 1998, pp. 226-38, esp. p. 237 n. 12, where she doubts my interpretation of 'tragedy' and supposes that the term was not as rare and peculiar as I think, that I have continued my researches on medieval tragedy and have published three books on the subject: *Tragedy and Comedy from Dante to Pseudo-Dante*, Berkeley 1989; *Ideas and Forms of Tragedy from Aristotle to the Middle Ages*, Cambridge 1993; and *Chaucerian Tragedy*, Cambridge 1997. See especially the last-named book. pp. 40-45, in the section, '"Tragedy" in Late-Medieval England', for the mere handful of uses of the term, whether in Latin or English, that I have uncovered in fifteenth-century England. Readers of my articles will recall that I find the term to be important in the Croyland Chronicle because it helps to establish that the secular and monastic sections of the Second Continuation were written by the same author.
5. *Rotuli Parliamentorum*, vol. 6, pp. 240-41. I modernize the spelling and punctuation of the text. See also the edition by Mortimer Levine, *Tudor Dynastic Problems, 1460-1571*, London 1973, pp. 135-37.
6. See A. B. Emden, *A Biographical Register of the University of Oxford to A.D. 1500*, 3 vols, Oxford 1957, vol. 3, pp. 1177-79. Emden takes Stillington to be the author of the *Titulus regius*, citing H. C. Maxwell-Lyte, *The Registers of Robert Stillington, Bishop of Bath and Wells, 1466-1491, and Richard Fox, Bishop of Bath and Wells, 1492-1494*, Somerset Record Society, vol. 52 (1937), p. xi. Kelly, 'Last chroniclers', p. 145, notes that a Yearbook of 1486 names Stillington as author, citing Mortimer Levine, 'Richard III — usurper or lawful king?' *Speculum*, vol. 34 (1959), pp. 391-401, esp. pp. 392-93 n. 8.
7. *Liber Extra* 4.3.1-3, *Corpus iuris canonici*, 2 vols., ed. Emil Friedberg, Leipzig 1879-81, cols 679-680.
8. William Lyndwood, *Provinciale, seu Constitutiones Angliae*, Oxford 1679, repr. Farnborough 1968, pp. 270-71 and appendix, pp. 39-40. Lyndwood, writing in the 1420s, assigned the constitution he cites to Archbishop Reynolds in 1322, and was followed by his seventeenth-century editors, and by me in my *Love and Marriage in the Age of Chaucer*, Ithaca NY 1975, p. 167 n. 18. But C. R. Cheney, 'William Lyndwood's *Provinciale*', *Medieval Texts and Studies*, Oxford 1973, pp. 158-84, at p. 170, says that the constitutions in question "'are all descended from synodal statutes of an unknown English diocese probably composed between 1222 and 1225'.
9. Lyndwood, pp. [273]-274.
10. *Ibid.*, pp. 274-77.
11. Cheney, pp. 179-80.
12. *Liber Extra* 4.15.1-8, Friedberg, 2:704-08. For the gloss, see *Corpus juris canonici*, 3 vols., Rome, 1582 (I use the edition of Lyons 1606), vol. 2, cols. 1518, 1520, 1521,1523, 1525-26.

13. Gratian, *Decretum*, Causa 33, questio 1, cap. 4; Friedberg, 1:1148, 1150.
14. *Liber Extra*, 4.1.14 (Friedberg, 2:666): 'Quum [=Cum] locum non habeat consensus ubi metus vel coactio intercedit, necesse est ut, ubi assensus cujusquam requiritur, coactionis materia repellatur. Matrimonium autem solo consensu contrahitur, et, ubi de ipso queritur, plena debet securitate ille gaudere cujus est animus indagandus, ne per timorem dicat sibi placere quod odit, et sequatur exitus qui de invitis solet nuptiis provenire'.
15. H. A. Kelly, 'English kings and the fear of sorcery', *Mediaeval Studies, vol.* 39 (1977), pp. 206-38.
16. *Ibid.*, pp. 219-27.
17. See the *DNB s.v.* Richard Woodville.
18. Kelly, 'English kings', p. 233; for details, see George Lyman Kittredge, *Witchcraft in Old and New England*, Cambridge, Mass. 1929, p. 84.
19. See my articles listed in n. 4 above.
20. *The Crowland Chronicle Continuations: 1459-1486,* ed. Nicholas Pronay and John Cox, London 1986, 144-46.
21. Kelly, 'English Kings', pp. 230-33.
22. Emden, p. 1778, citing Maxwell-Lyte.
23. *Ibid.*, pp. 234-35.
24. H. A. Kelly, *The Matrimonial Trials of Henry VIII*, Stanford 1976, pp. 241-42.
25. Crowland Chronicle, p. 160.
26. *Ibid.*, pp. 168-70.
27. *Liber Extra*, 4.1.15, 28, Friedberg, 2:667, 671 (the second text has *potuit* for *posset*).
28. Kelly, 'Last chroniclers', p. 166 n. 33.
29. For more details, see Kelly, 'Croyland observations', pp. 340-41.
30. See the example I give from Henry VIII's legatine trial of his marriage: 'English kings', p. 233 n. 105; *cf. Matrimonial Trials of Henry VIII*, p. 90.
31. For the possibilities, see my 'Canonical implications of Richard III's plan to marry his niece', *Traditio,* vol. 23 (1967) 269-311, esp. p. 383, and 'Shades of incest and cuckoldry: Pandarus and John of Gaunt', *Studies in the Age of Chaucer* 13 (1991), pp. 121-140, esp. p. 137.
32. Kelly, 'Canonical implications', pp. 271-74. Pope Pius II had recently given such a dispensation to a count of Piacenza, *ibid.*, pp. 303-06; see also *Matrimonial Trials*, pp. 12-13.
33. Kelly, *Matrimonial Trials*, pp. 241-60, 281-82.

IX

STATUTES OF RAPES AND ALLEGED RAVISHERS OF WIVES: A CONTEXT FOR THE CHARGES AGAINST THOMAS MALORY, KNIGHT

The basic meaning of the Latin *raptus* and *rapere* is "seizing." The words were limited largely to two kinds of seizure, one preceding sexual violation, and the other preceding abduction. The English "rape" followed suit (it did not take over a third meaning of the Latin word, "rapture" in a spiritual sense), but eventually the sexual meaning prevailed, except in hallowed phrases like "the rape of Helen," "the rape of the Sabine Women," and Pope's *Rape of the Lock*.[1] In the Middle Ages, however, abduction was as common a meaning as sexual violation, though modern historians in treating abduction tend to use the French-based reflexes "ravish" and "ravishment" (these words had a similar range of meaning, but are now restricted mainly to a woman's sexual effect on men—"she was ravishing"). Historians also concentrate on the abduction of heirs, usually female, though in fact more male heirs were actually "ravished," often by the mother of the boy in question.[2]

There is, however, another kind of alleged offense that is generally overlooked, namely, the accusation of ravishing a married woman and abducting her (the charge usually includes the theft of her husband's goods). This is the first of three related crimes named by Peace in the Z, A, and B texts of *Piers Plowman*:

> And thanne com Pees into Parlement and putte up a bille,
> How Wrong ayeins his wille hadde his wife taken,
> And how he ravysshede Rose, Reignaldes love,
> And Margrete of hir maydenhede, maugree hire chekes.[3]

[1]See H. A. Kelly, "Meanings and Uses of *Raptus* in Chaucer's Time," *Studies in the Age of Chaucer* 20 (1998). I am grateful to all my associates who have advised me on the present article, especially Daniel Klerman of the University of Chicago Law School.

[2]Sue Sheridan Walker, "Free Consent and Marriage of Feudal Wards in Medieval England," *Journal of Medieval History* 8 (1982) 123–134 at 127 and n. 28. For mothers as ravishers of their sons, see n. 128 below.

[3]William Langland, *Piers Plowman: A Parallel-Text Edition of the A, B, C and Z Versions*, ed. A. V. C. Schmidt, 1 (London 1995) 148, B 4.47–50, agreeing in essentials with Z and A. One variant of B makes Rose Reignald's beloved daughter; see *Piers Plowman: The B Version*, ed. George Kane and E. Talbot Donaldson (London 1975) 296. All versions continue with Peace's property complaints against Wrong, ending with the charges that he beats him and lies with his maid (B 47). I am grateful to William Snell for pointing out the importance of this passage of *Piers*, in a paper read at the New Chaucer Society meeting in Los Angeles in July 1996: "'Feloun' and 'Felonye': Violence and Violent Crime in the *Canterbury Tales*."

The nature of the alleged offense is not always recognized, and we will see that the same is true of the similar real-life charge brought against "Sir"[4] Thomas Malory, knight, in the next century. The most recent editor of *Piers*, A. V. C. Schmidt, translates the passage thus:

> Then Peace entered the Parliament Hall, and brought forward a formal bill of complaint.
> Wrong, he said, had raped his wife,
> And abducted Rose, who was due to marry Reginald,
> And deflowered Margaret, however hard she struggled.[5]

The interpretation of the second line was doubtless influenced by the C version: "How Wrong wilfully hadde his wyf forleyen," which transforms the abduction into a sexual rape.[6]

J. F. Goodridge's earlier translation of the B text is more accurate:

> Then a man named Peace came to Parliament bringing in a petition
> Against one Crime. "He has run away with my wife," he said,
> "And assaulted Rosy, Reg's girl,
> And had his way with Margaret too, for all her struggling."[7]

Both of these renditions leave out the important point that Wrong's action is said to be against the will of the husband—and not against the will of the wife. And the husband here, Peace, does service for the king's peace, which is always included as a "victim" in such charges (*pax* is said to be broken, *fracta*). For the second offense, Goodridge sees an assault, presumably sexual, whereas Schmidt sees an abduction, but the line is ambiguous, like many trial records, and admits of both interpretations. And since abduction is a possible meaning (presumably of an heiress), we would do well to

[4]I put "Sir" in quotation marks to draw attention to two other questions that interest me. When was this title regularly applied to contemporary knights in third-person discourse? When, later on, was it exclusively applied to knights? In the fourteenth century, it seems to have been consistently used only for "knights of old," like Chaucer's "Sire Thopas." If there was a standard application of the title to contemporary persons, it appears to have been mainly limited to secular priests and the higher nobility (kings and princes), to go by the examples in the *Medieval English Dictionary.* One thirteenth-century text in which nearly contemporary knights are "sirred" is the *South English Legendary,* ed. Charlotte D'Evelyn and Anna J. Mill, 3 vols., Early English Text Society 235–236, 244 (London 1956–1959) 2.670ff., in the account of Thomas Becket's murderers; but the title is also given to Sir Geoffrey, earl of Brittany (p. 689 line 2405). We can doubtless agree that it was common to speak of contemporary knights as sirs by 1470, or 1485, to judge from the colophon of the *Book of Arthur,* as given in Caxton's edition ("For this book was ended the ix yere of the reygne of Kyng Edward the Fourth, by Syr Thomas Maleore, knyght," etc., *Caxton's Malory,* ed. James W. Spisak, 2 vols. [Berkeley 1893] 1.600); this fits with the earliest instance in the MED, 1476, in the Stonor letters. But whether the style was already customary in 1451 when the *miles* Thomas Malory was charged with *raptus,* I have not yet determined. In any case, the title was still being shared with other classes for much longer. We read in Shakespeare, for instance, "I had rather go with sir priest than with sir knight" (*Twelfth Night* 3.4 ca. 270). One thing does seem certain: it is anachronistic for historians to apply the title religiously to knights and only to knights in the thirteenth and fourteenth centuries.

[5]A. V. C. Schmidt, *Piers Plowman: A New Translation of the B-Text* (Oxford 1992). For this and the following translation, I have arranged the prose originals into lines corresponding to the original verses.

[6] The C text also changes Rose into a rich widow whom Wrong ravished by night (or, in one variant, he ravished Rose, the rich widow's daughter); and, according to the next verse, he (ravished) Margaret of her maidenhood as he met her late (or, in a variant, as she walked here late). For the variants, see *Piers Plowman: The C Version,* ed. George Russell and George Kane (London 1997) 276–277.

[7]J. F. Goodridge, *Piers the Ploughman,* rev. ed. (Baltimore 1966) 56.

supply (mentally) another "ravysshede" in the last line, this time in an unambiguously sexual sense, to signify the forcible deflowering of a virgin.

In these four lines, then, we have the whole gamut of rape charges. But the first of them, the abduction of a wife, will be the most important in showing the purport of the numerous "statutes of rapes" that were passed from the thirteenth to the sixteenth centuries. I will argue, as a hypothesis, that they were primarily concerned with abduction rather than sexual rape, and were not intended to alter the "appeal of rape," the criminal procedure already in place for the prosecution of sexual rape. I also hope to demonstrate that the wives who were allegedly kidnapped were often willing accomplices of the abductors on the relatively rare occasions when an abduction took place. But in most cases the wives were walkouts or runaways, who usually had good cause to be shut of their husbands.

Our first chore will be to study the texts of the pertinent statutes and the different ways they can be and have been interpreted.

THE LANGUAGE AND PURPORT OF THE STATUTES

In the excerpts given below, I will give the original text and English translation as edited in the *Statutes of the Realm*,[8] unless otherwise specified. This translation of the early statutes is attributed to the lawyer and poet George Ferrers, noted later for his part in producing *A Mirror for Magistrates*.[9] The translation of the statutes of Edward I was first published in 1534,[10] and later statutes into the reign of Henry VIII were added in 1543.[11] I will note any place where his text differs importantly from the corrected text of the editors.

[8] *The Statutes of the Realm*, 12 vols. (London 1810–1828; repr. 1963). I expand all contractions, use modern distinctions for i/ j and u/ v, and follow my own punctuation and capitalization, and, for the translations, modern spelling. H. G. Richardson and George Sayles "The Early Statutes," *Law Quarterly Review* 50 (1934) 201–223, 540–571, at 569–570, in speaking of the need for a new edition of the statutes, have this to say: "Valuable as is the first volume of the *Statutes of the Realm*, it has serious defects. . . . Highly as the editors regarded manuscript evidence, they had a greater regard for the printed word: for, as they envisaged their task, they were concerned with finding support for the received text rather than with constructing an historically faithful text. Their work reflects the labours of compilers in the closing years of the thirteenth and the early years of the fourteenth centuries, compilers working obscurely without official authority and with no precise standard of textual integrity." We may observe, however, that from the viewpoint of later interpretation of the law, the received text may be more important than the original text.

[9] Sidney Lee in his life of Ferrers in the *Dictionary of National Biography* (Oxford 1921–1922) 6.1247 says that he received a bachelor's degree in canon law from Cambridge in 1531; but A. B. Emden, *A Biographical Register of the University of Oxford, A.D. 1501 to 1540* (Oxford 1974) 203 says that this is based on a mistaken identification. After mentioning Ferrers's 1534 translation, Lee cites Leland's statement that he became a member of Lincoln's Inn, and that his oratory gained him a high reputation at the bar.

[10] *The Boke of Magna Carta / with diuers other statutes*, etc. (London 1534: STC 9272); microfilm available from University Microfilms International; see the catalog, *(Early) English Books, 1475–1640, Selected from Pollard and Redgrave's Short-Title Catalogue*, 3 vols. (Ann Arbor 1956–1980) 1. 5, reel 7, no. 326.

[11] STC 9301. The first of two volumes is titled, *In this volume are conteined the statutes made and established from the time of kyng Henry the thirde, unto the fyrste yere of the reigne of our most gratious and victorious soveraigne lorde kinge Henry the VIII* (London 1543). I use STC 9301.3: *Early English Books* 3.160, middle of reel 1752. The translation of the additional statutes in this and following editions was conjectured to be that of Ferrers by Cay in his edition of 1758; see *Statutes* (n. 8 above) 1.xxii, xxiv.

* *1236: Statute of Merton, 20 Henry III, Chapter 6*

De heredibus per parentes vel per alios vi abductis vel detentis, [seu maritatis], ita provisum est: quod quicumque laicus inde convictus fuerit quod puerum sic [detinuerit, abduxerit, vel] maritaverit, reddat perdenti valorem maritagii, et pro delicto corpus ejus capiatur et imprisonetur donec perdenti emendaverit delictum, si puer maritetur, et preterea donec domino regi satisfecerit pro transgressione; et hoc fiat de herede infra quatuordecim annos existente.

(Of heirs that be led away, and withholden, or married, by their parents or by other, with force against our peace, thus it is provided: that whatsoever layman be convict thereof that he hath so withholden, led away, or married any child, he shall yield to the loser the value of the marriage; and for the offense his body shall be taken and imprisoned until he hath recompensed the loser, if the child be married, and further, until he hath satisfied the king for the trespass; and this must be done of an heir being within the age of fourteen years.[12])

It is noteworthy that the offense to the lord who loses the marriage of the ward is called a *delictum*, "misdeed" (not translated by Ferrers), whereas the offense to the king is a *transgressio*, "trespass."

The above text is part 1 of the chapter. Parts 2 and 3 have nothing to do with abduction. Part 2 first speaks of heirs between the ages of fourteen and twenty-one who marry without license of their lords. There is no distinction of gender in the Latin of part 2, but Ferrers rightly stops speaking generically of "the child" and starts using masculine pronouns. However, in part 3, which deals with lords who marry their wards under fourteen to unsuitable partners, Ferrers continues to use the masculine gender, even though the provision is applicable to female as well as male wards.

There is no recognition in this statute of the canonistic rule that girls can legally consent to marriage at the age of twelve.

1275: Statute of Westminster I, 3 Edward I, Chapter 13

Et le rey defent qe nul ne ravie ne prenge a force damoysele dedenz age, ne par son gre ne saun son gre, ne dame ne damoisele de age, ne autre femme maugre seon. E si nul le fet, a la suite celi qe suiwera dedenz les quarante jours, le rey en fra comune dreyture. Et si nul ne comence sa suite dedenz quarante jours, le rey en siwera; e ces qil entrovera copables, si averont la prison de deus aunz, et puis serrunt reintz a la volente le rey. Etsil ne unt dount estre reintz a la volente le rey, si seient puniz par plus long prison, solum ceo qe le trespas le demande.

(And the king prohibiteth that none do ravish nor take away by force any maiden within age, neither by her own consent, nor without; nor any wife or maiden of full age, nor any other woman, against her will. And if any do, at his suit that will sue within forty days, the king shall do common right; and if none commence his suit within forty days, the king shall sue. And such as be found culpable shall have two years' imprisonment, and after shall fine at the king's pleasure; and if they have not whereof, they shall be punished by longer imprisonment, according as the trespass requireth.[13])

[12] *Statutes* 1.3. "Parents" is noted by the editors as a correction for "kinsfolks" in the translation, but Ferrers 1534 has "friends."

[13] *Statutes* 1.29.

J. B. Post in his study of Westminster I and II gives an edition of what he takes to be the earliest form of this statute, but the only substantial difference is that he removes *a force* ("by force") from the text and gives it as a variant, whereas the editors of the *Statutes* indicate in their apparatus that the words are missing in some manuscripts.[14]

We note that Ferrers translates the text on the assumption that the person bringing the suit is a man connected with the female victim. But there is a long tradition, starting at least as early as Edward Coke (1552–1634), of interpreting the 1275 statute as referring only to sexual rape, so that it would be the victim herself who would bring the suit in the form of an appeal, since the right of such appeal was restricted to the woman.[15] Coke bases his interpretation on his selective reading of a treatise called *Speculum justiciorum*, first heard of around 1550 (we will examine it below). He starts * out by saying, "For the better understanding of this and other statutes concerning rapes, it is first to be seen what this word 'rape' doth signify, and secondly, what offence rape was at the common law before this statute." He defines rape as "carnal knowledge of a woman by force"; the Latin *rapere* means "to ravish legally," that is by carnal knowledge; the offense is *raptus* and the offender *raptor.* The offense was a felony at common law, he says, but this statute converted it to a trespass, only to have the statute of Westminster II in 1285 convert it back to a felony.[16] William Holdsworth also takes the statute to refer to sexual violation, and in fact he holds that after the Conquest the term "rape" was no longer used for abduction but was reserved to *violentus concubitus.* (Not true, as we will see.) His interpretation of the statutes of Westminster is contradictory. First he says, "Appeals of rape were abolished by the Statute of Westminster I (1275), but were apparently revived by the Statute of Westminster II (1285)." But in his next volume he says, "The Statute of Westminster I lengthened the period within which the woman could bring her appeal to forty days, and increased the punishment if the guilty person was indicted. The Statute of Westminster II made the offence in all cases a felony."[17] Pollock and Maitland also read the statutes as referring exclusively to sexual rape.[18] Post, while recognizing that it includes abduction, sees it as dealing primarily with sexual rape, and he says of the 1275 enactment that "the appeal of rape was apparently extended to matrons as well as maidens."[19]

[14]J. B. Post, "Ravishment of Women and the Statutes of Westminster," *Legal Records and the Historian*, ed. J. H. Baker (London 1978) 150–164 at 162. The first sentence of his edited text reads: "E le roy defend qe nul ravyse ne prengne damysele de deinze age, par soun gre ne sanz soun gre, ne dame ne damisele de age, ne autre femme maugre soun" ("And the king forbids anyone to ravish or take a maiden of under-age, by her consent or without, or a wife or maiden of age, or other woman, without her consent").

[15]J. H. Baker, *An Introduction to English Legal History*, ed. 3 (London 1990) 603.

[16]Edward Coke, *The Second Part of the Institutes of the Laws of England* (London 1817) 179–181.

[17]W. S. Holdsworth, *A History of English Law* 2–3, ed. 3 (London 1923) 2.361, 3.316.

[18]Frederick Pollock and Frederic William Maitland, *The History of English Law before the Time of Edward I*, ed. 2 (Cambridge 1898; reissued 1968 with introduction and bibliography by S. F. C. Milsom) 2.490–491.

[19]Post (n. 14 above) 153. John Marshall Carter, *Rape in Medieval England: An Historical and Sociological Study* (Lanham 1985) 36, 39 seems to have a similar view of Westminster I chap. 13, but perhaps this impression is caused by the fact that, even though he acknowledges that *rapere* and *raptus* have a variety of meanings, he is interested only in the meaning of "sexual attack on females" (46 n. 1).

In my view, however, Post's emphases should be reversed. That is, the statute deals with abduction, and only secondarily, or not at all, with sexual violation. This is the way it is taken in modern times by Sue Sheridan Walker,[20] and it also seems to be the way that Ferrers took it, since his translation precludes reference to female appellants. Moreover, the fact that the statute referred to the offense as a trespass would imply a continuity with the Statute of Merton. The rest of the matter covered by the Merton chapter, dealing with relations between wards and guardians, is taken up in Westminster I in two further chapters, 21 and 22.[21] But unlike Merton, chapter 13 of Westminster I does not deal with the abduction of wards of both sexes, but only all females—which would, of course, include female wards. And while it seems to have been aimed primarily at unmarried but marriageable women, married women are also mentioned or implied.

The statute first designates underage damsels, referring either to the age of marriage or the age when wardship ended (which varied according to the condition of the woman),[22] and says that the prohibition holds whether the girl consents or not. It then deals with women of full age: damsels, dames (presumably married women, possibly of high social standing), and other women (widows? nuns? women of servile condition or low social standing?). It is clear that the prohibition covers all such women who do not consent to being "ravished or taken." The first of the words used, *ravie*, can hardly bear the full weight of Coke's interpretation of carnal knowledge *contra voluntatem*, since the statute speaks of possible consent; at most, it could mean, if it refers to sex at all, "willing or unwilling carnal knowledge." If so, the phrase "by force" certainly does not belong in the original text. The word would also mean "sex *in situ*," whereas the other word, *prenge*, clearly means "abducted for longer-range purposes." But by implicitly exempting consenting older women from the prohibition, the statute suggests that the long-range considerations are primary, and that *ravie* and *prenge* are not contrasting actions but synonyms, both meaning "take away," or sequential words, meaning "seize *and* take away," whether the female being taken is willing or unwilling. Force could still be used even in the case of those women who were willing, but the force would be against their keepers (parents, guardians, husbands) or their keepers' "close." It is obvious that damsels or widows who consent to being taken away may be thinking of marriage. But what are the implications of a married woman or a nun who consents to being taken away? As this statute stands, the abductor, or "conductor," is not liable for any punishment or damages. The 1285 statute would attempt to clarify some aspects of this question.

But first let us look at a statute that clearly dealt with sexual rape.

* [20]This is the way it is read by Sue Sheridan Walker, "Wrongdoing and Compensation: The Pleas of Wardship in Thirteenth and Fourteenth Century England," *Journal of Legal History* 9 (1988) 267–307, esp. 286.

[21]*Statutes* (n. 8 above) 1.32–33.

* [22]*Bracton de legibus et consuetudinibus Angliae*, ed. George E. Woodbine, trans. Samuel E. Thorne, 4 vols. (Cambridge, Mass. 1968) 2.250–251. Bracton places the age of a girl for marriage at twelve, in conformity with canon law, but in Westminster II, as in Merton, the age is given as fourteen without qualification when speaking of both boys and girls. Canonically, a girl's consent to marriage between the age of seven and twelve was a mere betrothal, or *de futuro* contract, and could be broken off when either party wished, as far as church law was concerned.

"1276": Office of the Coroner, assigned to 4 Edward I (1275–1276) (excerpt) *

Si autem aliquis fuerit appellatus de raptu, appellatus attachiari debet, si apellum recens fuerit, et videant signum veritatis, per ampnum sanguinolentu[m], vel hutesium levatum, et tales attachiari debent per quatuor plegios, vel sex, si invenire possint. Si autem apellum fuerit sine hutesio, et sine signo manifesto, tunc sufficiunt plegii duo.

(Further, if any be appealed of rape, he must be attached, if the appeal be fresh, and if they see apparent sign of truth by effusion of blood, or an open cry made; and such shall be attached by four or six pledges, if they can find them. If the appeal were without cry, or without any manifest sign or token, two pledges shall be sufficient.[23])

Here force is unquestionably used against the woman, not against any guardian. As Theodore Plucknett notes, there is no internal evidence for the date of this statute; in his study of the early interpretation of the statutes of the first three Edwards, he includes it in the list of statutes of uncertain time before the statutes of Edward III.[24] It was traditional, however, to assign it to 1275–1276, 4 Edward I, and Ferrers gives it this date. In the 1534 edition, it is in an appendix after the index, but in the 1543 edition it appears in its chronological position. I have not determined how old the dating tradition is, but it would, of course, be risky to rely on the early date to interpret either the 1275 or the 1285 statute. The coroner's statute does, however, undoubtedly correspond to early practice, specifically concerning evidence of sexual rape and the role of the coroner, as can be seen in Bracton.[25]

1285: Statute of Westminster II, 13 Edward I, Chapter 34 [B]
N.B. The first part of this chapter, which I designate as [A], is considered to be a last-minute French insert into the statute, modifying the original Latin provisions of chapters 34 and 35. I give the text of [A] after treating the Latin texts.

[B1] De mulieribus abductis cum bonis viri, habeat rex sectam de bonis sic asportatis.

([B1] And of women carried away with the goods of their husbands, the king shall have the suit for the goods so taken away.[26])

If this is a clarification of the 1275 statute, it adds nothing to the situation of the abducted wives themselves, and says nothing of abducted maidens. Post believes that this provision as well as the following two deals with "consenting sexual relationships."[27] But we will do well to suspend our judgment for the time being. The second Latin provision reads:

[23]*Statutes* (n. 8 above) 1.41, with corrected translation. In the Latin text, *hutesium*, translated here as "open cry," refers of course to the hue and cry. *Ampnum* presumably means *amnem*, and the phrase translates as "by a bloody stream." Ferrers in his translation (as in the 1534 ed., fol. 161v) follows the reading of earlier printed texts, *per effusionem sanguinis.* But the translation given above corrects Ferrers in other particulars, putting "if they can find them" for his "if he can be found"; and "if they see" for his "they must see." For the Latin text the editors follow British Library MS Harl. 667 fol. 222v, compared with MS Cott. Vesp. B 7 and the printed version in Pynson's *Vetera statuta*, 1508.

[24]T. F. T. Plucknett, *Statutes and Their Interpretation in the First Half of the Fourteenth Century* (Cambridge 1922) xxxiv, 14.

[25]Bracton (n. 22 above) 2.415; see also 2.394–395.

[26]*Statutes* (n. 8 above) 1.87.

[27]Post (n. 14 above) 157.

* [B2] Et uxor, si sponte reliquerit virum suum et abierit et moretur cum adultero suo, amittat imperpetuum accionem petendi dotem suam que ei competere posset de tenura viri, si super hoc convincatur, nisi vir suus sponte, et absque cohercione ecclesiastica, eam reconciliet et secum cohabitari permittat; in quo casu restituatur ei accio.

([B2] And if a wife willingly leave her husband and go away and continue with her advouterer, she shall be barred forever of action to demand her dower that she ought to have of her husband's lands, if she be convict thereupon, except that her husband willingly, and without coercion of the Church, reconcile her and suffer her to dwell with him; in which case she shall be restored to her action.[28])

Here of course it is quite clear that the provision does not concern abduction, but deals with a wife's spontaneous action of leaving her husband. However, it could easily be read as being an addendum to the first provision, and, in fact, in the 1810 edition of the *Statutes of the Realm* it is joined to it by a semicolon. And since the wife's adulterer is mentioned, perhaps there was the idea that the wife was, if not *abducta*, at least *seducta* by him. We must remember, of course, that the idea of the woman's consent and abduction, even forcible abduction, are not contradictory, since stealth and force might have to be employed against the woman's guardians.

A third provision in the original statute deals with the abduction of nuns:

[B3] Qui monialem a domo sua abducat, licet monialis consenciat, puniatur per prisonam trium annorum, et satisfaciat domui a qua abducta fuerit competenter, et nihilominus redimatur ad voluntatem regis.

([B3] He that carrieth a nun from her house, although she consent, shall be punished by three years' imprisonment, and shall make convenient satisfaction to the house from whence she was taken, and nevertheless shall make fine at the king's will.[29])

Therefore, even if a nun wished to leave her house of religion, any accomplice who "abducted" her, that is, helped her to escape—even, say, her mother—was liable to fall under the penalties of this statute.

Donald Logan argues convincingly that this clause was prompted by the notorious case of the knight Osbert Giffard's abduction of two nuns from the abbey of Wilton in 1284.[30] But his action seems to have been part of a family dispute rather than the sort of consenting sexual relationship that Post speaks of. Osbert's cousin Juliana Giffard was abbess of Wilton, and one of the nuns, Alice Giffard, was doubtless also his cousin. He may have had "designs" upon her, as Logan surmises—whether matrimonial or wardship designs—but the charge filed against him by Juliana, as reflected in the royal order, was that he "has violently taken a nun of Wylton and carried her beyond seas without licence and there detains her against her will."[31]

The bishops of the province of Canterbury objected to the provision as encroaching on church jurisdiction, but they were assured that it was not the king's intention to legislate concerning the correction of sin (*peccatum*) against abducted nuns and

[28]Ibid.

[29]Ibid.

[30]F. Donald Logan, *Runaway Religious in Medieval England, c. 1240–1540* (Cambridge 1996) 85–88.

[31]Ibid., citing *Calendar of the Fine Rolls* 1.207, November 1284.

their abductors.[32] In other words, that statute merely added to what the ecclesiastical authorities might do to the culprits.

In addition to this original version of chapter 34, a long statute, chapter 35, was added, dealing with the abduction of marriageable wards of both sexes and of all ages up to twenty-one, limited however to those whose *maritagium* belonged to someone other than the abductor:

1285: Statute of Westminster II, Chapter 35

> De pueris, sive masculis sive femellis, quorum maritagium ad aliquem pertineat, raptis et abductis, si ille qui rapuerit, non habens jus in maritagium, licet postmodum restituat puerum non maritatum, vel de maritagio satisfecerit, puniatur tamen pro transgressione per prisonam duorum annorum. Et si non restituerit, vel heredem post annos nubiles maritaverit et de maritagio satisfacere non poterit, abjuret regnum vel habeat perpetuam prisonam.
>
> (Concerning children, males and females, whose marriage belongeth to another, taken and carried away, if the ravisher have no right in the marriage, though after he restore the child unmarried, or else pay for the marriage, he shall nevertheless be punished for his offence by two years' imprisonment. And if he do not restore, or do marry the child after the years of consent, and be not able to satisfy for the marriage, he shall abjure the realm, or have perpetual imprisonment.[33])

The statute then formulates new writs to cover these provisions. We note that the offense is categorized as a *transgressio*, "trespass."

Now let us look at the French insert placed before chapter 34.

1285: Statute of Westminster II, Chapter 34 [A]: French Addition

> [A1] Purveu est que si homme ravist femme—espouse, damoisele, ou autre femme—desoremes, par la ou ele ne se est assentue ne avaunt ne apres, eit jugement de vie e de membre.
>
> [A2] E ensement par la ou home ravist femme—dame espouse, damoisele, ou autre femme—a force, tut seit ke ele se assente apres, eit tel jugement come avaunt est dit, si il seit ateint a la suite le rei, e la eit le rei sa suite.
>
> ([A1] It is provided that if a man from henceforth do ravish a woman—married, maid, or other—where she did not consent, neither before nor after, he shall have judgment of life and of member.
>
> [A2] And likewise where a man ravisheth a woman—married lady, damosel, or other—with force, although she consent after, he shall have such judgment as before is said, if he be attainted at the king's suit, and there the king shall have the suit.[34])

Plucknett conjectures that this clause is in French because it was "an insertion made at so late a moment that neither translation nor re-drafting was practicable." He adds,

[32]F. M. Powicke and C. R. Cheney, *Councils and Synods with Other Documents Relating to the English Church* 2.2 (Oxford 1964) 965 (no. 7), 967 (no. 10). See also 973–974: Giffard may have been absolved of his excommunication at a provincial council in February 1286.

[33]*Statutes* (n. 8 above) 1.88.

[34]Ibid. 1.87. The text edited by Post (n. 14 above) 164 is substantially the same.

"If that was the case, it seems likely that the amendment was made when the statute was laid before parliament."[35] It may, of course, have been added even later, as Post seems to suggest. He says that a Chancery clerk who referred to chapters 34–35 as *De uxoribus, pueris utriusque sexus abductis*, when jotting down some of the business of
* the Parliament, did not know of the French insert "because he did not identify the chapter by what eventually became its first clause."[36] His argument, however, assumes that the French clause would not have been interpreted as dealing with abducted wives. We must remember that the first type of woman mentioned in [A1] is a wife, *espouse*. Post also agrees with Plucknett that the clause was probably inserted at a stage too late for redrafting; he suggests that it was inspired by a case of sexual rape that came to the king and his council on the first day of Parliament, 4 May 1285. We will
* discuss this case below, but here we can note that since the statute was apparently not given a public reading until 28 June,[37] there would have been adequate time to get up a Latin text.

We have seen that this French provision [A1–2] was taken by Coke and Holdsworth as converting sexual rape from a trespass, as treated in Westminster I, chapter 13, into a felony. But since that earlier statute seems to have been speaking only of abduction, punishable by two years in prison, whereas the Coroner statute obviously continued to treat sexual rape as before, probably as a capital crime or the equivalent (mutilation), and since the original Latin version of the 1285 chapter 34 was also speaking of abduction, perhaps our first conclusion should be that the French text also refers to abduction, and makes it a more serious crime.

From a literal point of view, the supplemented 1285 statute has no direct reference to sexual violation except for what can be gathered from the French section, in the word *ravise*. We saw that this word (in the form *ravie*) in the earlier Westminster statute most likely did service for simple abduction without overtones of unwilling coitus. The Anglo-Norman word *ravir* has the same range of meanings as the Latin *rapere* and the English *ravish*,[38] and one can only determine its precise meaning by a sufficient context. If the context is not sufficient, one must leave likely options open. Here we find, as in the 1275 statute, the possibility of a ravishment that can be consented to, therefore not forced or *contra voluntatem mulieris*, except that now there is no age stipulation, and apparently no crime involved when the woman consents beforehand. It is only when there is no consent at all or only later consent that the harsh penalty

[35] T. F. T. Plucknett, *Legislation of Edward I* (Oxford 1949) 121–122. Plucknett seems to be relying on his memory of the statute, since he indicates that all of chap. 34 is in French, and he speaks of "the curious first sentence of this statute which treats of the abduction of a wife entirely in terms of the chattels taken with her—clothing and jewellery, in fact." Earlier on (n. 24 above) 11, he found that the only likely explanation for the use of French in chap. 34 and chap. 49 was a desire to make the provisions perfectly clear to the public, which Post (n. 14 above) 156 rightly finds improbable. English rather than French was the only universally understood tongue at this time; see R. M. Wilson, "English and French in England, 1100–1300," *History* 28 (1943) 37–60; W. Rothwell, "The Teaching of French in Medieval England," *Modern Language Review* 63 (1968) 37–46.

[36] Post (n. 14 above) 156, citing *Calendar of Close Rolls* (CCR), *Edward I*, 5 vols. (London 1900–1908) 2.333.

[37] Powicke and Cheney (n. 32 above) 955.

[38] See the new *Anglo-Norman Dictionary*, ed. Louise W. Stone, William Rothwell, et al., 7 vols. (London 1977–1992) s.v. *ravir* (vol. 6).

applies. Whether there is any significance to the fact that force is mentioned only for the latter situation (that is, where there is subsequent consent) is not apparent.

But whatever the precise intention of the French addition, the emended chapter 34, as well as Westminster I chapter 13, has been accepted in modern times as including the whole range of related offenses, from the sexual violation of an underage girl or a nun to the elopement of a mature woman with her new husband or the adulterous union of a married woman with her lover. We will discuss below the extent to which these varied interpretations can be found in early references to the statutes.

1382: Statute of 6 Richard II, Chapter 6 (October 1382)

> [1] Contra malefactores et raptores dominarum et filiarum nobilium aliarumque mulierum violencius et plus solito hiis diebus quasi in omni parte regni predicti invalescentes, ordinatum est et statutum quod ubicumque et quandocumque hujusmodi domine, filie, et alie mulieres predicte decetero rapiantur, et post hujusmodi raptum hujusmodi raptoribus consenserint, quod tam raptores sive rapientes quam rapte et eorum quilibet decetero inhabilitentur et inhabiles sint ipso facto ad omnem hereditatem, dotem, sive conjunctum feoffamentum post mortem virorum et antecessorum suorum habendum vel vendicandum.
>
> ([1] Against the offenders and ravishers of ladies and the daughters of noblemen, and other women, in every part of the said realm, in these days offending more violently and much more than they were wont, it is ordained and stablished, that wheresoever and whensoever such ladies, daughters, and other women aforesaid be ravished, and after such rape do consent to such ravishers, that as well the ravishers as they that be ravished, and every of them, be from thenceforth disabled, and by the same deed be unable to have or challenge all inheritance, dower, or joint feoffment after the death of their husbands and ancestors.[39])

The law continues by saying that immediately after such consent to *raptus* the next of kin of both ravisher and ravishee can claim their property, and that the husband of the woman, if she has one, or, if she is unmarried or widowed, her father or next of kin, can pursue and sue the ravisher:

> [2] Et quod statim in hoc casu proximus de sanguine eorundum rapiencium et raptarum, cui hereditas, dos, seu conjunctum feoffamentum descendere, reverti, remanere, vel accidere deberet post mortem rapientis vel rapte, habeat titulum inmediate, statim scilicet post raptum, intrandi super rapientem vel raptam ac eorum assignatos et terre tenentes in eisdem hereditate, dote, seu conjuncto feoffamento, et illa hereditarie tenendi; et quod viri hujusmodi mulierum, si viros habuerint, vel, si viros non habuerint superstites, quod tunc patres vel alii de sanguine eorundem propinquiores, decetero habeant sectam prosequendi, et sequi pot[ueri]nt versus eosdem malefactores et raptores in hac parte, et illos inde, quamvis eedem mulieres post hujusmodi raptum dictis raptoribus consenserint, de vita et membro convincendi.
>
> ([2] And that incontinently in this case the next of the blood of those ravishers or of them that be ravished, to whom such inheritance, dower, or joint feoffment ought to revert, remain, or fall after the death of the ravisher or of her that is so ravished, shall have title immediately, that is to say, after the rape, to enter upon the ravisher or her that

[39] *Statutes* (n. 8 above) 2.27.

> is ravished and their assigns and land-tenants in the same inheritance, dower, or joint-feoffment, and the same to hold in state of inheritance; and that the husbands of such women, if they have husbands, or, if they have no husbands in life, that then the fathers or other next of their blood, have from henceforth the suit to pursue, and may sue against the same offenders and ravishers in this behalf, and to have them thereof convict of life and of member, although the same women after such rape do consent to the said ravishers.[40])

Literally, the law gives the right to the next inheritor to assume title immediately after the ravishment rather than after the consent to the ravishment, or proof of the consent. It then gives the right of appeal to husbands or next of kin *even though* there is consent, which might argue that it also allows it when there is no consent.

But the intention is to focus on cases where consent follows, since the supposed need for this law is stated explicitly in the *Rolls of Parliament*: the Commons allege that heretofore punishment of life and member was not given by law to any party in cases where the said women consent afterwards ("punissement de vie et de membre n'est pas donez par la loy pur nule partie en cas qe les dites femmes se agreent et assentent apres").[41] This statement is true if stress is laid on the word *party*, for, as we have just seen, the penalty of death was indeed given in cases where the woman consented afterwards, but at the king's suit.

The 1382 concludes by stipulating that the defendant cannot be admitted to trial by battle but only to trial by inquest (that is, by jury):

> [3] Et ulterius concordatum est quod defendens in hoc casu ad duellum vadiandum minime recipiatur; immo rei veritas inde per inquisicionem patrie trietur. Salvis semper domino regi et ceteris dominis regni predicti de raptoribus illis, si fortassis inde convincantur, in omnibus escetis suis.

> ([3] And further it is accorded that the defendant in this case shall not be received to wage battle, but that the truth of the matter be thereof tried by inquisition of the country. Saving always to our lord the king and to other lords of the said realm all their escheats of the said ravishers, if peradventure they be thereof convict.[42])

The last part of this section may have meant, in practice, that the father of the ravisher was able to retain any escheats.[43] The first sentence was inserted, J. B. Post concludes, because of the envisioned inequality of age in combats between fathers and unwanted sons-in-law.[44]

For, even though nothing is explicitly stated in the statute about abducting the woman (or carrying off goods), Post has shown that this legislation was inspired by a case of elopement, construed as an abduction, of a young woman, Eleanor West, from the custody of her father, the knight Thomas West, by Nicholas Clifton, with implied but unmentioned matrimonial intent. Therefore, even though the law gives primary

[40]Ibid.

[41]*Rotuli Parliamentorum*, 6 vols. (London 1767–1777) 3.139–140; the petition is translated by J. B. Post, "Sir Thomas West and the Statute of Rapes, 1382," *Bulletin of the Institute of Historical Research* 53 (1980) 24–30 at 26–27.

[42]*Statutes* (n. 8 above) 2.27.

[43]I. S. Leadam, *Select Cases before the King's Council in the Star Chamber*, SS 16 (London 1903) cxi.

[44]Post (n. 41 above) 27.

emphasis to the situation of an already married woman consenting to live in adultery with her abductor, a principal intention of the statute seems to have been to counter the escape of heiresses from the control of their guardians. *

In the first letter that Thomas West and his wife wrote on the subject of their abducted daughter, a supplication addressed to John of Gaunt in the summer of 1382, they said simply that Clifton, armed and with the aid of armed attendants, "ravished" their daughter Eleanor, for which they prayed remedy.[45] On 10 August 1382, a commission was given to West and others to arrest Clifton and others for assaulting and robbing West's family and for ravishing Eleanor.[46] Words of felony were not used in either case, but in another petition, this time addressed to the king, after the passage of the statute in October—which they said was enacted at their petition—they charged that Nicholas Clifton "feloniously ravished and deflowered" their daughter, and they asked that the statute be made to apply retroactively to Nicholas and Eleanor, "if she consent at any time," and that Thomas be able to attaint Nicholas, "notwithstanding that the said Eleanor be now covert of the said Nicholas."[47] Thus, after leaving Eleanor's consent to the abduction (and to the deflowering) still in question, West seems to admit that she was already married Nicholas.

The marriage could, of course, have intervened before Nicholas deflowered her, and, in fact, since matrimony could be effected by a simple private exchange of consent between the couple, both marriage and deflowering could have occurred well before the abduction was planned or executed. But even though the statute did not stipulate an element of sexual violence in the *raptus*, and though none was mentioned in his original petition, West seems to have been concerned to incorporate such a reference into his subsequent request to have the statute applied to him, and to state it in such a way as to suggest that it occurred immediately, as part of the original assault. He did not, however, go so far as to say that the deflowerment was against Eleanor's will.

Whether West continued to pursue the matter is not clear. However, a few months after the passage of the statute, Clifton was given a pardon of the king's suit in the matter at the supplication of Queen Anne, on 14 March 1383, "for all felonies and rapes with which he is charged." Six or seven weeks later, on 1 May, now being described as "indicted of having made a new insurrection and perpetrated divers felonies and rapes," he received another pardon of all offenses.[48] He seems to have been knighted a year or two after this, and some years later, in 1395, Mrs. West at least, if not West himself, showed her favor to Clifton in her will.[49]

As we will see below, the Commons in the next regnal year after asking for the statute in 1382 repented of it and asked for its repeal on the grounds that it was too harsh, but their request was denied.

[45]Ibid. 25–26; Post gives only an English translation of the French text of the letter.

[46]*Calendar of the Patent Rolls* (CPR): *Richard II*, 6 vols. (London 1895–1909) 2.197.

[47]Post (n. 41 above) 27, translating the original French.

[48]CPR *Richard II* 2.237, 269. "Rape" in the calendars is simply a translation of *raptus*, without distinction between simple abduction and forced sex.

[49]Post (n. 41 above) 29.

1390: Statute of 13 Richard II, Statute 2, Chapter 1

> . . . Nulle chartre de pardon desore soit alow devant qiconques justices pour murdre, mort de homme occys par agayt, assaut, ou malice propense, treson, ou rape de femme, si mesme le murdre ou mort de homme occys par agait, assaut, ou malice perpense, treson, ou rape de femme ne soient especifiez en mesme la chartre.
>
> (No charter of pardon from henceforth shall be allowed before any justice for murder, or for the death of a man slain by await, assault, or malice prepensed, treason, or rape of a woman, unless the same murder, death of the man slain by await, assault, or malice prepensed, treason, or rape of a woman be specified in the same charter.[50])

The act goes on to give other details about the granting of pardons. These details were repealed three years later, 16 Richard II, chapter 6, while leaving the above provision in force.[51] The statute is in keeping with exemptions of murder and other crimes, including rape/ ravishment of women from the last year of Edward III, February 1377,[52] through the first years of Henry IV,[53] including 5 Richard II, November 1381 ("ravissementz des femmes");[54] 6 Richard II, October 1382 ("rape des femmes")—granted at the same Parliament that passed the statute of 1382 noted above;[55] 8 Richard II, November 1384 ("rapes");[56] 11 Richard II, February–June 1388 ("ravisours des femmes");[57] 13 Richard II, January 1390 ("rape de femme")—at the Parliament that passed this statute;[58] and 21 Richard II, September 1397 ("rapes des femmes").[59] At the 1381 Parliament, the formula to be used when granting a general pardon to an individual also excludes "rapes"—"proditionibus, murdris, raptibus mulierum exceptis."[60]

1453: Statute of 31 Henry VI, 1452–1453, Chapter 9

> Item, qe come en touz parties de cest roialme dyvers gens de poiar, moevez de insaciable covetyse encountre tout droit, gentilness, verite, et bone conscience, ont labores et trovez novelx invencions et eux asseduousment executes, alendaungereaunce, trouble, et mavailx traiter de toutz dames et gentilx femmes et autres femmes esteants soulz eiantz ascune substaunce des terres, tenementes, ou autres moebles biens deins cest dit reame, entendauntz la graunte innocencie et symplenesse de eux, voillent prendre ceux par force, ou autrement veinient a eux resemblauntez estre lour tresgraundez amis, promettantz eux leur loialle amite, et issint par graunde dissimulacion ou autrement gaignent eux en lour possession, conveiauntz eux en autielx lieux ou lez ditz meffeisours sount de plus poiar, et qant ascuns femmes par tielx moiens ou par ascune autre moien sont en leur governaunce, la dit mavailx dispose persone ou persones ne voillent suffrer eux daler

[50] *Statutes* (n. 8 above) 2.68.
[51] Ibid. 2.86–87. See Thomas Andrew Green, *Verdict According to Conscience: Perspectives on the English Criminal Trial Jury, 1200–1800* (Chicago 1985) 74–75.
[52] *Rotuli Parliamentorum* (n. 41 above) 2.365.
[53] Ibid. 3.445 (1 Henry IV, October 1399), 544 (5 Henry IV, February 1404).
[54] Ibid. 3.103
[55] Ibid. 3.140 sec. 44 (no. 26).
[56] Ibid. 3.202.
[57] Ibid. 3.248.
[58] Ibid. 3.268.
[59] Ibid. 3.369.
[60] Ibid. 3.119.

a large et estre a lour libertee, jusqes a ceo qe eles voillent obliger ceux a les ditz meffaisours, ou autre persone ou persones a lour oeps, en graundes sommes par obligacion ou obligacions sibien symplez come condicionelx, ou par obligacion ou obligacions destatute merchaunt faitz devaunt maire ou baillif eiant poiar aprendre tielx reconusauntz; auxi multz foitz ils voilent compeller eux destre marries par eux, contrarie a lour propre desires, ou autrement ils voillent faire lever la dit somme ou sommes de lour terres et biens et dendaunger lour persone ou persones a leur tresgraunde damage; qe ad este et est semblable estre universall prejudice al ley del Eglice et la ley de cest roialme, saunz ceo qe due remedie sur ceo soit purveu: nostre dit seigneur le roy, considerant les premissez, ad ordeigne et establie par lauctorite de cest present parlement, qe en toutz tielx cases desuisditz, la partie oblige poet avoit brief hors del chauncerie, conteignant tout la matier de leur deresonable entraiter.

(Item, whereas in all parts of this realm divers people of great power, moved with unsatiable covetousness, against all right, gentleness, truth, and good conscience, have labored and found new inventions and them busily do execute, to the danger, trouble, and mistreating of all ladies, gentlewomen, and other women sole having any substance of lands, tenements, or other movable goods within this realm, perceiving their great innocency and simplicity, will take them by force, or otherwise come to them, resembling to be their greatest friends, promising them their faithful friendship, and so by great dissimulation, or otherwise, get them into their possession, conveying them into such places where the said offenders be of most power, and when any women by such means or by any other means be in their government, the said evil-disposed person or persons will not suffer them to go at large and be at their liberty, until they will bind themselves to the said offenders, or other person or persons to their use, in great sums, by obligation or obligations, as well single as conditional, or by obligation or obligations of statute merchant, made before a mayor or bailiff having power to take such recognisances; also they will many times compel them to be married by them, contrary to their own likings, or otherwise they will levy the said sum or sums on their lands and goods, and put their person or persons in danger, to their great damage; which hath been, and is like to be, an universal prejudice to the law of Holy Church and the law of this realm, unless due remedy thereupon be provided: our said lord the king, considering the premisses, hath ordained and stablished, by authority of this present parliament, that in all such cases aforesaid, the party bound may have a writ out of the chancery, containing all the matter of their unreasonable entreating.[61])

The statute continues, giving details of enforcing the writ. We must note that even though the use of force is implied, at least in preventing escape, the word "ravish" is avoided and the action is not made a crime; nor is there a criminalization of extortionate methods used to force women into making bonds signing away their goods or "agreeing to marry against their will." The statute simply provides a way for "women sole" of voiding the bonds.[62] This, of course, is to happen once they are freed from captivity, or once they come to their senses after having been seduced by unscrupulous suitors or false friends. Looked at another way, it provided women a way of get- *

[61] *Statutes* (n. 8 above) 2.376–368; I follow the version of the translation found in the Rolls of Parliament (given in the footnotes of this edition), which is closer to that of the 1543 edition of the statutes than is the translation found in the Statute Rolls (given in the main text of the *Statutes*).

[62] See E. W. Ives, "'Agaynst taking awaye of Women': The Inception and Operation of the Abduction Act of 1487," *Wealth and Power in Tudor England: Essays Presented to S. T. Bindoff*, ed. E. W. Ives et al. (London 1978) 21–44 at 23–24.

ting out of an unsatisfactory marriage without resorting to traditional prosecutions and lawsuits (though of course an ecclesiastical annulment would still be required).

1487: Statute of 3 Henry VII, Chapter 2

Item, come femez, si bien pusels come veus et femez mariez, aiantz substances, ascunz en biens moeblez et ascunz en terrez et tenementz et ascuns esteantz heirs apparantz a lour auncestrez, pur la lucre dautiels substances, sont sovent foitz prisez par mesfaisours, contrairie a lour voluntie et apres maries a tiels mesfaisours ou as autres par lour assent, ou deflorez, au graunde displeasir Dieu et encontre lez leyz du roy et disparagement de lez dictez femez, et surquidious dolour et descomfort de lour amys, et a malvais example de toutz autres: il est pur ceo ordeigne, establie, et enacte par notre dicte soveraigne seigneur le roy, de lassent dez seigneurz espirituels et temporels et lez Comens en le dit Parliament assemblez et par auctorite del mesme, qe qeconqe persone ou personez de cy en avant qe ou quels preigne ou preignent ascune feme ensi encontre sa volunte illealment, cest assavoir pusell, veu, ou feme marie, qe tiels pruise, procurement, et abettement all mesme, et auxi receitement scientment mesme la feme issint prise encontre sa volunte, et sacheant le mesme, soit felonie; et qe tiels mesfaisours, preignours, et procurourz a icell, et recettours sacheantz mesme loffence, en forme avandicte, soit de cy enavant reputez et jugez come principals felons. Purveu toutz foitz qe cest acte nextende pas au ascun persone preignant ascune feme tantsoulement en claymant come sa garde ou feme villein.

(*An Act Against Taking Away of Women Against Their Will*

Where women, as well maidens as widows and wives, having substances, some in goods moveable and some in lands and tenements, and some being heirs apparent unto their ancestors, for the lucre of such substances, been oft-times taken by misdoers contrary to their will, and after married to such misdoers or to other by their assent, or defouled, to the great displeasure of God, and contrary to the king's laws, and disparagement of the said women, and utter heaviness and discomfort of their friends, and to the evil example of all other: it is therefore ordained, established, and enacted by our sovereign lord the king, by the assent of his lords spiritual and temporal and the Commons in this present Parliament assembled, and by authority of the same, that what person or persons from henceforth that taketh any woman so against her will unlawfully, that is to say, maid, widow, or wife, that such taking, procuring, and abetting to the same, and also receiving wittingly the same woman so taken against her will and knowing the same, be felony; and that such misdoers, takers, and procurators to the same, and receiptors knowing the said offence, in form aforesaid, be henceforth reputed and judged as principal felons. Provided alway that this act extend not to any person taking any woman only claiming her as his ward or bondwoman.[63])

We note that once again the ambiguous word "ravish" is avoided. The alleged reason for the act is that women of actual or potential wealth have often been abducted against their will and then married "by their assent" to unsuitable persons. The "by their assent" could be read of the abducted women, but perhaps more likely it is meant of the abductors who assent to have them married to others. The act also speaks of women who are abducted and then deflowered (*deflorez*)—therefore refer-

[63]*Statutes* (n. 8 above) 2.512. The translation is taken from the enrollment on the Parliament Roll (see the preface to vol. 2 of the *Statutes*, p. v), and therefore may be contemporary with the statute. The same translation appears in the 1543 edition of the English statutes, except that for "assent" it reads "advice."

ring to virgins. (The English translation, "defouled," makes it applicable to nonvirgins as well.) Such sexual violations, like the forced marriages to unsuitable persons, result in the woman's disparagement, meaning that she is socially degraded. It also means a devaluation of her *maritagium.* This is the point of Simon the Miller in Chaucer's *Reeve's Tale,* when he says: "Who dorste be so boold to disparage / My doghter, that is come of swich lynage?"[64] In the case of deflowerment without marriage, the disparagement would result whether it was consensual or not. In case of forced marriage, the union could be annulled, and the woman could conceivably emerge with her value intact, though it would be more problematic if the union were sexually consummated.

We should note that even though the act specifically includes wives, it seems clear that the first motivation given for abduction, marriage, could only literally apply to unmarried women or wives forced into a second, bigamous marriage, whereas the second, deflowerment, could only apply to virgins. But what the profit-motive could be in the latter case is not easily imagined. At any rate, the statute makes it a felony to kidnap any unwilling woman—seemingly even a woman without money, since the final clause indicates that the it could apply to the abduction of a bondwoman who is not being claimed as the abductor's property.

This act has been analyzed by E. W. Ives, who says that it makes clear that marriage made under duress is covered, whereas Westminster II speaks of consent (not marriage) following forceful ravishment. But he goes on to observe what we have just noted, that, literally, "the law could be held to extend felony to abduction *per se.*"[65] He suggests that the statute was a response to a particular incident,[66] much like the act of 1382. We will discuss below Ives's assumption that before this time abduction without sexual violation was not considered a felony.[67]

I add three more statutes from the sixteenth century, which needed no translation, since they appeared in English to begin with.

1540: 32 Henry VIII, Chapter 12: Concerning Sanctuaries, §2

> . . . From henceforth the said parish churches . . . shall not . . . give any manner of tuition . . . to any manner of person or persons which at any time hereafter shall perpetrate, commit, or do any manner of wilful murder, or which shall commit or do any ravishment of or to any woman, or which shall commit any manner of burglary, or which shall commit or do any manner of robbery in the highway ...

The statute goes on to include life-threatening robbery, robbery of churches, and felonious arson.[68]

The ambiguous word "ravishment" is used, but perhaps the "indenture English" of the statute means something for once, and ravishment "of" a woman refers to abduction, while ravishment "to" a woman refers to sexual rape. The inclusion of ravishment in the company of felonies exempted from general pardons clearly indicates that it too is considered a particularly heinous crime, as in the 1390 act.

[64]Lines 4271–4272, *The Riverside Chaucer,* ed. Larry D. Benson (Boston 1987) 83.
[65]Ives (n. 62 above) 24.
[66]Ibid. 26–30.
[67]See below at n. 157.
[68]*Statutes* (n. 8 above) 3.757.

1558: 4-5 Philip and Mary, Chapter 8:

> An Act for the Punishment of Such as Shall Take Away Maidens That Be Inheritors, Being Within the Age of Sixteen Years, or That Marry Them Without Consent of Their Parents
>
> (1) . . . It shall not be lawful to any person or persons to take or convey away. . . any maid or woman child unmarried, being under the age of sixteen years, out of or from the possession . . . and against the will of the father . . . or of such person or persons to whom the father . . . shall appoint . . . the order . . . of such maid.
>
> (2) . . . If any person or persons . . . above the age of fourteen years shall from and after the first day of April next coming unlawfully take . . . any maid or woman child unmarried, being within the age of sixteen years, out of or from the possession and against the will of the father or mother of such child, . . . every such person and persons so offending, being thereof lawfully attainted or convicted, . . . shall have and suffer imprisonment of his or their bodies by the space of two whole years without bail or mainprise, or else shall pay such fine for his or their said offense as shall be assessed . . . in the Star Chamber at Westminster.
>
> (3) . . . If any such person or persons . . . shall so take away. . . and deflower any such maid . . . or shall against the will . . . of . . . the father, . . . if the father be in life, or . . . the mother, . . . by secret letters, messages, or otherwise contract matrimony with any such maiden, . . . except such contracts . . . made by the consent of such person or persons as . . . have the marriage, . . . every such person or persons so offending . . . shall suffer imprisonment...of five years . . . or else pay . . . fine.
>
> (5) . . . If any woman child or maiden, being above the age of twelve years and under the age of sixteen years, do at any time consent and agree to such person that so shall make any contract of matrimony, . . . the next of the kin . . . shall from the time of such assent . . . have . . . all such lands . . . as the same woman child . . . had in possession . . . during the life of such person that so shall contract matrimony.[69]

The first paragraph begins by speaking of girls who stand to inherit property, but, as can be seen, the actual language of the act applies to all unmarried females under sixteen. The third paragraph goes on to specify that, of any forfeitures assessed by the Star Chamber, half goes to the king and queen and the other half to "the parties grieved," presumably those who have suffered financially by the deflowerment or unauthorized marriage of the heiress. The last part of the fifth paragraph makes it clear that it is the offending husband who is deprived of the heiress's property during his lifetime, and after his death the property reverts to whoever would have it if this act had not been made. Presumably that would include the heiress herself, if she survived the husband, and any children that resulted from the marriage.

Ives presumes that this act was passed in reaction to a judgment of 1556–1557, after two men and two accessories were indicted for feloniously taking a woman against her will, contrary to the form of the 1487 statute. But because there was no mention that either principal married her against her will or deflowered her, which the justices considered to be implied in the preamble of the statute as necessary to

[69]Ibid. 4.329–330. Para. 4 specifies that the Star Chamber and justices of assize may determine offenses, and para. 6 exempts orphans from the act.

make the offense a felony, all parties were discharged.[70] Ives concludes that the 1558 statute completely discards the 1487 law by eliminating all notion of felony for the offenses, but that it follows the 1382 statute. We should rather say that the 1558 statute follows only the section of the 1382 act governing the property of consenting heiresses, * at least with regard to the abductor, if not entirely with regard to her, but it does not, of course, follow the section making the abduction of heiresses a felony. By assigning abductors of girls only two years in prison and deflowerers of abducted girls only five years, the legislators show that they were also ignoring the 1390 and 1540 statutes.

1576: 18 Elizabeth I (1575-76), Chapter 7:

> An Act to Take Away Clergy from the Offenders in Rape and Burglary . . .
> (1) For the repressing of the most wicked and felonious rapes or ravishments of women—maids, wives, and damsels—and of felonious burglaries, and for the avoiding of sundry perjuries and other abuses in and about the purgation of clerks convict delivered to the ordinaries, be it enacted and ordained by the authority of the present Parliament, that if any person or persons shall fortune at any time after the first day of June now next ensuing to commit or do any manner of felonious rape, ravishment, or burglary, and to be found guilty by verdict of any such felonious rape or burglary, or that any person or persons shall fortune to be outlawed for any the offenses aforesaid, or upon his or their arraignment shall confess any such felonious rape or burglary, that in every such case every person and persons so being found guilty, outlawed, or confessing any of the said felonious rapes or burglaries, shall suffer pains of death and forfeit as in cases of felony hath been used and accustomed by the common laws of this realm, without any allowance of the privilege or benefit of clergy; any law, custom, or usage heretofore had, made, or used to the contrary notwithstanding.
>
> (4) And for the plain declaration of law, be it enacted that if any person shall unlawfully and carnally know and abuse any woman child under the age of ten years, every such unlawful and carnal knowledge shall be felony, and the offender thereof being duly convicted shall suffer as a felon without allowance of clergy.[71]

It seems clear that "ravishment" is given as a synonym for "rape" in this act, since the latter does service for both words as the first paragraph goes on. Neither word is used in section 4, when sexual intercourse with girls under ten is declared a felony without benefit of clergy. This clause may have been inspired by a case from a few years earlier when a man was charged with having feloniously ravished and carnally known a seven-year-old girl. He was found guilty. "But the court doubted of rape in so tender a child. But if she had been nine years and more, it would have been otherwise" ("Mes le court doubta del rape en cy tender puel, mes sel fuissoit 9 ans et ouster, auterment serroit").[72]

[70] Ives (n. 62 above) 25, citing William Dalison, *Les reports des divers special cases* (London 1689) 22, repr. in *The English Reports*, 171 vols. (Edinburgh 1900–1930) 123.242.

[71] *Statutes* (n. 8 above) 4.617–618. Sections 2–3 provide that persons allowed clergy and burned in the hand are to be discharged without being committed to their bishop, but they may also be imprisoned for a year.

[72] *Reports* of James Dyer, 2:304a, for 13–14 Elizabeth I (1570–1572), *English Reports* 73.683, from the annotated English edition of John Vaillant (1794), drawing on the French editions of 1592 and 1688. I cite the French from the 1672 edition: Jaques Dyer, *Les reports des divers select matters et resolutions des reverend judges et sages del Ley*, etc. (London 1672) fol. 304.

Summary of the Statutes

Now that the complete texts are given above, let us summarize their central provisions, so that we can the better deal with their overall import.

* 1236 (Merton, 20 Henry III): Those who forcefully abduct or detain heirs under fourteen must pay the guardian and be imprisoned because of the trespass to the king; a heavier penalty is due if the heir marries.
* 1275 (Westminster I, 3 Edward I): It is a trespass to ravish/ abduct (by force) any female, married or unmarried, against her will (or, in the case of an underage girl, even if she consents). If no one sues within forty days, the king will sue. Fine and two or more years in prison for convicted offenders.

"1276" (Coroner statute, 4 Edward I?): The person appealed of rape, if recent, as evidenced by blood or hue and cry, requires four to six pledges; otherwise, two.

* 1285 (Westminster II, 13 Edward II): (chapter 34) [A1] *Death penalty for ravishing a woman—wife, damsel, or other—without her consent* [A2] *or, at the king's suit, even if she consents afterwards* [French addition]. [B1] Husbands' goods taken with abducted wives are at the king's suit. [B2] Adulterous wives who leave their husbands lose their dower. [B3] Three years' imprisonment and damages for abducting nuns, even consenting nuns. (chapter 35) Two years and damages for ravishing/ abducting male or female wards, even without marriage, or, if marriage occurs, even if compensation is paid. Exile or life imprisonment for not returning the ward or for being unable to recompense the *maritagium.*
* 1382 (6 Richard II): [1] When men ravish women (maids, wives, widows) who later consent to the ravishment (*raptus*), both the men and the women lose their rights of inheritance. [2] The husband or closest male relative of the woman can sue the man and seek the death penalty. [3] The man thus sued cannot resort to trial by combat. Escheats of ravishers are reserved to the king.

1390 (13 Richard II): General pardons do not include premeditated murder, treason, or rape of women unless specifically mentioned.

* 1453 (31 Henry VI): Women conveyed by force or persuasion and detained until agreeing to property settlements or marriage can have such agreements voided.

1487 (3 Henry VII): Felony (death penalty) for taking away any unwilling woman (maid, wife, or widow), or assisting in such taking away, whether for purpose of forced marriage or deflowering, resulting in the woman's devaluation.

1540 (32 Henry VIII): No sanctuary privileges for those convicted of ravishment of, or to, any woman, or murder, robbery, or felonious arson.

* 1558 (4–5 Philip and Mary): (1) Unlawful to take girls under sixteen. (2) Persons over fourteen who take girls aged twelve–sixteen are liable to two years in prison; (3) or five years if they deflower or marry them. (5) The goods of a girl who consents to such marriage do not go to the husband, but after his death revert to normal succession.

1576 (18 Elizabeth I): (1) No benefit of clergy to those convicted of felonious rape/ ravishment of any woman. (4) Carnal knowledge of girls under ten is a felony without benefit of clergy.

Out of all of these laws, only the early Coroner statute obviously deals with forcible sexual violation. The other laws all deal primarily with the forcible or assisted removal of persons, usually female but sometimes male, from one place to another, for various purposes, whether marriage, adultery, freedom, or extortion. In only two cases, namely, the 1487 and 1558 acts, is there any overt reference to forced coitus, when it is said that the abducted women may be either deflowered (*deflorez*) or married—but even here that emphasis would seem to be on the loss in value that her *maritagium* * would suffer. The codicil to the 1576 act, dealing with under-ten-year-old girls, does of course refer to coitus, but not necessarily forcible coitus, since "abuse" may be taken in a moral rather than physical sense.

I conclude that in all probability Coke and others after him who have seen some or all of these statutes (apart from the exceptions just noted) as dealing equally, mainly, or solely with forced coitus are mistaken. This is not to deny, however, that the statutes were sometimes interpreted as dealing with forced sex.

EARLY SEXUAL INTERPRETATIONS OF THE WESTMINSTER STATUTES OF 1275 AND 1285

In the case of the the statutes of Westminster I and II we have no certain knowledge concerning the motivations that lay behind the passage of the laws, except perhaps for the provision of 1285 chapter 34 [B3] dealing with nuns. But Post, while believing that both the 1275 act and 1285 chapter 34 [A1] addressed women's appeals of sexual rape, suggests that the 1275 statute was prompted by a recent abduction case.[73] (The case in question involved a charge by William Hotot against a group of men of taking his wife Amicia *vi et armis* along with his goods, worth 15 marks, and detaining both wife and goods, for which he claimed £100 damages. They replied that Amicia had previously married (*desponsavit*) one Alexander, and that William had subsequently ravished (*rapuit*) her with force and against her will and taken her away, whereupon she sent to Alexander to come with others and bring her back. The defendants denied taking any of Hotot's goods and denied using force.)[74] A few years later, however, in 1279 or 1280, in another case that Post cites, in which Emma appealed Hugh of raping her of her virginity and doing it in felony ("et quod hoc fecit in felonia"), the jury

[73]Post (n. 14 above) 154: "The statutory extension of the appeal of rape to matrons therefore brought brought within the purview of an existent private action [i.e., a virgin's appeal of deflowerment] the problem of ravished wives, and may have been prompted by a Sussex abduction feud which had recently attracted the Crown's attention." Post's suggestion that the sexual rape of nonvirgins was previously held to be a crime punishable in the ecclesiastical rather than secular courts is not supported by the example he cites, a case in 1260 of a chaplain sued by a husband who charged him with forcing his wife, begetting a son on her, wasting and consuming his goods, and taking the wife away and keeping her. The priest denied force and injury, and, as for lying with and ravishing the wife, he held that this was rather a matter for the bishop. The jury agreed, since it concluded that the sex was at the wife's desire and not against the peace, and that his only offense was adultery, which belonged to the ecclesiastical forum. See H. G. Richardson and G. O. Sayles, *Select Cases of Procedure Without Writ under Henry III*, Selden Society (SS) 60 (London 1941) 131–132. In another case in the previous year, this time concerning the elopement of a daughter, a trespass was found in that the lover's emissaries entered without the father's knowledge (ibid. 109), whereas in the other case the wife's permission seems to have been sufficient to avoid the trespass.

[74]London, Public Record Office (PRO), JUST (Justices Itinerant) 1/923 m. 27. There is a brief reference to the case in CPR*: Edward I* 1.69, 6 July 1274: Commission to investigate an assault on the sheriff of Sussex and his men "and the rescue from their custody of Amice, wife of William de Hotot, whom they were bringing under safe-conduct" to the king's representatives.

found Hugh guilty, but since they said that Emma was not a virgin, Hugh was to be kept in prison for two years, according to the new statute ("custodiendum in prisona per duos annos secundum novum statutum"), and he made satisfaction to Emma.[75] In another case of the same time, a defendant was indicted and found guilty of forcibly raping a nine-year-old girl of her virginity against her will. He was committed to jail to serve the penalty of the statute, two years.[76] These cases show at least that the statute could be interpreted to cover sexual rape, whether or not that was its primary intention. We are told enough details about the first case, *Emma v. Hugh*, to see that it did not fit the terms of the statute, which called for two years' punishment on conviction at the suit of a private party or at the suit of the king after a private party failed to prosecute within forty days. Or it may be that the statute was intended to specify the two years' imprisonment only on conviction at the king's suit, with the penalty for private suits left unspecified except for the vague "common right." In Emma's case, * the jury was clearly prepared to give a felony punishment if her suit had succeeded; but since it did not, because she was found not to have been a virgin, they settled for two years' punishment.

Post cites another interesting case at this point, namely *Savage v. Clifford*, an appeal of rape before the King's Bench in Michaelmas term, 1282.[77] Rose, daughter of Nicholas Savage, accused John Clifford and unknown accomplices of kidnapping her on the Sunday before Saint Hilary, 8 Edward I (7 January 1280), and taking her to his house in another town and there raping her virginity, leaving her all bloody. He then kept her captive for almost two years, from the Sunday after Saint Hilary (so 14 January) to the feast of Saint Martin in 10 Edward I (11 November 1282). As soon as she escaped, she raised the hue and cry and sued him in the king's court. Her appeal was rejected by the court as defective, on grounds that she had not named a definite day and year and place when he was supposed to have raped her (from this distance, her * details look very definite, except for the variance in the Sunday, stated first as before and then after Hilary), and so, as usual in all cases of "abatement" (technical failure), she was committed to jail for a false appeal (a procedure that would be required by law in 1285).[78] Clifford was then required to respond to the king's suit, to which he pleaded not guilty. He failed to appear when, in May 1283, a jury found him guilty of taking Rose away "wickedly and in felony and assault aforethought" and raping her virginity. The justices accepted the verdict and ordered him arrested. He later appeared and "made fine with the lord king for ten pounds." Post cites the case as demonstrating the fact that "the courts were still cheerfully levying the monetary penalties which had characterised conviction at Crown suit previously."[79]

Since Post believes that indictments (presentments) for sexual rape did not occur before 1275 and were in fact authorized by this statute of Westminster I, the previous convictions at Crown suit that he speaks of are presumably convictions after abated

[75]Post (n. 14 above) 154–155, referring to JUST 1/371 m. 15d.

[76]JUST 1/784 m. 17d (1279–1280), referred to by Post 155 n. 1. The report of the sentence reads: "Committatur gaole. Habeat penam statuti, scilicet duos annos."

[77]G. O. Sayles, *Select Cases in the Court of King's Bench*, 7 vols., SS 55, 57–58, 74, 76, 82, 88 (London 1936-1971) 1.101–102.

[78]Statute of 13 Edward I chap. 12 (1285): when appeals fail, the appellors are to be put in prison for a year, to pay damages to the defendant, and to pay a fine to the king (*Statutes* [n. 8 above] 1.81).

[79]Post (n. 14 above) 155.

appeal, for which monetary fines were standard. True, Bracton claimed that sexual rape was an exception, and cited a case in 1222 in which death—the *ultimum supplicium*—was imposed after abatement.[80] Presumably, Bracton also held that, after death was replaced by blinding and castration,[81] this substitute punishment would be imposed after abatement, a point explicitly stated in the *Placita corone*, dating from 1274–1275.[82] But Bracton admitted that some authorities held that a pecuniary punishment was to be levied after abatement,[83] and cases like this are to be found at York in 1218–1219.[84] J. M. Kaye, editor of the *Placita*, shows that the same was true in Bracton's own day: conviction after abated appeals of rape resulted in fines "for the trespass" (*pro transgressione*), citing examples from 1241, 1248, and 1256.[85]

What is particularly interesting about *Savage v. Clifford* is that the jury found the defendant guilty of a felony rather than a trespass. It shows that the 1275 statute did not preclude convictions of sexual rape as felonies, and it was not taken to require imprisonment. (A slightly later version of the *Placita corone* says that conviction after an abated appeal—in this case for felonious wounding—would not entail blinding and castration, nor loss of life, but the defendant "will be imprisoned for his trespass, until such time as he shall have made amends to the plaintiff, and to the king in respect of the trespass.")[86] *Savage* is also of interest because it turns out to be the case of sexual rape that Post adduces as coming to king and council just as the Parliament of Westminster II opened, on 4 May 1285.[87] But the only purpose of bringing it up on that day was to advise that Rose be paid £10 by Clifford for the rape done to her, and it was so ordered.[88]

When the statutory provisions of chapter 34, concerning abducted or eloped wives and nuns, were read six weeks later, can we suppose that the *Savage* case was again recalled, with outrage at the way in which it was handled, and that the French addendum was hastily devised to provide fairer treatment in the future? If so, the language arrived at did not quite do the trick of reinstating the death penalty after an abatement of appeal, for it only provided for conviction at the king's suit when there was no appeal or private suit by the woman at all, that is, when the woman consented to the rape. And if sexual rape was already a felony before the 1275 statute and still a fel-

[80]Bracton (n. 22 above) 2.403.

[81]Ibid. 2.414–415.

[82]*Placita corone*, ed. J. M. Kaye, SS sup. series 4 (London 1966) 9.

[83]Bracton (n. 22 above) 2.403.

[84]Roger D. Groot, "The Early-Thirteenth-Century Criminal Jury," *Twelve Good Men and True: The Criminal Trial Jury in England, 1200–1800*, ed. J. S. Cockburn and Thomas A. Green (Princeton 1988) 3–35 at 12.

[85]Kaye (n. 82 above) xvi–xvii, xxxiv.

[86]*Placita corone*, Shorter Version (n. 82 above) 27. The base MS used is E, which gives a date of 1278 or 1279 for a woman's appeal of the death of her husband (28; see 32–33).

[87]Post (n. 14 above) 156.

[88]PRO KB 27/75 m. 22d: "Consultum est quod predicta Roesia haberet pro raptu ei facto decem libras de predicto Johanne, etc. Et preceptum est vicecomiti quod de terris et catallis predicti Johannis predictos [...?] etc." It is not clear whether an additional £10 was assessed to Rose, over and above the sum to be paid to the king. According to the preceding rehearsal of the case, after Clifford was convicted he came and pledged to pay half the fine of £10 on the quindene of the next Michaelmas term and the other half on the quindene of the following Easter term. Since no year is given, it may be that the future terms of 1285 and 1286 were intended, and that the payments were not yet due. *

ony after it—as demonstrated by the *Savage* case itself—then there would seem to be no reason to call it a felony again in the statute.

If, however, Parliament became indignant not only at the sexual rape but also at the abduction and long imprisonment of Rose Savage, to which the King's Bench jury did not refer, one could argue that this was the reason for inserting the addendum, since, if such a rape happened again, it would allow the father or the husband to prosecute the kidnapper as a felon. Perhaps too a need was felt to override allegations of subsequent consent in such a captivity; hence the codicil to the addendum [A2], giving the suit to the king in such cases.

We must acknowledge that the three unofficial treatises of the time, the *Mirror of Justices*, *Britton*, and *Fleta*, do treat the 1275 and 1285 statutes as dealing with sexual rape. The first two of these treatises, both in French, are especially problematic. The
* author of the *Speculum justiciorum*, or *Mirror of Justices*, perhaps Andrew Horn (d. 1328), who produced the only extant manuscript of the treatise,[89] is notoriously unreliable, being guilty not only of distorting facts but also of passing on deliberate falsehoods as facts. The work has done a great deal of damage to English legal history ever since it came to light in the sixteenth century, especially because of its eager and uncritical acceptance by "the credulous Coke," as Maitland calls him.[90] The author does not comment on any laws beyond 1285, and he has a "special grudge," Maitland notes, against Westminster II, chapter 34, our 1285 statute of rapes.[91] His first comment, in the section on "Sins against the Holy Peace," is as follows:

> Rap se fet en deux maneres, cest assaver de choses e de femmes. Cest pecchie est mis ja por ceo qe le Roi Edward le fist mortel par sa constitucion, qe plus est funde sur volunte qe sur descrecion. Car un est stupre, autre fornicacioun, autre avouterie, autre incest, e autre rap, pur proprement parler e le pecchie distincter, dunt le un pecche est gregnur de lautre. Stupre est a despuceler femme felounessement. Fornicacion est a porgesir femmes corrumpues nient espouses. Avouterie est a porgiser autri espouse. Incest est a porgesir cosine, parente, ou affin. Rap est proprement alopement de femme pur desire del mariage. Rap neqedent solom la volunte del estatut est pris pur un propre mot done pur chescun afforcement de femme de quele condicion qe le seit.

> (Rape is committed in two manners: it is either of things or of women. This sin is put here because King Edward made it mortal by his ordinance, which is founded rather on arbitrary will than discretion. For stuprum is one thing, fornication another, adultery another, incest another, and rape yet another, if we speak correctly and differentiate sins, of which some are greater than others. Stuprum is the felonious taking away of a woman's maidenhood. Fornication is the defiling of an unmarried woman who is already corrupted. Adultery is the defiling of another man's wife. Incest is the defiling of a person related by consanguinity or affinity; but rape is strictly speaking the abduction of a woman with intent to marry her. By the arbitrary words of the statute, however, the one word "rape" is used for every forcing of a woman of whatsoever condition she may be.[92])

[89] *The Mirror of Justices*, ed. William Joseph Whittaker, SS 7 (London 1895), "Introduction" by Frederic William Maitland, who discusses problems of authorship.

[90] Maitland ix–x.

[91] Ibid. xxiii.

[92] *Mirror of Justices* (n. 89 above) 28–29.

Apart from his unlawyerly practice of confusing sins with crimes—it becomes particularly ridiculous to identify mortal sins with capital crimes—he lists various sexual sins in which no force is required to make them sinful, and ends by assuming that all of them require force, not only the felonious deflowering of a virgin, but even fornication and elopement.

Coke contrives to ignore the statement that the proper meaning of rape is the "eloping" of a woman for purpose of marriage, and he cites only the last sentence of this entry. He then says that the *Mirror* has a better definition elsewhere, where indeed the author does contradict his notion that rape primarily means elopement:

> Appeal de rap se fet en ceste manere: Arnebourgh, ici, appele Athelin, illoec, de ceo qe cum, ecet., la vint celi Athelin e ceste Arnebourgh abati, aforcea, e purrust maugrie, felon, contre la pees. E pur ceo qe chescun rap ne soloit mie estre tenu pecche mortiel nestoit nule tiel appeal covenable si ele ne dist, "e soun pucelage le toli."

> (An appeal of rape is made in this wise: Arnebourgh, who is here, appeals Athelin, who is there, for that, whereas, etc., there came this Athelin and knocked down, forced, and corrupted this Arnebourgh, against her will, feloniously, against the peace. And because it was not every rape that was accounted a mortal sin, such an appeal was not in due form unless she said, "and took away her virginity."[93])

He shows that he is fully aware of a traditional meaning of rape as the sexual forcing of a woman. The idea that the sexual rape of virgins was punished more severely than the defilement of other women is confirmed by Henry Bracton earlier in the century, in one of the places cited above: he distinguishes the deflowering of virgins from the violation of other women: matrons, widows, nuns, concubines, prostitutes; but he does not specify what the appropriate punishments should be for each case.[94]

The *Mirror* in due course specifies the defense that can be pleaded against an appeal of rape: namely, that the woman assented, as proved either by resulting pregnancy or by lack of signs of violence, like torn clothes, bloodshed, and hue and cry.[95] This accords with the implicit recognition in the Coroner statute that conviction without physical evidence of forced coitus will be more difficult.

The *Mirror* author later confirms his view that the 1285 statute deals only with sexual rape when he says that the punishment of rape now in the time of King Edward is hanging, whether the ravished woman was a virgin or not, and with no regard to her rank, and whether it was at her suit or the king's, whereas, before this time, the penalty was blinding and castration.[96] Among his objections to the current law is the fact that rape is considered a mortal sin.[97] He probably means rapes of women other than high-class virgins. His next complaint is that rape includes nonvirgins.[98] He means "mortal-sin rape," since he himself spoke of less serious sexual rapes earlier on.

In the specific criticisms of statutes at the end of the *Mirror*, the author denounces the 1275 statute of rapes only for imposing prison sentences.[99] The 1285 statute

[93]Ibid. 59.
[94]Bracton (n. 22 above) 2.414–415.
[95]*Mirror of Justices* (n. 89 above) 103.
[96]Ibid. 141.
[97]Ibid. 172.
[98]Ibid.
[99]Ibid. 186.

about rape (the part we labeled chapter 34 [A1–02]) is reprehensible, he says, for no one can legislate a venial sin into a mortal without the assent of the pope or the emperor (!). He continues:

> Lestatut qe li roi eit suit en rap [A2] ou en allopement des femmes maries [B1] est repernable, car nul nest tenu a respondre a la siute le roi si non par apel ou par enditement. E ceo qe est contenu de femmes perdre doeire pur le pecche devoutire [B2] dust aussi comprendre ceus avoutres qe cleiment a tenir les heritages lur femmes par la lei d'Engleterre, si qe nule accepcion ne soit en persones. Lemprisonment des allopours de noneyns e la ranceon ovek [B3] nest mie lei, einz est errour en double manere, sicom avant est dit en plusours lus.
>
> (The statute giving the king a suit for rape [A2] and for elopement of married women [B1] is reprehensible, for no one is bound to answer to the suit of the king save upon appeal or indictment. And what is said about women losing their dowers by the sin of adultery [B2] should include adulterous husbands who claim to hold the inheritances of their wives by the law (courtesy) of England, that so there may be no acceptance of persons. The imprisonment, coupled with ransom, for the elopers of nuns [B3] is not law, but is error and twofold error, as has been already shown in many places.[100])

His comment on chapter 35, dealing with the "ravissours de mariages," or kidnappers of wards with marriage-rights belonging to others, criticizes only the statutory penalty and the form of the writs.[101]

The other anonymous, or rather pseudepigraphous, French treatise noted above, *Britton*, purports to be by Edward I himself.[102] It also identifies the sexual rape investigated by the coroner[103] with the offenses treated by the 1285 statute:

> Rap est une felonie de homme de violence fete au cors de femme, quele qe ele soit pucele ou autre; et de tiels felouns soit enquis. De la quele felonie qi qe soit atteynt a la sute de la femme par appel de felonie, ou a la nostre, si soit le jugement tiel cum pur mort de homme, le quel qe ele soit assentue puis la felonie fete ou noun; sicum est contenue en nos estatutz de Westmoster.
>
> (Rape is a felony committed by a man by violence on the body of a woman, whether she be a virgin or not. Of such felonies let inquiry be made; and whoever is attainted thereof, either at the suit of the woman by appeal of felony, or at our suit, shall have the same judgment as for the death of a man, whether the woman have consented after commission of the felony or not, as is contained in our Statutes of Westminster.[104])

Like the *Mirror* author, then, *Britton* specifies a right of appeal for the woman, and says further that this is called for in the statutes of Westminster. The author's use of the plural indicates that he is referring to the 1275 statute as well as the 1285 law, which is confirmed in a further comment:

> En dreit de apel de rap, voloms qe chescune femme, pucele ou autre, eyt sa accioun a sure la venjaunce de la felonie par apel en Countree de eynz quarante jours; apres quel tens ele perd sa sute; en quel cas si le defendaunt graunte le fet, et die qe ele conceust de

[100]Ibid. 195.
[101]Ibid. 196.
[102]*Britton*, ed. and trans. Francis Morgan Nichols, 2 vols. (Oxford 1856).
[103]Ibid. 1.2, pp. 9, 17.
[104]Ibid. 1.16, p. 55.

ly enfaunt en mesme le tens, et ceo puse averreer, voloms nous qe en ceo cas ne soit nule felonie ajuge, pur ceo qe nule femme ne peut conceyvre, si ele ne se assente.

(With regard to an appeal of rape, our pleasure is that every woman, whether virgin or not, shall have a right to sue vengeance for the felony by appeal in the county court within forty days, but after that time she shall lose her suit; in which case, if the defendant confesses the fact, but says that the woman at the same time conceived by him, and can prove it, then our will is, that it be adjudged no felony because no woman can conceive if she does not consent.[105])

Here it is quite clear that *Britton* takes the 1275 statute to be referring to the woman's right to appeal sexual rape. It is noteworthy that the author considers the victim's action to be one of felony, and some modern interpreters agree, for example Pollock and Maitland[106] and Bertha Putnam,[107] as well as Holdsworth, in his second assessment.[108] But unlike these writers, who say that conviction of sexual rape by indictment was made a lesser crime or trespass by the 1275 statute and a felony by the 1285 law, *Britton* envisages only an indicted defendant who admits the coitus but pleads consent on the woman's part. He does not need the 1285 French addition, then, to tell him that sexual rape is a felony; and the only indication that he knows of it is his reference to the woman consenting afterwards.

Fleta, the third anonymous treatise of the time, is in Latin.[109] It agrees with *Britton* in considering sexual rape a felony appealable by the victim (and in taking pregnancy as a sign of consent),[110] and also in assuming that sexual rape was the issue in the 1275 statute, specifically in reference to the forty-day limit for suing: "Women also who are ravished will in no wise be heard after forty days" ("Mulieres eciam rapte ultra quadraginta dies nullatenus audiantur").[111] Elsewhere *Fleta* includes ravishers of women ("raptores mulierum") and abductors of wives with husbands' goods ("abductores sponsarum cum bonis virorum") among those against whom the king may have suit when the injured parties do not wish to sue.[112] The second category is dealt with in the first Latin provision of the 1285 statute, chapter 34 [B1], while the first is treated in the 1275 statute and in the French introduction to the 1285 chapter 34 [A2], where reference is made to women consenting afterwards. He also draws on the final clause of chapter 34, that is, [B3], providing three years in prison for abducting a nun,[113] and he quotes chapter 35 verbatim, on the ravishing of male and female wards.[114]

If, as Post asserts, indictments (as opposed to appeals) for sexual rape occur only after 1275, and soon after 1275, we might be inclined to agree, in a *post hoc ergo prop-*

[105]Ibid. 1.25, p. 115.

[106]Pollock and Maitland (n. 18 above) 491–492 n. 6.

[107]Bertha Haven Putnam, *The Place in Legal History of Sir William Shareshull, Chief Justice of the King's Bench, 1350–1361* (Cambridge 1950) 129, 274 n. 320.

[108]Holdsworth (n. 16 above) 3.316.

[109]*Fleta*, ed. and trans. H. G. Richardson and G. O. Sayles, vols. 2–4, SS 72, 89, 99 (London 1955–1984). The introductory first volume has not been published.

[110]*Fleta* 1.33 (vol. 2.88–89).

[111]Ibid. 4.5 (3.59).

[112]Ibid. 2.1 (2.107).

[113]Ibid. (2.106)

[114]Ibid. 1.13 (2.29–30); referred to also in 1.12 (2.25) and 2.1 (2.106).

ter hoc kind of proposition, that the courts agreed with the treatises in interpreting the statute of Westminster I as referring to sexual rape. But Post gives no examples.[115] We might be able to see if such indictments were in general use in the first half of the fourteenth century by examining the instances of rape in jail delivery cases that Barbara Hanawalt refers to, but we need to look at the actual texts, since she treats sexual rape and abduction together.[116]

When we turn to commentaries on cases, we find, out of all of the yearbooks edited in modern times from the reigns of Edward I, Edward II, Edward III, and Richard II,[117] no contemporary discussion in which sexual rape is at issue and reference is made to the statutes. This may, of course, be due to the paucity of criminal cases discussed in the yearbooks of the fourteenth century: only one report in twenty-eight deals with criminal proceedings (it increases to one in fourteen in the fifteenth century), though there are considerably more in the reports of the four eyres held

[115] Post (n. 14 above) 154–155. He refers (155 n. 1) to PRO, JUST 1/784 m. 17d (1279–1280) in connection with what he says is an adaptation of the statutory procedure to cover "nonsuited appeals," that is, cases in which appeals have been ruled inadmissible. The entry is headed "De hiis qui rapuerunt damicellas," one of seventy-odd new articles of eyre adopted at this time: see Helen M. Cam, *Studies in the Hundred Rolls* (New York 1974) 98: III 15. The full version of this article in the *Capitula itineris* statute clearly reflects the 1275 statute: "Si quis rapuerit damicellas infra etatem sponte vel invite, seu alias mulieres plene etatis existentes contra voluntatem earum" (*Statutes* [n. 8 above] 1.237–237a). In the two cases that follow in the roll entry, the victims presumably could not appeal because they were too young. The presenting jurors say that John Luveday raped Matilda, who was eight years old, against her will and then fled. He is to be placed in exigents and outlawed. He had no chattels, nor was he in a tithing, because he was a free man. The next case is that of the nine-year-old mentioned above. The presenting jurors say that Walter Dek raped Meynda, and since he is in the vicinity, he is to be arrested. He comes and denies that he raped her against her will, and puts himself on the country. The same jurors, acting now as trial jurors, find that he raped her of her virginity against her will, and he is sentenced to serve the statutory two years in jail (as noted above). Another case of underage rape, from the 1293 Staffordshire eyre, has been pointed out to me by Daniel Klerman: the jurors present that Hugh this year raped Agnes, eleven years old, against her will; since he fled, he is to be placed in exigents and outlawed (JUST 1/806 m. 6). Professor Klerman also draws my attention to the Yorkshire cases, possibly from the Yorkshire eyre of 1293–1294, collected by one of the scribes of the Cornish eyre of 1302: *Year Books of the Reign of King Edward the First*, ed. and trans. Alfred J. Horwood, 3, RS 31a.3 (London 1863) 528–545 app. 2. In one of the cases (529-532, treated in Horwood's preface xliv–xlvii), a knight, Hugh, is indicted for having raped (*rapuit*) a certain girl and having taken her to his own manor and known her carnally against her will. He denies this charge of *raptus*, and the jury acquits him, finding that the woman was forcibly raped (*rapiebatur vi*) by Hugh's men without his consent. The justice asks the jury if the men knew the woman carnally, and they say yes, but with her consent (532). Earlier, the justice informed Hugh that if the woman herself were pursuing an appeal against him, he could have counsel, but since the king was suing *ex officio*, counsel was not allowed (530).

[116] Barbara Hanawalt, *Crime and Conflict in English Communities, 1300–1348* (Cambridge, Mass. 1979) 66, 104–110. One case from 1306 occurs in *Wiltshire Gaol Delivery and Trailbaston Trials*, 1275–1306, ed. Ralph B. Pugh (Devizes 1978) 148 no. 986: "Henry Hauwys of Chetterne raped the virginity of Alice Godhyne in William Lyngonor's house"; 162 no. 1139: "Henry Hawys of Chitterne, indicted and taken because he raped Alice Goudhyne in William Lyngener's house and carnally knew her." He pleaded not guilty and was acquitted. (Since the coitus was not said to be against Alice's will, perhaps it was determined to be a matter of simple fornication or clandestine marriage.)

[117] Yearbooks of Edward I: Rolls Series (RS) 31[a].1–5; Edward II: SS 17, 19–20, 22, 24, 26–27, 29, 31, 33–34, 36–39, 41–43, 45, 52, 61, 63, 65, 70, 81, 85–86, 104; Edward III: RS 31.6-18 (or 31b.1–15); Richard II: vols. 1–7, Ames Foundation (1914–1996). I have also consulted the older edition of yearbook cases from the time of Edward III, *Reports des cases en ley que furent argues en le temps de le tres haut et puissant prince, roy Edward le Tierce*, 3 vols. (London 1679).

between 1300 and 1330.[118] We do, however, find one case from the past, *Alice v. John*, which is mentioned in the reports of these eyres: the Cornish eyre of 1302 (included by two of the yearbook scribes) and the eyre of Kent for 1313–1314 (copied by one of the scribes). Let us look at the latter text first, in the Maitland-Harcourt-Bolland translation. We are told that Alice brought an appeal against John, saying that he had "ravished her virginity by force against the peace" ("a force ly ravist soun pucellage encountre la pees"). "And because it was found by inquest that he was guilty and that he had done such deed before the statute, if Alice, by advice of counsel, had not withdrawn her appeal, the judgment of the Court would have been that Alice should tear out John's eyes and cut off his testicles, as he was a married man. If he had been single the judgment would have been that he should marry her, or should suffer that penance."[119] The editors assume that the statute in question is that of 1285, that is, Westminster II chapter 34 [A], stipulating the death penalty. But the penalty in effect before this would not be mutilation but two years in prison, if the 1275 statute, like *
that of 1285, were taken as dealing with sexual rape. Therefore, the reference would have to be to the 1275 statute, as changing the punishment for sexual rape from mutilation to imprisonment.

This was the conclusion reached by Alfred Horwood for the earlier citation, if the manuscript readings were to be accepted as accurate. But he believed it more likely that the text was in error, and so he altered "before the statute" (*avant statut*) to "after the statute" (*pus statut*), taking the statute to be that of 1285 and interpreting the "judgment of life and member" named there to mean castration and blinding. He was persuaded to accept this alternative because a note in one of his manuscripts "states that the Inquest found John not guilty, and that Alice laid the commission of the crime before the statute of Westm. 2, and that in such case the punishment specified in the text would not follow."[120] That is to say, the punishment of mutilation would not follow under the 1275 statute, but it would follow under the 1285 statute. This note, however, though it may accurately represent the opinion of the scribe who authored it, contradicts the main text, which says, like the 1313–1314 version, that *because* the inquest found John guilty of the deed *before* the statute, he would have

[118] David J. Seipp, "Crime in the Year Books," *Law Reporting in England*, ed. Chantal Stebbings (London 1995) 15–34, esp. 16–17. He counts 810 criminal cases from 1300 to 1500, with another 485 from the eyre reports.

[119] *The Eyre of Kent, 6 & 7 Edward II, A.D. 1313–1314* (*Year Books of Edward II*, vol. 5), ed. and trans. F. W. Maitland, W. V. Harcourt, and W. C. Bolland (London 1910) 134–135. Another case of appeal of sexual rape is dealt with on 106–107; a county jury had indicted the accused man, Ralph Grace, saying that the woman, Marina, wife of Gilbert of Talgarek, had raised the hue and cry against him immediately after he had ravished her (that is, had carnal knowledge of her against her will), at the time and place stated in her appeal, in the twelfth year of the king (presumably Edward I, therefore 1283–1284). The justices of the eyre direct the jury "to make presentment of this appeal," and find fault with the county court for not taking sureties from the woman's husband as well as from her. No reference is made to any statute. This case, reported in four of the manuscripts of the eyre, is also reported in one of the manuscripts of the Cornish eyre of 1302, *Year Books of Edward I* 3 (n. 115 above) 506–509 app. 1, but while the name of the defendant is given as Ralph, as in the Kentish text, the woman is said to be Agnes, wife of W., and no date of the crime is given.

[120] *Year Books of Edward I* 3 (n. 115 above) 498–501 app. I. Professor Klerman points out to me that if this case really did come to the 1302 eyre, the offense would not have occurred before the previous Cornish eyre, which was held in 1284.

been mutilated if Alice had not withdrawn. Horwood reconciles the text with the note by making another change, altering "because" (*pur ceo qe*) to "if" (*si*). His text now says, *if* the inquest had found him guilty *after* the statute, he would have been mutilated.

If *Alice v. John*, as recounted in the yearbooks (minus Horwood's alterations), actually reflected a tradition of interpreting the 1275 statute as putting an end to the punishment of mutilation, we may still wonder whether the tradition went back to the time that it was passed. As noted above, the *Placita corone*, dated around 1275, has mutilation still in effect. We saw that such punishment was in fact not used after abatement of appeal; but neither Kaye nor Post has found any case of punishment of death or mutilation earlier in the century, except for Bracton's 1222 case, even when the appeal was not abated.[121] Kaye believes that the punishment was long obsolete, and he takes its survival here as a nod to nostalgic calls for law and order.[122] The most conservative copy of the treatise, MS A, was written at the turn of the fifteenth century, so we can readily see that obsolete forms could live a life of their own. The oldest copy, MS B, probably from the early fourteenth century, made what Kaye calls a half-hearted attempt to bring the text up to date by inserting two provisions of the 1275 statute, including chapter 13 on "rape." But it leaves out the last sentence, which refers to the offense as a trespass.[123]

When we find a student around the turn of the fourteenth century calling sexual rape a capital crime,[124] he might be seen as agreeing with the *Mirror of Justices* in interpreting the French insert of the 1285 statute as setting the death penalty for sexual rape. But it may simply mean that sexual rape was always considered a felony, with death now reinstated as the expected penalty, as with other felonies, after the practice and concept of mutilation had faded away. The student's further notion that a failed appeal of rape would not entail imprisonment is called into question in the case of a rape that allegedly took place in the year of the statute, 13 Edward I (1284–1285), reported by the scribes of the eyres of Cornwall (*Joan v. W.*) and Kent (*Joan v. E.*), who say the appellant was sent to prison for a defective count (narrative) of her alleged rape.[125]

Two copies of the Kent yearbook preface *Joan v. E.* with a note or rubric stating that, if a woman sues an appeal of rape before the justices within the term given her by the statute ("denz terme que done lui est par statut") and then withdraws from it, the appellee will go free *sine die*.[126] This shows at least that the author of the note

[121]Kaye (n. 82 above) xvi n. 6. Both Post (n. 14 above) 151–152 and Kaye xxxiv seem to think that the punishment in Bracton's case ([n. 22 above] 2.403) is mutilation rather than death, in spite of the phrase *ultimum supplicium.*

[122]Kaye xvii.

[123]*Placita* (n. 82 above) 9 n. 7 and xi.

[124]Student's workbook, dating from the last years of Edward I, edited by Edward Huse Dunham, Jr., appendix to *Casus placitorum and the Reports of Cases in the King's Courts, 1272–1278*, SS 69 (London 1952) lxxxv-lxxxix; for the date, see lxii. Note 33 (p. lxxxvii) reads, " Si femme face un nun syute en play de rap, purtant nestil pas enprisonable, tut touche il vie e membre," that is, "If a woman is nonsuited in a plea of rape, she is nevertheless not liable to imprisonment, even though it touches life and member."

[125]*Year Books of Edward I* 3 (n. 115 above) 520–521; *Eyre of Kent* (n. 119 above) 111. One manuscript * of the latter identifies the justice as Henry Spigornel, who was one of the justices of the Cornish eyre of 1302. He was justice of the King's Bench from 1301 to at least 1323. See John Sainty, *The Judges of England, 1272–1990* (London 1993) 23.

interpreted the 1275 statute as referring to a woman's appeal of rape, even though there is no mention of the statute in the case itself, and even though Joan did not withdraw but was nonsuited by the justices because of a faulty appeal. Moreover, although E. was acquitted of her appeal, he was not allowed to go *sine die* but still had to answer the same charge from the Crown (he was found not guilty when Joan admitted that he was the father of her child, which, in the court's view, entailed her consent).

Statutory Rape of Wives: Abduction with Husbands' Goods

Plucknett, in his 1922 study of the interpretation of the statutes by the courts in the period from 1300 to 1350, found that the first reported action upon the 1285 statute was in the case of *Latimer v. Constable*, 1304,[127] in which William Latimer brought a writ of trespass before the Court of Common Pleas against Robert Constable and his wife Lucy and others to answer why they came with force and arms on a certain day and ravished and took away ("ravyrent e amenerent etc.") Margery, William's wife, along with his goods and chattels, against the provision of the king and his statute. When exception is made to the form of the writ as not following the language of trespass, the plaintiff's side counters that it is founded on the statute, according to which the issue touches life and limb (showing that the French provision, [A], of the 1285 statute is being referred to). Another exception is entered: the 1285 statute gives the suit only to the king, when it says that "the king shall have the suit for the goods and chattels of the husband so carried away" (citing [B1]). The justices respond by saying that the suit was given to the husband by the earlier statute of Westminster I if he sued within forty days of the deed, and that the statute of Westminster II did not take away his suit. The defendants plead not guilty, except for Lucy, of whom it is urged that the writ does not concern her, for a woman cannot ravish another woman ("qe femme ne poet autre femme ravir"). It is ruled by one of the justices, William Howard, that even though she could not ravish, she could assent to it; and therefore she too enters a plea of not guilty.[128]

Plucknett notes that the judges "do not seem to have found any difficulty in the fact that Westminster I does not say anything about the carrying off of goods, but speaks only of the ravishment (for which a subject may sue within forty days, and the

[126] *Eyre of Kent* 111.

[127] *Year Books of Edward I* 4, RS 31a.4 (n. 115 above) 316–321; Plucknett (n. 24 above) 102. It is interesting that Plucknett, or his indexer, classifies this discussion under "ravishment of wife" (199), but classifies his earlier reference to the French text of Westminster II chap. 34 [A] on p. 11 (noted in our discussion of the statute above) under "rape" (xxxiv).

[128] For Justice Howard, see Sainty (n. 125 above) 60. His agreement that a woman could not ravish another woman may show that the sexual element of the word was recognized to some extent—while forgetting that the next chapter of the statute, chap. 35, uses *rapere* of male and female wards, and forgetting too that it was common for mothers to be accused of ravishing their sons. See Sue Sheridan Walker, "Widow and Ward: The Feudal Law of Child Custody in Medieval England," *Women in Medieval Society*, ed. Susan Mosher Stuard (Philadelphia 1976) 159–172 at 163–165; in n. 39 (171) she gives examples from 1278–1279, 1290–1292, 1303, and 1313, and in n. 40 a 1306 case in which the mother's sister-in-law is the accused ravisher.

king after). Nevertheless, they thought that the statutes covered common ground."[129] This common ground, we see, is the ravishment and abduction of another man's wife.

* If we can agree with these experts—the King's serjeants and justices of Common Pleas in the 1304 case—in saying that the 1275 and 1285 statutes were aimed at suits of ravishment and abduction rather than at appeals of sexual rape (brought by women), let us see where it leaves us. The 1236 statute of Merton made it a Crown offense to abduct underage female heirs. There seems to have been a private action available to husbands, to judge from a case of 1241: Philip Haket brings suit against his wife Maud for consenting to William Karenham's break-in and abduction of her against Philip's will. When she is reported not found, but living with William, William also is ordered to be arrested, to respond to the same complaint.[130] Another case, from 1255, shows a plaintiff suing for the recovery of a woman not said to be his wife or heir.[131] In 1294 (i.e., after the statutes of Westminster I and II), in a case of conspiracy and trespass brought against a parson who was accused, among other things, of abducting a daughter from her parents and having her bring a suit of novel disseisin against them, the plaintiffs were told that there was a common-law writ dealing with the abduction of a woman available from Chancery.[132]

But the 1275 statute extended the king's suit to the abduction of all women, including wives, after forty days, and in 1285 chapter 34 [B1], the husbands' goods abducted with wives were added to the king's suit. The French introduction, [A1–2], made the forced abduction of wives and all other women a capital offense and available to royal indictment, at least if the women later consented to the abductions [A2]. We can therefore see [A1–2] as intended to supplement [B1], which gave the husbands' goods abducted with wives to the king's suit. But [A1–2] had no application to the willing wives of the next clause [B2], which did not deal with abduction at all, or to [B3], concerning the abduction of unwilling or willing nuns, since three years' imprisonment was incompatible with the death penalty. Chapter 35 was also incompatible with chapter 34 [A1–2], since it provided two years' imprisonment for the abduction of certain women (viz., female wards).

Chapter 35 included various forms of writs covering different situations, whereas no writs were included in chapter 34. Post, who presumes that chapter 34 was directed at sexual rape, thinks that no writs were needed because no new private action was thought to be entailed. But soon afterwards, he speculates, there was felt a need for writs for abducted women other than the wards of chapter 35, especially for wives, and he concludes that the resulting form, *De uxore rapta*, was clearly based on chapter 34 [A1–2], even though the action of the writ was unrelated to forcible coition.[133]

[129]Plucknett (n. 24 above) 102.

[130]S. F. C. Milsom, "Trespass from Henry III to Edward III," *Law Quarterly Review* 74 (1958) 195–224, 407–436, 561–590, at 211. The case is printed in *Curia Regis Rolls of the Reign of Henry III* 16, ed. L. C. Hector (London 1979), nos. 1532, 1631 (both in Easter term), 1694 (Trinity term). Later in Trinity term, on 25 June, William shows up and agrees to pay a fine of 30 marks for himself and Maud to Philip (no. 1756). An entry of 10 May shows that William, whom we can assume to be the new husband, has a suit of trespass, listed as old (*vetus est*) against Philip (no. 2682).

[131]Milsom loc. cit.

[132]Sayles (n. 77 above) 3.22–23; cf. Milsom (n. 130 above) 587; Post (n. 14 above) 159.

[133]Post loc. cit.

But since we are now assuming that chapter 34 [A1–2] as well as [B1] dealt with abduction and not forcible coition, the question of the writ's relevance to the statute changes. If husbands already had an action to recover abducted wives, no further writ would be needed after the 1275 statute. But in 1285, the provision of chapter 34 [B1] giving the suit of the husbands' goods to the king was awkward, and perhaps it was this that prompted a new action, *De raptu uxoris cum bonis viri sui*,[134] and a new writ.

Let us look at the language of the writ, as it appears in the Bodleian collection of writs, compiled around 1320:

> *De uxore rapta.* Ostensurus quare vi et armis L., uxorem predicti A., apud B. rapuit et eam cum bonis et catallis predicti A. ad valenciam tanti abduxit et eam adhuc detinent et alia enormia, etc., ad grave, etc., et contra formam statuti nostri in hujusmodi casu inde provisi, etc.

Here is G. D. G. Hall's translation:

> *Seizure of a wife.* To show why with force and arms he seized L., wife of the aforesaid A., at N. and carried her off together with goods and chattels of the aforesaid A. to the value of so much, and still keeps her, and (inflicted) other outrages, etc., to the heavy, etc., and against the form of our statute provided therein for such a case, etc.[135]

This formula corresponds exactly to the earliest known instance of an action of this * kind, in *Durant v. Ashdown*, 1300: Gilbert Ashdown responds to a plea of Robert Durant of Dunstable that with force and arms he ravished Gilbert's wife Matilda at London and abducted her with Gilbert's goods and chattels and still keeps them from him, and committed other outrages, to his serious loss, against the peace and against the statute ("uxorem ... vi et armis ... rapuit et eam cum bonis et catallis ipsius Gilberti abduxit, et ea ei adhuc detinet, et alia enormia, etc., ad grave dampnum etc. et contra pacem et contra formam statuti etc.").[136]

The writ can be thought accurate in its claim to be based on the *form* of chapter 34, in that it includes mention of the husband's goods. The fact that the statute gives the suit of the goods to the king may have been interpreted—perhaps rightly so, to judge from the 1304 decision (*Latimer v. Constable*)—as simply meaning that the king would have the suit if the husband failed to sue in time, as stipulated in the 1275 statute.

A yearbook case of 1310, *Guise v. Baldwin*, concerning a charge of abduction of wife and goods under the rubric *De raptu mulieris*,[137] opens with the defendant's first

[134] This is the name of the action in *Novae Narrationes*, ed. Elsie Shanks and S. F. C. Milsom, SS 80 (London 1963) 328.

[135] *Early Registers of Writs*, ed. Elsa de Haas and G. D. G. Hall, SS 87 (London 1970) 181. The same register has five writs concerning the abduction of heirs and heiresses (243–244), beginning with *De herede rapto* ("Seizure of an heir"); only the fourth, *Aliter de herede* ("Otherwise concerning an heir"), speaks of the seized *heres* as female.

[136] Sayles (n. 77 above) 3.100. Sayles identifies the statute in question as West. II chap. 34 (1285).

[137] *Year Books of Edward II* 4, ed. F. W. Maitland and G. J. Turner, SS 22 (London 1907) 4. The record of the case, from the KB rolls, is translated on 205–206. Co-defendants with Thomas Baudewine are named; the jury finds all not guilty, and the plaintiff, John de Gyse (from Aspley Guise, near Woburn, Bedford) is to be amerced for his false claim. Another translation of the yearbook discussion is given in J. H. Baker and S. F. C. Milsom, *Sources of English Legal History: Private Law to 1750* (London 1986) 310–311.

lawyer denying that his client came with force and arms or violated the king's peace in any way; he also denies the ravishment (*ravissement*) and whatever was against the relevant statute, and all damages. The defendant's third lawyer, King's Serjeant Edmund Passeley,[138] asserts that the statute gives a suit to the husband only because of the chattels taken with the wife ("Statut ne don mye suyt au baroun si non par resoun de chateux enportez ovesque sa femme"). This confirms the above reading of conformity of the writ *De uxore rapta* to chapter 34 [B1]. It also indicates that chapter 34 [A] (the French prologue) was read as giving the suit to a husband because of the abduction of his wife.

The main defense in *Guise v. Baldwin* will be relevant to cases discussed below: namely, defendant Baldwin claims that the woman in question, Isabel, was only Guise's *former* wife, Guise having obtained an annulment of the marriage, whereupon Isabel married Baldwin; Guise then abducted Isabel forcibly from Baldwin, and Baldwin simply retrieved her: he found her, still dressed in the clothes Baldwin had given her, and she followed him. The jury agreed.[139]

* In his 1947 Ford Lectures, Plucknett found an earlier "case upon the statute" of 1285 chapter 34, namely, *Alice v. B.*,1292, which draws implicitly on clause [B2], depriving an adulterous wife of her dower. He cites a similar case from 1307, *Lord Greystoke's Widow v. FitzWilliam*,[140] and another from 1312. In the last case, the lower tribunal, a seignorial court, faulted the defendant for not specifying whether the claimant left her husband before or after the statute (now a quarter century old!). Judgment was given in her favor, which Common Pleas reversed.[141] A similar case dealing with adulterous elopement comes from 1308–1310.[142] No further references to Westminster II chapter 34 have been perceived in the later yearbooks, which report mainly on Common Pleas cases, until 1382, 6 Richard II, which we will deal with below.

But court cases that draw on the boilerplate language of the writ *De uxore rapta* do, of course, continue to refer to the statute. Most of the cases that have been studied come from the King's Bench, and one interesting example from 1314, *Trays v. Quenby*, cites the writ explicitly as a *breve regis de raptu*.[143] In this case the defendant accuses the plaintiff's lawyer of a malicious suit, since his alleged client, the injured husband, did not exist. Upon investigation, this was declared to be true. The defendant was declared to have been wrongly imprisoned, and the real culprits were prosecuted. Around the same time, in January 1315, in response to a petition from a Robert Askeby, the king and council in Parliament noted that, previously, when a person was

[138]John Sainty, *A List of English Law Officers, King's Counsel, and Holders of Patents of Precedence* (London 1987) 5.

[139]Plucknett (n. 35 above) 121 n. 2 concludes that the presiding judge, Roger Brabazon, chief justice of the King's Bench (Sainty [n. 125 above] 6), guided the discussion so that it would go to a jury rather than to the bishop's court.

[140]Plucknett (n. 35 above) 121 n. 1, citing *Year Books of Edward I*, RS 31a (n. 115 above) 1.182–183, 5.532–535

[141]*Year Books of Edward II* 12, ed. William Craddock Bolland, SS 33 (London 1916) 228–229. According to Plucknett (n. 24 above) 119 (cf. idem [n. 35 above] 121 n. 1), it was the Court of Common Pleas that insisted on the mention of the statute.

[142]*Year Books of Edward II*, vol. 2, ed. F. W. Maitland, SS 19 (London 1903) 145.

[143] See Sayles (n. 77 above) 4.59–62; also edited by Morris S. Arnold, *Select Cases of Trespass from the King's Courts, 1307–1399*, 2 vols., SS 100, 103 (London 1985–1987) 1.74–77.

impleaded through a writ of trespass *de raptu alterius et de bonis suis asportatis*, he was not released by mainprise, especially because if he were convicted, he should be judged to be hanged. Now, however, they declared that he should be allowed bail, if he was of good reputation. Furthermore, whereas the practice had been, in case of an acquittal, that the plaintiff would suffer no penalty for his false claim other than amercement, he was now to to be put in prison for a year, and longer if he could not pay the fine assessed by the king.[144]

Felony v. Trespass

This order of the council leaves the death penalty in place for abduction of wife and goods, thereby illustrating Plucknett's dictum that "all felonies are trespasses, although not all trespasses are felonies."[145] We have seen that the jurists in the 1304 case, *Latimer v. Constable*, saw no problem about a private suit having an issue, from the king's point of view, in capital punishment. It is hard to know how this matter was rationalized; but in those days there was not a clear distinction between civil and criminal trespass. By the time of Edward III, however, one sees, as Milsom says, "the increasingly civil character even of trespass *vi et armis*."[146] We get a hint of the jurists' views in 1339, when William Shareshull, justice of the King's Bench, says that the Crown has the option of considering a civil conviction to be a criminal indictment, triable as a capital offense.[147] The case that triggered Shareshull's remark was one of abduction of wife and goods, brought as a criminal rather than a civil trespass,[148] and it may be that the Crown's policy in this matter had an effect on the way in which abductions of wife and goods were treated. A few years later, in 1344, in a trespass case of wife and goods, the defendant, a Lombard, appeared and pleaded not guilty, and the question arose whether he should be allowed an attorney, since, if there was a guilty verdict, the king would take the verdict as an indictment of a capital crime, in which case the defendant was not allowed an attorney. The answer was that what the king might do

[144] *Rotuli Parliamentorum* (n. 41 above) 1.290 (8 Edward II, 1314 and 1315).

[145] T. F. T. Plucknett, "Chaucer's Escapade," *Law Quarterly Review* 64 (1948) 33–36 at 35.

[146] Milsom (n. 130 above) 584–585.

[147] *Year Books of the Reign of King Edward III*, ed. Luke Owen Pike, RS 31b.3 (London 1866) 65. See Post (n. 41 above) 25.

[148] Putnam (n. 107 above) 129 thinks that it was a matter of sexual rape, and that Shareshull was saying that "an action for rape at the suit of the injured husband was trespass only." She takes it to refer to sexual rape because, as we have seen above, she interprets both the 1275 and 1285 statutes to be about either the woman appealing for rape or the Crown bringing an indictment, and she notes that a husband's "suing" seems to fit neither statute (274 n. 320). But what seems to be going on in the 1339 case is that the husband, let's call him "Albert," requested a commission of oyer et terminer against "George," which produced a criminal indictment of trespass for having abducted Albert's wife "Maud" and his goods ("trespas de ceo qil ravist sa femme et enporta ses biens"), for which George was outlawed and then subsequently pardoned. Now then, Albert and Maud are back together again, and George is suing in assise of novel dissesin. Maud comes to court and objects that George is an outlaw because of the trespass detailed above. George produces his pardon. Maud's lawyer says the pardon is for trespass and not for felony, but he has admitted outlawry for a matter that would entail capital punishment. Shareshull then intervenes and says that in a private trespass suit brought by writ, if the defendant is found guilty, the plaintiff will receive damages. But then "the king may take such verdict for an indictment, and arraign him, and then, if he be found guilty, the judgment will be of life and limb."

was none of the plaintiff's business.[149] As Milsom observes, using this case as proof, "In an action at the party's suit it was irrelevant that the king might take the verdict for an indictment; and, unless statute provided otherwise"—which is not the case here—"the defendant was liable to no punishment except to redeem himself for the breach of the peace."[150] There seems to have been a subsequent tendency to seek a criminal indictment in the first place, judging by the peace-sessions cases presented by Bertha Putnam.[151] Her records range from 1338 to1478, and the first indictment for this offense comes at the very beginning, around 1338, and seems rather isolated. It is indicted as a nonfelony (therefore as a trespass), and only three more such cases follow, in 1357, 1360, and 1362.[152] But there are seventeen possible cases in which the indictments are handed down as felonies, beginning in 1357 and ending in 1414, at which time the records end abruptly (when they pick up again in 1474, no further cases of this kind are found). However, in ten of the cases, only *rapere* is used of the wife, without any explicit statement that she is carried away with the husband's goods.[153] Of the seven felony cases in which the abduction of the wife is explicit, three use *rapere*,[154] while the other four do not, beginning with the 1357 instance, from the Somerset sessions that produced the trespass indictment of that year.[155] None of the four trespass cases use *rapere*.

I should note here what we will discuss in more detail below, that most of these criminal indictments were probably not seriously intended. Edward Powell has found 278 trials for rape before justices of jail delivery in the counties of Warwickshire, Derbyshire, and Leicestershire in the period 1400–1429, which he classifies, rightly or wrongly, as felony cases. Since there was not a single conviction out of all of the cases, he concludes that the defendants were not really regarded as felons but were rather accused as such as a way of penalizing them for some other kind of sexual offense, like fornication or adultery, which fell outside the jurisdiction of the secular courts: "The punishment lay in the inconvenience and humiliation of indictment and arraignment. The trial itself was a formality and a foregone conclusion."[156]

Putnam does not analyze the cases of *uxor rapta* that she presents, and Plucknett in his commentary takes them up only under larceny:

[149] *Year Books of Edward III*, RS 31b.12, pp. 14–15.

[150] Milsom (n. 130 above) 584.

[151] Bertha Haven Putnam, *Proceedings before the Justices of the Peace in the Fourteenth and Fifteenth Centuries: Edward III to Richard III* (London 1938), with "A Commentary on the Indictments" (cxxxiii-clxi) and analytical index (468–482) by T. F. T. Plucknett.

[152] Ibid. 158.12 (ca. 1338); 183.18 (1357); 279.31 (1360); 361.369 (1362).

[153] Ibid. 353.175 (ca. 1362); 373.598 (1363); 287.34 (1364); 113.65 (1378); 120.195 (1378); 132.17 (1396); 135.31 (1396); 100.34 (1413); 325.141 (1413); 302.33 (1414).

[154] Ibid. 442.57 (1383); 406.18 (1395); 413.48 (1397).

[155] Ibid. 190.68 (1357); 142.69 (1395); 329.163 (1414); 329.165 (1414). The 1357 Somerset sessions also produced two indictments of sexual rape, one as a trespass (184–185.26), and the other as a felony (188.49). The word *rapere* is used here to mean "seize as a preliminary to sexual assault." In the first case, the perpetrator allegedly *rapuit* a widow and lay with her against her will; in the other case, the accused, it was charged, feloniously *rapuit* a woman, abducted her to a mill, and there lay with her against her will.

[156] Edward Powell, "Jury Trial at Gaol Delivery in the Late Middle Ages: The Midland Circuit, 1400–1429," in Cockburn and Green (n. 84 above) 78–116 at 104. In contrast, there were 135 convictions out of the 722 larceny trials (18.7%).

> Still more interesting is the firm insistence by husbands that it is larceny to steal their wives. It was thought that taking away a wife was a trespass at common law [citing Fitzherbert, *New Natura Brevium*, 53k], and in 1285 a statute [i.e., Westminster II, chapter 34] hinted that it might also be felony. The law seems to have been very obscure, although our indictments speak confidently of stealing "a wife and other chattels" and even of "eloping a wife by night" without mention of chattels, as felony. They give no hint whether the women in these cases were consenting or not, seeming rather to imply that it was immaterial, and so they do not raise those subtle questions of a wife's apparent authority to deal with her husband's goods which exercised theorists centuries later.[157]

We note that Plucknett says that the 1285 statute only hints that abducting another man's wife may be a felony. He is speaking of [A], the French addition, which explicitly names judgment of life and member—seemingly more than a hint! But perhaps he means that the implications were not seriously thought out, assuming, as he does in his later study, that it was an amendment made from the floor of Parliament. We note further that Plucknett speaks only of abduction, not sexual rape, in keeping with his earlier analysis of the statute.[158]

E. W. Ives believes that "mere abduction was a trespass only" and that "the requirement of physical violation always governed interpretation of this offence by the courts," citing a King's Bench yearbook case from 11 Henry IV (1409), *Nansegle v. Vide*. Here one of the justices asserts that ravishment without carnal knowledge is not a felony but a trespass.[159] If this was an actual policy, it must have been relatively new; it was ignored in *Nansegle* itself, as we will see, and it had no perceivable effect on the wife-and-goods charges in Putnam's quarter-sessions cases between 1409 and 1414. These and her earlier cases, which extend to 1396, belie such a simple dichotomy, as both she and Plucknett testify.[160]

These data indicate that the decision whether to pursue a case of abducted wife as a felony or a transgression was fairly arbitrary. Christopher Cannon, working especially on the King's Bench cases recorded in Richard II's third year, 1379–1380, similarly finds that abduction can be treated either as a trespass or as a felony: "The only alteration made in the language of ravishment cases prosecuted as felonies is the addition of *felonia* to the margin of the record or, more commonly, the use of

[157]Plucknett (n. 151 above) clii. In the case of the husband who "eloped" another man's wife (Putnam [n. 151 above] 65.46, 1351), it is noted in the margin that the charge was a felony.

[158]In his subsequent study (n. 35 above) 121, Plucknett finds the most significant feature of this chapter the provision that unfaithful wives are deprived of their dower.

[159]Ives (n. 62 above) 23. For *Nansegle*, see n. 205 below.

[160]Putnam (n. 151 above) cxvii, speaking of sexual rape, taking of goods, etc.; Plucknett (n. 151 above) clx, speaking of larceny (which, as we have seen, includes theft of wife and goods), sexual rape, etc. Plucknett notes "the possibility that some felonies could be reduced to the category of trespasses at the choice of the crown or of the prosecutor." But even if sexual rape could be indicted as a trespass rather than a felony, it is hard to understand the remark of a King's Serjeant, William Thorp (Sainty [n. 138 above] 6), in a 1342 appeal of rape before the King's Bench, when he said that "this suit was only a trespass at common law." He was responding to the assertion of the chief justice, William Scott (Sainty [n. 125 above] 7), that the judgment affected life and limb. Scott did not disagree with Thorp's rejoinder, but only with the procedure that, in Thorp's view, followed from it. *Year Books of the Reign of King Edward III, Year 16*, RS 31b.8, pp. 216–219.

the adverb *felonice* before the main verb in the description of the crime (i.e., 'felonice rapuit . . . ')."[161]

WHY ARE WIVES ABDUCTED? A QUESTION THAT BEGS THE QUESTION

Taking the accusations of abduction of wife and goods on face value as indicating that there was usually substance to the charge will prove very misleading, for in most of the cases that can be investigated, there turns out to be no forcible abduction at all, but rather a matter of the wife's voluntary departure from her husband, and the husband's effort either to get her back or to receive compensation. In other words, the charge is a legal fiction, to put it politely; or, to be more forthright, like Morris Arnold when characterizing civil trespass cases brought by writ, it is an outrageous lie. He says,

> The law in the area of injuries to domestic relations is easiest to divine in the relatively rare cases involving an alleged "rape" of the wife. Probably because the husband-wife relationship is so complex, and the lie in the writ so outrageous, special pleading seems more prevalent in this action than in any other; and, probably for the same reason, this was the action in which counsel joined in demurrers proportionally most often.[162]

In other words, we are able to find out what the defendants have to say in explanation and are able to get a view of the real circumstances involved. The situation is very different in the criminal indictments collected by Putnam, where we hear only the husband's side of the matter, the mainly stereotyped charges reported to the grand jury and approved by a majority of the jurors.[163]

All of Arnold's cases are from the King's Bench. Let us look at the earlier ones here:

1) *Upton v. Heydon*, 1308: The case goes to trial and the jurors say that the defendant did not ravish the wife with force and arms or against the form of the statute; rather, he was a servant in the house who had consensual sex with her and encouraged her to go to her father's house, taking goods worth £60. The defendant was ordered to pay this amount to the husband.
2) *Trays v. Quenby*, 1314: The husband who alleged the *raptus* was determined not to exist, but to have been invented by the lawyer claiming to represent him (treated above).
3) *Wattisham v. Strutting*, 1315: The defendant is the wife's father, who took her back into his house when her husband disappeared after being indicted for felonies.
4) *Cornwall v. Servant*, 1316: The defendant claims that he married the woman, Isabel, and that the plaintiff did not object to the banns but only later alleged that she had been previously married to him, and on this basis the plaintiff obtained an annulment of the defendant's marriage to Isabel. The plaintiff denies that the defendant ever married Isabel and, accordingly, he denies having obtained any such annulment; he reiterates his charge, and the matter goes to trial.

[161] Christopher Cannon, "*Raptus* in the Chaumpaigne Release and a Newly Discovered Document Concerning the Life of Geoffrey Chaucer," *Speculum* 68 (1993) 74–94 at 83.

[162] Arnold (n. 143 above) 1.xlv. He gives nineteen cases, numbered 8.1–19 (1.73–93).

[163] On the procedure, see J. H. Baker, *An Introduction to English Legal History*, ed. 3 (London 1990) 576–577.

5) *Sirich v. Beck*, 1316: Jurors find that the wife left her husband voluntarily, fearing that her husband would harm her because of her rumored involvement with the defendant. The defendant thereupon sent his servants to take her to his home, but she complied unwillingly, preferring to return to her husband and be punished by him. The only goods taken were the robe she had with her, worth one mark. But damages are assessed at £100.
6) *Bull v. Ward et al.*, 1316: The defendant is the wife's father; he claims that his daughter voluntarily left her adulterous husband.
7) *Welye v. Bodenham and Herring*, 1318: The defendants are the uncle and mother of the wife, who was married against her will to the plaintiff; she escaped from his house and is seeking an annulment in the Church court.
8) *Green v. the Parson of Newbold Pacey*, 1334: The defendant says he rightfully took her as his church's serf; the plaintiff loses the case by failing to appear at the trial.
9) *Moulsham v. Cook*, 1366: The defendant claims that the woman was his clandestine wife, whom the plaintiff later forcibly married; she escaped and secured an annulment in the Court of Arches and publicly married the defendant.
10) *Barber v. Devenish*, 1369: The defendant says that the plaintiff secured an annulment from his wife, alleging his previous marriage to someone else, in the court of the archdeacon of London, but then tried to reverse the decision in the bishop's consistory, with no success, whereupon the defendant married her
11) *Cantiloup v. Paynel*, 1369: The defendant is the brother of the allegedly abducted wife. He explains that his sister had been married to the plaintiff while under age and without consenting; she left the plaintiff to go live with her father while seeking an annulment from the official of York.
12) *Beaumont v. Writtle*, 1369: The defendant says that after the plaintiff had been overseas for three years, the wife, thinking her husband dead, freely went to the defendant and asked him to marry her, which he did, but put her away when he found that the husband was still alive. Plaintiff sticks to his charge, and it goes to trial.
13) *Billesdon v. Eyryk et al.*, 1377: The defendant says that the girl in question is his ward, and that, when she was under the age of eight, the plaintiff forcefully ravished ("vi et armis rapuit") her, whereupon the defendant took and abducted her back, she still being under eight.

When Sue Sheridan Walker says, "Women allowed themselves to be abducted in order to affirm their own choice of a husband and force their families to accept the relationship and they allowed themselves to be abducted in order to leave their husbands,"[164] it may be a fair characterization of the alleged abduction of unmarried wards, but, as is evident from the above cases, what she says about the alleged abduction of wives needs qualification. No clear case of wife-abduction occurs in any of these thirteen examples or in the remaining six (to be outlined below), except perhaps in number 5 above, where the wife, having already left her husband, would have preferred to return to him, and number 8, where the parish priest retrieves his servant. The re-abducted seven-year-old of number 13 could not be considered a wife. Usually

[164]Sue Sheridan Walker, "Punishing Convicted Ravishers: Statutory Strictures and Actual Practice in Thirteenth- and Fourteenth-Century England," *Journal of Medieval History* 13 (1987) 237–250, esp. 237–238.

the accused person—sometime the wife's father or even her mother—has not even accompanied the wife from the husband's house, except in number 3 above and number 18 below. In most cases the wife seems to have departed under her own steam some time before the alleged abduction was said to have taken place. But, as we have surmised, the husband who wanted her back, or who wanted damages for his loss, was forced to resort to the legal fiction of abduction because of the nature of the available writ, *De uxore rapta*. The statutory conception of a man taking another man's wife for the sake of keeping her in adultery, if she consented, or presumably of keeping her as a sex-slave if she did not consent, seems little in evidence in recorded cases.

Sometimes the explanation is a matter of helping a wife to escape from a brutal or unloved husband. Divorce, in the sense of the dissolution of a valid marriage, was ordinarily not possible, but legal separation could be decreed by church courts in cases of cruelty. Not by coincidence the canon law on this matter was set forth under the title, *De restitutione spoliatorum*, "On the restoring of despoiled items," in connection with cases in which husbands claimed that their wives had been wrongly taken or were being wrongly kept from them.[165] As we have just seen, these courts could also decree an annulment, if a lawful impediment could be proved to have existed at the time of the marriage.[166] Apart from Arnold's examples, one of Putnam's cases, an indictment handed down in the Wiltshire sessions of 1383–1384, stated that John Godfray and his brother Thomas along with others conspired in June 1381 to ravish Alice, who was the wife of Philip Ashley (*que fuit uxor Philippi*), and that they actually ravished her *vi et armis*. No allegation of asporting goods was made, but instead the defendants were charged with promising Alice that they would procure a divorce (that is, annulment) between her and Philip. The jury concluded that an annulment was never made, and that Thomas married Alice against the law of the church.[167]

THE SITUATION AFTER 1382; SPECIFIC CASES

We have followed the assumption of the fourteenth-century jurists that the statute of 1285, chapter 34, dealt with abduction, and provided the death penalty for abductors of all women, married or otherwise [A1], and, if they consented afterwards, the Crown could similarly seek the death penalty [A2]. The circumstances surrounding the passage of the 1382 statute also suggest that abduction was mainly intended, even though only *rapere* and not the traditional formula *rapere et abducere* was used. The

[165]See *Decretales Gregorii IX*, issued in 1234, bk. 2 tit.13 (*De restitutione spoliatorum*), chap. 8 (*Ex transmissa*): a wife is to be restored to a man who has proved marriage and consummation, unless she fears his violence. *Corpus iuris Canonici*, ed. Emil Friedberg, 2 vols. (Leipzig 1879–1881) 2.283.

[166]Another decretal in the title *De restitutione spoliatorum*, namely, chap. 13 (*Litteras*), concerns a case in which a man demands the restitution of a wife who claims an impediment of kinship. She is to be ordered restored (but without sexual relations) while proofs of kinship are being presented and adjudicated, unless the husband is of such savagery that she could not be safely left with him (Friedberg 2.286–288). Two decretals from bk. 4, which deals with marriage, tit. 19 (*De divortiis*), chaps. 4-5, require restitution of a spouse if both husband and wife can be proved to be adulterers, and another, chap. 6, requires a wife to return to a husband she has left on her own because of his heretical doings; in order to stay away from him legally, she needs approval of a church court (Friedberg 2.721–722).

[167]Putnam (n. 151 above) 386.43.8. This is the third of three indictments against John Godfray.

statute was designed to supplement or modify the [A2] provision, so that the wronged husband, or next of kin, could appeal the abductor of the "rape" as a felony, with penalty of death, without personal danger to the appellor, since trial by combat was ruled out.

If we take the presumed view of the woman who inspired the statute, Thomas West's daughter, the *raptus* in question would seem to refer neither to sexual violence against her nor to violence used in abducting her against her will (since she was willing), but to the violation of the security provisions of her keeper, namely, her father, and this violation may have occurred without violence on the part of her lover and soon-to-be-husband, Nicholas Clifton. However, the father's perspective would be more important for the meaning of the statute, since he is the one who must have lobbied for its passage. He charged Clifton with ravishing his daughter with the aid of armed attendants, or, in a later formulation, in which he recognized that Clifton was now married or possibly married to his daughter, he claimed that he ravished and deflowered her, without specification as to whether the deflowering came before or after he married her, and also without specifying whether she consented to the "abduction" from the very beginning. But it is questionable whether the legislators or even West himself would have wanted the statute so narrowly focussed that unwilling sexual intercourse was a prerequisite for the offense, since West would presumably wish the law to apply even if it should turn out that his charges were wildly contrary to fact, and that his daughter consented not afterwards but from the beginning and willingly eloped with her lover.

It is not known whether West succeeded in having the 1382 statute applied retroactively to him, nor is it known what immediate effect, if any, it had on prosecutions. The first known case to invoke the statute is *Nansegle v. Vide*, 1409, and the second, *Smith v. Malory*, 1451, both of which are treated below. But we do know that the Commons who petitioned for the passage of the statute soon changed their minds. In May 1384, a bare year and a half after the law was passed, they petitioned to have it repealed, as too harsh and rigid, and to have the old statute of the rape of women be enforced; but the young king (or his advisors) left it in place, except to decree that all forfeitures to him and to the lords of the realm would occur as they had before the statute was passed.[168]

We have observed that the 1382 statute, as framed, seems to have been directed primarily against abducted wives, since the husbands of the ravished women are named first as those who have the right to sue, and only then, in cases where the women have no husbands living, the next of kin are named. As we will see, the Malory case presents just such a situation, in which a husband appeals over an allegedly abducted wife.

What was the connection between the new statute, designed as a supplement to the 1285 statute, and the actions and prosecutions for abducting wives and husbands'

[168] *Rotuli Parliamentorum* (n. 144 above) 3.174 no. 26. Leadam (n. 43 above) cxi mistakes the purport of their request and concludes that the Commons successfully petitioned to have the statute remain in force. The relevant passage reads: "Qe plese a nostre dit seigneur le roy, considerant que la dite ordinance est faite a trop dure et redde loy as liges nostre dit seigneur le roy, ordener qe la dite ordinance soit en ce present parlement adnullee et annientie et tenuz pur nul, si bien de tout temps passe come du temps a venir; et qe l'auncien estatut fait de rape des femmes estoise en sa force."

goods, which drew on the 1285 statute? A suggestive discussion on the latter subject occurred just around the time that the statute was passed. In the yearbook of 6 Richard II, we find included among the cases of Trinity term—that is, June–July 1382—a note recounting that one of the four justices of the Court of Common Pleas, William Skipwith, declared that "in the writ *De muliere rapta cum bonis viri*, it is fitting for the action to be brought before the King's Bench; for, although the statute never uses the term *felonice*, the word *rapuit* sounds in felony, as when a man is indicted, *Quod furatus fuit unum equum* [for having stolen a horse], though the indictment does not explicitly say *felonice*, he will be hanged, because the word *furatus fuit* says as much in itself." The Court agreed on his interpretation of *furatus fuit*, but disagreed about *De muliere abducta cum bonis viri*, "which plea could well be held in the Common Bench."[169] According to an early abridgment, this exchange occurred in Michaelmas term—therefore, during the same time that the 1382 Parliament was held, or in the month following.[170]

Even if Skipwith made his remark at the time that the 1382 statute of rapes was passed, he must have been referring to the statute of 1285, which we have presumed was the statute named in the writ *De uxore rapta*. But even though the 1285 act does not use the Latin word *felonice* or its French equivalent, it does speak in terms of felony, like the 1382 statute, by specifying punishment of life and limb. His remark therefore only makes sense if we take him to be referring to the statute as cited in the writ, which states that the action charged, *rapuit*, etc., is *contra formam statuti*. The Court in its response, by saying *de muliere abducta* rather than *de muliere rapta*, shows that it takes the *rapta* of the writ to signify *abducta*, corresponding to section [B1] of the 1285 statute: "De mulieribus abductis cum bonis viri," etc.

In 1382, therefore, the very year that the 1285 statute was being supplemented by allowing a husband or father to bring a felony charge against an alleged abductor even when the wife or daughter consented afterwards, a prominent judge was disturbed about the felonious import of the civil writ. But these writs continued to be executed as before, as we will see from Arnold's later trespass cases—which, though all were brought to the King's Bench, issued only in monetary damages when the plea was sustained by the juries. Crown prosecution of such cases also proceeded much as before. Juries convened at quarter sessions by justices of the peace continued to indict them, mainly as felons, as Putnam's cases show. But rather than reviewing these cases in detail, let us look at three high-profile examples in which felony and trespass charges are combined: first, the case of a younger son of Henry Percy, earl of Northumber-

[169] *Year Books of Richard III* 2: *6 Richard II, 1382-1383*, ed. and trans. Samuel E. Thorne with Michael E. Hager and Margaret MacVeagh Thorne, commentary by Charles Donahue, Jr. (Cambridge, Mass. 1996) 33–34: "*Nota* qe Skip. dit, [en bref] *De muliere rapta cum bonis viri*, qil covient qe laccion soit pris en Bank le Roy, qar, coment qe lestatut ne parle my *felonice* uncore, ce parole *rapuit* sonne en felonie; come si home soit endite *Quod furatus fuit unum equum*, coment qe lenditement ne parle my expressement *felonice* uncore, il serra penduz, qar ceo parolle *furatus fuit* comprent a tant en ly mesme. *Ad quod Curia concessit*, mez auter est *De muliere abducta cum bonis viri*, quel plee poet bien ester tenuz *in Communi Banco*." The rendering given in the text above is my own. For the court calendar and list of judges, see Introduction, pp. *212–213*.

[170] Ibid. 33, from Harvard Law School MS 41. After giving the date ("Anno VI Ricardi, termino Michaelis") it repeats the entire yearbook entry practically verbatim, except that when it first cites the writ it has *uxore* for *muliere*. But of course when a *mulier* is mentioned with her *vir*, it means she is an *uxor*.

land; second, a case investigated by Geoffrey Chaucer; and third, a case in which a bishop was the accused rapist. We will then look at the purely civil cases.

A. Hotspur's Remarried Sister-in-Law, 1384:
Crown v. Halsham et al., Superseded by Crown
Crown v. Anonymous Felons, Superseded by Crown

Ralph and Thomas Percy, the younger brothers of Henry Hotspur, sons of Henry Percy (created earl of Northumberland in 1377), married the two daughters of David Strathbogie, earl of Athol, who were joint heirs to his estate, Thomas taking the elder, Elizabeth, and Ralph the younger, Philippa. Strathbogie's death occurred on 10 October 1369, but it was only in 1377 that the king delivered the pertinent lands and castles to Ralph and Philippa, she having proved her age before the escheators.[171] The age of inheritance for a girl may have been as young as fourteen, but, as we have seen above in discussing the 1236 Statute of Merton, canon law allowed girls to marry at twelve. Present-tense contracts could be made before that time, but they would have the force only of future-tense betrothals.[172] Whatever the circumstances of her marriage, an impediment must have been found to invalidate it, for she subsequently married John Halsham and remained married to him—but not without a fight from Percy, for he accused Halsham of abducting her.

On 15 February 1384, on Percy's complaint, commissioners of oyer and terminer were appointed to hear and determine an alleged trespass by John Halsham and others committed against Ralph Percy, knight, at Semere, namely, ravishing, abducting, and still detaining Philippa, wife of the said Ralph, with Ralph's goods and chattels, against the king's statute provided in such a case, with damages claimed of £3,000 (which was, of course, an immense sum).[173] On the next day the same commissioners were appointed to inquire what evildoers and breakers of the peace feloniously ravished Philippa, wife of Ralph Percy, and abducted her with goods and chattels of her husband and still detained them.[174]

The advantage of a trespass conviction was that the aggrieved husband could collect damages, whereas a felony conviction would entail not only capital punishment

[171]CCR*: Edward III*, 14 vols. (London 1896–1914) 14.506–507.

[172]*Decretales Gregorii IX* 4.2.7; 4.2.14. See my treatment of this matter in the case of Henry VIII, who at the age of thirteen (therefore before the canonical age for males of fourteen) married Catherine of Aragon *per verba de presenti*, and a year later repudiated it: H. A. Kelly, *The Matrimonial Trials of Henry VIII* (Stanford 1976) 104–105.

[173]PRO, C 66/317 m.21d: "Ex quadam querela Radulphi de Percy, chivaler, accepimus quod Johannes Halsham, ac quidam alii malefactores et pacis nostre perturbatores, Philippam, uxorem ipsius Radulphi, apud Semere, vi et armis rapuerunt, et eam cum bonis et catallis ejusdem Radulphi abduxerunt, et ea ei adhuc detinent, et alia enormia ei intulerunt, ad dampnum ipsius Radulphi trium milium librarum et contra pacem nostram ac contra formam statuti in hujusmodi casu provisi. Et quia transgressionem predictam, si perpetrata sit, relinquere nolumus impunitam, assignavimus vos," etc., dated 15 February 1384, but recorded after the other commission of 16 February; calendared in CPR*: Richard II*, 6 vols. (London 1914–1927) 2.424.

[174]PRO loc. cit.: "Ad inquirendum . . . qui malefactores et pacis nostri perturbatores Philippam, uxorem Radulphi de Percy, chivaler, apud Semere felonice rapuerunt et eam cum bonis et catallis ejusdem Radulphi abduxerunt et eam ei adhuc detinent et alia facinora ibidem perpetrarunt," etc. CCR 2.423.

but also royal confiscation of all property, though normally a pardon would intervene before matters arrived at this pass. Perhaps the purpose of adding the felony action without resorting to an appeal was that the prosecution mechanisms that accompanied it were more productive of results.

The trespass commission makes the standard reference to the appropriate statute, doubtless understood as that of 1285 (Westminster II chapter 34). Percy could have invoked the 1382 statute and attempted to secure a trial of felony by appeal, since there was clearly consent on the wife's part, seeing that she was now the wife of the alleged ravisher. The appeal procedure would not have been impeded by a pardon from the king, since such pardons only dismissed the Crown interests while leaving private actions still available. We shall see the husband in Malory's case pursuing this alternative, but there is no indication that Percy did so or contemplated doing so.

In the event, writs of *Supersedeas* suspending both commissions were issued on 28 May 1384.[175] In the writ addressing the trespass action against Halsham, the king states, "Being moved by certain reasons, we desire to find a remedy before us by way of agreement touching the debates between the said parties."[176] On 7 June, Halsham was given a pardon for the rape (*raptus*) of Philippa de Artheles (i.e., Athol), and all other felonies and trespasses perpetrated by him.[177]

But the wheels of justice were already grinding against Halsham. As we see from two further writs of *Supersedeas* issued on 10 July, Halsham had been indicted under the commission that was to search for felons, and steps had been taken to have him outlawed (he was "put in exigents") because he did not appear when subsequently summoned; and a similar process of outlawry had been ordered under the trespass commission.[178] In addition to the new orders to suspend the actions, another pardon was issued, for all rapes, murders, homicides, and other felonies, on the same day, 10 July, this time including the standard clause about still being obligated to stand trial if anyone should speak against him on the aforesaid.[179] Furthermore, still on 10 July, the

[175]PRO, C 54/224 m. 2d. The previous commissions are rehearsed in similar terms. See CCR*: Richard II*, 6 vols. (London 1914–1927) 2.452, where the offense named in the felony commission is summarized, "feloniously ravished Philippa . . . and abducted her," and in the trespass commission as "the rape and abduction of Philippa"; "rape" is also used in reporting a canceled copy of the trespass commission, C 54/225 m. 43d (p. 558)—which shows that "rape" in the calendar does not always correspond to the noun form (*raptus*) in the original.

[176]"Jam certis de causis nos moventibus, desiderantes super debatis habitis inter partes predictas in premissis per viam concordie coram nobis remedium apponere," etc.

[177]PRO, C 66/317 m. 12: "Sciatis quod de gracia nostra speciali, et ad supplicationem carissimi consanguinei nostri comitis Oxoniensis, perdonavimus dilecto ligeo nostro Johanni Halsham sectam pacis nostre que ad nos pertinet tam pro raptu Philippe de Artheles quam pro omnimodis feloniis et transgressionibus per ipsum quoquo modo perpetratis. In cujus, etc.," dated at Corfe Castle. CPR *Richard II*, 2.399.

[178]PRO, C 54/225 m. 51d; CCR: *Richard II*, 2.571.

[179]PRO, C 66/318 m. 37: "Sciatis quod de gracia nostra speciali, et ad requisitionem carissimi consanguinei nostri comitis Notyngham, dilecto ligeo nostro Johanni de Halsham sectam pacis nostre que ad nos pertinet, seu pertinere potuerit, pro omnimodis raptibus, murdris, homicidiis, communibus roberiis, et latrociniis, ac quibuscumque aliis feloniis unde indictatus, rettatus, vel appellatus existit, ac eciam utlagariam, si que in ipsum hiis occasionibus fuerit promulgate, et firmam pacem nostram ei inde concedimus. Ita tamen quod stet recto in curia nostra si quis versus eum loqui voluerit de premissis. In cujus, etc.," dated at Worth Manor. CPR *Richard II*, 2.439.

sheriff of York was ordered "to dearrest and deliver to John de Halsham and Philippa Dartheles his wife certain goods and chattels of theirs arrested in Dancastre."[180]

In an entry for 21 May 1388, we find Philippa still married to Halsham, while her sister Elizabeth is the widow of Thomas Percy.[181] Thomas had had two children by Elizabeth and had died in Spain shortly before. Ralph, who had had no children by Philippa or by any subsequent wife, was killed in the Holy Land in 1399.[182] It is not known whether he received any monetary satisfaction from John Halsham, who, if he did not actually abduct his wife from him, may at least have hijacked her affections.

B. Chaucer's Investigation of Rape, 1387: *Crown v. Lording et al.* *Lording v. Carshill et al.*; *Lording v. Bretford*; *Lording v. Collins*

Much attention has been given to Cecily Champain's 1380 release of Geoffrey Chaucer for all actions concerning her *raptus*,[183] but less notice has been taken of his appointment some years later as a justice to investigate an alleged *rapuerunt et abduxerunt* case. He was commissioned with others on 16 May 1387 to discover the identity of the malefactors who ravished and abducted the underage Isabel Hall, daughter of Thomas Hall, when she was in the custody of Thomas Carshill. On 1 August 1387, a twelve-man grand jury concluded that John Lording and two other men ravished and abducted the said Isabel on the previous 20 March, and they designated the offense as a felony, even though it was not so named in the commission's charge.[184] We recall that the statute of 1285 chapter 35 stipulated only two years in prison for abduction of a ward, but chapter 34 [A] made the abductions of all women capital, reinforced by the statute of 1382.

Lording appeared before the King's Bench in Trinity term (beginning 31 May) of the next year, 1388, not to answer the felony charge, but to bring a trespass suit on the civil side of the court against the alleged custodian, Thomas Carshill, and two others, including Alice Hall, perhaps Isabel's mother, for having previously ravished and abducted the same Isabel, who, it turns out, was his wife. The charge also included, in accord with the writ *De uxore rapta*, taking along Lording's goods. The date of the kidnapping was given as 1 October 1386. The suit quickly concluded in his favor in the same term (Trinity 1388), with all three defendants being fined.[185] So in this case, a wife really had been abducted, and abducted twice. First, Carshill stole her away from her husband, Lording, and then Lording seized her back again. The fact that he won his suit shows that Isabel really was his wife—and therefore was of age to be married. Whether or when she was of age to inherit is not made clear.

But matters did not end there. Lording's next step was to take measures to protect himself and Isabel against a man named John Bretford, and on 22 January of the next

[180] CCR: *Richard II*, 2.459.

[181] Ibid. 421.

[182] W. Hedley Percy, *Northumberland Families* (Newcastle 1968–) 2.14–15.

[183] I deal with this subject in "Meanings and Uses of *Raptus*" (n. 1 above).

[184] Martin M. Crow and Clair C. Olson, *Chaucer Life-Records* (Oxford 1966) 375–376. For a chronology of all the events of this case, see 382–383.

[185] Ibid. 379–380.

year, 1389, Bretford was forced to give heavy security in court, guaranteeing that he would not harm the Lordings. At the same time, Lording and the two other men indicted for the felony-ravishment of Isabel Hall were required to plead to the charge before the King's Bench (criminal side). They said not guilty, and the case was set for trial by jury. A jury was summoned for the Easter term, but then the case was postponed. But during the Easter term, Lording filed another suit, this time against a man named John Collins, for having ravished and abducted his wife Isabel, no date specified, and for still detaining her and his goods and chattels, to his damage and against the king's peace and against the statute,[186] that is, the statute of 1285 as referred to in the writ. We need not take this complaint literally, especially the part about Collins still detaining Isabel, since, as we have seen, the charge is the standard boilerplate.

In addition to, or instead of, these civil proceedings, Lording could have laid information against both Carshill and Collins, and any others who were connected with the affair, and attempted to have them indicted of felonious rape; or, if he had wished to allege that Isabel consented to the abduction in either case, he could have invoked the 1382 statute and appealed them of felony. Carshill on his side had no standing under the statute, since he was neither husband to the abducted and presumably consenting Isabel (since her husband was the alleged abductor) nor next of kin.

By employing the civil route, Lording was able to get immediate results against Carshill and his fellow-defendants. As for Collins, the sheriffs of London and Berkshire were unable to arrest him, and the writ for his capture was renewed early in 1390. In the summer of that year, two other men were forced to give guarantees that they would do no bodily harm to Lording. One was John Crishull, doubtless related to Carshill (whose name also appears as Creshill, Cressel, Kershull, and Kershill).[187] In addition, Bretford was still making a nuisance of himself, and in Michaelmas term of 1390 Lording brought a plea of trespass of unspecified nature against him.[188]

Meanwhile, the case of felonious rape and abduction against Lording and the other two defendants continued to be deferred from term to term and year to year until 1398, when they obtained a pardon from the king and were dismissed.[189] Perhaps the delay was caused by the difficulty or expense of obtaining a pardon, especially since rape had been made an exceptional crime in the 1390 statute. We will see that Thomas Malory would also be kept waiting for trial on indictments for the better part of a * decade before being pardoned, but in his case he had to remain in prison for most of the time. Furthermore, the reason for the delay is there stated to be lack of jurors, a common but easily superable problem,[190] except that in his case there is reason to sus-

[186]PRO, KB 27/518 m. 34: "Johannes Lordynge in propria persona sua optulit se quarto die versus Johannem Colyns de placito quare vi et armis Isabellam uxorem ipsius Johannis Lordynge apud London rapuit et eam cum bonis et catallis ejusdem Johannis Lordynge abduxit et ea ei adhuc detinet, et alia enormia, etc., ad grave damnum, etc., et contra pacem, etc., ac contra formam statuti, etc."

[187]Crow and Olson (n. 184 above) 381–382.

[188]PRO, KB 27/518 m. 49d: "Johannes Lordyng in propria persona sua optulit se quarto die versus Johannem Bretford de placito transgressionis. Et ipse [Bretford] non venit," etc.

[189]Crow and Olson (n. 184 above) 377–378.

[190]See J. B. Post, "Jury Lists and Juries in the Late Fourteenth Century, " *Twelve Good Men* (n. 84 above) 65–77 at 67–68: it was common to adjourn civil cases until a sufficient number of jurors showed up, but in criminal trials "the standard practice seems to have been to ensure the trial, without respite or adjournment, by recruiting talesmen" (that is, bystanders, *tales de circumstantibus*).

pect that his powerful enemy, the duke of Buckingham, was preventing the trial for fear of an acquittal.

We may well be dismayed at the weaknesses of a system that would allow a man to remain under threat of a felony prosecution for a dozen years, for seemingly having done nothing other than recover his wife from kidnappers. Canon law sensibly stated, "Even though it is said to be a question of rape when nothing is done about nuptials beforehand, a man should not be called a rapist who had the woman's assent and who betrothed or married her before he knew her sexually, even though the parents might object and claim that he raped her."[191] It was, however, a matter of timing, and canon law might agree with the English statutes in finding rape when the consent came only later. We have learned to be suspicious of men who claim women as their wives (I have not, however, presented the abundant evidence for suspecting persons who claim women as their wards). We have also seen that canon law recognized that sometimes a wife who has escaped or been taken from her husband should not be restored to him. Was there some merit to the felony charge against Lording? Was he possibly an abusive husband from whom a mother was rescuing her daughter? It would hardly seem possible, since Lording won his case against Isabel's self-proclaimed guardian and against his mother-in-law (or whoever Alice Hall was); he also had another accused abductor on the run, and he convinced the justices of the King's Bench to issue restraining orders against other potential molestors.

C. Charges of Rape Against the Bishop of Worcester, 1387: *Crown v. Wakefield*; *Crown v. Crown*

Henry Wakefield is characterized by his biographer, W. P. Marett, as a typical civil servant—that is, typically rising. He became bishop of Worcester in 1375, and "he was probably a good bishop, bringing the qualities of an adminstrator to the care of an important diocese, not seeking the limelight and probably no longer ambitious."[192] He is remembered "as a bitter opponent of the Lollards," but Marett himself thinks that "his attitude to the Lollards seems to have been unconcerned and even dilatory."[193] He did, however, issue a strongly worded prohibition against Lollard preaching on 10 August 1387,[194] and it may not be entirely coincidental that in October of the same year he was indicted by jurors of the various hundreds of Gloucestershire as having committed a series of outrages four years earlier against the daughter and wife of a certain John Henley of Whittington.[195]

The charges of the jurors, presented in Michaelmas term, 1387, are as follows:

[191] *Decretales Gregorii IX* 5.17.6, the decretal *Cum causam* of Lucius III: "Cum ibi raptus dicatur admitti ubi nil ante de nuptiis agitur, iste raptor dici non debet cum habuerit mulieris assensum et prius eam desponsaverit quam cognoverit, licet parentes reclamarent, a quibus eam dicitur rapuisse" (Friedberg [n. 165 above] 2.810).

[192] Warwick Paul Marett, *A Calendar of the Register of Henry Wakefeld, Bishop of Worcester, 1375–95*, Worcestershire Historical Society 2.7 (Leeds 1972) xliii.

[193] Ibid. xli, xliii.

[194] Ibid. 150-152.

[195] The court record is given in Sayles (n. 77 above) 7.53–54, *Coram rege* Roll, KB 27/507 m. 27 (crown), Hilary term, 1388. The indictments of the jurors were presented in Michaelmas term of 1387.

1) On 4 October 1383, he feloniously ravished (*felonice rapuit*) Joan Henley, daughter of John Henley, at Whittington, against the peace.

2) On 6 October 1383, he feloniously ravished (*felonice rapuit*) Joan Henley at Alvechurch.

3) On 5 November 1383, he ravished (*rapuit*) Katherine, the wife of John Henley, at Whittington and seized and carried away Henley's goods and chattels found there, namely, woolen and linen cloths and other household utensils, to the value of 40s.

4) On 8 November 1383, he ravished and abducted (*rapuit et abduxit*) Katherine, wife of John Henley, at Whittington, against the king's peace and against the form of the statute.[196]

We note that the offenses against the daughter are brought as felonies, and those against the wife as nonfelonies, that is, trespasses, contrary to the normal use in Putnam's quarter-sessions. For the last-dated trespass offense, "the form of the statute" is invoked, using the language of the civil-trespass writ *De uxore rapta.* The idea that Wakefield first ravished the wife and left her there while carrying away clothes and utensils, and then three days later came back for additional ravishment, followed by abduction, is bizarre, and is probably the crude way that the informants hit on of trying to get all the elements of the statutory law in place.

Marett is noncommittal in reporting the rape charges against Wakefield,[197] but in R. N. Swanson's view, the charges against him were "clearly fictitious."[198] However, they may have been the sort of fiction that we have already seen in connection with such accusations, and they may point to some sort of domestic strife. The bishop or his court may have helped to rescue Joan and Katherine from an abusive household, perhaps effecting a legal separation of Katherine for *sevitia*—a step that seems to have been comparatively rare at this time[199]—or an annulment because of an impediment to the marriage.

As it was, the bishop did not bother to contest or explain the charges, but simply submitted a pardon from the king, dated 4 November 1387, which dismissed the royal interest in any felonies and transgressions of which he might be indicted, accused, or appealed. Wakefield also submitted a close writ from the king, dated 18 February 1388, forbidding interference with the pardon. As a result, he was dismissed *sine die.* As usual, the pardon stipulated that the bishop would still have to stand trial in the king's court "if anyone wishes to sue against him with respect to the aforegoing matters."[200] An appeal of sexual rape by Joan or Katherine, if the facts or their inclination had warranted it, would not likely have been well received, coming four years

[196] I give the charges in chronological order; in the indictment they are presented in the order 2–4–1–3.

[197] Marett (n. 192 above) xl.

[198] R. N. Swanson, *Church and Society in Late Medieval England* (Oxford 1989) 81.

[199] R. H. Helmholz, *Marriage Litigation in Medieval England* (Cambridge 1974) 100–105, notes cruelty as an issue in Canterbury cases of 1373 and 1394 and York cases of 1374 and 1390. Charles Donahue, Jr., notes that, out of the eighty-eight fourteenth-century marriage cases surviving from the York consistory court, only three, one from 1349, and two from 1395, raise the issue of separation because of cruelty: "Marriage, Children, and Family," paper read at the Tenth International Congress of Medieval Canon Law, University of Syracuse, August 1996, to appear in the *Proceedings* (Vatican City ca. 1998).

[200] Sayles (n. 195 above) loc. cit.: "ita tamen quod stet recto in curia nostra si quis versus eum loqui voluerit de premissis seu aliquo premissorum." *Stare recto,* "to stand to right," means "to take one's trial." See R. E. Latham, *Revised Medieval Latin Word-List from British and Irish Sources* (London 1965) s.v. *rect/um.*

after the alleged crimes. Henley himself could have appealed Wakefield of "ravishing" his subsequently consenting wife, in keeping with the 1382 statute, if he had wished to pursue his campaign further. But here too the time-lag would have raised suspicions of fraud.

D. Arnold's Later Civil Trespass Cases, 1386–1390

Now let us look at the remaining civil cases in Arnold's collection, all of them, like the earlier ones, from the King's Bench:[201]

14) *Warwick v. Hothe*, 1386: The defendant says that the wife's marriage to the plaintiff had been annulled long before the supposed ravishment and abduction occurred.

15) *Wyatt v. Vicar of Swalcliffe*, 1388: The defendant is the wife's uncle, a priest, vicar of the church of Swalcliffe in Oxfordshire. He explains here in court that his niece left her husband and lived with him when given permission by the official of the archdeacon of Oxford. She was asking for an annulment on grounds of the husband's impotence, and she feared his violence. The only clothes in question were not taken by him but by her, namely, those she was wearing, and the same was true of the one ring that the husband complained of.

16) *Hamm v. Gilbert*, 1389: The jury agrees that there was no ravishing, no use of force on the part of the defendant, who was the woman's employer, but it finds that he did encourage her to leave her husband, and it assesses damages of 100s.

17) *Ware v. Halmard et al.*, 1389: The defendants, who turn out to be the wife's son, son-in-law, and cousin, claim that she left her husband during annulment proceedings, being authorized to do so by an interlocutory decree of the judge, the archdeacon of Westminster.

18) *Rose v. Newthorp et al.*, 1390: The defendant says that he himself had married the woman clandestinely long before the plaintiff knew her; she left the defendant's company, and he tried for a long time to obtain an annulment from the official of the archbishop of Canterbury; but then the archbishop advoked the case to his court of audience, where the marriage was declared valid and the defendant ordered to solemnize it; he therefore came and requested her to fulfill the decree, and he took (*cepit*) and led (*duxit*) her to London and married her. The plaintiff says that his own marriage to her had been solemnized; he had not been advised of any court proceedings beforehand, and he appealed against the decree when he heard of it.

19) *Hampton v. Montgomery and Child*, 1390: The defendants explain that the plaintiff's wife was no longer married to him at the time of the alleged violation: she had had her marriage annulled because of her previous marriage to another man, Walter, and after the annulment she had voluntarily left the plaintiff, without any force being used by any of the defendants. One of the defendants had represented Walter in court, and the other defendant had been of the wife's counsel in the annulment proceedings.

[201]Arnold (n. 143 above) 1.86–93.

E. Two Guilty Verdicts, 1403 and 1408

Sayles presents two civil cases of *De uxore rapta* before the King's Bench in which the jury accepted that the charge of "rape" was verified, but apparently giving no credit to the allegations of force and physical injury.

1) *London v. Overton.* In 1403, a cordwainer is accused of the standard set of offenses specified in *De uxore rapta*, that is, ravishing a wife with force and arms and abducting her with goods and still detaining them, against the peace and the form of the statute, with damages stated at £100. The defendant denies all. A jury finds him guilty of the *raptus* and of taking goods worth 12d, but not guilty of taking the rest of the goods alleged. They assess total damages at 21s, and add another 21s of costs. The Court finds the damages set for the *raptus* too low, and adds another 100s, rounding the whole assessment to 150s.[202] Presumably the defendant kept the wife and the 12d worth of goods.

2) *Barett v. Portherd.* In 1408, a man and two others are accused of a similar set of offenses, with damages stated at £40. Jurors find the defendants guilty of the trespass and assess the damages at 100 marks (i.e., ca. £67). But the court refuses to go beyond the plaintiff's estimate, and awards only the £40 he claimed.[203]

Nansegle v. Vide et al., Smith v. Malory et al., and the Statute of 1382

In Michaelmas term of 1409, the King's Bench considered a case in which one T. Nansegle sued an appeal against T. Vide and another man for ravishing his wife, in violation of the statute of 6 Richard II, which was recited. Vide first objects that the appellant has already taken out a writ for the same rape during that very term ("L'appellee dist que le plaintiff avoit autre breve pendent, retrait mesme cest terme de mesme le rape," etc.). The plaintiff's lawyer, Hals,[204] replies that he can choose between them, but Justice Tyrwhitt rules that the second writ is good because the first has not been enrolled. Then the defendants' lawyer, Rolfe, objects that, according to the plaintiff's charge, "we ravished her feloniously, but he does not declare that we ravished her carnally," and so the appeal is defective. Tyrwhitt rules that it is enough to say "ravished feloniously"; we cited his reason earlier: "because if he ravished her and did not know her carnally, it is never felony but trespass" ("car si il ravishoit et ne conustroit carnelment, ce n'est my felonie, eins transgressione").[205] We speculated that this principle may have been a new policy that had not yet taken effect. But it may also have been an older maxim honored in the breach as well as in the observance, like the principle enunciated by the chief justice of the King's Bench,

[202]Sayles (n. 77 above) 7.134–135.

[203]Ibid. 181–182.

[204]Probably John Hals, who became King's Serjeant in 1413 (Sainty [n. 138 above] 9). I have not identified the defendants' lawyer, Rolfe. The justices who comment are Hugh Huls and Robert Tyrwhitt (Sainty [n. 125 above] 26), and the chief justice is William Gascoigne (ibid. 8).

[205]*Nansegle v. Vide*, Yearbook of 11 Henry IV, Michaelmas term (1409), *Les reports del cases en ley que furent argues en le temps de tres haut et puissant princes, les roys Henry le IV et Henry le V* (London 1689; repr. Abingdon 1981), year 11, Michelmas plea 30, p. 13. See n. 159 above.

William Gascoigne, in 1406, "that if one were indicted at the king's suit one would not have counsel."[206]

Rolfe's next objection, that only one of the defendants should have been charged as principal, is overruled by Justice Huls.[207] Then Rolfe addresses the text of the 1382 statute, saying that Nansegle admitted in his charge that his wife consented after the ravishment, and if she did not consent, then the appeal would lie with both the husband and the wife, according to the statute of Westminster II, and would not fall under King Richard's statute. Huls and Tyrwhitt agree that it does in fact fall under the latter provision.[208] Rolfe's statement, by the way, is noteworthy for its assumption that the 1285 statute entailed an appeal by both husband and wife. This requirement was stipulated in a case of sexual rape two years earlier, in 1407: when a woman who was being held in Marshalsea prison told the Court that she had been raped by one of the prison servants, the Court told her that since she was married, *covert de baron*, she could not make her appeal without him.[209] The same requirement is perhaps to be seen in a case reported a century earlier by the scribes of the eyres of Cornwall and Kent.[210] But in the 1407 case the reporter refers to the statute of 1382 rather than that of 1285.[211]

Rolfe next asserts that his main client, Vide, was originally affianced to the woman that Nansegle claims as his ravished wife. What happened, Rolfe says, is that Nansegle later took her to a church and forced her to marry him against her will. And since she never agreed to that marriage, she went to Vide, and he, because of the first contract between them, married her in a certain church. Therefore, the appellant was never legally married to her, which the defendant is ready to prove. The plaintiff's lawyer, however, asserts that this statement is an admission that a marriage took place between Nansegle and the woman, and that Vide ravished her. (We note that there is no further reference to carnal ravishment.) Rolfe says that the admission was intended only as a preliminary protestation, but Chief Justice Gascoigne replies that one cannot use a protest that proves one guilty of felony.[212]

Rolfe says that he has consulted with doctors of church law, who hold the marriage of his client to be legal in spite of the previous marriage to Nansegle. Justice Tyrwhitt replies that until the first marriage is annulled in a church court, the second marriage must be considered null; but Justice Huls says that if the first marriage was forced, it is null *ipso facto*, and there is no need to have it annulled. Rolfe enters a plea that the plaintiff was never married, and it is accepted. A writ is granted to have the bishop of

[206] Seipp (n. 118 above) 24, citing Year Book of 7 Henry IV, *Reports*, year 7, Hilary plea 4, pp. 35–36, and the formulation of the principle in the Yorkshire case treated in n. 115 above, dating more than a century earlier. Another example of a principle that might be thought ineffective is, "Felony is malice aforethought," stated by a lawyer in a 1466 case (Seipp 27).

[207] *Nansegle* (n. 205 above) 13–14.

[208] Ibid. 14.

[209] Yearbook of 8 Henry IV, *Reports*, year 8, Easter plea 2, p. 21.

[210] See n. 119 above.

[211] Loc. cit. in n. 209 above: "Et sic nota d'appeal de home et son feme, etc. Vide statutum de anno 6 R. 2 cap. 6."

[212] *Nansegle* (n. 205 above) 14. At this point a comment is made by "Werhm." (unidentified), to the effect (it seems) that if a woman became a nun after such a betrothal and then left the nunnery to marry her fiancé, the marriage would be subject to annulment unless the betrothal were a precontract (that is, a present-tense agreement, which constituted a valid marriage). See Kelly (n. 172 above) 49.

Exeter try the validity of the plaintiff's marriage, which allegedly took place in Devon.[213]

But before this conclusion, there is more discussion of the statute. The plaintiff's lawyer, Hals, notes that the husband has the suit of such a rape ("le baron eit le suit de tielx rape"), if the woman has a husband. Rolfe says that, since conviction would entail the death penalty, it is an *action de droit*, a matter of strict right, and if the husband is not strictly a husband, *baron en droit*, he cannot have this action, but only a writ of trespass, of wife ravished with husband's goods ("breve de trespas de feme ravy *cum bonis viri*"), because this suit is not a matter of right ("pur ce que le suit ne trench my in le droit").[214]

Rolfe's assessment of the use of the writ *De uxore rapta*, by men who were only dubiously married to their allegedly ravished wives, is borne out by our findings above, and is not contradicted by the Court. But his position on 6 Richard II is contested: Justice Huls concedes that when a woman appeals a man for killing her husband, it is a valid defense to say that he was not really her husband; but in the present case, the woman is the *de facto* wife until a divorce (annulment) is effected, and so the statute gives the suit to him even if he is not her legal husband.[215] But, as we saw, the action was put on hold until the bishop decided this very point.

Our second instance in which the statute of 1382 was invoked is very well known, in that it involves the author of the *Morte d'Arthur*, but the "rape" part of the story has been much misunderstood.

One key document in the case was published and translated by Edward Hicks in 1928,[216] namely, indictments brought against Thomas Malory, on 23 August 1451, by two grand juries at an inquest held at Nuneaton in Warwickshire. A chronological list of the indictments, as explained by Albert Baugh,[217] is as follows:

1) 4 January 1450: he and twenty-six other armed malefactors lay in ambush in Coombe Abbey woods to murder the duke of Buckingham (nonfelony).
2) 23 May 1450: he feloniously broke the close of Hugh Smith at Monks Kirby (near Malory's Newbold estate) and feloniously ravished Smith's wife Joan and lay with her carnally ("felonice rapuit et cum ea carnaliter concubuit").
3) 31 May 1450: with help of his servant John Appleby he extorted 100s from Margaret King and William Hale of Monks Kirby (nonfelony).
4) 6 August 1450: he feloniously ravished Joan, wife of Hugh Smith, at Coventry and lay with her carnally and feloniously stole, took, and abducted her along with £40 worth of Smith's goods and chattels ("ac illam cum bonis et catallis . . . felonice furat[u]s fuit, cepit, et abduxit"), taking them to Barwell in the county of Leicester, against the peace, crown, and dignity of the king.

213Ibid.

214Ibid.

215Ibid.

216Edward Hicks, *Sir Thomas Malory: His Turbulent Career* (Cambridge, Mass. 1928) 93–97, English translation 102–106.

217Albert C. Baugh, review of Hicks, *Journal of English and Germanic Philology* 29 (1930) 452–457 at 455–456; idem, "Documenting Sir Thomas Malory," *Speculum* 8 (1933) 3–29 at 4–5. In the original presentments, the charges are in this order: 7, 8, 1, 9, 5, 3, 2, 4, 6. The first eight charges were presented by a jury of the Hemlingford Hundred, and the last (no. 6 chronologically) by a jury from the Knightlow Hundred, where Cosford lay. See P. J. C. Field, *The Life and Times of Sir Thomas Malory* (Cambridge 1993) 101.

5) 31 August 1450: with help of Appleby he extorted 20s from John Milner of Monks Kirby (nonfelony).
6) 4 June 1451: Malory and five others rustled 7 cows, 2 calves, 335 sheep worth £22, and a cart worth £4 from a property in Cosford (nonfelony).
7) 27 July 1451: after the duke of Buckingham, acting on a commission of 13 July, arrested Malory on 25 July, he escaped from prison (nonfelony).
8) 28 July 1451: with Appleby and ten others he broke into Coombe Abbey, did much damage, and feloniously took and asported goods worth £86.
9) 29 July 1451: with Appleby and a dozen other named men and about 100 more unnamed he raided Coombe again, assaulted the monks, and feloniously stole many more goods.

We note that only the last four charges are of recent vintage, while the others, including the two rape episodes, are from the previous year. Neither Hicks nor Baugh, nor more recent writers like William Matthews and P. J. C. Field, have noticed that the second alleged ravishment of Joan Smith also included an alleged abduction.[218]

The justices of the peace who assembled the juries were headed by none other than Henry Stafford, duke of Buckingham, the intended victim of Malory's alleged assassination plot in 1450 (charge number 1) and the person who first arrested him in 1451 (charge number 7).

After these indictments were handed down in August 1451, six weeks later, at the beginning of Michaelmas term (week of 5 October), the supposedly wronged husband, Hugh Smith, appeared before the King's Bench in pursuit of an appeal of rape and breach of the peace ("optulit se . . . de raptu Johanne uxoris ipsius Hugonis et pace nostra fracta, unde eos appellat") against Malory and three other men, namely, William Weston, gentleman, Thomas Potter, husbandman, and Adam Brown, weaver. He invoked the statute of 6 Richard II ("juxta formam statuti in parliamento domini Ricardi nuper regis Anglie secundi post conquestum apud Westmonasterium anno regni sui sexto tento editi").[219] No details are given as to when and where the alleged rape took place, but since Brown was said to be from Coventry, it was doubtless the later of the two charged offenses that was intended.

The citation of the 1382 statute confirms that the appealed *raptus* refers to the occasion of the abduction of the wife, since it applied only in cases in which the ravished woman consented to the ravishment afterwards, as was pointed out in *Nansegle*. Now since, according to the earlier indictments, neither of Malory's alleged sexual encounters with Mrs. Smith were said to have been against her will, are we to see the consent as coming very early (if there is any truth to the charges)? Perhaps, but that would make the charge faulty, since willing adultery on the wife's part would remove the activity from the secular courts and place it entirely within the jurisdiction of the church courts.

It is possible, or even probable, that carnal knowledge was specified in the indictments because Smith and his lawyers (and Buckingham and the other colluding justices) believed that sexual violation was necessary for the offense to be classified as a felony. We recall that this was the view of Justice Tyrwhitt in *Nansegle*. But it was not specified in the statute. The other parts of the statute, which were designed to prevent

[218]William Matthews, *The Ill-Framed Knight* (Berkeley 1966) 17, 45; Field 97, 106.

[219]Baugh, "Documenting" (n. 217 above) 6. It is puzzling that Baugh calls this "the original record of this action" (5), that is, more original than the indictment, even though it came after the indictment.

the abductor and his retroactively compliant victim from enjoying her property, would hardly be relevant, since both Mrs. Smith and Malory were already married. Most likely, then, Malory and his companions had simply assisted her to leave her husband, for one or other of the reasons that have surfaced in similar cases discussed above.

The effect of an appeal after the presentment of an indictment was to remove the case to the King's Bench,[220] and, sure enough, a writ of *certiorari* was issued at the same time as the appeal, advoking the Nuneaton indictments to the King's Bench,[221] where Malory pleaded not guilty (to the indictments) the next Hilary term (27 January 1452). Another effect of such an appeal was to keep the defendant imprisoned during the new process.[222] This may have contributed to Malory's long stay in prison, but no further action in the appeal is recorded, and the charge of rape is not singled out in any of the later records concerning the indictments; there are only general references to "the divers felonies, trespasses, insurrections, extortions, and oppressions of which he stands indicted."[223] His trial was constantly postponed, for lack of a jury, * until he finally obtained a pardon in 1460.[224] Field comments: "The fact that Malory was never brought to trial suggests Buckingham had doubts about the outcome of a trial even in the King's Bench, and that he chose to make an example of Malory by preventing that trial from taking place."[225]

Buckingham and Smith were well advised to change the venue of the indictments to the King's Bench. Trials of rape held in Warwickshire before justices of jail delivery in the period 1400–1429 had a 100% acquittal rate, and the same was true in the neighboring counties of Derbyshire and Leceistershire (and doubtless elsewhere in England). As we have seen above, this has led Edward Powell to suspect that there was in many cases no truth to the indictments, that is, no violent sexual assault or abduction. The large number of clergy among the defendants, 80 out of 114 in Warwickshire (70%), 14 of 49 in Derbyshire (24.5%), and 50 of 115 in Leceistershire (43.5%), suggests to him that the real grievance was clerical fornication or adultery, indicated also by a protest raised in the Convocation of Canterbury in 1411: clergy accused of sexual offenses "should not be indicted for rape before the king's judges like common thieves, without the consent of the ordinaries." He concludes: "There can be little doubt that indictment for rape at peace sessions or the sheriff's tourn was being used as a popular expression of disapproval of clergy who broke their vows of celibacy," and he adds: "It is possible that rape indictments were used in a similar way against laymen who had committed adultery."[226] He does not consider the possibility that some of the indictments were fueled by resentment against those who, without

[220]Christopher Whittick, "The Role of the Criminal Appeal in the Fifteenth Century," *Law and Social Change in British History*, ed. J. A. Guy and H. G. Beale (London 1984) 55–72 at 65–66.

[221]Field (n. 218 above) 101, citing PRO KB 9/265 m. 77, dating it 5 October.

[222]Whittick (n. 220 above) 69.

[223]Baugh, "Documenting" (n. 217 above) 7–13.

[224]Field (n. 218 above) 105–123. He may have written some of his Arthurian stories during these years in jail, but it was during a subsequent stint in prison that he finished the work, in 1469 or 1470.

[225]Ibid. 105–106.

[226]Powell (n. 156 above) 100–103, and see 111–112. More precisely, out of 278 trials, there were 272 acquittals, 3 pardons, and 3 insufficient indictments. During the same time there was only one appeal of rape in the three counties, and that was in Warwickshire (105 n. 77).

any sexual involvement on their part, had helped wives to get away or stay away from their husbands.

A later case invoking the 1382 law has been brought to light by Ives, from the decade after the passing of the 1487 statute. The indictments resemble the charges against Malory to some extent, but the accused rapist in this case is not a knight but a laborer, or yeoman, named William Smith, and the supposedly ravished woman is a widow, Matilda Mourton, whose husband had been a gentleman. The ravishment was said to have been against Matilda's will—an allegation not specifically made in the Malory case—but afterwards she supposedly consented, thus making her liable to the statute. The statute, however, was designed to be enforced by the woman's husband or next of kin. Ives concludes that the alleged rape never occurred; he considers the jury's action and that of another jury, which indicted the same couple of having previously poisoned Matilda's husband, to be "expressions of public condemnation of an unfaithful wife and her plebeian lover."[227] This is like Powell's judgment: "Criminal trial procedure was thus being used by local society in a sophisticated manner as a formal sanction against sexual impropriety."[228]

CONCLUSION; 1453 AND BEYOND

The inherent ambiguity of the language of rape made it inevitable that there would be confusion surrounding all legislation that that did not make it clear whether sexual violation, abduction, or both, was the primary object of a given law. Practically speaking, only one statute, the Office of the Coroner, about 1276, deals unambiguously with sexual rape, because blood is mentioned.[229] But I have found no indication that this section of the statute was ever recalled or appealed to. There were some early unofficial interpretations of the statutes of Westminster I (1275) and II (1285 chap. 34 [A]) as referring to sexual rape, but the statutes themselves seem designed with only abduction in mind, and subsequent judicial use confirms this impression.

Apart from the comparatively straightforward abduction of wards, especially as treated in 1285 chapter 35, the chief use made of the Westminster statutes concerned the accusation of abducting wives with their husbands' goods. A new law was passed in 1382 to allow private appeal in cases where the wife or heiress consented to abduction, since the 1285 law allowed prosecution only to the king in such a case. The incident that inspired the statute, the abduction of Thomas West's daughter, since it occurred before passage of the law, was not covered, but even in the years immediately following 1382 Crown prosecution of alleged abductions continued as before. So did civil actions against alleged perpetrators, in spite of the misgivings of Justice Skipwith in 1382 that the writ *De uxore rapta* implied a felony charge. The view enunciated by Justice Huls in1409, which restricted felonious abduction to cases in which sexual intercourse occurred, may have been the basis for the explicit charge of felonious

[227] Ives (n. 62 above) 26.

[228] Powell (n. 156 above) 104.

[229] It is, of course, possible for blood to be mentioned in cases not involving sexual rape. There is an example in Putnam (n. 151 above) 344 no. 68 in which a woman in 1362 complained of being beaten up by a man when she refused to marry him.

intercourse against Malory, and, if such an idea was operative earlier, it may also account for Thomas West's emended complaint after passage of the 1382 law, claiming now that his son-in-law deflowered his daughter when he feloniously ravished her.

Two years after Malory was appealed of felonious rape, that is, abduction, of a wife who consented to the deed, a new statute was passed, that of 31 Henry VI, in 1453, dealing with single women who were either abducted by force or taken away by their own consent. It provided that they could get out of any property agreements they may have made, whether through marriage or otherwise, without resorting to the process of criminal indictment for ravishment and abduction, or without claiming sexual rape and making an appeal of felony. If a forced marriage occurred, this law would provide only for separation of her property from her husband. To get out of the marriage itself, she would have to get a decree of annulment from an ecclesiastical court, after proving that the contract had been entered into under force and fear. The husband, of course, could counter with an action *De uxore rapta*, not against the woman but against a convenient male relative, friend, or assistant.

The 1487 statute, 3 Henry VII, returned to the criminal side of abduction and in effect reiterated the message of the 1382 law, namely, that it was a felony to abduct (using the expression "take away" rather than the "ravish" of the earlier enactment) any unwilling woman (maid, wife, or widow), or to assist in such taking away, whether for purpose of forced marriage or deflowering, resulting in the woman's disparagement or devaluation. It differs from the 1382 statute by not focusing on any subsequent consent of the woman, though it does have a phrase, "by their assent," probably referring to the abductors, which could be taken of the women.

One result of the 1487 law was the right of women to enter an appeal of felony for abduction without having to allege sexual rape. But this right was established "only after consultation between the justices of both benches" in a 1492 case, *Shelley v. Pennington and Dixon*.[230] In his analysis of this matter, Christopher Whittick indicates that the point of discussion was whether an appeal should be allowed under a statute that did not explicitly provide for appeals, and he says that the plea in this case was allowed "by analogy with the admissibility of appeals under the act of 1382."[231] But another point of contention could have been whether a woman was allowed to make an appeal of ravishment in a case where no sexual violation was at issue. We find a * similar appeal being made in 1504 by a young widow, Margery Kebell, against her abductor, after criminal indictments failed.[232] Her abductor, who had forced Margery to marry him, responded by suing her rescuers for ravishing his wife with his goods, only to be rebuked by the judge.[233]

The judges themselves seem to have been vague about the laws of rape. In a yearbook case of 1491, when the justices were discussing a charge of felony rape brought in a court leet, the whole Court agreed that the leet have no jurisdiction over felony, the same being true of the Common Bench; and since rape was not felony at common

[230] Whittick (n. 220 above) 62.

[231] Ibid.

[232] Ives (n. 62 above) 37–38. The appeal also failed, and, as Ives shows, only a direct resort to the king and his council proved effective.

[233] Ibid. 39. Ives mistakenly says that the abductor-husband drew on "the little known section of Westminster I chap. 13, *de uxore rapta cum bonis viri*."

law ("et pur ce que al common ley rape ne fuit felony"), it could not be inquired as such, for it was made felony by the statutes of Westminster II (1285) and Richard II (1382).[234] We have seen a similar statement about rape being only a trespass in common law in a 1342 case.[235] In 1504, Robert Brudenell, just appointed king's serjeant (he became a justice of the King's Bench in 1507 and chief justice of Common Pleas in 1520),[236] asserted that in an appeal of rape, it is necessary to say, *felonice rapuit*, even though rape in itself is felony ("Come appel de rape, covient aver *felonice rapuit*; uncore rape in luy mesme est felony").[237]

This brings us to the sixteenth century and George Ferrers's translations of the statutes. We have seen that his rendering of the 1275 statute interprets it to refer to a male suit for female abduction rather than to a woman's appeal of her own sexual violation. This interpretation, except for some sexual understandings at the turn of the fourteenth century, accorded with the standard fourteenth- and fifteenth-century view that the statutes of 1275 and 1285 centered about abduction, especially of wives.

The statute of rapes that was passed in 1540, not long after Ferrers produced his translation, removed the privilege of sanctuary from those found guilty of committing ravishment "of" or "to" any woman, thus paralleling the statute of 1390, which named *rape de femme* as one of the crimes exempted from general pardons. These and the other statutes that designated rape/ ravishment/ abduction as felony—those, namely, of 1285 (chap. 34 [A]), 1382, 1487—were contradicted in effect by the statute of 1558, which provided for only two years in prison for abducting girls under sixteen and only an additional three years for deflowering them.

The statute of 1576 reverted to the spirit of earlier statutes by removing benefit of clergy from rapists and burglars and from those who had sex with girls under the age of ten. The act affirmed that rape/ ravishment and burglary were considered capital crimes, but it did not indicate whether sexual violation, or abduction for monetary gain, was uppermost in the legislators' minds. John Bellamy in discussing this statute says that "it was common for the assailant during the abduction (which is what many sixteenth century rapes really were) to take some of the woman's personal possessions with him, which was then charged as burglary by the irate husband," and he notes that the same was also true in the Middle Ages.[238] This, however, may be giving too much credence to the stereotyped charges of the writ *De uxore rapta*.

Some rapes, of course, were clearly of the sexual kind, like *Ellen Lamb's Case*, an appeal of rape brought in 1561 before the justices of jail delivery. In this case, after the defendant was found guilty of having feloniously ravished and deflowered the appellant and carnally known her, some doubts were raised by the Keeper of the Great Seal on command of the queen, among them the fact that the appellant did not include the word "feloniously" in her charge, and did not assert her lack of consent to the rape, whether before or after it occurred. When there is no consent, "the suit by the statute of Westminster II chapter 34 is given to the party, and otherwise it is given to

[234] *Les reports des cases en les ans des roys Edward V, Richard III, Henrie VII, et Henrie VIII* (London 1679), 6 Henry VII, Trinity plea 4, p. 4.

[235] See n. 155 above.

[236] Sainty (n. 138 above) 13; idem (n. 125 above) 28, 48.

[237] *Les reports* (n. 234 above), 20 Henry VII, p. 7.

[238] John G. Bellamy, *Criminal Law and Society in Late Medieval and Tudor England* (Gloucester 1984) 159.

the king by way of indictment only" ("le suit per lesstatute de West. 2 cap. 34 est done al partie, et auterment il est done al roy per voy d'endictment *tantum*"). Another difficulty was that the conclusion of the count omitted the words, *contra formam statuti etc.*[239] No resolution was brought to these doubts. We recall that Brudenell in 1504 stipulated the need for the explicit mention of "feloniously," even though the rape was automatically a felony. Lack of consent was also a feature of rape by definition, but that, of course, need not have cut any ice with court procedure.

Especially interesting to us in this case is that the 1285 statute was interpreted as dealing with sexual rape and not with abduction (or, at least, it was considered to deal with sexual rape as well as abduction); and, furthermore, that the 1382 statute, the statute appealed to in the case of Thomas Malory, which gave the suit to a party other than the woman, that is, to an aggrieved husband or near male kin, when the woman consented afterwards, was lost to the memory the judges and the Lord Great Seal. Which shows that the interpretation and observance of statute law, like other laws and procedures, is liable to be capricious.

The abduction of married women was at the center of most of the statutes of rapes, but, practically speaking, most of the charges actually made of kidnapped wives seem to have been bogus, as is exemplified in three of our cases. The complaints of Ralph Percy in 1384 illustrate the common situation in which a has-been husband accuses his replacement of having abducted his wife. A twist in this plot is seen in the case investigated by Chaucer in 1387: the grand jury assembled by him and his fellow justices of inquiry indicted John Lording of the felonious ravishment of an underage heiress. But even though he proved to the Court in a civil countersuit that the alleged victim was his own wife whom his accusers had previously kidnapped, he still had to face the criminal charge, until he was pardoned a decade later. In Malory's case, there was no new husband involved in the alleged abduction, as far as we know. At least it was not Malory himself, for he was currently married to someone else. He was accused in 1451 of twice having had felonious sex with another man's wife and, on the second occasion, of feloniously abducting her. Later, the woman's husband accused Malory and named accomplices of ravishing her, and since he invoked the 1382 statute of Richard II, he was admitting that the wife consented to the ravishment. We do not know who was more in the right, the woman's self-proclaimed husband or Malory. But, given the track record of other such accusers, I put my money on Malory.

We may never know more about Malory's relations with the wife of Hugh Smith, but they may have been as complicated as those between Lancelot and Arthur's queen in the French romances that he would translate during his stays in prison, which he may have already read in 1450. One notable change that he made in his version of the expanded *Book of Lancelot* was to transfer the abduction of Queen Guenevere by Meliagance from early in Lancelot's career and put it close to his own abduction of the queen, when he saved her from death at the stake, near the end of the work. It is noteworthy that in the first episode, the abductor accuses the would-be rescuers of having consensual sex with the queen. In keeping with his sources Malory depicts this as a capital crime of high treason,[240] something that would not become statutory law in

[239]Dyer, *Reports* (n. 72 above) 2.201b–202a; *English Reports* (n. 72 above) 73.445–446.

[240]Malory, *Le Morte d'Arthur*, book 19, chapter 6, *Caxton's Malory*, 1.545; *The Works of Sir Thomas Malory*, ed. Eugene Vinaver, ed. 3 rev. P. J. C. Field, 3 vols. (Oxford 1990) 3.1133.

England until Henry VIII had disposed of his fifth wife, Catherine Howard, in 1542.[241] In Malory's day, however, even though adultery was simply a matter for the internal and external forums of the church, we have seen reason to suppose that it was brought into the secular courts under a false charge of sexual violence or abduction, but without the expectation of conviction.

In Malory's French source, Guenevere's second abduction is misreported to "the Apostle of Rome," that is, the pope. He hears that Arthur first left her and then was attempting to capture her and put her to death. He also hears, more accurately, that the misdeed charged against her had not been proved ("li Apostoles ot oï que on ne l'avoit pas prise provee el meffait que on le metoit sus"). He therefore orders Arthur to take her back and treat her well, under pain of excommunication and interdict.[242] Malory omits the legal basis of the pope's decision, perhaps only because because he was following his English resume, the *Stanzaic Morte Arthur*.[243] He says:

> So of this war that was between King Arthur and Sir Lancelot, it was noised through all Christian realms, and so it came at the last by relation unto the pope. And then the pope took a consideration of the great goodness of King Arthur, and of the high prowess of Sir Lancelot, that was called the most noblest knight of the world. Wherefore the pope called unto him a noble clerk that at that time was there present (the French book saith it was the Bishop of Rochester), and the pope gave [him bulls] under lead unto the king, charging him, upon pain of interdicting of all England, that he take his queen again, and accord with Sir Lancelot.[244]

We know what happened to Lancelot, Arthur, and Guenevere. We know something of what happened to Malory. But we know nothing of what happened to Malory's neighbor, Hugh Smith, and the wife with whom Malory may have been intimate in 1450, and whom he may have escorted from Coventry to Barwell. The husband only belatedly, over a year later, accused him of criminal rape and breaking the king's peace—and, incidentally, alienating her affections—a charge that trapped Malory in the toils of the central judicial system.

[241] 33 Henry VIII chap. 21, *Statutes* (n. 8 above) 3.857. See Kelly (n. 172 above) 275–276. In Chaucer's Arthurian story, the *Wife of Bath's Tale*, the Wife of Bath seems to find it a matter of wonder that forcible sexual violation of a woman should be punished by death: "Paraventure swich was the statut tho" (line 893), as if it were not true in her (and Chaucer's) time.

[242] *La mort le roi Artu*, ed. Jean Frappier, ed. 2 (Geneva 1954; third repr. 1964) 153 §117; *The Death of King Arthur*, trans. James Cable (Harmondsworth 1971) 145–146.

[243] *Le Morte Arthur*, ed. J. Douglas Bruce (London 1903) lines 2246–2253.

[244] Malory, book 20, end of chapter 13, Winchester MS version, *Works* (n. 240 above) 3.1194

X

Meanings and Uses of *Raptus* in Chaucer's Time

The question of Geoffrey Chaucer's connection with the *raptus* of Cecily Champain has greatly interested literary historians since the matter first came to light in the 1870s. A recent breakthrough in the discussions came with Christopher Cannon's discovery of a new and different version of a release that Champain made to Chaucer on the same day, May 1, 1380.[1] I wish to review some of Cannon's findings here and to offer further considerations, especially on the various ranges of meanings that were given to the term *raptus* in fourteenth-century England, in the hopes of throwing additional light on the episode and clarifying or expanding its hermeneutic possibilities.

Professor Cannon informs me that many readers of his article have come to the mistaken conclusion that he has proved that Chaucer sexually violated Cecily Champain. His actual conclusion is only that Champain released Chaucer from a charge of sexual violation. I will conclude below that Cannon is probably correct, even though his argument may have to be qualified to some extent, especially with regard to the meaning of *raptus* in legal settings. As we will see, the term was used to mean not only sexual rape but also abduction, short for "ravishing and abducting," sometimes in circumstances where there is no possibility of sexual implications, as when referring to the kidnapping of a male heir.

After reviewing the Champain releases and considering various interpretations of *raptus*, we will discuss ways in which charges of *raptus* were employed, sometimes for different purposes. That is, we will see

[1] Christopher Cannon, "*Raptus* in the Chaumpaigne Release and a Newly Discovered Document Concerning the Life of Geoffrey Chaucer," *Speculum* 68 (1993): 74–94. I am grateful to Professor Cannon (recently my colleague at UCLA) for discussing all aspects of the case with me and for helping me in various ways, including dealing with the Public Record Office at a distance. I am also grateful to Brigette Bedos-Rezak, Paul Brand, and Charles Donahue, Jr., for their very helpful advice on this study.

instances in which sexual violation or abduction, with or without forced sex, was alleged without any basis in fact, but simply in order to get other grievances, real ones, into court. On the other side, we will see that when there was a factual basis to the *raptus* charge, a fictitious charge of another kind was sometimes brought against the culprit, notably that of assault, regularly characterized as a savage beating that left the victim barely clinging to life. We will be particularly interested in the options that various kinds of females (underage wards, mature wards, those who owned their own marriage-rights, married women, widows) had in acting against men who wronged them.

My objective is not to come to any definitive solutions, which is not yet possible with the present gaps in our knowledge, but to move the discussion forward and to call for further research in the abundant unstudied archives of the law, following Cannon's admirable example.

I. Cecily With and Without *Raptus meus*

First let us summarize the bare facts of the Champain-Chaucer case and some of their implications. On May 4, 1380, Cecily Champain, identifying herself as "late the daughter of William Champain and his wife Agnes" ("filia quondam[2] Willelmi Chaumpaigne et Agnetis uxoris ejus"), came to Chancery to enroll a document (*scriptum*) stating that on May 1 she released Geoffrey Chaucer from all actions concerning her "rape" (*raptus*) and any other cause. Besides this copy of the release, three other documents seemingly connected with the episode have long been known; they too are enrollment copies, this time from the court of the mayor of London, and, to accept Theodore Plucknett's interpretation, they deal with friends of Chaucer who helped to finance a monetary settlement to Champain. On June 28, 1380, the cutler Richard Goodchild and the armorer John Grove released Chaucer from all actions of law that they had against him, and on the same day Champain similarly released Goodchild and Grove from all actions that she had against them. Four days later, on July 2, Grove acknowledged that he owed Champain ten pounds, payable at Michaelmas.[3] Martin Crow and Clair Olson, the editors of *Chaucer Life-Records*, conclude:

[2] For a discussion in 1330 of the meaning of *quondam*, see Donald W. Sutherland, ed., *The Eyre of Northamptonshire*, vol. 2, Selden Society [hereafter SS] vol. 98 (London, 1983), pp. 568–70.

[3] T. F. T. Plucknett, "Chaucer's Escapade," *Law Quarterly Review* 64 (1948): 34. Plucknett is commenting on P. R. Watts, "The Strange Case of Geoffrey Chaucer and Cecilia Chaumpaigne," *Law Quarterly Review* 63 (1947): 491–515.

No more is known as to the nature of this *raptus* than is contained in the records just given, nor have any additional records clarifying the case come to light. Two theories have been advanced to explain the situation: (1) that it was a case of physical rape or seduction; (2) that it concerned the kidnapping or abduction of a young person, possibly in order to make an advantageous marriage. According to either theory Chaucer could have been a principal or an accessory.[4]

As noted above, Christopher Cannon has made a major contribution to our understanding of this episode by discovering another quitclaim that Champain made to Chaucer: on May 7 she came to the Court of King's Bench[5] with a *scriptum* that she asserted was a release made to Chaucer on May 1. This document, however, does not mention her *raptus* but gives only a vague reference to various kinds of charges or actions. Specifically, in place of *omnimodas acciones tam de raptu meo tam de aliqua alia re vel causa* ("all kinds of actions not only concerning my rape but also concerning any other matter or cause"), there are these words: *omnimodas acciones tam de feloniis, transgressionibus, compotis, debitis quam aliis accionibus quibuscumque* ("all kinds of actions not only concerning felonies, trespasses, accounts, and debts, but also all other kinds of actions").[6]

Raptus in the sense of abduction could be charged by indictment of a (grand) jury either as a felony (a capital offense) or as a criminal trespass

[4] Martin M. Crow and Clair C. Olson, *Chaucer Life-Records* (Oxford: Clarendon Press, 1966), p. 345; Champain's release is given on p. 343, and the three other documents on pp. 344–45. In my citations of medieval Latin, French, and English I follow modern conventions for *i/j* and *u/v* and use my own capitalization and punctuation.

[5] This was the central court, usually called *Coram rege*, in the fourteenth century. The other central court, later called Common Pleas, dealt only with civil cases and private criminal cases (that is, appeals of felony), while the Crown side of the King's Bench handled criminal cases brought by the king, and the Plea side dealt not only with civil cases but also with felony appeals. See J. H. Baker, *An Introduction to English Legal History*, 3d ed. (London: Butterworths, 1990), pp. 45–46. Baker says that the name "Common Pleas" came into use only in Tudor times, but "Common Bench" can be found well before Chaucer's day. See, for instance, *Year Books of Richard II*, vol. 2, *6 Richard II (1382–1383)*, ed. Samuel E. Thorne et al. (Cambridge, Mass.: The Ames Foundation, 1996), pp. 33–34, where *Bank le Roi* is distinguished from *Comine Bank* (French) or *Communis Bancus* (Latin).

[6] Cannon, "*Raptus*," p. 89, citing PRO (Public Record Office), KB 27/477 (Easter term, 1380), m. 58d. Champain's release of Goodchild and Grove specifies *omnimodas acciones querelas et demandas tam reales quam personales* ("all kinds of actions, complaints, and demands, whether of property or person"), and Goodchild and Grove's release of Chaucer has *omnimodas acciones querelas et demandas . . . racione alicujus transgressionis convencionis contractus compoti debiti vel alterius rei cujuscumque realis vel personalis* (". . . by reason of any trespass, agreement, contract, account, debt, or any other real or personal matter"). The four formulas also differ in expressing the temporal coverage of the release; see below at n. 75.

(in later terminology, a misdemeanor). *Raptus* as abduction could also be charged as a civil trespass (a "tort," in modern terms) in a suit brought by someone who claims monetary damages (and at the same time seeks a fine for the king, enforceable by imprisonment). When *raptus* refers to a sexual offense, the victim herself could charge the alleged culprit by way of "appeal," as a felony. To my knowledge, no example has yet been found of a woman appealing sexual rape as a criminal trespass, or of suing it as a civil trespass. Though it has been asserted by John Marshall Carter that "if a woman had sexual relations with a man against her wishes, she could theoretically bring an action of trespass against the man," the single example that he gives probably has a different explanation. He describes the case thus: when an appeal of rape was brought by Margery, daughter of Emma de la Hulle, against Nicholas Whatcomb in 1248, the court found that he had carnal knowledge of her but that he did not "forcibly ravish" her; he was declared "in mercy for the trespass," and fined ten marks.[7] But it is likely that Margery originally appealed the crime as felony (with a penalty of death or mutilation), and that when her appeal was "abated" (that is, the charge was found to be deficient), the jury convicted him of a trespass, as happened in other cases of the time.[8] But in this instance, since consensual sex was only an ecclesiastical crime, punishable in the church courts, as is noted at the beginning of Chaucer's *Friar's Tale*,[9] the trespass would have to be something other than *raptus*, say, the forcible breaking of the mother's close "by force and arms" (a standard fictitious charge, as we will see).[10] When charged by way of indictment, sexual rape was usually designated a felony. However, in the quarter-session cases collected by Bertha Putnam,[11]

[7] John Marshall Carter, *Rape in Medieval England: An Historical and Sociological Study* (Lanham: University Press of America, 1985), pp. 39–40.

[8] See my "Statutes of Rapes and Alleged Ravishers of Wives: A Context for the Charges Against Thomas Malory, Knight," *Viator* 28 (1997): 361–419, esp. pp. 382–83.

[9] See my *Love and Marriage in the Age of Chaucer* (Ithaca, N.Y.: Cornell University Press, 1975), pp. 169–71. Thomas Aquinas, *Summa theologie* 2–2.69.1 ad 1, gives simple fornication as an example of a crime that is restricted only to the internal forum of confession and not a matter for the external forum; but in England, fornication was indeed prosecuted in the church courts. See my "Right to Remain Silent: Before and After Joan of Arc," *Speculum* 68 (1993): 992–1026, esp. p. 1003, n. 46.

[10] Carter's suggestion that the court reduced the charge when actual coitus could not be proved (p. 40) is belied by the record: coitus was found, but not forced coitus.

[11] Bertha Haven Putnam, *Proceedings Before the Justices of the Peace in the Fourteenth and Fifteenth Centuries* (London, 1938), with "A Commentary on the Indictments" (pp. cxxxiii–clxi) and analytical index (pp. 468–82) by Theodore F. T. Plucknett. Putnam has isolated fifty-three rolls of shire sessions of the peace from 1338 to 1475 and

there are a few examples in which words of felony were omitted—that is, the offense was charged as a trespass.[12]

Charging abduction as a felony or a trespass sometimes seems, from this distance, to be fairly arbitrary, a conclusion that Cannon reached concerning the abduction of wives in studying the court records of 3 Richard II, 1379–80.[13] A slightly later example of such apparent arbitrariness can be seen in the case of abduction that Chaucer investigated as a justice *ad inquirendum* in 1387. He and others were appointed to discover who the malefactors were who ravished and abducted Isabel, daughter and heir of William Hall, being underage and in the custody of Thomas Carshill. The jury indicted three men of the crime and declared their offense a felony: "felonice rapuerunt et abduxerunt,"[14] thus apparently going beyond the original allegation. But unless the jury was sold a complete bill of goods by Carshill, it is difficult to believe that it elevated the offense from a trespass to a felony because sexual rape was involved,[15] since one of the accused, John Lording, was Isabel's husband, and was so recognized by the King's Bench in civil suits that he brought against his accusers and others before and after he pleaded not guilty to the felony charge.[16]

printed excerpts from twenty of the rolls; and she also notes (p. lxii) that the sort of cases heard by the Justices of the Peace are identical to those that came before the Crown side of the King's Bench. For some of the formulas used in the cases under discussion, see under "Robbery: Wife and chattels," p. 473, and "Rape," p. 474.

[12] In 1357 (p. 183, no. 17)—cited by Plucknett, "Commentary," pp. clix–clx—a man designated as a common disturber of the peace was charged with abducting a female servant and forcing himself upon her: "cepit et abduxit et concubuit cum ea contra voluntatem suam et contra pacem." In a similar case from the same year and place (Somerset), the alleged victim is a widow, and there is no abduction noted (pp. 184–85, no. 26): "rapuit et cum ea concubuit contra voluntatem suam et contra pacem." In 1363, a rector (parish priest) was accused of the trespass entering a woman's property *vi et armis*, taking her and sleeping with her against the peace ("cepit et cum ea concubuit contra pacem"), with "against her will" doubtless being understood (p. 369, no. 526). Another rector was charged in 1375 (p. 119, no. 157) with the trespass of seizing a wife and forcing her against her will ("rapuit . . . et illam aforciavit contra voluntatem suam"). In 1391 (pp. 219–20, no. 35), a man was charged with the trespass of forcibly entering a house and deflowering a servant against her will ("en countre sa volunte parcocha, pargisa, et defoila") and the next night coming and taking her away to his own service against the statute (concerning the regulation of servants).

[13] Cannon, "*Raptus*," pp. 87–88.

[14] Crow and Olson, *Chaucer Life-Records*, pp. 375–76.

[15] A principle of this kind was enunciated by one of the justices of the King's Bench in 1409, *Nansegle v Vide*, Yearbook of Henry IV: *Les reports del cases en ley que furent argues en le temps de tres haut et puissant princes, les roys Henry le IV et Henry le V* (London, 1689; rpt., Oxford: Professional Books, 1981), year 11, p. 13; see Kelly, "Statutes of Rapes," pp. 397, 410–12.

[16] Crow and Olson, *Chaucer Life-Records*, pp. 379–81.

In a case earlier in the decade involving Ralph Percy, the brother of Henry Hotspur, commissioners of oyer and terminer were instructed to investigate and judge a ravishing-and-abducting case both as a felony and as a misdemeanor: on February 15, 1384, they were appointed to hear and determine a trespass alleged in a complaint by Percy against John Halsham, namely, ravishing his wife Philippa and abducting her with goods and chattels worth £3,000, and on the next day the same commissioners were appointed to find out what malefactors and breakers of the peace feloniously ravished Philippa, wife of Ralph Percy, knight, and abducted her with Percy's goods and chattels.[17] Like Lording, Halsham was revealed to be the current husband of the allegedly abducted woman.[18]

As noted, ravishing-abducting could be prosecuted not only as a (criminal) felony or a criminal trespass but also as a civil trespass. This is illustrated by Lording's civil suits, and, contrary to what we might conclude from the felony charge delivered by Chaucer's jury, it was also the common procedure in wardship kidnappings.[19] Only one explicit case of ward abduction is to be found in Putnam's criminal rolls: an indictment for ravishing, taking, and abducting an underage male ward; and it is not charged as a felony.[20] But though wardship pleas "sounded in tort rather than crime," as Sue Sheridan Walker puts it in modern terms,[21] there is nevertheless a criminal element in the charge, an allegation that the violence was *contra pacem domini regis*, though not prosecuted as such. This was true also of many other kinds of civil trespass cases, as can be seen in Morris Arnold's collection.[22] However, there was a principle enunciated in 1339 by William Shareshull, a justice of the

[17] PRO, C66/317, m. 20d, recorded in reverse order; briefly summarized in *Calendar of Patent Rolls {CPR}: Richard II*, 2:423–24; for a fuller summary, see *Calendar of the Close Rolls {CCR}*, 2:452: two writs of *Supersedeas* issued on May 28, 1384, suspending the commissions (PRO, C54/224, m. 2d). For published calendars of documents in the PRO, see E. L. C. Mullins, *Texts and Calendars: An Analytical Guide to Serial Publications*, 2 vols. (London: Royal Historical Society, 1978–83), 1:16–36, 2:3–12: Public Record Office Texts and Calendars.

[18] For more on the Percy abduction, see below, and for both Lording and Percy cases, see Kelly, "Statutes of Rapes," pp. 403–7.

[19] See Sue Sheridan Walker, "Wrongdoing and Compensation: The Pleas of Wardship in Thirteenth and Fourteenth Century England," *Journal of Legal History* 9 (1988): 267–307, esp. 286–90.

[20] Putnam, *Proceedings*, pp. 71–72, n.138 (1352).

[21] Walker, "Wrongdoing," p. 268.

[22] Morris S. Arnold, *Select Cases of Trespass from the King's Courts, 1307–1399*, 2 vols., SS, vols. 100, 103 (London, 1985–87).

King's Bench, speaking about a case of an abducted wife, that the Crown had the option of considering a civil trespass conviction to be a felony indictment.[23] It was not always easy to distinguish between criminal and civil actions.[24] We can perhaps be fairly sure that only criminal cases were heard by the justices of the peace (Putnam's cases), and we should be able to presume that only civil trespasses and private crimes (appeals of felony) were heard by the Court of Common Pleas. But in 1382, William Skipwith, one of the justices of Common Pleas, said that since the word *rapuit* ("ravished," "raped") in the writ *De uxore rapta* "sounded in felony," such cases should not be heard by Common Pleas but only by King's Bench.[25] This shows not only that the line between civil and criminal cases of abduction was hard to draw, but also that borderline felony cases were being heard by Common Pleas, and that, since Skipwith's fellow-justices overruled him,[26] the practice continued.

The "accounts" and "debts" mentioned in the May 7 version of the release could refer only to civil and not to criminal charges. Plucknett, in his comment on the May 4 version of the release—which, of course, was the only one he knew—concludes, for reasons to be discussed below, that the *raptus* in question could only be sexual rape, but nevertheless he also concludes that her advisers (who seem to have been skilled) believed that she had a civil remedy for rape, and that her release was a bar to it.[27] But this leaves the question unanswered, he says, of how such a civil release might affect criminal remedies, or whether one could simultaneously bring criminal and civil actions. According to Plucknett, the modern law on the matter goes back only to the seventeenth century, but E. W. Ives cites an interesting abduction case only a century after Chaucer's time, in 1502, which may be relevant in showing what actions a woman well connected with the legal profession could take.

The case is as follows. A twenty-five-year-old widow, Margaret Kebell, was abducted and forced to marry one of her abductors, Roger Vernon, whereupon her relatives secured a commission in London ordering investigations and arrests in Staffordshire, and they also laid

[23] *Year Books of the Reign of King Edward III*, Rolls Series, 31b, vol. 3, p. 65. See J. B. Post, "Sir Thomas West and the Statute of Rapes, 1382," *Bulletin of the Institute of Historical Research* 53 (1980): 24–30, esp. p. 25.

[24] See S. F. C. Milsom, "Trespass from Henry III to Edward III," *Law Quarterly Review* 74 (1958): 195–224, 407–36, 561–90, pp. 197 and 584–85.

[25] *Year Books of Richard II*, 2:33.

[26] Ibid., 2:33–34.

[27] Plucknett, "Chaucer's Escapade," p. 35.

information at various quarter sessions (presided over by justices of the peace). After indictments were presented and trials resulted in acquittals, the widow herself appealed her abductors of rape in two counties, and she also pursued several civil actions for trespass in King's Bench and in Common Pleas.[28]

The Staffordshire indictments of March 16, 1502, accused Vernon and his associates of feloniously breaking the close of William Basset with the intention of feloniously ravishing and abducting Margaret, and of actually feloniously ravishing her and taking and abducting her against her will by main force, and feloniously assaulting Basset.[29] An earlier Staffordshire indictment, of February 21, 1502, charged the designated perpetrators with breaking Basset's close, assaulting Margaret to near death, feloniously ravishing her and abducting and carrying her away against her will, and also feloniously taking away £100 of her goods and chattels; the breaking and entering is then counted as a felony, added to which is an assault on Basset, likewise to within an inch of his life.[30] The Derbyshire indictments of March 17, 1502, made accusations of congregating with force and arms at Thorp and causing great terror against the statute on riots and routs, and of

[28] E. W. Ives, "'Agaynst taking awaye of Women': The Inception and Operation of the Abduction Act of 1487," in *Wealth and Power in Tudor England: Essays Presented to S. T. Bindoff*, ed. E. W. Ives et al. (London: Athlone Press, 1978), pp. 21–44, esp. pp. 33–38. By the act of 3 Henry VII (1487), accomplices to the "taking away" of women could be charged as principals. The statute avoids the ambiguous words "ravish" and "ravishment" (see "Statutes of Rapes," pp. 376–77), but the court records continue to use the standard terms, *rapere* and *raptus*.

[29] PRO, KB 9/425 no. 29; KB 27/966 (Hilary term, 1503) Rex (at the end of the roll), m. 6; repeated in KB 27/981 (Michaelmas term, 1506), m. 109.1d (= dorso side of first of four membranes), when Richard Bargh and other defendants cite it (and their acquittal) as part of their defense against Margaret's appeal: according to the indictment, over 200 named and unnamed persons "vi et armis clausum et domos Willielmi Bassett armigeri apud Blore in comitatu Staff. noctanter ac burgulariter et felonice fregerunt et intravenerunt ad intencionem felonice rapiendi et abducendi Margaretam Kebell viduam ibidem existentem, et eandem Margaretam adtunc et ibidem inventam felonice rapuerunt et ipsam Margaretam adtunc et ibidem contra voluntatem suam manuforte abinde ceperunt et abduxerunt, et super predictum Willielmum Bassett adtunc et ibidem insultum fecerunt et ipsum maletractaverunt ita quod de vita ejus disperabatur, contra pacem dicti Domini regis, coronam, et dignitatem suas" ["by force and arms broke the close and homes of William Basset, esquire, at Blore in County Stafford by night and like burglars and feloniously, and entered with the intention of feloniously ravishing and abducting Margaret Kebell, widow, who was staying there, and the same Margaret being found then and there they did ravish, and did take her there and abduct her thence against her will by main force, and upon the said William Basset then and there they did make assault and did maltreat him so that his life was despaired of, against the peace of the lord king and his crown and dignity"].

[30] KB 9/426 no. 11 (Roger Vernon and others); KB 27/966, mm. 6–6d (Richard Bargh and others). The latter record goes on to relate that the king called in the indictments in

assaulting Margaret Kebell such that her life was despaired of, and of feloniously taking and ravishing her against her will and abducting her to *le Peek* in Derbyshire, against the recent statute.[31] A Leicestershire indictment of March 28, 1502, specifies riotous assault upon Margaret and felonious ravishing and abducting of her, against the recent statute, and it charges William Vernon with knowingly receiving the felons at Netherscheyll.[32] Another Leicestershire indictment, of October 3, 1502, accuses Roger Vernon and others of assaulting Margaret at Netherscheyll and feloniously ravishing and abducting her against the recent statute, and William Vernon of receiving them.[33]

On June 17, 1502, Margaret submitted a bill to the king's council: "To prove William Vernon, brother to Sir Henry Vernon, knight, guilty of felous taking and ravishment of Margaret Kebell, widow, and of the felous receiving by the said William Vernon of Roger Vernon and divers other parties privy to the ravishment." In the interrogatories that follow, "taking away" and "ravishment" are used as synonyms both interchangeably and together (by way of "indenture English").[34] Margaret does not refer to sexual interference or forced marriage, either in her bill or in her response to the statement of William Vernon.[35]

On December 9, 1503, Vernon and 109 others were pardoned of "all trespasses, congregations, burglaries and misdeeds for the taking, abduction, or rape" [*capcio, abduccio, vel raptus*] of Margaret Kebell.[36] On March 23, 1504, Vernon was required to give heavy surety to keep the peace toward Margaret, pledging to do no harm to her and specifically promising not to abduct her or cause her to be abducted without her consent ("et preterea quod idem Rogerus absque consensu et assensu ejusdem Margarete ipsam non abducet nec abduci faciet").[37]

January of 1503, and in Michaelmas term the four named defendants (Richard Bargh and three others) were acquitted. In KB 27/969 (Michaelmas 1503) Rex, m. 3 similar indictments of March 16 and February 21 are given against Thomas Folijamb, who is also acquitted.

31 KB 9/425 no. 34 (a supplementary indictment says that they led her further into Derbyshire and finally out of the county, to unknown parts); KB 27/969 Rex, m. 3d.

32 KB 9/426 no. 7.

33 KB 9/437 no. 10.

34 Printed by I. S. Leadam, *Select Cases Before the King's Council in the Star Chamber*, SS, vol. 16 (London, 1903), pp. 130–37, along with related materials (cf. pp. cx–cxiv) from PRO STAC 1/19/17, 1–3.

35 PRO, STAC 2/25/68.

36 *CPR Henry VII*, 2:336–337; the pardon is submitted as a defense in KB 27/990 (Hilary term, 1509) Rex m. 13.1d (see below).

37 PRO, C 244/153 no. 117 (no. 118 is identical).

Margaret's appeal accuses the culprits of premeditated assault against the king's peace and feloniously taking and abducting her, and she states that immediately after the said felons committed the said felony and rape they fled, and she in timely manner pursued them from vill to vill (in accord with the standard formula).[38] But most records simply specify her appeal as one of rape (*de raptu ipsius Margarete*).[39]

As for the civil suits, one of the King's Bench cases is at an advanced stage and therefore unspecific, referring only to Margaret's plea of trespass against Henry Crichelowe.[40] But another is a standard plea of assault, wounding, and imprisonment, brought against one Ralph Wheledon of Doweall in co. Derby.[41] He is number 48 and Crichelowe
* is number 105 of the men named in the pardon.[42] In Keilwey's report of the Common Pleas case, which he refers to simply as a trespass plea, he says that when Vernon tried to invoke spousal privilege, Margaret

[38] KB 27/981 (Michaelmas term, 1506), m. 109.1, gives a complete rehearsal of her appeal. The defendants are to answer "de raptu ipsius Margarete et pace domini regis nunc fracte unde eos appellat." She says that when she was in the peace of God and the king on February 1, 1502, at Blore at the sixth hour of the morning, the defendants "felonice ut felones . . . insidiando et insultu premeditato contra pacem ejusdem domini regis . . . predictam Margaretam Kebell . . . contra voluntatem suam vi et armis [the arms are specified] illicite et felonice ceperunt et abduxerunt contra pacem, coronam, et dignitatem dicti domini regis ac contra formam statuti ejusdem domini regis anno regni suo tercio apud Westmonasterium inde editi et provisi; et quam cito iidem felones feloniam et raptum predictos in forma predicta fecissent, fugierunt; eciamque Margareta ipsos recenter insecuta fuit de villa in villam usque quatuor villatas propinquiores et ulterius, quousque, etc." ["feloniously as felons . . . by way of ambush and premeditated assault upon the peace of the same lord king . . . the aforesaid Margaret against her will by force and arms . . . they did unlawfully and feloniously take and abduct against the peace, crown, and dignity of the said lord king and against the form of the statute of the same lord king issued and provided on this matter at Westminster in the third year of his reign; and as soon as the same felons had committed the aforesaid felony and rape, they fled; and likewise Margaret in timely fashion pursued them from town to town through the four nearest townships, whitherever, etc."].

[39] KB 27/979 (Easter 1506), mm. 44, 50–50d; 27/980 (Trinity 1506), mm. 65–65d; 27/983 (Easter 1507), m. 29d; 27/984 (Trinity 1507), m. 26; 27/987 (Easter 1508), m. 27d; 27/988 (Trinity 1508), m. 20.

[40] KB 27/983 (Easter 1507), m. 17.

[41] KB 27/987 (Easter 1508), m. 48: "de placito quare vi et armis in ipsam Margaretam apud Blore insultum prebuit et ipsam verberavit, vulneravit, imprisonavit, et maletractavit, ita quod de vita ejus desperabatur, et alia enormia, etc., ad grave dampnum, etc., et contra pacem domini regis nunc, etc." ["concerning a plea why he made assault upon her at Blore and beat, wounded, imprisoned, and ill-treated her such that her life was despaired of, and other enormities, etc., to the grave harm, etc., and against the peace of the lord king now, etc."]. Ives says there is another case on m. 40, but none appears there or in the vicinity. On m. 45, however, there is an entry referring to the Wheledon case.

[42] Wheledon's town is given in the pardon as Dowell, as in KB 27/979 (Easter 1506), m. 50, where *Roger* Wheledon is no. 50 of the 90 defendants in Margaret's appeal of rape.

responded by saying that the marriage was against her will, and occurred only after threats and harsh imprisonment, and she sought damages.[43] It is clear that she brought up the circumstances of her forced marriage in order to bar Vernon's privilege, but these circumstances may also have been the substance of her complaint. In the event, Vernon's defense was accepted by the justices of the Common Bench: Margaret was to be regarded as Vernon's wife until a Church court said otherwise.[44] Margaret eventually shook off Vernon's marital claims, while continuing her campaign to punish her kidnappers;[45] she obtained a dispensation to marry Ralph Egerton, and became the grandmother of Lord Ellesmere,[46] whose manuscript of Chaucer we all know about.

We see, then, that Margaret used both criminal and civil actions for assault, and she could have added civil suits to the criminal accusation of taking and carrying away goods. Other possible actions of civil trespass which could conceivably be taken in connection with sexual attack and abduction are (to draw on Arnold's categories): threats, besetting, and false imprisonment.

When Plucknett says, "Although compounding a felony was a crime, compounding a trespass was probably not,"[47] we should note that compounding felonies (agreeing with the accused criminal not to prosecute, or to withdraw from prosecution, in return for a consideration of some sort) does not seem to have been criminalized as yet in Chaucer's time,

[43] Robert Keilwey, *Reports d'ascuns cases qui ont evenus aux temps du roy Henry le septième* (London, 1688), fols. 52v–53, rpt. in *The English Reports*, 171 vols. (Edinburgh: W. Green, 1900–1930), 72:210–11.

[44] Ives, "'Agaynst taking awaye,'" pp. 38–39.

[45] Ives did not continue his search for records beyond the death of Henry VII in April of 1509. The last of the documents cited is KB 27/990 (Hilary 1509) Rex, mm. 13.1–13.2: the Staffordshire and Derbyshire indictments of 1502 are put to Richard Forman and others and they plead the pardon of December 9, 1503, for all crimes committed in the *capcio, abduccio, vel raptus* of Margaret Kebell, and also produce a writ dated February 1, 1509, ordering no interference with the pardon. But since the pardon did not cover the charge of taking the £100, they were ordered to stand trial on it a month after Easter. *

[46] Ives, "'Agaynst taking awaye,'" pp. 33, 43. Ives says that Egerton was her uncle, that is, her mother's half-brother, but the dispensation was for the third and fourth degrees of consanguinity, making them second cousins once removed. See *Historical Manuscripts Commission, Eleventh Report, Appendix, Part VII* (London, 1888), p. 137: dispensation of June 11, 1509, for Ralph "Eggerton" and Margaret "Rebyll." I should note that the uncle-niece relationship was not prohibited by the levitical degrees and so, at least by this time, would have been easier to dipense than, say, nephew and uncle's wife, but it would still have required special action in Rome. See my "Canonical Implications of Richard III's Plan to Marry His Niece," *Traditio* 23 (1967): 269–311.

[47] Plucknett, "Chaucer's Escapade," p. 35.

but only subject to a fine. At any rate, Cannon's new document seems to show Champain compounding felonies as well as trespasses.

J. B. Post says that in the previous century, before the Westminster statutes of 1275 and 1285, many defendants who were charged with rape (which he defines as forced coitus, sometimes connected with abduction)[48] "concorded with the appellatrixes, either by financial compensation or by marriage."[49] Post sees the situation as changed, at least theoretically, after 1285, when the woman's subsequent consent left the wrongdoer open to Crown prosecution. But the Westminster statutes seem to have been intended to deal primarily with abduction, with or without sexual violation, and they were certainly interpreted in this way in the fourteenth century.[50] It may be, then, that the earlier arrangements concerning appeals of sexual rape continued as before. Withdrawal of appeal would ordinarily entail Crown punishment or fine. For instance, in 1375, a widow named Matilda or Maud Cantilupe withdrew, with a fine, from an appeal of the murder of her husband, leaving the Crown to prosecute the same charge by indictment.[51] Punishment was also forthcoming to the appellant if the appeal was found defective, but the failed appellant nevertheless had the option of prosecuting the felony by grand jury. Furthermore, we see a lot of compromising in the fifteenth century, which Christopher Whittick sees as part of a gradual evolution from the beginning of the fourteenth century.[52]

Another consideration, as we will see, is that a felony could be pardoned by the king as far as the offense against his peace was concerned, with the implication that the aggrieved citizen could similarly pardon the personal offense (even if liable to a fine). If, however, after having promised Chaucer that she would not pursue criminal or civil actions against him, Champain went ahead and did so, Plucknett believes that Chaucer could have used her release only to impede civil cases, since it is "difficult to believe that the release diminished her

[48] J. B. Post, "Ravishment of Women and the Statutes of Westminster," in *Legal Records and the Historian*, ed. J. H. Baker (London: Royal Historical Society, 1978), pp. 150–64, esp. p. 158.

[49] Post, "Sir Thomas West," p. 24.

[50] Kelly, "Statutes of Rapes," pp. 391–95.

[51] G. O. Sayles, *Select Cases in the Court of the King's Bench*, vol. 6, SS, vol. 82 (London, 1965), pp. 174–75. For two other such cases, see ibid., 6:154–56 (1368); 7:215–17 (1413).

[52] Christopher Whittick, "The Role of the Criminal Appeal in the Fifteenth Century," in *Law and Social Change in British History*, ed. J. A. Guy and H. G. Beale (London: Royal Historical Society, 1984), pp. 55–72, esp. pp. 63–64, 71.

criminal remedies."[53] But we are told that releases were sometimes pleaded in response to appeals, and there is record of a widow receiving £20 as compensation for a royal pardon in 1360.[54] We can deduce that this latter was a case in which Milicent, widow of John Waryn of Lockesley, appealed the knight Thomas Shirley of her husband's death; the pardon he received from the king had the standard formula, "Ita tamen quod stet recto," etc. (that is, "So that however he should stand trial in our court if anyone should wish to speak against him concerning the aforesaid death"). The £20 was paid to the widow in two installments, and she executed two receipts, which Shirley kept in his possession, along with the pardon.[55]

Plucknett assumes that the Champain charge dealt with forced coitus because "if only abduction had been involved, then the release would have proceeded from the injured party, viz., the feudal lord, parent, husband or employer of Cecilia."[56] But a case of 1362 shows a woman, Joan, who had been the wife of Nicholas Hotoft, bringing a complaint on her own against Henry Willows and others on a charge of criminal trespass for forcibly entering her close and imprisoning her.[57] That her accusation was one of abduction becomes clear the next year, when another commission of oyer and terminer was set up to investigate her emended complaint. Now she specifies that after she was imprisoned she was taken to unknown places until she swore to marry Henry; and she also alleges that Henry and his accomplices had carried away her goods and assaulted her men and servants. This time she is not identified as having been the wife of Nicholas Hotoft, but simply as Joan Hoto[f]t.[58]

The complaints (*querele*) of Joan Hotoft may have been in the form of "bills." An interesting example of such can be seen in Putnam for 1362,

[53] Plucknett, "Chaucer's Escapade," p. 35.

[54] Whittick, "Role of the Criminal Appeal," p. 64. Whittick cites the 1360 case as a meager exception to the fact that the releases are never recited and that there is little evidence of their content. He also mentions a case around 1500 in which a master whose apprentice had beaten a child to death exacted "a release from the mother by means of imprisonment on a feigned plea of trespass" (p. 64). He cites another case in 1469 in which widows were forced to agree to make appeals and not to execute releases (p. 68).

[55] The letter of pardon and the two receipts are noted in the *Fifth Report of the Royal Commission on Historical Manuscripts* (London, 1876), p. 369, but Whittick says that the Shirley manuscript collection was later broken up and the three documents recorded in the *Report* have not been traced.

[56] Plucknett, "Chaucer's Escapade," p. 35.

[57] *CPR, Edward III*, 12:288: October 25, 1362; text of original, PRO, C 66/266 m. 20d, below, appendix, no. 1.

[58] *CPR, Edward III*, 12:363: May 2, 1363; text of PRO, C 66/267m. 22d in appendix, no. 2.

in which Alice Lord complained against Geoffrey Wolmonger and John Causton for coming to her by force and arms and demanding that she marry Geoffrey. When she refused, Geoffrey took her by force against her will ("la prist afforce en countre son gre") and threw her on a horse behind John, whereupon she fell to the ground and received such injury that she could not work or walk for two weeks afterwards; then the two men took her ("lamenerunt") to some woods, stopped her cries, and hurt her so much that she was all bloody. The indicting jury found that the things alleged in this bill were true ("in ista billa infrascripta sunt vera") and charged it as a trespass.[59]

In a case of 1379, a woman named Idonia Cophyn, not further identified, simply obtained a writ against Henry Aleyn of Colbrok, who was required by the king to appear before him "to show why with force and arms he took, imprisoned, and maltreated the said Idonia in the parish of St. Clement Without the Bar of the New Temple of London and inflicted other enormities upon her to her grave harm and against our peace."[60]

In a 1364 document we hear of a case of abduction in which the woman is identified only as someone's daughter (like Cecilia Champain), even though it turns out later in the narrative that she was married, or at least had been married at the time. Hugh Bonehomme of Bugthorp is pardoned for a number of offenses, including having abducted, with the help of accomplices, "Agnes, daughter of John Giles of York, and by coercion and threats made her consent to contract an unjust marriage with Simon Porter, and of having carried away goods of Thomas Gilling, then husband of the said Agnes"; the abduction is referred to later in the pardon as a "rape" (*raptus*).[61] A widow or "annulled wife" would presumably have more call to act for herself than a currently married woman, whether or not she owned her own "maritage" (*maritagium*) or marriage-right. (When women's husbands died, their right to remarry reverted to the king or to other feudal lords, but

[59] Putnam, *Proceedings*, p. 344, no. 68; see Plucknett, "Commentary," p. clviii.

[60] PRO, KB 136/5/3/1/2, first of the Middlesex writs for the octave of Martinmas. The writ is addressed to the sheriff, who, if Idonia gives him security for pursuing her claim, is to have Henry produce pledges for his appearance before the king, "ostendendum quare vi et armis ipsam Idoniam apud parochiam sancti Clementis extra barram Novi Templi London. cepit, imprisonavit, et male tractavit et alia enormia ei intulit ad grave dampnum ipsius Idonie et contra pacem nostram." Dated October 22, 1379.

[61] *CPR, Edward III*, 12:515: May 6, 1364; text of PRO, C 66/267 n. 7, in appendix, no. 3.

normally widows were able to marry whomever they wished on payment of a fine.)[62]

A similar complaint could conceivably be brought by an unmarried woman—even an heiress who had come of age, if she had purchased her maritage from her guardian.[63] Such a woman could be in her twenties or older, as would be the case of Cecily Champneys, daughter of the baker William Champneys and his wife Agnes, who was left 20*s*. by her father in 1360.[64] If the William Champayne whose seal survives from 1354 was Cecily's father, she may have used the same or a similar seal,[65] just as Thomas Chaucer used his father's seal in 1409.

Cannon says that since the original release of May 1 no longer exists (or has not been found), we do not know which of the two memoranda corresponds more closely to it. He leans toward the hypothesis that the May 4 version is the authentic one, and that Champain was persuaded to suppress the term *raptus*,[66] but this may not be a plausible solution. Let us assume that the preparation or at least reading of the original document of quitclaim was observed by the named witnesses on May 1 and then sealed by Champain with her seal, as stated in both May 4 and May 7 enrollments. The May 1 original could not have passed into Chaucer's possession on May 1 if it was to be used on May 4 and again on May 7 for the enrollments, unless Chaucer gave it back to Champain temporarily when she went to Chancery and to the King's Bench. Such maneuverings would not be necessary if the release were an indenture, with the text copied twice on the same membrane and half given to each party; but if this were the case, it would undoubtedly say so in the text, and the text would also say that Chaucer used his seal as well. Chaucer

[62] Sue Sheridan Walker, "Free Consent and Marriage of Feudal Wards in Medieval England," *Journal of Medieval History* 8 (1982): 123–34, esp. p. 126.

[63] See Walker, "Wrongdoing," pp. 292–93, 296. See pp. 289–90, for the case of an abducted male ward in 1378, whose *maritagium* was assessed by a jury at £10—though in this case the ward was recovered unmarried—while additional damages were set at £10. Cf. the £10 that John Grove owed to Cecily Champain.

[64] Crow and Olson, *Chaucer Life-Records*, p. 346.

[65] Roger H. Ellis, *Catalogue of Seals in the Public Record Office: Personal Seals*, vol. 2 (London, 1981), p. 23, entry P 1179. The seal has a shield of arms bearing "three bells and a lion passant in chief." Two other seals of persons named Champain exist from the fourteenth century, those of Margery [dame] de Chaumpaigne of county Kent, from 1336, and Ralph Chaumpayn of Cotton Manor, Suffolk, from 1367. See W. de G. Birch, *Catalogue of Seals in the Department of Manuscripts in the British Museum*, 2 (London: Trustees of the British Museum, 1892), pp. 629–30, nos. 8503–5. I am grateful to Brigette Bedos-Rezak for these references.

[66] Cannon, "*Raptus*," pp. 91–93.

executed an indenture of this kind with Roger Elmham in 1389; Elmham's original "counterpart" still exists in the Exchequer records, and so do the enrollments made by both Elmham and Chaucer.[67] Needless to say, one or other of the enrollments differs in minor ways from the original and the other enrollment (harder to explain are a couple of readings in which both enrollments agree against the original).[68]

Cannon rightly argues that the differences in the Champain enrollments could not be the result of careless copying. We should also reject the notion that Cecily did not have the original release when she went to the two courts but simply described the transaction to the clerk in charge of each office. The purpose of such enrollments was to provide an authentic copy of a document, which could not be done simply on someone's say-so. For the same reason she could hardly have altered the original release after May 4 by having some words erased and bulkier words squeezed in at one point and, at another point, erasing the names of two of the five witnesses and substituting *& aliis*, and expected it to be accepted for enrollment by the King's Bench.[69] It would also have been risky to forge the whole document anew, especially since she had already enrolled the original text in Chancery. It would have destroyed its value for use in court if the three named witnesses were summoned and interrogated separately about "the making, sealing, the time and the place, the manner and time, and the other necessary circumstances surrounding the said deed," including "the substance of the making of the said writing," as specified in a 1318 case in which a release was at issue—and failed to pass muster.[70]

The notion that the five witnesses were regathered some time between May 4 and May 7 and asked to witness a new or emended deed of release that still stated the date of May 1 does not seem very likely. More plausible is the possibility that Cecily Champain created two instruments of release on May 1, perhaps dealing with two different affairs or purposes: one was specifically connected with her *raptus*, which she registered at Chancery, and the other, which did

[67] Crow and Olson, *Chaucer Life-Records*, pp. 406–8.

[68] Ibid., p. 406: both enrollments omit *non depicte* (n. 8); both add *magna* (n. 9). In n. 6, the enrollments have *scomour* ("skimmer") for *soudour* ("solder") among the plumber's implements, but this could be a coincidence; both plumbing items appear further down in the original, under the manor of Eltham (p. 408).

[69] For examples of releases rejected in court because of bad Latin, erasures, and overwriting, see *Le second part de les reports des cases en ley que furent argues en le temps de . . . Roy Edward le tierce* (London, 1679), 24 Edward III (1350), pp. 35, 73–74.

[70] *Reynham v Hatton*, Arnold, no. 4.3 (a case of false imprisonment), p. 40. See below, at n. 164.

not require mention of *raptus*, was registered at the King's Bench.[71]

In any case, it remains probable that Cecily Champain had brought, or threatened to bring, a complaint of *raptus* against Geoffrey Chaucer. According to the summary of the *Life-Records* cited above, Chaucer could have been charged with one of four offenses:

1) Principal perpetrator in a case of forced sexual intercourse.
2) Accessory in such a case.
3) Principal abductor.
4) Accessory to an abduction.

Let us add two more possibilities:

5) Principal in an abduction that involved forced coitus.
6) Accessory in such a case.

Inspiration for these last two categories comes from the further documentation that Cannon provides in the course of his article.

As far as the abduction categories are concerned, we should note that Chaucer could have been a principal abductor of Cecily Champain even though he himself could hardly have intended to marry her, since he is on record in 1381 as still being married to Philippa.[72] We must remember that his own father, John Chaucer, was abducted around 1325 by a woman who wanted him to marry not her but her daughter. The abductor was his aunt, Agnes Westhale, who, along with her accomplice Geoffrey Stace (later her second husband), seized him in an effort to marry him to her daughter Joan. This scheme must have been doomed to failure from the beginning, not only because John was at least two years below the canonical age of valid marriage for boys, namely, fourteen, but also because a papal dispensation to marry his first cousin would have been virtually impossible to obtain for persons of their standing.[73] The culprits were reportedly fined £250 in 1330, but

[71] Paul Brand informs me that it was quite common to make several releases on one occasion, which were not necessarily identical.

[72] Crow and Olson, *Chaucer Life-Records*, p. 77.

[73] Dispensations of this sort (in the second degree of consanguinity) do not seem to have been given even to royalty at this date. Later in the century, Edward III's son Prince Edward was given a dispensation for a slightly lower degree (second degree mixed with third) when he was allowed to marry his first cousin once removed, Joan of Kent. See Karl P. Wentersdorf, "The Clandestine Marriages of the Fair Maid of Kent," *Journal of Medieval History* 5 (1979): 203–31, esp. pp. 217, 223; and see also my "Shades of Incest and Cuckoldry: Pandarus and John of Gaunt," *SAC* 13 (1991): 121–40, esp. pp. 128–29. Of course, the problem would not arise if Joan were only the stepdaughter of Agnes; perhaps Crow and Olson are suggesting this possibility when they identify Joan as "the daughter of Walter de Westhall" (p. 372, n. 1) rather than as "the daughter of Walter

this amount seems too great and may be a mistake, since the tenements of young John were valued at no more than 20*s.* a year.[74]

Both texts of Champain's release(s) of Chaucer, as well as Champain's release of Goodchild and Grove and Goodchild and Grove's release of Chaucer, express the temporal coverage of the respective release in slightly different ways, but all have the equivalent clauses limiting it to all actions in the past, present, and future perfect up to the day of making the document (*quas . . . habere potero . . . usque in diem confeccionis presencium*; "which I shall be able to have up to the day of the confection of the presents"). The future clause is not saying much, since it literally refers only to a small window of opportunity, a matter of hours or days, between the oral agreement and the witnessed sealing of the written version. However, such agreements did not propose to forgo all future actions of whatever sort, but rather to abandon all actions concerning events that may have occurred in the past up to the present. In other words, there were to be no new filings of old quarrels. We will see below an example of a release of ravishment accepted in court as a sufficient response to a civil plea of ravishment.[75]

II. *Raptus* and "Rape" in Law and Literature

Cannon cites documents to support his view that when there is a clear case of abduction only, the words *rapere et abducere* are used together, whereas in cases of forced coitus *raptus* is used alone. To judge from his examples, the active forms of the verb *rapere*, especially the perfect tense, *rapuit*, when used alone, would also seem to be limited to forced coitus. He does acknowledge that the past participle *raptus/rapta* is used to refer to abduction alone, as in the writs *De herede rapto* ("Concerning an abducted heir"—note the masculine form) and *De uxore rapta*, dealing with a charge that someone seized and abducted (*rapuit et abduxit*)

---

and Agnes de Westhall" (p. 3). Derek Pearsall treats the abduction of John Chaucer in *The Life of Geoffrey Chaucer* (Oxford: Blackwell, 1992) as having to do "with the securing of John's inheritance from Robert [John's father], now that his mother had remarried" (pp. 12–14). This would undoubtedly mean that John's mother was an unnamed co-conspirator in the project. By the way, if Pearsall is correct in assuming that the mother's new husband, Richard Chaucer, was Robert's cousin (Crow and Olson, *Chaucer Life-Records*, p. 2, suggest only a possible relationship), a dispensation would have had to be obtained, unless Robert and Richard were related only as fourth cousins or beyond.

[74] Crow and Olson, *Chaucer Life-Records*, p. 3.

[75] See below at n. 160.

another man's wife; but he believes that the noun *raptus*, which "has an independent grammatical existence and a separate history of usage," is not employed in this way.[76]

This may be true in the main, but, as will be seen below, there are enough examples available to show that *raptus* by itself can refer to non-sexual abduction. I do not mean to make it an either/or matter, of course. I support Cannon's caution: "The obsession in Chaucer criticism with making just such a distinction often loses sight of the fact that abduction in practice may easily shade over into something that is hardly to be distinguished from sexual assault."[77] We can add that the opposite is also true: an abduction may have a sexual element that is of secondary importance. An example can be seen in Chaucer's only use of the English noun "rape," when Pandarus tells Troilus, "It is no rape, in my dom, ne no vice,/Hire to withholden that ye love moost" (*TC* 4.596–97).[78] Since Troilus has long been having consensual sex with Criseyde, Pandarus must be speaking primarily about "unlawful detention" rather than sexual violence. It is not a question of abduction, exactly, but of holding back the woman who loves him most. This fits with Pandarus's original advice to Troilus:

> Go ravysshe here! Ne kanstow nat, for shame?
> And other lat here out of towne fare,
> Or hold here stille, and leve thi nyce fare.
>
> Artow in Troie, and hast non hardyment
> To take a womman which that loveth the
> And wolde hireselven ben of thyn assent? (4.530–35)

We see here that "ravish" and "take" are synonyms; the ravishing could consist either of taking her or of keeping her, and it would be done with her assent. In all three cases, the corresponding word in Boccaccio's

[76] Cannon, "*Raptus*," pp. 80 (n. 31), 82. Cf. the similar distinction made by Sue Sheridan Walker, "Punishing Convicted Ravishers: Statutory Strictures and Actual Practice in Thirteenth- and Fourteenth-Century England," *Journal of Medieval History* 13 (1987): 237–50, that the verb form *rapuit* refers to abduction and the noun *raptus* to forcible coitus, but with some blurring in a few cases (p. 237).

[77] Cannon, "*Raptus*," p. 88.

[78] Ed. Stephen Barney, *The Riverside Chaucer*, gen. ed. Larry D. Benson (Boston: Houghton Mifflin, 1987). (Unless otherwise noted, I use the *Riverside Chaucer* for all citations of Chaucer's works.) Needless to say, I exclude the homonym "rape" meaning "haste," which Chaucer also used; other homonyms in use in his time were "rape" meaning "a form of turnip" and "rape" meaning "an administrative district of Sussex."

Filostrato is *rapire.*[79] But Chaucer may have deleted "rape" in line 596 in a later revision and substituted "shame," the reading found in most of the manuscripts. Alternatively, the change may have been scribal, a correction of the mistaken reading "jape" in some of the manuscripts.[80]

Troilus first rejected Pandarus's suggestion because the Trojan war was started on account of this kind of forcible ravishment of women ("For ravysshyng of wommen so by myght" [line 548]). He is doubtless referring to the original ravishment of Hesione by the Greeks, where force was used against her, and to Paris's retaliatory ravishment of the complacent Helen, where any force used was doubtless directed against her husband, Menelaus. Later, when speaking to Criseyde, Troilus tells her that her father may try to talk her into marrying a Greek, either ravishing her with his words or using force: "ravysshen he shal yow with his speche, / Or do yow don by force as he shal teche" (4.1474–75).

Rape as a noun has a long though sparse history of meaning "the act of abducting a woman or sexually assaulting her or both," according to the *Middle English Dictionary*: the first entry is from 1291–92, the second c 1425, and we have seen another example in Chaucer's *Troilus.* The earliest application of the verb *rape* to a woman is by Osbern Bokenham and occurs as late as 1447: he uses it to characterize Pluto's taking of Proserpina. In the next entry, from a paraphrase of the Old Testament, c 1450 (a1425),[81] the word is used of a woman's seduction of a man; the third and last entry is from the anonymous second translation of Higden's *Polychronicon*, ?a1475 (?a1425): Europa was "rapte" (Latin *rapta*) by Jupiter in the form of a bull, that is, carried off by force. We should also note that the participle *raptus/rapta* is used of ecstatics and visionaries; for instance, St. Paul was *raptus* to the third heaven and *raptus* into Paradise (2 Cor. 12:2–4). The noun *raptus* is also used in this sense ("rapture," "ecstasy") in medieval Latin.[82]

In John Trevisa's slightly earlier translation of the *Polychronicon*, in Chaucer's time, he used not "raped" but the French-derived reflex

[79] *Filostrato* 4.64, 65, 73; see the stanzas given parallel to Chaucer's in Barry Windeatt's edition of the *Troilus* (London: Longman, 1984), pp. 380–84.

[80] See Barney's textual note to 4.596, p. 1173. Windeatt, p.385, says that the cruder *no rape in my dom* "may reflect Chaucer's translation process here" (assuming, that is, that he later changed it to the less crude *no shame unto yow*).

[81] In the *MED* notation, when a date is followed by another in parentheses, the first refers to the manuscript and the second to time of composition; *c* means *circa* and *a* means *ante.*

[82] The *Revised Medieval Latin Word-List from British and Irish Sources*, ed. R. E. Latham (London: British Academy, 1965), gives instances from c1250 and c1343.

"ravished," which, as we have seen, was also favored by Chaucer. In *The Merchant's Tale*, when describing how Pluto abducted Proserpine, referring to Claudian—meaning his *De raptu Proserpinae*—he makes "ravished" the synonym of "fetched" ("in his grisely carte he hire fette" [line 2233]). Diomede also uses these synonyms: the revenge taken by the Greeks "for fecchynge of Eleyne" will make everyone fear "to ravysshen any queene" (5.890–95). In *Boece*, "ravish" does service not only for *rapere* but also for *raptare, arripere, subripere*, and *rapidus* ("ravishing").[83] Chaucer does use the verb "rape" once, however, in a colloquial expression, to mean "grab": "al that ye may rape and renne."[84]

In this article I will be following the usual practice of the Public Record Office calendars and translate *rapere* as "ravish," the past participle *rapta/raptus* as "ravished," and the noun *raptus* as "rape," letting the context determine when or whether it can be narrowed to abduction or sexual violation or a combination of both, or must be left undecided.[85] To do otherwise, say, to reserve "rape" for cases of sexual violence and "ravishment" for cases of simple abduction, would be to distort the evidence and disambiguate records and events by guesswork.

Giving a broad meaning to "rape" has also been the traditional practice of English letters. When we speak of "the rape of the Sabine women," and, of course, "the rape of Helen" and "the rape of Proserpine," it is mainly seizure and abduction that is meant, even though sexual intercourse may have followed (sometimes *contra voluntatem*, sometimes not).

In one of the examples from *Boece* noted above, we could well speak of "the rape of Philosophy":

Cujus [Socratis] hereditatem cum deinceps Epicureum vulgus ac Stoicum ceterique pro sua quisque parte *raptum ire* molirentur meque reclamantem renitentemque velut in partem praedae traherent, vestem quam meis texueram

[83] *Boece* 1 pr. 3.34 (*raptum ire*), 2 pr. 5.69 (*raperis*), 2 m. 7.28 (*rapiet*), 4 pr. 5.23 (*rapiant*), 4 m. 6.37 (*rapiens*), 4 m. 7.34 (*rapuit*); 1 pr. 3.70 (*raptatur*); 5 pr. 6.91 (*arripuit*); 4 pr. 3.111 (*subripuisse*); 1 m. 5.4 (*rapido*), 1 m. 5.56 (*rapidos*), 2 m. 2.5 (*rapidis*), 4 m. 6.9 (*rapidos*). Cf. also 4 pr. 3.105: "ravynour by violence" (*violentus ereptor*).

[84] *CYT* 1422. See Skeat's note for the evolution of the phrase, in *The Complete Works of Geoffrey Chaucer*, 2d ed., 7 vols. (Oxford: Oxford University Press, 1899–1907), 5:431–32. *Rape* here comes from OE *hrepian* (seize), but it was probably influenced by the homonym *rape* (seize), from Latin *rapere.*

[85] One must, however, guard against assuming that every use of "rape" in the calendars corresponds to *raptus* in the original; see the Percy case below (n. 93) for an exception.

manibus disciderunt, *abreptis*que ab ea panniculis, totam me sibi cessisse credentes abiere.

[After him the crowd of Epicureans and Stoics and the rest strove as far as they could to *seize* his [Socrates's] legacy, carrying me off protesting and struggling, as if I were part of the booty, tearing my dress, which I wove with my own hands, and then went off with their *torn-off* shreds, thinking they possessed all of me.][86]

When viewed from this perspective, even *The Rape of the Lock* could be regarded as having an element of sexual violation.

III. *Raptus* as Short for Ravishing-and-Abducting

Cannon mentions two cases of abduction of wife with husband's goods from 3 Richard II (June 22, 1379, to June 21, 1380) using the formula *vi et armis rapuit et eam cum bonis et catallis abduxit* ("he ravished her by force and arms and carried her away with goods and chattels") but also employing the summary formula *de raptu predicto*,[87] "concerning the foresaid rape." We should note first of all that *vi et armis* was often a pure legal fiction from the very beginning of its use in trespass writs and actions.[88] Or, in another analysis, the phrase "was not fictional but rather a low threshold test," alleging some but not necessarily a great deal of force.[89] The cases we are dealing with here correspond to the usage of the title of the relevant writ, *De uxore rapta*,[90] or *De raptu uxoris*,[91] and the

[86] Boethius, *Consolation* 1 pr. 3, lines 21–27, trans. S. J. Tester; Loeb *Boethius*, new ed. (Cambridge, Mass.: Harvard University Press, 1973), p. 143. Chaucer's translation is as follows (omitting the glosses): "The heritage of the whiche Socrates whan that the peple of Epycuriens and Stoyciens and many othere enforceden hem *to gon ravyssche* everyche man for his part, they as in partye of hir preye todrowen me, cryinge and debatying therayens, and korven and torente my clothes that I hadde woven with my handes; and with tho cloutes that thei hadden *arased* out of my clothes thei wenten awey wenynge that I hadde gon with hem every del." I italicize the relevant words. *Raptum ire* can be parsed as the future active periphrastic infinitive of *rapere* (*raptum* being the supine of the verb), and *abreptus* is the past participle of *abripere* (from *ab* and *rapere*).

[87] Cannon, "*Raptus*," p. 87.

[88] Milsom, "Trespass," pp. 222–23.

[89] Robert C. Palmer, *English Law in the Age of the Black Death, 1348–1381: A Transformation of Governance and Law* (Chapel Hill: University of North Carolina Press, 1993), p. 159.

[90] Cannon gives the text of the writ on p. 82, from a register of ca. 1320.

[91] In a case from 1314, Sayles, *Select Cases*, vol. 4, SS, vol. 74, p. 60, the writ is referred to as *breve de raptu uxoris.* Similarly, the king's council at the same time refers to it as *breve de transgressione de raptu uxoris alterius et de bonis suis asportatis*, and refers in summary to the charge as "de hujusmodi raptu." See *Rotuli Parliamentorum*, 1:290.

corresponding action, sometimes called *De raptu uxoris cum bonis viri sui.*[92] That is, a wife who is *rapta et abducta,* meaning only "abducted" (literally, "forcibly seized and carried off"), is referred to by shorthand in the more common title only as *rapta,* or, in the alternative title, the alleged offense is referred to as *raptus,* as in the two cited *rapuit et abduxit* cases. The meaning of the term is clear from the context, but when the context is missing, as in the first Champain release, we have no reason, without further information, to conclude that the case refers to sexual rape; it could instead refer only to abduction, or it could be designating a combination of both offenses. A similar example can be seen in the Percy case, mentioned above: John Halsham, having been charged with ravishing and abducting Percy's wife (now actually Halsham's wife), was pardoned by the king (June 7, 1384) for the *raptus* of Philippa of Artheles and for all other felonies and trespasses.[93] We note that Philippa is not identified as anyone's wife and is only referred to by a distorted version of her toponymic (she was the daughter of the earl of Athol).

Cannon also notes a standard plea by defendants in Arnold's collection, in which rape is denied with no mention of abduction: *venit et defendit vim, injuriam, raptum.* He observes that the latest case of this sort comes from 1318, dealing with a father who denies *omnis raptus* of his daughter; that is, he denies categorically that he abducted his daughter.[94] But in a King's Bench case from 1389, *Wyatt v Vicar of Swalcliffe,* the defendant distinguishes between the charges of *raptus* of the woman with the husband's goods, on the one hand, and, on the other hand, the *abductio* of the woman with some of her personal items:

Quo ad raptum predicte Alicie, et [quo ad] bona et catalla predicta, preter pannos lineos et laneos, flammiola, et anulos, dicit quod ipse in nullo est inde cul-

[92] This is the usual form in the C version of *Novae Narrationes*, ed. Elsie Shanks and S. F. C. Milsom, SS, vol. 80 (London, 1963), which dates from the early years of Edward II and was frequently copied. See p. 328. One MS of Edward III's time, Rawl. C.49, has *De raptu mulieris cum bonis viri sui*, and another, Dunn 51, has simply *De raptu.*

[93] PRO, C66/317 m. 12. See appendix, no. 12; *CPR Richard II*, 2:399. Another pardon was given to Halsham on 10 July, for all rapes, murders, homicides, common robberies and larcenies and all other felonies of which he stands charged, PRO, C66/318 m. 37, *CPR Richard II*, 2:439. In the *CCR* summary of one of the original commissions (see above, n. 17), the phrase "rape and abduction" is used, whereas in the original record only verbs are used (*rapuerunt, abduxerunt*).

[94] Cannon, "*Raptus*," pp. 87–88, citing Arnold, *Select Cases of Trespass*, 1:77–80 (8.4–6). The same phrase is used in the 1314 case noted above in Sayles, *Select Cases*, 4:59, and *raptus* is used four other times to sum up the action. In the Year Book for 3 Edward II (1310), a similar case is summarized in the rubric as *De raptu mulieris: Year Books of Edward II*, vol. 4, ed. F. W. Maitland and G. J. Turner, SS, vol. 22 (London, 1907), p. 4.

pabilis. . . . Et quo ad abductionem predicte Alicie et pannorum, lineorum, et laneorum, flammiliorum, et anulorum, dicit. . . .

[As for the rape of the aforesaid Alice, and [as for] the aforesaid goods and chattels, except the linen and woolen cloth, the kerchiefs, and the rings, he says that he is in no wise guilty thereof. . . . And as for the abduction of the aforesaid Alice and the linen and woolen cloth, kerchiefs, and rings, he says. . . .][95]

The defendant is the wife's uncle, a priest, vicar of the church of Swalcliffe in Oxfordshire. He explains here in court that Alice left her husband ("a comitiva dicti Johannis recessit") and lived with him when given permission by the official of the archdeacon of Oxford: she was asking for an annulment on grounds of the husband's impotence, and she feared his violence. The only clothes in question were those she was wearing, and the same was true of the one ring that the husband complained of. The uncle concludes, "This is the way he 'took and abducted' her" ("ipsam in forma predicta 'cepit et abduxit'").[96] In thus denying the *raptus* of his niece, he is only denying any forcible seizure of her and of goods belonging to her husband. It is not likely that there was any nuance in the husband's charge of incestuous sexual violation, or that the vicar was responding to any such connotation.

Another defendant before the King's Bench in 1389 (in the case of *Hamm v Gilbert*) denies "asportation" of the husband's goods and chattels. As for the *raptus* of the wife ("quo ad raptum predicte Margerie"), he says that the husband sent his wife to work for him. The husband persists in maintaining that the defendant "ravished her and still detains her" ("rapuit et eam adhuc detinet"), without any consent or agreement on his own part, contrary to the defendant's allegation. The jury finds that the defendant used no force and arms concerning goods and chattels, but that he did encourage the wife to leave her husband, and that this was why she removed herself ("se elongavit") from his company, without, however, the defendant ravishing her ("absque hoc, quod . . . rapuit"); they assess the defendant's damages to the husband

[95] Arnold, *Select Cases of Trespass*, 1:87 (8.15). My translation differs from Arnold's in that where he says "ravishing," I say "the rape" (in keeping with the above-noted PRO practice of translating *raptus* as "rape") and put "the abduction" where he has "abducting." I have also inserted "quo ad" in brackets before *bona et catalla* to underline the fact that, grammatically speaking, the phrase is not governed by *raptus*, since *bona et catalla* is in the accusative rather than the genitive, even though the recorder's intention may have been to refer to "the seizure of the wife and the goods."

[96] Ibid.

(in effect, for alienation of his wife's affections) at 100*s*.[97] The action in this case commenced, according to Arnold's summary, on "a writ and count in common form for abducting the plaintiff's wife along with goods of his."[98] Once again, while it is possible that an element of forcible or unwilling sexual intercourse was included in the husband's charge, if not in the defendant's denial and the jury's negative finding, it seems more likely that the main or only concern was with the defendant's role in the departure of the wife from her husband's home. The husband would hardly have needed to argue that he did not consent to the *raptus* if it denoted forced adulterous sex.[99]

Another similar writ and count resulted in a King's Bench case, *Hampton v Montgomery and Child*, in the following year, 1390, which similarly avoided all use of the terms *abductio* and *abduxit*. The charges were brought by the cordwainer John Hampton against two clerks, Philip Montgomery and William Child. They pleaded "not guilty" concerning the use of force and arms and the goods and chattels ("quo ad venire vi et armis et bona et catalla"), and they gave an explanation concerning the *raptus* of his wife, Katherine ("quo ad raptum dicte Katerine"): her marriage to the plaintiff had been annulled because of her previous marriage to another man, Walter; one defendant, Philip, was Walter's counsel in the annulment proceedings before the archdeacon of the abbot of Westminster, and the other defendant, William, was the wife's counsel. Each defendant admitted that, after the annulment was granted, Katherine left John to seek Walter, but without either clerk ravishing her ("absque hoc, quod ipse dictam Katerinam rapuit"). John, however, continued to insist that Philip and William "ravished the aforesaid Katherine at Southwark, as he supposes by his writ and count" ("predictam Katerinam apud Suthewerk rapuerunt, prout per breve et narrationem sua supponit").[100]

[97] Ibid., 1:88–89 (8.16).

[98] Ibid., 1:88.

[99] In this case, the court postponed coming to a judgment after the jury delivered its verdict, but there is no reason to think that its hesitation had anything to do with suspected coitus, forced or unforced, between the defendant and the plaintiff's wife.

[100] Ibid., 1:92–93 (8.19). A 1389 case of "abducting the plaintiff's wife along with goods," *Ware v Halmard*, which also involved annulment proceedings before the archdeacon of Westminster, is given by Arnold, *Select Cases of Trespass*, 1:89–90 (8.17). The husband, Bartholomew Ware, armorer, charges three men with ravishing and abducting his wife Isabel: Thomas, Isabel's son; John, Isabel's son-in-law, married to her daughter; another John, Isabel's cousin. Their story is that when Bartholomew and Isabel found out that they were cousins, Isabel removed herself from Bartholomew, and Bartholomew applied to their ordinary, the archdeacon of the monastery of Westminster (the monk John

The writ for "rape of heir" in a 1337 case, *Bolling v Chestfield*, dealing with the abduction of an heiress, is called *De raptu custodie* and *De raptu de custodia*. Such a writ was allegedly secured by John Chestfield against John Bolling, who, he claimed, had ravished (*rapuerat*) his ward, Joan Lightfoot, out of his custody (*extra custodiam ipsius*).[101] The word *raptus* in such a writ, which was designed for male and female wards, would seem to have no primary reference to sexual violence—though, of course, it was sometimes applied in cases where sexual violence was charged.[102] Rather, it primarily referred to abduction, understood as forcible removal from one's proper custodian. Walker notes that cases of ravished male heirs were more common than those of ravished females; for instance, in 1354, the ratio was 46 to 21.[103]

In a 1391 case, *Lincoln v Simond et al.*, where a man, Thomas Lincoln, claimed the marriage-right of his own daughter, he accused two men and a woman of breaking into his home by force and arms, ravishing and abducting his daughter, Alice, and taking and asporting his goods and chattels—terms normally associated with the writ *De uxore rapta*. One of the defendants, Alan Simond, after protesting that he did not admit that Alice was Thomas's daughter or that Thomas owned her maritage, asserted that he had secretly espoused Alice before Thomas espoused her to another man of his own choice, and that the first spousal had been upheld in the ecclesiastical court (as a valid marriage). Thomas then insisted that this spousal should be adjudged, legally speaking, a *raptus* of his daughter ("et sic dicta affidatio predicte Alicie, sine licencia dicti Thome [patris sui] facta, in lege raptum Alicie adjudicare debet"), because he had thereby lost her maritage, since he could not marry her to anyone.[104] The court postponed coming to a judgment in

Stow) for an annulment, which was granted. But during the proceedings, Archdeacon Stow decreed that Isabel was to live in some honest place apart from the company of her husband, and she accordingly spent some time with her son, her son-in-law, and her cousin, the three men whom her husband was now charging with abduction.

[101] Ibid., 1:43–44 (4.6). A jury found that Chestfield had actually not obtained the royal writ *De raptu de custodia*, but had instead pursued his case by means of a bill, which, as we saw above, was a plaintiff's informal petition initiating proceedings in common law.

[102] See Walker, "Punishing Convicted Ravishers," for various circumstances accompanying charged abductions, including the alleged abduction of wives (see below).

[103] Walker, "Free Consent," p. 127 and n. 26.

[104] Arnold, *Select Cases of Trespass*, 1:96–98 (9.2); cf. p. xlv. Arnold translates *affidatio* and *affidatio sponsalium* as "betrothal" and "betrothal of espousals," but he should use a neutral term, since it was surely a question not of betrothals but of marriages. Betrothals (*sponsalia de futuro*) could be broken at will, unless converted into marriage by intercourse;

this case, but the normal solution would have been for the guardian to keep the property of the ward until he was paid the value of the marriage, or else to sue the ward for the amount.[105]

A similar situation in 1377 in Yorkshire resulted in a criminal indictment. John Woodhouse (de Wodehous) of Brathwait was indicted for feloniously ravishing Alice, daughter of Richard Jackman, at Woodhouse on August 11, 1377, and feloniously abducting her with goods and chattels of Jackman to the value of 20 marks. When brought before the justices of jail delivery on April 18, 1384, he produced a pardon, dated August 23, 1383, granted at the request of Lady Mohun, upon which he was acquitted. The pardon notes that he was indicted for allegedly having ravished Alice and taken, abducted, (and/or) imprisoned her, and he is pardoned the king's suit for the rape (*raptus*) and other above-mentioned felonies, with the proviso that Alice could speak against him concerning the rape and other aforesaid felonies.[106] It is important to note that, according to this pardon, Alice had the same ability to appeal her abduction as Margaret Kebell would have at the beginning of the sixteenth century. Woodhouse's pardon, like the pardon of Roger Vernon and his accomplices, did not include the taking away of chattels (specified in the Woodhouse indictment as belonging to Alice's father, but in the Vernon indictments as Margaret's own goods). But in Woodhouse's case, he was not held to answer for the chattels. And

---

marriages (*sponsalia de presenti*) could not, and it was only the latter that were at issue in the ecclesiastical cases of "precontract" (which means "previous marriage"). It would make little sense to sue over which of two betrothals came first; Alice could at any time have simply converted either betrothal into marriage on the spot by using the present tense. On precontract, see R. H. Helmholz, *Marriage Litigation in Medieval England* (Cambridge: Cambridge University Press, 1974), pp. 76–77; for the laws on clandestine marriage, see my *Love and Marriage in the Age of Chaucer* (Ithaca: Cornell University Press, 1975), pp. 163–76. See also J. A. Brundage, "Rape and Marriage in the Medieval Canon Law," *Revue de droit canonique* 28 (1978): 62–75: "Abduction of one's own fiancé . . . did not count as rape" in canon law (p. 70, citing *Decretales Gregorii IX* 5.17.6, and also Adhémar Esmein, *Le mariage en droit canonique* [Paris, 1891], 1:392, for the axiom *Non fit raptus propriae sponsae*). When Brundage says that "the abduction of one's wife by someone else was likely to be treated somewhat differently, as 'diversion,' for which both ecclesiastical and secular courts offered separate remedies," his statement needs to be modified for England, where this procedure does not seem to have been common. Brundage cites Helmholz, *Marriage Litigation*, pp. 109–10, but Helmholz here mentions only a single case, in which a man accuses another man in a church court of "subtracting" his wife with her consent, and no reference is made to secular remedies.

[105] *Bracton de legibus et consuetudinibus Angliae*, ed. George E. Woodbine, trans. Samuel E. Thorne, 4 vols. (Cambridge, Mass.: Harvard University Press, 1968), 2:257; Walker, "Free Consent," p. 123; Walker, "Wrongdoing," p. 291.

[106] PRO, JUST 3/80/1 m. 1. See appendix, no. 11.

whereas Margaret really was abducted, it may be that Alice went with Woodhouse willingly. In fact, there may be a reference to them as man and wife later in the same jail-delivery session: William Draper of Wragby, indicted for ravishing Alice wife of John de Wodehousses on June 28, 1379 (the nature of the alleged ravishment is not described), is found not guilty—like all the other defendants, none of whom had pardons to show.[107]

As we can deduce from the examples given above, plaintiffs routinely brought charges of ravishing-abducting against defendants in cases where there was not only no forced sex but also no abduction. In the cases where the plaintiffs claim the supposedly abducted women as their wives, they were following the language of the pertinent writ, *De uxore rapta.*[108] The writ itself purports to be following "the form of the statute," probably that of Westminster II, ch. 34 (1285), with its reference to the goods of the husbands abducted with wives.[109] The next chapter, ch. 35, deals with abducted children, male or female, whose marriage-right belongs to someone: "De pueris sive masculis sive femellis quorum maritagium ad aliquem pertineat raptis et abductis," and provides the necessary writs within the statute itself.[110] We have seen above that both kinds of abductions, of wives and of heirs, were referred to simply as *raptus*, and the same is true of a statute passed in October 1382—that is, two and a half years after Cecily Champain's release of Chaucer. The purpose of the statute was to give the right of appeal to the husband, if the abducted woman was married, or to the next male kin in other cases, when the woman subsequently consented to the "rape" ("post hujusmodi raptum").[111] The text of the Commons' petition in the Rolls of Parliament speaks of ravishment ("apres le ravisement"),[112] but when the Commons unsuccessfully tried to get the statute repealed less than two years later, they also spoke of rape ("apres tiel rape," "apres cel ravissement").[113]

The husbands who used *De uxore rapta* had usually lost their wives not through abduction but through the wives' voluntary separation from

[107] Ibid., m. 1d.

[108] See Cannon, "*Raptus*," pp. 82–83, and Kelly, "Statutes of Rapes," p. 393, for the text of the writ, as given in *Early Registers of Writs*, ed. Elsa de Haas and G. D. G. Hall, SS, vol. 87 (London, 1970), p. 181.

[109] *Statutes of the Realm*, vol. 1 (London, 1810), p. 87.

[110] Ibid., p. 88.

[111] 6 Richard II, Stat. 1, c. 6 (1382), *Statutes*, 2:27. See Kelly, "Statutes of Rapes," pp. 371–73, 400–402, as well as Post's two articles (I modify his conclusions somewhat).

[112] *Rotuli Parliamentorum*, 6 vols. (London, 1767–77), 3:139–40.

[113] Ibid., 3:174.

them. As Morris Arnold says, "Probably because the husband-wife relationship is so complex, and the lie in the writ so outrageous, special pleading seems more prevalent in this action than in any other."[114] In other words, it was necessary to allege the violence of *raptus*, both for ward and wife, with or without the possible sexual overtones of the word, in order to get the real complaint into court; once there, the actual circumstances could be explained and appropriate judgment hoped for. Our first instinct, therefore, should be to dismiss the alleged incident as mere boilerplate dictated by the writ. A final example: on March 3, 1379, the tailor John Mare obtained two writs against two East Greenwich men, John Totenham and Thomas Horn, accusing each of ravishing his wife Alice and abducting her and his goods and still detaining them. Since he does not accuse them of acting together, he seems to suggest that his wife could be abducted twice and detained in two places at once.[115]

IV. *Raptus/Rapere*: Seizure, With Coitus Now or Later

Of the documents illustrating appeals by women that Cannon transcribes in their entirety, the first, dealing with Isabel Mohun, taken from the *Coram rege* (King's Bench) rolls, is the most interesting and complicated, and I will analyze it at length below. The second and third are entries from the controlment roll of 3 Richard II (1379–80). Of these two, the second, Agnes Marchal's appeal against Robert Baral, is straightforward: she claims that he came like a felon and lay with her carnally against her will and thus feloniously ravished her (*et sic ipsam felonice rapuit*), and the offense is twice referred to later as "the aforesaid felony of rape" (*felonia predicta de raptu*). The first case, the appeal of Amicia Serle against Roger Snow, is similar in alleging no act of taking the woman away, but only forced intercourse; here, however, it is stated that "he feloniously ravished her of her pure virginity" (*ipsam de pura virginitate sua felonice rapuit*), where the word *rapere* seems to mean "violently deprive," referring to a taking away or destroying of her maidenhood.[116]

[114] Arnold, *Select Cases of Trespass*, p. xlv. I analyze all of his cases in "Statutes of Rapes," pp. 398–99, 409. Arnold uses "special pleading" in the nonpejorative seventeenth-century sense of the phrase, meaning the recounting of the peculiar circumstances of a case, as opposed to "general pleading."

[115] PRO, KB 136/5/2/3/1, gathered with the writs of Kent for the quindene of Easter, 1379.

[116] Cannon, "*Raptus*," p. 86, citing KB 29/32, m. 1 (*Marchal v Baral*) and m. 31d (*Serle v Snow*).

Sometimes the virginity is the direct object: he ravished her virginity (from her). The same idiom is found in French: "ravist soun pucellage."[117] In English, the usual verb used is *reve* (it survives today only in *bereave*). Chaucer uses it to describe the two rapes of virgins he portrays, that of Philomela ("he hath reft hire of hire maydenhede, / Maugre hire hed, by strengthe and by his myght" [*LGW* 2325–26]) and that of the maid in *The Wife of Bath's Tale* ("Of which mayde anon, maugree hir heed, / By verray force, he rafte hire maydenhed" [lines 887–88]). He uses the same verb, this time with a double object, for the third sexual rape that he describes, that of Lucretia, but in this case she was bereft not of her virginity, for she was a married woman, but of her life: "And therwithal she rafte hirself hir lyf" (*LGW* 1855). When her rape is recalled by Dorigen in *The Franklin's Tale*, the verb used is "oppresse": "she oppressed was / Of Tarquyn" (lines 1406–7), and the same word is used of virgins: "To been oppressed of hir maydenhede" (line 1385).

In other cases, *rapere* may mean only "seize." This is true of the writ *De uxore rapta*, in which *rapuit, abduxit, et adhuc detinet* means "seized, took away, and still detains." The same may be true in cases of forced sex, even in the formula *eam felonice rapuit et cum ea carnaliter concubuit contra voluntatem ipsius*, which would therefore mean, "he feloniously seized her and immediately lay with her carnally against her will." The latter formula occurs in a case from 1412, where a man was accused of so acting by the command and counsel of his mother.[118] But in such cases it is also possible that the *et* means *sive* or *id est*: so that the *et* joining the words would not mean "and in addition" but would simply add a synonym, in indenture- English style.[119] That is, *rapuit et carnaliter concubuit* could mean no more than *rapuit, id est, carnaliter concubuit.* This may be the meaning of the indictment against Thomas Malory in 1451: *eam felonice rapuit et cum ea carnaliter concubuit*,[120] but the charge also included abduction of wife and goods, and a subsequent appeal, citing the 1382 statute, implied the wife's consent.[121]

[117] As in the case of *Alice v John* reported in the 1302 eyre of Cornwall and the 1313–14 eyre of Kent; see Kelly, "Statutes of Rapes," pp. 389–90.

[118] Putnam, *Proceedings*, p. 99, no. 30: "Robertus, filius Thome Howet, . . . ex precepto et consilio Alicie Howet, matris sue, Agnetem, filiam Johannis Clerk, magistri sui, apud Gaddesby, felonice rapuit et cum ea carnaliter concubuit, contra voluntatem ipsius Agnetis."

[119] I owe this suggestion to Christopher Cannon.

[120] Edward Hicks, *Sir Thomas Malory: His Turbulent Career* (Cambridge, Mass.: Harvard University Press, 1928), p. 96.

[121] Kelly, "Statutes of Rapes," pp. 412–15.

A similar interpretation may be called for in the felony case of the countess of Lincoln in 1336, which Cannon analyzes as presenting an ambiguous meaning of *raptus*. According to the indictment, the defendants entered the castle by treachery and took hold of the countess ("comitissam ceperunt") and then took her away (abducted her) from her castle to another castle and there ravished her against her will and against the peace of the king and against the form of the statute thereupon provided, and they did their will concerning her ("et predictam comitissam abduxerunt extra castrum suum predictum usque ad castrum de Somerton et ipsam ibidem rapuerunt, contra voluntatem suam et contra pacem regis et contra formam statuti inde provisi, etc., et voluntatem suam de ea fecerunt"). One of the defendants pleaded not guilty to *capcio, abduccio, raptus, seu felonia predicta sibi imposita.*[122] The statutory reference, if it is to be taken as accurately citing a specific statute, is most likely to be the first part or French section of Westminster II ch. 34 (1285), providing the death penalty for ravishing a woman without her consent.[123] If the ravishment refers to forced sex here, as seems likely, *rapuerunt . . . et voluntatem suam de ea fecerunt* could mean either "seized her and then violated her sexually" or, taking the *et* as explanatory, "seized her, that is, violated her sexually."

However, in other cases the latter interpretation is not possible and *rapuit* appears to mean only "seized," or, at most, "seized with the intention of later violating"; as, for example, in an indictment from 1357 in which a man allegedly *rapuit* a woman, *abduxit* her to a mill, *et cum ea concubuit contra voluntatem suam.*[124] In another case from the same year, a tailor, labeled a common night-stroller and common malefactor and perturber of the peace in the indictment, *rapuit et abduxit* a wife and goods and then *carnaliter cognovit* the wife.[125] Sometimes, of course, one cannot tell whether there was coitus, or full coitus, or not. This is true even in a gruesome indictment from 1413 according to which a man took a ladder one night and broke into (*fregit*) a house and *rapuisset* a woman and *lasaraverit* her clothes (*pannos, lineos, et laneos*), whereupon she raised the hue and cry and the whole village came running, but not

Δ [122] G. O. Sayles, *Select Cases in the Court of King's Bench*, vol. 5, SS, vol. 76 (London, 1958), pp. 90–91, discussed by Cannon, "*Raptus*," pp. 88–89, n. 61. It is noteworthy that the term *felonia* is not used in the narration of the jury's presentment, but it is in the charge that is made against the accused ringleader when he appears in court.

[123] *Statutes of the Realm*, 1:87.

[124] Putnam, *Proceedings*, p. 188, no. 49.

[125] Ibid., p. 190, no. 68.

before he had suffocated and murdered her.[126] The pluperfect subjunctive *rapuisset* and the perfect subjunctive *lasaraverit* may indicate that the woman's cries interrupted his rape attempt before he could complete it.

V. An Appealing Widow and Rapist Husband: *Mohun v Yulecomb*

Let us discuss now the appeal of Isabel Mohun against Henry Yulecomb, the first case of forced coitus that Cannon transcribes.[127] This record, from the *Coram rege* rolls (the Public Record Office KB 27 series of King's Bench plea rolls), like the two controlment-roll entries just discussed, comes from the one year that Cannon thoroughly examined, namely, 3 Richard II (June 22, 1379, to June 21, 1380). The gist of it is as follows. Henry Yulecomb was attached, along with William Yulecomb, his brother, and Lawrence Drew, to respond to Isabel, "who was (*fuit*) the wife of John Mohun," and to her appeal of rape and of breaking of the king's peace (*de raptu et pace . . . fracta*). She claimed that Henry came with the two other men to Bedenek in Cornwall on the evening of November 26, 1376, and feloniously took (*cepit*) her and led (*duxit*) her
* to Stanerton in the county of Devon and there lay with her carnally against her will on December 1; she was forcibly detained from the aforesaid November 26, 1376, until February 20, 1378, on which day she escaped; and thus he feloniously ravished her (*et sic ipsam felonice rapuit*). William and Lawrence, whom she would also be charging if they were there in court, were present on the aforesaid day and year (i.e., November 26, 1376), aiding and abetting Henry in committing the *felonia predicta* (*de raptu* is not added). And as soon as Henry had committed the *felonia predicta de raptu*, Isabel pursued him from vill to vill (following the standard formula); and if he should deny that he committed the *felonia predicta de raptu*, she is prepared to prove it, as the court wishes.[128]

[126] Ibid., p. 102, no. 45.

[127] I give the expanded or regularized forms of the names here; Cannon read the husband's name in the manuscript as "Mann," but he agrees now that it should be transcribed as "Moun."

[128] PRO, KB 27/475 (Michaelmas term, 1379), m. 61, transcribed in Cannon, "*Raptus*," pp. 85–86. The day of the abduction is given as the next Wednesday after the feast of St. Katherine (that is, November 25, a Tuesday), in the fiftieth year of Edward III (that is, 1376); the day of the unwilling coitus is given as the next Monday after the feast of St. Katherine. The day of her escape is given as the twentieth day of February in the first year of Richard II (1378).

We see then that the term *rapuit* is first used after Isabel escaped from her fifteen-month imprisonment, as if the the entire ordeal comprised the felony. Then she seems to limit the felony, in which his accomplices participated, to the initial kidnapping. Finally, she returns speaking of the events of the whole period as a *raptus*. She mentions only one instance of forced coitus, five days after she was seized.

Appeal against a man on a charge of sexual violation was an action traditionally reserved to women, and it may be that this is why Isabel specified the single instance of unwanted sex over a period of a year and a quarter of captivity. There is, however, one early case, *Tolymer v Mounpynzoun* (1315), that may suggest that forced sex was not necessary to the charge. In this case, William Tolymer brings a civil suit against a woman, Christian Mounpynzoun, and a parson, Thomas Holm, saying that they took and abducted (*ceperunt et abduxerunt*) his daughter and heiress Catherine and married her against his (the father's) will to Edmund Mounpynzoun—presumably Christian's son.[129] One of the defendants' lawyers, William Herle, a King's Serjeant,[130] objects that the writ is faulty because the daughter could not be called heiress until her father is dead. Therefore, the writ of ravishment of ward (*ravisement de garde*) is not appropriate, and the father "ought not to have an action; or if there were any action it must be one of rape (*rap*), the suit of which is reserved to the woman."[131] Herle's argument against the writ was not accepted, but there was no challenge to his assumption that a woman could bring an appeal of rape in a case of abduction. But perhaps his assumption was also that she would have to charge, not the mother, but the son to whom she was married, and against whom she would have to allege forcible coitus. However, we have seen in *Jackman v Woodhouse* in 1377 that a daughter could bring an appeal of ravishment and abduction against a man with no explicit allegation of forced sex, and her right to do so was confirmed in the pardon of 1383. But it may be that the situation was different for married women and widows.

In the fifteenth century, in 1436 and 1439, special acts of Parliament were passed to allow abducted and forcibly married women to enter

[129] *Year Books of Edward II*, vol. 19 (9 Edward II), ed. G. J. Turner and William Craddock Bolland, SS, vol. 45 (London, 1929), Common Pleas report, p. 31.

[130] John Sainty, *A List of English Law Officers, King's Counsel, and Holders of Patents of Precedence* (London, 1987), p. 5.

[131] Loc. cit.; Herle repeats his objection on p. 32.

appeals of felony against their husbands.[132] After the turn of the next century, Margaret Kebell, discussed above, entered an appeal of "felony and rape" without specifying forced sex but naming the 1487 statute, "Against the Taking Away of Women." Christopher Whittick notes that the statute does not specify the right of appeal, but he points out that when a woman entered such an appeal in 1492, it was received, but only after consultation between the justices of both benches.[133]

We should note, by the way, that when a woman is identified as *que fuit uxor*, having been the wife of someone, we cannot safely conclude, without more evidence, that she is a widow. We know that Maud Cantilupe in the case noted earlier was a widow because her husband had been murdered; but there is a case from 1383–84 of a woman *que fuit uxor Philippi* in which Philip was still very much alive, at least in the summer of 1381, when the offense allegedly took place (June 16, 4 Richard II): a man was indicted for forcibly ravishing her, promising to get her marriage to Philip annulled, and then bigamously marrying her

[132] Leadam, *Select Cases Before the Star Chamber*, p. cxii, citing *Rotuli Parl.*, 4:497–98; 5:14–15. In the first case, the widow of a knight, Isabel Butler, says that William Pulle broke into her house with armed misdoers and "felonously and moste horribly ravished" her and led her, naked except for kirtle and smock, to the wilds of Wales, "for which rape" he was indicted before the king's justices of Lancaster, after order was given for his arrest and her rescue. She wants order given that unless he appears in two weeks, he will be attainted of high treason, "considering that the said ravishing is done in more horrible wise and with more heinous violence than any hath been seen or known before this time, and that the said William ravisher is, and of long time hath be, outlawed of felony for man's death by him foul murdered and slain." In a second petition, she described the event again: William Pulle and other felons lying in wait "felonously there then took and ravished" her and led her into the county of Chester [not to Wales], and there, "to exclude her of her suit and lawful remedy of the said ravishment," imprisoned her for a day (or a week), then forced her to marry him; thereupon he put her in a strong chamber till night, and then "felonously and fleshly knew and ravished" her. She asks that she might "pursue by attorney an effectual appeal . . . of the said ravishment" in spite of the espousals between her and William. In the 1439 case, the petitioner, again the widow of a knight, charges that one Lewis plotted "to ravish the said Margaret and to have her to his wife." He kidnapped her, forced her to undergo a marriage service, and then "against her will ravished her and felonly lay by her." She asks a writ requiring him to answer "the said felony and rape." She refers to his offense interchangeably as "the said ravishment" and "the said rape." Note that in both cases the coitus is said to come only after the forced marriage.

[133] Whittick, "Role of the Criminal Appeal," p. 62. Whittick says that the justices' decision was "presumably by analogy with the admissibility of appeals under the act of 1382." But that act gave suit only to the husband or next of kin in a case in which the woman later consented to the ravishment—the presumption being that the right of appeal by next of kin in cases where the woman did not consent was already granted in the Statute of Westminster II, ch. 34 (1285); *Statutes*, 2:27.

himself.[134] In the case of Isabel Mohun, we know nothing about the status of her former husband, John Mohun, but we will see that another husband, or would-be husband, was in the mix, namely, Henry Yulecomb himself, and that Henry suspected another man, Guy Brian, of masterminding Isabel's prosecution against him.

The record transcribed by Cannon comes from Michaelmas term, 1379, but the events described must be earlier, since Henry has been arrested but has not yet been indicted and has not pleaded. However, less than two months after Isabel's alleged escape, Henry had reportedly been indicted and had received a pardon from the king, or in the king's name (we must remember that Richard II was only eleven years old at this time). The pardon is dated April 9, 1378, and it recounts that Henry Yulecomb stands indicted of having feloniously ravished Isabel Mohun at "Bodennek" on December 22, 1376, but that at the request of the marshall of England, John of Arundel, he is pardoned any breaking of peace connected with the said *raptus*, while still remaining liable to Isabel's charge.[135]

We note that the date of the ravishment of Isabel in Cornwall is given as almost a month later than the one that appears in the document transcribed by Cannon; and we also note that the *raptus*, without any elaboration as to its nature, is said to have allegedly occurred at her residence in Cornwall, not additionally somewhere else later on.

We must not conclude from the terms of the pardon that Henry had admitted to any guilt to the charge of *raptus*, whether it involved only his seizing of Isabel in Cornwall or the full account of events as described in her appeal. Her account is an odd one, and on the face of it suggests something more than she was admitting. If the events of Isabel's appeal are taken to bear a general resemblance to the truth, we may conjecture that Henry's primary motive must have been abduction with a view to marriage, rather than sexual passion leading to forced coitus, and that possibly there had been an betrothal agreement between him and Isabel which she wished to back out of; Henry may have thought that if he could consummate the agreement with copula, it would trigger the canonical provision that betrothals *de futuro* followed by intercourse turned the contract into a marriage *de presenti*. We will

[134] Putnam, *Proceedings*, p. 386, no. 8.

[135] PRO, C 66/301; calendared in *CPR Richard II*, 1:182. For text and translation, see appendix, no. 4.

see below that Henry did in fact claim that Isabel was his wife and that she had lived with him, presumably voluntarily, for a year and fifteen weeks.

Four other related King's Bench records from 3 Richard II are noted by Cannon, but not transcribed or summarized. We will see from one of them that Henry was released on mainprise in the autumn of 1379 and ordered to appear again in court in the next Hilary term, that is, in January 1380, but that he failed to appear. Two of the records, which appear together on the same membrane, seem to record what happened at that time. The first concerns the jury hearing Isabel's appeal of *raptus* and *pax fracta*, and it records that the hearing was continued until Easter term.[136] (Easter occurred on March 25 in 1380, meaning that the term would begin three weeks later, on Monday, April 16.) The entry immediately following records Isabel's appearance against William Yulecomb and Lawrence Drew for the aforesaid rape (*de raptu predicta* [*sic*]). On their nonappearance, further order was given for their arrest.[137]

The next record of 3 Richard II unearthed by Cannon is an order to the sheriff of Somerset, apparently requiring him to bring in the three knights who were the mainpernors of Henry Yulecomb, namely, Matthew Gournay, Thomas Trivet, and Thomas Fichet, along with the £200 each had forfeited because of their failure to deliver him to court and to restrain him from trying to prevent Isabel from pursuing her appeal. He not only failed to appear, but he attacked Isabel with a band of miscreants as she was approaching the royal palace in Westminster by the Waterbridge, in order to prevent her from prosecuting her appeal.[138]

We should note that the number of pledges required for appeals of rape was stipulated in the so-called Statute of the Coroner: if the appeal

[136] PRO, KB 27/476 9Hilary 1380), m. 30d. See appendix, no. 5.

[137] Ibid. See appendix, no. 6. The Lawrence Drew who was Yulecomb's accused accomplice is identified as the son of Drugo of Wringworth; he may be the Lawrence Drew who was appointed King's Attorney (Attorney General) on September 9, 1381 (with a successor appointed on July 8, 1382); see Sainty, *List of English Law Officers*, p. 43, drawing on *CPR*. Drew is found acting as King's Attorney from 1381 to 1384 in *Calendar of the General and Special Assize and General Gaol Delivery Commissions on the Dorses of the Patent Rolls: Richard II (1377–1399)* (Nendeln, 1977). In 1380, he served as Justice of the Peace in Berkshire (*CPR Richard II* 1:473, 513, 579), and he is seen on commissions in 1382 and 1383 (ibid., 2:25, 290). From 1386 to the end of Richard's reign he served as JP at various times in Berkshire and Wiltshire.

[138] PRO, KB 29/32 m. 52d. See appendix, no. 7.

is recent, and signs of its truth are seen, like bloody clothes, or the hue and cry raised, four or six pledges are to be used, if possible; but if the appeal is without cry and without manifest sign, then two will suffice.[139]

The record of the indictment by the grand jury is the final entry from the King's Bench rolls cited by Cannon. The attempted interception is said to have occurred on Wednesday, April 18, 1380. This date, we may observe, is just three weeks before Cecily Champain came to the King's Bench on May 7 to record her May 1 release of Chaucer from all felony-transgression-account-debt complaints. The indictment against Henry must have been handed down sometime before June 22, 1380, to fall within 3 Richard II. The jury presented that when Isabel came to prosecute her appeal of *raptus*, accompanied by Guy Brian, knight, John Kentcomb, and John Shakel, she was attacked near the Watergate Bridge by Henry Yulecomb, William Yulecomb, Baldwin Yulecomb, John Luke of Bodmin, John Cole (saddler of London), John Fowy, and John Willing of Cornwall. The attackers were arrested by James Lyons, sergeant-at-arms, but the miscreants broke the arrest and escaped.[140]

Thus, in trying to prevent an appeal of rape from being prosecuted, Henry's new accomplices, like William Yulecomb and Lawrence Drew before, were also implicated in a crime of rape.

In faint additions to this entry, one can make out that in the following Michaelmas term, "the Monday after three weeks" (October 22, 1380), the saddler John Cole appeared, and he was mainprised by other saddlers; and outlawry seems to have been declared against the three Yulecombs and the three other indicted accomplices.

Meanwhile, however, Henry Yulecomb had resorted to another measure, namely, obtaining a papal injunction against Isabel's Watergate escort, the knight Guy Brian, whom he blamed for her prosecution of him. There were two knights at this time named Guy Brian, a father and a son, and either one could be the person in question; the father had been especially active in serving as a justice of the peace and performing other official functions in Devon, Dorset, and Somerset.[141] Henry

[139] *Statutes* 1:41. This pseudo-statute was based on Bracton; see R. F. Hunnisett, *The Mediaeval Coroner* (Cambridge: Cambridge University Press, 1961). But Bracton does not specify the number of pledges. See Kelly, "Statutes of Rapes," p. 367.

[140] PRO, KB 29/32 m. 43d, Watergate indictment: see appendix, no. 8. This entry is referred to by Crow and Olson, *Chaucer Life-Records*, p. 345, n. 2, citing only "KB 29/32, 3–4 Richard II" without specifying the membrane.

[141] See the *Calendar of Patent Rolls*. The elder Guy seems to have been knighted in 1346

himself managed to be knighted around this time, it seems. His emissary to Rome was probably the chaplain John Dawe, who made proclamation of the papal prohibition on August 5, 1380, in the churchyard of St. Paul's Cathedral in London, immediately after the sermon, in the following terms:

Dominus papa per bullas et processus inhibet domino Guidoni Brian, militi, ne se intromitteret prosequi contra dominum Henricum Yeuelcombe, militem, pro Isabella, uxore ejusdem Henrici, que fuit uxor ejus, et est, et permansit cum eodem Henrico per unum annum et quindecim septimanas, et quod predictus Guido falso et maliciose facit prosecucionem contra eum in curia domini regis ad suspendendum eum. Et qui vult habere inde copiam veniat ad ecclesiam sancti Martini, et habebit.

[The pope by bulls and processes forbids Guy Brian, knight, to intermeddle by proceedings against Henry Yeuelcombe, knight, on behalf of Isabella, the said Henry's wife, who has been, and is, his wife, who lived with the said Henry for one year and fifteen weeks, and the aforesaid Guy falsely and wrongly proceeds against him in the king's court to get him hanged. And anyone who wishes to have a copy hereof, let him come to St. Martin's church, and he shall have it.][142]

On the following November 17, Dawe was charged in the king's court at Northampton for making this proclamation, which he acknowledged; when asked to produce the bulls, he said that they were now in the court of Rome. This unlikely explanation was seemingly accepted, and he was eventually released on condition that he never again go overseas without special license from the king.[143]

We should expect Henry, in addition to the extraordinary resort to papal injunction, to follow the usual course of bringing a writ *de uxore rapta* against Brian, as Roger Vernon was to do against the rescuers of

(*CPR Richard II*, 1:248); he was dead by 1391 (ibid. 4:445, 447, 467) and perhaps by June 1386 (3:162). The son is referred to as knight as early as 1377 (*CPR Edward III*, 16:160); he was part of the earl of March's Irish expedition (*CPR Richard II*, 1:409, 449), but it did not arrive in Ireland until May 15, 1380 (Thomas Frederick Tout, "Mortimer, Edmund (II) de," *Dictionary of National Biography*), so that he could still have been available to escort Isabel in April.

[142] Ed. and trans. G. O. Sayles, *Select Cases in the Court of King's Bench*, vol. 7, SS, vol. 88, (London, 1971), pp. 21–22.

[143] Ibid.

Margaret Kebell,[144] and it is likely that such a writ remains to be discovered.

There would also, of course, have been writs from the other side. One such is dated November 29, 1381, addressed to the coroners of Cornwall, ordering the outlawry of William Yulecomb and Lawrence Drew for not appearing in the last Trinity term to respond to Isabel Mohun *de raptu.* The coroner who returned the writ did not receive it until March 28, 1382, but the return was not due until April 21 of that year.[145]

Later in 1382, on October 23, Henry and his brother William received a royal pardon, just as the Parliament that passed the new statute of rapes was winding down. Henry, because of service that he is undertaking for the king in Portugal, is pardoned the king's suit for the *raptus* of Isabel Mohun on which he stands indicted, charged, or appealed, and any decrees of outlawry against him are revoked, but he remains chargeable by others on the foresaid *raptus.* William receives conditional letters of pardon for the same *raptus.*[146] William, by the way, is on record as having been pardoned once before, along with his brother Baldwin, on April 4, 1376, after being indicted or appealed for the death of John Carlyl.[147]

We see then that Henry and William Yulecomb were pardoned for the alleged rape of Isabel, even though Henry had already been pardoned for the earlier incident, and even though, according to Isabel's own accusations, William was involved only in a successful abduction in 1376 and in an attempted abduction in 1380. For a similar case, we can think of Hugh Bonehomme, pardoned for rape in 1364, for having kidnapped Agnes, daughter of John Giles, to persuade her to marry Simon Porter in spite of her being the wife of Thomas Gilling.[148]

[144] PRO, KB 27/973 (Michaelmas, 1504) m.1 of warrants (at end of roll): "Staff. Rogerus Vernon ponit loco suo Thomam Skrimsher versus Radulphum Gell nuper de Blore [and seven others] de placito transgressionis contra formam statuti de muliere abducta cum bonis viri inde editi et provisi, etc." See Ives, p. 39, who sums up the yearbook discussions. Ives finds Vernon to be "using the little-known section of Westminster I c. 13, *de uxore abducta cum bonis viri.*" As we have seen, the action was not uncommon a century earlier.

[145] PRO, KB 136/5/5/3/1 (quindene of Easter, 1382), last writ. See appendix, no. 9.

[146] PRO, C66/313, m. 13, reported in *CPR Richard II*, 2:179. See appendix, no. 10.

[147] *CPR Edward III*, 16 vols., (London, 1891–1916), 16:258 (at the request of Thomas Symon, chivaler).

[148] See appendix, no. 3.

Henry and William were pardoned for impending service in Portugal. But just a month after the pardon, order was given to the constable of Dover to arrest the knight Henry Yulecomb and sixteen other men, including William and Baldwin Yulecomb and John Fawy (Fowy), for having rebelled against the king's uncle Edmund, earl of Cambridge, when on a voyage with him. Similar commissions were given to others in England, including Guy Brian, to arrest the same men.[149] Two years later there were more commissions for the same offense,[150] but in the following year all three Yulecombs were pardoned by the king at the supplication of the earl's wife, the countess of Cambridge.[151] In 1388, we find Henry being appointed to a royal commission of inquiry.[152] In the next decade he served as commissioner of array[153] and king's escheator in Cornwall.[154] In January of 1399, Henry finally had successful dealings with another Isabel, but only after she was dead: a royal grant was bestowed on him in virtue of his good service, during the course of which, "by God's visitation," he had gone blind; he was to receive the lands belonging to Isabel Cornewaill, deceased, tenant-in-chief, during the minority of her grandson and heir, Thomas, son of her son David Hendore.[155] Henry's blindness did not prevent him from being included in the duke of Exeter's expedition to Ireland: he received protection for the voyage on May 1 and

[149] *CPR Richard II*, 2:256 (November 24, 1382).

[150] Ibid., 2:494 (June 24, 1384, only against Henry and three others, not including his brothers and Fawy; they "behaved rebelliously and frustrated the completion of the expedition" of the earl of Cambridge); 2:348–49 (July 3, 1384, against thirteen men, including the four Watergate fugitives; they "behaved so rebelliously" the earl of Cambridge could not complete the object of his expedition).

[151] Ibid., 2:534 (February 18, 1385).

[152] Ibid., 3:468–69 (May 28, 1388. Henry Ilecome, knight, and others are to inquire if a certain man was an alien and possessed his land illegally).

[153] Ibid., 5:88 (March 1, 1392).

[154] Ibid., 5:653 (December 2, 1395); 6:15 (July 5, 1396), 241 (July 12, 1397). Cf. 5:651 (December 3, 1395): Henry accuses the mayor of Bodmyn, Cornwall, of breaking into his lands, destroying his property, and lying in wait to kill him.

[155] Ibid., 6:479–80, January 25, 1399, for Henry Ivelcombe (i.e., Iuelcombe), knight. There is no record of Isabel's marriage to David Hendore's father. On November 18, 1398 we hear of a vicarage in the diocese of Exeter in the king's gift by reason of the minority of Thomas, son and heir of David Hendor, tenant-in-chief (*CPR Richard II*, 6:447). Isabel was married to Edmund Cornewaille in 1373, and Edmund's mother was also named Isabel (*CPR Edward III*, 15:295–96); an entry in 1389 may indicate that Edmund is dead: Isabel is called both "his wife" and "formerly his wife" (*CPR Richard II*, 4:25).

June 17 of 1399.[156] After Richard II's deposition, his wardship grant was confirmed by the new king.[157]

Meanwhile, new writs continued to be noted on the Watergate indictment, with no notice taken of the pardons of Henry and William from the king's suit in 1382. John Cole eventually turned up again, "made fine," and was released through new mainpernors, and finally, perhaps as late as 1386, was pardoned and dismissed.[158] I have been able to find no further word of Isabel; perhaps we will have to wait until Christopher Cannon's next foray into the Public Record Office.

VI. Releases Undocumented and Documented

We have seen that the king pardoned Henry Yulecomb and his brothers twice for the *raptus* of Isabel, first in 1378 and then in 1382. Isabel herself could have pardoned him as well by withdrawing her appeal at any time. This, of course, would have subjected her to a fine, which she would likely have wished Henry to pay as part of the settlement, along with other considerations. He in turn would undoubtedly have wanted a release from her of the kind that Cecily Champain gave to Chaucer.

A case from the early part of the next century shows the dangers of not having such a release. It concerns still another widow Isabel, *Isabella que fuit uxor*, this time the former wife of Roger Waye. In the county of Devon in 1422, she had a man named Stephen Melya attached, to answer her plea that "with force and arms he broke the close of the said Isabella at Burston and depastured, trod down, and wasted with some beasts her grass, lately growing there, to the value of 40*s*., and inflicted other outrages upon her, to the serious loss of the said Isabella and against the king's peace." Her attorney, Thomas Foulhill, appearing for her in court and specifying that the incident occurred on July 1, 1420, elaborated on the charges and put the damages at £20. Stephen's attorney, John Burley, denied force and injury and pleaded not guilty. Both parties put themselves on the country. As for the *residuum* of the aforesaid trespass, Stephen's position was that Isabel ought not to have maintained an action against him, because a long time after the trespass was

[156] *CPR Richard II*, 6:540, 573.
[157] *CPR Henry IV*, 4 vols., (London, 1903–9), 1:65, November 8, 1399.
[158] Watergate indictment.

supposedly committed, namely, on October 3, 1420, the two parties through the mediation of friends had reached a compromise, promising that they would "stand in high and in low" (*stare in alto et in basso*) by the award of mutually agreed upon arbitrators in Cornwall "both concerning the aforesaid trespass as well as all other trespasses, plaints, and quarrels held, instituted, or to be instituted" ("tam de et super transgressione predicta quam de omnibus aliis transgressionibus, querelis, et debatis . . . habitis, motis, seu movendis"). The arbitrators decided that Stephen should give Isabel one gallon of wine in full satisfaction of everything, and she accepted the gallon of wine in accord with the award. Stephen asserted that he was ready to prove this account of events, but Isabel denied that she had ever made such an agreement, and the case was sent to a jury.[159]

We note that the form of the alleged Isabel–Stephen arbitration, referring first to a specific charge and then to all other actions, corresponds to the May 4 version of the Cecily–Geoffrey quitclaim, rather than to the May 7 version, which first refers generally to various kinds of actions, including felonies, and then even more generally to all possible actions. If Cecily Champain and Geoffrey Chaucer entered upon a similar arbitration with the assistance of friends—for instance, the acquaintances of Chaucer who witnessed the release on May 1—he was fortunate that she not only agreed to the award but also registered it in two courts of law.

An example closer to our interest here can be seen in a 1344 ravishment plea: "When the four defendants showed the court a quitclaim from the plaintiffs, in which they had remitted their action for ravishment, the plaintiffs were amerced for false claim and the ravishers went free."[160] If Cecily Champain had taken Chaucer to court in spite of her release, he would presumably have been on clearer ground if he could have shown the version of the release that mentioned *raptus* explicitly, but the vague language of the May 7 copy would undoubtedly have served just as well.

[159] Sayles, *Select Cases*, 7:257–58: KB 27/643 m. 59.

[160] Walker, "Wrongdoing," p. 287 (Professor Walker informs me that her PRO citation of this case is erroneous, and that she has not yet recovered the correct citation). The plaintiffs in this case accused the defendants of ravishing and abducting a girl, who was a minor in feudal custody, against the will of the plaintiffs, but the defendants showed a *scriptum* remitting and relaxing them.

In another case of ravishment in which a quitclaim figured, this one from 1342, a mother is sued for abducting her son from the custody of his guardian—a fairly typical complaint.[161] Henry of Ravenswath, knight, charges Elizabeth Spring in a writ of trespass with ravishing the heir from his possession ("breve de transgressione per quod ei imponitur ipsam rapuisse predictum heredem extra possessionem ipsius Henrici") on May 5, 1339; Henry claims to own the boy's maritage, the value of which has allegedly deteriorated by the amount of £300. Elizabeth responds by submitting a *scriptum* according to which Henry's father quitclaimed the manor in question to the heir's grandfather, and the terms of the quitclaim indicate that the land is held is socage, not feudal tenure.[162] She asks the court's judgment on whether the quitclaim vitiates Henry's suit. Henry denies that the *scriptum* is his father's doing. Both Elizabeth and Henry call for a trial by jury (*per patriam*) and by the seven witnesses named in the release (*et per . . . testes in predicto scripto nominatos*). Meanwhile the *scriptum* is given to the king's clerk for safekeeping, and he eventually delivers it to one of the justices. Elizabeth's case would have been strengthened, of course, if she could have produced a court enrollment of the release as well as the original. But even as it was, she won the case, at least temporarily—apparently because Henry failed to appear on the appointed day of trial—and was dismissed *sine die.*[163]

If the plaintiff had appeared, along with the witnesses named in the release, the witnesses would have been examined by the jury and possibly by the justices as well, as in a 1318 case of false imprisonment mentioned above, *Reynham v Hatton*: After the jury found the seven defendants guilty, with damages assessed at £100, four of the defendants produced

[161] Walker, "Widow and Ward: The Feudal Law of Child Custody in Medieval England," *Women in Medieval Society*, ed. Susan Mosher Stuard (Philadelphia: University of Pennsylvania Press, 1976), pp. 159–72, at 163–65.

[162] As Walker explains (ibid., p. 164), socage was "a free tenure closer to the peasant level in which the land and the heir were placed in the familial custody of a relative who could not inherit in the event of the child's death. . . . Mothers who acted as guardians ('next friends') were especially liable to be involved in litigation if their late husbands held any land by feudal tenure."

[163] PRO, CP 40/324 m. 252. Walker, "Widow and Ward," p. 171, n. 39, recounts a similar case from 1303: "Johanna, widow of Adam de Lorymer, went *sine die* in a plea of ravishing Walter, the son and heir. Johanna disputed the tenurial claims of the plaintiff and the jury supported her. Probably she had taken her son from the plaintiff but he had had no right to the custody, and hence there was no case against her."

a *scriptum* in which the plaintiff allegedly pardoned ("remisit, relaxavit, et omnino imperpetuum pardonavit") all actions and demands that he had against them by reason of trespass, conspiracy, and imprisonment. The plaintiff's attorney denied that the *scriptum* was authentic, and he offered to prove it by the country and by the witnesses. The witnesses were examined separately, their conflicting testimony was recorded in detail and rejected as frivolous, and the *scriptum* was declared false. The four defendants were assessed an extra £50 damages.[164] In a 1390 case, *Colehill v Hankin*, in which the charge was the taking and carrying away of goods and chattels, the defendant pleaded a release of all actions real and personal given him by the executors of the plaintiff's former husband, and he asked immediate judgment of the justices without putting the matter to trial.[165]

VII. Conclusion

Both Isabel Mohun and Cecily Champain seem to have been "women of independent means"; Isabel was the former wife of someone, while Cecily was the "former daughter" of others. Both acted for themselves, Isabel in an appeal of rape, and Cecily in an unknown action or series of actions concerning rape and perhaps other complaints.

We know more about Isabel's situation. She was a widow, or else her marriage to John Mohun had been annulled. Presumably she owned her own "remarriage"; at least, we do not hear of anyone else who did. Henry Yulecomb obviously desired to marry her, and either she resisted and he used force from the beginning, in November of 1376 (her date) or in December of the same year (his date), or else she did agree to marry him and later tried to get out of it, lying about the violence used to take her away and to force intercourse upon her—which, she claimed, occurred only once, even though he detained her for well over a year. It may be that she had to include the reference to unwilling intercourse in order to mount an appeal, or at least she and her lawyers may have believed that such a reference was necessary. Margaret Kebell in a similar situation a century later had an appeal accepted on a simple charge of *raptus*. On the ecclesiastical side, Isabel could have sought an annulment

[164] Arnold, *Select Cases of Trespass*, pp. 37–41, *Reynham v. Hatton* (4.3).

[165] Arnold, pp. 173–74 (13.45). This is a case of demurral, that is, denial that the other party has a case (see pp. xxvii, liii). The outcome has not been found.

on the grounds that the marriage was entered into under "force and fear." Back on the secular side, she could have followed the example of the widow Joan Hotoft in 1362, when she charged Henry Willows with criminally breaking and entering and imprisoning her (doc. 1 below), or the same Joan in 1363, when, acting as a nonwidow, she made the same complaints against the same man but added abduction and forced marriage to the charges (doc. 2). Both women could also have brought similar civil suits against the alleged perpetrators. But whatever civil punishments she may have contemplated, Isabel was determined to bring Henry to court as a felon. Perhaps she wished to seek the death penalty for him, as he himself complained about her assistant, Guy Brian. Henry avoided the danger to his neck from the king's side by securing pardons from the king, but the danger from Isabel remained. However, Whittick's study of the appeal process in the fifteenth century leads him to conclude that "the object of an appeal was not vengeance exacted by the defendant's death, but the return of a chattel or a financial settlement after the greatest possible harassment of the other party," a process that he compares to the use of the appeal of rape in the thirteenth century, as reported by Post.[166]

As for Cecily Champain, we are still left with the bare word *raptus* in the first version of her quitclaim, summing up a set of circumstances perfectly well known to the participants but not to us. *Raptus* can certainly mean a sexual violation, short for *raptus et carnalis commixtio contra voluntatem femine.* But *raptus* is also sometimes short for ravishing-and-abducting, and it was used of both male and female wards and also of married women. In the latter case, the terms of the writ *De uxore rapta* required reference to ravishing, abducting, and detaining, even though there was usually no seizure, no sexual violation, no abduction, no robbery from husband, no detention, and even, sometimes, no longer any husband: that is, in some cases the marriage had been annulled in a church court. Thus, even if Isabel Mohun Yulecomb had annulled a marriage to Henry Yulecomb on the grounds suggested above, that she did not give free consent, Henry could have resorted to using the *De uxore rapta* writ, naming Guy Brian as the person who ravished, abducted, and detained her, even though well aware that Brian had done none of these things, but at most, let us say, had only persuaded her to

[166] Whittick, "Role of the Criminal Appeal," p. 63, citing Post, "Ravishment of Women," for the thirteenth century.

leave Henry. We have seen Roger Vernon doing this in the case of his forced wife, Margaret Kebell.

Isabel identified herself as having been the wife of John Mohun and made no allusion to the fact that Henry Yulecomb claimed her as his wife. Cecily claimed to be lately the daughter of William and Agnes Champain. She too may have been keeping silent about a claim that some man was making on her as his wife, or she may simply not have mentioned a former or current husband, as in the case of Agnes Giles Gilling (doc. 3 below). By using *quondam* of her parents, she may have been saying nothing more than that they were dead; or, just conceivably, she may have meant to say that she was no longer underage, or that neither they nor anyone else owned her maritage. If her father had owned her maritage (as was the claim in *Lincoln v Simond*, 1391) and she were abducted, he could have referred to her abduction as a *raptus*, and obtained a writ *De raptu de custodia*. But if her father or mother or some other person did not own her maritage and she were abducted by a would-be suitor who enlisted Chaucer's aid, what could she do to obtain satisfaction or damages? On the criminal side, she could have brought an appeal against the perpetrators, whether alleging a real or fictitious element of sexual force, like Isabel Mohun, or not mentioning forced sex, like Alice Jackman, daughter of Richard Jackman, in 1377, where the civil writ *De uxore rapta cum bonis mariti* was altered, in effect, to a criminal appeal *De filia rapta cum bonis patris* (doc. 11 below), or Margaret, widow of Thomas Kebell, later on. She could also, like Joan Hotoft, and like Margaret Kebell's relatives, have laid information at quarter-sessions. Or, like Alice Lord in 1362, in acting against the disappointed suitor who kidnapped her and beat her up, she could have filed a bill of complaint, seeking an indictment for felony or trespass. She could also have brought the sort of civil suits, including assault, that Margaret Kebell did, or obtained a writ charging that she had been taken, imprisoned, and maltreated, like Idonia Cophyn in 1379.

If, on the other hand, Cecily's *raptus* were one of sexual violation, she could clearly have pursued both an appeal and indictment on the criminal side. As for civil remedies, though no examples have yet been found of damages being sought in such cases, one can easily imagine that actions of breaking and entering and assault would be readily available.

Given the inherent ambiguity of the word *raptus*, when abduction and not sexual violation was the main issue, even when both *rapere* and *abducere* were used, there was probably an implicit accusation of sexual violation where the circumstances admitted it: that is, whenever a woman was abducted by a man. If so, that presumptive aspect of the charge would have to be argued or explained away in court. This would clearly be true in criminal prosecutions, but it would also obtain in responses to civil suits of abduction. Such a convention would not have been necessary, of course, in the actions of account and debt mentioned by Cecily in the version of her release discovered by Cannon.

To sum up, given both releases, the one naming *raptus* and the other naming both criminal and civil actions, Cecily's main grievance could have been either abduction or sexual violation or a combination of both. There is more evidence of both criminal and civil remedies being used for abduction than for sexual violation, but it is plausible for the latter as well. If the charge were abduction, say, in the wake of a soured marriage negotiation, an additional charge of unwanted coitus may have been added or even emphasized, in order to make it more convincingly the subject of an appeal of *raptus*.

But whether the charge was meant seriously or fictitiously, whether it involved forced sex—in actuality or only as part of a conventional complaint—or only abduction (with or without an explicit or implicit charge of sexual violation) we must be on guard against concluding that she had proved it or could have proved it, or that it is likely to have been true. Our tours through the legal practices of Chaucer's time should teach us that there are often many complications lying beneath the literal surface of legal records. The grand jury's verdict of "not proven"—or, as they put it in those days, "ignoramus"—is usually the wisest conclusion. Still, it is likely that there was something to the charge, whatever it was, since Chaucer seems to have paid to make it go away. It is pleasant to think that Cecily, acting on her own in a man's world, was able to obtain financial reparations after he had done something actionable against her.

This study has been mainly linguistic and legalistic: I have tried to survey the terms used for the two kinds of rape, sex-rape and abduction-rape, and the realities and fictions that can lie behind them. The second kind of rape gives rise to all sorts of combinations and mixtures of motives and emotions: abduction for the purpose of sex; abduction for the purpose of marriage or arranging a marriage, because of the abductee's wealth or potential wealth; with the abductee willing beforehand or later, or never giving consent to the marriage or the sex that occurs within it. Such distinctions must be kept in mind not only in historical contexts but also in literature.

Let us end by considering Jill Mann's judgment that for Chaucer "rape remains a constant touchstone for determining justice between the sexes; in the *Canterbury Tales* as in the *Legend* [*of Good Women*] it appears as the definitive form of male tyranny, representing a fundamental imbalance between the sexes which human relationships must seek to redress."[167] She is, of course, speaking primarily of the two sexual rapes in the *Legend*, namely, those of Lucretia and Philomela (the latter a case of abduction for purposes of forced sex), and the single sexual rape in the *Canterbury Tales*, at the beginning of *The Wife of Bath's Tale*, where the rape is followed by the hue and cry ("swich clamour / And swich pursute" [lines 889–90]) and the death penalty. Chaucer seems to have the Wife of Bath wonder at the severity of this punishment: "Paraventure swich was the statut tho" (line 893), as if it were not true in her modern England. But, of course, death was the punishment for all felonies, and though it may not have been carried out very often for indictments of rape, in an appeal of rape by the violated woman after a hue and cry, execution should have been inevitable—unless, of course, the traditional compromise of letting the rapist off in exchange for marrying his victim was still feasible in Chaucer's time. That solution does not come into play here (unless we should wish to regard the raped maiden and the Loathly Lady as one and the same person!).

What other rapes is Mann thinking of for her broad statement? She brings up later the foiled rape of Constance in *The Man of Law's Tale* and the plot to make Virginia a sex slave in *The Physician's Tale*, and also, in *The Franklin's Tale*, Aurelius's efforts to secure the affections of Dorigen, which Dorigen thinks of in terms of classical threats of sexual rape. Mann is not concerned with the sex-minded seizers of more or less consenting women in the farcical tales—Nicholas, John and Alleyn, Daun John—but she does include a character in *The Merchant's Tale*, namely, Pluto, for his rape of Proserpine, even though, as we have seen, Chaucer uses the term "fetched" instead of "ravished," for Mann thinks that the grisliness of Pluto's cart makes the event "violent and horrific" and "evokes the terror of the scene." But it seems that any potential terror is

[167] Jill Mann, *Geoffrey Chaucer* (Atlantic Highlands: Humanities Press International, 1991), p. 45. She deals with rape on pp. 43–47 (Lucretia and Philomela), 64–66 (Proserpina), 87–89 (*Wife of Bath's Tale*), 97–98 (near-rape in *Pamphilus*), 115 (Dorigen), 137 (Constance), 145 (Virginia), and 167–68 (*Troilus*).

diffused by Chaucer's making Pluto not the god of the underworld but the king of Faery. And even though she says that Pluto's antifeminist remarks are the words of a rapist, she admits that he is "a hen-pecked rapist." We must also acknowledge that Chaucer portrays Proserpine as having long ago consented to her ravished state, like Helen in the *Troilus*, whose rape Mann also discusses.

Since Mann has admitted Pluto and Paris to her list of Chaucerian rapists, I suggest a similar candidate, namely, Theseus. For, not to mention his abduction of the willing Ariadne and Phaedra (and abandonment of Ariadne) in the *Legend of Good Women*, he conquered the Amazons in the land of Feminy by force of arms, and although his subsequent courtship of Hippolyta is omitted—in the *Theseid* he considers her fairer than Helen, whom he had previously abducted (1.130)—we do see the way he deals with his captured ward Emily. He does not give her much room to withhold her consent to marry the winner of the tournament; and, at the end of the story, when she has been a widow for some years, though he does ask her consent to remarry and take Palamon for husband, he does not wait for her reply. We must assume, however, since we are told that she was happy with Palemon, that she was ravished by Theseus's speech (the sort of ravishment that Troilus contrasts with physical force) and gave her full assent. We can, therefore, classify Theseus as a rapist, even a serial rapist; but, since he never refuses any request that women make of him, he approaches the hen-pecked status of King Pluto in the realm of Faery. We must also remember that Pluto's wife is not the only ravished spouse in *The Merchant's Tale*, for January is "ravished in a trance" every time he looks on May's face, and that in turn brings out the rapist in him: he begins to "menace" her in his heart, threatening to "strain" her in his arms harder than ever Paris did Helen (lines 1750–54). Both January and May, then, are victims of rape, but January is at a disadvantage, since he is the victim of a divine conspiracy: after Venus injured him with her firebrand, he was "so ravished on his lady May" that he was nearly mad and on the point of swooning.

One lesson to take away from all this is that the language of rape has a very wide range in the Middle Ages, and we must not let our hatred for the narrowed meaning of our modern word "rape" mislead us when dealing with past uses of the word, for it will betray us like the most insidious kind of false friend.

Appendix

Documents from the Public Record Office

1. Commission of oyer and terminer, October 25, 1362: Criminal trespass complaint of Joan Hotoft that Henry Willows and others entered her close and imprisoned her. PRO, C (Chancery) 66/266, m. 20d, calendared in *CPR*, *Edward III*, 12:288.

Audiendo et terminando. Rex dilectis et fidelibus suis Johanni de la Lee, Johanni Knyvet, Waltero de Aldebury, et Thome de Eston, salutem. Ex quadem querela Johanne que fuit uxor Nicholai Hotoft, accepimus quod Henricus atte Wylewes de London, Ricardus de Ardern de London, peltere, Ricardus atte Grene de Hakeneye, Johannes Hereward, Willelmus Hereward, Johannes Sprot, Willielmus Bakere, Willielmus Wyot de Hakeneye, Thomas Hore, peltere, et Ricardus de Tychebourn, et quamplures alii malefactores et pacis nostre perturbatores, clausum ipsius Johanne apud Braghyng vi et armis intraverunt et ipsam Johannem ibidem ceperunt, imprisonaverunt, et male tractaverunt, et alia enormia ei intulerunt, ad grave dampnum ipsius Johanne et contra pacem nostram. Et quia transgressionem predictam, si perpetrata fuerit, relinquere noluimus impunitam, assignavimus vos tres et duos vestrum, quorum vos, prefate Johannes Knyvet, unum esse volumus, justiciarios nostros, ad inquirendum per sacramentum proborum et legitimorum hominum de comitatu Hereford, per quos rei veritas melius sciri poterit de nominibus malefactorum predictorum qui una cum prefatis Henrico, Ricardo, Ricardo, Johanne, Willielmo, Johanne, Willielmo, Willielmo, Thoma, et Ricardo transgressionem illam perpetrarunt, et de transgressione predicta plenius veritatem, et ad eandem transgressionem audiendum et terminandum secundum legem et consuetudinem regni nostri. Et ideo vobis mandamus quod ad certos etc., quos etc., quorum etc., ad hoc provideritis inquisitionem illam facere, et transgressionem predictam audiatis et terminetis in forma predicta. F[. . .] etc. Salvis etc. Mandavimus enim vicecomiti nostro Hereford quod ad certos [etc.,] quos etc., quorum etc., ei sciri facere, venire facere coram vobis ut quorum etc., tot etc., per quos etc., et inquiri. In cujus etc.
Rex, apud Westmonasterium xxv die Octobris.

Hearing and determining. The king to his beloved and faithful John Lee, John Knyvet, Walter Aldebury, and Thomas Eston, greetings. From a

complaint of Joan who was the wife of Nicholas Hotoft we have taken it that Henry Willows of London, Richard Ardern of London, pelterer, Richard Green of Hakeney, John Hereward, William Hereward, John Sprot, William Baker, William Wyot of Hakeney, Thomas Hore, pelterer, and Richard Tychebourn, and several other evildoers and disturbers of our peace, entered the close of the said Joan at Braghyng by force and arms, took the said Joan there and imprisoned and maltreated her, and inflicted other enormities upon her, to the grave damage of the said Joan and against our peace. And because we were unwilling to leave unpunished the aforesaid trespass, if it were perpetrated, we assigned you, three and two of you, of whom we wish you, the aforesaid John Knyvet, to be one, as our justices, to make inquest by the oath of good and lawful men from the county of Hereford, by means of whom the truth of the matter can be better known concerning the names of the evildoers who along with the aforesaid Henry, Richard, Richard, John, William, John, William, William, Thomas, and Richard perpetrated that trespass, and the truth of the aforesaid trespass can be more fully known, and to hear and determine the same trespass according to the law and custom of our realm. And therefore we mandate you that to certain men etc., whom etc., whose etc., you shall provide to make the said inquest etc., and hear and determine the aforesaid trespass in the aforesaid form. [?] etc. Saving etc. For we have mandated our sheriff of Hereford that to certain men whom etc., whose etc., to make known to him, to make come before you, so that whose etc., so many etc., by means of whom etc., and have inquest made. In whose etc.
The king at Westminster, the 25th day of October [1362].

2. Commission of oyer and terminer, May 2, 1363: Criminal trespass complaint of Joan Hotoft that Henry Willows and others broke into her close, imprisoned her, took her and her chattels away and kept her captive until she took an oath to marry Henry. PRO, C 66/267, m. 22d, calendared in *CPR*, *Edward III*, 12:363.

Audiendo et terminando. Rex dilectis et fidelibus suis Johanni de Moubray, Johanni Knyvet, Thome de Ingelby, Johanni Chilterne, et Luce Vynter, salutem. Ex quadam querela Johanne Hoto[f]t accepimus quod Henricus Wylewes de London, draper, Richardus Ardern de London, pelter, Johannes Sprot de London, shereman, Thomas Hore, skynnere, et Richardus Tychebourn, skynnere, ac quidam alii malefactores et pacis nostre perturbatores, clausum et domos ipsius Johanne

apud Braghyng vi et armis noctanter fregerunt et ipsam Johannam ibidem ceperunt, imprisonaverunt, et male tractaverunt, et ipsam sic imprisonatam abinde ad diversa loca ignota duxerunt, et eam sic in prisona, quousque eadam Johanna sacramentum corporale quod se prefato Henrico maritari promittere prestitisset, detinuerunt, et bona et catalla sua ad valenciam quadraginta librarum apud predictam villam de Braghyng inventa ceperunt et asportaverunt, et in homines et servientes suos ibidem insultum fecerunt et ipsos verberaverunt, vulneraverunt, et male tractaverunt, per quod eadem Johanna servicium suum eorundem hominum et servientum per magnum tempus amisit, et alia enormia ei intulerunt, ad grave dampnum ipsius Johanne et contra pacem nostram. Et quia transgressionem predictam, si perpetrata fuerit, relinquere noluimus impunitam, assignavimus vos, quatuor, tres, et duos vestrum, quorum aliquem vestrum vos, prefati Johannes de Moubray, Johannes Knyvet, et Thoma[s], unum esse voluimus, justiciarios nostros, ad inquirendum per sacramentum proborum et legitimorum hominum de comitatu Hereford, per quos rei veritas melius sciri poterit de nominibus malefactorum predictorum qui una cum prefatis Henrico, etc., transgressionem predictam perpetrarunt [continues as above].
Rex apud Westmonasterium, secundo die Maji [1363].

Hearing and determining. The king to his beloved and faithful John Mowbray, John Knyvet, Thomas Ingelby, John Chiltern, and Luke Vynter, greetings. From a complaint of Joan Hotoft we have taken it that Henry Willows of London, draper, Richard Ardern of London, pelterer, John Sprot of London, shearman, Thomas Hore, skinner, and Richard Tychebourn, skinner, and certain other evildoers and disturbers of our peace, by force and arms at night broke the close and houses of the said Joan at Braghyng and took the said Joan there and imprisoned and maltreated her, and, thus imprisoned, took her to divers unknown places and detained her thus in prison until the same Joan had made a corporal oath that she promise to be married to the aforesaid Henry, and they took and carried away goods and chattels to the value of forty pounds found at the aforesaid village of Braghyng, and they made assault upon her men and servants there and beat and wounded and maltreated them, by which the same Joan lost her service of the same men and servants for a long time, and they inflicted other enormities upon her, to the grave damage of the said Joan and against our peace. And

because we were unwilling to leave unpunished the aforesaid trespass, if it were perpetrated, we assigned you, four, three, and two of you, of whom one of you, the aforesaid John Mowbray, John Knyvet, and Thomas, we wish to be one, as our justices, to make inquest by the oath of good and lawful men from the county of Hereford, by means of whom the truth of the matter might be known concerning the names of the aforesaid evildoers who along with the aforesaid Henry, etc., perpetrated the aforesaid trespass [continues as in document 1].
The king at Westminster, the 2nd day of May [1363].

3. Pardon, dated May 6, 1364, of Hugh Bonehomme for various offenses including manslaughter and *raptus*. PRO, C 66/269, m. 7, calendared in *CPR*, *Edward III*, 12:515.

Rex omnibus ballivis et fidelibus suis ad quos etc., salutem. Sciatis quod cum Hugo Bonehumme de Bugthorp indictatus sit, sicut intelleximus, de eo quod ipse die dominica proxima post festum translationis sancti Thome martiris anno regni nostri tricesimo sexto [July 3, 1362] felonice interfecit Gilbertum filium Johannis Grayve de Bugthorp, ac idem Hugo similiter sit indictatus per nomen magistri Hugonis Boni Hominis, aliter vocatus Hugo Bonehomme de Bugthorp, quod ipse simul cum aliis in carnipriveo anno preterito [February 15, 1363] apud Eboracum vi et armis cepit Agnetem filiam Johannis Gyles de Eboraco et ipsam rapuit et secum abduxit et ipsam per cohercionem et minas consentire fecit ad matrimonium injustam contrahendum cum Simone Porter, et bona et catalla Thome Gillyng, tunc mariti dicte Agnetis, ad valenciam viginti marcarum cepit et asportavit, et de eo quod idem Hugo die dominica in quinta septimana quadrigesime anno regni nostri vicesimo tercio [March 29, 1349] bona et catalla Gilberti filii Johannis Grayve ad valenciam duarum marcarum apud Bugthorp cepit et asportavit, et de eo quod prefatus Hugo cum aliis contra prohibicionem nostram sediciose asportavit ad partes transmarinas ducentas marcas sterlingorum in pecunia numerata, videlicet, ad festum sancti Andree anno regni nostri tricesimo primo [November 30, 1357], ac eciam de eo quod ipse ad festum Invencionis sancte crucis anno regni nostri vicesimo tercio [May 3, 1349] venit apud Knyteros juxta Skirpenbek, armatus cum scuto et lancia ad modum guerre, et vadiavit bellum contra Rogerum Clerc, nos de gracia nostra speciali et ad requisicionem tam

fratris nostri nuper regis Francie, cujus anime propicietur Deus, quam quorumdam cardinalium qui nobis ex causa specialiter scripserunt, perdonamus eidem Hugoni sectam pacis nostre que ad nos pertinet pro morte et raptu predictis unde sic indictatus, rettatus, vel appellatus existit, ac eciam utlagarias, si que in ipsum hujus occasione fuerint promulgate, et perdonamus similiter eidem Hugoni omnes alias utlagarias in ipsum occasione sedicionis et transgressionum predictarum promulgatas, et firmam pacem nostram ei inde concedimus; ita tamen quod stet recto in curia nostra si quis versus eam loqui voluerit de morte et raptu predictis, et stet etiam recto in eadem curia nostra tam ad sectam nostram quam aliorum de sedicione et transgressionibus antedictis. In cujus etc.
Rex apud Westmonasterium vi die Maji [1364]. [It is noted that on the following July 5 three mainpernors secured Hugh's release on good behavior.]

The king to all his bailiffs and faithful to whom [these letters may come,] greetings. Know that, since Hugh Bonehumme of Bugthorp stands indicted, as we have understood, for that he on the Sunday next after the feast of the translation of St. Thomas Martyr in the thirty-sixth year of our reign [July 3, 1362] feloniously killed Gilbert the son of John Grayve of Bugthorp; and the same Hugh stands similarly indicted, by the name of Master Hugh Goodman, otherwise called Hugh Bonehomme of Bugthorp, for that he along with others on the day of Carnival last year [February 15, 1363] at York by force and arms took Agnes the daughter of John Gyles of York and ravished her and took her away with him and by coercion and threats made her consent to contracting an unjust marriage with Simon Porter, and that he took and carried off the goods and chattels of Thomas Gillyng, at that time the husband of the said Agnes, to the value of twenty marks; and for that the same Hugh on the Sunday of the fifth week of Lent in the twenty-third year of our reign [March 29, 1349] took and carried off goods and chattels of Gilbert the son of John Grayve to the value of two marks, at Bugthorp; and for that the aforesaid Hugh along with others against our prohibition seditiously carried away to places beyond the seas two hundred marks of sterlings in numbered money, viz., on the feast of St. Andrew in the thirty-first year of our reign [November 30, 1357]; and also for that on the feast of the Finding of the Holy Cross in the twenty-third year of our reign [May 3, 1349] he came to Knyteros near Skirpenbek, armed with shield and lance in warlike fashion, and waged

a duel against Roger Clerk; we of our special grace and at the request both of our brother recently king of France, on whose soul may God have mercy, and of certain cardinals who have specially for good cause written to us, we pardon the same Hugh the suit of our peace that pertains to us for the aforesaid death and rape whence he stands indicted, charged, or appealed, and also outlawries, if any have been promulgated against him by virtue of this occasion, and we similarly pardon the same Hugh all other outlawries promulgated against him on the occasion of the aforesaid sedition and trespasses, and we grant him our firm peace thereupon. So that however he stand trial in our court if anyone should wish to speak against him concerning the aforesaid death and rape, and that he also stand trial in our same court both regarding our suit and that of others concerning the aforesaid sedition and trespasses. In whose, etc.
The king at Westminster, the 6th day of May [1364].

4. Pardon dated April 9, 1378. PRO, C 66 / 301, m. 21; calendared in *CPR Richard II*, 1:182.

Rex omnibus ballivis et fidelibus suis ad quos, etc. Sciatis quod, cum Henricus Yllecombe indictatus existat, ut intelleximus, de eo quod ipse, die Lune proximo ante festum Natalis Domini anno regni carissimi domini et avi nostri Edwardi nuper regis Anglie defuncti quinquagesimo, felonice rapuit apud Bodennek Isabellam que fuit uxor Johannis Moune, nos de gratia nostra speciali et de supplicacione dilecti consanguinei et fidelis nostri Johannis de Arundell, marescalli nostri Anglie, perdonavimus eidem Henrico sectam pacis nostre que ad nos pertinent pro raptu supradicto unde sic indictatus, rettatus, vel appellatus existit, ac eciam utlagariam si qua in ipsum ea occasione fuerit promulgata, et firmam pacem ei inde concedimus. Ita tamen quod stet recto in curia nostra si predicta Isabella versus eum loqui voluerit de felonia supradicta. In cuius, etc.
Rex apud Westmonasterium, ix die Aprilis.

The King to all his bailiffs and faithful subjects to whom, etc. Know that since Henry Yllecombe stands indicted, as we have understood, for having on the Monday before the feast of the birth of Our Lord in the fiftieth year of the reign of our dear lord and grandfather Edward, recently King of England, now deceased [i.e., December 22, 1376], feloniously ravished Isabel, who was the wife of John Moune, at Bodennek, we of our special grace and by supplication of our beloved kinsman and

faithful subject, John of Arundell, our marshall of England, have pardoned the same Henry the suit of our peace that pertains to us because of the aforesaid rape whereof he stands indicted, charged, or appealed, and also outlawry, if any for this matter should have been promulgated against him, and we concede to him our firm peace. So that, however, he stand trial in our court if the foresaid Isabel should wish to speak against him concerning the above-mentioned felony. In whose, etc.
The king at Westminster, the ninth day of April.

5. Continuation of jury to Easter term, 1380 (April 16). PRO, KB 27/476 (Hilary term, 1380), m. 30d.

Devon. Jurata inter Isabellam, que fuit uxor Johannis Moun, in propria persona sua appellatricem, et Henricum Yeuelcombe, de raptu et pace domini Edwardi nuper regis Anglie, avi domini regis nunc, fracte, unde eum appellat coram domino rege, ponitur in respectum usque a die pasche in tres septimanas, ubicumque, etc., per districtionem juratorum. Quia nullus, etc. Ideo vicecomes habeat corpora omnium juratorum, etc. Idem dies datus est partibus predictis, etc., videlicet predicto Henrico per manucepcionem suam qua prius, etc.

Devon. The jury between Isabel, former wife of John Mohun, appellatrix in her own person, and Henry Yulecomb, concerning rape and the breaking of the peace of the lord Edward, late king of England, grandfather of the present king, whereof she appealed him before the lord king, is placed in respite until three weeks after Easter, wherever, etc., for the distraint of the jurors, because no one, etc. Therefore the sheriff is to have the bodies of all the jurors, etc. The same day is given to the aforesaid parties, etc., viz. to the aforesaid Henry through his mainprise by which earlier, etc.

6. Arrest order. PRO, KB 27/476, m. 30d.

Eadem Isabella in propria persona sua apud se quarto die versus Willielmum fratrem predicti Henrici et Laurencium Drewe filium Drugonis de Wryngworth de raptu predicta [*sic*], et ipsi non venerunt. Et precatum fuit vicecomiti sicut pluries quod caperet eos. Et vicecomes retornavit quod ipsi non sunt inventi, etc. Ideo sicut pluries preceptum est vicecomiti quod capiat eos si, etc. Et salvo, etc. Ita quod habeat corpora sua coram domino Rege ad prefatum terminum, etc., etc.

The same Isabel appearing in her own person on her own behalf on the fourth day against William, brother of the aforesaid Henry, and Lawrence Drewe, son of Drugo, of Wryngworth, concerning the aforesaid rape, and they did not come. And request was made to the sheriff, as frequently before, that he arrest them, if, etc. And saving, etc. So that he have their bodies before the lord king on the aforesaid date, etc., etc.

7. Order to arrest mainpernors of Henry Yulecomb (after April 13, 1380). PRO, KB 29 / 32 (3 Richard II, 1379–80), m. 52d.

Somerset. Dominus rex mandavit vicecomiti Somerset breve suum clausum in hec verba: Ricardus, rex Anglie et Francie et Dominus Hibernie, vicecomiti Somerset salutem. Cum Matheus Gournay, chevaler, Thomas Tryvet, chevaler, et Thomas Fichet, chevaler, nuper in curia nostra coram nobis manuceperunt pro Henrico Yeuelcombe habendi corpus ejus coram nobis a die sancti Hillarii in xv dies ultimos preteritos ubicumque, etc. [. . .] esserimus in Anglia ad respondendum Isabelle que fuit uxor Johannis Moun de raptu et pace Domini Edwardi nuper regis Anglie, avi nostri, fracta, unde eum appellavit simul cum aliis, et ulterius quousque placitum predictum inter partes predictas terminaretur, et etiam de bono gestu ipsius Henrici erga dictam Isabellam et populum nostrum, et quod eadem Isabella per ipsum Henricum nec per aliquem per eum caperetur nec aliqualiter inclosaretur quin eadem Isabella appellum suum predictum versus eundem Henricum et alios homines appellare vel prosequi posset, quilibet manucaptorum predictorum sub pena ducentarum librarum, sicut per sufficientem redditum (?) et processus inde coram nobis habitos nobis constat, dictusque Henricus in curia nostra predicta ad diem sibi postea prefixum juxta manucapcionem suam predictam coram nobis venire contempsit, et dictam Isabellam quominus appellum suum predictum prosequeretur, aggregata sibi multitudine malefactorum, ipsam Isabellam apud pontem aquaticum palacii nostri Westmonasterii venientem versus curiam nostram in proteccione nostra.

The lord king sends to his sheriffs his writ close in these words: Richard, king of England and France and Lord of Ireland, health to the sheriff of Somerset. Since Matthew Gournay, knight, Thomas Tryvet, knight, and Thomas Fichet, knight, recently mainprised for Henry Yeuelcoumbe of having his body before us, wherever [. . .] we should be in England, on the quindene of Saint Hilary last past, to respond to Isabel, who was the wife of John Moun, concerning rape and breaking the peace of the late king lord Edward, our grandfather, whereof she appealed him along with others, and further, until such time as the aforesaid plea between them should be terminated, and also of the good behavior of the said Henry towards the said Isabel and our people and that the same Isabel not be captured or in any way inhibited by the said Henry or by anyone through him to prevent the said Isabel from appealing or prosecuting her aforesaid appeal against the said Henry and others, each of the aforesaid mainpernors being under pain of 200 pounds, as is clear to us by sufficient return and processes thereon held before us, and since the said Henry contemptuously failed to come before us in our foresaid court on the day later set for him, according to his aforesaid mainprise, and, [to prevent] the said Isabel from prosecuting her aforesaid appeal, with a multitude of malefactors gathered to himself, [he attacked] the same Isabel at the waterbridge of our palace of Westminster as she was coming towards our court, being under our protection.

8. Watergate indictment (before June 22, 1380). PRO, KB 29 / 32, m. 43d.

Midd. Jurata, scilicet [twelve names follow], isto eodem termino coram domino rege apud Westmonasterium presentat quod, cum Isabella, que fuit uxor Johannis Mohoun, prosecuta fuit quoddam breve domini regis de appello de raptu versus Henricum Yeuelcoumbe et alios in curia domini regis coram ipso rege, eademque Isabella habuit diem nunc in tribus septimanis Pasche in appello suo predicto, et quidam Guido de Bryen, chevaler, ipsam Isabellam de London usque Westmonasterio ad appellum predictum in curia regis, ut predicitur, prosequendum, et diem sibi per justiciarios domini regis secundum legem terre datum custodiendum, in quadem batella per aquam duxerit, predictus Henricus Yeuelcoumbe [^. . .] [168] <u>et Willielmus Yeuelcoumbe</u> simul

[168] The dim careted note (something like "ij cart. terro –m° a° xiij r.r.p°") seems to be a reference to the thirteenth year of the reign, which would be 1389–90.

cum quampluribus aliis ignotis armatis in loricis et aliis armaturis machinans ipsam Isabellam capere ipsamque ab appello suo predicto totaliter excludere, die Mercurii proximo post tres septimanas Pasche anno regni nunc tercio [April 18, 1380] apud Westmonasterium, videlicet, juxta pontem palacii domini regis Westmonasterii apud Portam aquaticam in presencia justiciarorum domini regis de banco ipsius regis, et manus super ipsam Isabellam miserunt, et ad ipsam capiendam, et in Guidonem de Bryen, chevaler, Johannem Kentcoumbe, et Johannem Shakel venientes cum ipsa Isabella ibidem insultum fecerunt et ipsos verberaverunt, vulneraverunt, et male tractaverunt.

Et dicit quod Jacobus de Lyons, unus servientium domini regis ad arma, immediate ipsos juxta officii sui debitum ipsos arestavit, et ipse Henricus arestum predictum fregit, et quo voluit ivit cum hominibus suis predictis, nullo habito respecto ad arestum predictum.

Item presentat quod Baldewinus Yeuelcombe, Johannes Luk de Bodmyn, Johannes [^. . .] Cole de London. Sadelere, Johannes Fowy, et Johannes Willyng de Cornubia predicto die Mercurii proximo post tres septimanas Pasche anno supradicto omnes transgressiones superius nominatas et declaratas simul cum predictis Henrico Yeuelcombe et Willelmo Yeuelcombe apud predictam portam aquaticam Westmonasterii fecerunt, etc. **Per recorda de anno tercio.**

Per quod preceptum est vicecomitibus quod capiant eos si, etc.

Middlesex. The jury . . . presents that, when Isabel, who was the wife of John Mohoun, prosecuted a writ of the lord king concerning appeal of rape against Henry Yeuelcoumbe and others in the court of the lord king before the said king, and the same Isabel had a day in the present three weeks of Easter for her aforesaid appeal, and a certain Guy de Bryen, knight, would have led the said Isabel from London to Westminster in a boat by water to prosecute the aforesaid appeal and to keep the day granted her according to the law of the land by the justices of the lord king, as is said above, the foresaid Henry Yeuelcoumbe [^. . .] and William Yeuelcoumbe along with several other unknown armed men in breastplates and other armaments, plotting to seize Isabel and completely exclude her from her aforesaid appeal, on the Wednesday next after the three weeks of Easter, the present third year of the reign [April 18, 1380], at Westminster, specifically next to the bridge of the palace of the lord king at Westminster near the Watergate, in the presence of the justices of the lord king of the bench of the said king, and they put hands upon the said Isabel, and, in order to capture her, they also assaulted Guy de Brien, knight, John Kentcoumbe, and John Shakel, who were accompanying the said Isabel to that place, and beat, wounded, and maltreated them.

And the jury says that James de Lyons, one of the sergeants-at-arms of the lord king, immediately arrested them in accord with the duties of his office, and the said Henry broke the aforesaid arrest and departed whither he would with his aforesaid men, having no respect for the aforesaid arrest.

Likewise it presents that Baldwin Yeuelcombe, John Luk de Bodmyn, John Cole of London, saddler, John Fowy, and John Willing of Cornwall on the aforesaid Wednesday following the three weeks of Easter in the above-mentioned year committed all the trespasses named and declared above along with the aforesaid Henry Yeuelcoumbe and William Yeuelcoumbe at the aforesaid Watergate at Westminster, etc. **By records of the third year.**

By which order is given to the sheriffs to arrest them, if, etc.

9. Writ to the coroners of Cornwall, November 29, 1381. PRO, KB 136/5/5/3/1 (last writ in packet).

Ricardus Dei gracia rex Anglie et Francie et dominus Hibernie coronariis suis in comitatu Cornubie salutem. Cum nuper vicecomitem nostrum comitatus predicti precepimus quod exigi faceret Willielmum fratrem Henrici Yuelcombe et Laurencius Drew filium Drugonis de Wryngworth de comitatu in comitatum [?] quousque secundum legem et consuetudinem regni nostri Anglie utlagarentur si non compararent, et si compararent tunc eos caperet et in prisona salvo custodio faceret, ita quod haberet corpora eorum coram nobis in octobis sancte Trinitatis ultimis preteritis [June 17, 1381], ubicumque tunc essemus in Anglia, ad respondendum Isabelle que fuit uxor Johannis Moun de raptu et pace domini Edwardi nuper regis Anglie avi nostri fracta, unde eos appellat, dictusque vicecomes noster ad diem predictum nichil inde nobis misit; ac jam exigente [?] predicta Isabella accepimus quod predicti Willielmus et Laurencius in comitatu predicto, accione predicta utlagati, existunt, per quod vobis precipimus quod, strictatis rotulis et memorandis vestris, si quam utlagariam in eisdem inveniretis versus predictos Willielmum et Laurencium accione predicta, [eam] mittatis coram nobis a die Pasche in xv dies [April 21, 1382], ubicumque tunc fuerimus in Anglia, ut ulterius inde fieri faciamus quod de jure et secundum legem et consuetudinem regni nostri Anglie fore viderimus faciendum, hoc breve emittentes.

Teste R. Tresilian apud Westmonasterium, xxix die Novembris anno regni nostri quinto [November 29, 1381].

[Dorse] Ego Noelus Padirda, unus coronarius comitatus Cornubie, recepi istud breve apud Lostwcchiel die Veneris proximo ante Dominicam in Ramis Palmarum [March 28, 1382]. Virtute hujus brevis, strictatis memorandis rotularum nostrorum [?] de tempore viso inveni quod Willielmus frater Henrici Yuelcombe utlagatus fuit de felonia die Lune proximo post festum sancti Mathei apostoli anno regni regis Ricardi quarto [September 24, 1380].

Et predictum Willielmum ad [. . .] non inveni postea infra comitatum Cornubie. Et quoad Laurencium Drew filium Drogonis de Wryngworth, de utlagaria sua nullo modo michi constare potest quoad presens, et ipsum ad capiendum non inveni in comitatu Cornubie. Et quoad capiendum Henricum nominatum in breve, nihil michi constat de [. . .] sua.

Noelus Padirda, Robertus Davudel, coronarii regis [?].

Richard by the grace of God king of England and France and lord of Ireland wishes health to his coroners in the county of Cornwall. Since we recently ordered our sheriff in the aforesaid county to put in exigents William brother of Henry Yulecomb and Lawrence Drew son of Drugo of Wryngworth from county to county, so that according to the law and custom of our kingdom of England they were to be outlawed if they did not appear, or if they did appear, that he put them in prison under safe custody so that he have their bodies before us on the octave of Holy Trinity just passed [June 17, 1381], wherever we were in England, to respond to Isabel who was the wife of John Mohun concerning rape and breaking the peace of Lord Edward late king of England, our grandfather, on which she appeals them, and the said sheriff on the aforesaid day sent us nothing; and now from the foresaid Isabella we have received that the aforesaid William and Lawrence, outlawed by the foresaid action, are at present in the foresaid county, in consequence of which we order you that if, upon examining your rolls and memoranda, you find any outlawry in them against the aforesaid William and Lawrence on account of the aforesaid action, you send it before us on the quindene of Easter [April 21, 1382], wherever we then may be in England, so that we may cause further action to be done in accord with what we see is to be done in the matter by law and according to the law and custom of our kingdom of England, upon your sending this writ to us.

Witness Robert Tresilian at Westminster, 29th day of November in the fifth year of our reign.

[Dorse: the Return] I, Noel Padirda, one of the coroners of Cornwall, received this writ at Lostwcchiel on the Friday before Palm Sunday [March 28, 1382]. In virtue of this writ, having examined the memoranda of our rolls in the time specified, I found that William brother of Henry Yulecomb was outlawed for felony on the Monday after the feast of St. Matthew the Apostle in the fourth year of the reign of King Richard [September 24, 1380].

And the foresaid William I have not found for [. . .] afterwards within the county of Cornwall. And as for Lawrence Drew son of Drogo of Wryngworth, nothing can be confirmed to me in any way concerning his outlawry for the present, and I have not found him to arrest him in the county of Cornwall. And as for arresting Henry, named in the writ, nothing appears to me concerning his [. . .].

Noel Padirda, Robert Davudel, coroners of the king.

10. Pardon of Henry and William Yulecomb, October 23, 1382. PRO, C 66/313, m. 13, reported in *CPR Richard II*, 2:179.

Rex omnibus ballivis et fidelibus suis ad quos, etc., salutem. Sciatis quod de gracia nostra speciali et pro bono servicio quod Henricus Ylcombe chevaler alias dictus Henricus Yuelcombe nobis in partibus Portingalie impendit perdonavimus sectam pacis nostre que ad nos pertinet pro raptu Isabelle, que fuit uxor Johannis Moun, unde indictatus, rettatus, vel appellatus existit, ac eciam, utlagarie, si que in ipsum ea occasione fuerint promulgate—et firmam pacem nostram ei inde concedimus. Ita tamen quod stet recto in curia nostra, si quis versus eum loqui voluerit de raptu supradicto. In cuius, etc.

Teste rege apud Westmonasterium, xxiii die Octobris. Per breve de privato sigillo.

Cond. litteras regis de perdonacione habet Willielmus Ylcombe frater Henrici Ylcombe chevaler alias dictus Willielmus Yuelcombe [careted: de raptu predicto]. Teste ut supra. Per idem breve.

The king to all his bailiffs and faithful subjects to whom, etc., good health. Know that of our special grace and for the good service that Henry Ylcombe, knight, otherwise called Henry Yuelcombe, is undertaking for us in the regions of Portugal we have pardoned him the suit of our peace that pertains to us for the rape of Isabel, who was the wife of John Moun, whereof he stands indicted, charged, or appealed, and also any outlawries that may have been promulgated against him on that occasion [have been revoked], and we concede him our firm peace. So that however he stand trial in our court if anyone should wish to speak against him concerning the aforesaid rape. In whose, etc.

Witnessed by the king at Westminster, 23 October. By writ of the privy seal.

William Ylcombe, brother of Henry Ylcombe, knight, otherwise called William Yuelcombe, has conditional letters of pardon of the king—for the above-mentioned rape.

Witnessed as above. By the same writ.

11. Acquittal of John Woodhouse by the justices of jail delivery, April 18, 1384. PRO, JUST 3/80/1, m. 1 (first membrane).

Ebor. Johannes de Wodehous de Brathwayte captus pro eo quod ipse die Martis proximo ante festum sancti Laurencii martyris anno regni regis Ricardi secundi post conquestum Anglie primo [August 11, 1377] apud Wodehous felonice rapuit Aliciam filiam Ricardi Jakman et eam cum bonis et catallis ipsius Ricardi Jakman ad valenciam viginti marcarum ibidem tunc inventis felonice abduxit, unde coram Johanne de Drousfeld et sociis suis custodibus pacis domini regis in Westr. in comitatu Eboraci indictatus est, venit, per custodem gaole ductus, et per justiciarios allocutus qualiter se velit de predictis acquietare, dicit quod dictus rex nunc de gracia sua speciali et ad supplicacionem dilecte sibi domine de Mohun perdonavit eidem Johanni sectam pacis sue que ad [se] pertinuit pro raptu et aliis feloniis supradictis per has ipsius domini regis nunc patentes, quas idem Johannes his profert et que sequuntur in hec verba:

Ricardus Dei gracia rex Anglie et Francie et dominus Hibernie omnibus ballivis et fidelibus suis ad quos presentes littere pervenerint, salutem. Sciatis quod cum Johannes de Wodehous de Braythwait indictatus sit, ut accepimus, de eo quod ipse Aliciam filiam Ricardi Jakman de Wodehous felonice rapuisse debuisset et eandem Aliciam felonice cepisse, abduxisse, imprisonasse contra voluntatem suam, et nos de gracia nostra speciali et ad supplicacionem dilecte nobis domine de Mohun perdonavimus eidem Johanni sectam pacis nostre que ad nos pertinet pro raptu [et] aliis feloniis supradictis unde taliter indictatus, rettatus, vel appellatus existit, ac eciam utlagarias si que in ipsum hiis occasionibus fuerint promulgate, et firmam pacem nostram ei inde concedimus, ita tamen quod stet recto in curia nostra si predicta Alicia versus eum loqui voluerit de raptu et aliis feloniis supradictis. In cujus rei testimonium has litteras nostras nostras [sic] fieri fecimus patentes. Teste me ipso apud Westmonasterium, vicesimo tercio die Augusti, anno regni nostri septimo.

Quarum litterarum pretextu predictus [Johannes] de Wodehous petit se a prisona domini regis deliberari et de raptu et feloniis predictis exonerari. Et inspectis litteris domini regis patentibus predictis consiliatum est quod ipse eat inde quietus, etc.

York. John of Woodhouse of Brathwait, arrested for that he on the Tuesday before the feast of St. Laurence the Martyr in the first year of the reign of King Richard the Second after the Conquest of England [August 11, 1377] at Wodehous feloniously ravished Alice, daughter of Richard Jackman, and feloniously abducted her with goods and chattels of the same Richard Jackman found there to the value of 20 marks, whence he was indicted before John of Drousfeld and his associates, keepers of the peace of the lord king, in Westr. in the county of York, comes, led by the warden of the jail, and, addressed by the justices as to how he wished to acquit himself of the aforesaid, says that the present lord king, of his special grace and at the supplication of the lady of Mohun, dear to him, has pardoned the same John the suit of his peace which pertains to him for the rape and other felonies above-noted, through these letters patent of the said present lord king which the said John here presents, and which follow in these words:

Richard by the grace of God king of England and France and lord of Ireland to all his bailiffs and faithful subjects to which these present letters may come, good health. Know that since John of Woodhouse of Braithwait was indicted, as we have been told, for that he allegedly feloniously ravished Alice, daughter of Richard Jackman of Woodhouse, and took, abducted, imprisoned her against her will, so we of our special grace and at the supplication of our beloved lady of Mohun have pardoned the same John the suit of our peace that pertains to us for the rape and other felonies above-noted whence he is thus indicted, aretted, or appealed, and also outlawries, if any have been promulgated against him on these occasions, and we grant him our firm peace thereof, so that however he stand to right in our court if the aforesaid Alice should wish to speak against him concerning the rape and other felonies above-noted. In testimony of this matter we had these letters patent made. Witness myself at Westminster, the 23rd day of August, the seventh year of our reign.

In virtue of these letters, the aforesaid [John] of Woodhouse asks to be delivered from the prison of the lord king and to be exonerated of the rape and felonies aforesaid. And after the aforesaid letters patent of our lord king are inspected, it is determined that he should go quit thereof, etc.

12. Pardon of John Halsham, June 7, 1384. PRO, C 66/317, m. 12, reported in *CPR Richard II*, 2:399.

Rex omnibus ballivis et fidelibus suis ad quos, etc., salutem. Sciatis quod de gracia nostra speciali et ad supplicacionem carissimi consanguinei nostri comitis Oxon. perdonavimus dilecto ligeo nostro Johanni Halsham sectam pacis nostre que ad nos pertinet, tam pro raptu Philippe de Artheles quam pro omnimodis feloniis et transgressionibus per ipsum quoque modo perpetratis. In cujus, etc.
Rex apud Castrum suum de Corf, vii die Junii. Per litteram ipsius regis de signeto.

The king to all his bailiffs and faithful subjects to whom, etc., good health. Know that of our special grace and at the request of our most dear kinsman the earl of Oxford we have pardoned our beloved liege John Halsham the suit of our peace that pertains to us both for the rape of Philippa of Artheles and for all kinds of felonies and trespasses committed by him in any way. In whose, etc.
The king at his castle of Corfe. By letter of the king himself from the signet.

ADDENDA AND CORRIGENDA

I: Inquisition and the Prosecution of Heresy

p. 442, n. 14, line 3: In his recent book, *Inquisition and Medieval Society: Power, Discipline, and Resistance in Languedoc* (Ithaca, NY, 1997), pp. 15–16, n. 41, James Given takes note of my views, but suggests that they should be compared with 'the careful survey of papal decrees relating to the powers of inquisitors' in Albert Clement Shannon, *The Popes and Heresy in the Thirteenth Century* (Villanova, 1949), pp. 48–89. Such a comparison will reveal, I trust, that I cover all of the valid points that Shannon makes and correct him on other matters.

p. 444, line 7: Innocent IV's *Cum negotium* was not included in Boniface VIII's *Liber sextus*. It is referred to later as an 'extravagant' decretal (see II, p. 422, n. 52), but it was not collected by Jean Chappuis among the *Extravagantes Communes* in his edition at the turn of the sixteenth century, which was incorporated into the Roman edition of 1582. See Emil Friedberg, *Corpus iuris canonici* (Leipzig, 1879–81), 2:lxiv–lxv.

p. 445, end of par. 1: We see torture being used in what clearly seem to be non-heresy cases in the court of St Antoninus, Archbishop of Florence, in the middle of the fifteenth century; see Gene Brucker, 'Ecclesiastical Courts in Fifteenth-Century Florence and Fiesole', *Mediaeval Studies* 53 (1991), 229–57, p. 234 (reprinted in his *Renaissance Florence: Society, Culture, and Religion,* Goldbach 1994, pp. *303–*331, esp. *308), citing Stefano Orlandi, *S. Antonino: Studi bibliografici*, 2 vols. (Florence, 1960), 2:286, 293, 294, 298. Functionaries were hired from the secular courts to apply ropes to prisoners, including a priest, in examining them. They were also used to administer whippings and miterings (placing of miters with descriptions of offenses on heads of malefactors) as punishments.

p. 445, par. 2: See the Introduction, pp. xiii–xxii, for further documentation of these statements about legal counsel.

II: Inquisitorial Due Process and Secret Crimes

p. 411, n. 12 etc.: In this article I wished to use 'Sext' as the standard English title for Boniface VIII's *Liber sextus*, but it was converted into an abbreviation, 'Sext.', in the editing.

p. 419, n. 43: For the principle that the Church does not judge secret matters, see also the Ordinary Gloss to Gratian, D. 32 c. 11 v. *secretorum* (*Corpus juris canonici*, Rome, 1582, 1:161) and the citations listed there.

p. 419, n. 45: The work by Lea referred to, *History of the Inquisition of the Middle Ages*, is not mentioned n. 4; see instead I 439, n. 1, and also the note added to VII, p. 217 below.

III: Right to Remain Silent

pp. 994, line 17–18: My accounts of Lambert's trial here are faulty; see the corrected account in V, p. 3, n. 9.

p. 1011, n. 91: For my revised views on the extant forms of the *modus procedendi* discussed here, see VI, p. 301, n. 75.

p. 1024, n. 160: On the question of stalled efforts for the canonization of Columbus, see the added note to IV, p. 208

IV: Joan of Arc's Last Trial

p. 208, par. 2: On my visit to the Archives of the Congregation for the Causes of Saints in April 2000, all that could be found on Columbus was a dossier containing external documents, notably the publications of Giuseppe Baldi and a series of journal articles by Isidoro Marchini that appeared in *La Liguria del Popolo*: (1) 20 March 1926, pp. 1–2; (2) 27 March 1926, p. 2; (3) 15 May 1926, p. 4; (4) 22 May 1926, p. 2; (5) 12 October 1928, p. 1. Marchini says that he has been involved with the canonization effort for Columbus for over fifty years, since 1875. He mentions some early champions, notably, Archbishop Donnet and Count Roselly de Lorgues, and says that the *Civiltà Cattolica* (first issue of October, 1876), in reviewing one of Roselly's books (*Satan contre Cristophe Colomb*), declared that the legitimacy of the union with Beatrice seemed clearly proved (article 2; in article 4 he cites the issue of 9 March 1876 for a similar declaration). He does not give any report of early deliberations by the Congregation of Rites, but does say that the centenary of 1892 stimulated new efforts: the queen regent of Spain charged Count Roselly with introducing the cause before Leo XIII, supported by a list of over 900 bishops in favor of it, but the case became stranded by the sudden death of Roselly in 1898 (art. 1). He quotes the *Lega Lombarda* of Milan in 1893 as asserting, after reporting that the Congregation of Rites suspended the discussion of the cause because of the doubt about Beatrice, that the postulator had succeeded in establishing the matrimonial nature of the relationship and that the cause was going forward with good hope of succeeding soon (art. 4).

I should also note that the Cuban novelist, Alejo Carpentier. in *El arpa y la sombra* (1979; translated as *The Harp and the Shadow*, San Francisco, 1990), gives the impression of knowing a great deal about Pius IX's and Leo XIII's interest in promoting Columbus's cause. He speaks of a first stalling of the cause in the Congregation because of the Beatrice question, and a later setback over objections to Columbus's proposals to enslave the natives in the discovered lands.

No doubt we can conclude that, whatever preliminary discussions may have occurred in the Congregation, no local inquisitions were ever authorized, and that the case never reached a point at which a promotor of the faith was appointed.

p. 214, last par., line 4: For 'Newman, thereafter' read 'John Henry Newman,'.

V: Wyclif And Wycliffites

p. 2, par. 3, line 4: For 'papal depravity' read 'heretical depravity'.

p. 27, n. 105: I reproduce here my review of Thijssen's book, *Censure and Heresy at the University of Paris*, which appeared in *Speculum* 75 (2000), 729–31.

In this brief book the author takes a new look at some celebrated cases of censure at the University of Paris. He puts more emphasis on censure than on heresy, for, rather than concentrating on questions of deviations from right religion (as most scholars have done), Thijssen is more interested in efforts to make the faculty and students toe the academic party line. In the first chapter, he examines the procedures of censure; in chapter 2, he deals with the Bishop Tempier's condemnation of 1277; the short third chapter takes up the action of the Faculty of Arts in 1340 against six logical errors of Ockham; and chapter 4 concerns the Faculty of Theology's campaigns to correct statements of Nicholas of Autrecourt and John of Mirecourt, culminating in 1347. A final chapter, 'Academic Freedom and Teaching Authority', examines the views of Servais of Mt.-St.-Eloi (= St. Eligius rather than Elias?), Godfrey of Fontaines, and William Ockham on the teaching authority of the bishop, and Peter of Ailly on the teaching authority of theologians. In his Conclusion he looks forward to fifteenth-century cases and the Faculty of Theology's increasing role as an outside consultant in censure cases, most notoriously in the case of Joan of Arc (its condemnation of Wyclif's errors, featured at the Council of Constance, can be added to his list). Following extensive backnotes, the Bibliography begins with essays on unpublished and published sources; the former is particularly important for getting a bearing on Thijssen's confusing references to various documents called *Collectio errorum*. Then comes a series of very helpful summaries of the above and other cases of censure (pp. 169–78), some of them [p. 730] procedurely more interesting than the ones treated here. The index (just over two pages) is very inadequate, listing only names of persons and no subjects.

Thijssen's efforts in chapter 1 to label some court actions as disciplinary rather than criminal is not convincing from the viewpoint of procedural law, but it does echo a distinction made by Ailly (in the John of Monzón case in 1387) between scholastic and judicial condemnations of heresy and error, which Thijssen takes up in chap. 5 (pp.107–11). However, when Ailly goes on to claim quasi-judicial powers for the Faculty of Theology, he is silent on the mechanisms involved (Charles du Plessis d'Argentré, *Collectio judiciorum de novis erroribus* [*CJ*]1:2:75–79). Thijssen's suggestion that the chancellor of Paris did not have the full powers of an ecclesiastical judge (p. 10) is unlikely, though it is true that heresy cases were generally thought to be reserved to the bishop. However, the oath taken by lecturers in theology stipulated that dubious teachings were to be reported either to the bishop or the chancellor (Heinrich Denifle, *Chartularium Universitatis parisiensis* [*CUP*] 3:120–21). But Thijssen rightly observes that the chancellor did not always follow judicial procedure. In the case of Denis of Foullechat, O.F.M., in 1364 (pp. 9–12, 19–20, 36–37), the matter begins as a regular inquisition, with *fama publica* initiating an investigation by the chancellor. The expected procedure would be for the chancellor to cite and charge Follechat, and then, acting as sole judge, after consulting with assessors (chosen at his discretion), to pass sentence. But Follechat anticipated a formal citation by volunteering his cooperation, and the chancellor simply joined with the other masters of the Faculty of Theology in decreeing a form of revocation. Foullechat at first agreed to the revocation, but then appealed to the Holy See 'against the sentence of the chancellor and masters', as if it were a judicial sentence, and requested 'apostles' (a formal response to an appeal). But the chancellor ignored this request and, together with the Faculty of Theology, turned the matter over to the bishop and the papal heresy inquisitor. Foullechat in the meantime walked his appeal to the papal curia, where it was accepted as such, and a commission was set up to deal with it (*CUP* 3:114–22).

In the 1387 John of Monzón case (a controversy over the Immaculate Conception between the University and the Dominicans), which is also adduced to illustrate procedure, the chancellor was by-passed altogether, but Thijssen does not tell us why: the University was feuding with the chancellor—and besides, the new chancellor, John of Guignecourt, was only a bachelor in theology (*CUP* 3:340–425, 480–81). Instead, the Faculty of Theology made a pronouncement, and then, with the other three faculties joining in, the University submitted it to the bishop. In later notarial references to this condemnation, the Chancellor's absence is noted: the errors were condemned by the bishop of Paris and the Faculty of Theology 'sine presentia aut auctoritate cancellarii ecclesie Parisiensis' (*CJ* 1:2:132–48). The judicial function of the chancellor is made clear three years later, after Ailly had swapped his way into the post: the pope orders the chancellors of Paris and Toulouse to proceed against all fomenters of trouble and errors connected with the 'question' between the University and the Dominicans (*CUP* 3:532–33). In contrast with the chancellor, the dean of the Faculty of Theology and the Rector *du jour* of the University manifest no judicial role in these and similar proceedings. Sometimes they speak of acting out of motives of fraternal correction (p. 10), but never in terms of the trial procedure of *denunciatio* established by Innocent III for this purpose.

In his discussion of the appeal process (pp. 35–39), Thijssen should have noted that an appeal can be made at any stage of a trial, not merely after sentence has been passed; furthermore, extra-judicial petitions can be made to superior judges. In Foullechat's case, after he voluntarily withdrew his appeal, he complained again to the pope that the chancellor, bishop, and heresy inquisitor were harassing him, and the pope responded by committing the matter to Cardinal John Dormans; shortly afterwards, the pope issued another [p. 731] commission to Dormans in terms hostile to Foullechat, obviously responding to a petition from the other side (which recounted that Foullechat had succeeded in getting two more papal commissions appointed to hear his case). Finally, the pope responded to another petition by Foullechat and prohibited the chancellor, bishop, and heresy inquisitors from arresting or harassing him, now that the case was in the hands of the cardinal (*CUP* 3:122–24).

The Foullechat case took on the look of civil litigation between opposing parties mediated by the pope, and the same is true of the Monzón case, in which the pope finally (in 1391) summoned 'all questions, controversies, and causes' between the University and the Order of Preachers to his own audience (*CUP* 3:533). In the case between the chancellor and the University in 1385, the chancellor, John Blanchart, insisted that, since abuses of office were being alleged, one of the four modes of criminal prosecution should be followed (*CUP* 3:393: 'Et sic opportet quod per unam viam: accionis [*lege* accusacionis], vel denunciacionis, seu inquisicionis, vel excepcionis, opponantur'); but the civil format continued.

In chapter 2, Thijssen analyzes the condemnation of 1277 as a purely disciplinary and non-punitive action, since the propositions were listed anonymously; but punishment would be meted out to anyone who subsequently defended them. Thijssen is illuminating in laying out the context of Tempier's declaration: the citing of Siger of Brabant and others before the heresy inquisitor in the previous year, the two papal commissions to Tempier, and his subsequent inquisition against Aquinas's disciple Giles of Rome (which Thijssen thinks the bishop called off).

In chapter 3, Thijssen gives only a very brief treatment of the Arts Faculty statute of 1340 against Ockhamist logic, and deals mainly with questions of timing and dating (and he does not return to the arts statute in his Conclusion). It is a fascinating example of a purely academic matter raised to the level of a religious imperative by the requirement of an oath of conformity. The statute only brushes lightly against religion when alleging that the implicated errors might give rise to errors about Holy Scripture.

In chapter 4 we learn that in 1340 Pope Benedict XII summoned Nicholas of Autrecourt and other members of the Faculty of Theology to an inquisition at Avignon, apparently following an earlier trial or trials on the same charges. Thijssen's suggestion that the trial was advoked to Rome is not supported by the content of the citation: it is framed in terms of a de novo inquisition based on *fama publica* (*CUP* 2:505). Autrecourt finally confessed to having held four erroneous propositions, which he had to recant both at Avignon and at Paris. In the case of John of Mirecourt, there is even less to go on, since only his two responses to charged errors survive, addressed to the archbishop of Embrun, probably a papal judge delegate. In addition, there is a statement by the chancellor, Robert de Bardis, doctor of theology, 'ceterique magistri actu regentes Parisienses in facultate theologie', prohibiting bachelors and other students from holding them (*RTAM* 53 [1986] 191). But this local condemnation, like Tempier's, is anonymous: Mirecourt is not named. His fate is unknown. In neither Autrecourt's nor Mirecourt's case,

Thijssen observes, did the incriminated errors seem to pose any danger to the faith, and he can only conjecture as to what triggered the actions against them.

This is a very valuable study that should stimulate further speculation about the attitudes, motivations, and methods of academic censure in the Middle Ages. It has already had this effect on the present reviewer, inspiring antitheses or alternative analyses to some of the author's theses and hypotheses, as noted above. It is to be hoped that further research will lead to a grand synthesis on the questions raised.

VII: English Kings and Sorcery

p. 210, end of par. 1: Lyndwood remained as official of Canterbury until at least 1431; see A.B. Emden, *A Biographical Register of the University of Oxford*, 3 vols. (Oxford, 1957), 2: 1192.

p. 211, last line: For the distinction between the Roman Inquisition and earlier heresy inquisitions by papal delegates, see I, p. 440.

p. 211, n. 16: The 'edition' by R.W. Dunning referred to is only a reprint with a new introduction by Dunning.

pp. 212–13: On the allowability of torture in heresy cases: note that torture was also permitted in other kinds of cases; see I, p. 445 and added note, above.

p. 215, at n. 30: See also Walsingham's *Historia anglicana* 2:160, where he says that Richard II was 'impeded' by the *maleficia* of a certain friar who was with Robert de Vere. See George B. Stow, 'Richard II in Thomas Walsingham's Chronicles', *Speculum* 59 (1984), 68–102, p. 87.

p. 217, line 3: Rymer places the writ to Bishop Repingdon of Lincoln, which is dated 2 January, in 7 Henry IV, that is, 1405/6. H.C. Lea, *A History of the Inquisition of the Middle Ages*, 3 vols. (New York, 1888; repr. New York, 1955), 3:467, citing Rymer, dates it 1407, and assumes that a similar writ was sent to every bishop; he also assumes that suspects were to be held in prison with or without trial, but there is nothing to support such a conclusion.

pp. 219–29: For the trials of Eleanor Cobham and her alleged associates, see Ralph A. Griffiths, 'The Trial of Eleanor Cobham: An Episode in the Fall of Duke Humphrey of Gloucester', *Bulletin of the John Rylands Library* 51 (1968–9), 381–99.

p. 222, par. 2: Griffiths, p. 221, shows that order was given on 12 July for Bolingbroke to be brought before the King's Council.

p. 222, n. 64, line 6 up: 'the single non-convocation trial recorded in the register': the trial of John Claydon in 1415, treated above, VI, pp. 294–96, also seems to have been held outside of convocation.

pp. 229–30:The historical Friar Thomas Bungay, a friend of Roger Bacon's, lived two centuries earlier.

p. 231, and n. 99: I have revised my views on the authorship of the *Croyland Chronicle*. See VIII, p. 331, p. 334, n. 4.

IX: Statutes of Rapes

Most of the following precisions on statutes and cases are based on suggestions by Paul Brand, to whom I am most grateful.

p. 364: Merton. The date '1236' and the term 'statute' should be in quotation marks, since this material was only put together as a statute by later compilers. The first five chapters and some of the later chapters were provisions made at Merton on 23 January 1336. The substance of Merton c. 6 is in Bracton, *De legibus*, book 2, fol. 91b (Woodbine-Thorne, 2:264), and referred to as 'provisio de communi consilio'. See *Early Registers of Writs*, ed. Elsa de Haas and G.D.G. Hall, Selden Society 87 (London, 1970), p. ciii n. 7. It is referred to in 1375 in Westminster I, c. 22, as 'la porveaunce de Merton', which Ferrers translates as 'the statute of Merton' (see IX, p. 366). The words I include in brackets in the Latin text of Merton c. 6 are given as variants in three manuscripts, and were clearly in the text translated by Ferrers.

p. 365: *Speculum justiciorum*: should be *justiciariorum*. As I explain on p. 384, this is a late-thirteenth-century or early-fourteenth-century treatise, which was 'first heard of' in the sixteenth century in the sense of being read and cited by jurists only at that time and later.

p. 366, n. 20: Omit 'This is the way it is read by' (repeats matter in text).

p. 366, par. 1, n. 21: Only Westminster I c. 22 refers to Merton c. 6. Westminster I c. 21 is directed at the obligations of lords to care for the lands of underaged heirs (not treated in Merton c. 6).

p. 366, n. 22: In the introduction to the *De legibus*, Henry Bracton or Bratton, a priest-judge-jurist who died in 1268, claims to have written the work, and, though his statement is usually held to be authentic, many legal historians do not believe him, or, at most, hold him to be merely a re-writer or redactor. See J.H. Baker, 'Bracton, Henry de', *Biographical Dictionary of the Common Law*, ed. A.W.B. Simpson (London, 1984), pp. 69–71. But even if he is taken to be only a reviser, we cannot safely assume that any passage was left unrevised by him, and therefore that it antedates his handiwork in the form in which it now appears.

p. 367: Office of the Coroner: a pseudo-statute based on Bracton: see below, X, p. 137, n. 139. Paul Brand suggests that the reading *per ampnum sanguinolentum* is a mistake for *per pannum sanguinolentum*, 'by bloody clothes', which would fit with the Cotton MS reading, *per pannos sanguinolentos*.

p. 368: [B2], Latin text: I expand *ten.* to *tenura*, but it should probably be *tenemento* or *tenementis*.

p. 370, n. 36: The Chancery clerk that Post cites was not writing after Parliament met but beforehand, listing things to be discussed.

p. 370, par. 1, line 3 up: The case referred to is *Savage v. Clifford*, treated on pp. 382–83.

p. 373, par. 1, line 3: 'the escape of heiresses from their guardians'. Rather I should say that a principal intention of the statute was to prevent daughters from escaping from their fathers, if it was based on the case of Thomas West and his daughter.

pp. 375–76: I say here that the intent of the 1453 statute was to provide a way out of forced marriages, but it was doubtless aimed primarily at voiding bonds made under duress with arrangers of marriages, before such marriages took place. See the explanation given below, p. 416.

p. 378: My stripped-down citation of section 1 of the statute of 1558 does not verify my statement that it 'begins by speaking of girls who stand to inherit property'. Let me just quote the beginning of the long preamble: 'Where maidens and women children of noblemen, gentlemen, and others, as well such as be heirs apparent to their ancestors, as other, having left unto them, by their father or other ancestor and friends, lands, tenements, and hereditaments or other great substances in goods and cattels movable, for and to the intent to advance them in marriage somewhat like according to their degrees and as might be most for their surety and comfort', etc.

When I speak of 'the last part of the fifth paragraph', I am paraphrasing a portion not cited above. It reads: 'And after the decease of such person so contracting matrimony, that then the said lands, tenements, and hereditaments shall descend, revert, remain, and come to such person or persons as they should have done in case this act had never been had ne made, other than to him only that so shall contract matrimony'. Literally this would seem to say that even the consenting heiress, if she survived the marriage, could regain her lands, but this was probably not the intention of the law.

p. 379, top: The 'consenting heiresses' of the 1382 statute are spoken of as consenting 'after' the ravishment, whereas in the 1568 act the consent seems to be thought of as coming before the taking away. The 1568 legislators can be said to 'ignore' the 1390 and 1540 statutes in the sense that they did not consider ravishment to be a serious (felonious) crime.

p. 380: Summary of the statutes:

'1236' (Merton): The purpose of the imprisonment is to insure payment of a fine to the king and recompensing the guardian; more recompense is due if the abducted heir has been married – namely, the worth of the maritage.

1275 (Westminster I): The longer term in prison is for those who are not able to satisfy the fine.

1285 (Westminster II c. 35): The second reason for being punished with exile or life imprisonment, 'for being unable to recompense the *maritagium*', is limited to one who marries the ward after the age of consent ('post annos nubiles').

1382 (6 Richard II): It is important to note that women who consent to such ravishment lose not only all right of inheritance but also dower and joint feoffment and forfeit what they already had. Note too that escheats are reserved to the king or relevant lord.

1453 (31 Henry VI): The detained women are forced to enter into penal bonds which are then used to force them into marriage or other undesired actions.

1558 (4–5 Philip and Mary): The act applies to the taking of any girl under 16; the limit of 12 (the canonical age for valid marriage) applies to those who marry. 'Contract matrimony' in the statute means 'marry' (not 'make a preliminary agreement to marry'). Girls who so consent lose not 'goods' (as stated in the summary) but 'lands'.

p. 381, line 4: I withdraw my statement that emphasis in the 1487 and 1558 acts seems to be on loss of value in the woman's *maritagium*; in the former, one could see such a meaning only by inference with regard to the disparagement suffered, but social devaluation is at the forefront (see p. 377), together with the sadness of friends; and in the 1558 act the main concern seems to be with loss of control rather than with financial loss.

p. 382, end of par. 1: In the case of *Emma v. Hugh*, I should rather say that the jury was prepared to *recommend* the punishment due for felony, and that it was the *justices* who settled for the two years' punishment, because she was not a virgin. But the implication remains: the statutory punishment of two years would not have been thought sufficiently severe if the victim had been a virgin.

p. 382, par. 2, line 11: The variance in naming the two Sundays would, of course, have been sufficient grounds for the failure of Rose Savage's appeal. My citing of the statute on failed appellants (see n. 78) is misleading, since the statute addressed not the technical failure of appeals but cases in which the accused persons were acquitted by a jury either in the appeal or at the king's suit.

p. 383, n. 88: The text of the membrane reads 'cons. est', which I interpreted as 'consultum est', but 'consideratum est' is more likely, since the fact that the case was brought before the king and his council (at the Parliament at which the statutes of Westminster II were enacted) probably means that it was discussed by them, even though the record shows only the judgment giving her damages. The £10 awarded to her would have been additional to the £10 previously payable to the king, since the king did not share out his fines.

p. 384, par. 3, line 4: For *justiciorum* put *justiciariorum*.

p. 389, par. 1, line 4 up: I say here that the penalty before the 1285 statute 'would not be mutilation but two years in prison, if the 1275 statute, like that of 1285, were taken as dealing with sexual rape'. However, if *only* the 1285 statute were taken to deal with sexual rape, then it could be interpreted as saying that now the penalty is death ('life and members'), whereas before it was mutilation. The same would also be true if the 1275 statute were read as stipulating the two-years' punishment only when the king sued, while leaving the penalty of mutilation in place when the woman appealed.

p. 390, n. 125: Spigornel was a justice not of the Cornish eyre of 1302 but of the Kentish eyre of 1313–14.

p. 392, line 3: I should say just 'serjeants', not 'King's serjeants'.

p. 393, line 1 after insets: 'the earliest known instance of an action of this kind', i.e., in 1300. Paul Brand has found an earlier case, from Michaelmas 1392, namely, *Robert son of Henry Belet of Brill v. John son of Ralph le Clerk of Brill.* The defendant is to say why with force and arms he *rapuit* Isabel, Robert's wife, and 'eam cum bonis et catallis predicti Roberti abduxit', etc., 'contra pacem et contra formam statuti regis in hujusmodi casibus provisi etc.' (PRO CP 40/96, m. 199d). He tells me that there is a series of earlier cases going back to Hilary 1291 making similar allegations of seizure of a wife with the husband's chattels but without citing the statute.

p. 394, par. 3: earlier citing of a case drawing on Westminster c 34 [B2], namely, 1292. Paul Brand tells me that he has almost a hundred cases citing this dower section of the statute from the period between 1285 and 1307.

p. 406, line 4 up and p. 414, par. 2, n. 224: I cite P.J.C. Field to substantiate my statement that Malory's trial 'was constantly postponed, for lack of a jury, until he finally obtained a pardon in 1460'. Field actually says that Malory was probably released from his latest stay in prison (where he had been since at least January 1460) after the Yorkist victory at Northampton on 16 July 1460, when Buckingham was killed and Henry VI captured; but he argues that it was only in 1462 that he received a pardon that proved effective. He believes that the pardon that Malory obtained from Henry VI on 24 November 1455 and submitted on 30 January 1456 was not allowed. He does, however, find it odd that there is no further record of arranging for a trial in a subsequent term, and concludes: 'The court seems at this point to have given up attempting to try the prisoner' (*The Life and Times of Thomas Malory*, pp. 116, 122–23, 128–29). But in fact the record shows that the pardon was accepted: Malory is to go *sine die* and the jurors are to be 'exonerated'. However, Malory is to remain in prison until greater security can be found. There is a Latin marginal note which Hicks translates thus: 'Letters patent allowed. *Sine die*' (Hicks, *Sir Thomas Malory*, pp. 99, 107). Field has interpreted the marginal note as a 'postscript', which he dates 1462, but it is undoubtedly only the usual marginal summary of the action detailed in the body of the text, therefore dated 30 January 1456.

As I have pointed out (p. 404), a royal pardon does not prevent interested persons from pursuing the pardoned individual in court on their own. We do not know if any of the allegedly injured persons named in the 1451 indictment did follow through in this way, except that in the controllment roll for Michaelmas term, 1457, Malory is said to be in prison not only 'for various causes pending against him' and for a judgment [of debt] to Thomas Greswold, but also because of a writ from Henry VI for finding surety of the peace towards the king and all of his subjects, especially the Abbot of Combe (Hicks, pp. 100–01). It is probable that the said writ was secured by the Abbot of Combe, whose monastery Malory had been charged with raiding, and he may have been responsible for Malory's continued imprisonment in 1456.

p. 416, n. 232: 'Margery' Kebell should more properly be Margaret Kebell (*Margareta* in Latin).

X: *Raptus* in Chaucer's Time

pp. 110–11, n 43: 'Keilway's report' on Margaret Kebell: Keilway's reports have been reattributed to John Caryll, and edited by J.H. Baker, *Reports of Cases by John Caryll*, 2 vols., Selden Society, 115–16 (London, 1999–2000). For this Common Pleas case, *Kebell v. Vernon*, dated Trinity term 1504, see 2:424–5. For a related case, *Bargh v. Basset*, King's Bench, Hilary term 1506, see 2:506–11, 519.

p. 111, n. 45: 'search for records beyond the death of Henry VII': J.H. Baker, in the above-cited *Reports of Cases by John Caryll*, which extends to 1522, does not note any additional activity in the Kebell affair.

p. 132, line 11 up: 'Stanerton in the county of Devon': Maryanne Kowaleski informs me that this is almost certainly Staverton, a small Dartmoor tin town.

INDEX

For Product Safety Concerns and Information please contact our EU
representative GPSR@taylorandfrancis.com
Taylor & Francis Verlag GmbH, Kaufingerstraße 24, 80331 München, Germany

www.ingramcontent.com/pod-product-compliance
Ingram Content Group UK Ltd.
Pitfield, Milton Keynes, MK11 3LW, UK
UKHW020942210926
475569UK00020B/24
9780860788393